LAND SYSTEN IN TAMILNADU
(c. A.D. 800-1200)

LAND SYSTEM
IN
TAMILNADU

[c. A.D. 800-1200]

By

J. SUNDARAM

BHARATIYA KALA PRAKASHAN
DELHI (INDIA)

First Published : 2009

Published by **C.P. Gautam**
BHARATIYA KALA PRAKASHAN
3421-A, IInd Floor Narang Colony, Tri Nagar,
Delhi-110035. Phone : 32967505, Telefax : 27393083,
E-mail : www.bkp3421@yahoo.co.in
Website : www.bkpboo.com.

ISBN : 978-81-8090-238-3

Laser Type Setting by
A-ONE GRAPHICS
Delhi

Printed By :
G.S offset Printer,
Delhi

CONTENTS

PREFACE

Auvaiyar, the Tamil poetess who is reputed to have belonged to the Sahgam age (1-15 centuries AD) is credited with a verse which purported to say that the higher the embankments of the fields, more water would stagnate therein leading in turn to a better crop prosperity of the husbandsman (kudi) and ultimately of the king. This reflected that during her pẹriod the essentials for promoting rice cultivation and the value of agriculture for the prosperity of the king had been grasped. This verse tells only about the husbands man and the king as the dependent on the land. It does not indicate any intermediary. Whatever may have been the theory behind the king's expectation of a portion of the yield of land. As per this verse, King's interest was in the yield rather than in the land and the dues payable to him were adjusted to the crop. About who these husbandsmen were, other Sangam poems indicated that there were both Brahmins and veḷḷāḷar. Neither of them is indicated to have had any ulterior purpose in holding land beyond enjoying the benefits from the yield.

So far as the land held by the Brahmins was concerned it can be surmised that it was what had been given to them by the kings for their maintenance on account of their adhering to their ordained duties. There is no reflection in the Sahgam literature that any special rights were enjoyed by these Brahmins holding land during the Sangam period. The Sahgam poems also indicate that during that period the area under agriculture (the main irrigated rice cultivation) was restricted to the basins of the main rivers Kāvēri and Tāmraparṇī-Vaigai. On the basin of the Kāvēri, in the upper and lower reaches the Chōḷa ad probably the Chēra respectively had established their kingships and on the basin of the Tāmraparṇī -Vaigai complex the Pāṇdya kingship was based. The archaeological excavations at Koṛkai near the confluence of the river Tāmraparṇl with the sea, have reached that irrigated-rice cultivation had been going on in that portion of the Pāṇdya country from very ancient times. Only these three kings, the Chēra, Chōḷa, and Pāṇdya are seen described as the crowned kings (mudi-mannar) of the Tamil country in these poems indicated that their primacy and power were due to their territories agriculturally developed. The beyond the base territories of these crowned kings were apparently underdeveloped or awaiting development. This is borne out when the Sangam poems while describing the exploits of Karikāla -Chōḷa (2nd century A.D). says that when he conquered the people Aruvāḷar, Oḷiyar etc. around the basin of the river South Peṇṇār (i.e.) the southern portion of the land to clear forest and settle Veḷḷāḷar there into bring that land under the agriculture scheme.

Though there are no indications above the origin of these three crowned kings available the Sahgam Classics, it can be surmised that they were part of the local population. As such they could have faced any problem (i.e) hostility from the local population, necessitating the devising of special measures and to keep them in good disposition and under control.

Subsequent to the 7th century a sizeable number of the records are available in the shape of inscriptions. It has is these records revel that more regions had been brought under agriculture. In these inscriptions the terms *dēvadāna, brahmadēyam, irai-ili* etc. begin to get mentioned Thus the land system has seen to have been institutionalized and based on land. These institutions are also seen to have given a new shape to the land system. The origin of this change is traced to Toṇḍaimaṇḍalam.

The region that came to be known as Toṇḍai-nāḍu or

Toṇḍai-maṇḍalam lay along the basin of the rivers Pālāṛu and its major tributary Cheyyāṛu. During the Saṅgam period though not unknown, this territory seems to have been only partially settled. The available source material does not throw any light on the land system that was in operation even in that settled portion (i.e.) the areas nearer the coast, though included in the Tamil country had stronger links with the Guntur-Nellore region in the north both politically and culturally. It might have served as a channel for the percolation of the cultural developments in the northern region to the core of the Tamil country in the south. Even so it is seen that the practice of issuing charters granting *brahmadēyam* which had started in the Guntur-Nellore region even in the 3rd century had not spread even to Toṇḍaimaṇḍalam till the latter half of the 7th century. This practice is seen to have been adopted in Toṇḍaimaṇḍalam in the 7th century under a special set of circumstances. By this time Toṇḍaimaṇḍalam had become the base territory of the Pallava rulers. This dynesty which was earlier based in the Guṇṭūr-Nellore region and which probably had portions of Toṇḍaimaṇḍalam as adjunct to its territory had been displaced from its original territory and had come to depend on Toṇḍaimaṇḍalam for supporting its political existence.

As a consequence they had not only to take measures not only to develop the economic and agricultural potential of the region but they had also to devise ways and means to secure Their control over the different localities in the region. It was in this context that they are seen to have issued the *brahmadēyam* charters.

Through the issue of such charters they entrusted the brahmins who were fortified with several rights and privileges. The position of the brahmins in society was further strengthened by the development of the institution of temples. Beginning with rock cut shrines, impressive structural temples were set up during the period. Worship in these temples required the presence of the brahmins. Sometimes villages were attached to the temples and such attachment is referred to as *dēvadāna*. These villages were often left in the charge of the brahmins. Thus *brahmadēyam* and *dēvadāna* became characteristic features of the land system in Toṇḍaimaṇḍalam under the patronage of the pallavas. Once developed in Toṇḍaimaṇḍalam these institutions are seen to have been adapted into the land system of the Tamil country to change the shape of the land system from 9th century onwards. Hence it has been found that to understand the ramifications of the land system in the Tamil country during the periodi AD800-1200, it is necessary to study systematically the shaping of the land system in Toṇḍaimaṇḍalam on the basis of *brahmadēyam* and *dēvadāna* during the period (c.AD 670-1000). Such a concentrated study is attempted here and has been cast under the following chapters : The first chapter deals with the physical background against which the land system was developed. It is pointed out how the limited natural resources in the region is evidenced to have been judiciously tapped to maximise their utility only during this period.

The second chapter discusses the sources that have been made available and utilised for the study. After pointing out how numerous inscriptions pertaining to this period have been brought to light and how they, in the main supply a good amount of information on the aspects pertinent to the present study, the chapter describes their character, types, format, etc. Then the publications in which the texts of these inscriptions have been made available are also detailed. The chapter also discusses the value of the studies pertaining to this region that have been brought out so far and how they have left scope for a study of this kind taken up here.

The third chapter deals with land-control as exercised by the kings. As the circumstances faced by the Pallavas who ruled in the area up to about -900 AD and the chōḷas who followed them differed, the discussion has been done under two sections. The first section contains a description of the charters issued by the Pallavas, the extent of control over land claimed and exercised by them, their association of the brahmins in the land-control scheme and the extent of control passed on to the brahmins by them as reflected in these charters. It has also been examined if the Pallava kings held any land under their direct management. In the next section dealing with the Chōḷa period in Toṇḍaimaṇḍalam, it has been pointed out how the Chōḷa kings inherited the territory with a set land system, how they found it convenient to shift the emphasis and to steadily bring' the land under their direct control. In the same chapter the extent of the involvement of the chiefs, some of whom figure as supplicators (*vijñapti*) and secretaries (ājñapti) in the charters, and officials, in the land control scheme has also been dealt with.

Chapter IV is devoted to a discussion about the role of the corporate bodies in the land-control scheme. The character of the control vested with and exercised by each one of these bodies, *nāṭṭār, ūr*, *naggrattār*. *Sabhā* and temple authorities have been dealt with in detail.

In Chapter V the place of the individual land-holders in the land-control scheme has been examined. It has been shown that the individual land-holders barring the brahmins in *brahmadēyam* do not at all figure in the records as transacting in land and how even the brahmins in *brahmadēyams* are reflected to have been restricted by their having been members of the corporate body, the *sabhā*.

Chapter VI deals with the role of irrigation in the land system evolved in Toṇḍaimaṇḍalam during the period. It has been pointed out how this irrigation system made the land system possi ble and how to work the same, corporate action by the villagers was rendered essential. The irrigation rights passed on to the brahmins and the manner in which the corporate body of the brahmins exercised then have been discussed. The reflection in the records on the irrigation rights possessed by the other corporate organisations *ūr* and *nagarattār* have also been dealt with. It has also been examined if some levy was taken from the landholders on account of the irrigation facilities provided.

Chapter VIII is devoted to a discussion of the taxes on land. It is pointed out that the records indicate that the taxes fell into two groups, one consisting those meant for remittance to the king and the other consisting such levies meant to be utilised for the provision of local services by the corporate bodies. The significance of the tax-terms used and how far they reflect on the theory underlying the king's claim for the taxes have been dealt with here. The information provided by the records on the rates and the manner of collection of the taxes and escalation in the number of taxes during the passing centuries has also been discussed. Whatever information can be gleaned on the price of land from the records of the period has also been given.

The concluding chapter summarises the salient features of the land system evolved in Toṇḍaimaṇḍalam ciuring the period c. 700-1000 A.D as brought out in the above study. Attention is drawn to the passing on of the control over the blocs of territories by the king to the brahmins and how they were enabled to exercise this control through the provision of various rights and privileges. Pointed mention is made about the devising of irrigation facilities for their benefit and the extension of exclusive privileges to them for the use of those facilities, all of which though designed to strengthen the hold of the brahmin still contributed to a phenomenal extension of cultivation in Toṇḍaimaṇḍalam. Reference is also made to the fact that while the Pallava king seems to have been content with a tribute like fixed payment from the villages, the Chōḷa kings are seen to have imposed an additional levy and to have undertaken the assessment of land in minute detail. The apparent steadiness in the price of land during the period is also referred to.

I was advised to undertake research on the present subject by Professor R.S. Sharma and he always kept himself available to me for consultation and guidance. The pointed suggestions made by him helped me a great deal. I am greatly indebted to him. I am also very much beholden to Professor R.L. Shukla, Professor and Head of the Department of History and Professor P.B. Mangla, Chairman, Board of Research Studies who took great interest and helped me in many ways to submit this thesis. I am also indebted to Professor D. N. Jha who always encouraged and enthused me in my research. Dr. P. Bhatia, my guide and supervisor spared no pains in making suggestions and trying to systematise my research. She showed great patience in going through minutely innumerable drafts of the thesis and in suggesting improvements. Mere words are not adequate to express my gratitude to her. I am also beholden to Dr. S.N. Prasad, at present Chief Editor, History Division, Ministry of Defence and Dr. K.N. Pandey, Director, Historical Section, Ministry of Defence for their encouragement. I must also express my gratitude to my colleagues in the Historical Section, Ministry of Defence, who are always ready to extend any help I may need. My gratitude is also due to Dr. Burton Stein, Dr. T.V. Mahalingam of revered memory, Shri K.V. Soundararajan, Joint Director General of Archaeology, Shri K.G. Krishnan, Retired Chief Epigraphist, Dr. R. Champakalakshmi of Jawaharlal Nehru University, Dr. Y. Subbarayalu of Madurai University, Shri K.S. Ramachandran of the Archaeological Survey of India and Shri V.R. Mani of U.P.S.C. for the invaluable help they rendered by either gifting to me their publications and off print of articles or in making books available to me in other ways. The library and research room facilities available at the University of Delhi Library, National Archives of India, National Museum and Archaeological Survey of India Jawaharlal Nehru University were used by me and I am indebted to the staff at these places for the unstinting help they extended. I am also greatly indebted to those who kindly agreed to type the thesis at draft stage as also at the final stage. Several friends like Shri B. Jayaraman, Shri S. Rajendran, Shri Madan Lal Sharma, Shrimati Vijaya Lakshmi and Late Shri S. Annāḍurai without showing any tiresomeness typed the several drafts. Shri Mahabir Singh Sharma typed the final thesis in the best manner possible in spite of the fact that the final draft carried numerous corrections in ink with innumerable directions. I am grateful to him for enabling me to present the thesis in this form. I shall be failing in my duty if did not acknowledge the generous help rendered by the staff of the History Department and of the Faculty of Social Sciences of the University of Delhi on every occasion. I fondly remember my wife who bore with me for the late hours so long as she was alive. After her demise my teenage daughters (Kumari Sitala and Kumari Bhooma) took over the burden of keeping the house and helping me carry on the research. They also helped in correcting the copies of the script. While I am grateful to them for this, I am equally if not more indebted to Kumari S. Padmalochana, their friend, who spared her leisure hours and carried (to help me carry) over the corrections to the copies and readying the script. I am also grateful to the ICHR for the grant towards the expenses on paper, typing charge and the preparation of maps for getting the thesis in the required form and coppies for submitting to the University.

I also thank Dr. S. Swaminathan, Deputy Superintending Epigraphist and Smt. V. Ambika Devi, Library & Information Assistant of the Epigraphy branch, Archaeologial Survey of India, Mysore for correcting the proof pages of this book.

Lastly, Mr. C.P. Gautam, Bharatiya Kala Prakashan, Delhi deserves all praise for this prompt and neat publications of this work.

7th May 2009 **J. Sundaram**
Mysore

LIST OF ABBREBIATIONS

AREp.	Annual Report on Epigraphy Annual Report on South Indian Epigraphy Annual Report on Indian Epigraphy
C.P. Ins. of AP Govt Museum	Copper Plate Inscriptions of Andhra Pradesh Government Museum.
EI	Epigraphia indica
IA	Indian Antiquary
IESHR	Indian Economic and Social History Review (Bombay).
IHR	Indian Historical Review
Ind. Feud.	Indian Feudalism (Sharma R.S.) - unless otherwise specifically indicated, the reference is to the 1965 edition.
ISHP	Indian Society: Historical Probings.
JAS	Journal of Asian Studies
JESHO	Journal of the Economic and Social History of the Orient. (Leiden).
JIH	Journal of Indian History
JNSI	Journal of the Numismatic Society of India
Mem. ASI	Memoir of Archaeological Survey of India
NCERT	National Council of Educational Research and Training.

PIHC or Proc}. IHC	Proceedings of the Indian History Congress
SIH	History of South India by KA Nilakantha Sastri.
SII	South Indian Inscriptions
Tr. Arch. Soc. of S.I.	Transaction of the Archaeological Society of South India.

TRANSLITRATION TABLE

In the present work there has been necessity to transliterate both Sanskrit and Tamil words as occurring in inscriptions.

The vowel sounds except for the short 2 and 2 are common to both Sanskrit and Tamil.

Of the consonants, except for the aspirates and soft sounds in the middle of each *varga* as also the last four letters in the following list, the others are common to both Sanskrit and Tamil.

Vowels		**Consonants**				
अ - a	क - ka	च - cha	ट - ṭa	त - ta	प - pa
आ - ā	ख - kha	छ - chha	ठ - ṭha	थ - tha	फ - pha
इ - e	ग - ga	ज - ja	ड - ḍa	द - da	ब - ba
ई - ī	घ - gha	झ - jha	ढ - ḍha	ध - dha	भ - bha
उ - u	ङ - ṅa	ञ - ña	ण - ṇa	न - na	म - ma
ऊ - ū		य - ya	श - śa		
ऋ - ṛi		र - ra	ष - ṣa		
ए - ē		ल - la	स - sa		
ऐ - ai		व - va	ह - ha		
ओ - ō*		anusvāra - ṁ			
औ - au		Visarga - ḥ			

Special Tamil Sounds

-	h	-	This is not diffe-
-	l̤a		rentiated from
-	ḷa	-	*na* in the present
-	ra		work.

The shortened form of these letters has a distinct function and place in the Tamil scheme and is distingushed by *e* and *o* without the script on top.

CHAPTER—1

PHYSICAL BACKGROUND

Tamil-nāḍu is the area in the extreme south of peninsular India where Tamil, a language of the Dravidian group, is spoken. Its northern most limit is traditionally described as the Vēṅgaḍam mountain (the hill feature now called Tirupati where there is the temple of God Veṅkaṭēśvara). To the east is the Bay of Bengal and to the south is the Indian Ocean. On the west, the northern portions of Tamil-nāḍu are bounded by the Mysore plateau and the southern portions were probably once bounded by the Arabian Sea. The northern and western portions of Tamil-nāḍu are interspersed with hills. In the north the disjointed eastern Ghat sends out some spurs almost upto the Bay of Bengal and in the south-west there are some hills which can be treated as extensions of the Western Ghats. The coastal region to the east, is plain without any interference from hills.

There are four important river complexes in Tamil-nāḍu. The river Kāvērī which almost flows through the middle of the country is the longest and most important river. Taking its source in the Western Ghats, which receives a good amount of rainfall and thus has a thick vegetation, this river, with its moderate water and alluvial potential has enriched the area along its course. In the extreme south there is the river Tāmraparṇī, which also takes its source at the extreme southern portion of Western (ghats) but its potential has got limited due to its short run before joining the sea. To the north there are the Pālār-cheyyār and South Peṇṇār river complexes. The potential of these rivers to influence the history of the region is limited as they take their source in the Eastern Ghats or in the rain-shadow portion of the Western Ghats. They usually carry water when there is some precipitation in their upper reaches. In between the rivers Kāvērī and Tāmraparṇī, in the south is the river Vaigai which is of even less importance than the two river complexes in the north. There are several regions away from these rivers where there are some minor streams but these mainly depend upon rain-fall only. Each of the above mentioned river complex regions as also the regions away from the rivers has its own peculiarity due to several factors and consequently has had its own history.

Of the above listed regions the region around the rivers Pālār and Cheyyār in the northern extremity, the land system in which is the subject of concentrated study here, is the less favoured in comparison to the Kāvēri and Tāmraparṇī regions but it has also some favourable features. This region is known to history as Toṇḍai-nāḍu or Toṇḍaimaṇḍalam. It is situated north of the region covered by the river south Peṇṇār and east of the Mysore plateau[1]. Its northern boundary is the same as that of Tamiḻnāḍu, i. e. the latitude of the Tirupati hill. The Bay of Bengal lies to the east. In modern terms, Toṇḍai-nāḍu was the area covered by the whole of Chingleput district and most of the North Arcot district (the Tiruvannamalai taluk was outside Toṇḍaimaṇḍalam) in Tamil-nāḍu and some southern portions of the Chittoor and Nellore districts of Andhra Pradesh. Around the period under study this area is seen to have been divided into 24 koṭṭams, a designation of a territorial division peculiar only to Toṇḍaimaṇḍalam[2]. Besides the Pālār-Cheyyār of this region there are some more minor rivers like Aḍayāṛu, Kūvam, Kiliyaṛu and Svarṇamukhi[3]. All these rivers carry water only during the rainy season and contain hardly any water for nine months in a year.[4] The fertility of the soil in the region is not highly rated. The Chingleput District Manual says[5] "in the district the land is generally too inferior' and 'if there is any tract in the Presidency where high farming is necessary it is the Chingleput district', the natural disadvantage being that the soil "where not sandy or mixed with soda or other alkali is stony. Rock is present near the surface. However it is also stated that there are some small portions which are free from these drawbacks but that even there the fertility of the soil is not comparable with that of the other areas. The North Arcot District Manual[6] describes the district as being hilly, the valleys between hills being more fertile as they receive rain water as also some alluvium through several streams. But the major portion of the district constituting the modern taluks of Walajahpet, Wandiwash, Arni and Arcot is stated to be having black and red clay mixed with sand and gravel. It is stated that in the Wandiwash taluk the soil is in parts much impregnated with soda which effloresces during the dry season rendering the soil sterile. However here also some areas are stated to contain favourable soil[7]. The notable favourable point about this region is that it is served by both the south-west and north-east monsoons. The clouds of the south-west monsoon as they escape through the gap in the Western Ghats at Palghat are flown east and north-east and as a result along with the Kaverī region, Toṇḍaināḍu is also benefited with a moderate rainfall during the months May to August. The north-east monsoon has its regime during October-December. This monsoon serves the areas nearer the coast better as it weakens with its progress in land. Thus the eastern portion of Toṇḍai-maṇḍalam receives somewhat better treatment from the monsoons.

The data collected by the Indian Meteorological Department as given below will elucidate this point.[8]

District	**Places with highest & lowest rainfall.**	**Annual rainfall**	**No. of rainy days**	**No. of years for which data has been taken.**
Chingleput (bordering the coast)	(District average)	46.70	54.0	——

-do-	Cove long (highest)	51.51	57.9	48 years
-do-	Tiruvallam (lowest)	42.38	54.3	71 years

(Rainfall goes on increasing May-June onwards with highest in November and lowest in March).

North Arcot (away from the coast)	(District average)	38.01	51.8	—
-do-	Wandiwash (highest)	44.81	53.4	71 years
-do-	Vaniyampadi (lowest)	30.38	50.1	63 years

(Rainfall is quite heavy in August to November and poor in January-April, goes on increasing thereafter).

The physical features of Toṇḍai-nāḍu as detailed above make it clear that the area has some moderate agricultural potential but that it was such that had to be developed to realise the benefits of the potential. One of the major requirements is a technology to harness the runaway waters of the storm-fed streams for even utilisation in agriculture. Such technology seems to have been introduced into the region only during the period under study (i.e.) subsequent to the 7th century. For, during the earlier period the potential of the region does not appear to have been systematically tapped. The archaeological data, literary sources and notices in the Sanskrit classics pertaining to the earlier period all indicate that only the eastern portion nearer the coast was settled[9] and was serving as the link between the cultures in the regions to the north and the core of the Tamil country to the south. It is seen to have been sometimes treated as an extension of the northern cultures, Kāñchīpuram, the chief town in the area having been known as a Centre of Sanskrit learning[10] rather than as a cradle of

Tamil scholarship as the capitals of the Chēra, Chōḷa and Pāṇḍya kings in the core of the Tamil country were. The available data indicate that there was some trading activity in that area[11] but there is no information on the commodity/commodities that were involved. Some literary sources indicate that the south-western portion of Toṇḍaināḍu that formed the basin of the river Cheyāru was still inhabited by people who were continuing in their tribal culture and had not emerged as a settled agricultural community.[12]

On the other hand subsequent to the 7th century sufficient evidence is available to inform that necessary measures for water management had started being taken. Water flowing spasmodically in the rivers, often going to waste was now being guided into reservoirs for even prolonged utilisation. The resultant phenomenal expansion of cultivation resulted in the spread of agricultural settlements evenly throughout Toṇḍai-nāḍu. Unlike in the earlier period, Toṇḍai-nāḍu began suppor-ting a monarchy which dominated the political scene in one half of Tamil-nāḍu for more than two centuries from the 7th. The reasonable prosperity the area had attained helped in the erection of several temples, a distinct style getting evolved in the process. While these monuments that have survived to this day are impressive enough, it can be however said that the irrigation works, that are still surviving or of which enough vestiges, are available which seem to have come up during the period 700-1000 are the more impressive as it was they that made the development of the agriculture in the area, of the temple as an institution, possible and pushed the area into the limelight.[13]

Further whereas there is no information on the land system that was in existence prior to the 7th century,[14] in the subsequent period the developmental works executed are seen to have helped in the evolution of a land system with its own characteristic features as dictated by the necessities of the area and the compulsions felt by the monarch. The institutions that got organised in the process during this period probably had far-reaching influence.

NOTES

1. According to the poetess Auvaiyār, Toṇḍai-nāḍu was the area bounded by Veṅgaḍam hill in the north (the traditional northern limit of Tamil-nāḍu), the sea (Bay of Bengal) to the east, Pinākai (the river south Peṇṇar) to the south and Pavalamalai (Eastern Ghats) to the west. (Mahalingam, T.V., *Kanchipuram in Early South Indian History*, p. 3, n. 9). In the course of the redesignation of the various regions in the territory under their control with the stamp of their titles during the 11th century, the Chōlas designated roughly the same area as stated by Auvaiyar to have been Toṇḍai-ṅadu except the northern fringes, as Jayaṅ-gonda-Chōḷa-maṇḍalam. This correspondence between the extent of Jayangonda-choḷa-maṇḍalam and that of Toṇḍai-nāḍu as described by the poetess Auvaiyār might have been due to this poem having been composed by a poetess of the 12th century, who bore the same name as the one of the Sangam period (cf. Subramanian, N. Chopra, P. N., and Ravindran, T.K.,' *History of South India*, p. 146). In the *Classicial Age* (ed. Majumdar, R.C., p. 255) Toṇḍai-nāḍu is described as the area lying between the river north Peṇṇār (Nellore region) in the north and the river north Veḷḷar (the northern limit of Chōḷa-nāḍu) in the south. This is further wide off the mark as while the evidence of the period under study indicate that the south Peṇṇar region even to the north of Veḷḷar river is known to have been distinctly separate from Toṇḍai-nāḍu, the north Peṇṇār region is described as Kammaka-rashtra (Chendalur plates of Kumāra-vishṇu II and Muṇḍa-rashṭra (Viḷavetti grant of Simhavarman) in the records of 5-6th centuries. A record of the year 39 (1109) of Kulōttuṅga I from Panṭrangam (Gudur taluk), Nellore district which is quite to the south of north Peṇṇār region assigns Pavittiri-kkoṭṭam, which must have been the northern-most division of Toṇḍai-nāḍu to Rājēndra-Chōḷa-maṇḍalam rather than to Jayaṅgoṇḍa-choḷa-maṇḍalam.
2. It is stated that the inscriptions refer to as many as 27 koṭṭams (Mahalingam, T.V., *Kanchipuram* in *Early South Indian History*, p. 3 and n. 11). But traditionally the number of the kōṭṭams was only twenty-four and the names of the kōṭṭams as listed by Kanaka*sabhāi*, V. *(Tamils Eighteen Hundred years ago*, p. 28-29) on the basis of *Toṇḍaimaṇḍaḷa-paṭṭayam,* a late work, were as follows :—
    1. Pulal-kōṭṭam

2. Maṉavir-kōṭṭam
3. Ikkāṭṭu-kkōṭṭam
4. Cheṅgaṭṭu-kkōṭṭam
5. Paiyur-kkōṭṭam
6. Eyil-kōṭṭam
7. Damal-kōṭṭam
8. Ūṟṟukkāṭṭu-kkōṭṭam
9. Kaḷaṭṭur-kōṭṭam
10. Chembur-kōṭṭam
11. Āmbur (Āmūr)-koṭṭam
12. Veṇkuṉṟa-kkōṭṭam
13. Palgunra-kkōṭṭam
14. Ilaṅgaḍu-kkōṭṭam
15. Kāliyūr-kkōṭṭam
16. Chengarai-kkōṭṭam
17. Paḷuvūr-kōṭṭam
18. Kaḍigai-kkōṭtam
19. Chedirukkai-kkōṭṭam
20. Kunravattana-kkōṭṭam
21. Veṅgada-kkōṭṭam
22. Vellur- kkōṭṭam
23. Ittūr- kkōṭṭam
24. Puliyūr- kkōṭṭam

These kōṭṭams are stated to have contained 77 or 79 *nāḍu* subdivisions (also Gopalan, R., *History of the Pallavas of Kanchi*, p. 147, n. 2).

3. cf. Spate, O.H.K. and Learmonth, A.T., *India and Pakistan*: A general and Regional geography, p 743.
4. *Ibid*.
5. *op. cit.*, pp. 4-5, 65.
6. *North Arcot District Manual,* pp. 303-449. The North Arcot district dealt with in this publication included portions of the modern Chittoor district in Andhra Pradesh also. But probably the orientation of the old district coincided with the western portion of Toṇḍaimaṇḍalam.
7. cf. Spate, O.H.K. and Learmonth, A.T., *op. cit.*, pp. 721, 743.
8. Memoirs of the Indian Meteorological Department, Vol. XXVII, pt. V; Spate, O.H.K., and Learmonth, A.T., *op. cit.*, p. 739.
9. Raman, K.V., (the Early History of the Madras Region, pp. 1-2) tells about how palaeolithic sites diminish as one goes from the

coast inland. Ramachandran, K.S., ("Megalithic Zones of India," Prof. K.A.N. Sastri *Felicitation Volume,* p. 253) indicates that the megaliths are found nearer the coast. (He says that Megaliths of South India including those in Toṇḍai-nāḍu when uncovered, are seen to contain rice, copper/bronze objects, personal ornaments consisting of beads of terracotta, semi-precious stones, necklaces, bangles of gold and iron objects of offence and defence besides skeletal remains. The date of these megaliths is brought down even upto the 1st century A.D.—K.A.N. Sastri, *SIH*, pp. 55-58—He however, prefers to date them between 700 and 400 B.C.). However, the excavations at Paiyampaḷḷi in North Arcot district has revealed that the western portion of Toṇḍai-nāḍu was not wholly neglected.

10. Sivaramamurtti, C., Foreword to Sri-*Varadarajasvami Temple* (Raman, K.V.; Srinivasan, C.R., *Kāñchipuram Through the Ages,* p. 9, n 13, *Mahabhārata* also refers to the people of Kāñchi *(Kāñchyaḥ)* distinct from *Āndhra* and *Drāvida*. The late-Saṅgam poetess Auvaiyār knew Toṇḍai-nāḍu as a region full of learned men (Mahalingam, T.V., *Kāñchipuram in Early South Indian History,* p. 3 and n. 9). Mayūra-śarman, the progenitor of the Kadambas who probably lived about the 4th century A.D. is also said to have resorted to Kāñchi for vēdic learning as per report in the Tāḷguṇḍa inscriptions of Kakusthavarman (Subrahmaniam, N., Chopra, T. N. and Ravindran, T.K., *History of South India,* Vol. I, p. 32).
11. The trading activity is evidenced by the find of a number of coins of the ancient period in the area. cf. Maloney Clarence, "Archaeology in South India, Accomplishments and Prospects," *Essays on South India* ed. Burton Stein, pp. 20, 28-29; it is stated that the punch-marked coins might have been in circulation prior to 2nd century AD. *Ind. Arch. A Review*, 1962-63, pp. 12-13; Sarma IK, Coinage of the Satavahana Empire, pp. 43-44, 137; Ramayya S. "The Puzzle of the Pallava coinage and Some New Pallava Coins", *JNSI.*, XXIX, p. 23. It is speculated that the region upto Cuddalore must have been included in the Satavahana empire and that the Pallavas inherited this portion of their empire having been there earlier as their viceroys. There is also a speculation that Toṇḍai-nāḍu might have formed part of the Mauryan empire (Mahalingam, T.V., *op. cit.*, pp. 5-10.
12. The Sangam Work *Śiru-bān-ārruppaḍai* tells about the people *Eyinar* inhabiting this region and their chief Nalliyakkodan

(Mahalingam, T.V., *op. cit.,* pp. 12, 14; Also *Ibid.*, p. 21) cf. Jayasval Suvira, "Studies in the Social Structure of the Early Tamils," *Indian Society : Historical Probings*, p. 146-147, 153.

13. Spate, OHK and Learmonth, AT *op. cit.*, p. 210, 721, 743. Also cf. Croele, *Chingleput District Manual* p. 209, 250. It will be appropriate to quote here that terms in which he expressed his appreciation for the irrigation works and his estimation as to how they had helped the agriculture in the district, "The natives of India undoubtedly possess a natural aptitude for hydraulic engineering which whether it arise out of or be merely stimulated by self-interest has when directed by persons possessing the vast authority and influence such as native governors or collectors produced many grand and successful works. In point of fact nearly every successful irrigation work in the south of India has been initiated if not entirely constructed by such agency. Tradition and History concurs in assigning the construction of the tanks and irrigation works to that period. Many of them now abandoned or in ruins evince the solicitude of those ancient monarchs for the extention of cultivation even in tracts not favoured by natural position or the quality of the soil. Almost every catchment basin, however, small still bears traces of having been bundled across and in many instances this was done in order to secure a crop of paddy on a few acres of stony ungenerous soil to which all the fostering care of the British administration has failed to induce cultivation to return. Larger and more extensive projects also were not neglected, some of which still bear witness to the enlightenment of these Hindu kings; while the absence of scientific instruments in those remote times compels the astonishment and admiration of the beholder who examines such monuments of a hydraulic skill, almost intuitive as is exemplified, for instance, in the Kambukal chann, which leaving the Pālār at an ancient some twenty or thirty miles west of Conjeevaram, was carried along a natural ridge as far as Sriperumbudur whence it dropped into the lower country of the Chingle put taluk in which there are vestiges of it as far as Tiruppōrur near the sea-coast and supplied countless tanks in its course of 50 or 60 miles. It could have been no petty or impoverished line of princes who designed and constructed such works and their existence justifies the conclusion which is indeed confirmed by the express assertion of Ptolemy that the country was in a highly flourishing state before the Christian era.

14. It may be significant that the Sangam poem *Perumbāṇ-ārru-ppaḍai*

which describes the various groups of people inhabiting Kāñchi does not mention the agriculturist class. (Gopalan, R., *History of the Pallavas of Kāñchi,* p. 29), whereas this class found a place in Puhār, the Chōḷa capital which is vividly described in *Silappadi kāram* (Sastri, K.A.N., The Chōḷas, pp. 81-82; also *Ibid.*, pp. 37-88) It is not known if the indications on the land system and agricultural practices found in the Sangam texts was applicable to the Toṇḍai-nāḍu region (Ṣastri, K.A.N, *SI.,* pp. 130-131, Pillai, K.K., *A Social History of the Tamils,* p. 161 f). It is noteworthy that Pillai (*op. cit.,* p. 187) also indicates on the basis of another Sangam work *Maduraikkāñchī* (286-288) that there were some areas in Tamil-nāḍu during that period where paddy was also grown by the process known as *jhum* cultivation.

CHAPTER. 2

SOURCES

The chief source of information for writing the history of South India is the large number of epigraphs mostly inscribed on temple walls and sometimes on stray stones and on a few copper plates.[1] There are few coins, some literary material and some references in foreign writings which, if at all, only go to supplement the information available from the epigraphs. The advantage of the epigraphs as a source material is that either they are dated or can be approximately dated on the basis of palaeography. The epigraphs are also mostly *in situ* and often contain information on the nomenclature of the region and findspot current during the period to which they belong. Even copper-plates which could be transported from place to place—some of them like the Kaśākkuḍi plates of Nandivarman II and Paḷḷankōyil plates of Siṁhavarman were found at places far away from the regions to which they belong—contain sufficient information on the region to which they pertain and hence there is no difficulty in their attribution. The epigraphs are usually precise. Sometimes they, no doubt, contain idiom which is now obsolete and hence obscure but it is possible to interpret them from the context in the same inscription or with the help of other material. Moreover the available epigraphs are either records of grants of land and other land transactions or of documents that were meant for public notice. Hence they are businesslike without exaggerations. They are usually reliable.[2] Because of these characteristics, the epigraphs constitute invaluable material for historical research. Though they are mainly records of transactions they also contain sufficient information on the social, political and economic conditions of the period to which they belong.[3]

Of the material used to inscribe the records, copper was costly. Hence it could be expected to have been sparingly used and by persons in authority. Advantage of copper plates is their handiness, portability and permanence. They could be handed over to individuals for safe keeping to be used as proofs of their rights and claims. Generally copper-plates contain records of grants of *brahmadēyam* or *dēvadāna*. Hence they provide one type of information about the land system. Once the stone temples began to be constructed in large numbers, they provided ample space for inscriptions. The stone inscriptions seem to have been meant to serve as everlasting public notices of any activity that merited such publicity. The subjects covered ranged from such significant activities like the construction of and making provision for the maintenance of reservoirs or sales of land etc. to insignificant gifts of a few sheep for the maintenance of a lamp in temples. The persons whose activities are reflected also belonged to all strata of the upper crust of society from the king to the minor landholders. In contrast to the copper plates due to the very range and scope of the material provided by these stone inscriptions, they are even more crucial for historical research.

For the purpose of present study some twenty one records on copper plates are available. Of them, 12 pertain to Toṇḍaimaṇḍalam region and to the relevant period and three others no doubt pertain to Toṇḍaimaṇḍalam and are inscribed in characters of the 8th-9th centuries but since they quote the reign period of kings who are known to have ruled in the period prior to the 7th century their genuineness becomes doubtful. Two more pertain to Toṇḍaimaṇḍalam but one of them belongs to the seventh century and the other to the eleventh century. They too are very pertinent to the present purpose. Four are records of grants pertaining to the region around Toṇḍaimaṇḍalam but as they belong to the period under study and were issued by Pallava Kings, they share the characteristics of the Toṇḍaimaṇḍalam grants and hence they are very relevant for the present study.

In the Tamil country it is the Pallava dynasty of rulers who began the practice of issuing copper-plate charters. In their charters the Pallavas of Toṇḍaimaṇḍalam introduced some innovations which made them different from the copper-plate grants of other regions in India. The difference was both in the form and content. Leaving alone the charters pertaining to central and northern India, the charters of the Pallavas of Toṇḍaimaṇḍalam issued in the seventh and following centuries do not even conform with the charters pertaining to the Guṇṭ ur-Nellore region issued in the 3rd-5th centuries by a set of Pallava rulers who were probably the ancestors of the Pallavas of Toṇḍai-maṇḍalam[4].

Unlike the charters of the Guṇṭur-Nellore region, the Tamilnāḍu charters beginning with the Kūram charter which is the earliest such charter in the Tamil country[5] usually give the text of the grant bilingually, both in Sanskrit and in the local language Tamil. Even the Pallavas of the Guṇṭur-Nellore region might have started this practice of issuing copper plate charters in imitation of the Satavahanas, who were probably their overlords originally. Though many of the charters of the Pallavas of the Guṇṭur-Nellore region state that they were issued from the victorious Kanchīpuram, the grants pertain only to the Guṇṭur-Nellore region and hence these charters cannot be considered as belonging to Toṇḍaimaṇḍalam. As for the role of the Pallavas in introducing the practice of engraving the grants on copper plates into the Tamil country, it is noteworthy that the Pallava copper-plates from Koṟṟanguḍi (Paṭṭattāḷmaṅ-galam) and Kumāraḍimaṅgalam, both the grants pertaining to the Chōḷa-maṇḍalam were also engraved only by *kāṣṭakāri*s who belonged to Kāñchīpuram (of the quarter called Aimbuṇai-chchēri as in the former or the Imaṇachchēri as in the latter-both were probably the same). In the earlier grant the engraver was distinguished by the adoption of some of the titles of the king to become part of his name. (He was named Videlvidugu Pallava-pperuntachchan which might have been rendered possible due to his enjoying royal patronage). In these two cases of the charters, though the engravers of the records (*kāṣṭakāri* actually means wood worker and even though the charter was engraved on Copper-plates, the process seems to have required the services of only the woodworker) are mentioned (it is to be noted that in the third Pallava charter pertaining to Chōla-maṇḍalam, the Tandantottam plates, the record is imcomplete) they were not allotted land or shares, as the *kāṣṭakāris* of the charters pertaining to Toṇḍaimaṇḍalam (where feasible) were allotted. This also may be indicative of their preference to reside near Kāñchīpuram. The Sanskrit portion in these charters gives prominence to the description of the exploits of the king, sometimes of a chief who is introduced as the interlocutor (*vijñapti*) for the grant, sometimes of the donee of the grants and sometimes of the village granted but dismisses the actual grant with a succint mention. On the other hand the Tamil portion does not expatiate on the details about the king and others already dealt with in the Sanskrit portion but describes the various aspects of the actual grant fully. This difference in the emphasis in the two portions seems to have been deliberate. This is evident from the absence in the Sanskrit text of the address by the king to the local authorities regarding the grant which is a feature of the Guṇṭur-Nellore charters. In the Tamil-nāḍu charters such address is found in the Tamil text. However there is also a difference in the number and character of the people addressed and in their expected function. On seeing these special features in the format of the Toṇḍaimaṇḍalam charters one understands that it had been adopted to accord with the situation in the region which was different from that in the other regions. For the same reasons the contents of the grants, the character of the grants, the nature of the accompaniments, the exemptions and privileges, in the Toṇḍai-maṇḍalam charters are also found to be somewhat different from that of the Guṇṭur-Nellore charters. The details of the copper-plate charters that have been utilised in the present study are as follows:—

Sl. No.	*Issuer/king*	*Date*	*Grant*	*Beneficiery*	*Refernces*
I.	**Grants pertaining to Toṇḍaimaṇḍalam and to the period c. A.D. 700-1000**				
1.	Four sets of plates from Udayendram, Gudiyattam Taluk, North Arcot District.				
	a) Nandivarman II	Year 21 (752)	Grant of 2 villages as *brahmadēyam* to	59 brahmins in Shares	*SII,* II, 74, p. 361f.
	b) Parāntakachola I	Year 15 (922)	Grant of a villages as *brahmadēyam*	A *brahmadēyam*	*Ibid.* 76
	c) Bāṇa Vikramāditya	(940-966)	(fragmentary). Probably confirmation of the enjoyment of the *brahmadēyam* by the brahmins		*EI.* III, p. 74 f.
	d) Prince Vīrachōḍa	?	Grant of one village as *brahmadēyam*	Brahmins (number not known)	*Ibid.* p. 79 f.
2.	Kaśākkuḍi (findspot, Kaśākkuḍi is in Pondicherry State) plates				
	Nandivarman II	Year 22 (753)	Grant of one villages as *brahmadēyam*	One brahmin	*SII,* II, 73, p. 342 f.
3.	Pullur (Polur Taluk, North Arcot District) plates				
	Nandivarman II	Year 33 (764)	Grant of four villages as *brahmadēyam*	95 brahmins; in shares	*EI,* XXXVI, p. 144 f.

4.	Vēlūrpāḷaiyam (Arkonam Taluk, North Arcot District) plates				
	Nandivarman III	Year 6 (852)	Grant of village (along with the tax income) as *dēvadāna*	a temple of god Mahādēva	*SII*, II, p. 501 f.
5.	Chiṭṛūr (Chittoor Taluk, Chittoor District) plates of				
	Nṛipatuṅga	Year 6 (865)	Grant of a villate as *brahmadēyam*	53 brahmins in shares	*Studies in Medieval* Deccan History (Plates of the State Museum, Govt. of A.P.) Vol. III, p. 3 f.
6.	Guḍimallam (Kalahasti Taluk, Chittoor District) plates of				
	Bāṇa Vikramāditya	(910-916)	Giving protection to the earlier grant of a village to brahmins		*EI*, VII, p. 1 f.
7.	Madras Museum plates of				
	Uttamachōḻa	Year 16	Arrangements made for the administration and utilisation of the income from *dēvadāna* lands in a temple at Kāñchī-puram		*SII*, III, 128

8.	Two sets of plates from Veḷāñjēri/Tiruttani Taluk, Chittoor District)				
	a) Aparājita	Year 9 (c. 877 or 884)	Grant of income from a village as *dēvadāna*	God Subrahmaṇya (village attached to a *sabhā)*	Noticed in *IHC,* XL Session (Waltair), Section V, Presiden-dential Address, pp. 15-16.
	b) Parāntaka-chōḻa I	Year 25 (932)	Grant of income from village as *dēvadāna*	God Subrahmaṇya	*Ibid*. p. 16
II.	**Grants pertaining to Toṇḍaimaṇḍalam but of doubtful date**				
1.	Udayēndram plates of				
	Nandivarman I	Year 1	Grant of four *araṇya-*kṣētram (wood-land) as *brahmadēyam*	One brahmin	*EI,* III, p. 142 f.
2.	Rōyakōṭṭāh (the findspot is in Salem District) plates of				
	Skandaśiṣya	Year 14	Grant of a village	One brahmin	*EI,* V, pp. 49-51
3.	Paḷḷankōyil (the findspot is in Tirutturaippundi taluk, Tanjavur district) plates of				
	Simhavarman	Year 6	Grant of village and separately some land in another village as *paḷḷichchandam*	Head of a Jain establishement	*Tr. Arch. Soc. of SI,* 1958-59, p. 41 f.

III. Grants pertaining to Toṇḍaimaṇḍalam but slightly outside the period under study.

1. *Kūram* (Kanchipuram taluk, Chingleput District) plates of

Paramēśvaravarman I	(670-700)	Grant of land for defraying expenses for worship in a temple and a village as *dēva-dāna-nimitta-brahma-dēyam*	1) Temple 2) 20 brahmins, 2 priests and a maṇḍapa in equal shares	*SII*, I, 151, pp. 144-155

2. Tiruvālaṅgāḍu (Tirutani taluk, Chittoor district) plates of

Rājēndra-chōḻa I	Year 6 (1018)	Grant of a village as *dēvadāna* after detaching it from the possession of a *brahmadēyam* village.	A temple	*SII*, III, 205

IV. Grants pertaining to the region outside Toṇḍaimaṇḍalam but relevant to the present study

1. Taṇḍantōṭṭam (Kumbakonam taluk, Tanjavur district) plates (fragmentary ?)

Nandivarman II	Year 58 (784)	Grant of a village as *brahmadēyam*	308 (?) brahmins in shares	*SII*, II, p. 530 f.

2. Paṭṭattāḷmaṅgalam (findspot : Koṟṟaṅguḍi, Tirutturaippundi taluk, Tanjavur district) grant of				
Nandivarman II	Year 61 (792)	Grant of a portion of a village as *brahma-dēyam*	15 brahmins	*EI*, XVIII, 14, p. 115 f.
3. Kumaraḍimaṅgalam (findspot : Karumtattāṅguḍi, Tanjavur taluk and district) grant of				
Nandivarman III	Year 10 (856)	Grant of a village as *brahmadēyam*	23 brahmins in shares	*M Somasekhara Sarma Commemoration Volume*. p. 193 f.
4. Bāhūr (Pondicherry State) plates of				
Nṛipatuṅga	Year 8	Grant of three villages as *brahmadēyam*	Attached to another *brahma-dēya* for the benefit of an educational institution (*vidyāsthāna*)	*EI*, XVIII, p. 5 f.

Of the 21 copper-plate charters 14 were those issued by members of the Pallava family who ruled over the Toṇḍai-maṇḍalam region from about the end of the third century till about the end of the 9th century. Five of them were issued by the *Chōḷa* rulers who succeeded the Pallavas as the sovereigns of this region[6]. Two of them were issued by Bāṇa rulers who assumed independence in the region during the period of confusion when the sovereign dynasties of the Pallavas or Chōḷas were in eclipse.

Not all of them are grants of land. Two sets of plates issued by the Bāṇa kings which are fragmentary, record only the confirmation of the enjoyment of the villages earlier granted, by obviously the successors of the original brahmin beneficiaries. The Madras Museum plates of Uttama Chōḷa records only the arrangements made for the utilisation of the income from the *dēvadāna* lands in a temple at Kāñchīpuram. All these three pertain to Toṇḍaimaṇḍalam.

Of the other eighteen, nine records pertaining to Toṇḍai-maṇḍalam (I-la, b, d; 2, 3, 5, II-l, 2; III-l) record grants of *brahmadēyam.* Of these three (1, 2, II, l, 2) are grants to single brahmins; four (I-la, 3, 5; III,—1) are grants to several brahmins in shares, one (I-lb) records an addition of a village to a *brahmadēyam* and one (I-Id) just says that *brahmadēyam* was granted to several brahmins, Four records pertaining to Toṇḍaimaṇḍalam (I 4, 8a & B, III, 2) record royal grants of *dēvadāna* to a Hindu temple and one (II 3) records the grant to a Jain establishment. All the four charters pertaining to the region outside *Toṇḍaimaṇḍalam* which were, however, issued by Pallava monarchs, record the grant of villages as *brahma-dēyam*. Three of them (IV, 1, 2, 3) were grants to several brahmins in shares and one of them (IV 4) is an attachment of three villages to a *brahmadēyam* for the upkeep of an educational institution.

Of these grants, the earliest is the undated record belonging to the time of Paramēśvaravarman (670-700), i.e.

pre-seventh century period, from Kūram which is partly a *brahmadēvam* and partly a *dēvadānam* grant. All the records issued during the 8th century by Nandivarman II (731-796) are *brahmadēyam* grants. One of them (Kaśakkuḍi) dated in his 22nd year (753) is a grant of *brahmadēyam* to a single brahmin. Two others pertaining to Toṇḍaimaṇḍalam (Udayendram and Pullūr) are grants to several brahmins in shares issued in that king's 21st (752) and 33rd (764) years. The other two grants (Taṇḍantōṭṭam and Paṭṭattāḷmaṅgalam) pertaining to Chōḷamaṇḍalam are also gifts of *brahmadēyam* to several brahmins issued in the same king's 58th (789) and 61st (792) years respectively. The Udayēndram plates of Nandivarman I (year 1) and Rōyakōṭṭah plates of Skandasishya (year 14), both of which refer to the reign periods of kings who should have ruled prior to the 7th century but are incised in characters of the eighth century record grants to a single brahmin. Thus, including these two, five of the thirteen *brahmadēyam* grants found in Toṇḍaimaṇḍalam can be said to have belonged to the 8th century. The Pallankoyil plates of Simhavarman is the sole record of the period (the characters of the writing belonging to the 8th century) recording the royal grant of *paḷḷichchandam,* i.e. grant to a Jain establishment.

In the 9th century, in Toṇḍaimaṇḍalam, three copper plate charters were issued by the Pallavas two of which were grants as *dēvadānam* (Vēlūrpaḷaiyam plates dated year 6-852—of Nandivarman III and Velanjeri plates dated year 9-877 or 884—of Aparājita) and the third—*Chiṭrūr* grant dated year 6-865 of Nṛipatuṅga is a *brahmadēyam* grant, which, however, also partakes of the character of *dēvadānam*. In the same 9th century, the Pallava kings issued two other charters granting *brahmadēyam* in the region outside Toṇḍaimaṇḍalam. One of them, the Kumaraḍimaṅgalam grant of Nandivarman III, year 10 (856), pertains to Chōḷanāḍu and the other meant for supporting a *vidyāsthāna* or educational institution at Bāhūr in the middle region is dated in the year 8 (867 A.D.) by Nṛipatuṅga. In the tenth century, there are two grants of *brahmadēyam*. One of them (Udayēndram plates dated in the 15th year (922 A.D.) of Chōla Parāntaka I) records an attachment of a fresh village as *brahmadēyam* to Udayachandramaṅgalam, an already existing *brahmadēyam* and the other probably belonging to this period (Udayēndram plates of Vīrachōḷa) records the creation of a *brahmadēyam*. The identical postscript attached to the Udayēndram plates of both Nandivarman I and II, dated in the 26th year (933 A.D.) of Parāntaka I just records the resolution of two *sabhā* villages, Udayachandramaṅgalam and Kāñchivāyil alias Igaṉmaṛai-maṅgalam to merge together and live as one. But it will be observed that both the records pertaining to the period of Parāntaka I, one, the subscript to the earlier two Udayēndram plates and the other, an independent set coming from the same village reflect the enlarging of the *brahmadēyam* village Udayachandramaṅgalam. The other set of plates from Udayēndram of Vīrachōḷa, which could possibly be ascribed to the reign of Parāntaka I probably created another *brahmadēyam* also adjacent to the same *brahmadēyam* village of Udayachandramaṅgalam, as this record was found at Udayēndram along with the other records.

As per these available copper-plate charters of the period recording grants of *brahmadēyam* in Toṇḍaimaṇḍalam, the following number of brahmins were granted *brahmadēyam* in the three centuries under study.[7]

Last quarter of seventh -	20	(apart from two temple priests) (*Kūram* grant)
8th century	155	(Udayēndram plates of Nandivarman II—59; Kasākkuḍi plates of the same king-l; Pullūr plates of the same king-95.
9th century	53	(Chitrur grant of Nripatuṅga)

The area covered by these few grants was as follows. There are five sets of plates from Udayēndram alone, four recording grants of *brahmadēyam* and one confirming the earlier grants. Udayēndram or Udayachandramaṅgalam is stated to have been situated in Mēl-aḍaiyāṟu-nāḍu in Paḍuvūr-kōṭṭam. In the modern context the village is in Gudiyattam taluk of the North Arcot District, the western portion of Toṇḍaimaṇḍalam. The Rōya-kōṭṭah plates also records a grant of the village Chārukūr in the same Paḍuvūr-koṭṭam thus making six grants pertaining to Paḍuvur-koṭṭam.[8] In the Pullūr grant four villages that went to constitute Nayadhīramaṅgalam are stated to have been in Palkun-ṟākkoṭṭam. The modern Pullūr obviously identical with Pullūr, one of the villages, granted is situated in the Polar taluk of the North Arcot District[9]. The two grant villages, as recorded in the Kūram grant and the Kaśākkuḍi plates were situated in Ūrrukkaṭṭu-kōṭṭam. Uṟṟukkāḍu or Ūttakkāḍu is a village in the modern Kāñchīpuram taluk of Chingleput district[10] and hence the kōṭṭam named after that village must have been part of the present-day Kāñchīpuram taluk. Kūram itself was in *Maṇaiyir*-kōṭṭam and it was there that the temple was built. Paramēsvaramaṅgalam, the new *brahmadēyam* created as per the Kūram grant is stated to have been in Ūṟṟukkāṭṭu-kkōṭṭam a *koṭṭam* different from the one in which the temple was built. But from the circumstances of the charter, it can be presumed that Kūram and Paramēśvaramaṅgalam were adjacent[10a] to each other. Chiṭṟūr of the Chiṭṟūr grant was also situated in *Maṇaiyiṟ*-kōṭṭam and this Chiṭṟūr was the ancient name of the modern Chittoor, the name of the village, taluk and district in Andhra Pradesh, all of which are north of the Kāñchīpuram taluk. Hence it can be concluded that Maṇaiyiṟ-kōṭṭam was an area north of Kāñchīpuram. Tiruvippirambēdu (Viprapīṭha), the village which was already a *brahmadēyam* and which the Bāṇa Vikramāditya confirmed in the enjoyment of the brahmins according to the Guḍimallam plates was in Silaināḍu of Tiruvēngadak-kōṭṭam. Gudimallam, obviously the same as the ancient Tiruvippirambēḍu is in the present day Kalahasti division of Chittoor District which again is situated north of Kāñchīpuram. The village Tirukkāṭṭupaḷḷi granted as *dēvadānam* to the god of the place according to the Vēlūr-Pālaiyam plates, was in Nāyaṟu-nāḍu of Pular-kōṭṭam which was also situated to the north-east of Kāñchīpuram.[11] Vēlañjēri, near Tiruttani which was asked to contribute *pañchavāram* to the temple at Tiruttani according to the two new sets of plates from the place was in Kunṟavattana-kkōṭṭam also in the region north of Kāñchīpuram having been in Chittoor district till recently. But Amaṇśerkkai in Perunagara-nāḍu in Veṇkunṟa-kkōṭṭam which was granted as *paḷḷichchandam* according to the Paḷḷankōyil plates must have been to the south-west of Toṇḍaimaṇḍalam as Veṇkunṟam, the village after which the kōṭṭam was named is stated to be in Wandiwash taluk of North Arcot district, eight miles to the west of *Uttaramallūr*.[12] As will be seen in the following pages, there were pockets of Jainas in the southern portion of the North Arcot district continuing probably till date.[13] Thus grants of *brahmadēyam* or orders regarding *brahmadēyam*, as reflected in the available grants pertaining to Toṇḍaimaṇḍalam and to the period under study were confined to five *koṭṭams*, Paḍuvur-kōṭṭam in Gudiyattam taluk of North Arcot district claiming maximum attention with six of the charters pertaining to it. Palkunṟa-kkōṭṭam wherein one village complex was granted in another charter also formed part of the modern North Arcot district. Ūṟṟukkāṭṭu-kōṭṭam in the modern Chingleput district (near Kāñchīpuram) figures in two charters granting *brahmadēyam*. Manaiyiṟ-kōṭṭam in the modern Chittoor district of Andhra Pradesh was the area of one grant. Tiruvēṅgaḍa-kkōṭṭam also in the Chittoor District figures in a confirmatory charter. Out of the four *dēvadāna* grants, one was of a village in Puḷar-kōṭṭam in Chingleput district, two were villages in Kunravarddhana-kkōṭṭam in the modern Chittoor district and one in Maṇaiyiṟ-koṭṭam[14] (the Tiruvālaṅgāḍu plates). One charter granting *paḷḷichchandam* pertains to Veṇkunṟa-kkōṭṭam in the modern North Arcot district.

In so far as the format of the above-listed charters is concerned, it is observable that each family of rulers, who issued the grants adopted a different pattern. The Pallava charters usually contain a Sanskrit and a Tamil section, the length of each somewhat balanced. However two of the charters containing grants by the Pallava kings that have come forth from Udayēndram do not conform to this pattern and even these two are not similar in pattern to each other. The one of Nandivarman I, entirely in Sanskrit has a draft in the pattern of the issues of the Pallavas of the Guṇṭur-Nellore region, though unlike those charters the king did not address his order regarding the grant to the local inhabitants and officials. The one issued by Nandivarman II is also entirely in Sanskrit but the text is very similar to the Sanskrit section in the bilingual charters of this family. However both these charters have a postscript with an identical text in Tamil dated year 26 (933) in the reign of the Chōḷa king Parāntaka I. The content of this postscript has nothing to do with the grant recorded in the preceding plates and such later addition in the sets of copper-plate charters is unique among the charters of Tamil country.

The two sets of plates containing the charters issued by the Bānas are fragmentary and the text is drafted entirely in Sanskrit. Of the charters issued during the Chōḷa period, only the Udayēndram plates of Vira-choda is entirely in Sanskrit. The other (sets of the) charters are (in a way bilingual) (but the Sanskrit portion just records a gist of the grant) but the Tamil section is elaborate.

The contents in these charters depict a definite pattern. To take first the Pallava charters, the Kūram plates of Paramēśvaravarman, Paḷḷankōyil plates of Siṁha-varman, Rōyakōṭ ṭah plates of Skandaśishya, Kaśākkuḍi plates of Nandivarman II, Pullūr plates of Nandivarman II, Vēlūr-pāḷaiyam plates of Nandivarman III and Chiṭṛūr grant of Nṛipatuṅga among the charters pertaining to Toṇḍaimaṇḍalam, the Bāhūr plates of Nripatuṅga pertaining to the territory adjoining Toṇḍai-maṇḍalam to the south and the Taṇḍantōṭṭam and Paṭṭattāḷmaṅgalam plates of Nandivarman II and Kumara-ḍimaṅgalam plates of Nandivarman III pertaining to Chōḷa-maṇḍalam follow a similar pattern in the draft of the charter.

The Sanskrit portion of the records initially describes the geneology and exploits of the king and subsequently often give such geneology and exploits of a chief who is introduced in the charters as the one who made the *vijñapti* or petition for the grant. Then the charters mention a person who is usually described as a minister or chief minister or the incharge of the treasury (*kōśādhyaksha*-Tandantottam plates) or *Uttarakāraṇika*—(*Kūram* plates) as the executor *(ājñapti)* for the grant[15]. The Udayēndram plates and Pullūr plates also mention the motivation for the grant. The Udayēndram plates say that the grant was made for recompensing the valour with the sword (*asi-dhārānishkriyārtham*) exhibited by the chief Udayachandra in the service of the grantor, the Pallava king Nandivarman II. The village was not granted to him but to a host of brahmins at Udayachandra's request. The same king, when he granted four villages to a number of brahmins in the Pullūr grant made it for fulfilling his duty *(dharma-krityārtham)*[16] having been requested by Avanichandra-yuvarāja for the purpose. In the VēlūrPālaiyam plates recording a *dēvadāna* grant, the excellence of the temple built by the *Vijñapti* is also described. In the Kaśākkudi plates where the grant of *brahmadēyam* to a single brahmin is recorded, the excellence of that brahmin is also described. Then the charters give the location of the grant village and specify whether it was granted as *brahmadēyam* or *dēvadānam.* Where the gift was made as *brahmadēyam*, the grants also say that the grant village got a new name ending in *maṅgalam*, an outline of the boundaries of the village is also given. At this point, the Kaśākkuḍi plates mention that the *dēvadāna-brahmadēyam* and *kuṭumbi* (original inhabitant?) at the rate of two paṭṭis each were excluded from the grant.[17] Then the records mention the beneficiary or beneficiaries if the grant was meant for several brahmins (their total number is also given). The Udayēndram plates of Nandivarman II which do not contain a Tamil text however, lists the brahmin beneficiaries of the *brahmadēyam* grant in the Sanskrit text itself. The Sanskrit texts of the charters also refer to the grant having been made with all exemptions (*sarvvāparihāra*) and with entitlement to irrigation rights. It is the Sanskrit portion which sometimes contains the statement that the gift was to endure till the sun and moon lasted as also the statement that the grant was made with libation of water[18]. In comparison with the elaborate text concerning the details of the grant in the Tamil portion of these records the grant portion looks much truncated in the Sanskrit portion making it appear that the latter was included just to satisfy the vanity of the king.

The reason why the business portion was set out, in detail, (in the portion) only in Tamil might have been because the local authorities and people who were to execute the orders and take cognisance of the grant understood only Tamil. This supposition is supported by the fact that the eulogy of the king is found only in the Sanskrit portion and the Tamil text concentrates on the grant portion after just mentioning the name of the king and the date.

The Tamil text, in most of the charters, after short mention of the name of the king and the date in his regnal year, is usually drafted in the form of an order to the *nāṭṭār*, the body of the *nāḍu* sub-division in which the grant village lay.[19] This body was asked to delimit the grant village by walking around the boundaries,[20] plant stones and the milk-bush to mark the same, then to give the proclamatory order, i. e. to proclaim to the people of the locality that such and such a village had been granted to such and such brahmin/brahmins/temple as also the document for the release, i. e. to release the land for the occupation of the donees.[21] (As this address to the *nāṭṭār* is found only in the Tamil text, it is understandable that this feature is absent in the charters of Toṇḍaimaṇḍalam which have only a Sanskrit text. The Udayēndram charter of Nandivarman I which is in Sanskrit in the form of Guṇṭur-Nellore region charters does not fully follow its prototype even to record the royal address to the locals for their information and necessary action.[21a] However this address to the *nāṭṭār* is also absent in the Kūram grant, probably the earliest of this series of copper-plate charters, as also in the Vēlūrpāḷaiyam plates both of which have a Tamil section. This cannot be explained in the context of the dependence of the kings of the Tamil country during this period on the *nāṭṭār* for local knowlege. It is noteworthy that even in the Vēḷvikkuḍi grant of Paṇdya Māṛañjaḍaiyan (c. 769-70 A.D.) pertaining to the Pāṇḍya country,[22] when a brahmin claimed that the village granted to his ancestor by the king's own ancestor was resumed by the Kalabhra during the interregnum and so must be restored to him, the matter was referred only to the *nāṭṭār* for verification. As according to the Vēlūrpāḷaiyam plates the village Tirukkāṭṭuppaḷḷi granted as *dēvadāna* was severed from the control of the *nāḍu* and made into a fiscal unit by itself, the *naṭṭār* was entitled to be posted with the information of the grant of the village in its nāḍu to the temple and its being taken off from its jurisdiction. Hence the absence of the reference to the address to the *nāṭṭār* in these cases might just nave been an inadvertent omission.

The Tamil section of these grants also refer to the petitioner *vijñapti*, who is sometimes referred to as a chief or as a chief minister, and to the executor *(ājñapti)* who was either a *mantṛī* or *kōśādhyaksha* or *uttaṛakāraṇika*.

Sometimes the Tamil text also gives the detailed description of the boundaries of the land or village granted. Obviously, the *nāṭṭār* in such cases must not have waited for the final issue of the charter to carry out the royal order regarding delimitation but were probably ready with the necessary details even before the draft of the charter was finalised and got engraved. The grant village is usually stated to have included land for pasture, for public purposes, waste land, house sites and such types of land which can be understood to have properly appertained to an agricultural village. Usually the Tamil section of the grants also mentions that *dēvadāna-brahmadēyam* and *kuḍi* at the usual rate of 2 *paṭṭis* in the grant village, has been as excluded from the purview of the grant. Then the Tamil texts refer to the character of the grant made, whether it was *brahmadēyam* or *dēvadāna*. If it was a *brahmadēyam,* the texts also specify if it was made to a single brahmin or to several brahmins in shares. The *gotra*, *sutra* in the case of each such brahmin as also the village from which each one hailed in most cases are detailed.[23]

Where the grant of *brahmadēyam* was made to several brahmins (Udayēndram plates of Nandivarman II, Pullur grant, Tandantōṭṭam plates, Kumaraḍimaṅgalam grant of Nandivarman III and Chitrur grant of Nṛipatuṅga), the charters also indicate the number of shares to which each one of them was entitled. However in the Kūram grant, though the charter says that the village Paramēśvaramaṅgalam was granted as *brahmadēyam* and that 20 of the 25 shares of the village was to be distributed to 20 brahmins, the names of these brahmins are not specified. It does not also specify the amount of shares each one was to receive.[24] In the Paṭṭattāḷmaṅgalam plates, the names etc. of the 15 brahmins who got sixteen *vēlis* of land are given but not the share of each, but the clause in the grant that the gift land would be enjoyed by the nominated brahmins in proportion to their share in the main village seems to have taken care of the proper distribution.[25] In these grants where there was a distribution of the *brahmadēyam* in shares to brahmins, apart from the shares given to the brahmins, whose *gōtra* and *sūtra* are given some shares were also set apart to deities, temples for whom were obviously to come up in the village as also to some miscellaneous persons. The rationale of allotting the shares to miscellaneous persons in the *brahmadēyam* village, however, is not clear. They were not apparently to serve the village. From the titles of such persons, *kiḷān*, *peruntiṇai* etc. it looks as if they were deliberately introduced into the *brahmadēyam* for supervision. Of these grants only the Pullūr grant, says that over and above the allotments of shares to the brahmins, fifteen shares were also set apart on account of village servants. The composer of the *praśasti* and the engraver of the record also were allotted shares in many cases (Kaśākkuḍi, Udayēndram plates of Nandivarman II;(?) and Chitrūr grants). Of these the Kaśākkuḍi plates which record the grant of a village to a single brahmin while saying that two *paṭṭis* of land, and a house-site were set apart for the carpenter-stone mason, do not specify as to where he was to get the land in the gift village or elsewhere.[26]

Some of these grants also refer to the grant as having

been made after changing the *kō* and seal (Paḷḷankōyil grant) or after changing the old possessors (Kaśākkuḍi plates) or after disposing the *kō* and seal and changing the old possessors (Pullūr grant) or disposing of the *kō* and seal (Paṭṭattāḷmaṅgalam grant[27]) or only changing the old possessors (Bāhūr plates and Chiṭṛūr grant of Nṛipatuṅga[28]). This feature is probably connected with the grant of the status of *kō* to the donees with the privilege of not paying the levies to the *kō* and to take and enjoy whatever the *kō* could levy. This phenomenon is discussed, in detail, under the chapter on land control. The *kō* in these cases does not appear to have referred to the king. Then the Tamil section also refers to the new name given to the grant village on its becoming a *brahmadēyam*. The new name had a suffix *maṅgalam* and a prefix referring to a title of the king. When the grant was made in honour of a chief in recognition of services rendered, the prefix in the new name of the village, was the name of the chief as in the case of Udayachandramaṅgalam. In one case i. e. the Udayēndram plates of Parāntaka I (Prithvīpati II) the suffix in the name of the new *brahmadēyam* complex was *chēri* instead of *maṅgalam* and the prefix in the name was a title of the king.

The Tamil section of the grants also contains the statement that the grants were made with *sarvva-parihāra*, but such mention is usually followed by a list of the *parihāras*. As will be discussed below, the reference to *parihāras* in these charters, does not seem to have been intended to signify only exemptions. Sometimes they are specifically stated to have been entitlements.[28a] In many cases the list includes the house, house-site, loom and such which were clearly entitlements. However, there are also items in the list which apparently were taxes and such levies. But even in respect of these items one cannot generalise that at least those were exemptions. Whereas the Kaśākkuḍi plates indicate that such items under the *parihāras* were such that were exempted from payment. Many of the other records refer to the items listed under the *parihāras* as levies which the *kō* could collect and enjoy, which, either it is said that he would not collect or that the beneficiary/beneficiaris in the grant would himself/themselves collect and enjoy. But in none of the charters, there is any item reflecting the land-tax, in the list of *parihāras*. Only the *Bāhūr* plates refer to the grant as having been made with *sarvva-parihāra* and at the same time protected from taxes (*a-karatvēnarakshitān*)[28b].

In the Tamil portion of the grants the list of *parihāras* is usually followed by a list of privileges sometimes referred to as *Vyavasthai* to which the donee/donees would be entitled. It usually includes the right to raise mansions with burnt bricks to live in, plant cocoanut and arecanut trees as also special flower plants, exercise their discretion in the matter of allowing toddy-tappers to utilise the cocoanut and palmyrah trees in the precincts of their village, etc. The grantees are also stated to have been granted the privilege to fill up wells and ponds, as necessary. The most significant among the privileges granted were the irrigation privileges, which included the right to cut channels from the river to the reservoir and therefrom and exercise exclusive jurisdiction over these channels that were dug at their initiative, and to fine transgressors. These privileges are seen to have been extended only where the grant was made as *brahmadēyam*. The implications of this feature is discussed under the chapter on land control. Some of these grants (Paḷḷankōyil, Kaśākkuḍi, Pullūr, Vēlūrpāḷaiyam, Bāhūr and Chiṭṟūr charters) state that they had been made as *paradatti*.[29]

Some of these grants also contain at the end, some imprecatory verses in Sanskrit extolling the merit of gifting land as well as of protecting the gift of another and the heavenly punishment ordained against anyone disturbing the gift.[30]

Though the charters issued by the Chōḷas, who succeeded the Pallavas in Toṇḍaimaṇḍalam are also bilingual, there is a difference in the pattern of the draft. It appears that this was due to the change in the character of the kingship. The Chōḷa monarchs concerned themselves with the details of the administration of land in every nook and corner of their territory in contrast to the Pallavas who seem to have left such details to local organisations. There was also a shift in the emphasis with regard to *brahmadēyam* and *dēvadānam*. This difference in form might also have been due to the difference in the type of the grant. In the two charters of Chōḷas pertainig to Toṇḍaimaṇḍalam and to the 10th century, one of them, the Udayēndram plates of Parāntaka I as already mentioned, records the addition of a village to the already existing *brahmadēyam*. The distinguishing feature of this grant of *brahmadēyam*, the non-mention of exemption and privileges accompanying the grant, might have been due to the implication that *brahmadēyam* of Udayachandramaṅgalam would enjoy those exemptions and privileges they were already enjoying, in respect of the additional village also. However this fact was specifically stated in the earlier Bāhūr plates óf Nṛipatuṅga which also referred to the addition of villages to an existing *brahmadēyam*. But unlike the latter, where in the purpose of attachment was stated, the Udayēndram plates of Parāntaka I do not indicate the purpose for which a village was added to Udayachandramaṅgalam. There is no address to the *nāṭṭār* but they were assembled to delimit the additional village granted. The other copper-plate record, the Madras Museum plates of UttamaChōḷa is not a grant but is a record of the arrangement made under royal direction for the proper administration of the income of a temple at Kāñchīpuram. This latter record is almost entirely in Tamil, a Sanskrit text probably giving the gist of the contents recorded in Tamil being a caricature. But the Tiruvālaṅgāḍu plates of Rājēndra I issued just after the turn of the tenth century in 1018, definitely marks a change in the pattern of the charters. Even by the end of the 10th century, there are evidences of the devaluation of the *nāṭṭār* probably consequent on the village organisations strengthening themselves in the local adminisrative set-up and taking over several of the functions of the *nāṭṭār*. In the Tirumālpuram stone inscription of the time of UttamaChōḷa (986) recording the royal decision on the possession of a bloc of land granted as *dēvadāna*, the *nāṭṭār* was assembled along with the village organisations probably only for consultation and for witnessing the royal decision. But all other functions regarding the execution and recording of the royal order was left to a host of officials. In the Tiruvālangāḍu plates of Rājendra I (1018) which also records the grant of a village as *dēvadāna*, the *nāṭṭār* are seen to have been expected to play only a minor role. Though it delimited the grant-village, its function was supervised by officials.

In the grants of Toṇḍaimaṇḍalam no mention is made as to how the donee would have the land cultivated, and whether artisans were attached for serving them. The admonition to the locals to desist from interfering with the gift and to obey the donees, a feature which forms part of the grants of central India is also absent in these charters.

INSCRIPTIONS ON STONE

The copper-plate charters of Toṇḍaimaṇḍalam supply a good amount of information on how the brahmins and temples were introduced into the land system but their scope is limited. For instance these charters do not clarify as to what was handed over to the brahmins—land or only rights over the land and where the grant was made in shares to brahmins, how they were to arrange to enjoy what was granted. Many of these gaps in information are filled by the numerous stone inscriptions of the period, which not only augment the information available from the copper-plate charters but also supply new information on the land system such as fertility of the land, preparation of the land for cultivation, land measures, yield, price of the land and taxes on land.

Some of the charter-like orders of the king are also found inscribed on stone. It is possible that these orders had also been committed to copper.[30a] But in the absence of the copper-plates in respect of these grants the information contained in these stone inscriptions becomes invaluable. For instance only the stone inscription from Kīḷ-Muṭṭugūr dated in the reign of Narasiṅgavarman[31] informs of the practice of the period to invest *brahmadēyam* rights in respect of land already held by a brahmin. The Tirukkalukkuṛam inscription of *Vaṭāpi-koṇḍa*—Narasimhavarman I[32] evidences the start of the practice of attaching villages as *puṛam* of a temple. But such stone inscriptions of the period are short without the frills of the copper-plate charters.[33]

A host of other stone records contain the details of transactions inland which are very helpful in understanding the land system of the period. They not only supplement the information available from the charters, they also help us to guage the meaning of the difficult phrases contained in the charters. They, being records of transactions, give us a picture of the land system in operation and the conditions obtaining at the time. They help us to estimate the spread of *dēvadānam* and *brahmadēyam* villages, the charters being a few and incomplete. It is only they that supply the information on the village organisations which were very much concerned with the land system. Only the stone inscriptions throw some light on the types of land-holding other than *brahmadēyam* and *dēvadānam*.

The inscriptions recorded on stone pertaining to Toṇḍai-maṇḍalam and to the period under study are quite a good number, but even so it was not found advisable to study them in isolation. For amplification and elucidation of the information supplied by the set of epigraphs from Toṇḍaimaṇḍalam, epigraphs not only of the immediately earlier and later periods from the same region but also of the immediately earlier contemporary and latter periods from the regions surrounding Toṇḍai-maṇḍalam has also been taken into account.

The stone inscriptions can be classified into two varieties on the basis of their provenance. One variety consists of the records inscribed on stray stones and the other is the large number of records inscribed on temple walls. Further classification of the epigraphs can also be done in several other ways on the basis of the contents of the epigraphs.

Those of the donative type can be further classified on the basis of who was the beneficiary and the class of the donor whether the beneficiary was a temple or an individual or groups of individuals in institutions or other institutions requiring public maintenance of whether it was the king who initiated the record or an official or a chief or an institution or an individual, etc. All these classes of the inscriptions provide material for the history of the period.

The inscriptions on stray stones are only a few but those on temple walls are a good number. By their very nature, the two sets of records differ in their purpose and contents. The stray stones contain records of the setting up of an irrigation reservoir[34] or of the endowment for its maintenance, both by kings[35] and others[36] or of heroic deeds performed by individuals (hero-stones)[37] or of a sacrifice made by an individual.[37a] As such, these stray stone records where they refer to gifts of land or to irrigation facilities give fresh and very pertinent information on the land system. The inscriptions on temple walls are plenty,[38] but they record almost invariably transactions connected with the temple, gifts of gold, sheep or land to the temple, by kings, chiefs, members of the royal family, village organisations and individuals and the scheme of utilisation of the income in the temple. The temple records incidentally throw a flood of light on the practices concerning land and on the functioning of the village organisations of whom information is not available from any other source.[39] The inscriptions on the temple walls sometimes also contain decisions on the organisational matters concerning the *sabhā*,[39a] whose meeting used to take place in the temple premises[40]. Sometimes records concerning community matters like benefactions for maintenance of reservoirs also found a place on the temple walls.[41]

The stone inscriptions invariably in Tamil so far as Toṇḍaimaṇḍalam was concerned are business like and give precise and pointed information. In the early period, till the advent of Rājarājāchoḷa I at the end of the 10th century when the king was began to be introduced in the record with an eulogy describing his exploits (*praśasti* or *meykirtti*)[42] the records usually started with just mentioning the name of the king and the date in his regnal reckoning and straightaway began giving the details of the transaction. Sometimes when the record inscribed, referred to a benefaction to carry out a service in the temple, it ended with the invocation of the protection to the benefaction by the bodies, *paṇmāhēśvarar or srīvaishaṇavar* or even of the *sabhā*.

With such a concentration of information in the epigraphs, a good part of it concerning the land system these records are very useful for writing the history of the land system.

However it can be pointed out that whether it was the copper-plate charters or the stone inscriptions all of them deal exclusively with the upper strata society, (i. e.) those that were in a position to make gifts of land or other commodities and their organisation.[43] While information on the technology employed in the cultivation is almost absent, there is complete absence of information on the labouring class and their relationship with the land. However, with the material available a fairly good picture of the system can be drawn. The inscriptions have been made available for study in various forms by the government. A systematic attempt at copying the inscriptions throughout the then Madras Presidency was taken up by the Government of that Presidency by appointing an Epigraphist in 1886. He used to collect the estampages of a good number of inscriptions each year and issue annual reports on the collection giving a detailed discussion on the important information contained in the collection in an introductory part and then just listing the inscriptions indicating the dynasty, king, date and character of the epigraphs. Slowly the remarks column against each number in the lists in the annual reports began to expand to give more details and the introductory part also took the form of a critical analysis of the information supplied by the epigraphs listed in the issue concerned. Some significant inscriptions were selected and were published in a series entitled "South Indian Inscriptions", the first volume of which was published in 1890. The first three Volumes of this series contained the full texts of the epigraphs included and their translation in English. For each number, an introduction was also given discussing the place of the epigraph in the history of South India. From Volume IV (published in 1923) however, the policy was revised to speed up the publication of the mounting collection by giving the bare texts of the inscriptions collected yearwise.[44] This policy was pursued uptil the VIII Volume of the series (published in 1937), With this volume only the collections uptil the year 1903 could be covered. In the post-World war II era, a different style was attempted to bring the bulk of important inscriptions before the students. Selections of the inscriptions were made dynasty-wise and published in the Volumes XII, XIII, XIV and XIX. The Volumes XII and XIV dealt with a selection of Pallava and Pāṇḍya inscriptions and the Volumes XIII and XIX, a selection of Chōḷa inscriptions which respectively quoted the reigns of merely a Rājakēsari or a Parakēsarivarman whose identities were in doubt. In this series, along with the texts, a short introduction to each number was reintroduced though no translation of the texts was given. Again there was a change in policy and the policy of making a haphazard selection was abandoned. Publication of the yearwise collection of the epigraphs was revived and the collection during the year 1903-04 was published in Volume XVII in 1964. The collections in the year 1906-07 have been published recently in a Volume XXVI. In this series also, the practice of giving the text of each inscription with a short introduction and doing away with the translation has been kept up.

In 1903 the epigraphy department of the Government of Madras was taken over by the Government of India under the Archaeological Department but still the Annual Reports of the Epigraphy Department were confined to reporting the collections in Madras Presidency only and they were designated as annual Reports on South India Epigraphy till the year ending 31 March 1945. Since the year 1945-46, a new series entitled Annual Report on Indian Epigraphy to cover all the inscriptions discovered and copied throughout India during the year instead of only in South India began to be issued.

A scholarly and critical appraisal of the year's collection in the midst of earlier collections and also in the light of literary and other material continues to be given in the introductory part.

Apart from the above, some epigraphs which appealed to a scholar as significant and important were edited in articles in *Epigraphia Indica,* Volumes and some other journals like *Indian antiquary*. Here also, in the earlier stages, the authors of the articles included translations of the texts of the inscriptions but this was dispensed with as time went by. Now there is a Department of Archaeology under the Government of Madras which also interests itself in the subject and there is also an Archaeological Society of South India which published the Proceedings of their meetings or Seminars which usually centre on inscriptions.

Literary material for the period and region under study can be said to consist of the panegyric *Nandikkalambagam* dealing with the exploits of Nandivarman III[45] and the hymns of the *Nāyanārs* and *Ālvārs*. whereas the former does not contain any reference to the land system except perhaps to a feeding house at Mylapore,[46] the latter could have provided useful material for the present purpose but unfortunately in the absence of a systematic and analytical study of them, it was not possible to utilise this source here.[47]

The history of Toṇḍaimaṇḍalam, as such not to speak of a specialised study of its land system, has not received the attention of scholars so far. Monographs both on the general history of south India and on some imperial dynasties have been written and they invariably include some chapters on the administrative, social, religious, literary and economic aspects.[48] Some independent treatises on the history of administrative, social, as well as the economic aspects including the land system of selected regions or again of the region south of the Vindhyas have also been written. One study is devoted to the study of land system of south India. But each one of them either treats the whole of peninsular India as one unit or covers long periods.

It was Prof. K.A. Nilakanta Sastri who first undertook the task of studying the social, economic and administrational aspects of the History of Tamilnadu. His "Studies in *Chōḷa History and Administration*" was published as early as 1932. But he himself had to modify his conclusions in his further publications, which while concentrating on the dynastic aspect of the history, also devoted due attention to the other aspects. His, *"The Chōḷas"* was first published in two volumes between the years 1935 and 1937. He balanced the work as between the political and other aspects and devoted as many as six chapters for the latter. Though in this work he has dealt with the different aspects of the land system, the very scope of the work which has covered the whole of Chōḷa dominion and the period from about the end of the 9th century to about the middle of the 13th century limited his treatment of the subject. His other work "*A History of South India from Prehistoric Times to the Fall of Vijayanagar*" (1966), which has devoted a chapter social and Economic condition (26 pages) suffers from the same limitation.[49]

The first dynastic history pertaining to the region "*The History of the Pallavas of Kānchī*" was published in 1928 written by R. Gopalan. This author covered the history of this dynasty from the time it was based in the Guṇṭur-Nellore region in the 3rd century A.D. to the end of the 9th century. In a chapter under the heading "Pallava rule in south India", he has devoted a section each for the subjects, administration, nature of village government, taxation and revenue. But as the work is devoted mainly to political history, only limited information on the other aspects is given.

Minakshi, C.'s "*The Administration and Social Life under the Pallavas*" (1938) is probably the earliest full length treatise devoted entirely to the non-political aspects of south Indian history. Under the section, administration, the chapters deal with Ministry: Revenue and Taxation; Weights and Measures; Water supply and irrigation; famines, provincial and local Governments and the economic life of the village. But like

Gopalan, she has also clubbed together the two periods of Pallava rule in the Guṇṭur-Nellore region in the 3rd-5th centureis A.D. and in the Toṇḍaimaṇḍalam region in the 6th to 9th centuries. However, as she has utilised all available material and has tried to interpret them her work is of some use for the present study.[50]

T. V. Mahalingam's *"South Indian Polity"*(1955) also covers the same region and period as does Sastri's *"History of South India"*. He has got a chapter on taxation under which a section has been devoted to land Revenue system and a chapter each on local government and kingship. Though a scholarly study, it suffers from the drawbacks consequent on the vastness of the region and period covered.

A. Appadorai in his *"The Economic Conditions in South India"* 1000-1500 A.D. (1936?) has confined himself mainly to the region south of Āndhra. He has utilised all available material. But has not paid attention to regional variations and to the evolutionary aspect of the institutions.[51]

Deepak Ranjan Das's *"The Economic History of the Deccan"* (from the first to sixth century A.D.) (1969) is a concentrated study competently dealt with. His idea of Deccan covers that part of South India north of 13° 49 north latitude, i. e. the region excluding the Tamil country. He has devoted a chapter each on land; Revenue System; Agriculture; Forests and Famine and Irrigation. However, he often refers to the institutions in the Tamil country and his conclusions even though pertinent to the region selected by him have some relevance to the present study.

Recently, A. Vaidehi Krishnamurtti has published her work *"Social and economic conditions in Eastern Deccan"* (1970) wherein she has restricted herself to a portion of the area dealt with by D. R. Das[52].

K. M. Gupta has tried to make a particular study of the land system in his *"Land Systems in South India* (800-1200 A.D.)" (1933) which, *prima facie*, appears to be very close to the present study. However in so far as he treats the whole of peninsular India as one region and has not systematically utilised the local source material available the usefulness of his work has been rendered for more limited than that of the other books mentioned above.[53]

Burton Stein has been writing several articles bearing on the agrarian system and society in medieval South India (i. e.) Tamilnāḍu. He contributed an article, "The State and Agrarian Order in Medieval South India—A Historiographical Critique," to and edited a collection of articles in "*Essays on South India*" (1975) and more recently came out with a publication, *Peasant State and Society in Medieval South India*. All these evidence the intense research he has made. But he has concerned himself mostly with the Chōḷa period of the History of Tamil-nāḍu, when several institutions founded during the Pallava period had reached the zenith of their activity and had probably passed their acme of glory. He has not devoted attention to the circumstances under which these institutions were reared during the Pallava period.

Apart from the above treatise, there is a short monograph "*Studies in the Ancient History of Toṇḍaimaṇḍalam*" by R. Sathianathaier (1944) being the lectures delivered by the author as the Sankara parvati Endowment lectures under the University of Madras in Feb. 1944. It contains some statistics on the *Mahāsabhā* and inscriptions dealing with *Mahāsabhā* in the body of the lecture and in two appendices which are useful. The Journal "Indian Culture", Vol. XII contains an article on "*The History of Irrigation in South India*" by V.R.R. Dikshitar (p. 71 f). Though covering the whole period from ancient times to the end of the Vijayanagar period, this article also contains some useful information.

In this context, one cannot fail to mention the great usefulness of the introduction or Part II included in each annual Report on Epigraphy published by the Government.

All the above works have dealt with vast regions as one unit and have also covered long periods.[54] Due to their very nature, they did not pay due attention to the fact that Peninsular India consists of different regions, each one differing from the others in geographical and other attendant conditions including historical influences which affected the course of their development. Though covering long periods the above treatises did not take into consideration the evolutionary aspect that was endemic with every human institution. However each one of them has made a contribution and has laid the framework for future researchers to proceed further and concentrate on tracing the course of the several aspects of history in selected regions and selected periods.

NOTES

1. There are no extant records of the period under study inscribed on palm leaves. The references to *ōlai* (communication conveyed through palmleaf) as in *kōn-ōlai* (the chief's letter containing his order or to Tirumandiraolai-nayakam) (the head of the department of royal orders) certainly point to the fact that the palm leaf was also in use even for recording royal orders but the royal direction in later records, that his order regarding a grant should be committed only to stone and copper evidences that the king was aware of the impermanence of the palm leaf and the limitations of its use for record purposes, (cf. *EI.* 31, 263-264 An instance of the loss of palm leaf record in a fire is also evidenced).
2. Though most of the epigraphs can be relied upon, some of these records are also capable of misleading the student. Hence they are to be accepted only after proper examination and evaluation. Usually they contain elements which, on careful study, will enable the student to assess their genuineness. For instance some of these records are later copies of original records, the re-engraving or reinscribing having been rendered necessary due to several circumstances. This fact is sometimes found recorded in a preamble to the record (e.g. *SII,* 74, 896; S.I.I., III, 43). In such cases sometimes the inscriber is seen to have tried to copy the palaeography of the old record. But ordinarily the scribe of the recopy adopted the style of writing pertinent to his own period. Even where the fact of recopying is not revealed in the record a study of the contents enables the student to understand the genuineness or otherwise the record. Still some records, like the

Kilmuttugur inscription of Narasingappottaraiyar or the copper-plate records like the Udayēndram plates of Nandivarman I, Rōyakōṭṭāh plates of Skandasishya and Paḷḷankōyil plates of Simhavarman, remain a puzzle for the student. Forgeries of copper-plate grants are also not unknown, (cf. Sharma, R.S., *Light on Early Indian Society and Economy,* pp. 110, 212; Marc Bloch, *Feudal Society* (1974), p. 91; Sircar, D.C.

3. cf. Sastri, K.A.N., *A History of south India*, p. 13; The *Chōḷas*, pp. 4f.
4. That the Pallavas did not belong to the Toṇḍaimaṇḍalam or Tamil-nāḍu region is made evident by their very names and approach to the problems of government. They introduced a new fashion in the Tamil country which was not confined to copper-plate charters, *brahmadēyam* and *dēvadāna* but also extended to names. Against Kaduṅgōn, Karikāla, Kōchcheṅgaṇān, Peruvaḷudi etc. of the Saṅgam period, subsequent to the eighth century even the purely Tamil kings of the Chōḷa or Pāṇḍya time bore names like Vijayāḷaya, Parāntaka, Rājarāja, Vīranarāyaṇa, Rājakēsarivarman etc.
5. The Udayēndram plates of Nandivarman I, the Rōyakōṭṭāh plates of Skandasishya and Paḷḷankōyil plates of Simhvarman, no doubt, purport to belong to the period earlier to the 7th century but they are incised in characters of 8th-9th centuries. It is possible that the grants were made in the reign-periods of the kings whose name and date are quoted therein and due to the loss of the original which was probably written on perishable material like palm-leaf they had to be copied in about the 8th century which was done on copper-plates in the characters pertinent to the time of recopying. But whereas the draft of the Nandivarman I's record is fully in Sanskrit and is also similar in form to the charters of The Pallavas of the Guṇṭur-Nellore region of the 3-5th centuries A.D. and hence seems to have been re copied *verbatim* from the original, the other two are bilingual and in form similar to other Pallava charters of 8-9th centuries, which suggests that they were not only recopied but also redrafted. On the other hand all the three records could be spurious. (Mahalingam, T.V., has tried to identify the Skandasishya of this record with Chitramaya, the rival of Nandivarman II Pallava to the throne (*Readings in South Indian History,* p. 33-41). It is noteworthy that all the charters from Udayēndram excepting the postscript dated in the reign of Parāntaka I engraved on the two charters of Nandivarman I and II and the other wholly issued by him, are entirely in Sanskrit.

6. There is an identical postscript dated year 26 (933) in the reign of Madiraikoṇḍa Parakēsarivarman (Parāntaka-Chōḷa I) in the Udayēndram plates of both Nandivarman I and II. It records only the resolve of the sabhās of Udayachandramaṅglam and Kāñchivāyil alias Igaṇmaṛaimaṅgalam to live as one *ūr*.

6a. But if these records are genuine and are only later copies, then these grants would pertain to the pre-seventh century period.

7. But it will be erroneous to conclude that these were all the brahmins introdudced into or granted land in Toṇḍaimaṇḍalam during the period. For instance, the inscriptions from Uttaramallūr or Uttaramēru-chaturvēdi-maṅgalam, as it was called under its *brahmadēyam* name has produced inscriptions from the year 7 (803) of Dantivarman (*SII.*, VI, 365). As even in this early record the *sabhā* of the place was well organised, the *brahmadēyam* and the *sabhā* must have been in existence for some time before 803. Though no charter granting this *brahmadēyam* has so far revealed itself, from the fact that earlier than 803, no stone inscriptions from this place have been found, it can also be surmised that this *brahmadēyam* was created not long before that date. So it must have come into existence in the 8th century. There is no information as to the number of brahmins who were settled originally in the village. On the other hand, it has been noted above that Paramēśvaramaṅgalam was created with 20 brahmins according to the Kūram plates. But as the brahmins were not named, it is likely that the 20 brahmins were to be chosen from the 108 *chaturvēdi* brahmins from Kūram, which is said to have had that number of brahmin families. Obviously the 20 brahmins introduced (?) into Paramēsvaramaṅgalam were not new imports. The families of *chaturvēdi* brahmins at Kūram must have been residing there since long before the reign of Paramēśvaravarman. But as it is likely that the practice of granting villages as *brahmadēyam* of the type to be discussed below, to the brahmins started only with the time of Paramēśvaravarman, 'the brahmins of Kūram were not in enjoyment of *brahmadēyam* rights of this special type. In the same way, the Kaśākkuḍi plates of Nandivarman II (753) also says that the lone donee of the *brahmadēya* grant, Jyēshṭapāda Somayaji hailed from Puniya, a *brahmalōkam* in *Tuṇḍaka rāshtra* (*Toṇḍaimaṇḍalam*). To gain the reputation of being a *brahmalokam*, there must have been a good number of brahmins residing at Puniya for

quite a long time previous to 753. It is noteworthy that neither Kūram nor Puniya is described as a *brahmadēyam*.

8. *SII.*, XII, p. 176. Paduvūr-kkōṭṭam is said to have contained parts of Arkonam, Walajahpet, Velur and Gudiyattam taluks of North Arcot District.
9. *Ibid.* Palkunra-kkōṭṭam is said to have contained parts of Ārṇi, Pōḷūr and Wandiwash taluks of North Arcot District.
10. cf. *SII.*, XII, p. 108.

10a. cf. S11, XII, p. 76 and *SII.*, XIX, p. 313. Nallimaṅgalam (same as modern Puduppakkam in Kāñchīpuram taluk of Chingleput district) is said to be situated in Merapaḷugūr-nāḍu in Maṇaiyir-kōṭṭam.

11. cf. *SII.*, XII, p. 103

11a. cf. *SII.*, XIII, p. 82

12. *Ibid.*, p. 176.
13. For instance there were Jain institutions at Pañchapāṇḍavamalai, Tirumalai etc.
14. In Tiruvālaṅgāḍu plates of Rājendra I, the Village, Paḷiyanūr, granted as *dēvadāna*, is stated to have been in Perumūr-nāḍu and no name of the *kōṭṭam* division under which this Perumūr-nāḍu came is given. But from the list of the kōṭṭams and the constituent *naḍus* given by Kanaka*sabhā*i (*op. cit.*, p. 29) it is ascertained that Perumur-nāḍu was situated in Manavūr or Maṇaiyir- kōṭṭam.
15. This term can be translated as one who took note of or took down the royal order and as one who executed the order. But he seems to have been rather the secretary to record the royal utterances or orders (Chōḷa records refer to a *Tiruvāykkēḷvi,* who heard-what emanated from the mouth of the exalted one and communicated the same to the concerned persons for execution. All the official procedures from the time the king uttered the order till it reached the proper person or body in-charge of the administration of the locality was his responsibility).

    The details of the execution was taken care of by the local bodies or authorities. But here, for convenience, he is referred to as the 'executor'. In the charters of the Pallavas of the earlier period pertaining to the Guṇṭur-Nellore region, whereas no *vijñapti* is referred to, the Gunapateya grant of Chārudevi (in Prākrit—where the *ājñapti* is termed as āṇatti as in Tamil records), Yesanta grant of Siṁhavarman, Rēyūru grant of Narasimhavarman and Vunnagu-ravāyapalem plates of Paramēśvaravarman refer to the *ājñapṭi* for the record. In the Vesanta grant he was a *rahasyādhikṛita* and in the Reyuru grant and Vunnaguruvāyapalaiyam plates the *ājñap tis* were the chiefs (*nripēsvara*) of Nandikuṟṟu.

16. cf., *EI*, XXXVI, p. 152, text-line 12. The phrase which has been read as *dharma-krit-arttham* reads clearly as *dharmma-krityarttham* on the facsimile published in the reference.
17. The Udayēndram plates of Nandivarman II refers to the annihilation of evil-doers before making a grant of the village (*anyān-adhaṛma-kritvān-vināśya*). However, its significance is not clear. It does not appear that other religions like Jains were exterminated for making the grant (Jayaswal, Suvira, 'Studies in the Social Structure of Early Tamils", *Indian Society—Historical Probings*, p. 151). If the grant of Nandivarman I from the same place is genuine, it will indicate that there was already a brahmin settlement at Kāñchīvāyil adjacent to the village Udayachandramaṅgalam granted as brahmadēyam by Nandivarman II. The grant village in the plates of Nandivarman II appears to have consisted of only virgin land before the grant.
18. The stipulations connected with the grant are not found in each charter. The Pullūr grant does not refer to the accompaniment of the exemptions and privileges in the Sanskrit text. The reference to the sun and moon is found only in the Chiṭṛūr and Paṭṭ attāḷmaṅgalam grants and to the libations of water only in the Pullūr plates.
19. In the Rōyakōṭṭāh plates of Skandaśishya, the *nāṭṭār* and *Kōṭṭattāṛ* (the body, of the main kōṭṭam division) were addressed and in the Kasākkuḍi plates the *nāṭṭār* of the kōṭṭam division itself were addressed.
20. The phrase employed to signify this operation is *piḍāgai-naḍandu* or *paḍāgai-vaḷañjeydu*. The term *paḍagai* or *piḍagai* in stone inscriptions meant a hamlet or attached sub-village. It might have been so called because it was at the boundary. It is not known if this term is connected with piḍi., the Tamil term for the she elephant which is stated to have been used in one instance (Rōyakōṭ ṭāh plates of Skandasishya) in Toṇḍaimaṇḍalam for negotiating the boundaries. In the Pāṇḍya copper-plate grants also there are references to the use of the she-elephant for the purpose. For demarcation of boundaries the *nāṭṭār* often took the help of a functionary of the nāḍu for recognising the boundaries. The functionary is referred to as *viyavan* which has been translated as

accountant, which seems reasonable, as Rōyakkōṭṭāh plates say that the *nāṭṭār* took the help of the she-elephant as also the *karaṇa* (which means accountant) of the temple. However, Dr. T.V. Mahalingam translates the word as headman (*EI,* XXXIV, p. 146). It is noteworthy that the term *viyayan* is used in the same context as the accountant of a *ūr* in an inscription of a Rājakēsari from Kāñchīpuram (*SII.*, I, 84).

21. The phrase used to indicate this direction, in the Pullūr, Chiṭṟūr and Paṭṭattāḷmaṅgalam grants, *viḍunda* by itself seems to have conveyed the intended meaning. There does not seem to be any necessity to amend it to *viḍu-tanda* (*EI.*, XXXVI, p. 157, 103).

21a. cf. Sharma, R. S., "Rajasāsana", PIHC, 37th Session (Calicut) 1976, pp. 72, 78; *Ind. Feud*, pp. 139-40 and Maity, S. K., *op. cit.*, p. 29-30. The information of the grant by the king to the village inhabitants and assembly has been interpreted as an indication of the community of rights as between the king and the villagers. The Pallava grants pertaining to the Guṇṭur-Nellore region are usually in the form of a royal communication directed to the *grāmēyakas* of the grant-village, not only for their information but also to ask them and the local officials to give effect to the exemptions granted to the donee and also to see to it that the donee was exempted and was allowed trouble-free enjoyment of the land (e. g. Vasanta grant of Vijayasimhavarman, C. P., *Ins. of A. P. Govt. Museum*. Hyderabad, Vol. II, p. 211f, Nedungaraye grant of yuvamahārāja Vishṇugōpa). But in the Toṇḍaimaṇḍalam charters, the role of the *nāṭṭār* who were addressed was restricted to the delimitation of the boundaries of the grant village and to giving publicity to the fact of the grant. Maity's conclusion (*op. cit.*, p. 63) that the formality of informing responsible village elders etc. of the grant was intended to ensure that they investigated the circumstances of the grant-land to see to it that no injustice was done, seems to be borne out by the Toṇḍaimaṇḍalam charters. However, Sastri, K.A.N., Minakshi and T. N. Subramanian think that it was the phrase *kuḍi-nīkki* occuring in a different context in the Toṇḍaimaṇḍalam grants referred to the anxiety of the king that the least harm was occassioned for the *kuḍi*. *(eg. TN Subrahmanian, Thirty Pallava Copper Plates,* p. 18)

22. *EI,* XVII, pp. 291f.

23. cf. Sharma, R. S., 'Rajasasana', Proc. IHC, 1976 (Calicut), p. 73.

24. The possible explanation for this has been discussed under the land control.

25. Actually, apart from the engraver who is said to have hailed from Aimpanai(punai)chchēri of Kachchippēdu and who is titled Viḍēlviḍugu-*peruntachchaṉ* of the sixteen persons mentioned, the last one Dēvarchadan Āinnūṟṟuvan is not credited with any gōtra etc. and hence does not appear to have been a *brahmadēya* recipient. Whereas for the first thirteen no share entitlement is specified, the last two of the fifteen brahmins are said to have been entitled to only half a share each.

26. The usual terms used is *kāṣṭakāri* which means actually wood worker or carpenter. It is possible that the writing was done in negative and embossed on wood first which became a mould on which the molten copper was poured whereby the writing was etched on the copper plates. But this would have been a laborious process. Hence it appears that the *Kāṣṭakāri* used to engrave the record straight on the copper plates.

27. Originally the editor of the plates had read this phrase as *kōvum poriyum tirandu* (*EI*, XVIII, pp. 122, 36-37) which on the plates actually reads as *atirndu* (Also cf. *EI* XXXVI, p. 143).

28. *Poṛi* means insignia or distinguishing mark, Minakshi, C., (*op. cit.*, p. 45.). quoting *Nandikkalambakam* (verse 11) says that the *pori* of Nandivarman III was *viḍel-viḍugu,* which was a title. Also *EI,* XXXVI, p. 134 and n. 1. The editor of the Pullur plates describes the seven *poris* or *lāñchhanas.* Also ibid., p. 143. A Panchalin gāla (Kurnool District, A. P.) inscription of Bhuvanaikamalla, (line 21-22) says that the king in Saka 990 (1068 A.D.) granted land to the god with *rājya-chinhas.*

28a. It is noteworthy that in the Kūram grant, while the Sanskrit text says that the grant was made with *saṛvva-parihāra*, the Tamil text lists some items which are said to have been such that the donees could enjoy in proportion to their shares. For the lists of parihāras in Central Indian charters, see Maity, S.K.., *op. cit.*, pp. 64-66.

28b. cf. Ghosal, U. N., The Agrariyan, systems in ancient India, pp. 46-48.

29. Discussed below under the chapter on land Control.

30. The verse *Bhūmidānāt param dāṇam* etc. was most popular and is quoted in Kūram, Kaśākkuḍi and Pullūr charters. The latter two quote the verse *sva-daṭṭām para—dattām vā* etc. in addition. The Kasākkuḍi charter cites in addition the verse *Bahubhirvasudhā* etc. which alone is quoted in the Royakkōṭṭah plates. The Pullūr grant gives a new verse *Rakshā pīṭi cha etc*. The Kumāradi-

manglam grant just records a request of Nandivarmmā to all rulers to protect the grant.

30a. Later kings of the Tamil country used to direct that their orders regarding grants be committed to both stone and copper, (e. g. *SII.*, XVII, p. 170)

31. *EI,* IV, pp. 177-78.

32. *AREp*, 1909, 65; MEM. A*SI.*, 17, pp. 19-21.

33. However some inscriptions like the Piḷḷaippākkam (Chingleput district) inscription of the period of Dantivarman (*SII.*, XII, p. 44) and the. Mallam (Nellore district) inscription of Nandivarman III cite *vijñapṭis* and *ājñaptis* for the grants. However the *parihāras* and privileges are not found in these records. These paraphernalia came to be featured regularly in the royal orders recorded on stone in later periods. In these later records the exemptions or entitlements were not termed *parihāra*. (Butterworth and Venugopal chetty, *Nellore District Inscriptions*, Pt. I, p. 429; also Kāñchīpuram inscription of Nandivarman III,—Madras Christian College Magazine, Vol. VIII, p. 102.

34. Mahēndravāḍi (Near Sholinghur, Walajahpet taluk, North Arcot district) inscription of Gunabhara (Mahendraverman I) (EI., IV, p. 152). This record says that the king excavated a reservoir (taṭāka) and, a Viṣṇu temple (Viṣṇu-griham).

35. Shōliṅghūr inscription of Parāntaka I (*EI,* IV, p. 221) which says that the king granted a field and the tax income from the same for the maintenance of *chōḷa-vāṛidhi*, the irrigation reservoir.

36. *SII.*, XII, p. 97 (Pōṛpandal); 102 (Kīḻppudūr). Both the records are from Chingleput district and are dated in the reign of Kampavarman. They refer to the arrangements made for the maintenance of the local reservoirs with a pro-rata levy from the fields utilising the water from the reservoirs, A Madam (Wandiwash Taluk, North Arcot District) inscription of the time of Kampavarman (*Ibid.* 110) records a grant. of land as *ērippaṭṭi* by a private person.

37. *EI,* IV, pp. 180-183. Two Āmbūr (Velur taluk, North Arcot district) inscriptions of the time of Nṛipatuṅga; *EI,* XXIII, p. 147—Mēlpaṭ ṭi (Gudiyattam taluk, North Arcot district) inscription of the time of Kampavarman.

37a. *SII.*, XII, p. 106—Mallam (Gudur Taluk, Nellore District) inscription of the time of Kampavarman which records the offer of his head to goddess Bhaṭāraki by an individual and a grant of land in commemoration to the goddess as *toṛupaṭṭi*.

38. The plentitude of the inscriptions on temple walls can be explained in two ways. One, the period 700-1000 witnessed a spate of temple construction, carving out temples out of rocks predominating in the period upto 700, structural stone temples taking over thereafter, thus providing ample space for inscribing the records of even a trivial gifts of sheep for a lamp to be burnt in a temple. The other factor was the religious revival during this period. On the one hand this spurt in religious fervour goaded the temple building activity and on the other impelled the people to make gifts to temples and temple based activities as recorded in these numerous temple wall inscriptions. From a study of the inscriptions of the period one would be tempted to conclude that the temple was the centre of social activity during this period.
39. A. R., Ep. 1898, pp. 1-2, A. R. Ep. 1929-30, p. 176; *SII.*, VI, pp. 292, 295, 344, 345, 362.
40. *SII.*, III, p. 156.
41. *SII.*, VI, pp. 290, 282, 344, 359, 370.
42. The term *meykīrtti* means true eulogy. To start with, the introduction was a list of the king's exploits drafted in a poetical composition. When later kings had no such exploits to recount, the *meykīrtti* degenerated into panegyrics.
43. Jayasval, Suvira, *op. cit.*, p. 151.
44. The order of the government of the Madras Presidency, No. 890 (Home education) dated 5 July 1918 laid down this policy.
45. cf. Sastri, K.A.N., *SI, H*, p. 22 and 374. He says that though trustworthy and containing material, the work, as at present available, contains much later interpolations.
46. Verse 40.
47. cf. Jayasval, Suvira, Studies in the Social Structure of the Early Tamils, Indian Society-Historical *Probings*, Ed. Sharma, R.S., pp. 141-42, 154-55. She says that "a systematic analysis of the Sangam literature for first of all recognising the strata in this mass of literature has yet to be done" and that "this remark equally applies to the literature, especially of the hymn of the saints (nāyanārs and āḷvaṛs). Also Nandi, R.N., 'Some aspects of the Nalayira-Prabandham', *Proc IHC*, XXXVII Session (Calicut), 1976, p. 118.
48. cf. Jayasval, Suvira, "Studies in the social structure of early Tamils" *ISHP*, p. 154. She has remarked "So far the primary concern of the historians of South India has been to provide a clear and continuous picture of the ancient political and administrative

institutions to which a treatment of contemporary social life is appended for the sake of completeness. "

49. *Ibid*, p. 151. She pertinently observes "Sastri does not make allowance for the fact that since our sources are mostly the documents of the privileged class, they do not reflect the conditions and reactions of the lower classes in general. "
50. cf. Sharma, R.S., and Jha, D.N., 'The Economic History of India upto A. D. 1200—Trends and Prospects, *JESHO*, XVII, Part I, pp. 58-59.
51. cf. Sharma, R.S. and Jha, D.N., *op. cit.,* p. 60.
52 *Ibid.*
53. More recently, Raman, K.V. has published a book on *"Sri Varadarajasvami Temple"* (New Delhi 1975), Mahalingam, T.V. has brought out "Kānchipuram in Early South Indian *History"* (1969) and Srinivasan, C.R. has authored one book *"Kāñchīpuram Through the ages"* (Delhi 1979) which are not very relevant to the research undertaken presently. Sharma, R. S. and Jha, D.N., *op. cit.,* pp. 59-60.
54. cf. Jayasval, Suvira, *op. cit.,* pp. 142-43. She observed that these studies "do not take into account" any variations or changes which a priori must have taken place because of the increasing infiltration of Aryan influence as well as the confrontation of the settled well organised communities with the primitive tribes surrounding them."

CHAPTER—3

LAND CONTROL—(A) KINGS, (B) FEUDATORY CHIEFS

PALLAVA PERIOD

In Tamilṅādu, the ancient kings of the different regions other than Toṇḍaimaṇḍalam seem to have sprung only from the local population. But when for the first time a ruler of the whole of Toṇḍaimaṇḍalam emerged in about the 6th century, he is seen to have been an outsider and a conqueror[1]. (This very fact conditioned his kingship) and determined his priorities in the exercise of the control over the region, The Pallava when he took over the region probably found the same inadequately developed. Having come to be based on this region, he had perforce to devise ways and means to strengthen the economic potential of the region[2]. For this purpose he seems to have himself introduced a system of irrigation based on reservoirs to store the available water and improved whatever was existing from earlier times. His efforts seem to have been effective. For it is seen that in comparison to the mention of very few agricultural settlements prior to this period, as the Pallava rule progressed quite a good number of settlements begin to be heard of.

Apart from securing such expansion, the Pallava, as a conqueror had also to devise a mechanism to ensure that his control was not disturbed due to latent antipathies. First he seems to have given recognition to the community of rights that the local people had in the land by allowing them to exercise local control[3]. Probably he also associated some feudatories, those of the region whom he had subdued, or those even from outside who had allied themselves with him or such whom he had favoured with some portions of the territory, in this same task of securing the loyalty of the people.[4] These measures do not seem to have sufficed for the intended purpose. Probably for this reason the Pallava is seen to have started building temples of impressive dimensions.[5] The worship in them according to *āgama* or *vēdic* regulations was probably intended to overawe the local population and to hold their attention. This was one of the ways in which the Pallava tried to ensue the acquie-scenstute of the local people to his control. Side by side with this he is seen to have introduced more brahmins into the aṛea and issued *brahmadēyam* grants. He is seen to have shaped this *brahmadēyam* to suit his purpose. Villages were granted to the brahmins along with several rights and privileges and some new irrigation facilities were also placed at their disposal. He is also seen to have started attaching villages as *Dēvadāṇa* to the temples. These *dēvadāna* villages also were placed under the charge of the brahmins. Through all these measures he is seen to have associated the brahmins in his efforts, to perpetuate his control. The relevant *brahmadēyam* and *dēvadāna* grants of the period which reflect this pattern of royal control over land and association of brahmins are as under:—

Sl. No.	The Charter	Details of the grant-village granted, character, recipients and and purpose	Whether addressed to *nāṭṭār*	Vijñapti	Ājñapti	Motivation for the grant-special phrases used	Accompaniments of the grants Parihara	Privileges	Types of land included.
1	2	3	4	5	6	7	8	9	10
A. Records of Toṇḍaimaṇḍalam:									
1.	A Pallava grant from kūram(Paramēśvaravarman-No date-last quarter of 7th century.	Paramēśvara maṅgalam as brahmadēyam 25 shares to 20 shares to 20 chaturvēdibrahmins (unnamed). 3 shares to two priests Ananta-śivāchāryya & Phulla-sarmā; one share for reciting Mahābhārata in the maṇḍapa, one share for fire and water in the maṇḍapa. (Sanskrit portion-Paramēśvara manglam was dēvadānanimitta-brahmadēyam). Independent provision for food offerings in the temple, Vidyā-vinita-pallava-Paramēśvara-gṛiham, built by Vidyā-vinita-Pallavā-dhivāja.	No address to *nāṭṭār*	Vidyā-vinīta Pallava-rasa	Uttara-kāraṇika Mahā-sena	Nill	A list of items which the recipients could enjoy in proportion to the shares.	Irrigation	Vaḷaiyilśūṟṟū (land around), Paramēśvara-maṅgalam was Proably on the outskirts of *Kūram* but in a different nāḍu and kōṭṭa
2.	Udayendram Plates of Nandivarman Pallavamalla year 21(752)	Kumāramaṅgala-vellattur-koṟṟs-grāman,(New name as brahamadeyam-Udaya chandra manga-	No address to nāttār (No tamil text).	Udaya chandra		Asidhāranishkyārttham for sakalarājya-pradātuh.	sarvvapa-rihāra; anyān-adharma-	Irrigation	Only the boundaries of the village are given.

1	2	3	4	5	6	7	8	9	10
		lam) to 59 brahmins all of whose original homes were outside the grant village. 129 shares unequally distributed, 3 shares to others.					krityān-yināśya		
3.	Kaśakkuḍiplates of Nandivarman Pallavamalla year 22 (753)	Koṭukōlli (name changed to Ēkadhīramaṅgalam when made into a *brahmadēyam*) to one brahmin; a somayāli with high qualification who was a resident of Puniya, a brahmakoka, i.e. full of high class in Tondakarāshṭra (Toṅḍaimanḍalam).	Nāṭṭār of Urrukkaṭṭam delimted and gave araiōtai?	1)Brahmaśrīrāja 2)Brahmayuvaraja	Gorasarmma	a) Kon-ōlai munpeṟṟarai māṟṟi c) dēvadāna-*brahmadēyam*-nikki. d) paradatti (sāmān yanivarttanadvayamaryyadaya nirastāpuratana-devadana-brahmadeyam nirastakutumbi).	Sanskrit portion refers to sarvvaparibara and the Tamil portion lists the same	Irrigation; mansions with burnt bricks	nīr-nilan (wet) punsey udumbōdiāmai tavalndadu (Sanskrit test: kshētram, ārāma, nishkuṭan = sha;
4.	Pullur Plates of Nandivarman II Year 33 (764)	Nelli, Pullur and Kudiyur in Kilve-nadu and Takkaru in Mandlai Kuḷānāḍu (all on the southern bank of Chēyāṟu) in Palkunrakkōṭṭam, (all toether got the name Nayadhurama-ramanalam consequent on their grant as brahmadeyam) to 95 brah-	Nāṭṭār are nōt said to have been addressed but they delimited with the help of nāṭṭu-viyavan releāsed and gave	Avanichandrayuvarāja, a samantamukhya	Nagasarmma alias Brahmadhiraja, a (mantrivara Excellent minister)	a) saḷilapūrvvam b) dharmakṛityartham. c) Kovum, poriyum tīrttu d) mun-perrāi māṟṟi e) kuḍi-nīkki f) ippaḍiyālepārchayyum paradattiyum	Yes	nādu-kāppānum viyāyanum pugāmai: ivargal seyaPālane ivarumivar valikkannārume seyvaragaum; irrigation;	boundaries, wet and dry land, woods, kaḷar and uḍumbōḍi-āmai-tavalndadu.

1	2	3	4	5	6	7	8	9	10
		mins in unequal shares. All the brahmins were outsiders.	araiotal.			selvadāga arulichche(y) duparadatti seydadu.		donees and māḷigai. Could plant seṅgaḷunīr damanagam.	
5.	Velūrpāḷaiyam plates of Nandiveraman III, year 6 (852)	Tirukkāṭṭuppaḷḷi with *pañchavāram* of 1000 *kāḍi* to god Mahādeva for whom a temple was constructed by Yajña-bhaṭṭa.	No address to *nāṭṭār*	*Chōḷa-vaṁśa chūḷāmaṇi* Kumārāṅ-kuśa	Naban (Iraiyūr-udaiyan)	*nāṭṭu-nīṅgalāy-utpuravāy; paradatti śenṛadu*	Yes	Could-raise *māḍam* and *māḷigai* with burnt bricks; could plant *damanagam, iruvēli, śeṅg-aḷunīr-uḷḷi,* cocoanut and arecanut; could fill up ponds and Wells; set up the big oil mill; Īḷavar could not climb cocoa-nut and palmyrah trees at the boundaries Without their consent.	
6.	Chiṭṛūr plates of Nṛipatuṅga year 6 (865)	Chiṛṛūr (named Piridi-Mahādevi-chaturvēdimaṅga-lam on being made a	To *nāṭṭār* of *Panmānāḍu* in Maṇaiyiṛ-	*Agatrayēśa Parañjaya* (Kadupatti	Dramilādhi-raja (Kadupatti	a) *mulnpeṛṛarai-māṛṛi* b) excluding	Yes	Could build mansions with burnt	boundaries; wet and dry land ur, uridugai, manai,

1	2	3	4	5	6	7	8	9	10
		brahmadēyam) to 53 brahmins (all outsiders) in unequal shares. The village was *dēvadāna* now made *brahmadēyam* and then asked to pay *pañchavaram* of 750 *kāḍi* as *dēvadana* to another temple. The former temple. The former temple was given another village in exchange.	kōṭṭam to delimit, release and give *aṛai-olai.*	Muttarai-yan)	Tamilppāra-railyan.	*paḷaiyaparam* and *brahmadēyam* c) *Paradatti śen-ṛadu*		bricks, could plant *daman-agam, iruveli,* *śeṅgaḷunir* and such, as also cocoa-nut; could fill up ponds and wells; could set up big oil mill; irrigation; Īḷavar could not climb cocoanut & palmyran trees on the boundaries of the village without the consent of the donees.	manaippadaippu, manru, kanrumey-pal, *kaḷam, kōtta-garam,* kiḍaṅgu, *kēṇi, kār, ōḍai, uḍaippū, nīrpūśi-neḍupparam, berindadu, uḍu-bōḍi-āmaitavaḷan-dadū ellām uṇṇi-lam oḷivinṛi.*
7.	Tiruvallam stone inscription of Nandivarman III year 17 (863)	Aimbūṇi Viḷattūr and devadanam-Amarunri-maṅgalam made into one village Viḍēlviḍugu-Vikramaditta-chaturvēdi-maṅgalam with a *sabhā* stipulating that the *sabhā* should continue to pay 2000 *kāḍi* of paddy and 20 *kaḷañju* of gold to the	No address to *nāṭṭār*	Vānarāyan *alias* Vikramā-ditya vāṇā-rāyan	Kāḍupaṭṭi Tamiḻppēra-raiyan	Nil	Nil	Nil	Nil

1	2	3	4	5	6	7	8	9	10
		temple of Tiruvallamuḍaiya-Paramēśvarar as was being done till then by *dēvadāna Amarunṛimaṅgalam*.							
8.	Gudimallam plates of Bāṇa Vikramāditya II (Vijayāditya)	Viprapīṭha given to brahmins (*dvijēndrāṇām*) by *nṛiparāṭ* Nandi. Was given protection (*rakṣā*) by the prince.	No address to *nāṭṭār*	Vikramādirya II	Nil	Nil	*Samasta-parihāra*	Nil	Nil
9.	Udayāndram plates of Parāntaka I year 15 (922)	Kaḍaikkōṭṭūr clubbed together with Uḍayachandramaṅgalam and made into a new *brahmadēyam*, Vīranārāyaṇachchēri.	*nāḍu* assembled to survey and fix the boundaries.	Śembiyan Māvaliväṇarāyar	Nil	Old *paḷlichchandams vichchādirappaṭṭi* and *dēvarpaṭṭi* excluded; with a *puravu* of 1000.	Nil	Nil	Boundaries; *uṇṇilamoḷivinṛi*.
10.	Udayāndram plates of Bāṇa Vikramāditya (friend of Kṛṣṇarāja-Kṛṣṇa III?)	Confirmation (?) of the village Udayendrmaṅgalam to the brahmins of the place.	Nil	Nil	Nil	Nil	Nil	Nil	Nil
11.	**Records of Doubtful dates :**								
	Kīḷmuttugūr inscriptopm of Vijaya-Narasiṅgavarman, year 18	The wet and dry land and *manai* held in Mukkuḍūr by Śattaiyanar were made over to him as brahmadēyam.	Nil	Nil	Nil	With oblations of water into his hand	Nil	Nil	Nil
12.	Rōyakkōṭṭānq plates of Skandaśishya year 14	Chārukūr granted to a single brahmin and named as Skandaśishyamaṅgalam.	*Kōṭṭattār* and *nāṭṭār* address. They took the help	Nil	Nil	-	The Tamil text lists some items and refers	Nil	Surrounding the village *chenṛu*, *ūḷupāḷ*, *ēttappāḍu kāḍu*, *piḍīligai*,

1	2	3	4	5	6	7	8	9	10
			of the *karaṇam* (accountant) and elephant of the temple for the delimitation of the boundaries.				to them on *sarvvabādhā-parihāra.*		*uḷukōllai, erikāḍu, manṟu, akkāi, akkarai, pariśu, karambu, talaippēḷai, uṇṇilam-oḷivinṟi, uḍum-bōḍi-amai-tavaḷ-ndadū.*
13.	Udayēndram plates of Nandivarman I (First years ?)	(Kañchivāyil and ?) 4 *āraṇyakṣētraṁ* in Kañchivāyil to one *brāhmaṇa* of Kañchivāyil.	Nil	Nil	Nil	1) *purvv-opabbukta-maryādayā* 2) *brahmadēya maryādayā* 3) *devabhogahala-varjjam* 4) For the increase of the kings *āyu-bala, vijaya-aiśvarya.*	*sarvva-parihāra* to be given effect to by (the local residents ?)	-	It was wood land.
14.	Pallankoyil plates of Simhavarman, year 6	1) Amaṇśērkkai was granted to the *guru* Vajranandi as *paḷḷichchandam* for arranging the *pūjā* of Jinēndra-Jainendramunindra 2) 16½ patti of land in Damar to the same guru as pallichchandam	*Nāṭṭār* addressed for delimitation and giving *aṛaiyolai.*	Nil	Narabhayan the *mantri* (Minister)	1) *kōvum-poṟiyum māṟṟi* 2) *Kuḍinikki* 3) paradatti-śenṟadu	-	-	boundaries; wet and dry land, *kaḷar, kanṟuney* *pāl* woodland, *piḍiligai, kiḍaṅgu, kēṇi, manaimanai-ppaḍappu uḍum-bōdiāmaitavaḷ-ndadu, uṇṇilamoḷi-vinṟi.*
15.	Udayaendram plates of Vīrachōḍa (Para-	Parakesari-chaturvēdi-maṅgalam to brahmins	No.	Vīrachola to Chola	-	-	Nil	Nil	*Śalyādi-śasya-*bhūshi-tam-panas-

1	2	3	4	5	6	7	8	9	10
	kesarivarman)	*(bhūsurēbhyah)* (number not available)		king Parakesarivarman on the advice of his *dharmmōpadēṣṭā*					āmr-ādisamyuktam pūg-ārama (continuation plate not available).
CHARTERS PERTAINING TO REGION OUTSIDE TONDAIMANDALAM									
16.	Tandantottam (Tanjavur District) plates of Nandivarman II, year 58 (789)	Village named Dayāmukhamaṅgalam given to 308 brāhmins (list incomplete due to missing plates).	-	Dayāmukha (*nivēdta* not *vijñāpya) adāpayat* (had it given)	Kumāra The *Kośadhyakṣa, niyōga-karmma-kuśalaḥ*	-	Yes	Irrigation; Damanagam *can be* planted, *māḍa*-maligai can be raised with burnt bricks, ponds and wells can be filled up. Arecanut and cocoanut can be planted, big oil mill can be set up. Īḻavar cannot climb cocoanut and palmyrah trees on the boundary without their consent.	Lost in missing plates.
17.	Paṭṭattāḷmaṅgalam of Nandivarman II, year	Of the 40 velis of Talikkoṛraṅguḍi, leaving out 24 *velis*	*Nāṭṭār* addressed to	Mangala-rāṣṭra	Visaiyanallulan of Ālappā-	1) *Kōvumpoṛiyum tīrttu*	Yes	Nil	*manai, manaippaḍappu,* tank,

1	2	3	4	5	6	7	8	9	10
	61 (792) (Findspot; Koṟṟaṅguḍi, Tanjavur District).	of old brahmadēyam the rest 16 velis were granted as *brahmadēyam* in two instalments of 12 and 4 velis in the years 59 and 61. The block of 16 *velis* was now constituted into the *brahmadēya*, Paṭṭattāḷmaṅgalam and was asked to be shared as per proportion pertinent to the *ūr (ūr-kkūrupuḻḻi-vaḻiyāl)* by 15 brahmins (in unequal shares)	delimit and give *aṟai-ōlai*	(janapada) bharttā (Mangala-nāḍāḻvan)	kkam	2) *kuḍinīkki*			*koṭṭagaram, uvari, Ūr-pāḻ*, wood, stream, *nīr-pūśine-ḍum-baram-berin-dadu, uḍumboḍi-āmai-tavaḻndadu.*
18.	Kumaraḍimaṅgalam (Tanjavur District) plates of Nandivarman III, year 10 (856)	Kumaraḍimaṅgalam granted to 23 brahmins.	*Nāṭṭār* addressed	Nayaparamangalapperaraiyam	Name not clear		Yes	Irrigation; donees could plant *damanagam* and *iruveli.*	Leaving out 1½ *mā* of cremation ground *uṇṇilam oḻivinṟi uḍumbōḍi-āmaitavaḷ-ndadu ellām.*
19.	Bāhūr (Pondicherry) plates of Nṛipatuṅga year 8 (867)	Cheṭṭupākkam, vilaṅgāttāṅkaḍuvanūr and Iṟaip-puṇaichchēri together made into a *brahmadēyam* and added to *brahmadēyam* Bāhūr to maintain a *vidyāsthāna* therein	*Nāṭṭār* addressed to delimit and give *aṟai-ōlai.*	Vesalipperaraiyan	Viḍēlviḍugu Kāḍupaṭṭi Tamilpperaraiyan	*paradatti śenṟadu*	same as enjoyed by Bāhūr; sarvaparihāra; *akaratvēna rakṣitān*	same as enjoyed by Bāhūr	Wet and dry land *ūr, ūrirukkai, manṟu, kanṟumēy-pāḻ; kuḷam* (?), *kōṭṭagaram, kiḍa-ṅgu, kēṇi, kāḍu, kaḷar, ōḍai, uḍai-ppu* including these *nīrpūśineḍu-mbaram-berinḍa-du uḍumbōḍi-āmai-tavaḻivinṟi.*

The significant portions of the charters which reflect the character of the royal control over the villages and the king's intentions in making the grants to the brahmins and temples, are:

(a) the reference to the original home of the donees as having been situated in the Guṇṭur-Nellore region of Andhra Pradesh or in different places in Tamiḷ-nāḍu;

(b) the nature of the village granted;

(c) the royal order to the *nāṭṭār* to delimit the land to be granted;

(d) the phrases referring to the mode of the grants one pertaining to the exclusion of *dēvadānabrahma-dēyam* and *kuḍi* from the grant, the other phrase indicating that the old possessors were changed *(mun-peṛṛārai-māṛṛi)*, the pharse indicating that the lord and seal were changed or done away with (*Kōvum-poṛiyum tīrttu*),

(e) the reference to the gift as having been made as a paradaṭti;

(f) the grant of *parihāraṣ* or exemptions

(g) the grant of exclusive privileges to the donees: (i) in respect of irrigation, (ii) barring the toddy tappers from climbing trees in the precinctṣ of the grant village (iii) setting up an oil mill, (iv) of planting fruit trees of commercial value and (v) of building mansions of burnt brick.

(h) the reference to the inclusion of several types of land in the precincts of the village in the grant.

In these charters it is mentioned that the *brahmadēya* donees hailed from other villages, many of which are found in Āndhra Pradēsh and some in different parts of Tamilnāḍu. This indicates that the donees were outsiders to the place and they were being fitted by the king into the villages probably newly constituted.[6] There is a possibility that the donee brahmins had migrated to the village earlier and the king's grant to them was to further facilitate their prosperity. But this possibility is ruled out when it is seen that a good number of brahmins were found together at one place for the purpose of the grant and that previous to the grant they could not have enjoyed any facilities for living.[7] In the light of this it appears that the king had brought in these brahmins just because he could rely on them to serve, his purposes. The king to have made the grant to the brahmins, must have enjoyed the right of settling anyone of his choice in the land; as if it was his property to dispose off at his discretion.

In all the charters referring to *brahmadēyam* grants, the grant was of a village or villages which had already a name indicating that they were already inhabited. But the royal order was addressed to the *nāṭṭār* or the administrative body of the *nāḍu* or a group of villages, to delimit the grant village, proclaim the grant of a village and give a release document. From this, one presumption can be that the village named, already had a cognisable entity along with the agricultural land, with definitely known borders, which the *nāṭṭār* were to confirm for the sake of the grant. This might be indicated by the fact that the king's order did not specify the extent of land that was to be handed over to the donees. This, will suggest that the village concerned was already under agriculture and was either taken away from the possession of the villagers who must have had some recognised rights and handed over to the donees or that the erstwhile landholders in the grant village were made the tenants of the donees by a royal fiat. Alternatively, it is also possible to interpret the effect of the grant not as one of interfering with the land rights of those already holding the land but of imposing a lord over those agriculturists in the village with the lordship of the donees restricted to receiving the royal revenue instead of the king. However there are sufficient indications in the stone records of the period referring to transactions in land in *brahmadēyam*, villages that the brahmins were in possession of land. There is no reference anywhere that at some stage the brahmins snatched the land for their immediate proprietorship from the villagers over whom they had been imposed as lords. None of the records refer to the workers in the land having been conveyed by the brahmins in their sales or gifts of land. The charters also do not contain any address to the villagers asking them to obey the donees.[9] However the question arises as to how the villages granted were already cognisable entities to have names and how it became possible for the king to grant the villages to the brahmins without infringing on the rights of the villagers who might have been there already resident. The explanation may lay in two alternatives.

It seems possible that though named there was only a vague recognition of the extent of the village involved in the grant and that either there was no organised agriculture in the village with definite plots of land remaining in the possession of each member of the village or only a portion of the land within the recognised village limits was under cultivation by the villagers with a major portion left uncultivated only the bloc that required to be got delimited to be granted to brahmins. The limit of the village might have been also elastic[10]. If the latter was the case the *nāṭṭār* must be understood, from the royal order specifying the number of shares to each brahmin and specifying the number of brahmins receiving the grant, to have been required to calculate the exact amount of land that was to be delimited and handed over to the donees at the rate of 2 *paṭṭis* per share. While so doing the *ṅāṭṭār* might not have been restricted by the then accepted borders of the village. It is noteworthy that the *nāṭṭār* usually employed a she-elephant who was made to walk the boundaries of the grant village. This might have been done either because the ground to be negotiated was uneven and full of wood or bush which must have been the case only if the land was undeveloped[11] or because it had a measured tread or because of both reasons.[12]

Considering that nowadays elephants are used to take the visiting sightseers around the wild life sanctuaries which are forest-land; it may be assumed that it was mainly for the former reason that the she-elephant was used in the case of the grants of land. There could be another possibility. There might have been no calculation necessary to compute the total area required to meet the requirement of shares granted as per charter (i. e.) that land per share amounted to 2 *paṭṭis* in many cases did not mean that in every case the share should consist of two *paṭṭis* of agricultural land. The village granted might have been of a definite area, which the grantee brahmins had to distribute among themselves at the rate of land per share as determined by the total land divided by the total number of shares. Thus though the total arable land in the village might not have been precisely defined, the *nāṭṭār* and *viyavan* (accountant ?), the latter of whom helped the former in the delimiting operation according to the Pullūr plates, or *kōyil-karaṇam* (accountant of the temple ?) who figures in this capacity as the helper of the *nāṭṭār* in the Rōyakōṭṭah plates must have had a definite idea of the boundaries of the village and done the circumambulation accordingly. In the light of the above it would appear that what was granted to the brahmins was land over which no other had any claim.[12a]

However, the phrases *mun-peṟṟārai-māṟṟi, kuḍi-nīkki dēvadāna-brahmadēyam-nīkki* and *Kōvum-poriyum-tirndu* or *māṟṟi* used in some of these charters indicate that some local persons had some rights over the land in the village granted which was taken away from them as a result of issue of the relevant charter. *Mun-peṟṟārai-māṟṟi* meaning " Changing those that had it before, is used only in the following charters—the Kaśākkuḍi grant of Nandivarman II which records the grant of a village as *brahmadēyam* to a single brahmin, the Pullūr grant of Nandivarman II which records the grant of four villages coalesced into one as *brahmadēyam* to a group of 96 brahmins and the Chiṭṟūr grant of Nṛipatuṅga recording the grant of the village Chiṭṟūr as a *brahmadēyam* to 53 brahmins, the grant village having been a *dēvadāna* of Perumbiḍugu-Pallavēśvaragṛiham previously and which on becoming a *brahmadēyam* was stipulated to contribute *pañchavāram* to the temple of God *Mahādēva* at Palaiyanūr-Tiruvālaṅgāḍu. Whereas in the case of the Chiṭṟūr grant it is known who had the land before the grant and from whose possession the village was taken away, in the other two cases there is no indication as to who had the village, previous to the grant.

The other phrase, *kuḍi-nīkki* used in some of the records actually means removing the *kuḍi* or Inhabitant. But this phrase usually occurs in the grants immediately after the phrase *"dēvadāna-brahmadēyam-nīkki"* which has been taken to mean "after excluding *dēvadāna-brahmadēyam*" from the purview of the grant. Hence the expression *kuḍi-nīkki* has to be interpreted to have meant that the *kuḍi* was excluded from the purview of the grant. This *kuḍi-nīkki* along with *dēvadāna-brahmadēyam-nīkki* occurs in the Kaśākkuḍi plates and also in the Pullūr plates. But significantly the Chiṭṟūr and Bahūr records substitute *paḷāiyavaram* in the place of *kuḍi* and leaving out *dēvadāna* refer to the exclusion of both *paḷaiyavaram* and *brahmadēyam (paḷāiyavaramum, brahmadēyamum nīkki)*. A *Paḷaiyavaram* means "old habitations", the use of this phrase in this context makes it appear that while granting the village Chiṭṟūr as *brahmadēvym*. the king took care to exclude already existing *brahmadēyams* as also old habitations from the purview of the grant.[14] On the same analogy it can be deduced that in other cases also the reference to *kuḍi-nīkki* meant that just as the *dēvadāna-brahmadēyam* was excluded from the purview of the grant, *kuḍi* or old inhabitants were also excluded from the purview of the grant.[14a] In the Kaśākkuḍi plates the exclusion on these two accounts is stated to have been limited to two *paṭṭis* or *nivarttanas*.[15] Though it can be supposed that for *dēvadāna* and *brahmadēyam* 2 *paṭṭi* could have met their needs, when it is seen that only two *paṭṭis* were excluded in favour the *kuḍis* whether it was their living quarters or living quarters with agricultural land, one is led to conclude that these *kuḍis* had not developed the rest of the land of the village to claim any right over that land. It is observable that it is in these same three sets of plates, Kaśākkuḍi, Pullūr and Chiṭṟūr, the phrase *mun-peṟṟārai-māṟṟi* meaning "the old possessors were changed" is used. This indicates on the one hand that *kuḍi-nīkki* could not have meant removing the kuḍis as it cannot be imagined that the same idea was conveyed in two sets of phrases. On the other it is clarified that *mun-paṟṟārai-māṟṟi* had a different significance. It appears that the intention behind the employment of this phrase was that whatever vague rights the villagers might have possessed in respect of the land that remained after the exclusion in their favour and in favour of *devadāna* brahmadēyam were derecoegnised and definite rights with regard to that land were conferred on the donees.[16] However it is seen that in the Paḷḷankōyil plates of Simhavarman granting a village as also 16½ paṭṭi of land in another village to the guru of a Jain establishment there is no mention of *mun-peṟṟārai-māṟṟi* or of *dēvadāna-brahmadēyam- nīkki*. *Kuḍi-nīkki* is however mentioned. The text of the record as incised is dubious. It is impossible to say if the processes *kovum poriyum marri* and *kuḍi-nikki* mentioned in the record applied to the whole village or to the 16½ *paṭṭi* of land in another village both of which were granted as *paḷḷichchandam*. It is possible that in the second village, Dāmar, after excluding the land of the *kuḍi* only 16½ *paṭṭi* was available for the grant. But the phrases might have been applicable to both the whole village and to the second bloc also of land granted. However *kuḍi-nīkki* in the context of grants of land to religious institutions might have had a revenue significance rather than indicating the removal of *kuḍis* or reservation of land for the original inhabitants[16a].

It would appear that the non-use of these phrases in the other charters was due to the absence of the necessity for the same. Hence it will be seen that though the villages granted as per these charters bore names most part of them was still apparently undeveloped and none in the village had any visible right over that portion. However, the Paḷḷankōyil plates of Simhavarman as also the Pullur plates of Nandivarman II recording the grant of four villages as *brahmadēyam* to 96 brahmins refer to some other rights over the villages granted as already existing which had to be nullified before the king made over the land to the donees. They say that the grant was made after changing the *kō* and *poṛi* (*kōvum poṛiyum māṟṟi)* as in the former or after disposing of the *kō* and *poṛi (kōvum poṛiyum tīrndu*) as in the latter. The other set of plates of Nandivarman II from Chōḷamaṇḍalam, the Paṭṭattāḷmaṅgalam-grant, recording the grant of 16 *velis* of land as *brahmadēyam* to 15 brahmins also refers to the grant as having been made after disposing of the *kō* and *poṛi*. *Kō* means the 'lord' and *(poṛi'* means the 'seal'. To understand the identity of this *kō*. some other clauses contained in the grants help. Of the above-mentioned three grants the Pullūr and Paṭṭattāḷmaṅgalam grants give an itemised list of exemptions (*parihāras*) to which the *brahmadēya* grantees were entitled and the latter concludes the list saying that these and other such which could be enjoyed by the *kō* would not thereafter be enjoyed by him. The Taṇḍantōṭṭam (Chōlamaṇḍalam) plates of Nandivarman III and the Chiṭṟūr grant of Nṛipatuṅga, both recording grants of *brahmadēyam* as also the Vēlūrpāḷaiyam plates of Nandivarman III recording the grant of a village as *dēvadāna* also refer to the levies exempted under *parihāra* exemplified by an itemised list, as those which the *kō* was entitled to enjoy, which he would cease to enjoy consequent to the grant and which the donee would enjoy thereafter. Moreover the Kaśākkuḍi plates say that the transgressors of the irrigation facilities given to the grantees, would be fined as could be done by *kō*. This *kō* which means 'lord' mentioned in these contexts could not have been the king as the levies from which exemptions were granted were miscellaneous ones and the list did not include the main land tax which was payable to the king. It must be observed that the list of the exemptions at the end states that all that *kō* could take were exempted and if *kō* had referred to the king, the itemised list should have had the *iṟai* or land tax at the head, which was not the case.[17] Hence this *kō*, must have been a local lord with an entitlement to miscellaneous levies only.[18] Consequently the *kō* figuring in the expression *kōvum-poṛiyum-tīrttu* or *kōvum-poṛiyum-māṟṟi* must have been the same local lord entitled to the miscellaneous levies and the effect of the phrases used as a manner of the grant must have referred to the severence of the grant village from his authority. It is possible that this meant the same thing as 'changing the old possessors' (*mun-peṟṟārai-māṟṟi*). Though in the Pullūr grant only both the expressions are used, **in the other charters only either of them is used. This** *kō* might have been a local chief whom the Pallava king subjugated but allowed to continue in the territory under his authority. By the grant of the land to the brahmins or the temples, the king seems to have displaced the *kō* in respect of the bloc involved in the grant and thus granted the position of *kō*, to the grantee/grantees,[18a] not only in respect of the bloc granted to them but in respect of the whole village including the portion not involved in the grant. Otherwise the authorisation to them to collect and enjoy whatever the *kō* normally could have had no meaning. In this way the people that were already in the village prior to its grant as *brahmadēyam* seem to have been subjected now to the *brahmadēya* donees, as the former were required to pay the several levies payable to the *kō* now to the latter. Hence it can be said that the use of the expression, *kōvum-poṛiyum-tīrttu* in the grants also indicated the king's discretionary powers with regard to the gifting of the land and setting aside the authority of local lords.[19]

Thus the various expressions used in these grants of Toṇḍaimaṇḍalam while defining the manner of the grant seem to point to the king's right to grant as *brahmadēyam* or *dēvadāna* the portion of the viilages within his territory, which till that date remained undeveloped. While the above said features suggest that the king did not interfere with existing rights while exercising his control or associating the brahmins in the process, the other details found in these grants also give a definite indication that the local population was otherwise placed in a position of subjection or dependance under the grantees of these charters. Such a feature is the grant of *parihāras* to the donees which is normally succinctly stated to be all inclusive (*sarvva-parihāra*) in the Sanskrit portion of the grants but itemised in the Tamil text whereever such a text is found given.[20] They are usually said to be what the *kō* could take and are capable of being classified as i) facilities ii) right to take the best in the village iii) levies for local administration iv) levies for services provided; v) levies on professions/ professionals vi) levies on trades/traders/ bazar. vii) levies due on occasions or for occasions viii) levies based on land utilisation, ix) mines and treasures (x) fines (xi) Miscellaneous. These *parihāras* are included in the grants of *brahmadēyam* to a single brahmin, to groups of brahmins, as also of *dēvadāna* to a temple as per the two charters available. The *Kaśākkuḍi* plates and the Pullūr plates refer to the *parihāras* as such that were exemptions from payment authorised to the concerned donees[21] which seems to have meant that whether the donees collected these levies or not, they in their turn need not pay it to *kō*? The Paṭṭattāḷ-maṅgalam charter granting *brahmadēyam* to a group of brahmins says that the *kō* would not be entitled to collect the charges listed under the *parlhāras*, obviously from such of those chargeable with the said taxes and resident in the village. The other charters (the Chiṭṛūr, Taṇḍantōṭṭam and Kumaraḍimaṅgalam) granting *brahmadēyam* to groups of brahmins as well as the *dēvadāna* grants as contained in the VēlūrPālaiyam and Tiruvālaṅgāḍu plates make a definite statement that not only the *kō* would not collect these levies listed but that instead, the donees, the groups of brahmins or the temple would be eligible to collect and enjoy these charges. The charters while listing these levies under the *parihāras* also indicate that the list was only illustrative and not exhaustive as some of these charters (Taṇḍantōṭṭam and Paṭṭattāḷmaṅgalam grants of Nandivarman II, Kumaraḍimaṅgalam plates of Nandivarman III all these pertaining to the Chōḷa country and the Chiṭṛūr grant of Nṛipatuṅga pertaining to Toṇḍaimaṇḍalam which are all grants of *brahmadēyam* and the Vēlūrpāḷaiyam plates of Nandivarman III and the Tiruvālaṅgāḍu plates of Rājēndra I recording grants of *dēvadāna)* wind up the list of the items under the *parihāras* with the statement that including these items mentioned (*uḷḷiṭṭu*)[22] all such which *kō* could enjoy were either exempted from payment or were authorised to be enjoyed by the stated donees instead of the *kō* (the actual phrase is *kō-kkoḷḷa- pperā-de* which means "without the *kō* getting these"). It is not known if this investment of vagueness to the list was deliberate or the phraseology was just a flourish of language without any serious implication. It is also noteworthy that one could not expect all the classes of artisans, professionals and tradesmen on whom the charges were mentioned as leviable would have taken up residence in each of these grant villages. It is also to be noted that mostly the rate of the levies is also not mentioned as it was probably to be governed by convention. However, whatever the manner of mention, the implication of authorising these levies to the donees by a direct stipulation or saying that the concerned village was exempted from the payment of these levies seems to have been that these were normal levies taken wherever the concerned people were there to pay them and that these charges leviable on such persons becoming resident in their village would not be payable to the *kō*. The donees could collect and enjoy them at their discretion. Thus the classes of people who could be expected to pay these levies also seem to have been placed under the authority of the donees.[23] In all these charters it is also seen that the donees, both the single brahmin and the groups of brahmins as well as the temple in the two charters were authorised under the *parihāras* either *maṇṛupāḍu* (Chiṭṛūr grant of *brahmadēyam,* Vēlūrpāḷaiyam grant of *dēvadāna* in Toṇḍaimaṇḍalam, Paṭṭ attāḷmaṅgalam and Kumaraḍimaṅgalam grants of the *brahmadēyam* in Choḷā-nāḍu and Tiruvālangāḍu plates granting *dēvadāṇa* in Toṇḍaimaṇḍalam but pertaining to early 11th century) or *karaṇa-ttaṇḍam* and *adhikaṛaṇa-ttaṇḍam* (Kasākkuḍi plates) or *Upakaraṇa-ttaṇḍam. adhikaraṇa-ttaṇḍam* and *(āṛappuṛā?)-ttaṇḍam* (Pullūr plates).[24] While the ṭaṇḍam which means fines, with the prefixes indicating the place where the fines were imposed and collected, is easily identifiable, *maṉṟupadu* has to be understood as an imposition in the *maṉṟu* or form which could have been only fines. But a stone inscription from Tiruvaḍandai (Chingleput district) dated in the year 6 of a Parākēsarivarman,[24a] clarifies that it was a special fine apart from *daṇḍam*, the proceeds of which went only to *kō*.[24b] It seems possible, however, that *manṟupāḍu* was a general term indicating all kinds of fines levied in whatever forum was there in the village for imposition and collection and that the Kaśākkuḍi and Pullūr plates only referred to them severally instead of collectively. Though according to these charters the *brahmadēyam* recipients were exempted from fines, the Tiruvaḍandai inscription indicates that the *sabhā* of the *brahmadēyam* portion of that village was also liable to the fines under special circumstances. However an inscription dated year 37 (944) in the reign of Parāntaka[24c] I indicates that the kuḍis could be punished with *manṟupāḍu* if found to be guilty (*kuṟṟan-dōsham*). In all these authorisations and exemptions granted to the *brahmadēyam* donees and to the temple getting a village as *devadāna*[24d] a running theme is seen that the benificiaries of the grant were authorised to do everything as a *kō* could do. So it will be apparent that the effect of these grants was to invest the brahmin/brahmins/temple with the authority of *kō*[24e] (i. e.) the lordship of the village, village complex as explicitly mentioned in the charters 24f or over a wider locality centering around the bloc granted as *brahmadēyam* though not identified in the charters. The latter possibility is suggested by the *parihāras* the right to collect the levies on artisans/ professionals and tradesmen, which would have had any meaning only if there was a wide enough field for collection. The *kō*-ship conferred on the *brahmadēyam* donees seems to have been sought to be embellished with a right to reside in suitably impressive mansions as the charters say that the donees could build mansion with burnt brick.[24g]

Among these charters the Paḷḷankōyil plates of Siṁhavarman granting *paḷḷichchandam* the Vēlūrpāḷaiyam plates of Nandivarman III granting a village as *dēvadānam*, the Bāhūr plates of Nripatūnga granting three villages as *brahmadēyam* for the benefit of a *vidyasthāna*, the Kaśākkuḍi and Pullūr plates of Nandivarman II granting villages as *brahmadēyam* and Chiṭ ṛūr plates of Nripatuṅga granting a village as *brahmadēyam*, say that the grants were made as *paradatti*. The significance of this *paradatti* has been discussed below. It seems to have signified only the extension to the donees the right to alienate what was granted to them rather than to have indicated the king's right to endorse the grants by the subordinate chiefs.[24h]

The control of the king over land in his territory and his passing on the control to the donees in his charters are also reflected in the rights and privileges he extended to the donees in the grants. To take first the irrigation rights, it is seen that in the Kūram grant of Paramēsvaravarman (end of 7th century) the brahmins granted the *brahmadēyam* of Paramēsvaramaṅ-galam were authorised to cut channels from the river Pālār to the Paramēsvarataṭāka, the reservoir probably dug for their benefit and claim all the land constituting the channel as belonging to their village. Probably the grant of the rights *kōl-agalam* and *puḷudipāḍu* meant an authorisation to have the channel dug to the width of one *kōl* and to deposit and utilise the mud dug while cutting the channel and later during the dredgings[25] as fertilisers or otherwise. These plates as well as all the other plates say that while digging the channel from the river to the reservoir or from the reservoir to the fields as the case may be, the natural course, the water would take following the grain of the country *(nir-inda-vaḷiyāl)* could be adhered to (i.e.) there was no set instruction from the king as to the land through which the channel was to be cut but the grantees could cut the channel as would be most convenient to conduct the water. The Pullūr plates further say that the donees could also change the course of the channels, and filling up the bed of the abandoned channels. Moreover the Vēlūr-pāḷaiyam and Chiṭ ṛūr plates pertaining to Toṇḍaimaṇḍalam and the Taṇḍantōṭṭām plates pertaining to Chōḷamaṇḍalam authorised the donees to fill up wells and ponds *(kiṇaṟu and turavu)* probably if found at inconvenient places. The Pullūr and Chiṭṛūr grants also say that the *brahmadēyam* donees would have the first fill of water from the water courses (*nīr-kōkkum-aḷavuṅ-kokkappēṛuvadā-gavum)*.

Transgressors into their irrigation rights were punishable with fine either by the *kō* or the donees. (This is stated in the Kasākkuḍi and Pullūr plates). All these rights given over by the king to the donees must have been his rights ordinarily. For laying the irrigation works he could utilise any land depending upon the conveneience and feasibility and he could regulate the use of the irrigation water. He could stipulate the width of channels that the users of the irrigation water could cut to take the water to their fields. He could punish unauthorised users of the irrigation water. He had this right to have the mud dug deposited—at the place of his choosing and use the mud as he thought fit.

This grant of irrigation rights also placed the *brahmadēyam* grantees in a position to control the locality. If it was a new irrigation facility that was provided for the benefit of the donees or even if it was a facility already existing the donees were given exclusive and monopolistic rights over them. It is understood that the *kuḍis* who were allocated two *paṭṭis* or the other inhabitants already in the locality would have liked to benefit by the new innovations in agriculture introduced in the area and would have required the water for their agricultural purposes. Further it is seen that in due course the common land in these *brahmadēyam* villages was made available to *kuḍis* to retain later on.[26] Moreover it is also seen that sometimes the villages around were attached with the status of *brahma-dēyam* to some of the *brahmadēyam* villages. Probably these attached villages were to be fed by the irrigation system attached to the main *brahmadēyam,* village and the land therein was worked by tenants of the members of the main *brahmadēyam* village. All these would have been dependent on the irrigation facility over which the donees had exclusive authority. Consequently they would have come under the control of the donees.

The other privileges granted to the donees in the grants were to plant coconut and arecanut trees and some special plants. Of the charters from Toṇḍaimaṇḍalam, the Vēlūrpāḷiyam plates of Nandivarman III and the later Chiṭṛūr grant of Nṛipatuṅga mention the grant of the privilege of planting coconut and arecanut trees. Among the records from Chōḷamaṇḍalam, even the earlier grant of Nandivarman II as contained in the Taṇḍantōṭṭam plates mentions this right. The Kaśākkuḍi and Pullūr grants of the same king pertaining to Toṇḍaimaṇḍalam refer to a levy on the planting of the cocoanut, arecanut and other fruit trees which had been authorised as one of the entitlements of the *kō* which was exempted in the case of the *brahmadēyam* donees. Further the Pullūr, Vēlūr-pāḷaiyam and Chiṭṛūr plates pertaining to Toṇḍaimaṇḍalam and the Kumaraḍimaṅgalam plates of Chōḷa-maṇḍalam record the grant of the donees of the privilege of planting the flower plants, *seṅgaḷunir* and *damanagam*. All of these except the Pullūr grant record further the making over of the right to plant another plant *iruvēli* and the Vēlūrpāḷaiyam plates alone add the right to plant *uḷḷi* (onion or garlic). The Taṇḍantōṭṭam plates restrict the right to the planting of *damanagam* only. The fact that the king granted those rights to the donees implied that the king controlled the utilisation of the land. It seems that diverting the land away from food crops needed special permission from the king. The list of exemptions reveal that these special plants and commercial trees were specially taxed by the *kō*, probably with the authorisation from the king. Now the donees were given the privilege and thus were again placed in a pre-eminent position. As they had been authorised to levy the tax on the planting of these trees and plants just as the *kō* could do as per the *parihāṛas*, they seem to have been privileged to control the use of land by the other residents in the locality. Among these charters there is no reference to the right to the mines.[27] It is seen that only the Pullūr plates mention an item *sāḍīppon,* literally 'jar-gold' or gold in jars among the exemptions granted to the donee brahmins, which might have meant the treasures buried in jars that might be struck and brought up during ploughing and digging.[28] The donees were authorised to appropriate the same for themselves. But this may appear as one of the rights of the *kō* transferred to the donee brahmins rather than the right of the king. But it is noteworthy that it was the king who made over the right to the donees which indicates that the right to the treasures was his which he might have made over to the *kō* first and in the *brahmadēyam* grant to the donees. He could transfer the right at his discretion. In the same way another right of the king for salt manufacture seems to be referred to in the *uppu-kkō-chcheygai* "the operation for salt by *kō*" mentioned among the *parihāras* only in the Taṇḍantōṭṭam and Paṭṭattāḷmaṅgalam plates pertaining to the Tañjāvūr district, where also it was a right earlier authorised to the *kō*. It would appear that in Toṇḍaimaṇḍalam the income under these heads was insignificant and hence the king had allowed these to be enjoyed by the *kō* and did not deem it necessary to grant the same to the *brahmadēyam* donees. The same charters also list the types of land and facilities that were included in or that went with, the granted village. This feature also evidences the control over the villages inherent in the king and his intention that the grantees in his charters should act in his behalf in the localities. Some of the items stated to have been included refer to the water sources in the village—tanks, wells and channels (and probably *kōṭṭagaram*, *uḍaippu* and *taḷai-ppēḷai*).[29] They might either have been such that were already there in the village serving the inhabitants or they might have been such that were expected to be provided after the settlement therein by the *brahmadēyam* donees.

Whichever was the case, as these water facilities mentioned as included in the grant seem to have been meant to cater for the whole village, the people other than the donees, who would live in the village, as mentioned above must have become dependent on the grantee brahmins[30] probably even for drinking water. The charters issued by Nṛipatuṅga (third quarter of 9th century) as also the Tiruvālaṅgāḍu plates of Rājēndra I, (first quarter of 11th century), the former recording grants of villages as *bṛahmadēyam* and the latter the detachment of a village from a *brahmadēyam* and its grant as *dēvadāna,* apart from maṇai and mannai padaippu both mention *ūr* and *ūr-irukkai* (which mean the residential sites and the kitchen gardens), among the types of land included in the village granted. In these cases such reference to the residential sites twice cannot be rationally explained unless it is supposed that the different terminology used in each case was meant to differentiate the residential sites of two different classes of people. As the latter set, *maṇai* and *maṇai-ppadaippu* almost invariably occurs in all these charters, it can be surmised that these terms had relevence to the residential sites meant for the recipients of the charters. Hence it can be inferred that the former, *ūr* and *ūr-irukkai* referred to the quarter including the residences and attached land of those in the village other than the donees. Whereas the reference to the inclusion of residential sites for the donees in the grant is understandable, the inclusion of the quarters of the others in the grant, could only have signified that the grantor king expressly wanted to place the others in the village under subordination to the donees.[31] Thus when the charters on the one hand indicate that the *dēvadāna* and *brahmadēyam* already existed in the village and the *kuḍi* were excluded from the purview of the grant, the exclusion seems to have meant only that they could continue to hold whatever they were holding previously without any risk of being deprived of the same by the donees but on the other, the inclusion of *ūr* and *ūr-irukkai* among the types of land that formed part of the village granted to the donees of the charters, indicated that these people were however to come under the overall authority of the donees. It is quite possible that as there is no other reference to the quarters of other normal residents of a village, artisans, professionals and tradesmen, *ūr* and *ūr-irukkai* covered their quarters also.

In consequence of this understanding, the implication in the Tiruvālaṅgāḍu plates seem to be that *manai* and *manai-ppaḍaippu*, the localities of the superior class of people who might have taken up residence there when it was part of a *brahmadēyam* as well as *ūr* and *ūr-irukkai,* the localities of all other classes of people Palaiyanūr were to come under the authority of the temple. It is possible to understand that the handing over of *ūr* and *ūr-irukkai* to the donees implied the handing over of a lower order of people to the charge of the donees for their utilisation but in that case the absence of these among the included types and facilities in the other grants excepting these three charters will become inexplicable.[32]

Such subordination of the erstwhile residents and those that might colonise the village later to the donees is also indicated in the inclusion of several other types of land besides arable land in the grant-village. Some of the charters refer to the pasture land (*kaṉru-mēypāḻ*). forests *(kāḍu)*,[33] manṟu (market-place or forum?), waste land common to the village (*ūr-pāḷ* found only in the Paṭṭattāḷmaṅgalam grant) as the included types of land. The utility of these types of land to the villagers besides the donees, is clear. By including these in the grant the king made evident his intention about associating the donees for the control of the villages and villagers, the grants made sure that there was no inadvertent ommission by winding up the lists with the statement that all land high and low in the village (*uḍumbōḍi-āmai-tavaḷndadu-ellām*) could be deemed to have been included. Such statements about the included types of land as also the statement that Īḻavar or todāy tappers would not climb palmyrah and coconut trees in the precincts of the village without the consent of the donees and the grant of the right to levy and appropriate fines, all indicate the extent to which the king had control over the land and how the donees were associated in this control. It is also seen that some of the *brahmadēyam* charters as described above evidence the association of the *brahmadēyam* donees with the temples. The Vēlūrpāḷaiyam plates granting the village Tirukkāṭṭuppaḷḷi as *dēvadāna* with *parihāras* and privileges resembling a *brahmadēyam* grant, does not specify to whom the grant village was entrusted. From the prefacing of the grant with the statement that the *pañchavāram* of Tirukkāṭṭuppaḷḷi was 1000 *kāḍi*, it becomes evident that the village was already developed and occupied. It is not known if it was already a *brahmadēyam* village. From the trend of the record it appears that the builder of the beneficiary temple, a brahmin-resident of the village Tirukkāṭṭuppaḷḷi got the charge of the village. However it can be observed that the Kūram grant says that the *brahmadēyam* Paramēsvaramaṅgalam was created as a *dēvadāna-nimitta-brahmadēyam* or a *brahmadēyam* for the purpose of *devadāna*. In the light of the fact that the same charter says that for the temple constructed at Kūram, for food offerings separate provision had been made and for the maintenance of the temple in good repair and for the priests, a few shares had been set apart in the new *brahmadēyam* what purpose of the temple the whole new *brahmadēyam* was to serve is not clear. In the light of the clarifications in the Tamil text, the statement in the Sanskrit text that the *brahmadēyam* had to provide for worship etc. *(pūjā, snapana-kusuma-gandha, dhūpa-dīpa-havi-upachāra-bali-sañkha, paṭāh-ādi-pravarttan-ārttham*) is only puzzling. It appears that the purpose of the *brahmadēyam* was to serve as a brahminical buttrers for the temple. The Chiṭṛūr grant is more specific. The village Chiṭṛūr was a *dēvadāna* of the temple called Perumbiḍugu-Pallavēsvaragṛiham but was made into a *brahmadēyam* with the name Pirudi-Mādēvi-chaturvēdi-maṅgalam after the grant of a exchange village to that temple. But the record goes further to say that the *brahmadēyam* village would pay a *pañchavāram* of 750 kāḍi of paddy as *dēvadāna* for the expenses of a *chhatra*. (feeding house?) attached to the temple of Paḷaiyanūr-Tiruvālaṅgaḍu. These facts provided by these records can be studied in the light of the stone records of the period which reflect that some *sabhā* villages which were obviously *brahmadēyam* were in the *dēvadāna* or *puṛam*, of some temples and that some villages granted as *dēvadāna* were attached as *brahmadēyam* to other *brahmadēyams*. Though as will be shown below some villages under *ūr* are also found mentioned as belonging to the puṛam, it appears that the tendency of the Pallava king of the period was to entrust to the brahmins or *brahmadēyams* the villages he had granted for the temples also.

While the grants as discussed above, give in detail the rights conferred on the donees, they contain no explicit reference to the grant of exemption to the brahmadēyam donees, from the payment of land-tax, the collection of which usually indicated the king's exercise of his control over land. This has engaged the attention of some scholars and it has been speculated that such a tax was not levied by the Pallavas. But it has been seen that in the Chiṭṛūr grant the newly created Pirudi-Mahādēvi-Chaturvēdimaṅgalam was asked to pay 750 *kāḍi* (of paddy) as *pañchavāram* to the temple of god Mahādēva at Paḷāiyanūr-Tiruvālaṅgāḍu. This was referrred to as the *dēvadāna* of that god. This 750 *kāḍi* was probably the land-tax assessed on the village and this land-tax when it became the entitlement of temple, seems to have been termed as *pañchavāram*. The Vēlūrpaḷaiyam plates also refer to *pañchavāram* assessed on the village Tirukkāṭṭuppaḷḷi granted as *dēvadāna* as amounting to 1000 *kāḍi*. On the other hand, the Udayēndram plates of Parāntaka I (or Prithvipati II) mention that the village Kaḍaikkōṭṭur which was attached as *brahmadēyam* to another *bramadēyam* Udayachandramaṅgalam was stipulated to pay the *puravu* of 1000 (*kāḍi* or *kalam* which, however is not specified). Again it may be seen that the Kāṇḍiyūr (Tanjavur District) inscription of Nṛipatuṅga seems to explain the term *pañchavāram*. This record while mentioning the exemptions granted on land allotted to the temple by the *sabhā* refers to *pañchavāram* in the place where other inscriptions mention *iṛai* (the land-tax). Hence it can be concluded that the *puravu* used in the Udayēndram plates of Parāntaka I and *pañchavāram* used in the other plates all were synonyms for *iṛai* which term was more commonly used to denote the main land tax.[36] Since some *brahmadēyam* like Chiṭṛūr were asked to pay *pañchavāram* to a temple[37] it can be presumed that where there were no specific instructions diverting the payment, the holders of the *brahmadēyam* were expected to pay to the king the land tax which might have been termed as *pañchavāram* or as *puravu* or as *iṛai.*[38] This did not find mention in the *brahmadēyam* grants obviously because there was no intention on the part of the king to free the land from this commitment.[39] But it is noteworthy that in the above instances of Pallava grants, the *paṇchavāṛam* was given in round figures and as an assessment on the whole village. It is not certain if this assessment was the expectation of the king' of revenue from the whole village without particular reference to land or other assessable items in the village or it was actually an approximate estimation of the king's share of the produce from the land in the village. On the face of it, it looks like a tribute claimed from the village by the king without reference to land or any other taxable item.[40] Whatever was taken from the villagers by the king was for his enjoyment at his discretion. There does not seem to have been a policy whereby the revenue was taken into a royal exchequer to be returned to the people in the form of welfare measures. If the king undertook any schemes for public welfare like provision of irrigation facilities, he undertook them not as state policy but at his pleasure and for his personal merit. Construction of temples was not undertaken as a welfare scheme but as a personal venture of the king in order to enhance his glory and to acquire merit for himself. The levies which are listed under the *parihāras* either as exemptions from payment or as authorisation to the *brahmadēyam* donees to collect and enjoy the proceeds were the entitlement of the *kō* who, as has been pointed out above, could not have been the king but was probably his agent. They were also miscellaneous levies on professions and occasions and hence not related to land which the king seems to have permitted the *kō* to collect and enjoy. The above mentioned charters granting both *brahmadēyam* and *dēvadāna* do not however refer to the grant as having been made till the sun and moon[41] lasted or for the welfare of the king.[42] Only the Udayēndram plates of Nandivarman II state that the king made the grant of the *brahmadēyam* as a token of gratitude for the valour of the chief Udaya-chandra (*asidhāra-nishkriyārtham*) who had exerted himself on behalf of the king. Probably by the grant of the village named after the chief as *brahmadēya*, the king wished to enhance the merit *(puṇya)* of the chief. The Pullūr grant says that the king made the grant for fulfilling his duty for doing dharma (*dharma-krit-arttham*). The Chiṭur grant also seems to indicate that the *brahmadēyam* Prithvīmahādevi-chaturvēdimangalam was created by the king at the request of a chief, who in turn had been requested by his?) queen who in turn had been approached by the brahmins.[43] Hence it can be assumed that though not expressed in the charters, the other grants of *brahmadēyam* or *dēvadāna* were also made for gaining personal merit by the king apart from the above stated purposes.

Some of these grants, the Udayēndram plates of Nandivarman I, Kūram, Kasākkuḍi, Pullūr and the Rōyakōṭṭāh plates contain some verses (attributed to Vyasa in later grants and to Brahma by the Udayēndram plates of Nandivarman I) praīsing the gift of land and sometimes containing imprecations against resumpition of land gifted (Udayēndram plates of Nandivarman Kaśākkuḍi and Pullūr grants). The quotation of such imprecatory verses naturally implied that the makers of these gifts did not reserve for themselves the right to resume the land.[44] The imprecations were against others who were to succeed them so that they might not resume the land. That the hazard of such resumption was quite real, is probably indicated by the Gudimallam (Kalahasti taluk, Chittoor district) record of Bāna Vikramaditya II—(910-916)[45] and the Udayēndram plates of Bāṇa[46] Vikramaditya III (friend of Krishnaraja—940-966). The Bāṇa chief in the Gudimallam plates was one who had asserted his independence for a shortwhile early in the tenth century when the Pallava power had declined and the Bāṇa chief of the Udayēndram plates was the one who had come into his own consequent on the patronage of the Rāshṭrakūṭa Krishna III, who dealt a staggering blow to the Chōḷas. The former record states that the Bāṇa gave protection (*rakshā*) to the brahmans residing in Viprapīṭha (in other records in Tamil the same village was named Tīruvippirambēḍu which was evidently the earlier name of Guḍimallam) and the latter which is incomplete seems to record the grant of such confirmation by the Bāṇa chief to the residents of Udayēndramaṅgalam (Udayachandramaṅgalam). That such confirmation became necessary in these cases showed that the conqueror could have disturbed the holdings of these brahmins if he had chosen to do so. But such possibility was an aberration as such confirmations are not otherwise evidenced in the whole range of records of the Chōḷas who succeeded the Pallavas in the rule of Toṇḍaimaṇḍalam except perhaps in the Tirukkaḷukkunṛam inscription of Rājakēsarivarman (Aditya I—870-907)[47] by which the king confirmed the enjoyment of probably the village Tirukkaḷukkunṛam by the temple on the hill at that place as granted by earlier kings. It would appear that the conquerors retained the right to set at naught the grants by earlier rulers, but they seldom exercised these rights. When it is seen that even conquerors hesitated to exercise this right there was no question of a ruler resuming a gift he himself had made except perhaps by giving an exchange as indicated in the Chitṛūr and Tiruvālaṅgāḍu plates.

Thus from an analysis of the contents of the Copper plate grants of the Pallava kings, the following conclusions emerge with regard to the land rights on the king;

(1) The king had the right to grant land as *brahmadēya* or *dēvadāṇa*.

(2) The land granted as *brahmadēya* was probably the undeveloped land in the villages.

(3) Probably he did not interfere with the land rights of those who held cultivated land in their possession.

(4) He could alter the tenure of the holding of land held under *dēvadāna*.

(5) He could transfer the lordship of villages at his pleasure.

(6) He had control over the irrigation facilities and for devising these facilities he could utilise any land as he found it convenient.

(7) He depended upon the body called *nāṭṭār* the administrative organisation of the *nāḍu* (the intervening territorial devision between the village and kōṭṭam) to work out the details of the supervision of land utilisation.

(8) There was an inherent right of the conqueror to resume land granted by earlier rulers.

CHŌḶA PERIOD

The Chōḷas conquered this region from the Pallavas by about the end of the 9th century. But unlike for the pallavas, for the chōḷas, Toṇḍaimaṇḍalam was not designed to be base of their kingship. It was only an adjunct to their base, the Chōḷa territory to the south. This very character helped them to modify the land control system in accordance with their requirements. They must have found the system as it was existing in good working order. However, they introduced changes in the manner of exercising royal control over the villages. One of the chief features of this modified scheme of control was the shifting of the emphasis from the brahminism. For the control of land they are seen to have brought a host of their adherents from Chōḷa-maṇḍalam to administer the different localities of Toṇḍaimaṇḍalam as their officials. They engaged them for surveying the land and they posted them to temples to over-see the management of the temples and their lands. Their claim to more intimate control over the land seems to have extended to the assessment of land plotwise. This changed land control scheme is best reflected in three records of their period.

The Tirumālpuram stone inscription, though dated year 14 (984) in the reign of Uttamachōla,[47] records a series of land transactions beginning from about the end of the 9th century.[48]

It says that Siṟṟiyāṟṟūr in maṇaiyil-nāḍu in Manaiyil-kōṭṭam was made *dēvadāna-iṟai-ili* (tax-free d*ēvadāṇa*) of God Mahādēva of Tirumālpēṟu and entrusted as *dēvadān a brahmadēyam* to the *sabhā* of *brahmadēyam*, Puduppākkam in Purisai-nāḍu in the same kōṭṭam in the year 21(892) of the *uḍaiyār,* who died at Toṇḍaimān-Āṟṟūr (Āditya I). However while Siṟṟiyāṟṟur was so granted, the *kāṇi* of the *kiḷāṇ* of Sankarappāḍi[49] was excluded from the grant. It was stipulated that the *sabhā* of Puduppākkam would pay to the temple a *puravu* of 3000 *kāḍi* (of paddy?), an *iravu* (what is demanded benevolence?) of 561 *kāḍi* (of paddy) and a gold levy of 26 kaḷañju and 11 *mañjāḍi*. But the charter for the same was issued only in the next year after delimitation (*piḍagai-naḍandu)*. Further this grant was not entered in the tax register *(variyilaḍādey*) till the year 4(911) of the succeeding reign of Parāntaka I. Probably after these formalities were completed, the said *sabhā* was making the payments to the temple as stipulated. In the meanwhile in the year 36 (943) of Parāntaka I again, the 3000 *kāḍi* (of paddy, the *puravu* that was accruing as the *mudal* from the *kāṇi* of the *kiḷān* of Sankarappāḍi[50] was also granted as *dēvadāna-iṟai-ili*[51] and was so entered in the tax-register. The *sabhā* of Puduppākkam was reported to have seized this *kāṇi* of Sankarappādi-kiḷān also but to have been refusing to pay the *iṟai* in respect of that land (to the temple). This was the subject matter of the complaint by the *dēvakanmis* (administrators of the temple), *uṇ-ṇāḷigai-uḍaiyār* (priests of the sanctum and *pan-māyēsvarar* (of the temple) to the king when he camped at Kāñchīpuram. The king summoned both the parties, the complainants and the complained, made an enquiry and learning that the accusation was substantiated, fined the *sabhā (daṇḍaṇgondu)* but confirmed the *sabhā* on the possession of the said *kāṇi* and directed them to pay the 3000 *kādi* (of paddy) in respect of this *kāṇi* also to the temple (i. e.) in respect of the whole of Siṟṟiyāoṟṟūr the *sabhā* of Puduppākkam had to pay 6000 *kāḍi* (of paddy) as *puravu*. 561 *kāḍi* (of paddy) as *iravu* and 26 *kaḷañju* and 11 m*añjāḍi* as gold levy[52] to the temple, the whole village thus becoming *dēvadāna-*

brahmadēyam. The king ordered the contents of this order to be incorporated in the tax-register and a host of officials starting with the king's secretary (*nam-karumam-ārāiginṛa)* attested the entry.

The second record is the Udayēndram plates of Parāntaka I year 15 (922)[53]. It says that the *Perumānaḍigal* (the king) made a *brahmadēyam* named after him as Vīranārāyaṇachchēri by adding the village Kaḍaikkōṭṭūr in Mēlaḍaiyāṛu-nāḍu in Paḍuvūr-kōṭṭam to the (already existing *brahmadēyam)* Udaya-chandramaṅgalam. The *nāḍu* was assembled to delimit the boundaries and mark the same with stone, and milk bush.[54] Two *paṭṭis,*[55] one *Vichchādira* (vidyādhara)ppaṭṭi, the old *paḷḷichchandam* and *devarpatti* (land in the enjoyment of a Hindu temple?) were excluded from the grant. But otherwise all other types of land in the village were included in the grant. It was stipulated that (in respect of the village added) thousand (units of paddy) would be the *puravu*. The grant was made at the request of Sembiyan Māvali-vāṇarāyar (Ganga-Prithvīpati II Hastimalla), who also gave the proclamatory order and committed the grant to a charter.[56] The third record, the Tiruvālaṅgāḍu plates of Rājēndra I (year 6 (1018) is also very relevent for the present discussion of the king's rights. It contains an order of the king[57] from a secluded place in Muḍikoṇḍa-chōḷapuram[58] to the effect that Paḷaiyanūr, in Mēl-malai-ppaḷaiyanūr-nāḍu, which was coming down as *brahmadēyam* of the *sabhā* of Singaḷāntaka-chchatur-vēdimaṅgalam-in Naduvin-malai-pparumūr-nāḍu had been detached from the *sabhā* with a promise to the *sabhā* to give an exchange and brought under *veḷḷān-vagai* with the *iṛai*. payable being permanently settled.[59] After getting this order duly registered by his officials, the king further ordered that the paddy and gold payable by that village stood diverted from the year 6 to pay for the different *nibandham* (specified expenses for the services) in the temple of God Mahādēva of Paḷaiyanūr-Tiruvālaṅgāḍu.[60] This order was again registered by the same officials. Then the record details the boundaries of the grant village, the *parihāras*, the miscellaneous levies which *kō* could take and which subsequent to the grant, instead of the *kō*, the God (temple) would take, and the privileges including that of the enjoyment of the irrigation water. The proclamatory order (*arai-ōlai*) was issued by the *nāṭṭār* of Mēl-malai-ppaḷaiyanūr-nāḍu after taking the she-elephant around for delimitation and marking the boundaries with stones and milkbush. An official was present during this process and he also issued the proclamatory order. It was attested by the *sabhā* of Singaḷāntaka-chchaturvēdi-maṅgalam as also of Nittavinōda-chaturvēdimaṅgalam, which was one of the villages bordering Paḷaiyanur. The record says that the *ūr* of Palaiyanur also attested the document along with a string of officials.

Two of the above three records pertain to the attachment of villages with the status of *brahmadēyam* to another *brahmadēyam*. The third witnesses the detachment of such a village earlier attached as *brahmadēyam* to a *brahmadēyam* from that *brahmadēyam* and then the bringing of that village under the non-*brahmadēyam, veḷḷānvagai* tenure. Two of them are records of grants for the benefit of a temple and the third appears to have been an addition of the village to a *brahma-dēyam* just for its benefit. Two of the records witness the change brought about in the manner of grants of villages for the benefit of temples, during the 120 years from the grant by Āditya I to the grant by Rājēndra-chōḷa I. These records actually show three stages in such a change. In 892 Āditya made Siṟṟiyāṟṟūr a tax-free *dēvadāna* and attached it as *dēvadāna-brahmadēyam* to *brahmadēyam* Puduppākkam. In the year 943 Parāntaka I added the *puravu* from the *kāṇi* of Sankarappāḍi-kiḷān in Siṟṟiyāṟṟūr excepted earlier, for the benefit of the temple, again as tax-free *dēvadāna* but did not make it over to the *sabhā* of Puduppākkam. In 984 Uttamachōḷa was considerate enough to the same *sabhā* in allowing them to retain the said *kāṇi*. which, had been appropriated by them probably out of a conviction on the strength of the earlier practice that what was granted *dēvadāna* automatically became their entitlement as *brahmadēyam* which however was not intended. In the year

1018 the opposite extreme of a village in the possession of a *brahmadēyam* with the status of *brahmadēyam* being disassociated from the *brahmadēyam* is witnessed.

On an examination of these records it will be seen that the mode of exercise of control of the land by the king had begun to change under the Chōḷas. First of all it is seen that the king's association of *nāṭṭar* in the land scheme began changing. Whereas in the Pallava charters the king addressed himself to the *nāṭṭār* and depended on them to execute several functions regarding the grant all of which showed that there was a sort of community of rights between them, in the earlier copper-plate charter of the Chōḷa period as cited above the king did not address himself to the *nāṭṭār* that body's role got restricted to the delimitation of the grant village.[61] In the 11th century charter also the *nāṭṭār* is said to have delimited the grant village but their performance was attested by an official. No doubt in this latter charter as well as in the Tirumālpuram inscription, the operative part of the record opens with what looks like an address to the local bodies but herein the *nāṭṭār* was not unique but was clubbed together with the Kiḷavar of *brahmadēyams ūrgaḷitār* of several types of villages and the *nagaraṅgaḷiḷār* The communication was also in the nature of a conveyance to them for their information the royal decision.

Whereas even in his addressing of the royal communication, the *kiḷavar* of *brahmadēyams* are seen to have been placed on the same pedestal as the *nāṭṭār, ūrgaḷilār* and *nagaraṅgaḷilār*, the contents of these records further reflect that the king's dependence on the brahmins for exercising the local control was diminishing. It is seen that in 892 the king Āditya-chōḷa I is stated to have attached as *brahmadēyam* the village Siṟṟiyāṟṟūr which he had granted as *dēvadāṇa,* to another *brahmadēyam* evidencing the continuation of the practice of the Pallavas to associate the brahmins in the control of the village. But even then it is witnessed that there was a sizable bloc of land which was the *kāṇi* of a Saṅkarappāḍi-kiḷān which was kept out of the purview of the grant. Kāṇi having denoted land granted for possession against service, this exclusion signified that the king made sure that others who held land from him were kept out of the control of the temples or brahmins. However the circumstances under which this kāṇi of the kiḷān was decided to be granted as *dēvadāṇa* to the temple is not clear, but when it was done later that bloc was not made *brahmadēyam.* Though the *sabhā* of Puduppākkam seizing and enjoying this side, the king enquired into the matter and confirmed them in the possession on condition the *sabhā* contributed the stipulated revenue to the temple, the very fact that the king sat in judgement over them and fined them showed the extent of the royal control over land at the time of Uttama-chōḷa.

This degree of royal control and the king's ceasing to depend on the brahmins are pointedly brought out in the Tiruvālaṅgāḍu record of early 11th century when the king decided to cancel the *brahmadēyam* status of a village before granting the same to the temple.[63]

In the above records it is seen that it was the king's officials who carried out the several processes of the grant, evidencing that the king had assumed direct control of the localities in his dominion with the help of his appointed officials. Often these officials appear to have been chiefs, both petty and big. It might be a Madhurantan Gaṇḍarādittanār enquiring into the dimension of worship in the Tiruvallam temple[64] and fining the errant *sivabrāhmṇās*[65] or a Pudukkudaiyān Ēkadhīran bringing to order or regularising the affairs of Āmūr-nāḍu they are seen functioning away from what might have been their lordship-territory and only in an official capacity, without any involvement in the land where they were functioning.

The Chōḷa king on consolidating his position in Toṇḍai-maṇḍalam, also set about ascertaining his exact entitlement from the land just as the Britishers did eight centuries later. For the first time in the Tamil country land survey is recorded to have been understaken by Rājarāja I and his successors periodically resurveyed the land. It is not known how far the survey covered the other parts of the country but Rājarāja I claimed to have done a thorough survey of Toṇḍai- nāḍu. While this undertaking evidenced the intimate control the Chola claimed over the land, it is also seen that for this he did not depend upon any local organisation but his own officers.[66] He also made any local manipulations impossible by standardising the measuring rod and having specimens of that engraved on temple walls for loclal comparison and adherence.[67]

The details of the survey operation as was done in Toṇḍaimaṇḍalam is not available but the information contained in some of the Tañjāvūr inscriptions[68] can give an idea as to how this survey was conducted and the land was assessed. The total land of the village was measured in the minutest detail. Then from this the extent of land occupied by channels, land allowed for the burning ghat, the habitations of the paṛaiyas or the labouring class etc. which usually were entitled to be exempted from the payment of *iṛai* was deducted and the balance of land was declared as assessable and assessed. As a result the tax dues of villages ceased to be quoted in round figures but began to be given in fractions to a minute degree.[69] Probably the waste land in villages was also assessed but was expected to pay the taxes on reclamation, which is why it is found that the land sold by the village organisations for reclamation and endowment to temples had to be got freed from the burden of *iṛai* by payment of sufficient capital to the village organisation if the endower so desired. There are no records to show what discrepancies in the extent of the land in villages and in the corresponding tax assessment were found during the survey. However some temple records as uusual indicate the resultant action taken. The Tiruvallam inscription of the time of Rājarāja I, year 22 (1007)[70] says that the *pañchavāram* payable by a *dēvadāna* village under the management of a *sabhā* to the temple at Tiruvallam was increased. Probably this was the consequence of correct measurement and assessment.[71] Whereas the inscription of the time of Parāntaka I from Piḷḷaippākkam cited above says that the defaulters in tax payments would not be eligible for selection to the committees, the inscription of Rājarāja I (year 24 (1009) from Ukkal[72] authorised the sale of the land of the defaulters. Where necessary probably when influential persons or bodies were complained against in regard to misappropriations of land, the king himself seems to have sat in judgement as evidenced in the Tirumālpuram inscription.

All these operations undertaken by Rājarāja I were obviously based on his claim for receiving the correct tax from the land in the villages. Whether this claim to the tax on land was based on his superior ownership of all the land in his territory, it is not possible to say. Whereas the terms used earlier, *pañchavāram* and *puravu* do not reflect the basis on which the king made the claim, the term *iṛai* generally used to denote the main land tax, in later records, it seems to have been derived both from the verb, *iṛu*-to pay, and from the same word, *iṛai* meaning the 'Lord' indicating that the tax was construed as the lord's portion. In Tamil, the word *iṛai* is applied to both God and king. Tiruvalluvar whom one scholar places in the 1-2 century A.D.[73] and another places in the epoch 500-750 A.D.,[74] in the didactical work, Tirukkuṛaḷ[75] defined the king as the *iṛai* (God) of the people because he regulated and administered the law and protected the people. It thus implies that the king's role was that of the protector and hence his entitlement, the portion of the yield of land due to *iṛai* was in the form of fees to the protector and not as the portion payable to the supreme land-lord. This is also proabably indicated by the reference to the dues of the king (*nṛipa-dēyam*) froṃ the land as one sixth (*aṛu-kūrināḷ*) in the Shōliṅghūr inscription of Parāntaka I.[76] The inscriptions of Rājarāja[77] I however refer to the royal due from the land as *iṛai-kaṭṭina-kāṇikkaḍa*ṇ which can be roughly translated as "the due on account of the *kāṇi* as assessed tax". The word *kāṇi* is used to denote an allotted right to do a particular service, as in *muppadu-vaṭṭattu-kkāṇi*—"the right to have the turn in the cycle of thirty" used in respect of temple worship. The land allotment against that service was also called *kāṇi*. Otherwise also *kāṇi* is used to indicate land allotted against a service as in *tachcha-kkāṇi* the *kāṇi* of the carpenter[78]. Hence the reference to the royal dues as *kāṇik-kaḍan* might have indicated that all land was deemed to have been held by the individuals as *kāṇi* from the king and the taxes became payable in fulfilment of the contract between the king and the land-holders.[79] But it appears that what is quoted in the Tañjāvūr inscriptions as *iṛai-kaṭṭina- kāṇi-kkaḍan* did not represent the due on account of *iṛai*, the main land tax alone. Even from the time of Aparājita- Pallava it has been seen that a gold levy had been added to the *puravu* due from land. The Tirumālpuram inscription indicates that an *iravu* had been further added to the burden of the land.[80] The Tiruvakkarai inscription of the year 16 (1000-1001) of Rājarāja[81] I again refers to the levy Paḷḷippēṛu instead of *iravu,* as payable by the village in addition to *pañchavāram* and *kāsu* (in gold). The Tiru-vālaṅgāḍu plates refers to the permanent *iṛai* fixed as payable by the village granted as *dēvadāna* included *paḷḷi*. Hence the *iṛai kaṭṭina, kāṇi-kkaḍan* must have been the consolidated due. From the details provided in the Tānjāvūr inscriptions it becomes clear that the *iṛai-kaṭṭina kāṇikkaḍan* in respect of a *vēli* was either 100 *kalam* (approx) of paddy (in the case of *sabhā* and *ūr* villages) or 10 *kaḷañju* (approx) (in respect of *nagaṛam* villages). In the light of the information provided by the Shōliñghūr inscription of Parāntaka I and the discussion above, it can be concluded that this approximately 100 *kalams* of paddy demanded as *iṛai- kaṭṭina-kāṇi-kkadan* from a *vēlī* of land could not have formed just 1/6 of the produce. It might have been half or 1/3 of the produce representing a consolidated levy. Thus from the study of the tax-structure in respect of land under the Chōḷas it becomes clear that they exercised more intimate and strict control over land under their dominion.

A. Royal Demense and Association of the members of the king's family in Land control.

There is no evidence of the king in Toṇḍaimaṇḍalam, whether he was the Pallava or Chōḷa, having possessed land in the villages as royal demense worked under his own arrangement or having associated the members of the royal family in the control of land.[82]

There does not seem to have been any necessity for royal demense as the receipt of grain and gold in the form of taxes must have met his needs. Though as has been seen above the king had the right over the uncultivated land in villages, he exercised his right over such land only by gifting it to brahmins.

When the connection of the king with the land was overall and supervisory the question of his giving land to members of the royal family for their personal management could not have arisen. However two records of even the Pallava period evidence that the king could exercise controlling interest in respect of temple land and that the queens were also associated in the matter of making grants to temples. An inscription from Kūram (Chingleput district)[83] is dated[84] during the reign of Nandivarman III (840-869) and records a royal order to the *sabhā* of Kūram in respect of a plot of 6 *paṭṭi* extent which is described as *akkala-nimmaḍi-poṟṟipaḍi* in their *ūr*. The order referred to the changing of the possessors of that plot of land (*mun-peṟṟārai-māṟṟi*). The latter portion of the inscription is damaged but from the extant portion it is clear that the land was meant to be utilised for the worship of god Mahādēva and was vested with a priest for doing the worship as also for maintaining himself. First the designation of the plot of land as the *pōṟṟipaḍi* of *akkaḷa-nimmaḍi* suggests that the land had some connection with Aggaḷānimmaḍi, the queen of Dantivarman and the mother of Nandivarman III.[85] Poṟṟipaḍi (poṟṟi=praise; paḍi=allotment) may have been the plot, the revenues of which were earmarked to meet the expenses of the prayers for the welfare of the dowager queen. As the plot was known as such even at the time of the record under discussion, it is indicated that this plot had been earmarked for the purpose stated even earlier. It is not known if it was the king or the dowager queen that had granted the land and if the worship for the welfare of the queen originally was intended to be conducted in the same temple of

Mahādēva which finds mention in the present record. It is also not known as to who had been placed in charge of the land earlier from whose possession it was taken away and given over to the priest indicated in the present record. From the fact that the present royal order was addressed to the *sabhā* of Kūram, it is also clear that the land was under the administration of that *sabhā* but still was under the direct control of the king. It is possible that the concerned plot was of the share set apart for the temple of Mahādēva at the time of the creation of the *brahmadēyam* as was done in Chiṭṭrūr alias Pirudi-Mahādēvi-chaturvēdimaṅgalam and such land even in the *sabhā* village was under the control of the king who could direct as to with whom the land was to be vested.[86] He could also earmark that land for particular services. Alternatively, it is possible that the plot of land concerned was out of the cultivable waste of the village over which the king had joint control with the *sabhā*[87] and that in exercise of that right, he had earlier allocated the land for service in the temple for the merit of his mother or the queen in her own right or with the authorisation of the king had allotted the land for her own merit. The king's right over that land continued and so by the current order he div\erted a change in the possession of that land. An inscription from Kāñchīpuram dated during the reign of a Nandivarman (whether he was the second or third of that name depends on the date which is, however, damaged) also says that the queen Dharma-Mahādēvi assigned a small village Nāyivaṭṭi-kuḷattūr, a *dēvadāna* of god Māṇikkadēva in Dharma-Mahādevi-Iśvaragṛiham as *Tiruvāṇṇāḷigaippuṛam*. The village consisted of only 10 *paṭṭis* of land. The temple named after the queen was probably raised by her and the god Māṇikka-dēvar probably named after one of her titles as indicated by a string of her titles given in the same record (line 3) was probably the main deity in that temple. The reference to the village as the *dēvadāna* of the god suggests that the king or the queen herself had granted the village as *dēvadāna* earlier and now the queen specified that the village was meant for the purpose of maintaining the priests as also the services in the temple. The land in the village granted was not waste land as at least, a part of the village seems to have been under cultivation and in the possession of one Kaṇṇandai (*Kannaṇdai-kudippāḍu-uḷpaḍa)*. However, as in the Kūram inscription discussed above, there is no mention in the inscription that the old possessors were changed *(mun-peṟṟārai-māṟri)*. Hence it would appear that only the royal income from that village granted as *dēvadāna* was involved in the transaction.

However during the Chōḷa period the queens do not seem to have had the right of granting land on their own to the temple. For instance there is a gift of land by a queen of the enigmatic ruler Parthivendravarman of the later half of the 10th century recorded in an inscription from *Uttaramallūr*.[88] This record states that the queen Villavan-mahādēvi raised a shrine for Tiru-ayōddhyai-pperumānaḍigaḷ in *Uttaramallūr* and endowed 2920 *kuḷi* of land of the first sort in three plots for the *sribali* and *archchanā-bhōgam* of that god. The land was in *Uttaramallūr* and the queen paid *pūrvvāchāram* to the *sabhā* of the place to get the land freed from taxes. There is no mention of the land having been purchased by the queen. The fact that the land was classified as the first sort indicates that the land was already under cultivation and in that *sabhā* village must have been in the possession of a brahmin. It seems that the non-mention of the purchase of the plots by the queen was just an omission in the record. It may be due to the record having been drafted as a statement of the proceedings of a meeting of the *peruṅguri-sabhā* declaring the land tax-free on the receipt of *pūrvvāchāram*, where there was no necessity to state how the land had been endowed. This is probably clarified in another record from the same place dated in year 12 of the same king.[89] It states that another queen Tribhuvana-mahādēvi purchased six plots totalling 2495 kuḷis (the classification of which, however, is not mentioned) from the *kuḍimakkaḷ* of the *ūr*,[90] for endowment to the god in Srīvēli-vishṇugṛiham. She also got the land freed from taxes by paying *pūrvvāchāṛam* to the *sabhā*. The temple had been raised by a Koṅgaraiyar who was probably related to the queen.

In the period of Rājarāja I (985-1014) and later also the few references to queens connected with endowments to temples also indicate that the queens had no independent possession of land. For example, the Tiruvakkarai (South Arcot District) inscription of the year 17 (1001-02) of Rājarāja[91] I records that Sembiyan Māhadēvi, mother of uttama-chōḷa, the king's predecessor, built a temple and for that Rājarāja I made the village Maṇali, the *dēvadāna* the *ūrār* of the place being directed to contribute the *panchavāram* etc. to the temple. An inscription of the year 9 (1021) of Rājēndra I from Perumbulippākkam (North Arcot District)[92] says that his senior queen Malaiyan Kundavaiyar alias Sembiyan Māhādevi purchased land from the *ūrār* for endowment to the temple.

Regarding the queen's involvement with land, the above evidence would indicate that only during the Pallava period they were authorised some rights. Though private brahmin ladies are seen to have possessed some land allotted to them as their *angamaṇi*, the queens and ladies of the royal household probably did not enjoy the privilege.[93] Where it is seen that the kings themselves are not evidenced to have owned royal demense lands, there does not seem to be any question of the king's family being allotted land for their maintenance. But they could induce the kings to exercise their privileges on their behalf. Otherwise they seem to have possessed gold (cash) which they could utilise either by directly endowing it or for purchasing land for endowment to gods to earn merit.

Regarding the rights of princes with regard to the land, there is no evidence during the period under study. For the Pallava period, the records do not at all refer to princes. Princes of the Chōḷa family are, however, mentioned but they are invariably seen endowing gold only to temples. However, there is a stray reference to a *kāṇi-nāyakam* officer of prince Rājāditya, heir-apparent of Parāntaka-chōḷa I in two inscriptions from Vālikaṇḍapuram in Tiruchirappaḷḷi District.[94] *Kāṇi* usually denotes land allotted, against service and the desingation *kāṇi-nāyakam* seems to indicate that the officer was the agent of the prince managing the princes' lands. But in the epigraphs cited, the officer concerned is seen making only benefactions of gold. Hence it becomes doubtful if the term *kāṇi* in the designation of the officer denoted land held by the prince. Otherwise some of the Chōḷa princes are known to have held viceroyalties under the monarchs and in Toṇḍaimaṇḍalam there is evidence of such holding only in the Udayēndram plates of Vīrachōḷa.[95] The identity of this Vīrachōḍa, who is referred to as *nṛipēsvara* is Prithivīpati II but the contents give an indication of the limitations to the rights of this *nṛipēśvara* who was obviously a viceroy prince.[96] This prince was advised to grant land to brahmins for the purpose of elevating his forefathers to heavens. He approached the Chōḷa king requesting for permission (*anugrahaṃ*) to grant a village in the territory held by him *(mad-dēśe)*. He promised him that the village granted would be named after the king as Parākēsari-chaturvēdimaṅgalam. This leads to the conclusion that the princes, though allotted territories for administration, did not enjoy any right to dispose of land as it pleased them. For any gift of land, they had to seek the permission of the king.

B. Feudatory chiefs—Vijñapatis, kō, uḍaiyāṉ etc

The records of the period both those quoting the reign period of the Pallavas and the reign period of the Chōḷas refer to some personages who either from the express mention or from the context of mention can be understood to have had some connection with the land and to have been associated with the king in the control of land. Some of them were chiefs in the region around Toṇḍaimaṇḍalam who did not owe their existence to the kings of Toṇḍaimaṇḍalam and who seem to have allied themselves with the kings in a subordinate capacity and helped them to come to power. Some others seem to have been such who had been made into chiefs by the kings in return for services rendered. Some appear to have been officials who had been associated with the land as a fee for their functioning.[97] (The character and quantum of control over land in association with or in subordination to the king, the personages in each category had are indicated in the context where they get mentioned.) It is observed that there was a difference in the position of the subordinates as between the Pallava and Chōḷa periods.

The copper-plate charters as well as some stone instriptions recording the grant of *brahmadēyam* or *dēvadāna* refer to some chiefs or chief-like personages as having made the request to the king regarding the grant. They are called the *vijñapti* or supplicator in regard to the grant. They also refer to an official who is sometimes referred to as *mantri* (minister) as the executor or recorder of orders or *ājñapti* of the grant. It is usually understood that the supplicator was actually the one who had control over the region in which the grant villages lay and it was he who had made the grant of *brāhmadēya* or *dēvadāna* as recorded and his supplication to the king was for obtaining ratification for the grant from the king as it was he who had the overall control. It is pointed out that the reference to the grant as a *paradatti* (taken to mean "given by another)" in some of these grants definitely indicated this character of the record.[98] The position can be examined by an analysis of the contents of the records mentioning the *vijñaptis*.

In the Kūram grant of Paramēsvaravarman (670-700), the supplicator (*vijñapti*) was Vidyāvinita Pallavādhirāja and the executor *(ājṅapti)* of the grant was one *Uttarakāranika* Mahāsēnadatta. The village Paramēsvaramaṅgalam newly created and granted as *brahmadēyam* lay in Panmānāḍu in *Maṇaiyiṛ-* kōṭṭam. The temple for which this village granted as *brahmadēyam* was to be an adjunct, was in Kūram which was prosperous with 108 *chaturvēdi-kulam* in Nirvēḷur-nāḍu in Ūṛṛukkāṭṭu-kkōṭṭam. The temple had been built by Vidyāvinīta Pallavādhirāja, the supplicator for the *brahmadēya* grant, on land purchased by himself. The gift village was named after the king as Paramēsvaramaṅgalam and the irrigation reservoir authorised was also similarly named. A1l these circumstances indicate that Vidyāvinīta-Pallavādhirāja might have been a chief but his territory did not lay in the region of

Kūram. He could not be deemed to have purchased land in Kūram for the temple and at the same time to have himself granted a neighbouring village as *brahmadēyam* and approached the king for ratification of the same.

In the Udayēndram plates of Nandivarman II (year 21 = 752 A.D.) the supplicator was Udayachandra, who was excellent in intelligence *(dhī-varah)* a punisher of the circle of enemies (*para-chakra-daṇḍī)* born of Pūchān-kula, the chief of Vilvalapura, one who belonged to a family hereditarily attached to the Pallava dynasty (*Pallava-kula-paramparāgata)*, lord of Vegavatī-nadī and who fought battles on behalf of the king. He made the request to his lord *(svāmiṇ*) who made the grant of the village to the brahmins naming it after the requestor as Udaya-chandramaṅgalam in honour or as a recompense for his swordmanship *(asi-dhārā-nishkṛiyārtham)* which probably helped the king to retain his kingdom *(sakala-rājya-pradātuḥ)*[99]. The grant village lay in *Paschimāsrayānadi-vishaya* (Mēl-aḍaiyāṟu-nāḍu in Paḍuvūr-kōṭṭam). There is no executor mentioned. Here it is not likely that the king's ratification of a grant by Udyachandra alone gave expression to the former's gratitude to the latter.

The supplicator in the Kaśākkuḍi plates of the same king (year 22=753 A.D.) was Brahmasrī-rāja (also called Brahma-yuvāraja?), a chief minister devoted to Nandi. The Tamil portion of the grant is prefaced with the statement that it was a communication of the *(kō)* to the *nāṭṭār*. There was an executor by name Gōrasarmmā. The grant village Kōṭukoḷḷi was in Ūṟṟukkāṭṭu-kkōṭṭam and was named Ēkadhīra- maṅgalam on becoming a *brahmadēyam*. In the Sanskrit text of the grant there occurs a phrase, *svayam-evaprasādāt* after *brāhmaṇāya* and before *Undiravaṇa-kōshṭakē* in the sentence ending with *datta iti*. After this occurs the sentence *vijñaptiḥ = Brahma-yuvarājasya*. The phrase svayameva-*prasādāt* could mean either that the grant was made by himself out of grace, i. e. by the king[100] or that Brahma-srīrāja first got the land granted to himself by the king and thereafter he made the grant with his own heir as the requestor for the grant. It was a *paradatti* made in the presence of *nilai-kkalattar adhikāṛis* and those that took down the royal utterances *(vāyil-kēṭpār)*. The noteworthy detail about the *vijñapti* is that he was the chief minister of the king. There is no indication that he was a chief. His title reminds one only of the brahmin commanders of the Chōlas who were titled as *brahmādhirāja*.

In the Pullūr grant of the same king (year 33 = 764 A.D.) the request was made by Avanichandra-yuvarāja, the Vilvala-purēsvara, a *sāmanta-mukhya* and a *Pallava-bhakta*. He was obviously of the same family as the *vijñapti* of the Udayēndram grant and like the second *vijñapti* of the Kśākkudi grant, execution of a meritorious deed *(dharmma- krityāṛtham)*, when

he was surnamed yuvarāja He made the vijñ pana when the king was seated in his court. There was also an *ājñapti* by name Nāgasarmman alias Brahmādhirāja who was excellent both as a brahmin and as a minister *(dvija-vara* and *mantri-vara)*. Four villages, Nelli, Pullūr and Kuḍiyūr in Kiḷvē-nāḍu and Takkār in Maṇḍaikuḷa-nāḍu, all in Palkunṛakkōṭṭam were clubbed together and named Nayadhīra-maṅgalam after the name of the king and gifted as *brahmadēyam*. It was made as *paradatti* having been made eligible for *pāṛchāttu* and *paradatti*.

A stone inscription from Mallām, Gudur Taluk, Nellore District in Andhra Pradesh dated year (746 A.D.) in the reign of Nandivarman (probably the second) seems to record that the king granted the gold yield of *pañchavāram* to god Subrahmaṇia at Tiruvānpūr. Chalukki-araśar is said to have been the executor. The supplicator for the grant was an Āḷuvārasar.[101] This shows that the supplicator and executor were also cited in grants where land was not involved.

In the Rōyakkōṭṭāh plates of Skandasishya, the request was made by Mahābali-Vāṇarāja and there was an "*ājñapti* by name Mahēsvara-bhaṭṭar. The gift village Chārukūr was situated in Mēl-aḍaiyāṛu-nāḍu in Paḍuvūr-kōṭṭam. In the Vēlūrpālaiyam plates of Nandivarman III (year 6=852 A.D.) it is said that a

Chōḷavaṁsachūḷāmaṇi, named Kumāraṅkuśa, who was a *kṛitaj ñah* (grateful person) was made the supplicator for the grant *(vijñaptimātrā-kṛita)*. There was also an executor by name Namban, a *mantri* who in the Tamil portion is referred to as Iraiyur-uḍaiyan. The record definitely says that the king *(Iśvaraḥ)* gave the village Tirukkāṭṭuppaḷḷi in Nāyaṟu-nāḍu in Puḷaṟ-koṭṭam as *dēvadāna*. It was declared as *paradatti*.

In the Tiruvallam inscription of Nandivarman III, year 17 (863 A.D.), the Bāṇa chief Viḍēlviḍugu Vikramāditya is said to have been the supplicator and a Kāḍupaṭṭi Tamilppēraraiyan was the executor. Three villages, one of which was already a *dēvadāna* were clubbed together to form a new *brahmadēyam* named after the Bāṇa chief. The villages lay in Mīyāṟu-nāḍu in Paḍuvūr kōṭṭam[102].

The Kāñchīpuram inscription of Nandivarman III (year 18= 864)[103] records the grant of a licence to the traders of Viḍēlviḍugu-kudirai-chchēri to carry on trade in all goods from camphor to shoes and for this grant the supplicator was Anutta-rappallavaraiyan and executor Kāḍupaṭṭi Tamil-ppēraraiyan.

In the Chiṭṟūr plates of Nṛipatuṅga (year 6= 865 A.D.), the supplicator was Kāḍupaṭṭi Muttaraiyan[104] and executor Kāḍupaṭṭi Tamiḻppēraraiyan. The village granted as *brahma-dēyam* was in Panmā-nāḍu in Maṇaiyiṟ-kōṭṭam and the village was named Prithvī-mahādēvi-chaturvēdimaṅgalam (probably after the queen).

In the Udayēndram plates of Parāntaka I (year 15= 922 A.D.) the king added a village Kaḍaikkōṭṭūr to Udayachandra-maṅgalalam and created a new *brahmadēyam* after his own name on the request *(vijñapṭi)* of Śembiyan Māvalivāṇarāyar, i.e. Gaṅga- Prithvīpati II. The village lay in Mēl-aḍaiyāṟu-nāḍu in Paḍuvūr-kkōṭṭam. A stone inscription from Sholinghur, (916) of Parāntaka I[105] records the grant of the royal dues from a field (or hamlet) for the maintenance of the local tank called Chōḷāvaridhi. In the Sanskirt portion of the record, it is mentioned that Hastimalla by which title Gaṅga Prithvīpati II was known acted both the supplicator and as the executor for the grant. The Tamil portion, however, says that Vīraśōḷan Hastimallan (Gaṅga Prithvīpati II) gave the field so that the tank might get the *puravu* (the land assessment) *āyati* (other royal incomes from the village) and gold levy in respect of that field.

In the Udayēndram plates of Vīrachōda, it has been seen how the prince Vīrachōda petitioned the king for granting a village in his own nāḍu to the brahmins.

In an inscription from Paḷankōyil (Polur Taluk, North Arcot District) dated year 6 = 976 A.D. in the reign of Parakēsarivarman Uttamachōḷa[106] it is stated that Kamban Irāman alias Uttamachōla Pirudigaṅgaraiyar, who had Pangala-nāḍu petitioned the king when he was camped at Kāñchīpuram for the grant of Odiyampallam, a hamlet of Pudānadappāḍi to god Mahādēvar of the place, all of which was situated in his own nāḍū and got the favour *(prasādam)* granted by the king through a recorder of royal utterances *(vāśal-kēḷvi)* and with the knowledge *(jñānam)* of another official who probably committed such grants to memory. The village was freed from taxes and it was so entered in the register on the orders of the king. Thereafter the Pirudigaṅgaraiyar made the hamlet a *dēvadāna* free from *irai* after duplicating the same formalities of having his own official make the request, with his own recorder of utterances taking down the order and with one official acting as the one committing this to memory[107].

In another inscription from Pañchapāṇḍavamalai (Polur Taluk, North Arcot District) dated in the year 8 (993 A.D.) of Rājarāja I[108], Vīrachōḷa Ilāḍaraja, who as a feudatory was evidently holding the territory under his own charge, while making a remission of levies from a *paḷḷichchandam* land was requested for this purpose by his own consort (*dēvi*) and when he had the order committed to writing, he had his own agent *(karṇam)* as the executor. Evidently, the chief Ilāḍarāja did not involve his sovereign because the levies he remitted was within his own competence.

It may be seen that of the above-listed instances wherein the king is stated to have acted on being supplicated for the grant by a *vijñapti,* in one instance, i.e. in the Kāñchīpuram inscription of Teḷḷāṟṟeṟinda Nandivarman III, (year 18 = 864) the transaction involved in the record was the grant of a licence to traders. It does not appear as if the right of granting licence for trade was vested in a chief and the king's intervention was to ratify the grant of such licence by the feudatory, Anuttara-ppallavaraiyan. Even if it is supposed that Anuttara-Pallavaraiyan had an entitlement to the fee-proceeds from the issue of licences, in other cases where the feudatory of official granted such levies or exemptions from such levies he did not go to the king for ratification. The inscription of the year 4 (889) of Aparājita from Satyavēḍu recording the grant of *puravu* and *pon* from Tuṟaiyur to God Mahādēva of Tirumadaṅganpaḷḷi by Kumarandai Kurumbarādittan and the grant of exemption from the levies *kaṟpūravilai* and *anyāya-vāva-daṇdam* in respect of land held as *paḷḷichchandam* by a Jain establishment by Vīrachōḷa Ilāḍarāja in the year 8 (993) of Rājarāja I as per the Pañchapāṇḍavamalai inscription noticed above did not involve ratification by the king. In the Vēlurpāḷaiyam plates the record says that for the grant of *dēvadāna* by the king, the Chōḷavamsachūḷāmani Kumārāṅkusa was made the *vijñapti*. In the case of the Udayēndram plates of Nandivarman II, the grant of *brahmadēyam* by the king was to reward a feudatory for having helped the king to emerge as successful ruler of Toṇḍaimaṇḍalam. This feudatory is mentioned as the *vijñapti* for the grant. If the feudatory was the actual grantor of the *brahmadēyam* and the king only ratified the same, this ratification could not have amounted to a reward worth mentioning. It is also noteworthy that except in this case as well as in the case of the Tiruvallam inscription of Nandivarman III, in the other cases of the grants in Toṇḍaimaṇḍalam the grant village was named after the king again indicating the king's connection with the land granted. In the Shōliṅghūr inscription of Parāntaka I, the same chief, Hastimalla was the supplicator as well as the executor of the grant which indicates that the terms *vijñapti* and *ājñapti* referred to the official function of the persons named. Also whereever the territory controlled by the chief is mentioned in the record, it appears that the grant village was not included in that territory. In the Kūram grant it may be observed that the chief Vidyāvinīta Pallava had to purchase land in Kūram for constructing the temple. The village Paramēśvaramaṅgalam granted as *brahmadēyam* must have been adjacent to Kūram and as such was not within the territory held by the *vijñapti* feudatory.[109] It can also be seen that in the Pullūr plates the formalities of the grant are stated to have been carried out when the king was seated in his court. The grant was made for carrying out the duty (*dharmma-kṛityartham*) by the king and not by the *vijñapti*.

It does not also appear as if the term *paradatti* used in some of these grants to describe the character of the grant indicated that the *vijñapti* made the grant and sought the ratification of the same by the king. It may be observed that of all these grants quoting a *vijñapti*, only the Kaśākkuḍi plates and the Pullūr grant,[110] both recording the constitution of a *brahmadēyam* and the Vēlūrpāḷaiyam plates granting the income from a village as *dēvadānam* refer to the grant as having been made as a *paradatti*. The mention of this *paradatti* only in those three grants as also in the Paḷḷankōyil plates wherein no *vijñapti* is quoted for the grant of the village and additional land as *paḷḷichchandam* to a Jain establishment, point to the term having meant something else than that the grant had been made by another, requiring ratification by the king. The expression *paradatti śelvadāga* or *paradatti-śenṛadu,* i. e. that the grant went as *paradatti* as employed in the record also seems to indicate that in the cases where mentioned the expression was used to record the authorisation extended to the grantees to part with the land[111]. It appears that the non-mention of *paradatti* with reference to the grant in the other cases meant that the donee (donees) were not invested with the authority to part with the land to another either by gift or by sale[112]. Thus all the evidence points to the conclusion that the expressions used in the charters while describing the mode of the grant of the land or village, *vijñapti, ājñapti*. and *paradatti,* did not signify the existence of joint control in respect of the grant land/village involved in the said respective grants as between the king and a feudatory. The *vijñapti*[113] and *ājñapti* in the grants though they might have been chiefs even enjoying some territory allotted to them by the king, in so far as the relevant grant was concerned, fulfilled a court procedure and *paradatti* referred to an authorisation granted to the donees.

However, some of the records pertaining to the region outside Toṇḍaimaṇḍalm indicate that the land/village involved in the grant lay within the territory in the enjoyment of the chief who is cited as the one who made the request regarding the grant. It is noteworthy that the phraseology used to denote their function in these grants was somewhat different though derived from the same verbal root *(jñap* with the prefix Vi). It is in these records that there is evidence of the joint control with regard to that land involved in the grant held by both the king and the feudatory. The two charters of the period of Nandivarman II from Chōḷamaṇḍalam and the charter of Nṛipatuṅga from the middle region belong to this category of charters. In these, the grants of land are reflected to have actually been made in the territory of a subordinate chief at his initiative with the concurrence of the overlord monarch. In the Paṭṭ attālmaṅgalam grant of Nandivarman II, though the Tamil section makes a succinct mention that the grant of *brahmadēyam* was made with Maṅgala-nāḍaḷvan as the *viṇṇappam* (supplication) and Alappākka-Nalluḷān as the *āṇatti* (executor), the Sanskrit text gives a more illuminating description of the process of the grant. It states that the *Mangala-rāshṭra (janapada)-bharttā*, a servant *(bhṛitya)* of the Pallavēndra humbly requested or informed *(vijñāpya)* his master *(svāmin)* and gave the 16 vēlis in the village Taḷikkoṟṟangudi as *brahmadēyam*. The gift is said to have been a *datti* of the said chief. The record, however, is not described as *paradatti*. The Tamil section is drafted in the form of a royal order to the *nāṭṭar* of Tenkarai-Arvalakkūṟṟam in Chōḷa-nāḍu, who honoured the royal letter, marked the boundaries of the bloc of land granted as *brahmadēyam* and issued the proclamation (*arai-olai*). In the Taṇḍantōṭṭam plates of the same king, the Sanskrit draft is similar. Dayāmukha, the chief of the territory is stated to have informed (*nivēdya*) the king and got a village named after himself as Dayāmukhamaṅgalam given (*adāpayat*) as *brahmadēyam* to 308 brahmins. Though the leaves of the set of plates containing the Tamil portion of the text referring to the *vijñapti* etc. are missing, even in the Sanskrit text extant, the royal involvement in the grant is prominently indicated by the mention of a chief of the treasury (*kōśadhyaksha*) named Kumāra as the *ājnāpti* of the grant. In the Bāhūr plates of Nṛipatunga pertaining to the south Pennar region, the Sanskrit text conforms to the former two. A chief who is described as the "sun of the Vēśāli family" informed or requested (*vijñāpya*) the king and got three villages in his own territory (*rāshṭra*) (approved) for the grant of *brahmadēyam* for supporting an educational institution. The king made the allotment through an executor. The Tamil text refers to the *Vesālippāḍi-araiyan as the viṇṇappam* for the grant. This grant is stated to have been made as *paradatti*.

It will be seen that in these charters pertaining to the region outside Toṇḍaimaṇḍalam, there is a clear-cut evidence of the existence of the joint control of territories by the king and his feudatories. There is no evidence to enlighten us on the background of the chiefs mentioned. Even in the Chōḷa country the chiefs mentioned in the two grants detailed above do not appear to have had any connection with the Chōḷa family.[115] As such all these chiefs seem to have owed their position to the king who might have granted them the territory to administer. But the above detailed records show that they were not authorised to gift away or part with the land in the same territory on their own. Not only permission of the king was necessary to gift the land but also the forms of the gift was made to appear as if it was a gift by the king. The grant of *brahmadēya* privileges also seem to have been a reserved right of the king.

In one case where similar characteristics are also evidenced in a grant of land within Toṇḍaimaṇḍalam during the Pallava period the circumstances seem to have been peculiar to that region. In this case, however, the grant land lay within Toṇḍaimaṇḍalam but bordered on Perumbāṇappāḍi or Vaḍugavaḷi (the path of the northerners- 12000, just north of Toṇḍaimaṇḍalam that the territory of the Bāṇas, a longstanding minor dynasty of rulers who often allied themselves with one of the chief powers of the region, tilting the balance of power.[116] The records from Paḍuvūr-kōṭṭam describe how the Bāṇas gradually gained control over this territory of the Pallavas. When Nandivarman II issued his charter granting Udaya-chandramaṅgalam in Paśchimāśraya-nadī-vishaya (Mēl-aḍaiyāṛu-nāḍu) in Paḍuvūr-kōṭṭam as *brahmadēyam* in his year 21 (752), there is no evidence of the area being controlled by anyone other than the king. The *vijñapti* in that grant Udayachandra, the chief of Vilvalapura does not seem to have had any rights over this territory. But the Rōyakōṭṭāh plates recording a grant by Skandasishya of a village in Mēl-aḍaiyāru-nāḍu in Paḍuvūr-kōṭṭam to a single brahmin refers to a Mahābali-Vāṇarāja as the *vijñapti* of the grant. The date of this Skandasishya is uncertain but, however, it is to be noted that there is no indication in the record that this Bāṇarāja's function in the grant was any more than that of the other *vijñaptis* of Toṇḍaimaṇḍalam records. There is also no evidence in the record of any close association of the Bāna with the land. But a record dated in the year 62 (793) of Nandivarman II[117] indicates that the Bāṇa had gained hold of the territory even by that time. This record from Tiruvallam which was in Miyāṛu-nāḍu in Paḍuvūr-kōṭṭam, after referring to the king refers also to Māvalivāṇarāyar as ruling Vaḍugavaḷi-12000 without, however telling how he and Vaḍugavali were connected with Tiruvallam. However, his hold over the territory is made clear by the statement that the Bāṇa delimited *(valañ-jeydu)* a plot of land purchased and endowed by a private person. In this record it is noteworthy that the Bāṇa is introduced in such a way that it is made clear that with regard to his home territory Vaḍugavali-mēṛku, he was without obligation to anyone[118]. But in respect of Paḍuvūr- kōṭṭam he was subordinate to the Pallava king who had his overall controls the Bāṇa having only an associate status, either as a result of conferment or encroachment. How strong these associate rights of the Bāṇa came to be in due course is hinted at in the record dated in the year 17 (863) of Nandivarman III from the same Tiruvallam.[119] This record does not refer to Māvali-vāṇarāyar as the ruler of Vaḍugavaḷi-mēṛku. The text says that three villages Aimbūṇi, Viḷattūr and Amarunṛimaṅgalam were joined together to form a new chaturvedi- maṅgalam at the *viṇṇappam (vijñapaṇam)* of Māvalivāṇarāyan Vikramāditta-vāṇarāyan and with Kāḍupaṭṭi Tamiḻppēraraiyan[120] as the *āṇatti* (*ājñapti*). However, it is seen that the involvement of the Bāṇa with the grant was not of the same kind as that of the *vijñaptis* of the other Toṇḍaimaṇḍalam grants though the pattern of the text is similar to the other such grants. The new village was named after the Bāṇa as Viḍēlviḍugu-vikramāditta-chaturvēdimaṅgalam, but it is noteworthy that there is no statement as in the Udayēndram grant that the king named the new *brahmadēyam* after the chief as a mark of appreciation and recognition of his valour. There is also no hint of such subservience on the part of the Bāṇa as exhibited by the feudatories in the grants of Chōḷamaṇḍalam and the middle country. Though in those cases also the grant village was named after the feudatory, it is only in the Tiruvallam record it is seen that the naming of the *brahmadēyam* village after the Bāṇa had a greater significance. For understanding the implications of the grant one has to study this record in the context of the other later records that have come to light from Tiruvallam. These later records from the place cite only the Bāṇa without mentioning any overlord king.[121] One of them actually refers to him as ruling the world then. Further the Udayēndram plates of Parāntaka-chola I of the early 10th century indicates that the Paḍuvūr-kōṭṭam area was part of the Bāṇa territory that was conquered and handed over to Gaṅga Prithvipati II by Parāntaka I. So, in the light of all this it can be stated that by the time of Nandivarman III the area around Tiruvallam had come under the control of the Bāṇa and that was why the newly constituted *brahmadēyam* was named after him.[122] His *viṇṇappam* to Nandivarman was obviously due to an acknowledgement of the fact that in respect of this territory within Toṇḍaimaṇḍalam the Pallava king still retained some control. The reference to the Pallava king may have also been due to the fact that the Bāṇa could not interfere with the land revenue collection from the area as it is seen that the record refers to the arrangement regarding such land revenue.

Other chiefs and their Role :

Apart from the chiefs who figure in the land grants as *vijñaptis* as detailed above, who sometimes seem to have had control over portions of the territory within the domain of the Pallavas jointly with the king, some stone inscriptions recording donations evidence the existence of some minor chiefs in the Pallava territory, having control over some areas with an interest in the development of the land. They had probably been allotted the land by the king under certain circumstances. But being creations of the monarch, they seem to have had only a minor role in respect of the land. Some of them seem to have had connections with the Bāṇas and were probably given the territory out of deference to the influence of the main line Bāṇa with the king. One Viṇṇakōvaraiyar Eṟṟukkunṟanār is stated to have donated 16 *kaḷañju* of gold to goddess Bhaṭāri in Aruvākūr in the year 6 (802) of Dantivarman according to an inscription from Toṇḍur, Gingee Taluk, South Arcot District.[123] Aruvakūr was in the Kīḻvaḷi of Śingapura-nāḍu. This Vinnakōvaraiyar was of a family of a chiefs which continued to hold the territory for at least two centuries as evidenced by two inscriptions of a Parakesarivarman (10th century) from the same place.[124] They refer to a Viṇṇakōvaraiyar Vayirimalaiyan who gave his name to the *nāḍu* (Viṇṇakōvaraiyar-nāḍu) and claimed it as "his nāḍu". It is noteworthy that the Viṇṇakōvaraiyar of Dantivarman's record made only a donation of gold, but that in the later records, the chiefs either made a donation of land or made an arrangement with the nāḍu organisation for maintaining the local reservoir evidencing their intimate connection with the land in this nāḍu. Probably, during the earlier period, the chief's rights were restricted to receiving the revenue from the villages in the area allotted to him without any right to transfer land. Further, two concubines of a Vāṇakōvaraiyar are recorded to have made gifts of gold to the god at Tiruvoṛṛiyur in the reign of Aparajita.[125] There are no means to know the exact position of this Vāṇakōvaraiyar and if he was connected with the family of Viṇṇakōvaraiyar. It would appear that both these families originally were of Bāṇa extraction but later had become distinct and prominent in the Peṇṇār (south) region to warrant a portion of the region to be known as Vāṇagōppaḍi. Another personage connected with the Bāṇa is also mentioned as having an interest in the land in an inscription from Kīḷputtūr, Chingleput District, dated in the reign of Kampavarman (year 11 = 881).[125a] One Mādēvanār who is stated to have been the son of Perumbāṇan Sakkaḍi-araiyar arranged with the *ūr* of Kīlppudūr in Kāliyūr-kōṭṭam to levy a *kāḍi* of paddy per *paṭṭi* of cultivated land in the village for the upkeep of the local tank.

Just as the Bāṇa it is also seen that though the chiefs of the Gaṅga family are not quoted as the *vijñaptis* in any of the grants of the Pallava period and they are not seen to have claimed, any land within Toṇḍaimaṇḍalam as having been held by them under the overlordship of the Pallavas, there were others who seem to have had connections with the Gaṅga family and who either claimed to have had a nāḍu within the Pallava territory under them or just are seen to have had some interest in the land in particular localities. Pṛithiyaṅgaraiyar or Pṛithvigaṅgaraiyar figures first in a record of Kampavarman, year 17 (887) from Tippasamundram, Velur Taluk, North Arcot District,[126] and refers to himself as *in-nāḍu-uḍaiya* (the one who had this nāḍu). That "this nāḍu" referred to was Paṅgaḷa-nāḍu. in Palkunṛakkōṭ ṭam and this tract continued as the *nāḍu* of the Pṛithigaṅgaraiyar chiefs for more than a century thence, is known from other records.[127] If it is remembered that Gaṅga- Prithvipati I of the main family made the supreme sacrifice on behalf of Aparājita at the battle of Śrīpurambiyam against the Pāṇḍya in c. 885,[128] it can be surmised that a close association had developed between the Pallava and Gaṅga at about this time.[129] Probably as a consequence, a member of the family of the Gaṅga was provided a principality within Toṇḍaimaṇḍalam. But the terms of conferring the principality to him involving a joint control over the land between the Pallava and Prithiyaṅgaraiyar is not known. The Prithiyaṅgaraiyar of the Kampavarman's record was interested in the development of the land and he set up a channel from the river to the reservoir in Valivala-kkamaṅgalam (modern Tippasamudram?). Apart from the Pṛithivigaṅgaraiyar there is also a reference to one Amanigaṅgaraiyar's son as one who was ruling Viṭṭūr in an inscription of Nandivarman III from Paḷḷikoṇḍa, Velur Taluk, North Arcot District.[130] Nothing more is heard about him or his family. Nothing much is also known about one Koṅgaraiyar Ninṛaperumān, who figures in an inscription of the time of Nṛipatuṅga from Marudāḍu, Wandiwash Taluk, North Arcot District[131] as one who set up a weir. All these were obviously of Gaṅga extraction and were subordinate chiefs under the Pallavas but the extent of control enjoyed by them vis-ā-vis the king is not known.[132]

OFFICIALS :

It has been seen that in the charters recording royal grants, the *vijñapti* apparently fulfilled an official function and that he was invariably a chief. However as this function was just *ad hoc,* it is not known if these chiefs figuring as *vijñaptis* had other official functions in the service of the king. On the other hand in the same charters one *ājñapti* , an executor of the royal order or recorder of the royal order also figures, and the charters usually refer to his official position also. Among the charters of the Pallava period, the *ājñapti* in the Kūram grant was an *Uttara-kāraṇika* in the Paḷḷankōyil plates, a *mantrivara* or the choicest among ministers, in the Taṇḍantōṭṭam plates a *kōśādhyaksha* (chief of the treasury) and an expert in *niyōga-karmma.* In these cases there is no indication in the names of these persons that they were chiefs or had been installed as the lords of particular territories in remuneration for their official function.[133] However in the Vēlūrpāḷaiyam plates the *ājñapti* was one Iraiyūr-uḍaiyān, whose official position is however not indicated. His title might be construed as the possessor of Iraiyūr or one who hailed from Iraiyūr. If it had the former significance it is not known if he had been given the control of Iraiyūr as a fee for any official function. His position can be compared with that of the *ājñapti* of the Paṭṭattāḷmaṅgalam grant, who was Ālappākka-viśaiya-Nalluḷān who was not described as the uḍaiyan of Ālappakkam.[134] In the Tiruvallam and Kāñchīpuram inscriptions of Nandivarman III as also in the Chiṭṛūr and Bāhūr plates of Nṛipatunga, the *ājñapti* was one Tamil-ppēraraiyan. His ending in *araiyan* (derivative of *rājā*) on first sight suggests that he was a chief, but on close look it appears that it was more a title reflecting his expertise in Tamil.[135] In this case however his official attachment to the Pallava monarch is reflected in the other titles, Kāḍupaṭṭi and Viḍēlviḍugu, actually the titles of the king, attributed to him. Apparently all these persons figuring as *ājñaptis* were important personages in the official hierarchy whether specifically stated so or not. However there is no information if they were associated by the king in the control of the land while remunerating them for their services.

It has been stated above that the charters also refer to a *kō* as one entitled to receive some miscellaneous levies and fines. There is no reflection anywhere on his identity. There is a likelihood that he might have been a functionary under the king and his entitlements as reflected above were what had been conferred on him for his official function. It is significant that there is no indication in the records regarding the mode by which the king's revenue was collected from villages and as to how, especially, the collection in kind was disposed off.[136] The *kō* might have been such an agent for collection of revenue as well as the instrument of control for the locality.[137]

In this context it may be mentioned that some of the

persons found making endowments of sizable amounts of paddy for local purposes might have been officials and the paddy they endowed might have been out of the revenue collected in the locality in kind or out of what they themselves could appropriate as fees. For instance one Saḍaiyan is stated to have endowed 1000 *kāḍi* of paddy for dredging the reservoir at Ukkal in the year 15 (885) of Kampavarman.[138] This interest of Śaḍaiyan might have been as an instrument of the king's policy to utilise the whole or part of the collection in kind for local welfare measures or it might be that the paddy endowed was part of the collection that was the due of Śaḍaiyan. If the latter was the case, his interest in having the local reservoir maintained might be indicating that he had some interest in the land also. This may further indicate that apart from authorising their officials to retain a part of the collection of revenue for their own use as remuneration, the Pallava king also allowed them to get some control over the land.

Though in the above instance the position of Saḍaiyan is left for surmise, in another inscription of the period, there seems to be evidence of the Pallava king having authorised the paddy collection from a village to be appropriated by some royal servants. An inscription from Vayalaikkāvūr (Kāñchīpuram taluk, Chingleput district) dated year 2 (798) in the reign of Dantivarman[139] says that five persons, Kaṇḍi, Pūran, Śiṟu-nambi, Aduri and Āyiravan, who described themselves as having the bedchamber *(paḷḷi-kkaṭṭil-udaiya)* were entitled to three *kūru* (portions) of the paddy in the village Vayalaikkā and that they endowed the same for food offerings and perpetual lamp of God Bhaṭāra of the village. The endowers might have been officials of the royal bed chamber[140] and the portions which they endowed might have been only a part of what they had been authorised as they had to retain a good portion for their own maintenance.

Another record of the period also evidences that one person had the right over the entire revenue from a village. An inscription dated year 4 (889) of Aparājita from Satyavēḍu

(Ponneri taluk, Chingleput district)[141] records that one Kāḍu-paṭṭi pperaraiyan Kumārandai Kurumbar-ādittan who hailed from Chēra- nāḍu (*Chāra-nāḍu-uḍaiya*) gifted the *puravu* and *pon* (revenue in kind and cash) from the village Tuṛaiyūr for God Mahādēva of Tirumadaṅganpaḷḷi in Tekkūr-nāḍu in Paiyūr-iḷangōṭṭam. Significantly the record does not say that the endower gifted the village nor does it indicate that the gift was made in perpetuity. The record does not also say that he got the permission of the king for the grant of the revenue. What is said and what is not said in the record it can be inferred that this person from Chēra-nādu had an important position in the service of the king, that he had full rights over the entire revenue of some villages, apparently during the period of his service and that he had no control over the land. In the light of this it seems possible that the gold seem to have been endowed by persons whose names suggest their connection with chiefs, were also part of their entitlement from the village or locality authorised to them as fee by the king for their service.[142]

Thus it is seen that the records of the Pallava period indicate that there were subordinates of the king holding some territories outside and inside Toṇḍaimaṇḍalam. There were also officials. the chiefs who seem to have held territories in the outlying areas of the Pallava dominion wielded more control over land but they did not have independent powers to gift land. Some people especially officials seem to have been remunerated with the revenue of villages without any control over the land in those villages, about the others who figure in the records as those who might have had interest in the land no more information is available.

CHOḶA PERIOD

In the Chōḷa period also there are good many references to controllers of land subordinate to the king. Some were very important chiefs like the Gaṅga of Irukkuvēḷ, who had their own standing among the chiefs. Some were of the medium type like Ilāḍattaraiyar or Paṅgḷanādu chiefs. There were a good many *araiyan*, *kiḷān*, *uḍaiyān* etc who might have held the village or territory reflected in their titles. Most of them are seen engaged in official tasks, but at places which had no relationship with the territory indicated in their titles. The records describe how all of them were associated in the control of land but under strict limitations consequent on the nature of the kingship of the Chōḷas.

Just as in the Pallava period some chiefs figure as *vijñaptis* in the charters. In the earliest charter of this period (i. e.) in the Udayēndram plates of Parāntaka I (922), Gaṅga Pṛithvipati II given charge of the Bāṇa territory[143] which at this time might have included a portion of Paḍuvūr-kōṭṭam, is stated to have been the *vijñapti* in that record for the constitution by the king of a new *brahmadēyam* formed by adding a village to the already existing *brahmadēyam* of Udayachandramaṅgalam. The new *brahmadēyam*, which was apparently situated within the territory given over to the control of the chief was named after the king as Vīranārāyaṇa-chchēri. In this naming of the new *brahmadēyam* the king's control over the land even in such territory which might have been held by a chief is evidenced. Further the chief quoted as the *vijñapti* is also seen put incharge of the execution of the grant by giving the proclamatory notice *(aṛai-ōlai)*. Evidently he was carrying out a royal order even though the Sanskrit text of the charter says that he made over the village to the brahmin chaturvēdi-maṅgalam. The same chief was again quoted as both the *vijñapti* and *ājñapti* for the grant by the king of the royal income from a field for the maintenance of a reservoir, Chōḷavāridhi as recorded in the Shōlinghūr inscription of Parāntaka I dated in his year 9 (916)[144]. In this record it is the Tamil text which says that the chief made over the field for the reservoir. These two records indicate that under the Chōḷa administration, the control of a feudatory within the Chōḷa territory did not extend to the right of alienation of land or diverting the revenue from land. This fact is more pointedly brought out in the Paḷḷaṅkōyil inscription of the reign period of Uttamachōḷa year 6 (976).[145] Pṛithvī-gaṅgaraiyar, who had Paṅgaḷa-nāḍu[146] and who had added the name of Uttamachōḷa to his own to show his subordination to the king, is stated to have approached king Uttamachōḷa when he had camped at Kāñchīpuram and requested *(viṇṇappam-vijñāpana?)* that the village Pudānaḍappāḍi in his own nāḍu (Pangala-nāḍu) might be granted to god Mahādēva in the same village. The king was pleased to sanction *(prasādam)* the request, and he further directed his 'recorder of King's utterances (*vāśal-keḷvi*)" and mnemonic assistant (*jñānam*) to note down his grant of the village with tax-free status and further got the same entered in the tax-register (*variyiliḍu*). Though the record goes on further to say that the Prithivīgaṅgaraiyar enacted the same drama in his own court before granting the village to the temple, his role vis-a-vis the king is made clear that though he was holding the territory he could not grant away land in it without the permission of the king. The disposal of the revenue income from land within that territory was exclusively the privilege of the monarch. If the feudatory held his own court and repeated the procedure of the royal court it must have been for his own edification.

Thus even though these records reflect that after the Chōḷas took over the administration of Toṇḍaimaṇḍalam there was a semblance of joint control of land between the king and feudatories continuing they also indicate that the feudatories had only usufructary rights with regard to the land they might have got from the monarch. The feudatory could not disturb the tenures within that territory under his jurisdiction nor could he alter the revenue structure. However, there would not have been any meaning to their holding the territory if they had not been entitled to receive the revenue from it. Hence it can be surmised that the king's control over such land was exercised to see that the feudatory did not disturb the land arrangement in that territory as it had to conform to the pattern set by the king in territories which were under his direct control. However another record indicates that the entitlement of the feudatory to the land allotted to him was restricted to the appropriation of miscellaneous levies. The Pañchapāṇḍavamalai (Polur taluk,

North Arcot district) inscription dated in the year 8 (993) of the powerful Chōḷa king Rājarāja I[147] says that one Vīrachōḷa Ilāḍarāja on the representation from his wife remitted the levies *kaṛpūravilai* and *anyāya-vāva—danḍam* in respect of Kūragan-pādi, the *Paḷḷichchandam* of the (Jain establishment) at Tiruppanmalai. The chief's order was recorded by his own agent *(kanmi)* who is referred to as the *ānatti* (*ājñapṭi*). There is no mention in the record that the chief referred the matter to his overlord. Obviously, the levies were his own entitlement as the record also says that an earlier Ilāḍaraja began levying the taxes in respect of that land, also. Hence it appears that the other grants referred to earlier had to be made only by the king even though the grant village was included in the territory under the enjoyment of a feudatory, because the feudatory had no right over the chief taxes on land and that in the last case the king's intervention was not sought because what was granted was within the competence of the feudatory.

The records of the Chōḷa period in Toṇḍaimaṇḍalam as available do not throw much light on the extent to which other chiefs and officials were associated in the control of land. There are only three rare references to military commanders and others having had a village as their maintenance.

An inscription dated in the year 4 of a Rājakēsarivarman from Veṇbākkam (Kāñchīpuram taluk, Chingleput district)[148] records the setting up of a sluice by a Kēraḷan Rājādittan alias Nanivichchādiramārayan who is said to have had Vala-kkōnmaṅgalam in Kunṛa-nāḍu in Ūrrukkāṭṭu-kkōttam as his maintenance. It is not known as to what for he had got the village as his maintenance. Probably he was a military commander. There are no further records from the village to enlighten more.

Two inscriptions from Pōdavūr, Kāñchīpuram taluk, Chingleput district, dated in the year 6 and 9 (later half of tenth century) of Pārthivēndravarman[149] refer to the holding of Mērpiḍavūr in Puriśai-nāḍu of Maṇayiṛ-kōṭṭam as her maintenance by a lady Tennavan Mādēviyār. But the records say that her brother got some land by purchase from the *ūravar* having had the same exempted from all taxes. Obviously, these details given in these records clearly indicate that the lady had nothing to do with the land and that her interests in the village were confined to the revenue from the village. It is not clear, however, as to what for she got the village as maintenance. In the same way, an inscription dated year 5 (1068) of Vīra-rājēndra from Maṇimaṅgalam (Chingleput district)[150] states that a *brahma-mārāyar,* described as a *sēnapaṭi*, had *jīvitam* in that *sabhā* controlled village. This also indicates that the *sēnāpati* had an interest only in the revenues of the village.[151]

Apart from the above information the records of the Chōḷa period in Toṇḍaimaṇḍalam which refer to several chiefs and chief-like persons functioning in various capacities do not indicate the extent to which they were associated by the king in the control of land.

NOTES:

1. The theories claiming local origin for the Pallavas are unconvincing (Mahalingam, T.V., Kanchipuram in Early South Indian History pp., 21-24).) The facts that indicate their having come into the region from the region to the north are: (1) their claiming to belong to Bharadwaja-gotra (2) their Sanskritic names (3) their fostering of Sanskrit learning and (4) their introduction of the practice of issuing *brahmadēyam* and *dēvadāna* charters. Such characteristics were not found in any other ruler of the Tamil country at and before their time.
2. Organised agriculture (in the territory) was the main source of power in the pre industrial revolution days. Cf. Maity, S.K., The *economic Life* of *Northern India* in *Gupta Period* (A.D., 300-500), pp. 23-29.
3. Sharma, R.S., Ind. Feud, p. 136.
4. *Ibid.*, p. 28, 264.
5. Cf. Nandi, R.N., Religious Institutions and Cults *in* the Deccan, p. 1-2. Though Kōchcheṅgaṇān, the Chōḷa who might have ruled in about the 4-5 th centuries A.D., is reputed to have constructed 70 fine temples of Siva, there are no details available

about them. It is not possible to know if the worship in them was brahmin-based and if *the dēvadāṇa* grants were made for them. There is no information on when those temples were built. So far as Toṇdaimaṇḍalam is concerned in the period earlier to the coming of the Pallava there is only one mention of a temple at Kāñchipuram that of Tiruvehka in the Sangam Perumbāṇārṟuppaḍai. This too is said to have been situated in the quarter of the Mallas and hence does not seem to have required the brahmin for conducting the worship. As far as tangible evidence goes it was Mahendravarman I Pallava (580-630) who made a start in this direction by excavating temples out of monoliths. Structural temples came later. The earliest available record for the attachment of a village to a temple is probably the Tirukkaḷukkunṟam inscription of Narasimhavarman I Pallava (630-668) *(Mem.* AS I, 26, p. 10- 11).

6. It is doubtful if the brahmins were granted the *brahmadēyam* on the basis of their qualifications. It is seen that brahmins whose surnames might have indicated their high qualifications were treated often on par with those without Such quantication surnames and those with the same surnames were not treated equally, A list indicating the places of origin as well as their surnames of the brahmins who received shares of *brahmadēyam* in Toṇḍai-maṇḍalam charters is given in Appendix -I.

7. This can be compared with the record of the grant of *brahmadēyam* rights in respect of the wet and dry land as well as the housesite already in the possession of a brahmin Sattaiyanār at Mukkuḍūr. Apart from the fact that here the *brahmadēyam* was obviously what is usually understood by the term. It is noteworthy that this grant was only a benefit in addition to that he was already in enjoyment in the village. In every way the cases of the brahmins of the charters referred to above was different.

8. cf. Sharma, R.S., Ind. Feud, pp. 220-22. Also pp. 55, 267, 270, 281, 284, 286.

9. This order to the villagers to obey the orders of the brahmin grantees seems to have been a speciality of central Indian charters, cf. *Ibid.*, pp. 3, 115, Maity, SK., _op. _cit., p. 63-64. Cf. Ramesan, N., 'The Vesanta grant of Pallava Simhavarman' *CP., Ins., of A. P., Govt. Museum*, Hyderabad, Vol. I., pp. 214, 233. He says that the *grāmēyakaṣ* and other officials in the

locality were asked to obey the royal order with regard to the seeing to it that the grantee was not interfered with in the enjoyment of the land and that he was enabled to enjoy the benefits of the *parihāras*. Though the concerned lines (18, 22-24) do not warrant the use of the words 'obey, even so the obeying if at all was there was only to the royal order and not with reference to the donees, Also cf. Sharma, R.S., *Ind. Feud*, p. 3, p. 53f.

10. cf. *Ibid.*, 220-222, 267.

11. cf. Sharma, R.S., Ind, Feud., pp. 113-14, Ghosal, U.N., The Agrarian Systems in Ancient India, p. 121.

12. The explanation for having an elephant preceding the boundary-marking partly could have had a ceremonial significance but it must be pointed out that every ceremonial formality had a utilitarian beginning. An inscription from Tiruchchendurai (Tiruchirappali district) which neither quotes a date nor cites a king (*SII.*, VIII, 633.) says that to raise a Viṣṇu temple, the land was dug up, filled with sand and trampled with the elephant indicating that the elephant was used to harden the ground.

12a. Lallangy, Gopal, *op., cit.,* pp. 4, 8, Udgaonkar, Padma B, '*The* Political Institution and Administration of Northern India during Medieval Times (A-750-1200 A.D.), pp. 181-182.

13. cf. Ramesan, *op., cit.*, p. 63. He interprets the phrase as meaning getting rid of the old taxation and the old *brahmadēya* obligations. The Bāhūr plates of Nṛipatunga which records the grant of three villages as *brahmadēyam* for a *vidyāsthāna* also employ identical phrases as the Chiṭṛūr grant of the same king.

14. *Palaiyavaramum brahmadēyamum-nīkk*i employed both in the Chiṭṛūr and Bāhūr plates of Nṛipatuṅga, has the *mūrdhanyara* in the latter part of the word paḷaiyavaṛam and hence it is possible that the word indicated *paḷaiya*-old; aṛam-charities. However, as *kuḍi-nīkki*. is not mentioned in these charters *kuḍi* being a feature which could be expected in any locality, till there is some evidence to point the other way *paḷaiya*vaṛam can be interpreted to mean old puṛam or habitation. Also cf.,the detached Tamil inscription of the 10th plate of Tiruvālaṅgāḍu plates.

14a. In the Udayēndram plates of Parāntaka I, *nīkki* is actually equated with *vihāya*—leaving out—in the Sanskrit text. The absence of the mention of the exception of *dēvadāna*-

brahmadēyam in the Pullūr plates might be due to the non-existence of such lands in the four villages concerned in the grant. But *kuḍis* seems to have been there and their land was excepted.

15. Cf., Minakshi, C., (op. cit., p. 122) understands *kuḍi-nīkki* to mean 'excluding houses (of the ryots)'. Also *SII.*, II, p. 360. The editor of the Kasākkuḍi plates says that three categories *dēvadāna-brahmadēyam,* and *kuḍi* were jexcluded. While the *brahmadēyam* granted during the period referred to whole villages, and does not seem to have referred to exemption from the taxes to the king, the plots referred to as *brahmadēyam* and excluded in these charters seem to have been the type where the land enjoyed all excmptions (cf. Kīl-Muttugūr inscriptions of Narasiṅgavarman *EI.*, IV, pp. 177-178.

16. Cf., Sastri, K.A.N., *Studies in Cola History and Administration*, p. 104. He says 'several instances can be cited in which all the previous owners of the lands in a certain locality were bought out and the existing leeses for cultivation terminated by payment of compensation in order that an absolutely unencumbered *ḍēvadāna* might be made or a fresh *brahmadēya* usually a chaturvedimaṅgalam might be formed. ' T.N. Subramanian (Tr., Arch., Soc., of. *SI.*, 1958-59, p. 72) repeats the same interpretations of the phrases *mun-peṟṟārai-māṟṟi* and *kuḍi-nīkki*. Apart from other things it is not known what suggested to them that there were purchases and payment of compensations. Moreover they would make it that the tenancy conditions were bad enough in those times that not only the king had to purchase the land but also had to displace the tenants, the fact becoming worthy of mention in the record.

16a. cf. Tiruviḍaimarudur inscription of a Parakesari (*SII.*, III, 203). The status of the land whether it was *kudi-nīkki* or *kudi-nīṅgā* determined whether the contribution from the land to the temple was to be more or less.

17. This is verified when it is seen that in the Chiṭṟūr grant which says that the village granted as *brahmadēyam* with the entitlement to enjoy whatever the *kō* could collect it is stated that the *brahmadēyam* should contribute 750 *kāḍi* as *pañchavāram* to the temple at Paḷaiyaṅur-ttiruvālaṅgāḍu. Obviously this *pañchavāram* was not an entitlement of the *kō*. The Kaṇḍiyūr (Tanjavur district) inscription of Nṛipatunga (*SII.*, V, 572) seems

to equate *pañchavāram* with *iṛai*, the land tax. That the *brahmadēyams* in Toṇḍaimaṇḍalam paid *iṛai* is verifiable in various ways.

18. Udgaonkar, Padma B., *The politlcaḷ Institutions and Administration of Northern India During Medieval Times* (from 750-1200), p. 187.

18a. cf. Mahalingam, T.V., EI XXXVI, p. 148. He says that *Kōvum-poṛiyum-tīrttu* had the implication of having removed the authority of the king and his officers. Subrahmanian, T.N. (*Tr, Arch. Sec., of SI.,*. 1958-59, p. 71) interprets the expression as meaning 'that the gift village was completely freed from the administrative control of government and that it secured an independent status. It may be seen that the Pullūr plates say that whatever the *nāḍu-kāppāṉ* and *viyavaṉ* (the protector of the nāḍu and accountants?) could do the grantees and their successors would do, thus indicating the replacement of only these two by the body of the donees, *Nāḍukāppāṉ* might have indicated the *kō*. The position of this *kō* vis-a-vis the *vijñapti*s (supplicator) who are described as chiefs and figure in these same records is discussed below.

19. When the king granted the revenue of villages to his officials, he does not seem to have conferred on them the position of *kō*. cf. *SII.*, Ill, 30. This inscription of the 11th century from Maṇimaṅgalam (Chingleput district) says that *sabhā* village was the *jīvitam* (maintenance) of a *brahmādhirāja*, a *sēnāpati*; *SII.*, XII, 86. This inscription of the time of Aparājita from Satyavēḍu, Chingleput district reflects that a Kumarandai Kurumbaradittan of Chēranāḍu, probably an official had the tax in kind and cash *(puravu* and *pon)* from Turaiyur at his disposal. These were probably in the position of *kō* and the *kōs* referred to in the charters were similar persons.

20. The items included under the *parihāras* in these charters and their significance are discussed in Appendix II to this chapter.

21. The Kasakkudi plates however contains a statement which seems to authorise the enjoyment of the levies by the donee brahmin as they were not payable to the *kō* thereafter.

22. cf. Sharma, R.S., *Ind. Feud*, p. 123. The Pāla grants are said to conclude the list of taxes which the grantees could levy from the villagers with the term *ādi* (et cetera) allowing room for the grantees to impose fresh taxes besides the ones mentioned.

23. Yadava, B.N.S., *op. cit.*, pp. 147, 148.
24. The absence of these in the earliest charter, Kūram grant, could be explained as having been due to the character of *brahmadēyam* and *dēvadāna* not having taken a definte shape in Toṇḍaimaṇḍalam and in the Udayēndram plates of Nandivarman II due to the absence of a Tamil text, only which in the other charters contains the details of the *parihāras* (probably the reference to *sarvva-parihāra* in the Sanskrit text covered these items also). But the absence of any of these in the Tandantōttam plates is inexplicable except as an inadvertant omission or as having been covered under the sweeping clause referring to all that the *kō* could enjoy. In the Royakottah plates also such reference to fines is absent.
24a. *SII.*, III, 125.
24b. The record indicates that *manṛupāḍu* was levied apart from *daṇḍam* which was to be paid at *dharmmāsanam.*
24c. *SII.*, III, 12.
24d. In the Vēḷūrpāḷaiyam plates, the grant portion opens with a mention of the assessment (*pañchavāram*) on Tirukkāṭṭuppaḷḷi which was the village granted as *dēvadāna* as per the charter. This suggests that the effect of the grant was that this *pañchavāram* alone became payable to the temple from the date of the charter. In the same way it is also seen that Siṟṟiyāṟṟūr which was attached as a *dēvadāna-brahmadēyam* to *brahmadēyam* Puduppākkam (SII, 111, 142) and Palaiyanur whose assessment was permanently fixed by the king (*Ibid.* 205) were also asked to pay only the amount of tax revenue to the respective temples. As such it would appear that the rights of the landholders in the villages granted as dēvadāna were left untouched. It is also noteworthy that the entitlement of the God under the head, *parihāraṣ* or exemptions was also only to the levies from several classes of people. The temples rights were not linked to the holding of the land. However the Veḷūrpaḷaiyam charter while listing the privileges granted to the God refers to the construction of mansions with burnt bricks. This, and such other privileges are usually found in the *brahmadēyam* charters where the grant of such a privilege could have made sense. Hence it seems possible that though the Veḷurpaḷaiyam record does not state so, the village granted as *dēvadānam* the status of *brahmadēyam* just as *Sirriyaṛrūr*. (the brahmin who constructed the temple for

which the *dēvadāna* was made by the king belonged to that village. If that was the case the entitlement to levies under the head *parihāras* mentioned in the record would have pertained to the holders of the *brahmadēyam* and the God's entitlement might have been restricted to the *panchavāram*.

24e. The identity of this *kō* has been discussed in appendix

24f. The stone inscriptions recording transactions involving the *sabhā*, evidence that in the case of some *brahmadēyams,* several villages/hamlets around the main *brahmadēyam* had been placed under the authority of the *sabhā* of the main village with the status of *brahmadēyam*.

24g. cf. Sharma, R.S., Ind. Feud., p. 207.

24h. cf. Mahalingam, T.V., 'Pullūr plates etc.', EI, XXXVI, p. 145 Subramanian, T.N. 'Pallava Jaina CP Grant from Paḷḷaṅkōyil', Tri. Arch. Soc. of SI, p. 72. Both of them interpret the term *paradatti* to mean 'a gift by some other person (the *vijñapti* of the records) which the king ratified (declaring the lands or villages tax free). That some other person who made the gift is usually taken to have been the *vijñapti* or the chief who made the request for the grant to the king. This aspect is dealt with in detail under feudatories. Here it suffices to point out that in the Paḷḷankōyil plates, the *paḷḷichchandam* is not stated to have been granted at the instance of a *vijñapti* or any other but still the grant is stated to have been made as *paradatti* (ll. 63-64)

25. It has been discussed above as to how this distribution might have taken place, how the *karai* system might have had its genesis in this apportionment of villages in shares. The operation of the *karai* system in the Tanjavur district and the types of villages, *yajamān, pasūngarai* and *arudīkaṛai*, found in the Chingleput district in the 19th century by the British administrators, has been discussed above.

26. An inscription dated year 4 in the reign of a Parakēsari Rājēndra from Uttaramallūr (*SII.*, VI, 336) records the entrusting of the land earmarked for God Subrahmaṇia-dēvar in their *ūr* by the *sabhā* of the place to a sivabrāhmaṇa enjoining on him to carry on the worship of the God as before. Though it is not known if the plot of land involved was the entitlement of the temple against the share set apart for it in the charter, it appears that till this date of the grant, the *sabhā* itself had been managing the land and maintaining the worship in that temple.

27. The word *kuḍi* was probably capable of being applied to all categories of such inhabitants—independent landholders, tenants and serfs.

27a. cf. Croele, *Chingleput District Manual,* pp. 213-214 Also Jha, D.N., Presidential Address, IHC, 1979 (Waltair), p. 25.

28. cf. *EI,* XXXVI, p. 149 and n 4.

28a. The inscription of Māṛañjaḍaiyan form Mānūr (Tirunelveli district) *SII.,* XII, 37) also fefers to possession of *srāvaṇai,* even if it had been acquired as gift or dowry, as the eligibility condition for taking part in the deliberations of the *(sabhā)* at that place.

29. cf. Sastri, K.A.N., The *Chōḷas,* p. 493, it is possible that where there was a sizable landholding population outside the *brahmadēyam* in the same village/village complex, the former might have organised themselves into a *ūr*. In such cases the relationship between the two segments of the village might have been one of co-operation rather than of subordination of one to the other. Also cf. *SII.,* III, 180.

30. The character of the *yajamān-grāmam* as found by the British administrators in the 19th century has been described above. But it may be seen that they did not say that these villages were *brahmadēyams*. The *mirāsi* rights exercised by the *yajamāns*. however resembled the *brahmadēyam* rights.

31. However, there is, no evidence to conclude that his subordination of erstwhile residents to the *brahmadēyam* donees amounted to enjoining them to serve the donees (cf. Sharma, R.S., Ind. Feud., pp. 45, 55 f). It is however possible that *ūr* in these contexts referred to the group of people who had not yet fully emerged from their tribal background and claimed land for agriculture and that the service of these poeple were placed at the disposal of the donees. This may explain the differentiation between *ūr* and *kuḍi* in these charters.

32. cf. Shrama, R.S., Ind. Feud., pp. 146, 153.

33. The forests provided the leaf-manure as well as firewood. Also Sharma, R.S., *op. cit.,* p. 225 f. But is is noteworthy that while many the items listed under the *parihāṛas* in these charters are taxes and levies payable by artisans and professionals as charges on their avocation. Some are levies for meeting charges on local administration and these and some others seem to have been payable by all residents. The Kūram plates in the Tamil section does not refer to the term, *parihāra,* but gives a list of

items including even house-site and house garden which the 25 shareholders (only 20 of whom were *brahmadēya* recipients) would enjoy proportionately.

34. Ghosal, U.N., The *Agrarian Systems in Ancient India*, p. 46-48, also Dr. Das, *op. cit.*, p. 53-54. Das rightly questions the statement of Ghoshal but he has not cited any Toṇḍaimaṇḍalam record to buttress his arguments. Ghosal has not also explained as to how the Pallava king sustained himself and his kingship.

35. cf. Tirumālpuram inscription of Uttamachōla (*SII.*, III, 142) where the levies on the village were classified under the three heads *puravu*, *iravu* and *pon*.

36. Among the records from Toṇḍaimaṇḍalam, the earliest use of the term *irai* is probably found in the Tiruttaṇi inscription of the time of Aparājita, year 18 (903) (*SII.*, XII, 95) or the Tiruvoṟṟiyūr inscription of Kampavarman (*Ibid.* 105). Which of them preceded the other is a matter of speculation in spite of the recently found Vēḷañjēri plates.

37. As another instance of a *brahmadēyam* being asked to contribute to the temple, the Tiruvallam inscription of the time of Nandivarman III can be cited, (*SII.*, III, 43).

38. That this was the character of the *brahmadēyam* of the period in distinction from that reflected in the Kiḷmuṭṭugūr inscription and in the exclusions in the *brahmadēyam* grants is very well indicated in some inscriptions of the period which figure the transactions of the *sabhā*.

39. cf. Sharma, R.S., *Light on Early Indian Society & Economy,* p. 72. "Further it seems that in most cases the rulers (Sātavāhanas) retained their control over some sources of revenue accruing from the lands granted by them." Also Jha, D.N., *Revenue Systems in Post Maurya Gupta Times,* p. 125 (12 b). Generally on the basis of the several texts he suggests that the brahmin should be exempted only from tolls and miscellaneous levies and only *srōtriyas* who strictly followed a brahmin's duties should be exempted from taxes and forced labour because they paid taxes in the form of pious acts. Even if *srōtriyaṣ* in the Tamil nāḍu context can be understood as those holding *srāvaṇai* generally held as the land-share, there is no indication of pious acts they were engaged in which could have earned them the exemptions, cf. Mahalingam, T.V., *op. cit.*, p. 148. Also Subramanian, N., *Sangam Polity,* p. 203.

40. cf. Ghosal, U.N., The *Agrarian System in Ancient India*, p. 8-9. He refers to *bali* or the entitlement of the king from the subjects as an appellation coming from *Vedic* items denoting both the contributions to the king from the subjects as well as the tributes to him from conquered enemies. This indicates that originally *bali* was meant to be the tribute both from the subjects and conquered enemies and the meaning of the term was modified slightly later to denote a share of the produce from the land. Also cf. *SII.*, III, 57, wherein the miscellaneous levies are seen to have been related to the land tax and taken from the landholders, cf. Subrahmanian, N. *History of Tamilnādu*, p. 323.

40a. cf. Sastri, K.A.N., *The Chōḷas*, p. 512.

41. The exception was the Paṭṭattāḷmaṅgalam grant. This record states that the donor king wished that the grant might last till the earth, the sea, the sun and the moon lasted. The Chiṭṟūr grant also in the corrupt Sanskrit text expected that the grant made as *brahmadēyam* to last so long as the mountains, seas, etc. lasted.

42. Though not stated in the charters, the grants of *brahmadēyam* by the kings seem to have been impelled by the desire of the king to gain merit. The incomplete set of the Udayēndram plates of Vīra-Chōla (whose identity and date are uncertain) (*EI,* III, p. 79 f) states that prince Vīra Chōḍa was advised by his religious preceptor (*dharmmōpadēshṭā*) to grant *brahmadēyam* to excellent brahmins *(dvijēndrēbhyō*) for elevating all his ancestors (*gurūṇām)* to heaven.

43. Text lines, 5-6 third plate, first side and 2nd side lines 1-2. Also Ramesan, N., *op. cit.*, p. 24-25. It is pointed out below how it does appear that the queen Prithvīmāṇikkam was rather the consort of the king rather than of Parañjaya who was the *vijñapti* for the grant.

44. The 13th century inscription citing the reign of (Kōnērin-maikoṇḍān from Pērūr, Coimbatore district (*SII.*, V, 232) records the confiscation of the lands of one Tiribhuvana-siṅgadēvan who had turned traitor (*drōhi*) and grant of the same to the temple by the king. It is possible that even lands granted to brahmin's were liable to be confiscated for treachery. Attachment of a brahmin's land for failure to honour his commitments to the temple is probably indicated in the Tiruvallam inscription of Rājarāja I, year 13 (*AREp.*, 1921, 208).

45. *EI,* VII, p. 1f. Also Balambal, V., *Feudatories of South India* (1978), p. 51.

46. *EI,* III, p. 74 f. Also Balambal, V, *op. cit.,* p. 55. The placing of the chief in the 12th century as done by the editor is untenable.

46.a EI, III, p. 277.

46b. Chōḷa Karikāla of the 1-2 century A.D. is stated to have reclaimed land in the forest region north of Chōḷa-nāḍu and settled Veḷḷāḷar therein. (Pillai, K.K., *A Social History of the Tamils,* p. 186). It is seen that the *ūr* with definite rights over the locality is first heard of only in this region (*SII.,* XII, 42) 802 A.D. Āddoṇḍai-chakravartti is also known in tradition to have settled Tuḷuvā-veḷḷālas with *mirāsi* rights in Toṇḍaimaṇḍalam (Croele, *Mannuaḷ of the Chingleput District*, p. 300). It is also seen that it was the Chōḷas who introduced the service of singing of the hymns of Tamil saints in temple (cf. *SII.,* III, 43. Though this inscription is dated in the regin of Nandivarman III, being a recopy, it appears that the contents of the original record were modified). The Chōḷas and Pāṇḍyas patronised only Tamil poets.

47. *SII.,* III, 142.

48. The king addressed himself to and drew the attention of the *nāṭ ṭār brahmadēya-kkiḷavaṛ ūrgalilār of dēvadāna-ppallichchanda-kaṇi-muṛṛūṭṭu-veṭṭappēṛu* and *nagaraṅgaḷilār* of Maṇaiyil-nāḍu and Maṇaiyil-kōṭṭam, wherein the grant village lay.

49. The quarter of mixed castes?

50. The expression *mudalay-varuginṛa puravu* probably meant the consolidated assessment (on the land).

51. The effect of the statement is that the said *kāṇi* (holder) would pay the *puravu* to the temple and hence for the purpose of official register of the assessment of the king, the land would be shown as tax-free *dēvadāṇa*.

52. It is noteworthy that the charges *iravu* and *pon* were not payable by the *kāṇi* of Saṅkarappāḍi-kiḷān, though they were payable by the rest of the land in Siṛṛiyāṛṛūr, though that part had been given the status of *brahmadēyam*.

53. The record is known as Udayēndram plates of Prithvipati II Hastimalla.

54. Detailed boundaries are given.

55. It is not known if the *paṭṭi* mentioned here denoted the plot of the definite area of 1200 *kuli* as defined in the Kūram grant or just a plot of land.

56. *SII.*, III, 205.
57. The king drew the attention of the same bodies as were addressed in the Tirumālpuram inscription cited above except that under the *ūrgalilar, palavaram* and *śāḷābhogam* were also included. Of course, the bodies pertained to a different nāḍu-Mēlmalai-ppaḷaiyanūr-nāḍu in which the village involved in the transaction lay.
58. Paḷaiyāṛu near Kumbhakonam.
59. The record details this process of change of the tenure from *brahmadēyam* to *veḷḷānvagai* and fixation of the assessment. The details of this process as given is too much involved that their significance is rendered obscure.
60. The village is in Tiruttani taluk of Chittoor district.
61. The Tiruvallam inscription of Nandivarman II, year 62 (793) (*SII.*, III, 42) witnesses that delimitation was not the yardstick for guaging the importance of the *nāṭṭār* in the locality. This was reflected more prominently in their giving the release and proclamatory order, which were done by the feudatory in the Udayēndram plates.
62. *Kāṇi* usually denotes an allotment of or against service. It seems possible that the particular bloc of land had been granted earlier by some king to the *kiḻān* for some service, as a privileged holding as only the *puravu* is said to have been due from that bloc whereas in respect of the rest of the village even though it was given the status of a *brahmadēyam*, *iravu* and *pon* levies had to be paid in addition. Further the record suggests that whatever the circumstances of the original grant, this bloc of land had lost its original significance as land held against a service and was available to the king to be granted to the temple. It is also seen that it was not the *puravu* from that land above that was available for the grant but the land itself, as it is stated to have been seized by the *sabhā* and enjoyed. There is no reflection in the record if the holder of the *kāṇi* was compensated when the land was granted to the temple. The instance where Nandivaraman III is reflected to have had controlling rights over the land set apart for temples (*SII.*, VII, 44) as detailed below seems to reflect a different kind of right of the king.
63. It is not impossible that king Rājēndra I took away the village Paḷaiyanūr from the *sabhā* of Siṅgaḷāntaka-chaturvēdimaṅgalam with a view to help them as the *sabhā* was probably finding it

difficult to get the land cultivated and pay the taxes as stipulated. Though the record says that the king promised to the *sabhā* another village in exchange, it is not known if the exchange was actually given. However the king's rights in regard to the villages is very clear in the record. The control exercised by the Chōḷa king in the affairs of even brahmin villages is also evidenced in the records which tell about the laying down of regulations for selection to the various committees in the *sabhā* villages at royal direction and in the presence of a royal official (*AREp*. 1898, 2, 1 (919 and 921) respectively of the reign of Parāntaka I; *Ibid*., 1929-30, 176; pt. II, p. 78-Piḷḷaippākkam-Chingleput district—inscription of the year 19 -926- of Parāntaka I).

64. *SII*., III, 49

65. *AREp*. 1921, 218.

66. Such officials seem to have been designated as *nāḍu-vagai—cheyginṛa* (*SII*., I, 40) Also cf. Sastri, K.A.N., *The Chōḷas* pp. 456, 472, 527-28, 555. Probably the other official referred to as *i-vvāṇḍu-nāḍu-cheyginṛa* -the one doing the nāḍu, in this year-in an inscription of Parāntaka I from Vēdāraṇyam (Tanjavur district) (*SII*., XVII, 478) had a different function. Rājarāja I, who started this practice of the survey of land in the villages especially in Toṇḍaimaṇḍalam assumed the title *Toṇḍai-ṇāḍu-vagai-cheyda-uḍaiyār*—the lord who brought Toṇḍai-nāḍu to order (by his year 16 (1001) as reflected in an inscription from Tirukkarugāvūr, Tanjavur district (*AREp*. 1961-62, B. 393).

67. A specimen of the standard measuring rod is found engraved in the temple at Sīyamaṅgalam, North Arcot district (*SII*., VII, 440—inscription dated year 19-1004 of Rajaraja I). Such engraving was done probably for the information and use of the villagers. The reference to a mark on the *upāna* of the temple at Vēlūr as representing the 16 span rod probably belongs to the period of Rājarāja I though the inscription beside the mark is dated in the reign of Parāntaka I (*AREp*. 1933-34, 66).

68. *SII*., II, 4, 5.

69. It is seen that the Tiruvakkarai inscription of the year 16 (1000-1001) of Rājarāja I (*SII*., XVII, 222) still quoted the *pañchavāram* payable by the village Manali in round figures, However the other taxes *paḷḷippēṛu* and *kāsu* payable in addition are given in fractions. It is not known if such a rounding of figures was

resorted to when the taxes were made payable to temples. But it is also noteworthy that the Tañjāvūr inscriptions do not indicate that the other taxes besides *irai-kaṭṭina-kāṇi-kkaḍan* were payable by the villages mentioned. Here it seems possible that these figures were given after consolidation of all the taxes and that is why the fractional nature of the other taxes got reflected in the consolidated amount. In the Tiruvālaṅgāḍu plates also the permanent *irai* fixed as payable to the temple which is in fractions is stated to have included *paḷḷi* which might have been the same as *paḷḷipperu* of the Tiruvakkarai record. It is also seen that in the Toṇḍaimaṇḍalam region conversion from *kāḍi* to *kalam* also resulted in fractional figures. It is noteworthy that even after the survey and assessment the basis of assessment was still the village.

70. *AREp*., 1921, 219.
71. cf. *AREp*., 1924, 326. This inscription of Rajarāja I year 27 (1012) from Mēlappaḷuvūr, Tiruchirappalli district refers to the increase in the assessment of the village by 900 *kalam* of paddy as a result of survey.
72. *SII.*, III, 9.
73. Pillai, K.K., *Studies in the History of India (with Special Reference to Tamilnadu)* (Madras, 1979), p. 188 and n. 11 (p. 228). Also *ibid*. p. 220.
74. Sastri, K.A.N., *SI.*,H, p. 366.
75. Chapter 39, Verse 8; Also chapter 44, Verse 6.
76. *EI,* IV, p. 221 f. The text (line 19) runs as follows : *aṛukūrināl puravum, ādyadivum ponnutn perumāṛu* which may indicate that the king was entitled to 1/6 of all the earnings of the subjects. It does not seem likely that *puravu*, *pon* and *āyadi* together formed the 1/6 of the produce from the field *mūṅgilvari* granted for the upkeep of the tank *chōḷavāridhi*. The one sixth probably applied only to the *puravu*, obviously 1/6 of the produce of the land, and ā*yadi* and *pon* were extra levies. In the Sanskrit text (verse 4 lines 9),. this income from the field is referred to as *vamsavāri-janitan-Nṛipadēyam*. Kautilya who speaks about crown lands worked with slaves labourers and prisoners (Dr. Das, op. cit., p. 23) also says that the king's share of the produce from other lands was 1/6th (*Ibid*., p. 54). This indicates that the 1/6 norm applied to land which was not directly owned by the king.

77. *SII.*, II, 4, 5.
78. *SII.*, III, 35. Also *SII.*, VIII, 16. This inscription of the time of Kulōttuṅga I from Seyyūr, Chingleput district says that the village was the *kāṇi* of a *Sēnāpati*.
79. cf. *SII.*, III, 9—this inscription of the year 24(1009) of Rajaraja I from Ukkal (North Arcot district) refers to those who held the land in the villages *(urs)* of *savanar, Vaikhānasas* and brahmins and were paying *iṛai* as those having *kāṇi* in the villages. Also *SII.*, VIII, 668. This inscription of a Parakesari from Āndanallūr, Tiruchirappalli district refers to *dēvadāna-kāṇikkaḍamai* (i.e.) the *dēvadāna* land held as *kāṇi* and the dues *(kaḍamai)* paid as stipulated.
80 The *iravu* quoted as one of the items of dues from the village Siṟṟiyāṟṟūr in the Tirumālpuram record is not mentioned in the case of other villages.
81. *SII.*, XVII, 222.
82. Contra, Minakshi, C., *op. cit.*, p. 140. 'Her statement that "Pallava kings were owners of personal farms in villages" is unsupported by evidence. If she had based her statement on the mention of *rāja-vastu* land having been granted to a brahmin in the Chendalur plates of Kumāravishṇu II it must be noted that this grant pertains to the Guṇṭur-Nellore region and to an earlier period and that significantly the grant is stated to have been made by the'rule of the plough' *(hala-ṇyāya)* which definitely indicates that the land was virgin and had or was to be reclaimed by the grantee.
83. *SII.*, VII, 40.
84. The date portion of the record is damaged. Only this much is clear that the date was above twenty in the king's reign.
85. *AREp*. 1911, page 62, para 8. This information is supplied by the Vēlūrpāḷaiyam plates of Nandivarman III. She is said to have been a Kadamba princess.
86. This can be compared with a record of Rājēndrachōḷa I from Naṅgāvaram, Tiruchirappalli District (*SII.*, VIII, 644) which records an order of the king addressed to the *sabhā* of Aṛinjigai-chchaturvēdimaṅgalam and to the authorities who were incharge of the temple of the place, reallocating the *kāṇi* (land for maintenance against service) meant for the temple drum-beaters (*uvachchar*) of the temple of Tirumaravan-Iśvaram in the village. This record also exemplifies the 11th century Chōḷa king's right

over the land in village set apart for services in the temples. Another inscription from Andanallūr in the same district dated year 19 in the reign of a Parakēsari (10th century) (*Ibid.* 668) refers to some land in that *ūr* -controlled village as *kāṇippāḷ* land which probably was land earmarked for allotment of *kāṇi* against service in the temple which was under the authority of the king. The local Irukkuvēḷ chief requested the Chōḷa king and got 3 *vēli* of that land for allotment to a particular person for making contribution to the temple. The territory had been under the authority of the Irukkuvēl chiefs but it is seen that the *kāṇippāḷ* land was controlled by the Chōḷa king. It is also seen that a royal official presided over the apportionment and allocation of temple lands to the various servants of the temple, which process was called *nibandham* (*SII.*, XVII, 243,) Mēlsēvūr inscription of Rājarāja I, year 18.

87. It is seen in a Uttaramallūr inscription dated year 8 (878) of Kampavarman (*SII.*, VI, 288) that the *sabhā* of the place allotted land which was lying unutilised (*madhyamamāy-kkiḍanda*) as *aṛchchanābhōgam* to the god of Srī-Gōvardhana and vested the land with the priest to utilise for his own as well as the god's benefit. The *sabhā* declared the land *iṛai-ili* or tax-free on their own.

87a. *SII.*, IV, 827.

88. *SII.*, III, 193.

89. *Ibid.* 194.

90. *cf. Tiruttaṇi Inscription of the time of Aparājita (SII.*, XII, 95). It says that one Nambi Appi purchased land from the *kuḍimakkaḷ* of that *sabhā* village for endowment to the god at Vīraṭṭānam in the village. '

91. *SII.*, XVII, 222.

92. *AREp.* 1968-69, B. 182.

93. The statement in the Chinese account of Jan Yun Hua "Hui Chao's Record on Kashmir", (Kashmir Research Biannual, No. 2, pp. 119-20 as quoted by Sircar, D. C. in *landlordism and Tenancy in Ancient and Medieval India as Revealed by Epigraphical Records,* pp. 38-39 and Sharma R.S. *Indian Feudalism,* pp. 58-59) that the king, queen and the royal consorts have their respective villages and their folk, probably applied to Kashmir or the place which Jan Yun Hua visited. This Chinese account has been ascribed to 732 A.D.

94. *AREp*. 1943-44, Nos. 255, 261.
95. *EI,* III, p. 79 f.
96. cf. The Rēyūru grant of Narasimha II and Vunnaguru-vāyapālem plates of Paramēsvaravarman. These cite the *Nṛipēsvara* of Nandikuṟṟu as the *ājñaptj* of the grants.
97. cf. Sharma, R.S., *Ind. Feud*, p. 14-29.
98. Mahalingam, T.V., "The Pullūr plates of Nandivarman II, Pallavamalla, year 33, EI , XXXVI, p. 145; Minakshi, C., *op. cit.,* p. 141). Subrahmanian, T., "Pallava Jaina grant from Paḷḷankōyil", *Tr. Arch Soc.* of S.I. 1958-59, p. 41
98a. Mentioned in the Sanskrit text only.
99. cf. Sharma, R.S., *Ind. Feud.*, p. 87.
100. Subrahmanyam, T.N., (Thirty Pallava Copper plates, pp.145-179) translates this phrase "out of what was received by him (the *vijñapti).*"
100a. cf. With the name of the *vijñapti* of the Kasākkuḍi plates.
101. cf. Butterworth, Inscriptions of Nellore District, Part I, p. 429. The translation of the inscription given in this reference which has been adopted by Minakshi, C. (*op. cit.*, p. 121) is defective. What has been given above is the only possible interpretation, (cf. Minakshi, C., *op. cit.*, p. 121.) cf. Salatore, B. A., *Ancient Karnaṭaka Vol. 1—History of Tuluva* p. 207-11; Ramesh, K. V., *A History of South Kanara* p. 63-64.
102. *SII.,* III, No. 43.
103. *AREp*. 1895, 12. Published in *Madras Christian College Magazine*, Vol. VIII, p. 102.
104. Evidently Parañjaya, described as *aga-trayēsa* (III plate, 1st side, lines 1-2) and *saila-tray-ēndra* (*Ibid* line 8) who made the *vijñapti* to the king (III plate, 2nd side, line 2) for the grant according to the Sanskrit text of the Chiṭṟūr plates was the same as Kāḍupaṭ ṭi Muttaraiya on whose *viṇṇappam* the king made the grant according to the Tamil section. 0 (cf. Ramesan N., *op. cit.*, p. 29). Probably the (Kaduve)tti-Muttaraiyan who is referred to as (Dantivarman from Piḷḷaipāḷaiyam, Kāñchīpuram Taluk, Chingleput District (*SII.*, XII, 44), belonged to the same family.
105. cf. *Ibid.*, pp. 23-24. Though the somewhat involved Sanskrit text on the III plate of the Chiṭṟūr grant introduces the wife (*vadhū)* named prithvīmānikka who made the request to the king for the grant to brahmins on being approached by the brahmins for the same, just after mentioning Parañjaya, it does

not seem as if that she was the queen of Parañjaya. For, the text says that she was the *vadhu* of the Prithvībrit, which appellation is neither applied to Paranjaya in the text (cf. *Ibid.*, line 1 verse 12 starts with asmin= mahim=avati—while he was ruling the earth-where the he stands for Nṛipatunga) nor to any other feudatory, in a record of his suzerein. Hence it seems reasonable to assume that Prithvīmāṇikka, the queen of Nṛipatunga, approached her lord king for the grant and in the same way as Kumārāṅkusa was made the *Vijñapti* in the Vēlūrpālaiyam plates Parañjaya who has been clumsily introduced in the text was, or was made the *vijñapti* for this grant. Hence it is also reasonable to assume that the measure, Prithvīmāṇikka referred to in an inscriptions of Nṛipatuṅga from Tiruvālaṅgāḍu (*SII.*, XII, 66) cf. the temple Bhuvani-māṇikkavishṇu-gṛiham mentioned in another inscription of Rājakēsari (Āditya I ?) from Ukkal (*SII.*, III, l) named after the queen of the Pallava king rather than of Parañjaya.

106. *SII.*, XIX, 169.

107. In the copper plate grants of the Pāṇḍya kings also the *vijñatis* and *ājnaptis* are cited among the officials connected with the grant.

108. *EI,* IV, p. 139.

108a. *SII*, XII, 86.

109. Though in these instances the chiefs cited as *vijñati* for the grant do not appear to have controlled the territory in which the grant land/village lay, they seem to have held some other territory within Toṇḍaimaṇḍalam probably allotted to them by the king. For instance the *vijñapti* of the Udayēndram grant of Nandivarman II is described as the lord of Vilvalapura and as the chief of the Vegavatī-nadi. Though Vilvalapura has not been identified, the other title involving Vegavati-nadī indicates that the chief had got some territory allotted to him within Toṇḍaimaṇḍlam as Vēgavatī-nadī for the most part flows through Toṇḍaimaṇḍalam.It stands to reason that this chief who is described in the record as having been attached to the Pallava family hereditarily and as having fought the king's wars, was allotted some territory by the king in recognition of his services and adherence to the cause. There are no records to indicate if his rights in respect of the allotted land was restricted by the overall rights of the king.

110. In the Pullūr grant it is stated that the grant was made with the entitlement to *pāṛ-chāttu* and *paradatti* (lines 111-12). Mahalingam (*op. cit.*, p. 149) understood *pāṛchāttu to mean "effecting or entry of the division or apportionment of the land and village granted"*, (sic).

111. Actually for authorisation to the donee to part with the land the expression should have been *paradēyam*. But it is possible that originally the expression had the significance of a gift to or by another but in course of time without any rational explanation the term came to be applied for a gift with an authorisation for alienation. This *paradatti* can be compared with *vaisyadatti* used to denote a grant of honours and a village connected with a mercantile town to a *setti (srēshṭi)* by a Nolamba chief in a record from Nelappali, Punganur taluk, Chittoor District (A.R.Ep., 1912, 328; *Ibid.*, pt. II, p. 103; also Balambal, V., *op. cit.*, p. 87.

112. Under the *akshayanīvi* system of the western Indian context, the donee was authorised only to enjoy the proceeds from land without the right to part with what was conferred on him. cf. Sircar, D.C., *Land Lordism and Tenancy*. etc., p. 26; also Das, Dr., *op. cit.*, pp. 42-43.

113. The Pullur grant actually says that the *vijñapti* Avanichandra-yuvarāja made the request to the king when he was seated in the audience hall. The king is stated to have readily responded and made the grant of the villages through an executor. The court function of these chiefs is well brought out in the Rēyūru grant of Narasimha II and VunnagurvāyaPālam plates of Paramēsvara-varman I both pertaining to the Nellore region. The former cites one Rājāditya, son of Somaditya and the latter to Kulavarmmā, both belonging to a family of Nṛipēsvara of Nandikuṛṛu as the executors *(ājñapṭi)* for the grants. The grants of this region do not cite *vijñaptis* for the grants.

114. It is noteworthy that the employment of this word and the context of its use are entirely different from that of *paradatti*.

115. It is doubtful if Maṅgala-rāshṭra-bhartta, Dayāmukha and Vēsalippāḍi-araiyan were aboriginal chiefs raised to the position of vassals (cf, Sharma, R.S., Ind. Feud., pp. 277-85). Kumār-āṅkusa, who is described as Chōḷa-vamsa-mārttāṇḍa and as the *vijñapti* in the royal grant of *dēvadānam* to the temple at Tirukkāṭ ṭuppaḷḷi as recorded in the Vēlūrpāḷaiyam plates of Nandivarman

III must have belonged to the Teluguchōḍa family. This grant pertained to Toṇḍaimaṇḍalam.

116. The Bāṇas were the *āpta-sāmantas* of the Pallava monarchs (cf. Sharma, R.S., Ind. Feud, p. 28.)

117. *SII.*, III, 42.

118. The Bāṇās seems to have secured some rights over the Toṇḍaimaṇḍalam territory bordering on his own. A similar citation of the Pallava king Nandivarman (III) (year 23) and the Vikramāditya-Māvalivāṇarāyan as the ruler of Vaḍugavaḷi-mēṟku together is also found in the Gudimallam inscription (*EI,* XI, p. 224). Gudimallam was in Silai-nāḍu of Tiruvēṅgaḍakkōṭṭam. cf. *AREp.*, 158-59, B 15, 16, 17, 26; *Ibid.*, 1959-60, B 5, 10. In these records from Tadpatri taluk in Anantapur district of Andhra Pradesh, the Western Chāḷukya kings with their regional years are quoted and the Bāṇa is also mentioned prominently either as the ruler of Gaṅga-Rēnāṇḍu or Suramara-vishaya or Vaṅganūr-nāḍu or Vaṅgaru-vishaya. These records pertain to the period earlier to 750 when the Bāṇa had not shifted his loyalty from the Western Chalukya to the Pallava. Tadpatri taluk of today must have been known by several designations as noted above and that territory was to the Tamils *Vaḍugavāḷi-Mēṟ*ku-12000.

119. *SII.*, III, 43.

120. Kāḍupaṭṭi Tamiḻpēraraiyan seems to have been an important official of Nandivarman as he figures as the executor in Kāñchīpuram record of Nandivarman III, dated in his year 18,(Ulagaḷanda-perumāl temple Kāñchīpuram-inscription of the King's year 18) besides the Tiruvallam inscription. He also figures as the executor in the Chiṭṟūr grant of Nṛipatuṅga.

121. *Ibid.*, 44, 45, 46, 47, 48. Of them 44 is dated Saka 810 (888) and 45 says that the Mahābalivāṇarāyar was ruling the world.

122. The intimate connection of the Bāṇa came to have with the area is also evident from the name of a suburb of Tiruvallam and the reservoir attached to the village (Vāṇapuram and Vāṇasamudram). cf. Govindaswami, M.S., *The Role of Fedudatories in Pallava History,* p. 25. He says that the Bāṇas were hereditary rulers having a status higher than that of a governor.

123. *SII.*, XII, 42.

124. *Ibid.*, XIX, 80-81. Both are dated in the year 3 of Parakēsarivarman.

125. *SII.*, XII, 87-88.

125a. Subbarayalu, Y., *Political Geography* of the *Chōḷa Country*, p. 77. Govindaswami, M.S., (*op. cit.*, p. 25) however thinks that Perumbāṇappāḍi extended from Vaḍugavali-Mēṟku in the Cuddapah-Anantapur districts of Andhra Pradesh to South Arcot district in Tamiḻnāḍu.

125b. *SII.*, XII, 102.

126. *EI*, XXXIII, p. 23 f.

127. *Ibid*, also *SII.*, XIX, 169.

128. Sastri, K.A.N., *SI.*, H, p. 175.

129. cf. *EI*, IV P 177-78. On the basis of the swan and elephant engraved below the inscription of a Visaiya Narasingavarman at Kīḻmuttugūr, Gudiyattam taluk, North Arcot district, the king of the record is associated with the Gaṅga family. Also *SII.*, XII, p. 50 (Introductory remarks on No. 107). On the basis of the name of a village Rājamalla-chaturvēdimaṅgalam, probably identical with the modern Brahmadēśam, Cheyyar Taluk, North Arcot District the area is connected with Western Gaṅga Rachamalla.

130. *SII.*, XII, 45.

131. *Ibid.*, 65.

132. An inscription from Mēlpaṭṭi, Gudiyattam taluk, North Arcot District dated in the reign of Kampavarman (*EI*, XXII, p. 147) witnesses the conflict between Prithigaṅgaraiyar and a Vāṇarāyar in Kāvanūr in Miyāru-nāḍu in Paḍuvūr-koṭṭam. The Kuldikki, Gudiyattam taluk, North Arcot district inscription of Nandivarman III (*Ibid.*, pp. 110-113; *Tr. Arch. Soc. of SI.*, 1958-59, pp. 15 f) also witnesses a similar conflict. Only in the latter a Pallavaraiyan is also introduced. From this it seems that the control of the soverign over the area had become nominal by the middle of the 9th Century and the minor chiefs were fighting it out to grab the territory.

133. Among the charters issued by the Pallavas in the period 3-5th century pertaining to the Guṇṭur Nellore region only the Vesanta grant of Vijya-Simhavarman refers to an *ājñapti* who was a private secretary *(rahasy-ādhikṛita)*. In the two charters pertaining to the same region issued by the Pallavas in the 7th-8th century (Unnaguruvayapalem plates a of Paramēsvaravarman-aṅd Reyuru grant of Narasimhavarman), the *ājnapti* is stated to have been a chief (*nripesvara*) of Nandikurru. In these charters no Vijñapti is cited

134. cf. *EI*, XI, p. 154 f.,
135. *Nāṭaka-ppēraraiyan*. expert chief in dramatics (*AREp*. 1965-66, B437)
136. In this respect the inscriptions of the Chōḷa period throw some light. An inscription of the year 21 (1006) of Rajaraja I from Agaram, Villupuram taluk, South Arcot district (*AREp*. 1922-379) refers to the *tālam* (treasury) at Kāñchīpuram where the proceeds of the sale of land of defaulters had to be sent. The cash collection(in the form of taxes)could have been similarly remitted to the central treasury. An inscription of the year 19 (1031) of Rājēndra I from Tanjavur (*SII*., II, 20) indicates that there were local bhandaras (store houses). As the king is stated to have authorised the drawal of paddy from the same for a local benefaction it is suggested that revenue collected in kind was stored in such store houses and utilised for local disbursements. The practice might have been the same earlier under the Pallavas.
137. Again an inscription of the year 17 (1002) of Rājarāja I from Ukkal (*SII*., III 6) mentions a *kiḷavan* who or his father had the right of collection in that village (*emmūr-taṇḍa-uḍaiyārgaḷ*).
138. *SII*., III, 5.
139. *SII*., XII, 39.
140. cf. *AREp*. 1937-38, 382. This inscription from Kodukkappaṭṭu, Tirukkoyilur taluk, South Arcot district, dated year 15 (1000) of Rājarāja I records a gift of land probably by the king to a *Paḷḷi-kkaṭṭil-ēṟiya Nāṭṭ*upperaiyan.
141. *SII*., XII, 86.
142. e.g. *SII*., XII, 66, 69, 99, 100 etc. In these cases the chiefs or chief-like persons endowing gold seem to have held some territory independent of the service to the king but to have got authorisations for the collection of the revenue in gold from some villages as fee for their service.
143. Sastri, K.A.N., The *Chōḷas*, p. 126,127.
144. *EI*, IV, p. 221 f.
145. *SII*., XIX, 169.
146. The Tamil word used to indicate "had" is *uḍaiya* which does not always seem to have meant possession. As in the Satyavēḍu inscription cited above some times the word also indicated that the persons concerned "hailed from".
147. *EI*, IV, p. 139.

148. *AREp*. 1923, No. 419
149. *Ibid*., 69, 68; also *Ibid*, Pt. II, p. 122, para 90.
150. *SII.*, III, 30. Obviously the entitlement of this *brahmamārāyar* was different from that of the *brahmādhi-rāja* who was allotted four shares apart from the *brahmadēya* grantees in the Pullūr grant. It is noteworthy that in the Pullūr grant the executor Nagasarmā had the surname brahmādhirāja and is described as *mantrivara*. *Brahmādhirāja* in the Chōḷa period was a title applied to brahmin military commanders. The title was the same as that of Pallava-adiaraiyan, Kāṭaka-adiaraiyan etc, with only this difference that brahma added as the prefix instead of Pallava or Kātaka indicated the caste of the concerned person.
The requestor of the Kasākkuḍi plates was Brahma-srīrāja, who was a *mukhya-mantri*. The *adiaraiya* of *adhirāja* seems to have only indicated the exalted position in the official heirarchy held by the one having that title. The *brahmādhirāja* figuring among the recipients of shares in the same Pullūr plates was probably a village functionary, the strongman of the village, and belonging to a category different from the executor who had the same title, A Śivabrāhmana is also seen entitled *brahmādhirāja* (*SII.*, III, 50 inscription dated year (992) of Rājarāja I from Tiruvallam).
151. cf. Drākshārama inscription of Kulōttuṅga I (1070-1120) (*EI,* XXII, No. 23) which states that the kings had bestowed extensive gifts including land on his commander.

CHAPTER—4

COMMUNAL CONTROL IN THE LAND SYSTEM

It has been seen above that the Pallava kings, in their charters, associated the *nāṭṭār* or the body of the *nāḍu* in their grants of *brahmadēyam*. It has also been seen that four of the six charters granting *brahmadēyam* issued by the Pallavas were made in favour of whole groups of brahmins rather than to individual brahmins. One of these charters says that the grant of *brahmadēyam* to a group of brahmins was for the benefit of the temple *(dēvadāna-nimitta)* and another such says that the new *brahmadēyam* with 53 brahmins would pay *pañchavāram* as *dēvadāna* for a temple. After the take over of the region by the Cholas near the end of 9th century, the first Chōḷa king (Āditya I) to rule over Toṇḍaimaṇḍalam is stated to have attached a village granted a *dēvadāna* to a temple, to another existing *brahmadēyam*, giving the same ṣtatus of *brahmadēyam* to the *dēvadāna* village. His son and successor Parāntaka I issued a charter attaching one village to an already existing *brahṃa-adēyam* constituting a new *brahmadēyam* complex. While the above records evidence the tendency of the monarchs of the period to place the account on the people (landholders) of the different localities forming themselves into corporate groups, the stone records describing transactions in land during the period, also refer to *sabhās* of *brahmadēyams, ūrs* and *nagarams*., all corporate organisations, dealing with land-affairs as a group in each case. They also refer to some of the *sabhā* and *nagaram* villages as having attached villages/hamlets. All in all, from the information provided in the records of the period it is evident that the people of the different localities in Toṇḍaimaṇḍalam had formed themselves into corporate groups either out of necessity as dictated by the character of the land-system or as a result of the intentions in the matter of the king who preferred to place his reliance on such groups for helping him to consolidate his control over land and to recognise his community of interests in respect of land only with such groups. It is also evidenced that when the Chōḷa king got his buracratic machinery organised, he began relying on these local organisations less and less towards the end of the 10th century.

Now the character and functions of each of these corporate organisations can be studied in detail. *Nāṭṭār.*

This body obviously was of the *nāḍu* or territorial subvidision into which each *kōṭṭam* or main division had been divided.[1] This is the earliest local body to be mentioned in the records of Toṇḍaimaṇḍalam. When the earliest such record, the Kaśākkuḍi plates (753) refer to the *nāṭṭār* as having been addressed by the king with regard to the grant, it is indicated that this body had been there in Ūṟṟukkāṭṭu-kkōṭṭam even before the date of this grant.[2] Beginning from this charter, this body figures in each of the *brahmadēyam* grants of the period. The role of the *nāṭṭār* as described in these records was also similar to each other. Only in the later half of the 10th century, a body also named *nāṭṭār* gets mentioned in a different context, with no definition of its role in respect of the grant or transaction as recorded.

When it is considered that the *nāṭṭār* organisation had been existing in the localities even before the year 753 and in the charters it was expected to carry out certain specific functions with regard to the land in the villages granted, two possibilities regarding its origin and identity suggest themselves. One possibility is that it was a vestige of the tribal organisations of the localities in Toṇḍaimaṇḍalam, which as per the references pertaining to that earlier period had been occupied by tribal groups.[3] With the advance of agriculture this organisation might have assumed a general supervisory role in the division which came to be known as *nāḍu* without any specific of intimate involvement with agricultural land. As only some pockets in these *nāḍus* might have been agriculturally developed in the earlier period, the *nāṭṭār* might have been formed with representatives from each of the localities in these *nāḍus* and might have had a vague control over all the land, both such that had been developed and such that still remained to be developed. It might have developed a jealous feeling of possession over all the land in the *nāḍu* with a disinclination to pass any land within that *nāḍu* to any outsider.[4] The king might have established a rapport with the *nāṭṭār* by recognising a community of interests with regard to the undeveloped portion of the land in the *nāḍu* between himself and the *nāṭṭār* and might have had the intention of overcoming its anti-alienating feelings by associating it in the grants.[5] It is observable that unlike in some of the Guṇṭur-Nellore charters of the earlier period[6] of the north Indian charters[7] the *nāṭṭār* or people of the locality involved in the grant was neither just informed of the grant[8] nor was asked to ensure that the grantees were exempted as directed by the king[9] nor was asked to obey the king's grantees[10] but to delimit the grant village,[11] mark the boundaries,[12] release the land for the occupation of the grantees[13] and give the notice proclaiming the new occupation of the land within that nāḍu. Considering that the king must have had the coercive power to instal anyone of his choice in the localities without seeking the approval of the local inhabitants, the fact that he decided to associate the *nāṭṭār* in the way indicated above, shows that he had due appreciation of the feelings of the locals. He might have also intended that the *nāṭṭār* should ensure that existing rights over land inside the bloc granted by him were not interfered with.[14]

Another possibility is that the *nāṭṭār* was an association of only those who already held some land under their occupation in the localities concerned. When it is seen that Veḷvikkuḍi grant of Naḍuñjaḍaiyan(1.769-70)[15] which is very near the dates of the charter of Nandivarman II and which pertains to the Pāṇḍya country also refers to the *nāṭṭār* as a body depended upon by the king for the verification of claims with regard to land, it appears that the formation of the body, *nāṭṭa*r evidently with a membership of those concerned with land in the localities was an age-long general practice of Tamil country. Whether it was in the Pāṇḍya country or in Toṇḍaimaṇḍalam, in the charters the *nāṭṭāṛ* is seen to have possessed the local knowledge, not only casually but institutionally, of the land-affairs, and as such this was utilised by the king as the agency for the administration of land. But the Toṇḍaimaṇḍalam charters reflect that the *nāṭṭār* there, had also the authority to delimit villages, make over the same to the donees in the king's charters and also issue a proclamatory notice. Hence, though in the Pāṇḍya country also this body might have originated in the tribal background of the people, of the localities in Toṇḍaimaṇḍalam it seems to be more clearly indicated that the *nāṭṭār* represented an organisation that had come to play a role in the control of the localities and had a community of interest with the king in the control of localities.

While the evidence suggests that the *nāṭṭār* had a communal control over land in the *nāḍu,* this control is seen to have been different in character from the control exercised by the organisations at the village level that is discussed below. The body is not seen to have possessed common land to be developed at its initiative, nor is it reflected to have had the charge of the local irrigation works[16] nor is it known to have been in charge of the collection of revenue. This body is never known to have freed land from taxes on being paid a captial against the same.[17] But, it seems to have had some responsibility for local administration and local policing at least in some areas. The Kaśākkuḍi plates refer to a charge termed *nāṭṭu-vagai* (on account of nāḍu), the Paṭṭattāḷmaṅgalam grant refers to *nāḍukāval* (the watch of the nāḍu) and the Velūrpāḷaiyam, Kumaraḍimaṅgalam, and Chiṭṛūr plates to *nāḍ-ātchi* (the administration of the nāḍu) and *nāḍukāval* among the exemptions. While these charges were apparently meant to defray the expenses of local administration by *nāḍu,* it is noteworthy that these charges are mentioned as those payable to *kō*. Hence it is to be surmised that either the *kō* was a functionary of the *nāḍu* or if he was distinct from this body he collected the charges and made the proceeds available to the *nāṭṭār* to run the local administration.[18]

While the *nāṭṭār* of the Pallava charters are seen to have been a body with substantial control over land in the localities, when Toṇḍaimaṇḍalam had passed under the rule of the Chōḷas, this body is seen to have got its control truncated. When Chōḷa Parāntaka I issued a charter in 922 (Udayēndram plates of Parāntaka I) adding a village to *brahmadēyam*, Udayachandra-maṅgalam, the order was not addressed to *nāṭṭār*. The *nāṭṭār* was utilised to delimit the grant village. The execuōtion of the royal order was left to the feudatory Gaṅga Prithvipati II, who had been given charge of the nāḍu. It was this feudatory who issued the proclamatory notice. Again in 1008 Rājēndra I granted a village as *dēvadāna* (Tiruvālaṅgaḍu plates of Rajēndra I) but he did not address the order to the *nāṭṭār*. The *nāṭṭār* however delimited the village and issued the document of benefaction *(aṛavōlai)*but under attestation by a royal official.

However, in the Tiruvālaṅgāḍu plates as well as in the Tirumālpuram inscriptions of Uttamachōḷa (year 14 -984) the records are prefaced with a statement that they were addressed to the *nāṭṭār* of the respective *nāḍus* in which the villages involved in the transactions lay, the elders (*kiḷavar*) of *brahma-dēyams*, *ūragaḷilār* of villages under special tenures—*dēva-dānam*, *paḷḷichchandam*, *kaṇimuṛṛūṭṭu* and *vēṭṭappēṛu* as in the latter, these same plus *paḷavaram* and *sālābhōgam* as in the former and *nagaraṅgaḷilār* (all obviously within the same nāḍu). Of these only in the former record the *nāṭṭār* is stated to have carried out the function as mentioned above. Otherwise the *nāṭṭār* in the latter record and the other bodies are not witnessed to have carried out any function. Hence it appears that the address to them by the king was only for their information. Further on a perusal of the list in the preface, it is apparent that the bodies other than *nāṭṭār* mentioned were made of representatives of the specified villages and not the whole body of landholders. Hence it appears that the *nāṭṭār* mentioned in the same context was also a representative body and that too of villages other than those represented by the other bodies.[19] In the light of this it becomes doubtful if the *nāṭṭār* mentioned as having carried out the delimitation in the Tiruvālangāḍu plates was the same as that mentioned in the preface. In these two records unlike the Pallava charters, several royal officials are found carrying out definite functions. Hence it appears that at least by the late tenth century the king's control over the land was manifested through his officials and the *nāṭṭār* was tolerated and allowed to carry on some functions as of old but under supervision of the royal officials. It is possible that another kind of *nāṭṭār* representing strictly such villages which were not under special tenures had also come into being by that time making the position of the original *nāṭṭār* a bit farcical.

VILLAGE ORGANISATION

Ūr

While *nāṭṭār* as a body is found having some overall control over the localities that were the *nāḍu* subdivisions, *ūr*, *nagaram* and *sabhā* are mentioned in the records of the period as having had communal control over villages in Tonḍaimanḍalam. The *nāṭṭār* did not probably owe their organisation to the king's action. But of the village organisations the *sabhā* seems to have been organised at royal initiative through grants to groups of brahmins and the *nagaram* that came into the land scheme at the end of the 10 th century was also probably formed under royal encouragement. Both of these seem to have been integral parts of the land control scheme of the kings of the period. But the background against which the organisation *ūr* witnessed to have had some communal control over villages came into being is not known. *ūr* in Tamil meaning a settlement (a corruption of pura?), there is a possibility to understand the 'term as used during the period, as indicating the villagers in their severally. As if to lend plausibility to this understanding even *sabhās* are sometimes seen referring to themselves as *urōm*.[1] However, the records indicate that in some contexts the term *ūr* as used referred to a more substantial distinct body rather than such a generality.

Such *ūrs* gave undertakings and we asked as a corporate body of villages, performing a role some what similar to the *sabhās*. How these *ūrs* came to be what they were, might be indicated in the account contained in the Sangam classics referred to above, about the 2nd century Chōḷa king settling *Veḷḷālar* in newly reclaimed land. There may be some indication of this in the traditional claim of the *Tuḷuva-veḷḷaḷār* in Toṇḍaimaṇḍalam that their ancestors had been settled in the region with what came to be known as *mirāśi* rights by one Adoṇḍai-chakravartti.[2] However though there is no indication anywhere in the records as to whether *ūr* was composed of only landholders of a village, some records also indicate that there was no peculiarity about the landholding in a village where the *ūr* is found functioning.[3] For instance it is seen that an *ūr* of Palaiyanur is seen attesting the document contained in the Tiruvālaṅgāḍu plates of Rājēndra I,according to this document Paḷaiyanur was attached as *brahmadēyam* to the *sabhā* of Siṅghaḷāntaka-chaturvēdimaṅgalam earlier, but was taken off from the charge of the said *sabhā* and after cancelling its *brahmadēyam* status was brought under *veḷḷanvagai* (the tenure of the agriculturist?)[4] before being granted as *dēvādāna* to God Mahādēva of Paḷaiyanur-Tiruvalaṅgāḍu. From this narration it will be clear that the *ūr* was there in Paḷaiyanur even while it was being held as *brahmadēyam* by the said *sabhā* and that the *ūr* being found in that village had no relationship with the village being under *veḷḷāṇvagai* which was accomplished only as a result of this document. Similarly an inscription of the year 11 (891 ?) of Kampavarman from Kīḻpputtūr (Kanchipuram taluk, Chingleput district)[5] says that in the village Kilppundūr which had an *ūr*, the types of landholding included *dēvabhōgam*, *paḷḷichchandam*, *vaijya-bhōgam* and *pāppaṇ-paṭṭi* (bloc held by brahmins). In the same way the above said Tiruvālaṅgāḍu plates as well as some 10th century inscriptions refer to the *ūrgaḷilār* of *devadāna, paḷḷichchandam, kaṇi-muṟṟuṭ ṭu, veṭṭippēṟu, paḷayaram* and *śālābhōgam* (villages) apart from *the kiḷavar* of *brahmadēyam* and *nagaraṅgaḷilār*. Of them the reference to *paḷavaram* as having *ūr* organisation recalls to mind the exclusion from the *brahmadēyam* granted as per the Chiṭṟūr and Bāhūr plates of Nṛipatuṅga. It had probably reference to old settlements, *Dēvadāna* in this context seems to have had reference to such villages granted to temples which had not been made *brahmadēyam* and entrusted to *sabhās*.The phenomenon has been discussed below, p*aḷḷi- chchandam* was a village/land granted to a jain establishment, *kaṇi-muṟṟuṭṭu* seems to have meant the village/land which fed the *kāṇi* to the full and *veṭṭappēṟu* was the village/land in the enjoyment for or by *vēṭṭam*. These two defy proper interpretation.[7] *Sālā-bhōgam* referred to the village/land in the enjoyment of *śālās*, either free feeding-houses[8] or some other establishment for its maintenance. The reference to *ūrgaḷilār* of these villages may be indicative of the villagers in their severalty. But considering that in some of the *dēvadāna* villages, it is seen a body called *ūr* was in control[9] it seems possible that in all these villages under special tenures there was the body *ūr* in control.[9a] That it is also likely that the corporate body *ūr* was formed only in these special types of villages and not in other *non-brahma-deyam* villages, is indicated by the non-mention of the *ūr* of other villages in the same context. *ūr* might have been already there in these villages granted special status by the king or *ūr* might have come into being subsequent to the grant. The other body *nāṭṭār* mentioned in the context might have represented those villlages, which did not come under the control of a *ūr*.

Hence the evidence does not give any definite indication if the *ūr* was a body specifically resulting from a design to exercise control over the localities. However, it is seen that it was an important limb on the organisation of village localities, important enough for the *ūr* of Vāṇapuram to be described as a *ṭaṇkūṟṟu* (a revenue division by itself).[11] *ūr* is also evidenced to have controlled the common land in villages as also had the charge of the maintenance of the irrigation works pertaining to the village. The following records will illustrate the point. The earliest reference to an *ūr* in inscriptional records is found in the Toṇḍur (Gingee Taluk, South Arcot District) inscription of the year 6 (802) of Dantivarman.[11a] The *ūr* of Aruvākūr in Śingapura-nāṭṭu-kkīḻvaḻi just south of Toṇḍaimaṇḍalam accepted a deposit of 6 *kaḻañju* of gold for undertaking to maintain some services in a temple.[12] This indicated that the *ūr* needed gold and that they were in a position to invest the gold in a manner that it might give them some income required to be contributed to the temple.

Ūr is known to have been associated only with the agricultural activity in the village and so the only productive area they could have thought of must have been land. They might have utilised the gold in developing the common land, the cultivable waste in the village. Though the investment could have been directed towards the development or improvement of the irrigation facilities or such general works for the improvement of the agricultural prospects in the village, as a whole, this possibility is discounted when it is seen that there is no evidence of their getting a return from the villagers for such improvements without which, it was impossible for them to pay the interest to the temple. That the *ūr* held such common land and directed its efforts for reclamation of the same is indicated by the sales of such land by the *ūr* at the end of the 10th century and later. An inscription of the year 16 (1001) of Rājarāja I and another of the year 3 (1015) of Rājēndra I from Tiruvallam[13] witnesses such sales by the *ūr* of Vāṇapuram. The former specifically says that the land involved was the *mañjikkam* (land on the outskirts of the village?) of the *ūr*. Of course, the land sold was for endowment to the temple. For the maintenance of the irrigation works etc. they probably did not depend upon taking deposits from the temple funds. Such responsibilities entrusted to the *ūr* were financed otherwise. Two inscriptions of the time of Kampavarman (year 2 = 872 and year 11=881) from Pōṟpandal and Kīḻpputtūr (both in Chingleput district)[14] record the undertaking by the *ūr* of the place to maintain the local reservoir with the levy of a *kāḍi* of paddy per *paṭṭi* of land in the village which raised crops utilising the water from the reservoir. Someone seems to have donated the amount necessary for the capital works as the records say that the *ūr* sold the undertaking to that someone.[15] Further the role of the *ūr* as a body meant to manage land is brought out in some references to *ūrs* being incharge of a *dēvadāna* village. Vaikkāṭṭūr, one of the villages in the *dēvadāna* complex of Tiruvorriyur was under the charge of an *ūr*[16] and another *devadāna* village Tiruvaḍavandai in Paḍuvūr-ṅāḍu in Āmūr-kōṭṭam (chingleput District) was jointly in the charge of a *sabhā* and an *ūr*, according to an inscription dated in the reign of Parthivendravarman from the place.[17] An inscription from Allur in Tiruchirappalli district dated in the year 4 of a Parkēśari-varman[18] and recording an order of the Ilangōvēḷ points to the *ūr* of the place being put in charge of the cultivation of land purchased from them, reclaimed and endowed to the temple, i.e. the *ūr* as a community was enjoined to undertake the routine process of cultivation also in respect of some land besides being incharge of the regulation of the agriculture in the whole village. In these instances of sales of land by the *ūr*, the corporate body also made the land purchased and endowed tax-free on being paid the commensurate amount against the same. This indicates that the body was also in charge of the collection of royal dues from the villagers on behalf of the king.[19] One can appreciate the fact that the importance of the corporate body of the village would get accentuated when the cultivated land in the village had been rotated periodically among the villagers and this process was to be presided over by the corporate body. There is no evidence if this procedure of rotation was in vogue in *ur*-controlled villages[20] except a reference to *karai*, the blocs into which the land in the village was divided at redistributions, in the *ūr* of Karuṅgāli and an officer Munaippadi-Mūvēndavēḷān who was in charge of the same[21] in an inscription dated year 26 (965) of Kṛishṇa III from Chintāmaṇi, Ponneri taluk, Chingle-put district.[22] All this evidence leads to the conclusion that *ūr* a corporate body of one type of villages had some community rights over the land in the village, a supervisory right over the whole land as well as direct rights over the common land and cultivable waste in the village. However, the involvement of *ūr* in the management of land does not seem to have been of the same type as of a *sabhā*. There is no evidence about the existence of different committees associated with the management of land as was the case in a sabhā village.[23]

Further *ūr*, though seem to have had control over villages and in some cases is known to have been in a position to make allotment of land after making it tax free, to a temple[24] is sometimes reflected to have been subordinated either to a temple or to a *brahmadēyam*. It has been mentioned above that several villages under *ūr* were in the *puṛam* or *devadāna* complex of temples. The temple to which these villages paid the taxes which normally would have gone to the king thus became the 'lord' of these *ūrs*. This 'lord' temple also could probably take additional levies from these villages as it thought fit. Otherwise it is not understandable why an inscription from Takkōlam dated in the year 21 (928) of Parāntaka[25] I found it necessary to record an agreement by the *ūr*, of Kayattūr in that *puṛam* complex to pay to the temple *ṣiddhāyati* including *āṭṭ ukkarai*, *tokkaikunṛi* besides *puravu* (the main land tax) to the temple. Probably the *Siddhāyatis* were additional levies which the temple chose to take from that *ūr*. It may be it was this adjustability of levies when the *devadāna* village was put under *ūr* management that prompted Rājarāja I to give Maṇali under *ūr* as *dēvadāna* to the God at Tiruvakkarai.[26] Apart from this the *ūr* was also in the position of a tenant in the temple land. An inscription from Tiruvaṇṇāmalai, Tiruvannamalai taluk, North Arcot district dated year 19 (1031) in the reign of Rājēndra I[27] says that the *ūr* of Kīl-aṇṇāttu purchased (?) land from the temple and undertook to work (*uḻdu*), the land and pay into the temple's treasury the paddy due as *mēlvāram*. *Mēlvāram* is the landlord's share a tenant has to pay to his lord. The *Allūr* inscription of Parakēsarivarman as cited above[28] also placed the *ūr* of *Allūr* in the position of tenant of the temple though the land concerned had been purchased from that *ūr* and endowed as *dēvadāna*.

In the Tiruvālaṅgāḍu plates it is stated that Paḷaiyanūr was a *brahmadēyam* attached to the *brahmadēyam* of Singaḷāntaka-chaturvēdimaṅgalam and through the record it was brought under *veḷḷānvagai* before being granted as *dēvadāna*. The record also refers to the *ūr* of Paḷaiyanūr. Obviously Paḷaiyanūr must have been under *ūr* even while it was attached to the *brahma-dēyam* of Singaḷāntaka-chaturvēdimaṅgalam and as such it must have been subordinate to that *brahmadēyam*. It is not known as to what benefit accrued to the *brahmadēyam* of Siṅgalāntaka-chaturvēdimaṅgalam from having this village with an *ūr* under its 'lordship', in view of the fact that the record suggests that the said *brahmadēyam* was paying the *iṛai* tax and gold levy in respect of Paḷaiyanur to the king or to the temple. It seems possible that Paḷaiyanūr was in the *devadana* of the God at Tiruvālaṅgāḍu even before the date of the charter and that this charter only altered its status. If Paḷaiyanūr had been in the *dēvadāna* earlier also then the *brahmadēyam* mentioned must have been an intermediate 'lord' between the *ūr* of Paḷaiyanūr and the temple at Tiruvālaṇgāḍu. As will be discussed below, it may not be that the *brahmadēyam* in such temple-complexes itself was under the authority or control of the temple. It seems possible that the *brahmadēyam* had at least a part in controlling the temple itself in which case it has to be understood that *ūrs* like Paḷaiyanūr attached to temples though having communal control over the village in their charge, were themselves under the communal control of a higher body, the *brahmadēyam* or/and the temple.

NAGARAM

The *nagaram* in the Tamilnadu was a locality or village

with a predominent population of traders and the *nagarattār* as a corporate body of the traders. This main activity in which these traders were engaged and for what purpose the corporate body was formed is not reflected in the records. The *nagarattār* gets mentioned in the context of land control only by about the end of the 10th century. How this body of traders came to perform this role is not known. In the records of the earlier period the *nagarattār* figure in several contexts.

Probably the earliest reference to *nagarattār* is found in an inscription of Nandivarman II, year 65 (796) at Mahābalipuram.[29] It says that one among *(iḍai)*[30] the *nagarattār* of Māmallapuram, Valañjān Kaṇḍan purchased land from the son of the *kilār* of Kunṟattūr and endowed it as pasture land for cattle *(kanṟu-mēy-kaḷani)*. This indicates that during this early period the *nagarattār* or its members did not have land under their control. Several other records refer to benefactions of paddy or gold made by one or more members of the trading community. A *vāṇigan* (trader) of Uḷakkuni endowed 6400 *kāḍi* of paddy as capital for the dredging, the big reservoir at Payinūr, in the year 37 (768) of Nandivarman II.[30a] In the year 17 (863) of Nandivarman III the *Śeḷiya-vāṇigar* of Kunrattūr in Puliyūr kkuḍi-kkōṭṭam seem to have made an endowment for a service in the temple at Māṅgāḍu.[31] Three inscriptions dated year 15 (885), 18 (888) and 21 (891) in the reign period of Kampavarman from Uttaramallūr[32] also refer to endowments of gold and paddy made by two merchants resident in the merchant quarter of the village for the dredging of Vairamēgha-taṭākam. In one of them[33] however there is a hint that one of those merchants held land in the village as it is stated that he was exempted from paying extra-*iṛai* (*puṛa-iṛai)* like *maṇaippoṇ*, *alapi*ṛai and *śōṛumāṭṭu* and was asked to pay only the bare *iṛai* by the *sabhā* in appreciation of his endowment. But there is no indication as to how he came to possess land in the *sabhā* village and if he was under the discipline of *nagarattār*. His possession of land might just have been an accident. Even as late as the 3rd quarter of the 10th century in the period of Pārthivēndravarman merchants hailing from Kāñchipuram are only seen paying *pūrvvāchāram* (capital against taxes?)[33a] to the *sabhā* of Uttaramēru-chaturvēdimaṅgalam to free the land endowed or belonging to the temples in that village from taxes.[34] Apart from this, a *nagarattār* probably of the merchant quarter in the village is seen associating itself with the priests *(padi-pādamūlattār)* in giving an undertaking to contribute ghee for a lamp in the temple of Tiruvūral-mahādevar, against sheeps endowed in the year 5 of a Parakesarivarman.[35]

But suddenly in the reign period of Rājarāja I, the *nagarattār* of Mahābalipuram and Mēlpāḍi *alias* Rājāśraya-puram are seen controlling land in those villages. The inscription dated year 25 (1010) of Rājarāja I from Mahā-balipuram[36] records the elaborate arrangement made for the distribution of land among the 100 houses (*maṇai*) of the merchants in the *nagaram* (of Mamallapuram[37]) and the rate of taxes to be levied on such of the merchants that lived in the village but did not possess land. This arrangement was done by the *nagarattār* and *pēriḷamaiyār* under the supervision of a royal official, who was organising or regulating (*vagai-śeyginṛa)* Āmūr-kōṭṭam, the division in which Māmallapuram lay. In that *ūr* all land paying taxes *(iṛai-nilam)*, including the wet land, dry land (*veṇ-nilam*), garden land, kitchen-garden-land (*kōllai-ṇilam*),[38] was divided into four blocs *(kūrūs)* for allotment to the 100 houses. Of this, one bloc was set apart for the 25 houses of *śaṅkarappāḍiyār* of Kāḍumbiḍugu-chchēri (the quarter of that name) in that *nagaram*. The rest three blocs were allotted to the remaining 75 houses. Subject to the arrangement of (regulations pertaining to) the bloc, the house-sites and the land were capable of being sold, mortgaged and endowed (*dharmma-dānam*). The fruit trees standing in each bloc were to go to the one who had the bloc. Otherwise, such trees standing in the *mañjikkam*[39] were to be enjoyed as per *kūru* by all the 100 houses. Those above 16 years of age and doing trade (obviously such who did not have a claim to land as they did not belong to the bodies mentioned) were to be taxed ½ *kalañju* of gold. Those that were working as labourers were also to be taxed ½ *kalañju* of gold and those that had the plough and hired it (with themselves to operate it?) *(variśaikku-mūvār)* were liable to pay ¼ pon. The details of the *kūru* were to be recorded and the document was to be issued (to the *kūru*-holders?). The record further says that consequent on this new allocation, the old earlier document (*lakshaṇam*) along with annexures (*sāṅgam*) concerning the same were cancelled. This indicates that the *nagaṛattār* had been holding land under such *kūru* arrangement even earlier than the period of the record. The land allocation system described in the record is typically similar to the *karēyīḍu* system in the Tamil country found in the 19th century by the British administators.[40] This Mamallapuram record belonging to early 11th centry draws pointed attention to the following facts : (1) The members of the body *nagarattār* in Mamallpuram which was an important trade centre were not mere merchants but merchants holding agricultural land. (2) The eligibility to hold land in the village was restricted to some members of the village only, the reasons for which are not known. There were others in the village engaged in trading activities but were not of the 100 houses eligible to get the share of the land. This fact as well as the fact that the land was distributed to those 100 as per norm indicate that just as in the case of grant of *brahmadēyam* to several brahmins in shares, the merchants also might have been given land in the village by the king in shares[41]. On the other hand, it is also possible that they were given the whole village and the distribution of land among the membership was left to be guided by their own norms. (3) There were three distinct bodies in the village, the *nagarattār,* the *per-iḷ-maiyār* and *śankarappāḍiyār.*[42] The latter two also seem to have belonged to the same group of traders but only the *per-ilamaiyar* is seen to have had the eligibility to associate itself with the *nagarattār* in the exercise of control over land. The last, *śankarappāḍiyāṛ* was dependant on the former two, but was given due consideration by the traders who allotted one bloc to this group. The record mentions that there were in the village some persons engaged in trade without having any land in their possession. This heterogenous traders might have been such who did not originally belong to the village and thus had missed being included in the group that was granted the village at an earlier time. The record also evidences that there were free labourers possessing only a plough and were ready for engagement (4) The *nagarattār* and *pēriḷamaiyār* had control over all groups in the village. They determined the distribution of land in the village but it is not known on what basis they allotted the different types of land mentioned among the four *kūrus*. They could fix the taxes payable by non-landholders in the village. (5) While the record refers to the trees in the *mañjikkam* of the village as belonging to all the 100 houses involved in the redistribution, it does not reflect that the body of *nagarattār* as such retained some land for control as common land. Of the types of land listed to have been involved in the redistribution *veṇṇilam* or white land might have signified the saline tract and as such what was lying waste. But as there is no mention of land for dry crops in the list *veṇṇilam* might have indicated only dry land. Whether it meant the waste land or land under dry crops this *veṇṇilam* was part of each of the four *kūrus* and not land common to the whole village. It is likely that the mention of common land was omitted in the record just because such land was not involved in the transaction recorded.

Two inscriptions of Rājarāja I dated in his year 29 (1014) from Mēlpāḍi (Chittoor District)[43] give more details on the role of the *nagarattār* in the control of land. One of these[44] says that the *nagarattār* of Mēṛpāḍi alias Rājāśraya- puram made land available for raising a temple called Aṛiñjigai-Iśvaram by the king in memory of his grandfather as also for setting up residential quarters for the persons engaged in the worship in the temple, for raising a flower garden, etc. This record also refers to the allotment of *kūru* in the village and the mesuring rod used in the process. Further the *nagarattār* authorised the temple to take a channel ¼ *kōl* broad from the river *Nugā* for irrigating of land allotted to the God. Another inscription from the same place dated in the same year[44a] says that the same *nagarattār* granted all the land including wet land, garden land and forests in a hamlet of the village, Pulikkunram (*of the nagaram*) to the same god. The hamlet is stated to have been one of such *ūrs* which the village had got and that it had remained common land as it had not been apportioned (*kūr-iḍādu*) among the houses. The *nagarattār* also made the land tax-free on their own as there is no mention of any capital payment against the taxes by anyone. Obviously they undertook to pay the taxes on the land granted to the temple. It is also possible that the king had excused the taxes in respect of that land as the land had been granted to a temple raised by him. Thus these two records from Mēlpāḍi evidence that the *nagarattār* had under control not only common land in the village but also hamlets attached to the village. The body had the authority to grant away such land and hamlets as also to make the land tax-free.

One of these three records discussed above is from Māmallapuram which was well known as a trading centre from even the 8th century. The other two are from Mēlpāḍi which had an alternate name Rājāsrayapuram to denote its importance as a trading centre.[45] The earliest inscription from this place, however is dated only in the year 14 (999) of Rājarāja I.[46] All these records indicate that the control over land in these villages that the *nagarattār* possessed was something which that body had already been enjoying. Significantly the Māmallapuram record also refers to the cancellation of the old document on the allotment of *kūru* as it had become redundant after the redistribution recorded. But no record is available to enlighten on when the *nagarattār* came to be associated with land control. In the case of Mamallapuram also between the years (796 and 1010) there are no records. But some details available from 11th century inscriptions from other places it can be deduced that the *nagarattār's* induction into the land-system could have taken place only sometime before if not in the early years of Rajaraja I. Tirukkalukkunṛam, where the earliest inscription recording the endowment of *Vaḷippāṭṭu- ppuṛam* by Pallava Narasimhavarman[47] I (630-668) and the inscription dated year 27 (898) of Rājakēsarivarman (Aditya I)[48] recording the confirmation of what was given to the God as *iṛaiili* earlier do not indicate any association of *nagarattār* with the village, is stated to have had an alternate name Ulag-aḻanda-chōḻapuram with an association of nagarattār in the year 16 (1028) of Rājēndra I.[49] In the same way Takkōlam where the 10th century inscriptions[50] refer to the God of the place as Tiruvūral-Mahādēva and mention several villages, 4 under *sabhā* and two under *ūr* as having been under the *puram* of that God is found to be referred to as *nagaram* with an alternate name Kshatriya-śikhāmanipuram in an inscription dated year 26 (1011) of Rajaraja I[51] and two other inscriptions of Rājēndra I dated year 3 (1015)[52] and 20 (1032)[53] in his reign. An inscription of the year 9 (1021) of Rājēndra I from Tirukkōvalur in South Arcot District[54] again says that a village Śivapuram, in the *dēvadāna* of the God of the place was under the control of *nagarattār*. The evidence of these records makes it clear that during the reign of Rajaraja I and his son, the body of traders had an ascendency in the land-system. This acquisition of a role in the land-system by the *nagarattār* could not have been an accident. This body of traders was probably favoured by these kings with grants of land in the villages where they were predominant, with an authorisation to apportion the land among themselves and have control over the village in all respects. Just as hamlets and villages were attached to *brahmadēyams*, for their control, similar attachments of hamlets are also seen to have been made to *nagarattār* villages. This body as seen above had all the characteristics of a *brahmadēyam* village, with land held in shares, control over common land, rights over the irrigation system and right to collect taxes from those in the village. This body could not have got all these rights unless through a royal grant.[55] However the old centres of temple complexes, might have passed under the control of this body due to its money power.[56] But whatever control this *nagarattār* of temple centres got must have been different from the control which the *nagarattār* of trade centres like Māmallapuram and Mēlpāḍi had. Apart from the characteristic features of control the latter had, this *nagarattār* is also seen to have had an establishment with an accountant *(karaṇattān)* who took down and recorded the proceedings and orders of the *nagaṛattāṛ*.

SABHA

The earliest mention of *sabhā* amongst the epigraphy of Tamilnadu is found in the Tiruvaḍi (South Arcot district) inscription of the year 3 (673 or 731) of Paramesvaravarman.[57] Again a *sabhā* is mentioned in the Velvikkudi grant of Neḍuñjaḍaiyan[58] (c. 769-70) pertaining to the Pandya country. Whereas in the former the *sabhā* is found associating itself with the body śrī-Panmāhēśvarar to assure protection to an endowment entailing contributions from land to the temple, in the latter the *sabhā* is stated to have accorded approval to the distribution of portions of the village granted to him by the king by a brahmin amongst his relatives and others. As such the nature of the composition and the role of the *sabhā* in these records is not clear. However they do not appear to have been related to the communal control of land in the village and of the same nature as of those of Toṇḍaimaṇḍalam. In Toṇḍaimaṇḍalam the earliest mention of a *sabhā* is found in an inscription of the year 7 (803) of Dantivarman from Uttaramallūr[59] selling common land for digging a reservoir, a role characteristic of the *sabhā* found in later inscriptions of Toṇḍaimaṇḍalam and of Tamilnāḍu.

The *sabhā* of Toṇḍaimaṇḍalam was a corporate body of brahmin landholder which is seen associated with the control of four types of villages :—

(1) Those which are described as *brahmadēyam*.[60]

(2) *brahmadēyam* villages which are stated to have been meant for *(nimitta) dēvadāna*.

(3) Villages given the status of *brahmadēyam* and given

as (*devadāna* or for an educational institution and attached to the *brahmadēyam* of the first type.

(4) Villages in the *puṛam* or *dēvadānam* complex of a temple.

All the above types were *brahmadēyams* In so far as these whole villages are described as *brahmadēyam,* the character of this *brahmadēyam* is seen to have been different from the *brahmadēyam* of plots of land.[61] The Kaśākkuḍi plates refer to the exclusion of *brahmadēyam* to the extent of 2 *paṭṭis* from the purview of the grant of the whole village *Ēkadhīramaṅgalam* as *brahmadēyam* as per that charter. Obviously the *brahma-dēyam* character of these 2 *paṭṭis* must have been different from that of *brahmadēyam* of the whole village granted as per the charter. Probably this *brahmadēyam* of these two *paṭṭis* was the same as the *brahmadēyam,* that was granted in respect of the agricultural land and house site already possessed by a brahmin Sanmāduran Tamaḍi Vārāndara Saṭṭaiyan, of Mukkūḍūr, by Narasiṅgavarman as per the Kilmuttugūr inscription.[62] Further the whole village or bloc of land in the posession of several brahmins, by being described as *brahmadēyam* was also different from the *pāppān- paṭṭi*, the bloc of land with brahmins referred to in an inscription of the year 11 (881) of Kampavarman from Kīlputtur.[63]

The *sabhā* seems to have been organised only where these whole villages had been granted as *brahmadēyam* to brahmins. When other villages either granted as *dēvadāna* or for suppor-ting a *vidyāsthāna* were attached to *brahmadēyams*, they actually came under the control of the *sabhā* of that *brahma-dēyam*. The raison d'etre for the *sabhā* and the character of the communal control entrusted to it have therefore to be sought in the charters granting these villages as *brahmadēyam*. However, though the records of the period refer to the *sabhā* of 89 villages, the charters constituting all of them as *brahma-dēyam* have not come further for study, As pointed out above only seven charters recording grants of *brahmadēyam* in Toṇḍaimaṇḍalam during the period under study are available.

Of the seven charters two—the Kaśākkudi plates of Nandivarman II and the Rōyakkōṭṭah plates of Skandaśishya record the grant of a village to a single brahmin, four—the Kūram grant of Paramēśvaravarman, the Udayēndram[64] plates and Pullūr plates of Nandivarman II and the Chiṭṟūr plates of Nṛipatuṅga—record the grant of a village or a group of villages made into a single complex, with a new name, to several brahmins in shares, and one—the Tiruvallam stone inscription of Nandivarman III[64] just says that three villages including a *dēvadāna* village were clubbed into one *chaturvēdimaṅgalam* and that this *chaturvedimaṅgalam* had a *sabhā* acting on behalf of the complex. The two villages granted to single brahmin, Kōṭukoḷḷi in the Kaśākkuḍi plates and Chārukūr of the Royakottah plates are not otherwise figuring in records and it is not known if a *sabhā* had been formed in them. However in view of the fact that there is no evidence of other brahmins having been holding land in these villages prior to the grant or of the single brahmin granted the village as *brahmadēyams* having distributed the land in the village to his relatives or other brahmins,[65] it does not seem possible that there was any ground for the formation of *sabhā* in those villages. In due course when this single brahmins descendants multiplied and began holding shares in the village as their inheritance, they could have formed a *sabhā* to facilitate the exercise of the control vested in them due to the village being a *brahmadēyam*.

Of the four *brahmadēyams* granted in shares to several brahmins, Paramēśvaramaṅgalam granted as per *Kūram* record was probably meant to be merged with Kūram. For, the temple for which this *brahmadēyam* is stated to have been meant to be an adjunct (*dēvadāna-nimitta-brahmadēyam)* had been constructed. This village *Kūram* is stated to have had 108 *chat urvēdi* (well versed in the four vedas) brahmins. While constituting the *brahmadēyam*, Paramēśvaramaṅgalam, the record just says that the village was constituted with 25 shares and that 20 out of the 25 shares were meant for 20 *chaturvēdi* brahmins without specifying the names of the recipients, while, however, naming the brahmin priests in the temple, who were to take 3 shares out of the twentyfive. Hence from the non-specification of the *chaturvēdi* brahmins who were to be given the 20 shares, it appears that the intention of the king was that the body of brahmins of Kūram should take over this new *brahmadēyam*, nominate twenty among their own membership to take over the twenty shares in Paramēśvaramaṅgalam in addition to what they might have possessed in Kūram and also administer the whole *brahmadēyam*. The record also speaks of a reservoir attached to Paramēśvaramaṅgalam and of a feeder channel to it to be cut from the river Pālāṟu, which indicates that the land in the new *brahmadēyam* was to be developed before the shareholders could benefit from the land. This co-operative effort, needed to share the new village into an agricultural unit was probably expected to be provided by the brahmins of Kūram. Kūram is known to have had a *sabhā* even during the period of Nandivarman III (846-869) as per a record from the place[66] and it was to this *sabhā* that the king addressed an order regarding the disposal of a bloc of land designated *akkaḷanimmaḍi-poṟṟipāḍi*. It is also noteworthy that in a record of the time of Rājarāja I[67] Kūram is described with an alternate name as Vidyāvinīta-chaturvēdimangalam.[68] As it was the subordinate chief Vidyavīnita-pallava who purchased land in Kūram and constructed the temple and made the supplication to the king for the grant of Paramēśvaramaṅgalam as *brahmadēyam*, this record of the period of Rājarāja I strengthens the surmise that Paramēśvaramaṅgalam was constituted with a view to attaching it to the *brahmadēyam* Kūram.[69]

Whether the *brahmadēyam* Paramēśvaramaṅgalam was meant to be an independent unit or was to form part of the village Kūram, this charter evidences the character of the communal control that was vested with the holders of this *brahmadēyam*. As the whole village was *brahmadēyam* and as only the recipients of the 20 shares, the *chaturvēdi* brahmins, were eligible to receive *brahmadēyam* the priests who were entrusted with three shares and whoever held the other two shares set apart for the reciting of *Mahabharata* and the provision of fire and water in the *mandapa* at *Kūram* must have been intended to come under the control of the whole body of the 20 *chaturvēdi* brahmins. The irrigation rights and the entitlements which were to be shared by all the 25 share-holders mentioned in the record must have also been vested only with the body of these 20 *chaturvēdi* brahmins.

Udayachandramangala was granted in unequal shares to 59 brahmins as *brahmadēyam* as per the Udayēndram plates of Nandivarman II (752). In this *brahmadēyam* apart from the brahmins, a person (also named) who was to attend to the medical needs of the villagers got two shares and the composer of the eulogy (*praśasti*) also got a share. In this charter, which has got only a Sanskrit text the irrigation rights and the *sarvva-parihāra* (all exemptions) accruing to the *brahmadēyam* are very pithily stated. That to work this *brahmadēyam* a communal organisation was necessary and was formed are clearly stated in the subscript dated year 36 (943) of Parāntaka I, which says that this Udayachandramaṅgalam had a *sabhā* and for some reason, Kañchivāyil alias Igaṇmaṟai-maṅgalam which also under a *sabhā*[70] had decided to merge with the village Udaya-chandramaṅgalam and become a single village. Besides this, some more information is available on the progress of this village. In his regnal year 15 (922) (i. e.) earlier than the date of the subscript referred to above Parāntaka I is stated to have added one more village, Kaḍaikkōṭṭūr, to this *brahmadēyam* to make a new *brahmadēyam* complex. It is not known if on the merger of Kāñchivāyil the *sabhā* of that village ceased its existence and how this merger affected the scheme of communal control. But Kaḍaikkōṭṭūr must have only been controlled by the whole community of Udaya-chandramaṅgalam. Though the record of the 15th year of Parāntaka I says that with the addition of Kaḍaikkōṭṭur, the *brahmadēyam* was renamed as Vīranārāyaṇachchēri, it is observable that the subscript dated year 36 of the same king refers only to the *sabhā* of Udaya-chandramaṅgalam.

Nayadhīramaṅgalam was granted as *brahmadēyam* in unequal shares to 95 brahmins as per Pullūr grant of Nandi-varman II and Piridivimādēvi-chaturvēdimaṅgalam alias Chiṭṟūr was granted again in unequal shares to 53 brahmins. Again the land content of each share is not specified. In these two grants also some shares were set apart for a few persons other than those eligible to receive *brahmadēyam*. In the Pullūr plates 15 shares were also set apart for securing the services necessary for the village. In both these records some shares were also set apart for temples. Yet as the whole village in each case was designated as *brahmadēyam* it seems to have been implied that the *brahmadēyam* donees, as a body, would control the whole village and have the holders of the shares set apart for miscellaneous persons, under their authority. In both these charters several types of land as already referred to above are stated to have been included in the grant. Extensive irrigation privileges were also granted, all this seems to have been meant to secure for the *brahmadēyam* recipients communal control over an area beyond the village granted to them. These villages do not figure in any further records to enlighten us as to the organisation of these villages; and whether the *brahmadēyam* recipients had formed a *sabhā*.

With regard to the *brahmadēyam* Viḍēlviḍugu-Vikrāma-ditta-chaturvēdimaṅgalam created as per Tiruvallam record of Nandi-varman III, it is stated therein that a *dēvadāna* village Amarunṟimaṅgalam was amalgamated with two others, Aimbūṇi and Viḷattūr to form that *brahmadēyam*. There is no information provided in the record as to which of the two latter villages was the original *brahmadēyam* village to which the other two were added and as to how many brahmins were there and if the original village had been distributed in shares.[71] It is apparent that at least the *dēvadāna* village added to the *brahmadēyam* was not meant to be divided among the brahmins but was to be managed by the collective body of the brahmins, the *sabhā* of the whole complex, the Viḍēlviḍugu-Vikramāditta-chaturvēdimaṅgalam. It was this *sabhā* which was asked to contribute the stipulated amount of paddy and gold to the temple of Tiruvallamuḍaiyār in respect of the *dēvadāna* village Amarunṛimaṅgalam given to its charge.

Out of the seven *brahmadēyams* constituted according to the available charters, only two are evidenced to have organised the *sabhā* in the village. In the case of Udayachandra-maṅgalam further records in respect of that village have become available and hence it could be known that a *sabhā* had been formed in that village. In the case of Viḍelviḍugu- Vikramāditta-chaturvēdimaṅgalam, even the record constituting the village refers to the *sabhā* of the village. However when the character of the grant where *brahmadēyams* were constituted with a group of brahmins, is studied, it becomes evident that the grantees had to organise themselves into a corporate body to function in and benefit from the *brahmadēyam*. The village was granted as *brahmadēyam* in unequal shares. Though the major portion of the shares was given to the brahmins some shares had also been set apart for others. The extention of irrigation rights alone with the grant of *brahmadēyam* suggests that the village was to be brought under the plough afresh. Plots were not also earmarked for those granted the shares and no norm for the distribution of land to them was laid down. In consideration of all this, it appears that the intention of the grantor king was that the brahmin community of shareholders should arrange for the cultivation of land in the village and divide the yield among themselves and the other shareholders in proportion to the shares.[72] Further the grant of *brahmadēyam* was accompanied by a bundle of rights. Several types of land and irrigation facilities which may have been required by others in the locality to serve their needs also, had been placed under the authority of the groups of *brahmadēyam* donees. Several privileges like the setting up of the oil press laying out cocoanut and arecanut groves and allowing the toddy tappers to climb cocoanut and palmyrah trees had also been authorised to these groups of brahmins, under the head *parihāras*, the donees also appear to have been authorised to collect several miscellaneous levies from the other villagers and enjoy the proceeds.[73] The exercise of all these rights and privileges by the donees could have been possible only if they got together and acted as a single body.[74] Further at some stage the brahmin donees seem to have divided the land itself among themselves as per share as some inscription refer to the sale of land by the individual brahmins of *sabhā* villages.[75] As all the land in the village could not have been of equal fertility and enjoying equal facility, some organisation must have been necessary to distribute the land equitably among the share-holders and also probably to rotate the land among them periodically to avoid burdening anyone with inferior land permanently.[76]

This distribution of land seems to have resulted in a residue of land, probably what could not be immediately reclaimed, remaining which also had to be taken charge.[77]

Thus it is seen that corporate action by the donees of shares in *brahmadēyams* was rendered necessary for two purposes— one to work the land in the village and benefit from it and the other to exercise control over the locality. This seems to have been the genesis of the *sabhā* of the period, though it cannot be averred with certainty that all the *sabhās* witnessed to be functioning during this period had been organised only in such *brahmadēyams* granted in shares.[78]

That the *brahmadēyams* of the period were designed to exercise communal control over the locality is clearly brought out when it is seen that villages were attached with a status of *brahmadēyam* to the already functioning *brahmadēyams* with *sabhās*. It is not clear as to what motivated the attachment of Kaḍaikkoṭṭūr to Udayachandramaṅgalam as recorded in the Udayēndram plates of Parāntaka I. As the *nāṭṭār* were assembled to demarcate this village, it is possible that the same was in an undeveloped state and the attachment to the *brahmadēyam* Udayachandramaṅgalam was done to get it developed through the efforts of the latter[79] acting as a group. As the record refers to the *puravu* of 1000 it appears that the *brahmadēyam* Udaya-chandramaṅgalam was expected to manage the attached village and pay the *puravu* to the king. Probably, the brahmins of this period and region were known to possess the expertise. But Amarunrimaṅgalam, which was amalgamated with two other villages and made into a new *brahmadēyam* according to the Tiruvallam inscription of Nandivarman III was a *dēvadāna* village and is stated in the same inscription, to have been already under cultivation and contributing 2000 *kāḍi* of paddy and 20 *kaḷañju* of gold to the temple of Tiruvallam- uḍaiyār. The *sabhā* of Viḍēlviḍugu-vikramāditta-chaturvēdi-maṅgalam was asked to continue paying the same amount to the temple obviously in respect of that *dēvadāna* village. The benefit accruing to the *brahmadēyam* village from the amalgamation must have been over and above such contribution that they had to make either to the king or to the temple.[80] That benefit to the *sabhā* of holding the *dēvadāna* village must have been the proceeds from miscellaneous levies.

Of the above two cases in one a village was merged with a *brahmadēyam* without any statement of purpose and in the other three villages one of which was a *dēvadāna* were again merged and constituted into a *brahmadēyam* the *sabhā* of the new *brahmadēyam* having been obliged to make a contribution to a temple in respect of the *devadāna* village. It has been seen that in the Udayēndram and Pullūr plates of Nandivarman II also 3 and 4 villages respectively were merged together to form a new *brahmadēyam* but the difference between these two *brahmadēyams* and the new *brahmadēyams* created as per the Tiruvallam inscriptioin of Nandivarman III and Udayēndram plates of Parāntaka I was that in the former the merger was complete and the whole *brahmadēyam* village was granted in shares to the brahmins and in the latter two the villages merged seem to have been meant to be maintained with their separate identities. At least in the Parāntaka I's charter it is reflected that the added village was to be held in its entirety by the whole body of the *brahmadēyam* with which the new village was attached. In the latter two cases the *brahmadēyam* village is seen to have been under the control of a *sabhā* and hence it can be understood that it was this sabhā, which got the control of the additional village.

Such entrusting of village/villages for the control of a *brahmadēyam* for specific purposes is also witnessed in the Bāhūr plates of Nṛipatuṅga which pertains to the middle country. Three villages without any apparent merger were granted as *vidyābhōgam* to the *vidyāsthānattār* (as enjoyment for education to those of the educational institution) but were made *brahmadēyam* and attached to *(eṛi)* Vākūr. The grant included several types of land, wet land, dry land, *ūr*, *ūr-irukkai*,[81] *maṇai*, *manai-ppaḍappu*,[82] forum,[83] pasture-land, waste, tank, *kōṭṭagaram, kiḍaṅgu*,[84] wells, forests, *(kaḷar)*[85], channels and rivulets (carrying rain water) and all land covered with water or lying waste (*nīr-pūśi-neḍum-beramberindu*) or crept by tortoises and frequented by iguanas, within the boundaries as marked by *nāṭṭār*. The exemptions and privileges that were under enjoyment by Vākūr were eligible to be enjoyed in respect of this village also. The Sanskrit text further says that the villages granted through this record were protected with a tax-free status (*a-kara-tvēna-rakshitān*). Thus Vākūr which got the villages had full control over the villages attached to it with an obligation to maintain the *vidyāsthāna* which was also probably under its charge. Vākur is stated to have had a *sabhā*[86] or maha *sabhā*.[87] Hence it was the *sabhā* of Vākūr which must have exercised the control over the villages meant for the *vidyāsthāna*. During the Chōḷa period there are references to two attachments of villages to the *sabhās* of *brahmadēyams*. The Tirumālpuram inscription of Uttamachōḷa, year 14 (984)[88] refers to the entrusting of the village Śiṟṟiyāṟṟūr as *dēvadāna-brahmadēyam* to the *sabhā* of *brahmadēyam* Puduppākkam in the year 21 (892) of Āditya I (*Toṇḍai-mānāṟṟūrtuñjina (udaiyān)* While so entrusting the village Siṟṟiyāṟṟūr the *kāṇi* of Śaṅkkarappāḍikiḷān was excluded. In respect of what was entrusted to it the *sabhā* had to pay to the temple at Tirumalpēṛu, a *puravu* of 3000 *kāḍi* of paddy, an *iravu* of 561 *kāḍi* of paddy and a gold-tax of 26 *kaḷañju* and 11 *mañjāḍī*. This amount of dues from the *sabhā* is seen to have remained unaltered till 984 and later. Thus the *sabhā* is seen entrusted with a *dēvadāna* village with a *brahmadēyam* status which must have entailed control over the locality minus the kāṇi of Śaṅkarappāḍikiḷān. But the *sabhā* seems to have been so confident of its position in the village that it assumed that when the *kāṇi* of Śaṅkarappāḍikiḷān was granted as *dēvadāna* at a later date it was automatically entitled to take possession of that bloc of land also. The record goes on to say how the king who enquired into the complaint about this, disabused the *sabhā* of this assumption, fined it for seizing this *kāṇi* but probably out of consideration allowed it to continue in possession and contribute the stipulated dues to the temple in respect of this bloc also.

The Tiruvālaṅgāḍu plates state that Paḷaiyanūr had been attached as *brahmadēyam* to the *sabhā* of *brahmadēyam* Siṅgalāntaka-chaturvēdimaṅgalam. When this attachment took place and what for it had been done are not stated. But the record refers to the gold due as iṛai (*iṛai-kaṭṭina-pon*) fixed as payable by Siṅgalāntaka-chaturvēdimaṅgalam. Paḷaiyanūr might have been a *dēvadāna* and the gold stated as payable by the *sabhā* might have been the fixed contribution due to the temple. But Rājēndra I in his year 6 (1018) ordered the disassociation of Palaiyanūr from its *brahmadēyam* status and attachment to the *sabhā*. It is stated that the *sabhā* was promised an exchange, whether such a replacement was actually given or not is not reflected. When the record goes further to say that the village Palaiyanur with the tenure altered to v*eḷḷāṇvagai* and with the *iṛai* due to the temple permanently fixed was granted to the temple at Tiruvālaṅgāḍu it highlights the change in the royal thinking regarding the essentiality of the link between a *sabhā* and temple.

While the above-quoted records furnished the instances of attachment of whole villages, either granted as *dēvadāna* or with a purpose unspecified as *brahmadēyam* to the *sabhās* of *brahmadēyams* some stone inscriptions refer to villages with *sabhās* as having been in the *puṛam* of some temples. When it is seen that the Tirukkalukkurram inscription records the grant of *vaḷippāṭṭuppuṛam* (*puram* meant to maintain the worship) for the God of Mūlasthāna on the hill by *Vātāpikoṇḍa* Narasiṁhavaṛman (I—630-663)[89] and some other inscriptions refer to the land set apart for specific services in the temple as the *puṛam*[90] and in consideration of the fact that these same villages in the puram of the temples are referred to as *dēvadāna* villages in later inscriptions[91] it can be concluded that *puṛam* signified a *dēvadāna* complex. Such *sabhā* villages in the *puṛam* were as follows :

Maṇali[92] and Ādambākkam[93]	-	Tiruvoṛṛiyūr-puṛam
Rājamārttāṇḍa-chaturvedi-maṅgaḷam[94], Aparājita-chaturvedimaṅgalam[95], Pōndaippākkam[96] and Parundūr.[97]	-	Tiruv*ū*ral-puṛam (Takkōlam)
Rājamalla-chaturvēdimaṅgalam[98] and Añjashṭaśatam.	-	Tiruvekamba-puram

Apart from this one village Mandiram alias Jayameru-śrī-karaṇamaṅgalam with a *sabhā* is stated to have been a *dēvadāna* of the temple of Tiruvallamuḍaiyar.[100]

All these above-mentioned villages stated to have been in the *puṛam* or *dēvadāna* of a temple seem to have been such as had been granted as *brahmadēyam* and held by several brahmins who had formed the *sabhā*. The communical control exercised by these *sabhās* must have been of the same order as enjoyed by the *sabhās* in *brahmadēyam* villages which are not seen to have been so attached to temples[101] only with this difference that the former had to direct their contributions to the temples of which the villages held in their charge were *dēvadāna*. Regarding the contribution due to the temples from such villages, an inscription of the year 22 (1007) of Rājarāja I refers to the *pañchavāram* due to the temple of Tiruvallam-uḍaiyar from the *sabhā-* managed *dēvadāna* village Mandiram. But in the 11th century such *sabhā* villages seem to have been obliged to pay in addition several miscellaneous levies just as any other ordinary village to the temple as indicated by an inscription of the year 2 (1072) of Kulōttuṅga I from Tiruvoṛṛiyur.[102] So it would appear that *sabhā* had come under subordination to a temple. But some records from Takkōlam and Brahmadēśam which refer to the villages in Tiruvūralpuṛam and Tiruvēkambapuram, indicate that at least one of those *sabhā* villages in each complex was preeminent and as such might have also been in control of the temple-administration. Rāja mārttāṇḍa-chaturvēdimaṅgalam in Tiruvūralpuṛam is referred to as a *tan-kūṟṟu* village, which designation was reserved for such important villages which were fiscal divisions (*kūṟṟam or nāḍu*) by themselves. Rājamalla-chaturvēdimaṅgalam in the Tiruvēkambapuṛam complex, though not specifically described as a *tan-kūṟṟu* in the extent records, is stated to have had an *āḷuṅga ṇattār.*[104] A body, *gaṇa-vāriya*-ppe*rumakkal,* is stated to have been changing annually to look after the temple within Brahmadesam.[105] Apparently this body was contributed by the *sabhā* of Rajamalla-chaturvēdimaṅgalam. The inscriptions from Tiruvorriyur refer to the *amrita-gaṇattār* along with the sabhā, as of Ādambākkam one of the villages in the puram of Tiruvoṛṛivur.[106] So it appears that each of these villages in the puṛam complex not only had control over the concerned temple but also over the other villages in the complex both such that were under *sabhās* and such that were under *ūr* organisation.

In the instances cited above it has been seen that in one instance a village was added to a *brahmadēyam* with a *sabhā* without specification of the purpose for which this was done and in several other instances a *dēvadāna* village had been placed under the charge of the *sabhā* of an existing *brahmadēyam* apparently for maintaining the temple of which the attached village was *dēvadāna*. Apart from this the records of the period also reflect that some villages/ hamlets were attached to some *sabhā* villages. The records for such attachments are not available. Some times such attached villages are also seen to have been under the management of a *sabhā* or *ūr.* This feature brings out the fact that all *sabhā* villages were not of the same category. It appears that such *sabhā* villages which had attachments of villages around, that were given the status of *tankūrṛu* (*tani-ūr*) or of being a fiscal division by itself, though in every case of a *tankūrṛu sabhā* village, the attachments are not evident. The *sabhā* of such villages are referred to as *mahā-sabhā*. It appears that in such villages apart from the *sabhā* a governing body, *ālunganattār* had also been formed, the purpose of such formation, however is nowhere made clear. Ukkal referred to in the records as *uṭkar*. Śivachūḷamaṇi-chaturvēdimaṅgalam, Aparājita-chaturvēdi- maṅgalam and Śri-vikramābharaṇa-chaturvedimaṅgalam is first referred to as taṇkūṟṟu in an inscription of the year 16 (955) of Kṛishna III[108] and is seen to have had one hamlet Sodiyambākkam attached to it. Uttaramēru-chaturvēdimaṅgalam had 27 villages/hamlets attached to it.[109] One of these attached villages is stated to have had a *sabhā* and two *ūr*[110] An inscription dated year 7 (963) of Madirai-konda Rajakesari (Sundara-chōḷa)[111] and another dated in the reign of Pārthivēndravarman from Veḷichchēri (Saidapet taluk, Chingleput district refer to the *mahasabhā* of Veḷichchēri[112] and another dated year 5 (961) of the reign of the former king records[113] a benefaction by a member of the *āḷuñgañaṭṭāṛ* of the place. This village is reflected to have had at least one hamlet, *karagam* attached to it.[114] Singaḷāntaka- chaturvēdimaṅgalam and Nittavinōda-chatur-vēdimaṅgalam mentioned in the[115] Tiruvālaṅgāḍu plates are stated to have had several hamlets attached to them but as the two *sabhā* villages do not figure in any other records more details about them are not ascertainable. Tennēri (Kanchipuram taluk, Chingleput district) inscriptions dated in the reign of Rājarāja I (985-1014)[116] refer to Sri-Uttamachōla-chaturvēdi- maṅgalam as a *tankūrru* but if these were any attached villages, their details are not available. Two inscriptions dated in the reign of Pārthivēndravarman from Tiruvaḍandai (Chingleput taluk and district)[117] mention Talaiśayanapuram alias Taiyūr in Āmūr-kōṭṭam as a *tankūrṛū* but no details about this village have come forth. Kāvirippākkam or Kavidippakkam alias Amani-nārāyana-chaturvēdimaṅgalam is never referred to as a *tankūrṛu* but an *āḷuṅgaṇattār* of the place is referred to[118] and an inscription of the time of Parthivendravarman from Tiruppāṛkaḍal[119] suggests that this latter village was attached to the former. Guḍimallam (Kalahasti taluk, Chittoor district) inscriptions[120] indicate that Tiruvippirambēḍu had a governing *gaṇa* and also an *āḷuṅg-aṇattār* of Veppambōḷappāḷ. The latter might have been an attached village of Viprapīṭha or Tiruvip-pirambēḍu. As it appears that villages in which committees had been formed were also such which had attached villages, Ninṛavūr mentioned in an inscription of the time of Parāntaka I from Piḷḷaippākkam (Chingleput district)[121] was also another such village with attached hamlets though the details of such hamlets are not available.[122] Kūram to which probably Parmēśvaramaṅgalam was attached is stated to have had an *āḷuṅgaṇa*ttār.[123]

The records of the period reflect that the *sabhās* of villages freed land purchased and endowed to temples from taxes on being paid commensurate capital against the same indicating that they might have been the agency through which the king collected the taxes from villages. Sometimes they are also seen to be controlling some common land in villages which they sold for being reclaimed and endowed to temples.[124] They are also seen to have had the charge of the maintenance of the local reservoir[125] and control over the irrigation system.[126] But in the case of such villages which are stated to have been *tankūṛṛ*u or to have been presided over by *mahāsabhās,* the extent of control over the land in the village and locality possessed by these brahmin organisations is brought out very prominently. The *mahāsabbās* of these villages held some land as common at their disposal. The *sabhā* of Ukkal announced its readiness to make over such land which was common in the village (*madhyamamāy-kkiḍanda*) to any *kuḍi* expressing readiness to reclaim it and pay *iṛai*.[127] Inscriptions from Uttaramallūr refer to land which had fallen to the lot of the *ūr* and was not paying *iṛai*[128] or *ūr-viḷuliyāy-kkiḍanda-nilam*[129] or *pūndi* which had not been apportioned (kūriḍāde).[130] The *sabhā*s sold part of this land on their own for reclamation and endowment. The *sabhā* of Uttaramallūr is seen to have had the charge of the maintenance of the reservoir meant for this *ūr* and also had control over the system.[131] The *sabhā* in Uttaramallūr is stated to have allotted land as *vyākhyāvṛitti* and *vishahara-bhōgam* (the maintenance of one providing the extraction of poison services) and at least in one case the record reflects that the *sabhā* had the authority to entrust land meant for a temple.[132] Probably the plots of land involved were what had been set apart for the purposes mentioned in the charter (which is absent) and hence had remained under the control of the *sabhā*. When Nandivarman III directed the *sabhā* of Kūram to transfer a plot of land designated *aggaḷanimmaḍi-poṟṟipaḍi,* land meant for service in the temple of God Mahādeva, he recognised the control the *sabhā* had over that plot[133] The *sabhā* of Kūram *alias* Vidyā-vinīta-chaturvēdimaṅgalam is known to have allotted land as *uṇaṅgaṟpiḍi* for maintaining a service in the temple of Subrahmanyadeva in its *ūr* making it tax free as per an inscription of the period of Rājarāja I.[134] While these instances evidence the control of the *sabhā* over land within the main *brahma-dēyam,* its extensive control over land in the attached villages is significantly brought out in some records. An inscription of the year 37 (944) of Parāntaka I from Ukkal[134a] says that the *sabhā* of that *tankūrru* village Uṭkar allotted a hamlet called Śōdiyambākkam to the north of their *ūr* to the god of their *ūr* with the stipulation that the land in the hamlet including wet and dry land, a reservoir and residential sites, could be reclaimed through *kudis*, and that the *sabhā* of Uṭkar undertook not to show *iṟai* or land tax against that hamlet and to prevent its committees in charge of annual, reservoir and garden functions from taking *veṭṭi* (free labour or payment in lieu) *vēdinai* and *vālakkāṇam* (both these apparently were charges in the same category as free labour) from the *kuḍis* of that hamlet. It is also stated that the criminal jurisdiction over those *kuḍis* was made over to the temple. For the *sabhā* to make over all these rights to the temple and grant the exemptions it must have first possessed these rights with regard to that hamlet or such hamlets. The freedom from *iṛai* granted in respect of the land might have been done on the basis that they themselves had got the hamlet from the king on these terms or they might have been authorised to direct the *iṛai* to the temple, if they so chose. However the name of the temple Bhuvanimāṇikka-vishṇu-gṛiham[135] suggests that it had been constructed by the king. Hence he might have directed the making over of the hamlet to the temple by the *sabhā* and the tax-free status accorded to the village was an effect of his order in the matter. It is also indicated by the circumstances that the *sabhā* of Uṭkar had been allotted the hamlet for development but being unable to do so they took recourse to the allotment to the temple or were directed to entrust the charge to the temple. But they seemed to have had continued authority in that hamlet even though it had been allotted to the temple. Another inscription from the same place dated in the year 16 of a Parākēsari (obviously a Chōḷa king with that title who came after Parāntaka I)[136] records that Chakrapāṇi Nambi, who was managing the temple (*śrīkāryam)* approached the *sabhā* of Ukkar for getting an assignment of land for the potters supplying pots to the temple and that the *sabhā* duly assigned ½ *vēli* of the newly reclaimed land in Śōdiyambākkam and two other plots for the purpose. Obviously, this was an apportionment of the income from the land in that hamlet for a stated purpose connected with the temple as originally the *sabhā* had allotted the whole village to the temple, as the land was meant to be developed by the kuḍis, the intention of the original allotment of the hamlet must have been that the *kuḍis* would contribute to the temple only the taxes as the village had been freed from that burden by the *sabhā*. It is reasonable to assume that the *kuḍis* must have claimed a sizeable portion of the yield to compensate them for their efforts in reclaiming land. In the second inscription, the tax income from half a *vēli* out of that hamlet was obviously apportioned to maintain the potter. Though this evidence points to the *sabhā* as having had control over that hamlet even after the allotment to the temple, it was the temple which was the lord in so far as the *kuḍis* were concerned as it had criminal jurisdiction over them too. The sequence of these transactions reveals that when originally the hamlet was allotted to the *sabhā* of Uṭkar, the land in that hamlet was not meant to be distributed among the brahmins of Uṭkar but was to be held by the whole body of the *sabhā*. The *sabhā* could engage or lease out the land to kā*ḍis* for development which right it transferred to the temple as per the inscription of the time of Parāntaka I. The hamlet was apparently on par with the common land in the village of *Uṭkar* itself, which also according to another inscription from the same place dated year 16 (955) of Krishna III,[137] the *sabhā* declared its readiness to sell to *kudis*, who would undertake to develop and pay *iṛai*. On the *kuḍis* coming forward also, the *sabhā* must have enjoyed criminal jurisdiction over them in the same way as in Śōdiyambākkam, where such jurisdiction the *sabhā* seems to have enjoyed and later conveyed to the temple along with the land. In the same way the *mahāsabhā* of Veḷichchēri (Chingleput district) in the year 7 (963) of *Madiraikoṇḍa* Rājakēsari[138] is also stated to have sold some land of unspecified area in the eastern hamlet Karagam under the reservoir Adambuḷān-ēri, which they seem to have received for reclamation to two *veḷḷāḷa* (agriculturist) brothers with all exemptions (*sarvva-parihara*). Here however this is stated to have been done after taking sufficient price for the same. The two brothers reclaimed the land and made it over to the *śivabrāhmaṇas* of the temple. The *sabhā* undertook not to reflect in their records that *iṛai* and other levies were due from that land. There is no evidence if the *sabhā* continued to exercise some rights over that land even after the sale but probably they had resigned such rights by making the land exempt in every way against the monetary consideration.[139]

The *mahāsabhā* of Uttaramallūr is also recorded to have allotted land in an attached locality or hamlet to a temple and to have made the same tax free without waiting to be provided a capital against the same. An inscription[140] of the year 8 (878) evidences such an allotment in Malliyan-kārāṇai, probably a hamlet or locality attached to the main village, which was lying *madhyamam* (uncultivated common land ?). The *Mahāsabhā* of Kavidippākkam, when it allotted alternate land in the place of the land already allotted getting sand logged due to floods, for the temple at Tirukkarapuram (Tiruppaṛkaḍal) which was probably an attached village, it made the land tax free on its own. The *mahāsabhā* of Veḷichchēri, however sold land in a hamlet, Karagam attached to it and made it taxfree apparently against payments[141] for the reason that the purchase had no religious purpose behind it.

When it is thus seen that the three *sabhās* granted a whole hamlet or land in a hamlet attached to it to a temple after freeing it from taxes, it appears as if, in some instances, when hamlets were attached to *sabhās,* the *sabhās* were not expected to contribute any levy to the king in respect of those hamlets and that is why they had been enabled to act in the manner noticed. However an inscription from Uttaramallūr indicates that at least in some other instances the entitlement of the *sabhā* from an attached village was restricted to the miscellaneous levies. This recalls to mind the provision in the charters where while entitling the body of the donees, with the *paṛihāras*, it is stated that they could take and enjoy whatever the *kō* could. The inscription of the year 23 (962) of Krishna III from Uttaramaḷlur[142] refers to several miscellaneous levies as those which the *mahāsabhā* of Uttaramēru-chchaturvēdimaṅgalam was entitled to take from Tiruvuḷḷiyūr, the southern hamlet *(pidāgai)* which it endowed to the temple of god Mahādēva at Tiruvuḷḷiyūr for maintaining the players on instruments *(uvachchar)* attending the *śrībaḷi* service in the temple. In this case the indication is that either the hamlet had been already developed and was attached to the *sabhā* of Uttaramēru-chaturvēdimaṅgalam with the stipulation that the listed miscellaneous levies paid by the landholders of the hamlet could be retained by the *sabhā* or that the *sabhā* which had received the charge of the hamlet for development on their initiatives had given away the hamlet to the *kuḍis* for development. The miscellaneous levies gifted to the temple were probably only a part of their entitlement from that hamlet.

In these villages which had a *mahāsabhā* controlling them and had some villages around attached to them several committees are mentioned as managing some definite departments. That these committees are found functioning in these villages makes it appear that they had relevance with regard to the management of the attached villages and as such were the instruments of their control over those attached villages. Probably in the early days there was only one committee referred to as *vāṛiyar* in charge of the main function connected with the irrigation reservoir[142a] The *Uttaramallūr* inscription dated year 9 (805) in the reign of Dantivarman[143] may be the earliest to mention the *vāriyar*. The record says that a Śaṭṭ adaraiyar Dānavēndan made a provision for the dredging of the reservoir, Vairamēgha-taṭāka, and that the *sabhā* gave the necessary undertaking and ordered that the respective *vāriya*r of the period should carry out the dredging every month. It is noteworthy that the record says that it was the *sabhā* which gave the undertaking but it ordered the subordinate committee to carry out the task. As the activity of attaining villages to *brahmadēya sabhās* seems to have reached its zenith in the later half of the 9th century and in the 10th century which period also seems to have witnessed the multiplication of their functions, the *sabhā* appears to have set up more committees with specialised functions. More and more committees are heard of since the reign of Kampavarman in the last quarter of the 9th century and the 10th century records refer to a good number of them. The Committees immediately concerned with agriculture were the 'reservoir committee' *(ēri-vāriya-pperumakkaḷ)*. 'sluice committee' (*Kaliṅgu-vāriya-pperumakkal*). Agricultural fields committee' (*kaḷani-vāriya-pperumakkaḷ*) and 'gardens committee', (*tōṭṭavāriya-pperumakkaḷ*).[144] Of these the 'reservoir committee' and the 'sluices committee' can be understood as those looking after the irrigation system under the control of the *sabhā* for the general welfare of the community. So was probably another committee, 'the annual committee' (*samvatsara-vāriy*a-*pperumakkaḷ*).[145] From the evidence of the Ukkal inscription cited above, it can be deduced that the three committees in charge of the reservoir, gardens and annual affairs were entitled to take free labour or payment in lieu and some other levies *vēdinai*, *vāḷakkaṇam* etc. for their purposes from the villagers of the attached villages. It is not certain if they could also levy these charges from the land-holding members of the *sabhā* itself or were to levy the charges only from the *kuḍis* engaged to develop the land in the main village and attached hamlets. It is also conceivable that the gardens and groves were held in common in the village and the "gardens committee" was necessary for looking after their common interest. But the exact function of the "agricultural fields committee" is not clear. It is possible that this committee was in charge of the management of cultivation in the attached villages only.[146] Apart from these committees, there were some committees concerned with the administration of the village. There was the 'accounts committee' (*kaṇak*ka-vāri*ya-pperummakkaḷ*) and the 'measures and pathways committee' (*taḍi-vaḷ*i-*vāriya-pperummakkaḷ*). The *pañchavāra* committee was probably in charge of the *pañ*chav*āram* payments from the *dēvadāna* villages attached to the *sabhā* village. The *saṁvatsara-vāriya-pperumakkal* were also probably in charge of the collection of the taxes.[147] There were also committees in charge of the administration of the local temples in the charge of the village. These committees were entitled *vāriya-pperuimakkaḷ* with the designation of the temple prefixed, like Krishṇa-*vāriya-pperumakkal* or simply as the *ganattār* of the temple like *Śātta(Śāṣtā)-ganattar*.[148] There was also a 'committee on charities' (*dharma-vāriyaṭ pperumakkal)*.[149] One committee for the assaying of gold, probably such that was collected as levies, was also constituted, for which, however, the non-brahmin quarters in the village were also authorised to send members.[149a]

The committees did not have any independent existence apart from the sabhā. Sometimes the *sabhā* is seen catering to their needs.[150]

The existance of the committees evidently helping the

mahāsabhā in the exercise of control over land in the main *brahmadēyam* village or in the attached hamlets is understandsable. But not so well understandable is the existence of the *āḷuṅgaṇattār* or governing body in these villages.[151] The composition or role of this body is nowhere reflected. Only some members of this body are mentioned in the records as having endowed gold to temples[152] or having purchased land for the same purpose. As the records reflect that this body was aloof and separate from the *sabhā* and its committees, it appears that it was a superior body supervising the functioning of the village. It might have been a select body made up of the more important or richer members of *sabhā*. It might have also been a body not connected with *sabhā*. It is seen that the members of this body are referred to as *kiḻār* or elder.[153] Of the charters granting *brahmadēyam* during the period the Pullūr plates say that in the new *brahmadēyam* Nayadhīramaṅgalam one share was meant for the kiḷān of Śāttaṅgudi, two shares for Kāriśarmman of Kāśyapa-gōtra administering Parambūr and one share for the *perun-tinai* of Kaḍaṅgāḍu among other such recipients of shares who did not belong to the main body of brahmins eligible to receive *brahmadēyam*.[154] The allotment of shares to these persons is not explainable. However the designation of one of these as the kiḷān of Śāttaṅgudi suggests that he was introduced into the *brahmadēyam* for exercising some supervision over the working of the *brahmadēyam*. It seems possible that *āḷuṅgaṇattār* was made up of such persons introduced into the *brahmadēyams* even at the time of its creation to act as a check.

An inscription of the time of Parāntaka I from *Uttaramallūr* says[155] that the *sabhā* of the place was enjoined to act on the basis of the order of *mahāsabhāi-ttiruvaḍi*. It looks as if *tiruvaḍi* was added to *Mahāsabhāi* to indicate the dignified position of the whole body of the *mahāsabhā*. But when the Piḷḷaippākkam (Chingleput district) inscription of the time of Parāntaka I[156] says that Bāhūr-ttiruvaḍi presided over the deliberations of the *sabhā* of Ninṛavūr, it is definitely indicated that the *tiruvaḍi* was a concrete single person. He seems to have been a person in authority in Bāhūr, a *brahmadēyam* in the middle country, figuring in the charter of Nṛipatuṅga and other stone records. It is not known if such *tiruvaḍis* were members of the *āḷuṅgaṇattār*.

So it appears that though through the charters the king had invested the *brahmadēyam* recipients with extensive means for the control of the localities in which the *brahmadēyams* granted to them were located, he had also, at the same time devised a machinery to keep a check over them. But as these persons so introduced into the *brahmadēyams* were also probably brahmins, they might have in due course, merged with the other brahmins of the *brahmadēyam* or *sabhā*.

After the Chōḷa take over of the administration of Tondaidalam the records indicate that a stricter check on these *sabhās* was maintained. Three inscriptions of Parāntaka I two from Uttaramallūr, one from Piḷḷaippākkam and one of Rājarāja I from Teṉnēri, all the three places being situated in the Chingleput district record the laying ḍown of regulations by the *sabhās* of these villages for the constitution of the various committees. In the first inscription[157] dated year 12 (919) of Parāntaka I from Uttaramallūr it is stated that the proceedings were initiated on the order of the king and conducted in the presence of an official, Tattanūr-Mūvēndavēḷān. The second one is dated year 14 (921) of that king[158] and records some liberalisation of the rules earlier laid down again under royal order and in the presence of an official, Kāñchai-Koṇḍaya-kramavitta-bhaṭṭan *alias* Sōmāsi-pperumaṉ. The Piḷḷaippākkam inscription dated year 19 (926) of the same king[159] is damaged but this much is clear that the regulations were drafted by the *sabhā* of Niṉravur in the presence of Bāhūr-Tiruvaḍi who was probably specially deputed by the king for the purpose. Probably this was also done under royal order. The fourth one from Tennēri dated year 11 (996) of Rajaraja I[160] refers to somewhat similar regulation laid down by the *mahāsabhā* of Uttamachōla-chaturvedimaṅgalam.[161] Probably this was also done under royal orders.

In the last mentioned record it is stated that the regulations formulated were to apply for eligibility to participate both in the *sabhā* and the committees. Apparently in the earlier cases also the qualifications for participation in the *sabhās* of those villages were to have been the same as these laid down for the committees.[162] If that was so, then it becomes apparent that for being a member in the *sabhā* in the 10th century, it did not suffice that the brahmin aspirant was one of those granted a share in the *brahmadēyam* or was a descendant of one such. All the above-quoted records except the Piḷḷaippākkam inscription say that a good knowledge of *mantra-brāhmaṇam* (at *Uttaramallūr* the higher qualifications laid down earlier (i.e.) deep knowledge of *vēdas* and *śāstras* was scaled down later) was essential. The *Uttaramallūr* inscriptions further prescribed the possession of ¼ (*vēli*) of (agricultural) land,[163] residence in a house built on a house-site belonging to himself, being above 35 years of age but below 60 and purity in conduct as the essential qualifications. Hence it can be concluded that the *sabhās* of 10th century, which exercised communal control over land were elitist bodies.

TEMPLES AND LAND CONTROL

It has been seen above that during the period under study, the *sabhā* often was in control of the plots of land allotted to minor temples in the village administered by it and also of some *dēvadāna* villages allotted to prominent temples. The other village organisation *ūr* has also been seen controlling some temple villages. However in the cases of some of the temples that figure in the records of the period there is no information on who controlled the land or village granted to them. For instance it is not known as to whose control the land set apart for supplying the food offerings to the temple at Kūram was entrusted. In the same way there is no indication in the Vēlūrpāḷaiyam charter of Nandivarman III as to who took over the village Tirukkāṭṭuppaḷḷi granted along with several rights to the temple constructed therein. Apart from this, though in some of the villages controlled by it, the *sabhā* is stated to have nominated committees to administer the minor temples and is suggested to have had control over the administration of some prominent temples with which it was connected through holding the villages in the temples *dēvadāna*, in many cases there is no indication as to the person or persons in charge of the temple who were to take over the contributions accruing to the temple and maintain the worship in the temple. However there are also cases where some temple-bodies are reflected to have been concerned with the conduct of worship with the contributions. Some times these bodies are indicated to have been in control of temple-land also. Such bodies seem to have been of two kinds. One of them is reflected to have been composed of the administrators of the temple. The other was composed of the priests of the temple.

The earliest mention of such a body is found in the inscription of the year 12 (808) of the reign of Dantivarman from Triplicane (suburb of Madras).[164] It refers to the *kulaṅgilār* of Tiruvallikkēṇi as having mortgaged the temple-land. The name of this body is composed of *kulam* which might have indicated the *dēvakulam* or temple and *kiḷār*-elders. It is doubtful if the priests were referred to with this designation. They might have been an influential body holding the temple land and arranging for the worship in the same.[165] It is not known if Tiruvallikkēṇi to which this body belonged referred to the village or temple. In the same way an inscription of the year 18[166] (903 ?) of Aparājita from Tiruttani refers to the *dharmis* of the *ūr* who were entrusted with the land, purchased from the *kuḍimakkaḷ* of the *ūr*, got freed from taxes by the *sabhā* of Tiruttaniyal and endowed for services to the God at Tiruttaṇiyal by one Nambi Appi.[167] The *dharmis* were under the supervision of the *sabhā* and were to arrange for the intended services with the proceeds from the endowed land. As this body *dharmis* is said to have been of the *ūr* there is a suggestion that it might have been a committee of the *sabhā*.[168] But if the *sabhā* of Tiruttaṇiyal had constituted such a body to administer the temples in the village it is not explainable why when king

Aparājita in his year 9 (894?)[169] made a grant of the *pañchavāram* of a thousand *kadi*[170] as payable by the *sabhā* of Meliruñjēru in respect of the village Pudūr attached to it for the purpose, to God Subrahmaṇia on the hillock in Tiruttaṇi he did not say that the contribution would be paid to the *dharmis* of the *ūr*. An unfinished record of the year 17 of a Rājakēse-rivarman from Uttaramallūr[171] suggests that the *dharmis* was a body of the priests of a Śiva temple. It says that a Kāṭakaḍi-araiyar raised a temple each for Iśvara *(Iśvar-ālayam)* and Vishṇu (Vishṇu-gṛiham) and made some provision for the *dharmis* and *vaikkānasar* (priests in a *vishṇ*u temple) worshipping the respective deities. But as the Tiruttani record says that the *dharmis* was of the *ūr* and not of the temple of God Mahādēva, it is indicated that it was a body different from the body of priests.[172]

Another body *dēvakanmis* which term literally means the secretaries of God[173] gets mentioned as 'intimately connected with the temple from about the last quarter of the 10th century. Among the records of Tondaimaṇḍalam this body first figures in the Tirumālpuram inscription of Uttama Chola, year 14 (984),[174] wherein it is stated to have been one of the bodies that went to the king to complain about the unauthorised seizure of the *kāṇi* of Śaṅkarappāḍi-kiḷān by the *sabhā* of Puduppākkam. But an inscription of the year 4 (1016) of Rājēndra I from Tiruvallam[175] states that the *dēvakanmi*s of Tiruvallam-uḍaiyār were associated along with the Śivabrāhmaṇas who had *kāṇi* in Kukkanur, a *dēvadāna* of God Tiruvallam- uḍaiyār in a sale of land in that Kukkanūr. Obviously this association of the *dēvakarmi*s in this sale was due to the overall control this body had in respect of that land though the land was within the village which was the *kāṇi* of *Śivabrāhmaṇas*. This position of the *dēvakanmi*s in so far as Kukkanūr was concerned is confirmed in another inscription dated year 6 (1018) of the same king[176] which says that 1500 kuḷi of land which was yet to be reclaimed was endowed for Goddess Durgā by the *ūr* and the *dēvakanmi*s. As the record says that the land was handed over to a *śivabrāhmana,* though in Kukkanūr, this plot of land must have been outside the *kāṇi* of the *sivabrāhmanas*. From this village Tiruvallam several more earlier inscriptions have been brought to light but the *dēvakanmis* did not figure in them. Even as late as the year 7 (992) of Rājarāja I[177] an enquiry is stated to have been conducted by a royal representative Madhurāntakan Gaṇḍarādittanār to fix responsibility for the dímunition of worship in the temple but the *dēvakanmis* were not in the picture. He is stated to have summoned both the *sabhā* of Tiruvallam and *Śivabrāhmaṇas* and not the *dēvakanmis* for that purpose. Hence it appears that the body *dēvakanmis* was constituted in respect of the temple at Tiruvallam only in between 992 and 1016. This position of the *dēvakanmis* in so far as Kukkanūr was concerned, the composition of this body *dēvakanmis* is not indicated in the records. It does not seem 'to have been a body of the priests as in the above instances this body was distinguished from the body of priests, the *śiva-brāhmaṇas*. It might have been composed of influential local landholders. It might have been organised for the temple at Tiruvallam under the king's direction, as during Rājarāja I's time the temple affairs were found in disarray and the appointment of a supervisor of the temple in the person of Araśūruḍaiyān Irayiravan Pallavaraiyan alias Mummuḍi-sōḷa-pōśan[178] was thought necessary and he is seen to have been continued there till the year 4 (1016) of Rājēndra I.[179] In that same year the temple's accounts are stated to have been audited by another official.[180] But as in that same year the *dēvakanmis* are also mentioned, it is not clear as to how far the *dēvakanmis* were allowed to exercise control over the temple land and its affairs.[181] Probably the royal control was still present and the control of the *dēvakanmis* was subordinate to that of the king and his officers.[182] Thus of the three administrative bodies that have been reflected as having had control over temple land only the *kulaṅgiḷār* might have had some sort of independant control. The others were subject either to the *sabhā* or to the king's officers.

Whereas in the above instances the *kulaṅgiḷār*, *dharmis* and *dēvakanmis* appear to have been administrative bodies, the priests of the temple as corporate bodies also seem to have been entrusted with the control of temple land as well as the worship. The land allotted to this body was both for the maintenance of the members (i.e.) as fee for the services in the temple as well as for maintaining the services with the yield of the land. Beginning from the Kūram charter there are several instances found in the records whereby one or two priests were entrusted shares or land for both maintaining themselves and worship in the temple given to their charge. The charge was given to them for hereditary possession.[183] In such cases it is possible that by inheritance the descendants came to possess control over that land and worship as a body. It seems more possible that some of the prominent temples required the services of several priests to officiate in the worship in rotation and these priests had formed themselves into a corporate body to facilitate the exercise of their control. However such prominent temples seem to have been supported by the grant of whole villages which had their own corporate organisations. The priests of those temples do not seem to have been concerned with the land in those villages. The Tiruvallam inscription of the year 17 (863) of Nandivarman III[184] indicates that the *śivabrāhmaṇas* of the temple of Tirutīkkālivallam-uḍaiyar were maintained with 500 kāḍi of paddy out of the contribution made by the *sabhā* of Viḍēlviḍugu-Vikramāditta-chaturvēdimaṅgalam to which Amarunrimaṅgalam, a *dēvadāna* village of the temple had been entrusted. The Tirumālpuram inscription of Uttama-chōḷa, year 14 (984)[185] also indicates that the *uṇṇāḷigai-uḍaiyār* (the priests of the sanctum) did not have anything to do with the village granted as *dēvadāna* to the God of Tirumālpēru in those temple they were serving. However it is noteworthy that in these instances the priests, *śivabrāhmaṇas* or *uṇṇāḷigai-uḍaiyār* are referred to collectively. This body of priests seem to have become responsible for the administration of worship in the temples concerned as it was the *śivabrāhmanas* as a body whom the royal official Madhurāntakan Gaṇḍarādittanār summoned to enquire about the dimunition of worship in the Tiruvallam temple and it was them he fined in the year 7 (992) of Rājarāja I.[186] However the inscription of the year 4 (1016) of Rājēndra I [187] witnesses that this body of *śivabrāhmanas* had been entrusted one village Kukkanūr in the *dēvadāna* of the Tiruvallam temple as their *kāṇi* (portion for service). The record reflects that the *kāṇi* of the village was given to them not only for maintaining themselves but also for contributing for some services in that temple of Tiruvallam-uḍaiyār.

So whatever the background for the formation of a collective body of the priests, towards the end of the 10th century this body was recognised and entrusted with the plots of land endowed for various services in the temples. Of the temples also there is only one rare instance of the body of priests in a *vaishṇavite* temple. As an example of such a rare instance, an inscription of the time of Rājēndra II (11th century) from Śōmaṅgalam (Chingleput District)[188] can be cited. It records the *pariśu* (document) drawn by the *mahāsabhā* of Śōmaṅgalam alias Rājaśikhāmaṇi-chaturvēdimaṅgalam detailing the services in the temple that the *śrīvaikhānasar* as a body were to carry out, by taking over or managing the plots of land endowed for the specific purpose. But it is the *sivabrāhmaṇas* or the body of priests in *Śaivite* temples who figure frequently in the records as holding land of the temple for maintaining themselves as well as the worship in the temple[189] or as having been entrusted with plots of land endowed by benefactors.

A record from Guḍimallam (North Arcot District) dated in the year 4 (989) of a Rājakēsari (Rājarāja I)[190] says that Madhurāntakan Gaṇḍarādittanar purchased from the brahmins of the village two *paṭṭis* of land which was got freed from taxes on payment of the required *pon* to the *sabhā* and endowed it for meeting the expenses of the services to a deity Kūtta-pperumāḷ (Naṭarāja) set up by himself in the temple Paraśura-mīśvaram in Tiruvippirambēḍu and for a festival in the main temple. The *śivabrāhmaṇas* who had the *kāṇi* in Tiruvippirambēḍu undertook to take the *bhōgam* or the landlord's share from the land and conduct the intended services as stipulated by the donor (*nibandham*). A Tiṇḍivanam (South Arcot District) record of the year 11 (996) [191] of the same king refers to the *srī-kōyil-uḍaiyār* (those that had the temple) of Tiṇḍīsvaram as having taken over two plots of land (named) and attached well, purchased and endowed by one Ārkkāḍu-kiḷān for conducting the worship of the deity Gaṇapati in the temple.

An inscription from Bāhūr (Pondicherry) dated in the year 12(997) of Rajaraja I[192] also records the making over of land (3-3/8 *vēli* and one *mundivigai*) by the *sabhā* of the place for the goddess of the mint (Poṛsālai-naṅgai) undertaking themselves to pay the taxes on the land and entrusting the land to the body of the *sivabrāhmaṇas* who had the temple of their *ūr* for carrying out the benefactions after themselves having the land cultivated (*payir-ēṛṛi*). They were to be under the supervision of *pēriḷamaiyār* of the mint. A Tiruvallam (North Ārcot Disctrict) inscription of the year 7 (992) of Rājarāja I[193] records that one Vikramādittan *alias* Kīrttimārttāṇḍa-brahmādhirājar, himself a *sivabrāhmaṇa* of Nartuṅga-chatturvēdimaṅgalam in Karai-nāḍu in Paḍuvūr-kōṭṭam set up the deity Kuttāḍum-peru-mānaḍigaḷ (Naṭarāja) in the temple at Tīkkālivallam in Mīyāṛu-nāḍu in Paḍuvūr-kōṭṭam and for a perpetual lamp and food offerings to that deity, he got the *sabhā* of Mandiram alias Jayamēru-srīkaraṇa-maṅgalam, a *dēvadāna* of the temple at Tīkkālivallam, allot 1700 *kuḷi* of land in their village after paying them the price money (*vilai-dravyam*) and deposit against taxes (*iṛai-dravyam*). The land was handed over to the *sivabrāhmaṇas* of the temple at Tīkkālivallam to manage and enjoy the land (*anubhavittu*) and carry out the services. Another inscription dated year 3 (1055) of Rājēndra II from the same place[194] records the taking over of 25 *kaḷañju* of gold endowed by a member of the *gaṇattār* of Aimbūṇi, by a *sivabrāhmaṇa* (probably a mistake for the plural *sivabrāhmaṇa*) having the *sthāṇam* of the temple of Tīkkālivallam who undertook to have the worship done (*bujippikka* mistake for *pujippikka*) in the temple by a brahmin (*avanai-iṭṭu*)who was initiated *(dīkshita)* in *vēdam* and *āgamam*.

There are also two inscriptions of the year 3 and 4 of Parakēsari Rājendra[195] from *Uttaramallūr*, which record the entrusting of land to the body of *sivabrāhmaṇas* by the *sabhā* for having the worship conducted. The one dated year 3 and 334th day[196] says that the *perunguṛi sabhā* of the place allotted 2920 *kuḷi* of land in 12 plots after making the same tax free for the purpose of *archchanā-bhōgam*, food offerings, 2 lamps at each *sandhi* and two perpetual lamps for God Kayilāyam-uḍaiyār of their *ūr* and stipulated that the *sivabrāhmaṇas* (the body) conducting the worship *(archchikkum)* in the temple of Brahmīsvaram-uḍaiyār would do the worship in this temple also (taking over the land allotted?). The other dated year 4 tells[197] of the allotment as per the stone record (making the earlier grant against which the *sabhā* was now making the allotment) of 2546 -*kuḷi* of land by the *mahāsabhā* of the place after making the same tax-free for the worship of Tiruppuli-valam-uḍaiyār of their *ūr,* so that the *sivabrāhmaṇas* could have the worship done by a brahmin well versed in the vedas and capable.

Thus it is seen that the *sivabrāhmaṇas* had been entrusted with the whole village as *kāṇi* in one case and in several other cases with plots of land meant for carrying out specified services in temples. However the control that this body had over such land was subordinate to the control of *dēvakanmis* or of the *sabhā* where plots of land in *brahmadēyam* villages were entrusted to this body. Further the control over land entrusted to this body was conditional. It had to maintain the services in the temple for which the land concerned was endowed.

There seems to have been different types of the holding of land by the community of *sivabrāhmaṇas*. One type was the holding of a whole or major part of a village as evidenced in the sole case of Kukkanūr. Just as in a *sabhā* village there was some land in this village which was awaiting reclamation and which was in the common holding of the *sivabrāhmaṇas*. It is stated that when this body sold that land, it authorised the purchaser to clean unwanted growth and prepare the land *(vettiyun-tiruttiyum)*, lay out irrigation facilities (*ēri- kaṭṭiyum)*[198] and grow any crop the purchaser chose. It is reflected that this land also had been earmarked for a service in the temple. Probably the *śivabrāhmaṇas* did not support that service with this land before this sale.[199] The purchaser was told that he should contribute for the specified service and whatever of the income that remained after this could be utilised by him for instituting any additional service in that same temple of Tiruvallam-uḍaiyār. The record reflects that this body had leased out the land to others for cultivating and contributing an income to the temple as well as to it. For it is stated that it excused this land from paying levies including *veṭṭi* (free labour or payment in lieu) *kūrṛu-nel* (share of the paddy) and *aḷpam-iṛai* (minor taxes?). The only features that differentiated this holding from that of the *sabhā* were: l) the *dēvakanmis* had to be associated in the sale 2) the land had to contribute to the temple apart from the contribution to the *sivabrāhmaṇaṣ*. The other inscription from the same place dated year 6 (1018) of Rājēndra I might also indicate that as in villages attached villages Kukkanūr had its own village organisation *ūr*[200] and the control of the *śivabrāhmaṇas* was comparable to that of the *sabhā* but it is noteworthy that when the *ūr* gifted land they did not associate the *sivabrāhmanas* in the transaction but only the *dēvakanmis*.

Another body connected with the temple is also seen to have been treated as a group and sometimes entrusted land for communal control. This group is referred to as those serving with the drum in the Kūram grant (*paṭaha*) drum-beaters *(ṭaṭṭaḷi kōṭṭigaḷ)* in the Taṇḍantōṭṭam plates, those beating (the drum at the presentation to the God of food offerings during) *śrī-bali* (*śrī-bali- kōṭṭuvār*) in the Tiruvallam inscription of the year 17 (863) of Nandivarman III[201] and *uvachchar* in later records. This group of *uvachchaṛ* seems to have consisted of not only drumners but also others playing on different instruments. All of them together were to provide a sort of orchestra at the presentation of food offerings at *śrībali* service to the God.

Of the three records mentioned above only the Taṇḍantōṭṭam plates records the provision of one share in the newly created *brahmadēyam* for the *taṭṭaḷi-koṭṭigaḷ*.[202] This record pertains to Chōḷamaṇḍalam.[203] Of the other two records which pertain to Toṇḍaimaṇḍalam, though the Kūram grant in the Sanskrit text says that the new *brahmadēyam* Paramēsvaramaṅgalam was created for the various services including the drum-beating in the temple newly constructed at Kūram in the Tamil text detailing the distribution of shares, does not refer to any allotment of share to the drumbeater/beaters. Probably it was intended by the monarch that either the two priests, allotted three shares or the *chaturvēdi* brahmins allotted twenty shares in the *brahmadēyam* would arrange for the drummers probably paying them an allowance in paddy, out of the yield of the land given to their charge. That this was the practice in Toṇḍaimaṇḍalam at this time seems to be indicated in the other record from Tiruvallam which says that the *sri-bali kōṭṭuvār* group out of the contribution made by the *sabhā* of Viḍēlviḍugu-Vikramāditta-chatārvēdimaṅgalam holding the *dēvadāna* village Amarunṛimaṅgalam. Probably this service was as important as the main worship as the record says that the *śivabrāhmaṇas* were also to be given only 500 *kāḍi* of paddy. This practice of making available an allowance instead of land seems to have lingered on in Toṇḍaimaṇḍalam even to the time of the year 23 (962) of Krishṇa III. This record from Uttaramallūr, a *sabhā* village,[204] says that the *sabhā* allotted the proceeds from some miscellaneous levies (listed) to which they themselves were entitled from the hamlet Uḷḷiyūr, as the maintenance of *uvachchar* beating the *srī-bali* in the temple of Iśvara-bhaṭārar in that hamlet (Tiruvuḷḷiyūr). In all these cases where the *uvachchar* in the temples situated in *brahmadēyam* villages are seen to have been allotted either shares or a paddy allowances, control on them must have been exercised by the *sabhā* of that village.

But it seems that in a non-*brahmadēyam* village land was given to the *uvachchar* for their maintenance. An inscription of the year 2 of Vairamēghavarman[205] from Kīḻpulam, Arkonam taluk, North Arcot district[206] records that the *ūr* of Palkalam in Damar-kottam alloted two fields named (uḷ*uvān*) and *Ūruvadi* with all exemptions (*saṛvva-paṛihāra)* at the instance of one Ādittan Āḷi of Muḷḷikkuḍi probably an official, to arrange for the beating the *srī-bali* all the three times daily, with five persons including one beating the gong. The fields were entrusted to one *uvachchaṉ* named Arayaṇi-chchingam probably for his individual holding as it is stated that he was to do *ēr* (plough) and *amañji* (?) himself and that he could draw water of a fixed quantity *(ōrāḷi*) at his turn for irrigating the fields given to him. It seems he was responsible to pay and provide the other four accompanists in that group who were to perform at *srī-bali* service. The record however, mentions that two priests of the temple (*i-ttirukkōyil-uḍaiya*) who were brothers, Kūḷisivan and Madisūdasivan would present the food offerings to the God and blow the *kāḷam* at that time. It is not clear if these *kāḷam* blowing was part of the *uvachchar* service for which provision was made and if these two priests were to receive a remuneration from Arayaṇi Siṅgaṉ for doing this part of the service. Thus this record witnesses the entrusting of the land meant for the *uvachchar* group to a single contractor. It is not indicated if he was authorised to hold the land hereditarily.

The Madras Museum plates of Uttamachōla dated year 16 (985-86)[207] which records the apportionment of the income from various sources accruing to a temple at Kāñchīpuram singles out the *uvachchar* numbering nine as those eligible for receiving 150 *kāḍi* of paddy payable as interest by *uḷai-ūr*. This record also says that this group was also entitled to two *paṭṭi* of land specified. This entitlement is stated to have been of the whole group of nine and not of one who was to arrange for the other eight. The above stated two *paṭṭi* of land was pur-chased from the *nagarattār* of Kāñchīpuram, probably by the temple administrator for this purpose. It is not indicated if the group of the nine *uvachchar* was to hold the land together as a group or to distribute it among themselves and if they could hold it hereditarily. The *uvachchar* are not named. Hence there is a possibility that the *nagarattār* were themselves to administer it and pay the nine *uvachchar* engaged.[208] There is no indication in the record if the said land had been freed from taxes.

NOTES :

1. It has been mentioned above how Toṇḍaimaṇḍalam was divided into 24 kōṭṭams and how each kōṭṭam contained a few nāḍus. Apparently the *nāṭṭār* was of each such nāḍu division. The kōṭ ṭam division does not appear to have been organised to form a body of all these records only the Rōyakōṭṭah plates mention the *kōṭṭattār* as having been addressed along with the *nāṭṭār*.
2. In the Toṇḍaimaṇḍalam charters this addressing of the royal order to the nāṭṭār/*kōṭṭattār* is found only in the Tamil texts of the grants probably because members of these bodies did not know Sanskrit. There is a variety in the character and role of the nāṭṭār figuring in the Toṇḍaimaṇḍalam charters. In the Kaśākkuḍi plates of Nandivarman II the nāṭṭār of Ūṟṟukkāṭṭu-kkōṭṭam were addressed and the grant village Kōṭukoḷḷi is stated to have been in their *nāḍu*. In the Pullūr plates recording of the grant of four villages joined together to form the new *brahmadēyam*, three of the villages lay in Kīḻvēnāḍu in Palkunra-kkōṭṭam and the fourth lay in Maṇḍaikuḷa-nāḍu (not Manaḷai-kuḷa-nāḍu as read by the editor) which was also in the same *kōṭṭam*. There is no express statement that an order was addressed to any *nāṭṭār* but the *nāṭṭār* is stated to have carried out the processes as if they had been addressed. The *nāṭṭār* that carried out the processes was single body and hence it is to be surmised that the *nāṭṭār* was of Palkunṟa-kkōṭṭam and not of each of the two ṇāḍu in which the grant villages lay. Thus in the two instances noticed above the *nāṭṭār* was the body of the Kōṭṭam, the higher division rather than of the nāḍu subdivision. In the same Nandivarman II's period in the Paṭṭattāḷmaṅgalam grant pertaining to Chōḷa-nāḍu the king addressed his order to the *nāṭṭār* of Tenkarai Ārvalakkūṟṟam (It is tempting to identify *Kūṟṟam* of Chōḷa-ṅāḍu with the *Kōṭṭam* of Toṇḍaimaṇḍalam. But cf. Subbarayalu, Y., *op. cit.*, p. 19). In the other set of plates from Cholamaṇḍalam issued by Nandivarman II, the Taṇḍantōṭṭam plates, though the plates containing the iniitial portion of the Tamil section which usually starts with the

statement that the king addressed the *nāṭṭār* are missing, from the later portion of the grant as extant it is ascertainable that the nāṭṭār was of Tenkarai-Naraiyūr-nāḍu and that this body had done the delimitation (obviously this nāḍu had nothing to do with the Naraiyūr-*kūṟṟam* in the South Arcot District. Cf. item Nos. 186-87 of the list of ṇāḍus given by Subbarayalu, Y., op. cit.) In the Rōyakōṭṭāh plates of Skandasishya of doubtful date, the king addressed his order to both the *nāṭṭār* and *kōṭṭattār*. The grant land lay in Mēlaḍaiyāṟu-nāḍu in Paḍuvūr-kōṭṭam. Here the two bodies of the *nāḍu* and *kōṭṭam* were differentiated. In the same way, in the Paḷḷankōyil plates of Simhavarman which again must have been engraved about the 8th century, the king addressed his order regarding the grant to the *ṇāṭṭār* of Perunagara-nāḍu in Veṇkunra kōṭṭam. In the Chiṭṟūr grant of Nripatuṅga the king's order was addressed to the *nāṭṭāṛ* of Panmā-nāḍu in Naṇaiyiṟ-kōṭṭam. In the Bāhūr plates of Nṛipatuṅga pertaining to the middle country, the king's order was addressed to the *nāṭṭār* of Vāhūr-nāḍu in the Kīḻvaḷi of Aruvā-nāḍu. In the Kumaradimaṅgalam plates of Nandivarman III, the king addressed his order to the *nāṭṭār* of Tenakkaraiga-nāḍu in Tenkarai Chōḷa-nāḍu. In the Udayendram plates of Parāntaka I, the record says that the *nāḍu* apparently of Mēl-aḍaiyāṟu-nāḍu in Paḍuvūr-kōṭṭam was assembled just to demarcate the boundary and fix the boundary stones. In the Tirumālpuram inscription of Uttamachōḷa, year 14 (984) (*SII.*, III, 142), the *nāṭṭār* was one among the bodies representing all types of villages in *Maṇaiyil-nāḍu* in *Maṇaiyil-kōṭṭam* that were informed of the proceedings of a royal enquiry and decision on misappropriation of land by the *sabhā*. In the Tiruvālangāḍu plates also the *nāṭṭ ār* and other bodies representing various types of villages in Mēnmalai-ppaḷaiyanūr-nāḍu are stated to have been informed of the royal grant and a *nāṭṭār* is also seem to have done the delimitation.

3. Kosambi, D. D., *An introduction to the Study of Indian History,* p. 291, Sharma, R. S., *Ind Feud.* 39-42, 140, 222-223; Narayanan, MGS "The Vedic Puranic,Sastric Element in Tamil Sangam Society and culture. Proc IHC, 75, p. 84.
4. Sharma, R. S., Ind. Feud., p. 137.
5. If the above was the background for involving the *nāṭṭār* of the localities, it is not known why the *nāṭṭār* was not associated in the grant of *brahmadēyam* under the Kūram charter.

6. The grants of Guṇṭur-Nellore region issued by the Pallavas of the earlier period are also drafted in the form of orders to the local agencies. Among them only the Hirahaḍagalli plates of Śivakhandavarman with the text drafted in Prakrit which could be assigned to about 4th century A.D. refers to *raṭṭhaka* who might have been *rāshṭrikaṣ*, people of the *rāshṭra* equivalent to the *nāṭṭār* of Tamilnāḍu context, among the host of officials and dignitaries to whom the king addressed his order regarding the grant. Otherwise in these grants the royal order was addressed to the villagers (*grāmē-yakaṣ*) either alone or along with a list of officials stationed in the region (*adhikrita-najyōgikaṣ and vallabhas*). The address to the *gṛamēyakas* is understandable as at least in one case it is definitely indicated that in the grant of land as *brahmadēyam*, the king exercised his joint right over the cultivable waste in the village and the villagers were rightly informed of this. The relevant charter, the Chandalur, plates of Kumaravishnu II, recorded the grant of 432 *paṭṭikā* of *rājavastu* land out of the total of 800 *paṭṭikā* of land in the village, according to *halanyāya*, the principle pertaining to the bringing land under the plough, to a brahmin. In the other cases also, it is likely that only such land that was not under the plough was granted to the brahmins as *devabhōga* and *hala* land were excluded from the purview of the grant (cf. Minakshi, *op. cit.*, p. 93 n f. It is better to take *devabhōga* or land under the enjoyment of the temple and *hala*-land under the plough-as two categories). As such, the villagers were entitled to know about the grant. From the Viḷaveṭṭi grant of Simhavarman it is further learnt that the villagers were made to pay some miscellaneous levies to the donee brahmin. Hence the order of the king to the villagers was in the context of the conveyance to the donees of the entitlement to the miscellaneous levies from the villagers. It is also noteworthy that these charters enjoin the *grāmēyaka*s and the officials to see that the exemptions granted to the donees were given effect to and also admonish that anyone causing obstruction to the donee's enjoyment would deserve corporal punishment.
7. Sharma, R. S., *Ind Feud.*, pp. 139, 276. Also Maity, S.K., *op. cit.*, p. 63-64, 28.
8. Sharma, R. S., *op. cit.*, pp. 139, 225.
9. cf. The Guṇṭur Nellore charters; Sharma, R.S., *op. cit.*, p. 3.

10. Sharma, R.S., *Ind. Feud.*, pp. 3, 235: *Light on Early Indian Society and Economy*, p. 79.
11. In the Rōyakkōṭṭāh plates of Skandasishya, the *nāṭṭār* and *kōṭṭ attār* are stated to have taken the help of the temple elephant and the accountant (*karaṇattan)* of the temple for circumambulating the boundaries. In the Pullūr and Kaśākkuḍi plates the *viyavan* (accountant ?) of the *nāḍu* is stated to have indicated the boundaries. The operation for going round the boundaries is indicated by the phrase *piḍāgai-naḍandu* or *valam-vandu.* Here *piḍāgai* (which is also used to denote a hamlet) might have been derived from *piḍi*—the she-elephant which was usually used for going round the boundaries.
12. The usual phrase used is *kallum-kaḷḷiyum nāṭṭi,* i.e. planting stones and milk bush. Both were probably used only to mark the boundaries of the village and not for individual fields at that time.
13. The term used is *viḍunda or vīdu-taga*. As in every case only *viḍunda* is used; there is no basis to assume that *viḍunda* is a mistake for *vidutada* (Mahalingam, *EI,* XXXV1, p. 157, line 103)
14. Sharma, R.S., Ind. *Feud.* (2nd Edn., 1980), p. 219.
15. *EI,* XVII, p. 291 f.
16. Cf. AREp., 1965-66, B-175. This record in characters of 9th century from Brahmadēyam in Coimbatore District tells about declaration by the Cherukkali-*nāṭṭār* to protect a lake, shrine and channel named after *Nāṭṭān*.
17. Cf. Subbarayalu, Y., *op. cit.*, p. 39. The instance he cites (*SII.*, XVII, 549) to show that the *nāḍu* freed land from taxes on receiving the commensurate deposit belongs to the 13th century. Also, cf. Mahaliagam, T.V., 'Village communities in South India," *Readings in South Indian* History, p. 95. Also Stein, Burton, Integration of the Agrarian System of South India', Land Control and Social Structure in Indian History (ed. HE Frykenberg) p. 177 f.
18. Cf. Mahalingam, T.V., South indian Polity, p. 168 the 14th century guru of the Vijayanagar ruler advised the collection of the contribution due to several agencies by the king's man and their later distribution to them. Also Jha, D.N., "Temples as Landed Magnates, ISHP, p. 210.
19. Cf. Subbarayalu, *op. cit.*, p. 33-36. There does not seem to be

any justification for the conclusion that *nāṭṭār* was a body of *veḷḷānvagai* landholders or individual husbandsmen. *Veḷḷān-vagai* is not referred to in Toṇḍai-maṇḍalam records before the Tiruvālaṅgāḍu plates of Rājēndra I.

VILLAGE ORGANISATIONS

1. e.g. *SII.*, VI, 324, 344.
1a. As pointed out above, this reclamation by *karikāla* seems to have been restricted to the middle country where he had vanquished the Aruvāḷar and Ōḷiyar. Significantly the first *ūr* is heard of in Aruvākur situated in this middle country (*SII.*, XII, 42).
2. Their class name suggests that they hailed from the *Tuḷu* region on the West Coast. The presence of chiefs hailing from the west coastal region in Toṇḍaimaṇḍalam during the period understudy is attested by the Mallam inscription of Nandivarṇan III ?) (Butterworth and Venugopal chetty, V., op, *cit.*, and the Satyavēdu inscription of the time of Aparājita (*SII.*, XII, 86,89).
3. cf. Subbarayalu, Y., 'The Place of *ūr* in the Economic and Social History of the Early Tamilnāḍu, A.D., 760-1350' *Rangavalli*, p. 172.
4. This term is first heard of only in this document only.
5. *SII.*, XII, 102.
6. Cf., *SII.*, III, p. 427. In the light of the Chiṭṟūr and Bāhūr plates *paḷayaṟam* and *śālābhōgam* are to be construed as two separate words.
7. *Muṟṟūṭṭu* can be compared with *pūrnōpajīvi* occurring in the Piṭhāpuram plates of Vīra-chōḍa (*EI*, V, p. 70 f). For a discussion on *veṭṭippēṟu* and the identity of *kāṇi* see Subrahaniam, T.N., "Chola Jaina C.P. Grant, *Tr. Arch.* Soc. of *SI.*, 1958-59, p. 87 f).
8. *SII.*, III, 151. *Kaṇi-muṟṟūṭṭu*, *vēṭṭa-ppōṟu* and *sālā*, *bhōgam* seem to have been some special types of tenures. But beyond some stray references to them not such information is available on them.
9. e.g. *SII.*, V, 1375.
10. Subbarayalu, Y., The Political Geography of Chōḷa Country), p. 35 f.
11. *SII.*, III, 51.
11a. An inscription dated in the reign of Pārthivēndravarman from

Moranam (North Arcot District) *AREp*. 1965-66, B. 154) records that the *ūrār* of Pulavay-puttur executed an agreement *(ottōtai)* in favour of the *ūrār* of Morāṇḍattur in respect of rights of irrigation.

11b. *SII.*, XII, 44.

12. Such deposits of gold with either a *sabhā* or *ūr* or *nagaram* was an *akshaya-nīvi*, unending or indestructible capital. An inscription of Rājēndra I (year 16 = 1206) from Vēppaṅguḷan (Kāñchīpuram Taluk, Chingleput District) (*SII.*, VIII, 5) which records the taking over of gold from the temple by several *sabhā* undertaking to contribute paddy to the temple as interest also records their undertaking that they would not ask the temple to take the gold back. This undertaking though not recorded in other instances must have been a thing understood by the very nature of the transaction.

13. *SII.*, III, 51, 53 respectively. Also Podavur (Chingleput District) inscription of year 9 of Pārthivēndravarman (*AREp.*, 1923, 68).

14. *SII.*, XII, 97, 102 respectively.

15. cf. *Ibid.*, 34.

16. *Ibid.*, 103. The village is actually stated to have been in the puṟam of Tiruvoṟṟiyūr that this appellation *puṟam* denoted *dēvadāna* is indicated when several other villages stated to have been in the puṟam of Tiruvoṟṟiyūr in the 9-10 century. Inscriptions are referred to as the *dēvadāna* of villages of the God at Tiruvoṟṟiyūr in 11th century inscriptions *(AREp.* 1912, 102, 131). Another village, Igaṇai-ūr in the same Tiruvoṟṟiyūr-puṟam complex is reflected to have been under *ūr* management in a eleventh century inscription (*SII.*, II, 64). In the same way Kayattūr and Siṟūr in the Tiruv*ū*ralpuram complex are also stated to have been under the control of *ūr* (*SII.*, v, 1366; 1375; *AREp.*, 1921, 257 Menalur in Tlrukkaṟṟaḷippuṟam is also stated to have had an *ūr* (*SII.*, I, 84). Kukkanār in the *dēvadāna* of the God Tiruvallamuḍaiyār also probably had an *ūr* (*AREp.*, 1921-217). An inscription from Takkōlam what the *ūr* of the village in the puṟam complex was to contribute to the temples (*SII.*, v, 1375).

17. *Ibid*, III, 180.

18. *Ibid.*, VIII, 692.

19. Vāṇapuram, adjacent to Tiruvallam, had gained the status of a taṇ*kūṟ*ṟu (self-administered fiscal unit) in the reign of Rājarāja I (*SII.*, III, 51) and its importance was such that it could convey

sarva-parihāra (all exemptions) in respect of land sold by it for endowment, of course on being paid the required capital, (*Ibid*. 53).

20. However, the 19th century evidence indicates that even till that time in all the villages in Toṇḍaimaṇḍalam the land was redistributed at periodic intervals though practice had been discontinued in some villages (Croele, op. cit., IA, III, p. 65) Also Mahalingam, T.V., 'Village communities in South India', Readings in South Indian History (ed. Ramachandran, K.S.), p. 101.
21. In the *kareyiḍu* system of the rotation of land, the land was divided into main blocs called *karai* and each bloc was in charge of a *karaiyāḷan*. For a description of the *karayīḍu* system in the 19th century, see IA, III, p. 65 f.
22. *AREp*. 1933-34, 19 and Pt. II, p. 32 para 9
23. The employment of the phrase *vārigappaṭṭōm* with reference to the undertaking by the *ūr* of Aruvākūr in the Toṇḍūr Inscription of Dantivarman (*SII*., XII, 44) seems to have been employed only to indicate an undertaking and not that the *ūr* would form a *vāriyam* or committee for managing the endowment recorded in the inscription.
24. *SII*., XIII, *Ibid*., VIII. 67.
25. *SII*., V, 1375
26. *SII*., XVII, 222.
27. *Ibid*., VIII, 66
28. *Ibid*., 692.
29. Mem. *ASI*., 26, p. 9.
30. This participle *iḍai* could also mean "from" (cf. line 11 in the same record) but as further on, the record states that the land was purchased from Kaṇḍan, the son of the kiḻār of Kunṟattūr, it is not possible to interpret the content of the record as a purchase of land from the *nagarattār*,

30a. *SII*., XII, 34.

31. *Ibid*., 53.
32. *Ibid*., VI, 375, 348 and 369 respectively.
33. *Ibid*., 369.

33a. Ibid., III.

34. *Ibid*., III, 155, 157, 162, 170 etc.
35. *SII*., V, 1369. Another inscription from the same place dated in the reign of Parthivēndravarman (*Ibid*., II, 166) records an endowment of gold by the *nagarattār*.

36. *Ibid.*, I. 40.
37. The actual name of the village must have been Māmallapuram. It might have been so named after the group of people, Mallas stated to have been occupying a quarter in Kāñchīpuram in *Perumbāṇārṟuppaḍai*. The Pallava kings also bore *malla* titles—Mahāmalla (Narasimhavarman I—630-668) Pallavamalla Nandivarman II (731-796).
38. The differentiation between garden land and kitchen garden land was probably that the former contained commercially profit-yielding trees.
39. The editor interprets *mañjikkam* as the cause-way between rice-fields. He connects it with the urdu word mangil meaning destination. This derivation will be anachronistic. But from the contexts of the occurrence of this word, it can be deduced that it referred to the outskirts of the village. Several other inscriptions of the period refer to the land in the *mañjikkam* as the common land of the village awaiting reclamation.
40. *IA*, III, p. 66 f. The Kareyīdu described herein pertains to the Tañjāvūr district. Also e.g. *AREp*. 1912, 441; *Ibid.*, 1913, pt. II, p. 108. An inscription of the year 12 (1190) of Kulōttuṅga III from Tiruppālatturai (Tiruchirappalli district) also evidences the redistribution of land among *sāliya-nagarattār*.
41. Sharma, R.S., *Ind. Feud*, p. 71.
42. While *pēr-iḷamalyār* could be understood as a body of junior traders or apprentices. The identity of the Sankarappāḍiyār is not clear. If sankarappāḍi was a quarter of mixed castes or if those whose caste had become blurred due to intercaste marriages, it is not known why such people should have linked themselves with traders without however merging with them, cf. *SII.*, III, 19. One Saṅkarappāḍiyan figures in this record of the period of Rājarāja I from Mēlpāḍi, as a resident of Arumolidēva-pperumteru in Rājāśrayapuram (*Mēlpāḍi*). *Perunterus* usually were the quarters of traders. This Saṅkarappāḍiyan is stated to have individually taken charge of land endowed to the temple after purchase from the *sabhā* of Tiruvallam. It is not knwon if there was a group of *sankarappāḍiyar* in Mēlpāḍi also and if this body had been allotted a bloc of land as evidenced in the Māmallapuram inscription. Also cf. *Ibid.*, 65. This record of Rājakēsari Rājēndra (Kulōttuṅga I), (year 2= 1072) from Tiruvālaṅgāḍu

says that the king settled 25 kuḍis) of saṅkarappāḍi in a locality named after the king as Rājēndra sōḷappāḍi and asked them to contribute ghee for 15 perpetual lamps in the temple. It is not known if the Sivapuram where from the king's order was issued was the same as the *dēvadāna* village of the God at Tirukkoyilūr which was under the control of *nagarattār* Also *AREp*. 1964-65, B. 298, 300.

43. *SII.*, III, 15, 16.

44. *Ibid*. 15.

44a. *Ibid.*, 16.

45. The inscription of Nandivarman II from Māmallapuram and the Inscription of Rājarāja I from Mēlpādi refer to *peruvaḷi* or highway among the boundaries of the land involved in the transactions. This feature itself indicated their importance.

46. *Ibid.*, 19. This record refers to the street Arumoḷidēva-pperunderu in the village. It was evidently named after Rājarāja I. This and the fact that the king had set up the temple as a memorial to his grandfather and the name of the other God of the place indicate that this village might have been brought into the limelight by Rājarāja I.

47. Mem. ASI., 26, p. 10-11.

48. *EI*, III, p. 277-280.

49. *SII.*, V, 464. The same alternate name and *nagarattār* are associated with the village in the inscriptions of Rājādhirāja I and Rājēndra II from the same place (*Ibid.*, 465, 466 respectively), An inscription of the year 21 (1011) of Kulōttuṅga I (*Ibid.*, 473) records the delimitation of the village herein referred to as *dēvadāna-brahmadēya* but makes no mention of the alternate name nor to *nagarattār* which do not also find mention in any of the later inscriptioms.

50. *SII.*, III, 190; *Ibid.*, V, 1366, 1371, 1375; *AREp.*, 1921, 252, 255, 257

51. *AREp*. 1921, 259.

52. *SII.*, V, 1378

53. *AREp.*, 1921, 256.

54. An inscription dated year 3 of Pārthivēndravarman from the same place (*SII.*, III, 166), refers to an endowment of gold by a *nagarattār* without mentioning its location and another of Parakesariverman, dated in his year 5 (*Ibid.*, V, 1369) records an undertaking given by the *nagarattār* in Takkōlam in

association with the priests *(padi-pāda-mūlattār)* for contributing ghee against an endowment of sheep. But in these cases there is no reflection that the *nagarattār* controlled the village.

55. Though favoured by the king it is doubtful if the traders received all the rights and privileges that a group of brahmins has been seen to have been entitled to. cf. Sharma, R.S., *Ind. Feud.*, pp. 70-73; Maity, S.K., *op. cit.*, p. 158

56. cf. Maity, S.K., *op. cit.*, pp. 159-60 while it is quite possible that the traders got control of the centres of *dēvadāna* complexes through lapses of mortgages of land to them or through direct purchases of land, it has also to be noted that such control of these centres by the *nagarattār* seems to have been only temporary as evidenced in the Tirukkalu-kkuṇṛam inscriptions cited above. However the Paiyanūr inscriptions cited above indicate that the merchants had got possession of paddy. The other inscriptions which tell about the benefactions of merchants for the maintenance of irrigation works suggest that the merchants had an interest in the well-being of agriculture in the different villages. This might have been due to the agricultural products having been their main item of trade. As such their trading interests might have led the merchants to purchase and possess land instead of merely the prestige associated with the possession of land. The *Chiramēḷi guilds* of the 12-13 century might not have been guilds of agriculturists but of traders in grain who had got control of the source of their trade (cf. Mahalingam, T.V., *Readings in South Indian History,* p. 105-109.

57. *SII.*, VIII, 331. It is not certain if the king mentioned in the record was the first or second Pallava ruler of that name. However the possibility is that he was the second Paramēsvaravarman.

58. *EI,* XVII, p. 291 f.

59. *SII.*, VI, 365.

60. This appellation describes the character of the whole village. As brought out below, it does not seem proper to describe this village as of brahmin landholders.

61. Cf., Das, Dr., Economic History of the Deccan , p. 32-33; also Sharma, R.S., *Light on Early Indian Society and Economy*, p. 79.

62. *EI,* IV, p. 177-78.

63. *SII.*, XII, 102.

64. *SII.*, III, 43.

65. cf. Velvikkuḍi grant of Neduñjaḍaiyan, (c. 769-70) (*EI.*, XVII, p. 291 f.). The single brahmin granted the village, apportioned it among his relatives and others, in this context a *sabhā* is mentioned but its identity and role are unknown.
66. *SII.*, VII, 40.
67. *SII.*, VII, 32. Also *Ibid.*, 34.
68. It is likely that though the new *brahmadēyam* was named after the king as per the Kūram grant, the personality of the subordinate was more prominent in the minds of the people and in course of time he came to be honoured by the attachment of his name to the main village.
69. Such attachment of villages as *brahmadēyam* to already existing *brahmadēyams* is witnessed in the Bāhūr plates of Nṛipatuṅga, Udayēndram plates of Parāntaka I, and Tirumālpuram inscription of the time of Uttamachōḷa (*SII.*, III, 142). The Tiruvālaṅgāḍu plates of Rājēndra I also refers to such an attachment.
70. The Udayēndram plates of Nandivarman I refers to the grant of virgin land in Kañchivāyil to a brahmin who was resident there. If this village had already been granted to brahmins as *brahmadēyam* it is not understandable as to why this virgin land had not been included in the *brahmadēyam* and when the *sabhā* of the village emerged.
71. Aimbūṇi is referred to as Viḍēlviḍugu Vikramāditya-chaturvēdimaṅgalam in a record dated year 6 (1080) of Rājendrachola I from Tiruvallam (*AREp*; 1921, 220). This may indicate that Aimbūṇi was the centre and was the original *brahmadēyam*. Cf. the case of Kūram being characterised as Vidyāvinīta-pallavamaṅgalam as referred to above.
72. Cf. Mahalingam, T.V., Village Communities in South India, Tr. *Arch. Society* of _*SI.*, 1955, p. 34. He points out that in England also such a stage of common proprietorship of land in the villages had been there.
73. It is however seen that out of the three *brahmadēyams* constituted with a group of brahmins in Chōḷa-nāḍu during this period (Taṇḍantōṭṭam, Paṭṭattāḷ-maṅgalam and Kumaraḍimaṅgalam) none have produced records to confirm if *sabhā* were formed in those vilages.
74. The *parihāraṣ* or exemptions granted by the king to the *brahmadēya* donees only meant that the king would not expect the items of levies listed to be paid to him by the village. The

donees were, however, free to collect the same and enjoy the yield in proportion to the share as clearly indicated in the Kūram grant.

75. The facts that the individual brahmins in a *brahmadēya* village held land and that such holding was an essential qualification for taking part in the Committees of the *sabhā* are well brought out in the two Uttaramallūr records *(AREp.* 1898, pp. 1-2). An inscription of the year 21 (817) Dantivarman from Uttaramallūr (*SII.*, VI, 344) refers to the kuḍimakkaḷ, who had the land of the *ūr* and the help rendered by the *sabhā* of the place to them for reclaiming land. That this *kuḍimakkaḷ* were the brahmin holders of the land rather than tenants is indicated by other records (*SII.*, XII, 95; *Ibid.*, VII, 32, etc.). Inscriptions of Nandivarman III (846-869) *(SII.*, VI, 356), and Kampavarman (*Ibid.*, 285, 287, 294, 347) from the same place also refer to the land held as per share by the brahmins in that *sabhā* village. Other Uttaramallūr inscriptions of the later half of 9th century (*Ibid.*, 285, 293 etc.) also refer to sales of land by the brahmins of the place with the share rights.

76. That such reallocation of land was done periodically in *sabhā* villages seems to be indicated in two inscriptions of the 11th century from Maṇimaṅgalam (Chingleput District) (*SII.*, III 30-31). These refer to the order of the *ṣabhā* regarding land allotted to the temple at the time of *kaṛai* (*karai-iṭṭa-kkarai-ppōndu*). *Karai-Iḍu* referred to such a system of periodical redistribution (IA, III, p. 65 f.). Probably the Pullūr grant itself referred to the rotation of land with a periodicity of 12 years, when it refered to *pannīr-āṭṭai-kkarai* among the exemptions (here *karai* may be a mistake for *kaṛai*—cf. Mahalingam, T.V., The Pullur Plates etc; XXXVI, p. 148*)*, However it cannot be explained why a periodical rotation which was a necessity in these villages was exempted in respect of this *brahmadēyam*.

77. An inscription of Dantivarman dated year 7 (803) from Uttaramallūr (*SII.*, VI, 359) indicates that even at that early period, the practice of distribution of the land to the share-holding brahmins of the *sabhā* and the leaving of some land with as common land, in the *brahmadēya* villages had started. This record says that the *sabhā* of Uttaramēru-chaturvēdi-maṅgalam sold to one Chaturvēdi-Sōmayāji the land reserved for the reservoir for dredging and strengthening the embank-ment. Referring to the land sold, the record says that it was not

common land. This indicates that the *sabhā* was vested not only with common land but also with such land which had been earmarked for specific purposes. The control of the *sabhā* over the non-allotted common land is indicated among others in an inscription from Ukkal dated year 16 (955) in the reign of Krīshna III (*SII.*, III, 7). The *sabhā* of the place expressed their readiness to sell the land which is referred to as common or middling land (*madhyamamāy-kkiḍanda*) in their village to any *kuḍi* who would undertake to reclaim the same and pay *iṛai*. Another inscription from Mēlpāḍi (Chittoor district) dated year 14 (999) of Rājarāja I (*SII.*, III, 19) records the sale of *1000 kuḷi* of land in their *mañjikkam* by the *sabhā* of Tiruvallam for endowment. The land was entrusted to a member of the *saṅkarappāḍi* of Rājāsrayapuram.

78. Cf. *SII.*, VIII, 5. This inscription dated year 16 (1028) in the reign of Rājēndrachōḷa I from Vēppaṅguḷam, Kāñchīpuram Taluk, Chingleput District, lists the *sabhās* of four villages which took the deposits of gold from the temple for contributing the interest in the temple of Tirukkāraikkāḍu-uḍaiyar in Kāñchīpuram. Of these, only one, the village Siṛukachchippēḍu, in Eyil-nāḍu in Eyil-kōṭṭam is referred to as *brahmadēyam* whereas the three others, two described as chaturvēdimaṅgalam and the other only as maṅgalam are not described as *brahmadēyam*. May be, the differentiation between the first and other villages was deliberately stressed indicating that all *sabhā* villages or villages where brahmins were then predominant landholders need not have been *brahmadēyams*. Or this differentiation had no significance and the appellation *brahmadēyam* was optionally attached to the name of the villages even though in actual fact the village might have been a *brahmadēyam*. It is possible that the appellation *brahmadēyam* was attached to Siṛukachchippēḍu just because it did not have the distinguishing epithat *chaturvēdimaṅgalam* as the others. cf. The Tiruvālaṅgāḍu plates of Rājēndra I as discussed above.

79. However the two *paṭṭis* or blocs of land, Vichchādira-ppaṭṭi and dēvar-paṭṭi excluded from the purview of the grant probably formed the developed part of the village.

80. The Bāhūr plates of Nṛipatuṅga witnesses that sometimes such attachments were made to a *brahmadēyam* for it to manage and maintain an institution like a *Vidyāsthāna* and not to make any contribution to anyone.

81. *Ūr* and *ūr-irukkai* in this context seem to have referred to the residential quarter and attached garden-land of the inhabitants other than *brahmadēyam* donees in a village. This has been discussed above.

82. *Manai* and *manai-ppaḍappu* seem to have similarly referred to the residential sites and kitchen garden land of brahmins.

83. There were probably the same as the section of the village that came to be known as *ūr-nattam* in eleventh century and later inscriptions. An inscription of the year 18 (1030) of Rājēndra I from Tiruvaṇṇāmalai (*SII.*, VIII, 67) refers to the extension of the privilege of residing in the *ūr-nattam* to the cultivators of the land sold to the God of Tiruvaṇṇāmalai by the *ūr* of Āḍaiyūr. The Tañjāvūr inscriptions of the time of Rājarāja I (*SII.*, II, 4-5) say that the *paṛai-chchēri, Iḷachcheri. kammāṇa-chchēri* apart from *ur-nattam* or *ūr -irukkai* as types of land that were *iṛai-ili* in villages. Also *cf.* Gopalan, R. History of the Pallavas of Kāñchi, pp. 28-29 On the basis of the account in the Sangam work *Perumbāṇaṟṟuppaḍai* of Rudraṅgaṇṇanār he says that the quarters of the brahmins were separated from the *paḷḷis* of the *iḍaiyaṇs* and the *paṛai-chcheri*s of the *Eyinars*, which were at the extremity of the village, ie. the city of Kāñchīpuram. Also see Madras Museum plates of Uttamachōḷa (*SII.*, III, No. 128) which refers to various *chēri*s in Kāñchīpuram. But *chēri* was sometimes used to describe brahmin quarters also (cf. Udayendram plates of Parāntaka I which refer to the *brahmadēyam* as Vīranārāyaṇachchēri). Another locality in many villages called śaṅkarappāḍi was probably the quarter of tradesmen who did not form part of the *nagarattār*. It is possible that Sañkara meant the intermingled caste.

83. That *maṇṟu* was the forum of the village used as a judicial institution also, is indicated by the word *manrupāḍu* meaning a fine (cf. Tiruvadandai-Chingleput district—inscription of the year 6 of a Parakēsarivarman—*SII.*, III, 125). *Maṇṟupāḍu* was what was levied as the *maṇṟu*. The word *maṇṟu* itself has been used in a verbal form to refer to the process of fining as in the phrase, *maṇṟa-pperuvadāgavum*. (another record from Tiruvaḍandai dated year 8 (966)—of *Vira-pāṇḍiyanai-talai-koṇḍa* Rājakēsarivarman—*Ibid*, 186) or *maṇṟa-oṭṭi-kkuḍuttōm* (pāḍi-Tiruvalidāya Chingleput district—inscription of the reign of Pārthivēndravarman—*Ibid*, 181). The function of the *maṇṟu*

though often was related to such judicial acts, it was not probably meant to be confined to that. The Mānūr (Tirunelveli district) inscription of the time of Māṟanjaḍaiyan (10 century?) (*Ibid.*, XIV, 37). employs the term *manral-āduvadaṟku* in the sense of taking part in the deliberations at the forum.

84. *Koṭṭagaram, (Kōshṭagara)* and *kiḍangu*, both mean a godown. But as both are mentioned here one might have referred to the store house for the sheeś of corn and *kidaṅgu* to the warehouse for storing grains. The Bāhūr plates also included *kidaṅgu* and *kōttagaram* among the types of land According to Appadorai, A (*op. cit.*,75) *kīḍaṅgu* meant ditches and *kōttagaṅ* a vast expanse

85. As *kaḷaṟ* follows kāḍu (forest) it might have meant shrubs, cf. Appadorai, A., *Economic Conditions in South India*. 1000-1500 AD, p. 87. He draws attention to the *kalam* mentioned as one of the types of land in the village Anbanur, whose tax payments were diverted to the tmple at Tanjavīr, which were left of account *irai-ili* land, as per the Tanjavur inscription of the reign of Rājarāja I (985-1014) (*SII.*, II, 5) and relates it to *khala* in Sanskrit which means threshing floor. But kaḷam might have also meant the field or location as in *pōr-kkalam* meaning battle-field. *Aḷin-jiṟ-kaḻam* mentioned in an inscription of the time of Nandivarman II (*SII.*, III, 42) referred to a field. An inscription of the year 20 (866) of Nandivarman III from Pillaippākkam (Chingleput district) (*SII.*, XII, 72) refers to *kalam* as a particular site in the village reserved for doing something with paddy *(neṭṭattuvār)* in that village.

86. *SII.*, VII, 802.

87. *Ibid.*, 805, 809, 811.

88. *SII.*, III, 142.

89. Mem *ASI.*, 17, p. 19-21; *AREp.*, 1909, p. 72.

90. *Avi-ppuṟam* or land for supplying the *havis* or food offerings (*SII.*, VI, 356) *Ibid.*, XIV, 118); *maḍappuṟam* or land for the expenses in the temple -kitchen (*Ibid.*, 200, 259; *Ibid.*, XVII, 625, 628, 730, 759); *tiruviḷakkuppuṟam* or provision for maintaining lamp in the temple (*Ibid.*, XIV, 239; *Ibid.*, XVII, 448, 537, 555 604); *tiruviḷāppuṟam* or land to meet the expenses of conducting festivals. (*Ibid.*, VII, 32).

91. *AREp.*, 1912, 131; *SII.*, V, 1381.

92. *SII.*, XII, 70 (Nripatunga); 90 (Aparājita); 99, 105 (Kampa-varman).

93. *Ibid.*, 87, 88, 91 (Aparājita).
94. *Ibid.*, III, 190 (Pārthivendravarman).
95. *AREp.*, 1921, 255 (Rājakēsarivarman).
96. *SII.*, V, 1371 (Parāntaka I).
97. *AREp.*, 1921, 252 (Parāntaka I).
98. *Ibid.*, 1915, 217 (Parāntaka I), 189 (Pārthivēndravarman), 192 (Rājarāja I), 237 (Rājakēsarivarman), 219.
99. *Ibid.*, 226 (Parāntaka I), 195, 208 (Pārthivēndravarman).
100. *SII.*, III, 50; *AREp.*, 1921, 219.
100a. cf. *SII.*, XIII, 292. This inscription dated year 20 (891 ?) of Rājakēsarivarman (Āditya I) tells about the endowment of land out of his holding for feeding a brahmin in the temple daily by a member of the governing body *(āḷuṅgaṇattār)* of Rājamalla-chaturvēdimaṅgalam.
101. *SII.*, XII, 105. Dated in the year 19 (889) of Kampavarman, this record from Tiruvorriyūr witnesses the sale of land by the *sabhā* of Maṇali in Tiruvoṟṟiyūrppuṟam. Apparently it was the common land held by the *sabhā*.
101a. *AREp.*, 1921, 219. This record actually seems to record an upward assessment of the dues from that village.
102. *AREp.*, 1912, 131; *Ibid.*, 1913, pt. II, p. 104. This records clubs together Manali alias Simhavishṇu- chaturvēdimaṅgalam, Ambilavāyil, Igaṇaiyūr, Veḷśāṟu and Piṟaippākkam as the *dēvadāna* villages of the God of Tiruvoṟṟiyūr and reflects that each of them had to pay to the temple besides *pañchavāram, pu-ppon; vēlikkāśu, ūr-vilai, veṭṭi muṭṭai-āḷ, echchōṟu* and *kūṟṟu-nel*. It is observable that Maṇali of these villages was under a *sabhā* and Igaṇaiyūr under *ūr.*
103. *SII.*, III, 190.
104. *Ibid.*, XIII, 292; *AREp.*, 1915, 219.
105. *Ibid.*, 204; also 207, 208 etc. However, the temple of Tiruvēkamba of which these villages were *puṟam* was probably the Ēkāmranātha temple at Kāñchīpuram. An inscription of the year 21 (1006) of Rajaraja I from Tiruvottūr (Cheyyar taluk, North Arcot district) (*SII.*, VII, 110) seems to describe Tiruvottūr which is said to have had a *sabhā* and *āluṅgaṇattār* as a *tankūrru dēvadāna*.
106. *SII.*, XII, 87, 88, 91.
107. The inscription from Tiruvaḍandai dated in the reign of Pārthivēndravarman (*Ibid.*, III, 186) refers to the *sabhā* and *ūr*

acting jointly in that *dēvadāna* village, Tiruvidavand. It is likely that the village was the dēvadāna of the temple of śrī-Varāhadēvar in that village which the *sabhā* and *ūr* were controlling. An inscription of a Parakēsarivarman from that same village *(Ibid.*, 125) mentions only *ūr*. Similarly in Tiruvāmāttur in South Arcot district it is stated to have been a *dēvadāna* of the Perumānaḍigal of that village and to have had a sabhā, and *dēvakanmigal* all of whom acted in concert to assure protection to an endowment of gold for a perpetual lamp in the year 3 of a Parakēsarivarman (*Ibid.*, 95).

108. *SII.*, III, 7. It is referred to as a *tani-ūr* in an inscription of the year 29 (1014) of Rājarāja I (*Ibid.*, 4). The earliest inscription from the place is dated year 15 (885) of Kampavarman (*Ibid.*, 5).

109. The earliest inscriptions from Uttaramallūr belong to the period of Dantivarman (year 7—*SII.*, VI, 365; year 9—*Ibid.*, 359; year 21—*Ibid.*, 344). But the earliest reference to the village as *tan-kūrṟu* is found only in an inscription of Kampavarman, year 8 (878) (*Ibid.*, 285).

110. The records from Uttaramallūr specifically state that the following six were its hamlets (*piḍāgai)*.
   1. Aḍumā (southern hamlet) (*SII.*, VI, 323).
   2. Perūṅgāttēri-kkiḷ-Aiḍalam-pūṇḍi (Southern hamlet) (*Ibid.*, 368).
   3. Puliyūr (southern hamlet) (*Ibid.*, 285).
   4. Tiruvuḷḷiyūr (southern hamlet) (ur?) (*Ibid.*, 324). Tiruvullaur (*Ibid.*, III, 186). (s. a. ?) Tiruvunniyūr (*Ibid.*, 158).
   5. Tiṭṭattūr (southern hamlet) (ūr) (*Ibid.*, 286). (s. a. ?) Tittātil (do) (do) *(Ibid.*, 318).
   6. Puṅgōdaippūṇḍi (western hamlet) (*Ibid.*, 297). Apart from this, in the case of the following which were either distinct localities within Uttaramēru-chaturvēdimaṅgalam or hamlets, it is merely stated that they were of the *ūr*.
      1. Tiruppulivalam (*SII.*, VI, 346).
      2. Vāmana-chchēri (*Ibid.*, 287; *AREp.*, 1923, 163).
      3. Malliyan-kārāṇai (*SII.*, VI, 288).
      4. Kuman-pāḍi (*Ibid.*, III, 168, 169).

It is observable that Tiru-vuḷḷa-ūr which is probably the same as Tiruvuḷḷiyūr, stated to have been the southern hamlet, is also referred to as of the *ūr*. The following which were either localities or hamlets with distinct identities also find mention in the records.

1. Madisūdana-chchēri (*Ibid.*, VI, 287.
2. Tirunāraṇa-chchēri (*Ibid.*) (s. a. ?) Nārāyaṇa-chchēri (*AREp.* 1923, 167).
3. Vīshṇu-chcheri (*SII.*, VI, 347).
4. Kēśava-chchēri (*Ibid*).
5. Mādhava-chchēri (*sabhā*) (*Ibid.*, 292).
6. Dāmōdara-chchēri (*sabhā*) (*Ibid.* III, 159).
7. Panmai-chchēri (*Ibid.*, 195 ; *AREp.*, 1923, 186).
8. Gōvinda-chchēri (*AREp.* 1923, 166, 187, 190).
9. Hrishī-kēśava-chchēri (*Ibid.*, 164).

The records also mention the following merchant localities.

1. Terkil-aṅgāḍi (*SII.*, III, 172; *AREp.*, 1923, 189).
2. Naduvil-aṅgāḍī (*SII.*, III, 195 ; *AREp.*, 1923, 187).

The several other geographical features with names ending with *vati* mentioned in the records were apparently channels.

111. *SII.*, III, 116.
112. *Ibid.*, 191.
113. *Ibid.*, 114.
114. *Ibid.*, 116.
115. The case of Paḷaiyanūr with an *ūr* attached as *brahmadēyam* to Siṅgalāntaka-chaturvēdimaṅgalam has been dealt with above.
116. *SII.*, VII, 411, 412, 414.
117. *SII.*, III, 185,186.
118. *SII.*, XII, 82 (Nṛipatuṅga). An inscription from this place dated in the reign of a Parakēsarivarman (*Ibid.*, XIX, 177) refers to the *gaṇapperumakkaḷ* of Iḷamaṇḍagam. It is not known if the village Illamaṇḍagam was a hamlet or if it was another name of Kāvērippākkam.
119. *Ibid.*, III, 156.
120. *EI,* XI, p. 225 (Dantivarman); p. 224 (Nandivarman III); *Ibid.*, VII, p. 1 f. (Bāṇavikramāditya).
121. *AREp.*, 1929-30, 176; Pt. II, p. 78,
122. An inscription dated year 3 (1073?) of RājakēsariRajēndra (*SII.*, VII, 392) says that Śomaṅgalam (at present in Kāñchīpuram taluk of Chingleput district) had a *mahāsabhā*.
123. Probably *Mañjikkam* referred to land at the outskirts of the village, the extent of the area under the control of the *sabhā*.

123a. *SII.*, XII, 95 (inscription of the time of Aparājita from Tiruttaṇi);

Ibid., 105 (inscription of the time of Kampavarman from Tiruvoṟṟiyūr); *Ibid.*, VII, 420 (inscription of time of Kampavarman from Kāvantaṇḍalam.

124. *Ibid.*, 105; *Ibid.*, VIII, 9 (inscription of the time of Parāntaka I? from Śōḷapuram) *Ibid.*, III, 181 (inscription of the time of Pārthivēndravarman from Pāḍi-Tiruvalidāyam). The record refers to such land as *mañjikkam* of the *sabhā*. This *mañjikkam* might have indicated land at the outskirts of the village the extent of which might have been vague and adjustable at the discretion of the *sabhā*.
125. *SII.*, XII, 34 (inscription of the time of Nandivarman II from Payinūr).
126. An inscription probably dated in the reign of Parāntaka I from Śōlapuram says that the two *sabhās* of Kāñchivāyil and Niḍūr jointly authorised the taking of channels from the reservoir of their *ūr* for irrigating temple lands (*Ibid*,., VIII, 9).
127. *SII.*, III, 7 (inscription of the time of Krishṇa III from Ukkal).
128. *Ibid.*, 162 (inscription of the time of Parthivēndra-varman).
129. *Ibid.*, 182 (DO) *Viḷuli* might have had so special significance. It might not have meant waste land as the land is found graded.
130. *Ibid.*, VI, 368 (inscription of the time of Nṛipattuṅga) cf. *Ibid.*, III, 16.
131. Whereas several inscriptions refer to the role of the time of Pārthivēndravarman (*Ibid.*, 161) says that 15 *kūḷi* for the channel was added to a plot set apart by the *sabhā* as *Vyākhyā-vṛitti*.
132. *Ibid.*, VI, 336. A fragmentary inscription from the same place also evidences the same control of the *sabhā* of the place.
133. *Ibid.*, VII, 40 Also cf. *AREp;* ending 31 March 1923, p. 104., para 30.
134. *Ibid.*, 32. The term *uṇaṇgarpiḍi* has not been interpreted.

134a. *SII.*, III, 12.

135. cf. Prithivimāṇikkam, queen of Nripatuṇga (*SII.*, XII, 66). However the name of the temple Bhuvanimāṇikka vishṇu-gṛiham suggests that it had been constructed by the king, Hence he might have directed the making over of the hamlet to the temple by the *sabhā* and the tax-free status accorded to the village was an effect of his order in the matter.
136. *Ibid.*, 11.
137. *SII.*, III, 7.
138. *SII.*, III, 116.

139. A Chōḷapuram (North Arcot district) inscription of probably the time of Parāntaka I (*SII.,* VIII, 9) records the grant of channels to draw water from the reservoirs of their villages to irrigate land in the third village also under *sabhā* which had been purchased and endowed to a temple by the *sabhās* of Kāñchīvāyil and Niḍūr.

140. *Ibid.*, VI, 288. Also *Ibid.*, 339, 342.

141. *Ibid.*, III, 116. (142) *Ibid.*, VI, 324.

142. The *gaṇattār* mentioned as the body which received a deposit of paddy from a *vāṇigan* or merchant and gave an undertaking regarding the dredging of the big reservoir at payinūr (Chingleput District) as per an inscription dated year 37 (768) in the reign of Nandivarman II from that place (*SII.,* XII, 34) and the *Perumakkal* who gave a similar undertaking as per an inscription from Kaḷattūr (Chingleput District) 14 (860) in the reign of Nandivarman III (*Ibid.*, 51) were apparently the same as the *sabhā*. (contra. Mahalingam, TV., Village *communities in South India*, R*eadings in South Indian History* (ed. Ramachandran, K.S.), p. 101. The committees never took deposits or gave undertakings by themselves. In the same way the *gaṇapperumakkaḷ* of Śaileśvaram temple who took over a deposit of gold made by an individual to the temple and undertook to contribute interest for the food-offerings during mid-day services according to an inscription of year 16(875) of Nṛipatuṅga from Paramēśvaramaṅgalam (*Ibid.*, 69), might have been a similar body controlling the temple. The *vāriyarpperu makkal,* whose protection was invoked to an endowment of gold for a perpetual lamp in another record of the same year from Uttaramallūr (*Ibid.*, VI, 346) must have been different from the other committees of the *sabhā*.

143. *SII.,* VI, 359.

144. *Vāriyam* may be connected with *varyaḥ* Sanskrit which means "those that were to be selected." *Perumakkaḷ* meaning 'great men' was just a honorific. It is stated that the members of the executive committee of the towns in Rajputana during the coeval period were called *vārikas* (Udgaonkar, Padma, B. ; *The Political Institutions and Administration of Northern India during Medieval Times* (from 750-1200 A.D.), p. 158). The elders among merchants in Western India were called *vārika* in a record of A.D. 592 (*EI,* XXX, 30; Thakur, Vijaykumar, 'Forced labour in

Gupta Period' *Proc. IHC,* 38 session, Bhubanesvar, 1977, p. 148). Also Mahalingam, T.V., 'Village Communities in South India', '*Readings in South Indian History*' (ed. Ramachandran, K. S.), p. 98-99.

145. *SII.*, III, 12.

146. cf. *SII.*, III, 156. This inscription from Tiruppārkadal (North Arcot District) dated in the reign of Pārthivēndravarman (late 10th century) records an order of the Mahāsabhā of Kāviripākkam to the *kaḷanivāriya-pperumakkaḷ* to allot 1400 *kuḻi* from the *mañjikkam* land of the *ūr* to the temple in Tirukkarapuram in lieu of the temple-land sandlogged. This indicates that the said committee was in charge of cultivable waste also but it is not clear if this charge of the committee wa restricted to the attached villages one of which Tirukkarapuram must have been.

147. cf. *SII.*, VI, 291; *AREp.*, 1923, 105.

148. *SII.*, III, 6. An inscription of Rājarāja I, year 16 (1001) from Śiruvākkam (Chingleput District) (*AREp.* 1923, 66, Pt. II, p. 104) says that one *manrāḍi-vāriyam* had been constituted to supervise the correct receipt of the contributions from temple lands. It appears that the *amṛita-gaṇaṭṭār* mentioned along with the *sabhā* of Ādambakkam in the Tiruvoṟṟiyūr complex in the inscriptions of Aparājita only (*SII.*, XII, 87, 88, 89) were independent of the *sabhā*.

149. The *gaṇapperumakkaḷ* (*SII.*, XII, 69; *AREp.*, 1915, 204, etc.) or *gaṇa-vāriyappermakkaḷ* (*SII.*, XIII, 274, 322; *AREp.* 1915, 194, 198, 206, 207, 222) or *kōvil-variya-pperumakkaḷ (AREp.* 1915, 241) or *kovil-ārāyyōm*) (*SII.*, V, 1369) or the *puṇya-gaṇatta-pperumakaḷ* of the sri-mulasthānam (*SII.*, VII, 810) or *dhanma-vāriya-pperumakkaḷ* (*SII.*, III, 6) mentioned as bodies acting on behalf of the temple in the records probably were also committees of the *sabhā* as their names indicate or they might have been bodies formed of nominated numbers from the *sabhā* without any subordination to the same. (cf. Sastri, K.A.N., The *colas*, p. 511). These bodies can be compared with the *mūla-parishad*, a body of brahmins figuring in the records of the villages Tirukkuḍamukkil (Kumbhakōṇam) (*SII.*, III, 200, 204) and Tiruvallaṛai (Tiruchirappalli District) (*SII.*, XII, 12) both of which are said to have been *dēvadāna*. This body might have been the equivalent of the *sabhā* of a *dēvadāna* village in Toṇḍaimaṇḍalam instead of being a committee. Their role in the management of

the temple and its lands is not definitely indicated in the sources, (cf. Sastri, K.A.N., *The Chōḷas,* p. 513).

149a. *SII.*, VI, 295—*Uttaramallūr* inscription of Parāṇtaka I year 15 (922).

150. Eg. Ukkal inscriptions of Kampavarman of year 15 (885) *(SII.*, III, 5) which states that the *sabhā* of Uṭkar received a deposit of 1000 *kāḍi* of paddy for the maintenance of the local reservoir, and against this deposit the *sabhā* arranged for the *samvatsara-vāriya-pperumakkaḷ* to have the maintenance done. Obviously the capital of paddy must have been passed on to the committee to enable them to defray the expenses of the maintenance or even if the *sabhā* might have utilised the deposit for their own purposes they must have equipped the committee to fulfil their role. Also *SII.*, XIX, 297—Tiruppāṟkaḍal (North Arcot district) inscription of a Parakēsarivarman, year 12 which says that the gold received by the *sabhā* for providing a perpetual lamp and food offerings to the temple was handed over to the reservoir committee; Also *Ibid.*, 180; *Ibid.*, VI, 348.

151. cf. Mahalingam, T.V., village communities in South India, Readings in South Indian History, (ed. Ramachandran, K.S.), p. 101.

152. cf. *SII.*, XII, 107 (Inscriptions of Kampavarman, year 20- 890- from Brahmadēśam); SII, VI, 341, 372 (Inscriptions of the period of Parāntaka I from Uttaramallūr).

153. According to an inscription of the year 23 (873) of Nandivarman III from Guḍimallam (Kālahasti Taluk, Chittoor district) (*EI,* XI, p. 224 one Muḷḷir Kiḻār of the *āluṅgaṇattār* of Tiruvippirambēḍu purchased some land in an auction *(vilai-śrāvaṇai*) and endowed the same for a lamp in the temple. The land was handed over to the charge of the *sabhā* of the place. Another *kiḻār* of the same body of the same place endowed some land for the maintenance of the reservoir Veḷḷēri as *ērichcheṟuvu* according to an inscription of the year 45 (845) of Dantivikramavarman (*Ibid.*, p. 225). In some cases the *kiḻār* seems to have been the chief person or headman of the *sabhā* village, (cf. inscriptions of the period of Rājarāja III, year 8-1224—from Maṇimaṅgalam, Chingleput District—*SII.*, III, 35. This record refers to the *kiḻān* of this maṅgalam, i.e. Alagiyaśoḷanallūr-maṅgalam). Probably *kiḻavan* was a synonymn for kiḻār (*Tirukkuṟaḷ*. ch. 104, verse 9 refers to *kiḻavan* and the commentator Parimelagagar translated

it as 'one who had the right to the land indicated. ') A *kiḷavan* of Taṭṭūr is stated to have had the *kiḷamai* (eldership) in the *tankūrṛu sabhā* village Ukkal and he could also make some collections in the village according to an inscription of the year 17 (1002) of Rājarāja I from Ukkal (*SII.*, III, 6) (cf. Yadva BNS, 'Secular land grants of the post-Gupta period and some Aspects of the Growth of Feudal Complex in northern India', *Land System and Feudalism in Ancient India,* p. 32. He says that "in some regions the village headmen also became like petty chiefs.") The title *tiruvaḍi* also probably indicated the same as kiḷāṇ (cf. Bāhūr-ttiruvaḍi). While these references indicate that *kiḷan* or *kiḷavan* was an important person in a village, an inscription of the year 6 of Pārthivēndravarman from Pāḍi-Tiruvaliḍāyam (Chingleput District) (*SII.*, III, 181) refers to a bhaṭṭa styled as the *peruṅgiḷavan* of the place as taking down the order of the *sabhā* as village accountants usually did. A Paramāra inscription of A.D. 1067 is stated to refer to the grama-*mahattara* (i.e.) elder of the village (Udgaonkar, Padma B., *The Political Institutions and Admnistration of Northern India During Medieval Times*, (from 750 to 1200 A.D.), p. 155 and n 4.) In Bengal the *grāmapati* is known to have been the administrator of the village and such an administrator was also known as *Paṭṭakila* according to some *Paramāra* inscriptions (*Ibid.*, p. 159).

154. Allotment of shares to *madhyastha*s or arbitrators is mentioned but they were obviously subordinate to the brahmin donees cf. *AREp.*, 1929-30, 176.
155. *SII.*, VI, 292,
156. AREp. 1929, 30, 176.
157. *AREp.* 1898, 2.
158. *Ibid.*, 1.
159. *Ibid.*, 1929-30, 176, *Ibid.*, pt. II, p. 78.
160. *Ibid.*, 1922, 240; 241; *Ibid.*, pt. II, para 16.
161. Though this name indicates that the village was founded by Uttamachōḷa, it is not unlikely that an already existing *brahmadēyam* was renamed during the time of that king. cf. Ukkal inscriptions.
162. *SII.*, XII, 37 This inscription from Mānūr (Tirunelveli district—Pāṇḍya country) dated in the reign of a Māṛañjaḍaiyan records some restrictive qualifications for taking part in the

deliberations of the *manṟu* or forum laid down by the *sabhā*. It is not known if the *manru* mentioned here was the judicial organ of the *sabhā* or the *sabhā* itself.

163. The later inscriptions *(AREp.*, 1898, 1) said that if a person possessed only 1/8 (*vēli*) of land but was adept in one full *vēda* and was capable of expounding at least one of the four commentaries *(bhāshyam)*, he too was eligible.

164. *EI,* VIII, p. 290 f.

165. The *kulaṁ-giḷār* are not again mentioned in the inscriptions of Toṇḍaimaṇḍalam. Several inscriptions from Tiruvakkarai in South Arcot district, beyond Toṇḍaimandalam refer to this body. An inscription of Rājakēsarivarman (Āditya I) dated year 26 (897) (*SII.*, XIII, 317) records that the *kulaṅ-giḷavargaḷ* of Tiruvakkarai took over the paddy endowed to the temple and undertook to maintain the service intended. It is noteworthy that just as in the Triplicane Inscription, the body is said to be of the village and not of the temple. Another inscription dated year 10 (980 ?) in the reign of a Parakēsarivarman Uttamachōḷa ?) (*Ibid.,* XIX 240) lists four persons, who might have been priests as forming the body *kulan-giḷavar,* who had the charge of the worship *(archchikka-uḍaiya)* in the temples of kaṟṟali-paramasvāmigaḷ, and Vishnu-bhaṭṭālakar at the place had the entitlement to four shares probably in the village Tribhuvana-mahādēvi -chaturvedimaṅgalam, of which the *peruñguri-sabhā* made some arrangement for the allotment. It is noteworthy that the record mentions a separate arrangement made for the expenses of the worship in the two temples. This can be again compared with an inscription of the year 10 (1080) of Kulōttuṅga (*Ibid.,* XVII, 199) which mentions a *kulaṇ-giḷān* and a *śivabrāhmaṇa* separately, as having undertaken together to burn a lamp with the ghee yielded by sheep endowed. Some more inscriptions of the time of Kulōttuṅga I (1070-1120) and Vikrama-chōḷa (1118-1135) refer to a single kulaṅgilān (*Ibid.*, 199) or *kulamgiḷavan* (*Ibid.,* 203, 206, 224, 225, 229) as one who was of the temple (*Ibid.*, 199, 224) or one who had the *kāṇi* of the temple (*Ibid.*, 203, 206, 225, 229) who took over either *kāśu* or sheep for maintaining lamps.

166. *SII.,* XII, 95

167. This might have been the temple constructed by Nambi Appi (*Ibid.*, 94).

168. The records of the period mention several other bodies whose names suggest that they might have been committees of the *sabhā*. But all these bodies are stated to have only taken over gold deposited with the temple for carrying out some specified services. The *gaṇapperumakkaḷ* of the temple of Śailēśvaram is mentioned in an inscription of the year 16 (875) of Nṛipatuṅga from Pararmēsvaramaṅgalam (Chingleput district) (*SII*, XII, 69). This body was of the *mahasabhā*. *Āmṛitagaṇattār* figure in equal partnership with the *sabhā* of Ādambākkam in the inscriptions of the time of Aparājita (885-903?) from Tiruvoṛṛiyūr (*Ibid.*, 87, 88, 91). *Dhanma-vāriya-pperumakkaḷ* and *śātta-ganattār* (the group in charge of the temple of *śāstā* are mentioned in the inscription of the year 17 (1002 of Rājarāja I from Ukkal (North Arcot district) (*Ibid.*, III, 6). These two bodies are seen to have been intimately connected with the *sabhā* and in a position to order the making of arrangements for carrying on the worship in a temple. But an inscription of the year 27 (966) of Kṛishṇa III from Bāhūr (Pondicherry) (*Ibid.*, VII, 810) refers to *puṇya-gaṇaṭṭār* whose role was different from that of the other *gaṇattār* mentioned. This body gave an undertaking to carry out alone an endowment with land to be purchased and reclaimed with the money deposited by a brahmin member of the governing body *(āḷum-perumakkaḷ)* of that *sabhā* village. *Karma-kkiḷavar-āvima-urom* (the *ūr* composed of the elders of the administration) of Tiruvoṛṛiyūr who also undertook to carry out an endowment against a gold deposit, as per an inscription of the year 8 (893?) of Aparājita from Tiruvoṛṛiyūr (*SII.*, XII, 92) might or might not have been such body deputed by one of the *sabhās* of the *dēvadāna* villages of that temple. One body known as *Tirunāmakkiḷavar* of the quarter Ulaichchēri of the village Ūṛṛukkāḍu, undertook to burn a perpetual lamp with the gold and to present food offerings to the God with the land, both endowed by a *puśāli* (non-brahmin priest of a village deity ?) in the year 25 (895?) of Kampavarman. Ūṛukkāḍu is not known to have been a *sabhā* village. As the name is coupled with *nama* it suggests, this body might have been a specially constituted of the temple.

169. Proc. *IHC*. 1979 (Waltair), p. 1075. While the date has been equated as above on the basis of KAN Sastri's SIH. KG Krishnan equates it to c. 877.

170. cf., Velūrpāḷaiyam plates; Udayēndram plates of Parāntaka I.
171. *SII.*, VI, 376
172. On the other hand the bodies *thānattār* which finds mention in records pertaining to the region south of Toṇḍaimaṇḍalam, as one in charge of temples is reflected to have been composed of priests in some records it is not known if the *dharmis* were connected with *dharmāsanam* mentioned as the place where fines imposed on defaulters were paid.
173. In later inscriptions pertaining to siva temples, it is usual to find a deity, Chaṇḍikēsvara, to be cited as the secretary or agent of the main deity of the temple. Transactions connected with the temple are represented as have been carried on by that deity. But in so far as Toṇḍiamaṇḍalam is concerned, the first reference to the installation of this deity is found only in the year 8 (1126) of Vikrama-chōḷa in an inscription from Guḍimallam (*SII.*, VIII, 512). It is to be noted that this temple at Guḍimallam seems to have been in existence even during the period of Dantivarman. Hence the introduction of this deity seems to have been a planned innovation introduced in late 11th or 12th century, in respect of Toṇḍaimaṇḍalam. The *dēvakanmis* might have been a group constituted to administer the temple in the name of that deity. In Chōḷanāḍu this deity is cited even in 10th century inscriptions (*Ibid.*, 570, 576).
174. *SII.*, III, 142.
175. *Ibid.*, V, 489.
176. *AREp.*, 1921, 217.
177. *SII.*, III, 49.
178. *AREp.*, 1921, 208.
179. *SII.*, III, 54.
180. *AREp.*, 1921, 227.
181. An inscription of the year 6 (1018) of Rājēndra I from Vēppaṇguḷam (Chingleput district) (*SII.*, VIII, 6) cites the *dēvakanmis* as the authority representing the temple, who were to receive the contribution of ghee from a *manṛāḍi* who had taken over sheep endowed for a lamp. The latter was to take a receipt from the *dēvakanmis*. The *dēvakanmis* are found in the region south of the Toṇḍaimaṇḍalam to have been in charge of the temples and in a position to oversee the exemption of their commitments by those holding temple lands even from about the 10th century. An inscription of the year 2 of Para-

kēsarivarman from Uḍaiyārguḍi, South Arcot district (*SII.*, XIX, 15) records an undertaking by the *dēvakanmis* who were doing the administration of the temple *(śrī-kāryam)* at that time *(anṛu)* and who were connected with the temple treasury. However at Tiruvaṇṇāmalai (though it is now in the North Arcot district, this taluk itself is south of and outside Toṇḍaimaṇḍalam) the *dēvakanmis* are differentiated from the single person doing the temple administration *(srīkāryam)*, the latter of whom was to receive a daily wage whereas the former is referred to as a body receiving the proceeds from the temple-lands and utilising the same for the services and as the body representing the temple, identified with the temple and addressed by the king regarding the administration of the temple in an inscription of the year 27 (1039) of Rājēndra I (*SII.*, VIII, 68). But there is a difference noticeable between the address of the king to the *sabhā* in respect of temple land (cf., *SII.*, VII, 40) and the case cited above. (also *Ibid.*, XVII, 243). Whereas in the former case the order is couched in polite language, in the latter the king's official is seen commanding the *dēvakanmis* to carry out the wishes of the king. The inscriptions of the period subsequent to the dawn of the 11th century from Chōḷamaṇḍalam and Pāṇḍi-maṇḍalam exhibit the prominence of the *dēvakanmis* with regard to the administration of the temple and its lands (*SII.*, VIII, 571, 683, 677, *Ibid.*, XIV , 191).

182. There was another examination of the temple affairs and apportionment of its income under royal auspices in the year 3 (1070) of Ādhirājēndra (*SII.*, III 57).

183. Two Uttaramallūr inscriptions, one dated in the reign of Kampavarman (year 8 (878) (*SII.*, VI, 288) and the other in the reign of Parakesari Rājendra. (*Ibid*,339) There are also some instances where the *sabhā* or other individuals including local chiefs granted land to a newly raised temple and entrusted the same to a single priestly brahmin or more than one priestly brahmin. The records say that the priest or priests would enjoy the land hereditarily carrying on the worship and maintaining himself or themselves with the proceeds from the land. Three inscriptitions from Uttaramallūr dated in the reign of Kampavarman record such benefactions. The earliest of them dated in the King's year 6 (876) (*SII.*, VI, 347) states that one of the brahmins of the village granted land out of his share as

archchanā-bhōgam to god Mahāvishṇukkal in the temple Gōvardhanam in the village. The two others are dated in the king's year 8 (878). One of them (*Ibid.*, 288) records the gift of 1200 *kuḷi* of *madhyamam* land (common uncultivated land?) as *archchanā-bhō*gam to the same god by the *sabhā* of the place. The other one (*Ibid.*, 287) is again a grant as *archchanā-bhōgam* to the same god of land (960 *kuḷi* in four *pāṭakams*) by an outside individual after purchasing the same from members of the village. In all the three cases the land was entrusted to Dāmōdara-bhaṭṭan, son of Sridhara-bhaṭṭan, a *Vaikhānasan,* to be enjoyed hereditarily, supporting himself and the temple. Another inscription from the same place dated in the year 4 of a Parakēsari Rājēndra (11th century ?) (*Ibid.*, 336) records the making over of the land belonging to the god Subrahmaṇia-dēvar of the place to Iruṇi, alias Gangādharabhaṭṭan, a sivabrāhmana by the *mahāsabhā*. The priest was to hereditarily do the worship (*aṛchippānāga*) to the god in accordance with the *nibandham* already laid down. Two inscriptions from Chōḷapuram (North Arcot District) probably belonging to the period of Parāntaka I record the endowments of land probably to the same temple. In one, the god is described as the Perumāḷ in Nandikampisvaram (*SII.,* VIII, 9) and in the other as Mahādēva in the Piḍāra-kōyil (*Ibid.*, 10). In both the cases the temple is stated to have been situated in Kāṭṭuttumbūr and as having been taken over *(ēṛṛu-ppeṛṛa* by two persons, Gangādhara and Kara-puravanār who are described as the sivabrahmanas in the latter record. In the former, a private individual purchased 1600 *kuḷi* of land at the same time getting the land freed from taxes from the *sabhā* of Vēlūr alias Paramēsvaramaṅgalam and handed the same over to the above said two priests for hereditary posssession *(vaḷi)* for arranging for lamps and food offerings in the temple. In the latter, someone with a view to ensure the welfare (*nanṛāga*) of Prithvīgaṇgaraiyan granted 8 *paṭṭis* of land free of taxes to the temple and entrusted it to those same two persons for hereditary possession.

184. *SII.*, III, 43.
185. *Ibid.*, 142.
186. *Ibid.*, 49; *AREp.*, 1921, 217.
187. *SII.*, V, 489
188. *SII.*, VII, 392.

189. Where this right pertained to a saivite temple, it was termed a *sivabrāhmaṇa-kkāṇi* in 10th century inscriptions. In some inscriptions probably the same land was also designated as *aṛchchanā-bhōgam*. Some records (Uttaramallūr inscriptions of the time of Kampavarman (*SII.*, VI, 288, 347); Tiruvottūr, North Arcot District, inscription of the year 21-1006 of Rājarāja I, *SII.*, VII, 110 etc.) indicate that it was land given over to the brahmin both for his own maintenance as well as that of the worship in the temple. Some other records (e.g. Allūr, Tiruchirappalli District, inscription of the year 40 (947) of Parāntaka I, *SII,* VIII, 698 (also *Ibid.*, 694, 697) indicate that *archchanā-bhogam* was land given as fee for maintenance of the priest. Another inscription of the year 4 of a Parakēsarivarman from Naṅgavaram (Tiruchirappalli District) (*SII.*, VIII, 659) refers to a bloc of land as the *manyam,* 'grant for maintenance, of those that had the temple *(tirukkōyil-uḍaiyāṛgaḷ)*.
190. *Ibid.*, VIII, 521
191. *Ibid.*, VII, 841.
192. *SII.*, VII, 809.
193. *SII.*, III, 50.
194. *SII.*, III, 55.
195. *SII.*, VI, 339, 315 respectively. This king could have been the first of that name, in which case the date quoted will correspond to 1015 and 1016. But comparing the contents with that of the Tiruvallam inscription cited above which is also dated year 3 in the reign of Parakēsari Rājendra II, these records also could be assigned to the same reign period. Then the equivalents of the dates quoted would be 1055 and 1056 respectively.
196. *SII.*, VI, 339.
197. *Ibid.*, 313.
198. Another phrase used in this context, *pūṭṭai-iṭṭum* is not explainable.
199. However in the text *mudal-taram* has been doubtfully read by the editor, as an attribution of one of the plots. If that was so, then it would appear that of the land sold some plots were already under cultivation and graded as first sort. In that case it will be inexplicable as to why those plots came to be sold. As the purchaser looks to have been an official and the fact that the *dēvakanmis* were also involved it might also indicate that the sale was forced.

199a. *AREp.*, 1921, 217

200. The first two letters in the name of the village are damaged and left blank in the Annual Report, but as the village was *dēvadāna* of Tiruvallam- uḍaiyār and was in Tū-nāḍu it can be assumed that the village was Kukkanūr.

200a. *SII.*, III, 43.

201. The conclusion that they were a class of Jains does not seem to be justified (*SII.*, I, p. 88 n 5; Basham, A.L., *op. cit.*, p. 193.

202. This group has to be understood as the drum-beaters in the temple as the reference to the allotment to them is found in the same context of the allotment of shares to the temples in that *brahmadēyam*.

203. The practice of allotting shares in the *brahmadēyam* villages to the drum-beaters in the temples therein seems to have been prevalent in the area south of Toṇḍaimaṇḍalam even during the early period. The inscription dated year 10 (980?) of a Parakesarivarman (Uttamachōḷa?) from Tiruvakkarai (South Arcot district) evidences the allotment of 4 shares for *uvachchar* (it is noteworthy that the body of *kulan-giḻār* arranging for the worship was also given only equal number of shares) in respect of two temples in the *brahmadēyam* village Tribhuvana-mahādevi-chaturvēdimaṅgalam (*SII.*, ; XIX, 240).

204. *SII.*, VI, 324

205. The identity of this king is not settled. He seems to have belonged to the ninth century.

206. *SII.*, XII, 114

207. *SII.*, III, 128

208. The Mēlsēvūr (south Arcot district), inscription of the year 18 (1003) of Rājarāja I (*SII.*, XVII, 243). This record which details the *nibandham* arrangement for the services in the temple of Tiruttānṛōnṛippirān made by a royal official says that five *paṭṭi* (1100 *kuḷi* per *paṭṭi*) of land were earmarked in one of the *dēvadāna* villages taken up for the *nibandham* and another 2000 *kuḷi* of garden land (*kōllai-nilam* in two *dēvadāna* villages were added for allotment for the services of the *uvachchar*. The services required of the *uvachchar)* were : (one *timilai*, one *maṭṭalam*, one *karaḍigai*, handbell—one, and conch-two). Here also there is no indication if the land was entrusted to the body of *uvachchar* or if, though the land was earmarked, only the landlord's share (*mēl-vāram*) from the allotted land accrued

to the body of *uvachchar*. There is no indication in the record as to who was holding the said villages till the date of the record. If the connotation applied to the word *dēvadāna* in Toṇḍaimaṇḍalam was also applicable to Siṅgapura-nāḍu (*kīḻvaḻi*) then the entitlement of the temple and its functionaries from the *dēvadāna* villages could not have been the land but only the tax contribution, which probably was designated as the landlord's share from those villages. Then the reference to the earmarking of the said amount of land meant only that the taxes from that land would be utilised for the purpose stated. Again in the same context this *dēvadāna* land must have been tax-free in the king's accounts.

CHAPTER—5

INDIVIDUAL CONTROL

BRAHMINS IN BRAHMADEYAM

As discussed above the royal copper plate charters granting *brahmadēyam* in Toṇḍaimaṇḍalam during the period under study conferred two sorts of control on the brahmins—one was the control of the people of the locality centering round the *brahmadēyam* and the other the control of land within the *brahmadēyam*. These charters fall under two categories. One was the grant of a whole village as *brahmadēyaṃ* to a single brahmin as reflected in the Kaśākuḍi plates of Nandivarman II and the Rōyakkōṭṭāh plates of Skandasishya. The other was the grant of a village or a group of villages clubbed into one as *brahmadēyam* in shares to a number of brahmins as described in other charters, Kūram plates of Paramēsvaravarman, Udayēndram plates and Pullūr plates of Nandivarman II and Chiṭṛūr plates of Nripatuṅga, in the case of the former, no further records from Koṭukkoḷḷi or Ēkadhīramaṅgalam and Chārukūr or Skandaśishya-Maṅgalam, the villages granted as *brahmadēyam*, have come forth to enable one to guage the extent of control over land that was meant to be vested in the brahmins granted *brahmadēyam* in these charters and what was actually exercised by them in practice. However in so far as the Kaśākkuḍi charter of the two specifically says that land in respect of *brahmadēyam* and kuḍi was excluded, that the grantee brahmin Jyēshṭapāda-Sōmayāji was enabled to lay out channels etc. for irrigation and that he could have exclusive use of these facilities, it is indicated that he was given possession of the land in the village (with the exclusions as above) which was to be developed with the facilities authorised.[1] As this charter further states that the grantee was exempted from the remittance of certain levies (to the kō) and was authorised to enjoy the income from such levies, it becomes clear that the grantee was also enabled to have control over the people inhabiting or that might inhabit the village. Hence it can be understood that during the period when a single brahmin was granted a village as *brahmadēyam* the character of control vested in him had two aspects one proprietorship of the land in the village granted as *brahmadēyam* and the other control over other people in and around the block of *brahmadēyam*. The individual grantee might have engaged tenants to work the land for him, keeping all the land under his direct management or he might have distributed it to his relatives[2] and assumed the role of *yajamān* in relation to them.[3] Whatever mode was adapted by these brahmins to exercise the control each was in sole charge of the village concerned.

In the other type of *brahmadēyam* granted during the period also, it has been seen that irrigation privileges as also authorisation to receive miscellaneous levies and enjoy the proceeds, accompanied the grants.[4] But each of these grants says that the *brahmadēyam* had been granted in shares to a number of people. These recipients of shares in each of these charters belonged to two categories—one the main bulk of brahmins whose *gōtra*, *sūtra* (pedigree) and often attainments are given, the other, miscellaneous persons, temples etc. From the description of these categories of people, it is apparent at that the intention of the grant was to benefit the first category as it contained the brahmins entitled to receive *brahmadēyam*. The second category was probably meant to fullfil several purposes for the benefit of the first category. So it can be said that in each of these charters, it was the whole group of the first category of people which was given charge of the *brahmadēyam* with the control over land within the *brahmadēyam* which this body was to develop along with other rights and privileges incidental to the *brahmadēyam*. In so far as each individual brahmin in this category was concerned, he was restricted to the share specifically allotted to him in the charter itself. It has been seen that each one of these brahmins also did not get an equal allotment, some of them got only one share, some two and some others more. Thus each brahmin was not equal to the other even within this group. However even the one share belonging to a brahmin of this category was different in character from the share that was meant for the persons in the second category. The former share connoted a share of the control over the shareholders in the second category as the whole village was *brahmadēyam* to which only the former shareholder was entitled. Further the share of the former category also must have denoted the proportion of the proceeds from the collection of miscellaneous levies to which the *brahmadēyam* group was authorised. The share of the members in the second group could not claim the same privilege. Hence it can be deduced that each individual brahmin included in the groups of the first category of donees in the charters of the period enjoyed a special position in the *brahmadēyam* though he was not the equal of every other brahmin of the group. This special position was determined by the share which was however only a fragment of the whole *brahmadēyam* (i.e.) whatever rights and control were pertinent to the *brahmadēyam* were the belonging of the community as a whole only. Hence, even the brahmin in the group entitled to the maximum number of shares in the *brahmadēyam* could not have claimed to have been the holder of the *brahmadēyam* in the same way as Jyēshṭ apāda Sōmayāji or Mādhava-sarma-bhaṭṭa who received as a whole *brahmadēyam*, the villages Ekadhīramaṅgalam and Skandaśishyamaṅgalam respectively.

While the charters say that the individual brahmin of these *brahmadēyams* was allotted share/shares, they do not specify if and how the share was related to the land in the *brahmadēyam*. As stated above it is deduceable that the land in the villages granted as *brahmadēyams* as per these charters, was meant to come into the possession of the body of the grantees and was unoccupied and awaiting development. The grantor king might have originally intended that the grantees should posseses and work the land as a body and share the yield as per the entitlement of each. However from the information provided in the records pertaining to the *sabhā* villages of the period which seem to have been such as had been granted as *brahmadēyam* to groups of brahmins (out of the four *brahmadēyams* constituted as per the charters mentioned above, Udayachandramaṅgalam is stated to have come to have a *sabhā* in the post script in Udayēndram plates of both the first and second Nandivarman), it is seen that each of these brahmins came to possess land in these villages. Not only that, the tenth century inscriptions from Uttaramallūr[6] indicate that the possession of a minimum quantum of land was a *sine qua non* for the participation of the brahmins in the activities and probably the rights pertaining to the *brahmadēyam*. It is not known as to when and how such a distribution of land in the *brahmadēyam* village was effected. As the land was probably virgin the brahmins as a body might have reclaimed the land, marked out the plots and then distributed the land as per entitlement in which case on the strength of the reclamation, the rights of the communal body would have been prominent. On the other hand, it is also possible that even initially after laying out the plots, the land had been distributed to the shareholders and each one was left to his own devices for developing the land. Of course he might have been helped in the process by the irrigation rights etc. that were conferred along with the *brahmadēyam* to the whole body. In this case the individual brahmin who developed the land must have become eligible to claim some special rights with regard to that land.

Regarding how this distribution of land to the share-holders was effected, an inscription of the year 6 (876) of Kampavarman from Uttaramallūr[7] gives a hint. It refers to the share *(paṅgu)* as having consisted of a house-site *(manai)* and *srāvaṇai*. From the context it can be understood that *śrāvaṇai* referred to agricaltural land.

Literally the term *srāvaṇai,* being derived from the verbal root *sru*-to hear, refers to what was made to be heard. As such, as applied to the land held by the brahmin, it might have meant that it was got after making others, especially the king, hear the recitation of the *vēdas*.[8] But in the above cited reference the brahmin concerned is stated to have held a share which consisted of the house-site and agricultural land of which only the latter was termed as *srāvaṇai*.[9] Whatever might have been the basis for the king's grants to the brahmins such grants were designated as *brahmadēyam.* It is not imaginable that the different parts of the grant, the house-site and the agricultural land were designated differntly.[10] Hence obviously the term *srāvaṇai* as applied to the agricultural land held by the brahmin must have described the special characteristics of the land. It seems to have indicated that the brahmin had got the land after making another hear (i.e.) bidding for it.[11] This procedure to invite the brahmins to bid for the land commensurate with their shares seems to have been the method by which the communal body of the brahmins had solved the problem inherent in the distribution of land in the village which must have consisted of different types of land with Various types of facilities like nearness to the residential quarter[12] water resources etc., There was also another method available to allot plots of land to the share-holders after a draw of lots, it cannot be said with certainty that only the former of these methods was adopted and the other was not resorted to.

Even if in all the *brahmadēyam* villages, the share-holders had been allotted land only on the basis of their bidding for it, equity could not have been achieved in the distribution. In this context three inscriptions pertaining to the llth century[13] might be indicating the method adopted to secure justice for each one of the brahmins. All these records come from the Kāñchī-puram taluk of Chingleput district. Two of them from Maṇi-maṅgalam[14] refer to the orders issued by the *sabhā* of the place at *karai* (*karai-iṭṭu-kkaṛai-ppōndu*—laying down the *karai* and *karai* having been done). An inscription from Tennēri[15] mentions the Committee (*perumakkaḷ*) of *karai-iṭṭukkarai-ppōnda*. A *kareyidu* found in operation in a village in Tañjāvūr district in the 19th century, referred to the process of reallocation of land to the villagers in a particular year.[16] On this analogy the *kare-yīḍu* of the 11th century must have also had reference only to this Periodical redistribution of land among the shareholders. This process must have ensured that none of the shareholders was burdened with inferior or unattractive land permanently. However it is not known if this process was adopted in each of the villages granted in shares to the brahmins. If in some villages, the land had been allotted to the shareholders even initially before development and if the individual brahmin had been responsible for bringing the plots allotted to him to a satisfactory agricultural state, he must have acquired some special rights in respect of that land and he might not have been willing to exchange it at a later stage. But even then in the same village there must have been shareholders, who had not found the land to their satisfaction, hence, as there was no reason why anyone of the shareholders should be permanently burdened with land which placed him at a dis-advantage only a periodical rotation of the land among the shareholders might have secured justice to them especially in view of the fact that the charters did not forcibly tie each one of them to specified plots of land. But even though holding only a share of the *brahmadēyam* and land against the share interchangeable at the reallocations the individual brahmin is seen to have enjoyed the rights pertaining to the proprietorship of land, the right to bequeeth it in inheritance to gift it or sell it. However in such transactions, the link with the share was often found stressed.[17]

Whether the brahmin conferred these *brahmadēyams* were authorised to bequeeth the land, gift it or sell it, the available charters make no clear mention. Among the available charters only the Chiṭṟūr grant pertaining to Toṇḍaimaṇḍalam and the Paṭṭattāḷmaṅgalam grant pertaining to Chōḷa-maṇḍalam state that the grants of *brahamadēyam* made were to last so long as the sun, moon, stars etc lasted, thus authorising the group of brahmins to pass on the *brahmadēyam* to their progeny. Regarding the authorisation to part with the *brahmadēyam* as discussed above, there is no reference in the charters. However the term *paradatti* mentioned among the enabling clauses in the Kaśākkuḍi, Pullūr and Chiṭrūr plates could have meant the conveyance of such right to gift or sell the *brahmadēyam*. It is not known why these provisions were not included in each of these charters—if it was an omission or if it was deliberate. Moreover all rights and privileges in the *brahmadēyam* were granted to the whole group of brahmins. It is not known how these rights and privileges could percolate to the individual brahmins holding only a share, as in making the grant of *brahmadēyam*, the king seems to have had a definite purpose of securing the control of the locality through the agency of the brahmins and further seems to have placed his reliance on a particular group of brahmins, he would not have wished that each in the group could go his own way. Hence, even if it can be supposed on the strength of the land transactions in the *sabhā* villages during the period, that the enjoyment of the *brahmadēyam* in perpetuity and the authority to gift or sell were implied in the grants whether specifically referred to or not in the charters, the communal body of the grantees would have been expected to keep a watch and ensure that the actions of the individuals in the group did not disturb the harmony and effectiveness of the purpose of the whole *brahmadēyam*.[18]

As land allotted to each brahmin on the strength of the share was a tangible commodity for transactions and at the same time it symbolised the share there might have been the involvement of the community in the shape of regulation of the transactions in land by the individual brahmin. The community could have had no locus for interference where the individual brahmins bequeethed the land along with the share to their progeny, excepting to wish that the successors would prove useful members in the community and help in maintaining the character of the *brahmadēyam*. But in gift and sales the community could be expected to have had the right to be consulted. However in such transactions as wistnessed in the *sabhā* villages, there is no evidence of such consultation having been made by the individual brahmins. The reflection of the responsibility of the individual brahmin in respect of the share allotted to him is found only in the frequent mention of the connection of the share with the land involved in the transactions.

An inscription of the year 6 (876) of Kampavarman from Uttaramallūr[19] refers to the endowment to the temple of a whole share (excluding one *pāṭakam*) including house-site and agricultural land *(śrāvaṇai)* by a brahmin who says that the share was his own *(tāṇ- uḍaiya)*. He had apparently inherited it. Here it appears all the rights pertaining to the share were transferred along with the land. The same record also refers to the endowment of a plot by another brahmin but here no reference is made to the share.

Another inscription of the year 19 (880) of the same king from the same place 19a records an endowment of a plot of land by a brahmin, who was one of the governing body *(āḷunganattār)* of this *sabhā* village. The plot was part of what the endower's father had got as per his share *(paḍaittuḍaiya pangin-vaḷi)*.[20] Probably in this instance it was only the income from the land that was claimable for the purpose of dredging the *Vairamēgha* reservoir. Whereas in these cases the brahmins themselves are seen to have gifted their own share land[20a] in the following records the brahmins are stated to have sold land for endowment. Another record from the same place dated year 15 (922) of Parāntaka I[20b] refers to plots of land endowed to God earlier by two brahmins out of their holding and in that connection mentions 'by way of share'. It may have meant that the plots had become theirs on the strength of their share or that they had conveyed the rights proportionate to the plots sold out of the shares.

A record of the year 24 (870) of Nandivarman III from Uttaramallūr again[21] says that a brahmin lady *(brāhmaṇi)* and two other brahmins each separately sold plots of land which are described as *paṅgin-vaḷi-mudal-iṭṭu* to a *madhyasthan* for endowment to God Mahādēva.

Another record of the year 8 (878) of Kampavarman from the same place[22] however reflects that a brahmin who was a member of the governing body *(āḷuṅgaṇattāṛ)* had purchased two *pāṭakam* of land from a brahmin (of the village) by way of the share *(paṇgin-vaḷi)* and that the same had been endowed for God Mahādēva. It is noticeable that in the former two cases the share is referred to only while particularising the land involved in the sale and in the present instance the sale is stated to have been effected by way of the share. This may signify that in the last instance the proportion of the other rights appertaining to the share had also been conveyed along with the land.

An inscription dated year 15 of a Parakēsarivarman from Tiruvāṇḍārkōyil (Pondicherry state) in the middle country[23] gives more elaborate details regarding the sale of land by way of the share. It says that a member of the *āḷuṅgaṇattār* of *brahmadēyam* Tribhuvanamāhadēvi-chaturvēdimaṅgalam endowed a share excluding the house-site for God Paramasvāmigaḷ of the temple of Tiruvārai-Nakkan-kōyil and entrusted it to a brahmin priest of the temple of Paramēsvara-bhaṭṭ ārakar of *brahmadēyam* Tiranalāṛu.[24] This share which the endower had purchased consisted of several shares as follows:— A share each from three brahmins of the village, one of the shares is described as what the brahmin concerned had got on the strength of being a *śāsana-baddha*. The two other shares are stated to have belonged to the two brahmins concerned who were *śāsana-baddha*.[25]

Three quarters of a *paṅgu* each from two brothers who are stated to have been the relatives with rights *(ñati)* of one of the above said brahmins and to have got the share as their portion *(kūru)*.[26]

Another share was also such that another brahmin had got as his portion *(kūru)*.

In this record, as there is no reference to land and only to the shares the intention of the purchaser seems to have been to get all the rights pertaining to the shares concerned and vest them in the priest of the temple to whom these shares were coagulated into one and entrusted.[27]

In the following instances of sale of land by the brahmins in *brahmadēyam* villages there is no reference to the *paṅgu* or share but they throw interesting light on inheritance and sale procedures in *brahmadēyam* villages.

Another inscription of the year 8 (878) of Kampavarman from Uttaramallūr[28] records the purchase of several plots of land for endowment by Tēpramāṇi, the *Araiyan* of Atiaraiya-maṅgalam and in the case of one of the plots it is stated that it was purchased from a (group) including (*uḷḷiṭṭār*) Sivadāmōdara-chaturvēdi. Though it is not stated, the plot of land must have been a fraction of a share, which had been inherited by the said brahmin as one of the heirs and the description of the transaction indicates that the plot forming a fraction of the share could only be sold with the consent of the holders of the other fractions of the share. However the other plots purchased by Tēpramāṇi were also the possessions of other brahmins of the village and it is not known why there is no mention of the association of any other than the seller in these transactions. The only explanation could be that those seller brahmins were the sole inheritors of the share.

A damaged inscription dated year 13 (983?) of Parakēsari-varman from Tirumālpuram[29] records the purchase of land for endowment by the wife of a Mūvēndavēḷān. The land seems to have belonged to a group of two brothers and the wife of a third brother (probably deceased), the last of whom, however, is stated to have had her eldest brother-in-law as her guardian *(mudu-kaṇ)*.[30] Apparently the land involved in the transaction was part of a share over which all the three, the two brothers and another brother's wife had joint rights. It is also possible that the land involved belonged to the brahmin lady and the brothers of her huasband were brought into the transaction of the strength of their holding the other fractions of the share. probably the eldest brother was a member of the governing body *(āḷunganattār)*. This record evidences that even a lady (wife of a shareholder or of the heir to a fraction of a share) could hold a portion of the share, only she had to have a guardian.[31] It is not known if she was enabled to participate in the other rights pertaining to the share.

There are some references to sales of land in *sabhā* villages where no reference to the share is made. An inscription of the year 18 (903?) of Aparājita from Tiruttaṇi[32] refers to the purchase of land from the *kuḍimakkaḷ* (obviously the landholding brahmins as the village was under a *sabhā*) by one Nambi Appi for endowment to God Mahādēva of Tiru-viraṭṭānam. The land of the extent of 1000 *kuḷi* was entrusted to the *dharmis* of the village for carrying out the stated purpose of the endowment. The *sabhā* of the place asked to oversee the same. An Uttaramallūr inscription of the year 8 of a Rājakēsari-varman[33] records the purchase of land in the southern hamlet Aḍuma from the brahmins who had the land, by one Arattuṇai-puttan,the Kiḷān of Kalumbar-Pallavamaṅgalam. The land was endowed for feeding brahmins in a temple in the main village. It is stated that the purchase was made by the process of *Kuḍi-kkuḍiyān-vilai* which might be indicative of an auction of land, wherein even after sale the land would remain with the seller, who would thenceforward direct his contribu-tions to the temple.[34]

In the above two cases, the non-mention of the share with reference to the land might have been due to the land involved having been held outside the share. It is seen that at least in the second case the land is stated to have been situated in a hamlet which apparently was not under consideration when the village Uttaramēru-chaturvēdimaṇgalam was granted as *brahmadēyam* in shares. As it has been seen above that when villages/hamlets were attached to *brahmadēyams* they were held by the whole body of the *brahmadēyam,* this record might be providing a rare instance wherein the brahmins of the *brahmadēyam* had individually taken over land in an attached village also.

Thus it is seen that in *sabhā* villages, which seem to have been such as had been granted as *brahmadēyam* in shares to groups of brahmins, the brahmins held land and had the right to pass it on to their progeny in inheritance, gift it or sell it. Though the land in his holding was probably subject to reallocation periodically he could play the role of a landholder in a village.[35] Having been one of the members of the *brahmadēyam* the individual brahmin might have also enjoyed the right to utilise land for raising special flower plants like *damanagam, iru-vēli seṅgaḷunīr* and setting up groves of cocoanut or arecanut trees, the authorisation of which is seen to have been conferred on the whole body of the donees in the Chiṭṛūr plates among the charters of Toṇḍaimaṇḍalam and in the Taṇḍantōṭṭam plates pertaining to Chōḷa- maṇḍalam.[36] Apparently the brahmins did not engage themselves in cultivation. They might have had serfs or might have engaged labourers though there is no indication in the records to that effect.

But this holding of land by the individual brahmin was on the strength of the share which reflected his association in the control of the land. Even the enjoyment of facilities for cultivating the land must have been regulated by his entitlement as per the quantum of his share. These regulations were, however, administered by the communal body which also presided over the periodical redistribution of land. Hence though the individual brahmin held land, his individual control over that land could have been only a reflection of the control vested with the whole body. That is so long as the brahmins in a *brahmadēyam* were organised in a communal body, the individual brahmin could not have had individual control independent of the communal body. As a participant in the communal body he was only a part of the scheme for the control over land. It is also seen that the communal body could also lay down conditions for the participation of the individual brahmin in the control exercised by the community. As by inheritance, gift or sale the holding of some individual brahmins came to consist of dimmunitive plots the *sabhā* or the communal body is seen to have restricted the participation in the community only to those having a minimum amount of land The two Uttaramallūr inscriptions[37] dated in the reign of parāntaka I (year 14-921 and year 12-919 respectively) laid. down that for being eligible to compete for membership in the committees, the brahmin should have possessed ¼ or 1/8 (*vēli*) of tax-paying land[38] (the latter smaller holding was possible if the concerned brahmin was exceptionally qualified in the *vēda*s) as well as a house on his own site. Evidently these regulations were equally applicable for participation in the *sabhā* itself and as such in the claiming of his portion in the benefits that accrued to the whole body of the *brahmadēyam*. So the control that was inherent in a *brahmadēyam* was based on land and each individual participant also had to possess sufficient land and vedic knowledge to maintain his dignity. Divested of land, the individual brahmin had no part in the *brahmadēyam*.[39] However the communal body had no means to control or influence the dealings of the individual brahmin with regard to land. It could only safeguard its dignity and prestige by restricting its membership to those that could even individually command respect with a minimum quantum of land against his share and vedic knowledge.

BRAHMIN PRIEST

It has been discussed above as to how the land scheme as devised by the Pallavas in Toṇḍaimaṇḍalam was based on the control exercisable by the brahmins. Sometimes the brahmin's control was based on temples,the villages or land granted to which having been placed in the charge of brahmin. But it is seen that the brahmin priests, in these temples themselves did not play any significant part in the land control scheme. The priests mentioned in the records of the period were brahmins but they were distinct from the brahmins, who are seen to have received *brahmadēyam* during the period.[40] This distinction is evidenced even in the earliest available charter pertaining to Toṇḍaimaṇḍalam (i.e. the Kūram grant (670-700) which mentions Anantasivaācharyya, son of Kūrattācharya and Phullasarmma, as the persons who were given the charge of 3 shares in *brahmadēyam* Paramēsvaramaṅgalam for doing the worship in (*dēva-karma*) and keeping in good repair (*nava-karma*) (the temple built at Kūram), apart from the 20 *chaturvēdi* brahmins, to give *brahmadēyam* to whom the village was constituted. The Chiṭṛūr grant of Nṛipatuṅga, while enumera-ting the recipients of the shares in *brahmadēyam* Prithvi-Mahādēvi-chaturvedimaṅgalam says that the *Ācharyyan* (hailing from) Ālaṅgāḍu, the priest put in charge of the Śiva temple in the village would get ½ a share. None of these had any claim for equal status of the *brahmadēyam* brahmins. However the right to conduct worship in temples seems to have become the monopoly of this class of brahmins and even when the worship was desired to be done by a brahmin trained in vēdas, the priestly class had adopted the agamic mode of worship, the charge for getting the same done was entrusted to the priestly class of brahmins.[41]

As already referred to, these priestly brahmins were some-times given some shares in *brahmadēyam*, or were sometimes entrusted with land meant for temples, to be held hereditarily both for maintaining the temples and themselves.[42] Sometimes land endowed for carrying out some specified special services was also entrusted to them.[43] Again as already discussed the priests in some temples had also organised themselves into distinctive bodies, holding temple land as a body.

In whatever way these priests were entrusted with temple-land they are seen to have been subject to the control of either a body, of a *brahmadēyam* or the administrative body of the temple. Their holding of land was also against a stated purpose and obviously they could hold the land only so long as they carried out the purpose.[44] In every respect their standing in respect of land was very different from that of the head of a Jain establishment given charge of land/ village and the brahmin given *brahmadēyam*. The Paḷḷaṅkōyil plates of Simhavarman, which might have belonged to a period just anterior to that under study,[45] records the grant of village Sraman-āsrama or Amaṇsērkkai to the *guru* (in charge of the Jain establishment) Vajranandi who belonged to the order of Nandi-saṅgha. The Tamil portion in the record further says that 16½ *paṭṭi* of land in (the village) Tamar was also granted to him. All was given as *Paḷḷichchandam*. Obviously this *Pallichchandam* was meant to maintain the worship in the Jain place of worship as also to maintain the monastic order which was headed by Vajra-nandi that had charge of the establishment. This *paḷḷichchandam* was an independent unit and was not part of a *brahmadēyam*. Further there was no question of the granted land/village getting fragmented as the *guru* entrusted with the village was a celebate monk. The village would have passed on in its entirety to the successor in the guruship. There is no evidence of the *guru* having been questioned about the proper utilisation of the land. The *brahmadēyam* granted to a brahmin or group of brahmins was also an independent entity. There is no reference in the records to this grant having been made to the brahmins for carrying out a stated purpose or of their being questioned about their mode of carrying out the purpose. On the other hand the grant of *brahmadēyam* implied the passing of the control of the locality to the brahmins who were authorised several rights and privileges for the purpose. While it is seen that the priestly brahmins never got control of land in the same way as the *guru* of the Jain establishment or the brahmin of the *brahmadēyam*, it will be evident from the above cited charters that the priests granted shares in the *brahmadēyams* Paramēśvara-maṅgalam and Prithvi-mahādēvi-chaturvēdimaṅgalam were subject to the control of the *brahmadēyam*. For, from all appearances, it is seen that the grants of *brahmadēyam* were mainly meant for the bloc of brahmin who were versed in the vēdas. This control of the body of the *brahmadēyam* brahmins over the land allotted as per share to the priestly brahmins within the *brahmadēyam* village seems to be well brought out in several inscriptions, from Uttaramallūr. They refer to the allotment of land to the priests of temples by the *sabhā* of the place[46] on to the entrusting of land meant for a temple to a *sivabrāhmaṇa* or priest, of the Siva temple.[47] It appears that the land concerned was already earmarked for the temples concerned as per the share allotment in the charter and *sabhā* had the discretion in its allotment to the priests.[48] These allotments seem to have been different in character from the allotments made to priests by the *sabhā* on its own.[48a] This control over land meant for temples exercised by the *sabhā* is also made evident in the Tiruppāṟkaḍal inscription of the time of Pārthivēndravarman[49] which tells about the *sivabrāhmaṇa* of the temple of Perumānaḍigal of Tirukkarapuram appealing to the *sabhā* of Kāvirippākkam to give land in exchange for that which was in the enjoyment of the above said temple and which had sandlogged due to the river breaching its banks. The Tirumālpuram inscription of Uttamachōla[50] highlights the helplessness of the *sivabrāhmaṇas* and the *dēvakanmis*.

In the one instance, where the *sivabrāhmaṇas* of the temple of Tiruvallam are reflected in the inscription of the year 4 (1016) of Rājendra I,[51] to have been in control of a *dēvadāna* village, in the same way as a *sabhā*, this body of priests is seen to have been tied up with the *dēvakanmis* the administrators of the temples. (There were other villages in the *dēvadāna* of the temple and two of them Amarunṛi- maṅgalam[52] and Mandiram[53] are known to have been under *sabhās* and one Kukkanūr[54] under an *ūr* organisation. In the reign of Rājarāja I (year 7-992)[55] they were subjected to an enquiry by a royal representative and the relevant record cites that the *sabhā* of Tiruvallam also were involved in the matter. Probably the *sivabrāhmanas* were under the supervision of the *sabhā* of Tiruvallam. They were subject to be fined as evidenced in a record of the same year.[56]

Though the priestly brahmins in their holding of land on

behalf of temples were not independent, even within those limitations they are seen to have had some usual sort of control over land. It has been stated above that in the *brahmadēyam* charters and in other records when land was entrusted to the priest for maintaining worship in the temple (i. e. keeping the deity in the temple in worship) as well as himself he was authorised to hold (enjoy) the land hereditarily. A record belonging to the 13th century coming from Āragal, Salem district [57] which indicates that it was actually the right to worship which went down in inheritance, that the right to worship was constituted into units corresponding to the days in the month *(muppadu-vaṭṭattu-kkāṇi)* and that these units could be inherited even by ladies, might be describing the general practice in the matter throughout the Tamil country including Toṇḍaimaṇḍalam even during the earlier period which is under study. Though not indicated in the reference the holding of the right to worship can be taken to have been inclusive of anything that was earmarked as maintenance of the priests for conducting the worship. Though such a thing earmarked could have been anything, [58] the practice described must have been equally applicable to the land set apart as fee for conducting the worship or to the land allotted to the priest for maintaining the worship as well as himself. The division of the right to worship into the 30 units must have been done to facilitate the inheritance of the full right to worship by several succeeding heirs and the land earmarked must have also been correspondingly divided into units.[59] The cited reference states that 3 1/8 days' worship was in the right of a lady. Apparently this lady must have hired other priests to conduct the actual worship on her behalf as it is not seen anywhere that ladies officiated in the worship. The record also evidences that this share of the right was attachable and saleable and when sold, the purchaser/purchasers engaged the priests holding the remainder of the shares in the worship to take over the responsibility for worship against this share also.[60] While the record tells only about the divisions of the right to worship and does not even mention what had been held as fee for this conduct of worship, it stresses that the land or any income that was the fee could never be divorced from the duty in the worship.

It is also seen that it was the *māhēsvaras* and chief officers of the temple, that sold the *kāṇi* of 3 1/8 days' worship out of the whole 30 days' worship in a month (*muppadu-vaṭṭa-ttu-kkāṇi*) belonging to a lady. These authorities of the temple could arrest and confine the priests.[61] All this again highlighted the subordination of the priests to the temple authorities.[62]

In the one case discussed above where the *sivabrāhmanas* or priests in a siva temple as a body is seen to have held a temple village, also the position of the individual priest could not have been different. This record from Tiruvallam dated year 4 (1016) of Rājendra I, stresses that the first charge on land in a *dēvadāna* village was the service in the temple against which it is earmarked and that the priests' holding of land was under the authority of the *dēvakanmis*.

Some record found in the regions outside Toṇḍai-maṇḍalam indicate that the priests who held land on behalf of the temple could have themselves carried on the agricultural operations. A record of the year 12 (997) of Rājarāja I from Bāhūr says that the *Sivabrāhmanas* would themselves raise the crop (*payir-ēṛṛi*) in the temple. Another from Allūr (Tiruchirappall district) dated year 3 of a Rājakēsarivarman[63] says that the priests *(i-kkōyil-paṭṭu-uḍaiyār)* would themselves plough (*uḻudu-koṇḍu)* the land endowed. The phrases used in the above records might have been just figurative and might have meant that the priests would get the land cultivated. But a record of the year 25 (11th century) of Māravarman Vikrama-chōḷapāṇḍya, from Āttur (Tirunelveli district)[64] states that the priests (*aga-nāḷigaiyār*) undertook to raise the crop *(payir-ēṛṛi* and have the crop raised (*payir-eṛṛuvichchum*) on the land endowed. This differentiation between the two modes of utilisation of the land in the same records suggests that at last some times the priests in the regions to the south of Toṇḍaiman-ḍalam themselves took to the plough.This might have been the case in Toṇḍaimaṇḍalam also. However the abovecited Tiruvallam inscription of Rājēndra I, year 4, indicates that at least when the *sivabrāhmaṇas* had organised themselves into a body they might have engaged tenants *(kuḍis)* to cultivate the land in the *dēvadāna* village in their charge. The record suggests that they collected from the *kuḍis, veṭṭi.kūṟṟu-nel alpam-iṟai* and appropriated the proceeds among themselves.

While the holding of land by the priests was invariably under the authority of a superior body there was an outstanding feature about such land. During the period and in the region under study, it has been seen that land entrusted to the priest for maintaining himself and the temple was got freed from taxes, on the strength of a commensurate, capital against the tax liability deposited either by philanthropist[65] or by the priest himself.[66] The *sabhā* of Uttaramēru-chaturvēdimaṅgalam is also seen to have freed the land endowed and entrusted to a priest by itself.[67] Apart from this among others, the Uttaramallūr inscriptions especially dated in the reign of Pārthivēndravarman refer to several instances of the *sabhā* freeing land allotted to temple from taxes on being paid *pūrvāchāram* by a trader or some other.[68]

In some instances at least such land allotted to temples might have been entrusted to priests,[69] where the land allotted was for the maintenance of the priest as well as of the temple, if the land was freed from taxes such privilege could be construed to have been meant for the benefit of the priest also. However where the priest was entrusted with land freed from taxes for carrying out specific services in the temple, in such cases also the priest could have derived some profit due to the land being free from tax obligations, as whatever of the yield of the land remained after meeting the obligation to the temple must have been his or his own enjoyment.

OTHERS

While in respect of *brahmadēyam* villages (which seem to have been the same as *sabhā* villages), some details about the activities of the individual brahmins in them are available which enables one to make an assessment of the extent of their control over land, the individual landholders in other villages never even figure in inscriptions. Among these other villages, it has been seen that some were under the administration of the village organisation, *ūr* and some others under the organisation of traders designated as *nagarattār*. It appears likely that there were villages which had not organised themselves into one of these village bodies.[70] As for *ūr* villages,the Chintāmani (Chingleput district) inscription of the year 26 (965) of Krishna III refers to the village Karuṅgāli with an *ūr* administration and to a Mumaippāḍi- Mūvēndavēlan as administering the *karai* in the locality.[71] The reference to *karai* suggests that there was a periodical redistribution of land in *ūr* villages also. If it was so, it can be surmised that in *ūr* villages also the individuals held land against shares. For them to have held land against shares, they must have been the beneficiaries of grants which might or might not have been accompanied by rights.[72] However, as discussed above, such organisation might have been confined to those under special tenures, *vēṭṭappēru Kaṇimuṟṟūṭṭu* etc., then the beneficiaries from these villages must have been some favoured persons including temples, and the landholders in them must have been subordinate to such favoured persons. Hence in the light of the available evidence it is impossible to say if the landholders in these villages had any special control over land beyond such which enabled them to work the land and bequeath it to their progeny. It is observable that there is not a single record of a sale or gift by an individual landholder in *ūr* villages.

In the case of the *nagarattār* villages in early 11th century, as pointed out above the Mahābalipuram record[73] gives a definite indication that there was a periodical redistribution of land in that village. The record says that the individual members of this body of *nagarattār* could sell, mortgage and gift the land, apparently what had come to their possession at the time. The purchaser, mortgagee or beneficiary of the gift must have been made aware of the liability of the land to be exchanged at the next reallocation. That the *nagarattār* like *brahmadēyam* holding *sabhās* also got the benefit of attachment of villages to them and the members could apportion the land in the attached village is indicated in the Melpāḍi, inscription.[74] Beyond this there is no information on the individual trader's control over land in those villages and if it extended beyond the land as in the case *brahmadēyam* holders. Though there are several instances of traders purchasing land from *sabhā* or individual brahmins, there is no instance of a trader selling or gifting land out of his own holding.[75]

NOTES :

1. However, there is no specific mention in the charters that the grant land was virgin and was to be reclaimed by the donees. Only in the Udayēndram plates of Nandivarman I (*EI,* III, p. 142 f) whose genuineness, however, is not beyond question, it is said that four *aranya- kshētram* or forest land was granted as per "the right of erstwhile enjoyment" (*pūrvv-opabhukta-maryyādayā*) to a single brahmin of Kañchivāyil. Only among the charters of the Pallavas pertaining to the Guṇṭur-Nellore region, in the Chendalūr plates of Kumāravishṇu II there is reference to the grant of 432 *pattika* of land which was *rājavastu* in the village by halanyāya or the rule pertaining to the first bringing of land under the plough to a single brahmin.
2. cf. Veḷvikkuḍi grant of Pāṇḍya Neḍuñjaḍaiyan, c. 769-70, (*EI,* XVII, p. 291 f); also Udgaonkar, Padma B, *op. cit.*, p. 157.
3. Croele (*op. cit.*, p. 208) describes the character of the "yajaman's" control in *mirāsi* villages in Toṇḍaimaṇḍalam in the 19th century.
4. *Ibid.*
5. When the earliest of this group of charters, the Kūram grant says that the rights and privileges were to be shared in proportion by all the shareholders the twenty *chaturvēdis* getting twenty shares, the two priests with three shares and the purposes in the mandapa at Kūram financed by two shares, it can be presumed that it was unique in that charter only.
6. *AREp.*, 1898, 1-2.

7. *SII.*, vi, 347.
8. It does not appear that the word had reference to the learning of the brahmin which entitled him to get the gift of the land. To convey that meaning, the word should have been *śrāvaṇai, Śrāvaṇai* does not also seem to be connected with *srōtriyam* which referred to land granted to a learned brahmin who kindled the sacred fire, i. e. who strictly followed the brahminical observances, which pious acts formed the taxes to the king in respect of the land (Jha D.N. *Revenue System in Post-Mauryan*-Gupta Times, p. 125). Cf. Monier Williams, A, Sanskrit-English Dictionary, p. 1103 Col. 1. 2. Also cf. Amarakōśa, II, 7,6—*Srōtriya-chchandasau-samau-śrōtriya* was the same as *chchandasa* i. e. who recited *Vedas*.
9. cf. *SII.*, XII, 37. This inscription from the Pandya country refers to the full *srāvanai*. Here also the term seems to refer only to the agricultural land eligible against the share.
10. cf. *EI*, IV, p. 177-78. This inscription from Kīlmuṭṭugūr says that the king granted the *brahmadēyam* status to all the land, house-site, wet-land and dryland, held by the brahmin Vārāndara Śaṭṭaiyanār, the younger brother *(tamaḍi)* of Sanmāduran.
11. cf. *EI*, XI, p. 224. In this record, land is stated to have been purchased by '*vilai-srāvaṇai* causing the price to be heard; Here the phrase is clearly indicative of an auction.
12. Cf. Rōyakōṭṭah plates of Skandaśishya. It refers to one type of land as *senru-ulu-pāl,* waste land that had to be reached for ploughing indicating probably the land on the outskirts of the village. Also cf. Mukhia Harbans, Presidential address-Medieval India, Proc, IHC, 1979 (Waltair), p. 234.
13. While the Uttaramallūr inscriptions of Pārthivēndravarman and some such indicate that shares allotted to temples might have been included in the category for being meted out justice. It is doubtful if the shares allotted to other miscellaneous persons including those set apart for doing servive to the village (Pullūr plate) were eligible to be treated on an equal basis.
14. *SII.*, III, 29-30. They are dated year 4 (1056) of Rājēndra II and year 5 (1068) of Vīrarājēndra respectively. Also *SII.*, II, 22.
15. *Ibid.*, VII, 412, this is dated year 2 (10. . .) of Rājarāja I.
16. A full description of the procedure adopted is given in *Indian Antiquary* (III, p. 65 f.).
17. cf. Mahalingam, TV., "The Pullur Plates etc. " *EI,* XXXVI, p.

149 n 4. He indicates that even till recently, the link of land with share was remembered in Tañjāvur district.

18. *AREp*. 1921, 159. This inscription of the year 28 (967) of Krishna III from Kāvanūr records a regulation made by the *sabhā* of the place to the effect that the seller and purchaser as well as the mortgager and mortgagee of land in the village should belong to the same community.

19. *SII.*, VI, 347.

19a. *Ibid.*, 294.

20. The phrase actually runs. as follows : *padaittuḍaiya-paṅgiṇvali-mudaṛ-kudumbittu-nālām pāṭakam*. Here *mudar- kuḍumbittu* might be indicative of the location of the plot or character of the land (cf. *Ibid.*, 347, 356).

20a. An inscription of the year 3 of a Parakēserivarman from Tiruppāppuliyūr (South Arcot district) *(SII.*, VII, 742) records the grant of 15 *kōllai* (garden land of 15 kuḷi?), 2 mā, of the field in Milalai *(milaḻai-pulam)* ¼ (*vēli*) of the field under the reservoir *(eri-ppulam)* 700 arecanut and 300 cocoanut trees in the groves in the field of *vēlan* (*vēlan-pulam*) as *brahmadēyam* for 5 brahmins by a brahmin of the place. The grantor brahmin however stipulated that the recipients could neither sell nor mortgage what had been given to them.

20b. *Ibid.*, VI, 291.

21. *Ibid*. 356.

22. The significance of the phrase is obscure. cf. *Ibid.*, 294 above.

22a. *Ibid*. 285.

23. *Ibid.*, XIX, 373.

24. *Ibid.*, p. 195. The interpretation of the text as given in an introduction to the text of the inscription seems to be defective.

25. *Śāsana-baddha* seems to signifiy that the brahmin who sold the share was either one of the group of the original grantees of *brahmadēyam* or such one's descendant. This seem to have been employed here to differentiate these brahmins from the three others, mentioned as also having sold shares, who were only *ñatis* and had got the shares only as *kūru*. Also cf. *SII.*, XIX, 405—This inscription of the year 16 (986) of Parakēsarīvarman (*Uttama-chōḷa*) says that the queen-mother entrusted gold endowed for feeding on the day of her birth asterism in the temple, with *śāsana-baddha*-chaturvēdi-bhattādāna-peru-makkaḷ

26. cf. Velivikkuḍi grant of Pandya Neḍunjaḍaiyan (*EI,* XVII, p. 291 f).
27. In these cases where the land or share is stated to have been purchased by a member of the governing body or *madhyasthan*, it appears that the transactions concerned were distraints couched in a polite language. An inscription of year 23 (869) of Nandivarman III from Gudimallam (EI, XI, p. 224) actually employs the term *vilai-śrāvanai* which seems to have meant an auction, with reference to the purchase of land by a member of the *āluṅgaṇattār* from a member of the *gaṇattār* for endowment. It is noteworthy that the price paid is never mentioned. Two inscriptions from Tañjāvūr district, one dated year 17 of a Rājakēsarivarman, (*Ibid*, V, 573) and the other dated year 4 (960) of *Pāṇḍiyanai-talai-koṇḍa* Parakēsarivarman (*Ibid.,* 574) which refer to sales of shares in favour by temples (in the second record such purpose is not clear) by members of the governing body themselves, specifically mention the price in gold received. The records describe in detail how these members of the governing body got the share. Only one share involved is stated to have been received on the strength of the charter *(śāsana-baddha*) by the father of the concerned member of the governing body. All the others are stated to have been such as had been purchased by the concerned brahmin or his father (cf. *AREp*., 1922, 379; *Ibid*., 1923, pt. II, p. 103.).
28. *SII.,* VI, 287.
29. *SII.,* XIX, 318.
30. cf. *Ibid*., 404. This inscription of the year 16 (986) of Parakesarivarman (Uttama-chōḷa) from Tirukkōlambiyūr, Tañjāvūr district used the terms *mudu-kaṇ* in two senses the land that was given to a lady for her support or maintenance (lines 2,8) and the guardian (line 9).
31. cf. *SII.,* VI, 356 cited above. In this record the brahmin lady is stated to have held a share. There is no mention of a guardian for her. Brahmin ladies are also seen to have held land on two other accounts—what they got as *śrī-dhanam* (*Ibid*., VIII, 617; *Ibid*., XIX, 404 -both these records are from the Chōla country) or as *aṅgamaṇi* (*Ibid*., XIX, 321; *Ibid.,* VIII, 331). *Aṅgamaṇi* probably denoted any material given to a lady for maintenance (*Ibid*; VI, 314; also cf. *Ibid*., XVII, 640—this inscription dated year 30-937 of Parāntaka I from Tiruchirappall district refers to

a garden received by a lady from her husband for food and clothing as *(śōṛu-kūrai)*.

32. *Ibid.*, XII, 95.
33. *Ibid.*, 323.
34. *Kuḍi-kkuḍiyān-vilai* might have also indicated an auction wherein only the other *kudis* of the village were authorised to bid (cf. *Ibid.*, 111,9). However in the above case it was an outsider who purchased the land. Also cf. *AREp.*, 1921, 159.
35. In spite of the fact that the land was only an accompaniment of the share and no plot of land could have been claimed as his permanent possession by any of the brahmins, the land in the brahmin's possession at a time seems to have been capable of being treated as his asset and of being attached to meet his liabilities. The various cases where the governing bodies *(āḷuṅga-ṇattār)* or other governing agencies are stated to have purchased land for endowment, it might have been such an attachment of land. In this connection three inscriptions of the period of Rājarāja I (one from Ukkal—*SII.*, III, 7, another from Tiruvallam—*AREp.*, 1921, 208 and another from Agaram—*Ibid.*, 1922, 379; *Ibid.*, 1923, Pt. II, p. 103) reflect such capability of the attachment of the land with the brahmins. In cases, where such land attached and auctioned was only a part of the holding of the concerned brahmin, how far such sale affected his standing in the *brahmadēyam* and if the purchaser could claim the proportion of the *brahmadēyam* rights in respect of that land are not ascertainable.
36. *SII.*, VII, 412. An inscription of the year 2 (.) (1005-1014) of Rājarāja I from Tennēri, Chingleput district records a resolution (*vyavasthai*) by the *sabhā* of the place that from the succeeding year till another ten years lands where plantain and arecanut trees had been planted would be required to pay only ½ the *iṛai* and thereafter also the/lands with arecanut would pay only two *kaḷañju* pon (?). As the record refers to the plantains rotting in a particular year the said concession seems to have been extended to encourage continued planting of plantain trees.
37. *AREp.*, 1898, 1-2.
38. It has been pointed out above how, the land in a *brahmadēyam* was liable to pay tax.
39. While it can be envisaged that the heirs of the original *brahmadēyam* grantee must have intherited the control inherent

in the *brahmadēyam* scheme, as governed by the share, though fragmented further and further by successive generations, it cannot be said if such share in the *brahmadēyam* control got transferred when the land of the individual brahmin was sold or gifted. If the purchaser or receiver of such land as gift was a brahmin and was sufficiently qualified, he might have acquired the rights by the shape pertaining to the portion of the land he got (cf. *SII.*, XII, 37). When the land in the share of a brahmin was gifted to a temple or was sold to any one for such endowment that portion of land must have lost its right to be represented in the communal body. However in the three cases (*Ibid.*, VI, 285, 291; *Ibid.*, XIX, 373) where the conveyance is stated to have been made through the share, it might have been intended that the beneficiary temples could get the other benefits that could accrue to that share or portion of the share. In any case, the communal body's control over that land within the *brahmadēyam* could not have ceased.

40. It is seen that the priestly brahmins were themselves of two classes, the *vaikhānasas* in charge of worship in Viṣṇu temples and *sivabrāhmaṇ*as in charge of Śiva temples.
41. *SII.*, III, 55. Tiruvallam inscription of the year 3—(1055) of Rājēndra II; *Ibid.*, VI, 313 ṣ Uttaramallūr inscription of the year 4 (1056 ?) of Parakēsari Rājēndra (II ?); *Ibid*, 355.
42. *Ibid.*, 287, 288, 347, 336; *Ibid.*, VII, 32.
43. *Ibid.*, III, 50; *Ibid* VII, 809, 841; *Ibid.*, VIII, 521.
44. Cf. *SII.*, II, 66—This inscription of the year 29 (1014) of Rājarāja I from Tañjāvūr clearly states as to what was to be done if there was failure to do the stipulated service against the *kāṇi* allotted, by the priests.
45. *AREp.*, 1958-59, p. 4.
46. e. g. *SII.*, III, 170. This inscription is dated in the reign of Pārthivēndravarman (second half of the 10th century), As several records from this place dated in the same king's reign refer to allotments of land to temples in that village by the *sabhā,* the context might have been a rotation of land. The records usually state that the transactions were carried out by the *peruṅguṛi sabhā*. Among several inscriptions an Ukkal inscription dated year 4(1016?) of Parakēśari Rājēndra (I?) (*Ibid.*, III, 10) when it records a sale of land by auction by the *sabhā* refers to the order in this regard having been issued in the *kuṛi* and written down

by a *karaṇattān*. Hence it can be surmised that kuṛi or *perunguṛi* was a functional assembly by the *sabhā* for executing some special type of transactions with reference to land. (Also *Ibid*., 156, 181, 182). Cf. *SII*., XVII, 627—This inscription of the year 48 (1119) of Kulōttuṅga I from Kallaperumbur (Tañjāvūr district) refers to the constituting of the *peruṅguṛi*; *Ibid*., XIV, 37, from Mānūr in Tirunelveli district dated in the reign of Māranjaḍaiyan specifically says that the *Mahā-sabhā* assembled the *peruṅguṛi (peruṅguṛi-śāṛṛi,)*: another inscription from the same district also refers to the assembling of the *peruṅguri*; on the other hand three inscriptions from Tirumejñānam (Tanjāvūr district) dated in the reign of Parakesarivarman refer to *mahā sabhāi-pperuṅguri-pperumakkaḷ*. Also cf. Sastri, K.A.N., *The Chōḷas*, p. 502.

47. *Ibid*., VI, 336.
48. It may be observed that in the Pullur plates pertaining to Toṇḍaimaṇḍalam and the Kumaraḍimaṅgalam plates pertaining to Chōḷamaṇḍalam the charters do not name the priests to whom the shares in the *brahmadēyam* allotted for temples in those villages were to be entrusted. Apparently the allotment was left to the discretion of the *brahmadēyam* grantees. Also *Ibid*., VI, 339.
48a. *SII*., VI, 288.
49. *Ibid*., III, 156.
50. *Ibid*., 142.
51. *SII*., V, 489.
52. *Ibid*., III, 43.
53. *AREp*., 1921, 219.
54. *Ibid*, 217.
55. *SII*., III, 49.
56. *AREp*., 1921: 218.
57. *AREp*. 1913, 439; *Ibid*., 1914, p. 93.
58. cf. *SII*., III, 43.
59. It cannot be ruled out that this organisation of the worship into 30 units circulating among the priests had been done due to the requirement of several priests as in the case of big temples to take charge of the worship. However here also this division might have been a consequential arrangement to accommodate several inheritors of the right to worship.
60. cf. Tirukaḷār (Tañjāvūr district) plates of Rājarāja (II?), year 18

(1164?) (*SII.*, III, p. 472-473). It states that even the endowment (of what is not indicated) for a specific service in the temple taken charge of by several people could be divided into shares and bequeathed to heirs. The legal point that came up for decision was whether ladies could inherit the endowed commodity and contribute interest towards the service. One Kanakarayar probably the administrator of the temple and *Śrī-māhēśvaras* arbitrated in the matter and decided that the endowment would be so inherited.

61. As it is stated that a defalcation of temple jewels was detected. Probably all the priests were put in confinement to elicit from them the information on the person responsible for the defalcation. They must have put the blame on the lady.
62. Also cf. Tirukkalar plates of Rajaraja II cited above.
62a. *SII.*, VII, 809.
63. *Ibid.*, VIII, 694.
64. *SII.*, XIV, 191.
65. *Ibid.*, III, 170; *Ibid.*, VIII, 9-10.
66. *Ibid.*, VI, 287, 347; *Ibid.*, VII, 32.
67. *Ibid.*, VI, 288.
68. *Ibid.*, III, 155, 157, 158 etc.
69. e. g. *Ibid.*, VI, 336.
70. In early 19th century, on investigation the British administrators found that common holdings and payment of government dues in kind were the salient features of revenue administration in Hindu period (Croele, *Chinglepuṭ District Manual*, p. 202).
71. *AREp.*, 1933-34, 19, *Ibid.*, Pt. II, P-32 para 9
72. This recalls to mind the *Saṅgam* account about Karikāla- Chōḷa reclaiming land and settling veḷḷāḷar therein and the tradition about Ātoṇḍai-chakravartti settling Tuḷuva-veḷḷāḷas in Toṇḍai-maṇḍalam. That the holding of land by these non-brahmin agriculturists in Toṇḍaimaṇḍalam might have been similar to the holding by the brahmins in *brahmadēyam* villages at least in early 19th century, is indicated in the descriptions of the land system in Toṇḍaimaṇḍalam by Croele (*op. cit.*, p. 50, 204-05, 208, 211-14). Also Mahalingam, T.V., *Readings in South Indian History* p. 101.
73. *SII.*, I, 40.
74. *Ibid.*, III, 16.
75. Mem A*SI.*, 26, p. 9. The record dealt with here is from Mahābalipuram and is dated year 65 (796) of Naṇdivarman II.

CHAPTER—6

IRRIGATION

In Toṇḍaimaṇḍalam prior to the period under study, the irrigation system as it was might have consisted of the rivers, wells and ponds or natural depressions collecting rain water. But this system was apparently inadequate as much scope was left for expansion of the system and agriculture in the period under study. The system reflected in the records of the period subsequent to 670 is found to have been based probably on the same old existing facilities but expanded and integrated together.[1] Probably the same old natural depressions were expanded with additional structures to enable them to take in more water to become the reservoirs of the period. Often wherever possible they are seen to have been linked to the rivers so that the runaway storm water in them could be stored for even, prolonged utilisation in agriculture. Sluices were provided to draw the water from the reservoirs and a net-work of channels, from the rivers to the reservoirs and from the reservoirs to the fields was laid.[2] The system by its very nature had to include a set up for constant maintenance as there was the ever present hazard of silting up in the reservoirs and channels.[3]

It was probably the Pallavas, the rulers of this region between the middle of the 6th century and the end of 9th century who were responsible for the devising of this reorganised irrigation system in Toṇḍaimaṇḍalam. Some of the reservoirs mentioned in the records bear their names. In one instance it is seen that the main channel feeding the reservoir from the river was also named after the Pallava king. It is not known if these kings themselves financed these constructions. It seems likely that a part of the system owed their origin to them and the other part was contributed by their subordinates or by local agencies. When in the latter half of the 9th century, some feudatories are evidenced to have controlled some territories in Toṇḍai-maṇḍalam, they are stated to have provided sluices and channels to the reservoirs. The maintenance of the system is seen to have devolved upon the local people and philanthropists. The latter provided the capital and the local organisations took charge of the task of maintenance. There does not seem to have been a governmental organisation to manage the system and there is no indication in the records that the king collected any additional levy for having provided the facilities. Probably he was satisfied that the irrigation system he had inspired to be provided resulted in the increase of the area under cultivation which automatically brought him suitable returns.

It has been pointed out that the Pallava king of the period had been forced to depend upon this region to provide the economic base for his ambitions. He also seems to have stood in need of a mechanism to keep under control the different areas. The irrigation system introduced by him seems to have been meant to achieve both the purposes. In the earliest mention of the construction of a reservoir, by a pallava king as provided in the Mahēndravāḍi inscription of Guṇabhara (Mahendra-varman I early seventh century[4]), the details regarding the purpose of the construction is not available. But by the end of the seventh century the *Kūram* charter linking the irrigation system with a *brahmadēyam* clearly indicates the purposes for which the system provided for *brahmadēyam* Paramēśvara-maṅgalam was devised.

This charter of Paramēśvaravarman (670-700) recording the constitution of the *brahmadēyam* Paramēśvaramaṅgalam, refers to a reservoir, Paramēśvara taṭākam, (probably cons-tructed at the initiative of the king in or near the village for the benefit of the new *brahmadēyam*) and says that the donee brahmins were given the right to dig the Perumbiḍugu-kāl (channel) from the river Pāḷāṟu to the Paramēśvara-taṭākam in their *ūr* and draw the channel from the same to the fields *(Uṟṟukkāl*[4a]) along the natural course following the grain of the country *(nīr-īnda-vaḷiyāl)*. The grant also says that the lands through which the channels passed, the *puḷudipāḍu*,[4b] the *talai-vāy* and *talai-ppēlai*[4c] would be treated as the land belonging to Paramēśvaramaṅgalam (i.e.) those lands would be under the authority of the *brahmadēyam*. A broken plate of the set also mentions *kuṟṟēttam* or small picottah. It is likely that as in later inscriptions the members of the *brahmadēyam* were authorised to fine anyone setting up the small picottah to draw water from the channels unauthorisedly. Thus it is seen that the donees of the *brahmadēyam* together were given extensive and exclusive rights with regard to the irrigation facilities.

In the Udayēndram plates the brahmins who got the *brahmadēyam* Udayachandramaṅgalam, were authorised two *jalayantra*s (picottahs ?)[5] as also the enjoyment of the water of the river and channels (*naḍī-kulya-jalābhōgyam*). On four of the eight quarters bounding the village there were water facilities, Stēkanadī, Uragahrada, Sinduvārahrada and Kshīra-nadī (Pālāru river).[6] Obviously the *jalayantras* were meant to be used to draw water from these rivers and ponds. In this charter there is no reference to the monopolistic privileges conferred. As such details are found only in the Tamil text of the charters, such non-mention of the privileges here might have been due to the absence of the Tamil text.

In the Kaśākkuḍi plates which records the grant of a village Ēkadhīramaṅgalam as *brahmadēyam* to a single brahmin, the water rights (*udaka-bhāga*) authorised are succinctly put in the Sanskrit text as that of blocking the rivers, Dūra- sarit, Vēgavatī and the reservoir Tīralayataṭāka as convenient *(yath-ōpapādam)*[7] and of drawing channels therefrom. The Tamil text however sets out the rights more eleborately. The donee could dig *āṟṟukkāl* (channel from the river to fill in reservoirs they might devise) and *veḷḷakkāl* (channel to catch the over-flow in floods)[8] from the rivers

Chēyāṛu, Vehka[8a] and the reservoir Tiraiyanēri[9] and take it along the grain of the country. For these channels the donees got the rights of *kōlagalam*[10] and *puludipāḍu*.[10a] The exclusiveness of their rights with regard to the irrigation facilities was also spelt out when the record says that those who (unauthorisedly) used baskets for bailing the water, or cut branch-channels *(kuraṅgaṛuttum)* or set up small picottahas (*kuṛṛ-ēttam*) would be fined (by the brahmin ?) in the same way as the *kō* could do.

In the Pullur plates, it is stated that the new *brahmadēyam*. Nayadhīramaṅgalam had two reservoirs, Pādiēri, Nēsalār-pūṇḍi-ēri and the river Chēyāṛu on three of the boundaries. The donee brahmins were authorised to draw channels by way of the grain of the land from the river and reservoirs. They could also probably fill up old channels and cut new channels as they found it fit. The record also states that the donees could take water to their fill from another reservoir, Nelli-ēri. For the reservoirs of the *ūr*, they could bring the water from the river by digging *ārrukkāl* again following the grain of the country. The other rights were similar to those contained in the Kaśākkuḍi plates except that in the Pullūr plates the transgressors were to be fined by the kō.

In the Chiṭṛūr grant the *brahmadēyam* granted Piridi-mādēvi-chaturvēdimaṅgalam, had two reservoirs on the boundaries, Panmāttuppēr-ēri and Kaḍumbaraiyianūr-ēri and a channel Maṇaiyiḻār-kāl. The donees could dig channels by damming (*aḍaittu*)[12](the river) and take water to their fill and till they had been served no other could bale water with baskets, set up the small picottah or take sub-channels.

In the Udayēndram plates of Parāntaka I, though there is no mention of any special irrigation rights having been granted, the village Kaḍaikkōṭṭur which was amalgamated with Udayachandramaṅgalam to form a new *brahmadēyam* complex Vīranārāyaṇa-chchēri had the river Pālāṛu on two boundaries, one channel Vayirakkāl a reservoir Gangeyan-ēri, and two ponds Kuraṅguṭṭai, and Tanakkōṭṭaikkuṭṭai on three other quarters. All these indicated that irrigation facilities existed at the place to help in the reclamation of the village. As the record does not give the details of other privileges also and as the charter records only the amalgamation of a village with an already existing *brahmadēyam* it seems to have been left to be understood that the privilege that must have been already under the enjoyment in respect of the original *brahmadēyam* village could be enjoyed in respect of the new villages also.

Thus also it is seen that in a charter belonging to the end of the seventh century a reservoir named after the king was provided for supporting a *brahmadēyam* or it was already there when the grant was made. But the channel from the river to feed this reservoir, though named after the king, was still to be dug only by the donees in the *brahmadēyam* who were authorised to take the channel. Among the other charters only the Kaśākkuḍi plates refer to a reservoir reflecting the name of an anicent king of the 2nd century A.D. Otherwise any irrigation reservoir associated with the names of the kings of the region are not mentioned. However some rivers, reservoirs, and ponds are found mentioned. It is noticeable that in each case the charters contain an authorisation to the donees to dig channels from the rivers. Probably they were expected to get the reservoirs and ponds expanded with the help of these channels from the rivers. Apart from such *brahmadēyams* regarding whose creation the few charters are available it is seen that other *brahmadēyams* in the region, regarding whose creation charters have not come forth, also had a water reservoir sometimes named after Pallava kings probably reflecting that they had been constructed by the king at the time of the creation of the *brahmadēyam*.[14] The famous Uttaramēru-chaturvēdi-maṅgalam had the *Vairamēgha-taṭākam*. The fact that the earliest inscription from this place is dated in the reign of Dantivarman Pallava coupled with the name of the reservoir, lead to the conclusion that both the *brahmadēyam* and the *taṭ ākam* came into existence simultaneously during the time of Dantivarman. The name of the reservoir suggests that it was constructed at royal initiative as Vairamēgha was a title of that king.[15] In the same way there was a *chitramēgha-taṭākam* supporting a Narasiṅgamangalam (Māmaṇḍūr or a village near Māmaṇḍūr near Kāñchīpuram)which was a part of Tiruvēkambapuram. Though the names of the reservoir and the *brahmadēyam* suggest that they had come into existence during the reign period of a Narasimhavarman Pallava,[15a] the earliest record from the place is dated only in the reign of Rājarāja I at the end of the 10th century.[16] Some other *brahmadēyam* villages of the period are also seen to have had a reservoir attached to them. But the reservoir is not found named. For instance Kāvidippākkam which had an alternate name Avani-Nārāyaṇa-chaturvēdimaṅgalam, which suggests that as *brahmadēyam* it had been founded by Nandivarman III who had the title *Avani-narayana*,[17] it had a reservoir to support the agriculture therein.[18] This might have been already there or might have been constructed simultaneously with the founding of the *brahmadēyam*. In the same way Kurattūr alias sri-Parāntaka-chaturve dimaṅgalam was included in a nāḍu in Pulal-kōṭṭam which had for its support a reservoir of Ambattūr (*Ambattur-eri-kil-nāḍu*). This reservoir could have come into existence when probably Parāntaka I founded the *brahmadēyam* named after him.[19]

On the basis of such information provided by these charters and other records it becomes evident that almost in every case a *brahmadēyam* of the period had a reservoir attached to it. Though in only some cases the records suggest that donor—Pallava king might have been responsible for the setting up of such reservoirs in the other cases also he is seen to have been responsible indirectly either for constructing the reservoirs or for developing the system through the authorisations to the donees of *brahmadēyam*. Though it can be supposed that these donees were relied upon in this task due to the king's knowledge about their expertise it is not possible to guage as to where he expected them to find the capital.[20] But in the event it is seen that whoever provided the capital the *brahmadēyams* got started.

What the king is clearly seen to have passed on to the donees with regard to irrigation was a set of rights -the right to dig channels through any ground as thought convenient and claim such land on the path of the channel as well as the land on which these facilities stood as their own, the right to have their fill of the water first before allowing any one else to use that water and the right to fine transgressors. Apart from this they were given exclusive rights over tanks,[21] channels and whatever facility existed in the village as also the right to fill up wells and ponds, probably those found at incvonvenient places. Though apparently these rights were conferred on them to ensure that they could carry on the development of the land without interference, it can also be seen that possessing such monopolistic rights over the water resources in the locality, they would have been in a position to control the local population already resident or that was likely to become resident in that locality which had to depend only on these same irrigation facilities for their agriculture.

These irrigation facilities pertaining to a *brahmadēyam,* excepting in the one clear case of a grant to a single brahmin as contained in the Kaśākkuḍi plates are also seen to have been placed in the charge of the whole body of the recipients of the grant. Hence the king seems to have intended that the recipient-brahmins should act in unison. As discussed in the previous chapter, the character of the grants seems to have necessitated the formation of the *sabhā* witnessed in the *brahmadēyam* villages. These *sabhās* are seen in several records to have either taken over gold from endowers with a promise to contribute the interest necessary to maintain an intended service in a temple or received the gold from the temple itself with an undertaking to contribute interest to the temple. So it appears that this entrusting of the task of developing the irrigation system to the whole body was done because it was envisaged that as a corporate body, the group of brahmins could command the capital necessary for the execution of the works. Probably it was also thought that these brahmins if obliged to act as a corporate body, could more efficiently administer the system.

Having been entrusted with such rights over the irrigation facilities in the locality, the body of the *brahmadēyam* recipients had also to shoulder some responsibilities with regard to that irrigation system. It is seen that maintenance of the system became a primary concern of the bodies of the villages. As a corporate body these brahmins are witnessed to have become an effective agency for the task. As a body the *sabhā* attracted deposits for probably the capital costs connected with maintenance, like the provision of boats[21a] and other equipment for dredging and the provision of lifts (picottahs) where necessary. In due course the *sabhā* is seen to have set up committees for the execution of the tasks connected with irrigation works. It was also enabled to take forced labour or payments in lieu from the landholders in this connection.

The earliest evidence of this corporate body being engaged in this task is provided by an inscription from Paiyaṇūr (Chingleput taluk and district) dated year 37(768) in the reign of Nandivarman II.[22] It states that the *gaṇattār*[23] of Payinur undertook to levy 16 *kāḍi* of paddy from each *paṭṭi* of land benefiting from the big lake of the place to pay for the dredging of the lake every year. This liability of the land could not cease even if it was sold or mortagaged and none could question this arrangement. Probably for the capital expenses connected with this dredging this *gaṇattār* had received a deposit of 6400 *kadi* of paddy measured by *por-kāl* from one Nāgan, an Uḷakkuni-vāṇigan, a resident of Mamallapuram. The interest from this capital in paddy probably was meant to meet the recurring costs on capital account.

Early in the 9th century, the *sabhā* is mentioned and this *sabhā* is seen to have developed executive organs for carrying out the several responsibilities, maintenance of irrigation works being one of them. But still the organisation seems to have been in a fluid state. Further at this time there seems to have been dependence on benefactors to provide the cost of the equipment connected with the task.

An inscription dated year 9 (805) of Dantivarman from

Uttaramallūr[24] says that the *sabhā* of the place undertook to have the digging or dredging *(kuḷi-kuttu)* of the *Vaira-mēgha-taṭāka* done every month against a deposit of 20 *kaḷañju* of gold and the proceeds of the sale of manure *(eru-vilai)* or a tax on manure from the cow-shed *(toru-nilai)*[25] at — va-chcheri as made available by one Śēṭṭadaraiyar (Dana) vendan of Kachchippēḍu, probably a merchant,[26] and that *the sabhā* entrusted the responsibility for carrying out the tasks to the committee of the time. Another record dated year 21(817)[26a] in the same reign also refers to a provision for the benefit of the same reservoir and the *sabhā's*[26b] connection with it but the terms used are obscure.

Towards the end of the ninth century also there was a dependence on private benefactions to equip the *sabhā* for its task. But the *sabhā* was getting the administration better organised. A committee on annual affairs as well as a committee for the reservoir seem to have been entrusted with the task of maintenance of the reservoir. An inscription from Ukkal (North Arcot district) dated year 16 (886 ?) in the reign of Kampa-varman[27] says that one Saḍaiyan deposited 1000 *kāḍi* with the *sabhā* of Uṭkar and that the latter undertook to have the local reservoir dredged every year.[28] The *sabhā* entrusted the task to the committee on annual affairs (*samvatsara-vāriya-pperumakkaḷ*).

However when three other benefactions were made for the dredging of the reservoir at Uttaramallūr the *sabhā* is seen to have entrusted the task to the reservoir committee. In the same king's year 10 (880[29] ?) one brahmin of the governing body (*āḷuṅ-gaṇattār*) endowed the income from one *pāṭakam* (of 240 *kuḷi*) out of his share (in the village) for this purpose and the reservoir-committee was asked to supervise the execution of the task with the income endowed. This committee was entrusted with a similar charge by the *sabhā* when one Maṇṇipākkiḷān-kōyil, a merchant living in the southern merchant street (*aṅgaḍi*) endowed 100 *kaḷañju* of gold each time in the year 18 (888[30]) and year 21 (891[31]) of the same king, to yield a total interest of 30 *kaḷañju* as also a gold levy from the standing houses in the northern row of the same merchant street for dredging and bringing the mud ashore. The *sabhā's* position in the village and in the irrigation system are pointedly brought out in these records which say that the *sabhā* greatly pleased with the merchant's generosity granted to him and his progeny the privilege of paying the bare *iṛai* without the liability to pay *puṛa-iṛai* including *manai-ppon, alapiṛai* and *śoṛumāṭṭu*. But in the case of two other benefactions of the same period when the *sabhā* is stated to have undertaken to have similar tasks carried out neither the reservoir committee nor the committee on annual affairs is mentioned in that connection. One of these was made in the year 15 (885) of Kampavarman by another merchant Devandai Kalukkunṛan of the merchant quarter (*aṅgāḍi*). He endowed 100 *kaḷañju* of gold and 28 *kāḍi* of paddy to yield an annual interest of 10 *kaḷañju* of gold and 3 *kāḍi* of paddy and the requirement was the dredging of Vairamēgha-taṭāka in the two months of *Vaikāśi* and *Āni* every year and bringing the mud ashore. The other was an endowment of 1000 *kaḷañju* made by one Aparājita, a servant *(aḍi)* of Pērumānaḍigaḷ[33] in the same year as above[34] out of which the *sabhā* was asked to take 200 *kaḷañju* and have the dredging done during the three months following *Āni* every year.

In the tenth century also the *sabhā* continued to receive benefactions of capital for the maintenance of the reservoir attached to the *brahmadēyam* village but there seems to have been a difference. An inscription from Takkōlam (North Arcot district) dated year 19 (926) in the reign of Parāntaka I[35] says that the *sabhā* of Pōndaippākkam in Tiruvūral-puram accepted 800 *kāḍi* of paddy measured by *eṇṇāḷi-kkāl* from Kōvattak-kuḍi-udaiyan (i.e. headman or resident of Kōvattakkuḍi in Tenkarai-nāḍu of Chōḷa-nāḍu) Śingan Pāḷi and undertook to contribute 100 *kāḍi* (at the rate of 4 *nāḷi* per *kāḍi*) as interest per annum and have the reservoir of their village dredged *(kalluvippōm)* every year. But it appears that the *sabhā* was not directly involved in the process as it is stated that the *sabhā* also undertook to feed the person coming to collect the interest twice daily. Further the record makes it out as if a duty was imposed on the *sabhā* after duly entrusting the paddy to them. The *sabhā* also cautioned itself by stating that it would incur great sin if it failed to carry out its commitment. Probably Kōvattukkuḍaiyān was an official and he was acting in his official capacity in the record and the depositing of the paddy with the *sabhā* was part of official policy of the time.[36] As such the tenor of the record with regard to the reflection on the position of *sabhā* is in contrast to the records of the earlier period. In the third quarter of the 10th century a sale of land by the *sabhā* to be endowed back for the maintenance of the reservoir is also witnessed. The record is from Kāvanūr (Gudiyattam taluk, North Arcot district) dated in the reign of Pārthivēndravarman. The 1000 *kuḷi* of land sold for the purpose by the *sabhā* to one Vayiramēgan Toruvatti Peruntaṭṭān probably remained with the *sabhā* for administration. Thus the *sabhā* got the sale money as also an endowment for the reservoir. The sale might have been necessitated to meet some contingency faced by the *sabhā*. In these records which are of 10th century the committees are conspicuously absent. Probably these villages were small *brahmadēyam* and there was no necessity for the *sabhās* of these places to take the help of committees. For, an inscription from Ukkal (North Arcot district) dated year 37 (944) in the reign of Parāntaka I[39] indicates that the reservoir committee as also the other committees for annual affairs and garden were still very much in the picture and that all of them were entitled to collect forced labour (*veṭṭi*) or a *vēdinai* and *vālakkāṇam* at least from *kuḍis* taking up land in the *brahmadēyam* complex for reclamation. Probably the institution of committees was special only for big *brahmadēyam* villages. But in the light of this record while the reservoir committee by its very designation could be understood to have been concerned with the irrigation system in the 10th century, it is not possible to guess how the annual or garden committees were also having something to do with that system and why the free labour and the other levies were required by them in that connection. It is not also certain if the latter two levies were also other sorts of forced labour or compounded payment in lieu of the two *vēdinai* may be a derivative of *vēdanā* or pain and as such may indicate a forced levy. But the other with the suffix *kāṇam* a low denomination coin seems to have been even originally a cash levy and could not have once indicated forced labour. However it might have been also a cash levy taken by the committees to meet the expenses of some services they were expected to execute.

It has been seen that apart from gold, paddy or land endowed by individuals to help the *sabhās* in the upkeep of the reservoirs attached to their villages, even from about the middle of the 9th century the *sabhās* of villages were entrusted with the gold endowed against different services in the temples on their undertaking to contribute the stipulated interest for the maintenance of the service intended by the donor. In a few instances in the tenth century the *sabhās* are recorded to have made such gold available to the reservoir committee for utilisation.[41] It can be observed that there were three ways in which the *sabhā* got committed with reference to the upkeep of the irrigation system on receiving a capital against the same. One of them was, apparently to invest the capital in procuring some capital equipment and for the routine maintenance to levy a regular ad hoc contribution from the users of the irrigation system. The second way was to take the capital endowed for the maintenance and contribute interest to pay for the charges of the upkeep. The third way was to take charge of gold endowed to the temple for temple purposes, utilise the same for the irrigation system and contribute interest to the temple for fulfilling the purpose for which the gold was endowed. In the latter two cases the *sabhā* had to invest the gold in such a manner as to ensure a regular income from it. One of the ways in which the gold was invested must have been to expand the irrigation facilities and secure an extension of cultivation, so that the yield of the newly reclaimed land could be made to pay the interest. The other was to utilise the amount fully in the irrigation system instead of the interest or a levy from the users but at the same time levy a regular *pro rata* charge from the users to pay the interest. It appears that one levy *nīr-vilai* (price of water) which is rarely mentioned in records of late 10th century and late period, was not such as was to be paid to the king but was the charge levied by the *sabhā* as a contribution taken from the users of the irrigation system to enable it to fulfil its commitments consequent on its taking a capital to maintain the system.

Levying free labour or computed cash payment from the users was probably in addition to the charges taken from the landholders as mentioned above. Probably this was taken to carry out tasks other than maintenance, like regulating the water supply etc. This free labour taken on other account seem to have been designated differently. Several tenth century inscriptions refer to a number of levies which from their designations could be deduced to have been several kinds of free labour or computed payments. Of these three *śennīr-amañji,*[43] *śennīr-veṭṭi*[44] and *sennīr-ppodivinai*[45] seem to have had reference to the supply of irrigation water (*sennīr).*[46] It is not known why so many kinds of free labour were required in connection with irrigation. It is possible that each had relevance for a particular process in the course of the supply of irrigation water to the landholders.

It appears that if it was the *pro-rata* levy or the *nīr-vilai* or the various kinds of free labour, all were equally leviable from all landholders including the brahmins holding shares of land in the village. This is indicated when it is seen that barring the *pro rata* levies, the others find mention in the exemptions granted in favour of temples in respect of land, which was sold by the *sabhā* or the individual brahmins out of their holding for the purpose. The explanation probably lies in the fact that these were required to work the irrigation system. The payment of these charges or contributing free labour to enable an arrangement for their proper use of the land could not have affected their rights with regard to the irrigation facilities. However it seems possible that the *sabhā* took some additional charge from non members that were utilising the water from the irrigation facilities especially meant for them. The *ēri-āyam* mentioned in an inscription from Bāhūr (Pondicherry state) dated in the reign of Rājarāja I[47] I might have been such a levy.

However the rights of the *brahmadēyam* shareholders in the irrigation system are seen reflected in the efforts the *sabhā* made to expand the irrigation facilities in the village and in the transfer and conferring of rights to the temples when land in their villages was endowed by the *sabhās* of some of the villages. While extending the irrigation facilities the *sabhā* had however to take the help of others. The gold that was taken as deposit in the several instances cited above might have been utilised for such expansion of the facilities. Actually such reflection of the *sabhās* activities in this respect is found only in some records from Uttaramērūr. An inscription dated year 7 (803) of Dantivarman[48] from the village indicates that in the village there was some land set apart for a sub-reservoir on Paramēsvaravati[49] which was under the control of the *sabhā*. The land, five *pāṭ akam* in extent is stated to have been sold by the *perunguri-sabhā* (a functional aspect of the *sabhā*), to one Svāmi-Kumāra-chaturvvēdi-Sōmayāji, probably a member of the *sabhā* and a shareholder of the village, for building the embankments for the sub-reservoir and for dredging it. But probably the requirement for the reservoir was more extensive that what is reflected in the record as the reservoir was authorised by the *sabhā* to be designated as Svami-Kumara-kuṭṭam after the purchaser of the land. Probably it was a natural depression in the land which Svami-kumāra had to deepen by excavation and bund it up. But even though the *sabhā* had sold the land ear-marked for the reservoir to Svami-kumara, it was not willing to permit the enjoyment of exclusive rights with regard to that reservoir by the purchaser and his off spring just on the strength of this purchase. Another record from the same place dated year 16 (923) of Parāntaka I[50] states that the *mahāsabhā* purchased strips of land from the member brahmins to take out a channel of 2 *kōl* width *(iru-kōl-agalam)*[51] from the main channel Paramēśvaravati. It seems to be indicated that this became necessary as the old channel had dried up and had overgrown with weeds. This purchase was made by order of the mahā*sabhā*ttiruvaḍi (either the *mahāsabhā* itself or the administrator). The land so purchased was made tax-free.[52] The execution of the task was entrusted to the garden committee probably because this channel was to serve the gardens in the village. While this later record evidences the use to which the *sabhā* must have put the gold that it was used to take from several sources, both of the above two record also indicate the rights enjoyed by the *sabhā* in the matter of laying out irrigation facilities though anyone might invest in the expansion of the facilities, the resultant advantage was for the whole village and none could claim exclusive rights. The *sabhā* could take out new channels and claim the land along the channel to be tax-free.

Another inscription from Uttaramallūr dated year 8 (878 ?) of Kampavarman[52a] refers to the *mañjikkam* land meant as *bahirbhūmi* (land in the precincts of the reservoir which could not be put to any other use?), earmarked for putting up a pavilion around the pond Kārigai-kkuṭṭam in the village and its sale by the *sabhā* to a member of the *āḷuṅgaṇattār* of the place, Kuravaśiri Rāmadēvabhaṭṭan and his two brothers, by the process of an auction. This suggests that the land concerned was in the charge of the *sabhā* for carrying out the necessary constructions but it could not do so and hence decided to auction the same to whoever was willing to undertake the construction. But in this case some exclusive rights *(bhattasamantu)*were given over to the purchasers. Anyone infringing on their rights (by spiking that land—the term used is *muḷ-kuttinār*) were to be fined five *kalañju,* which would become the due against free labour (*veṭṭi-mudal*) for the main reservoir, Vairamēghataṭākam.

That the *sabhā* had rights to transfer or confer a part of their rights over the irrigation facilities and the use of water to others especially temples is evidenced in several records of the period.

A Chōḷapuram (Velur taluk, North Arcot district) inscription probably belonging to the time of Parāntaka I[53] says that when the *sabhā* of Vēlūr alias Paramēśvaramaṅgalam sold land for endowment to a temple at that place the *sabhā* of Kañchivāyil and the *sabhā* of Nīḍūr gave channels from the reservoir of their *ūr* for the benefit of the land endowed. The Pāḍi (Tiruvalidayam) (Saidapet taluk, Chingleput district) inscription of the time of Pārthivēndravarman[54] says that when the *sabhā* of Kuṟaṭṭūr alias Parāntaka -chaturvēdimaṅgalam sold their *mañjikkam* land to God Mahādēva of Tiruvalidāyil, they authorised the temple to use the water of the reservoir and channels in the same way as they themselves could do. An inscription dated in the reign of *Vīra-pāṇḍiyanai-ṯalai-koṇḍa* Pārthivēndravarman from Uttaramallūr, which[55] is in the form of a transaction by the *perungurīsabhā,* lists several plots (400 *kuḷi* of III grade, 720 *kuli* of I grade and another 220 *kuḷi* of first grade) allotted by three brahmins (members of the village?) for maintaining the expounding of *vyākarana-śāstram,* as *vyākhyā-vritti* and seems to record the allotment of 15 *kuḷi* from the side of the *sabhā* for taking a channel to feed these lands.

The *sabhā* of another *brahmadēyam* village, Koṭṭūr *alias* Chōḷavidyādhara-chaturvēdimaṅgalam is also evidenced to have provided the facility of taking a feeder channel through their village for one Tribhuvamahādevi-ppēr-ēri at Kūvam *alias* Madhurantakanallūr according to an inscription dated year 5 probably in the reign of Rājēndra I from *Kūram* Chingleput district.[56] The land required was however sold by the *sabhā*.

While it has been seen that there were irrggation reservoirs attached to *brahmadēyams* or *sabhā* villages in Toṇḍaimaṇḍalam with those organisations having some special rights and responsibilities in respect of the irrigation system, some other reservoirs are also seen mentioned in the records of the period. In some cases there is no indication as to the type of organisation in the village benefitting from the reservoir and as to the way the irrgation system based on those reservoirs was administered. But some records also refer to reservoirs attached to *ūr* and *nagaram* villages. In these cases also there is no evidence to indicate as to when and how these reservoirs came into being and if the landholders in the *ūr* and *nagaram* villages also had been conferred rights with regard to the irrigation system. Their rights and responsibilities with reference to the irrigation system came to light in the records which refer to their exercise of these rights and responsibilities. Of them *ūr* is seen to have been having responsibilities for the maintenance of the reservoir attached similar to those of the *sabhā*.

Two records pertaining to the period of Kampavarman, one from Porpandal[57] and the other from Kilputtūr,[58] both situated in Kanchipuram taluk, Chingleput district record the sale of undertakings by the *ūr* of the place to take a pro-rata levy from the fields for maintaining the local reservoir. In the former dated in the king's 2nd year (882?) the *ūr* of Porpondal sold the undertaking to one Valiyāṇai (whose identity is not clear) but it is not stated for what consideration the sale was effected. The reservoir involved was described as Malaiveḷḷap-peruṅguḷam probably indicating that the reservoir stored the water of the floods from the hill, i. e. rain-water flowing from the hill.[59] They were to levy one *kāḍi* (of paddy) per crop *(pū)* per *paṭṭi*. Transgressors of this arrangement were to incur a fine and also to incur the sin of having destroyed Kachchippēḍu (Kāñchīpuram). In the latter dated year 11 (891?) the *ūr* of Kilppudūr is stated to have sold the undertaking to one Mādē-vanār, son of Perumbāṇan śakkaḍi-araiyar having received gold (the amount is not specified again). They were to levy a *kāḍi* per *paṭṭi* of cultivated land, whether it was *(iṛai)* vayal (land paying *iṛai*), *aḍai-nilam* (land mortgaged), *karai-nilam* (land on the borders) *ētta-ppulam* (land maintained by or maintaining picottahas) *dēva-bhōgam, paḻḻichchandam, vaijya-bhōgam* or *pāppanpatti* (land in the possession of brahmins). In effect no land was exempted from the levy for the maintenance of the reservoir. The reference to the sale of the undertaking by the *ūr* concerned to the individual mentioned probably implied that the latter had an interest in the land in the village and had given the amount of gold for capital expenditure connected with the maintenance.

The *ūr* organisation also either set apart land or sold land for being endowed for the maintenance of the reservoirs in their villages. An inscription from Madam, Wandiwash taluk, North Arcot district dated year 26 (896?) of Kampavaraman[60] says that one Jayavallavan, a *vāṇiyar* (merchant) of Kuḷattūr in Tennnaṟṟūr-nāḍu in Paḷkunṟa-kkōṭṭam purchased a *cheṟuvu* (a definite field) from the *ūr* of Kuḷattūr and endowed it as *ēri-paṭṭi*. Probably the land remained under the control of the *ūr* and they had the responsibility for the administration of the endowment. An inscription from Śiṟupākkam in Tirukkōyilur taluk of South Arcot district, dated year 3(959) of Vīra-pāṇḍiyanai-talai-koṇḍa-Parakēsari (Āditya II)[61] records the grant of land by the *ūr* of that village as *ēri-paṭṭi*.

Some records also evidence the enjoyment of the right to transfer or sell their irrigation rights and facilities by the *ūr*. The earliest such instance is probably recorded in an inscription dated year 12(897?) of Aparājita from Tiruvoṟṟiyūr.[62] It says that the *kiḷavar* of Igaṇaimudūr, who was also a *kūḍi* of that *ūr*, which was part of Tiruvoṟṟiyūr-ppuṟam sold some land to one Nirmmalan to enable him to endow the same for the temple called Chola-malliśvaragaram, raised by him and at the same time the kiḷavar gave two big picottahs or picottah operated by two. Considering that the *brahmadēyam* charters prohibited any one other than the donees to operate picottahs etc. to draw water from the channels authorised to the donees, it is to be presumed that the kiḷavar in this case was one who had been authorised to use the contrivance in respect of his land and that he had also the right to pass on a part of his right along with the land sold for endowment. It is not known if the *kilavan* carried out the transaction in his personal capacity or as a representative of the village organisation administering that village.[63] If the latter was the case it can be understood that the village organisation of a non-brahmadēyam type also had received such rights. The land involved also might have been the village common land awaiting reclamation.[64]

Such rights of the *ūr* in the irrigation system is more pointedly become evident in some later records. An inscription of the year 19 (1004) of Rājarāja I from Śīyamaṅgalam (Wandiwash taluk, North Arcot district)[65] records that the *ūr* of Śīyamaṅgalam in Tennāṟṟūr-nāḍu in Palkunṟa-kkōṭṭam sold land against gold endowed for two perpetual lamps in the temple of God Mahadeva in their *ūr* by a veḷḷāḷan. It is stated that the land 1415 *kuḷi* in extent measured by the 16 span rod was such that had to be reclaimed after clearing the woods, levelling the ground and marking the fields through the efforts of the endower.[66] To help in these efforts the *ūr* gave him authorisation to cut a branch channel (of the width of one *kōl* measuring four spans) from another branch channel taking off from the big sluice of the reservoir of the *ūr*. This conveyance of rights was not done *gratis*. The gold paid by the veḷḷāḷan is stated to have covered the price for such authorisation also.[67]

The Bāḍūr (Wandiwash taluk, North Arcot district) inscription of the year 9(994) Rājarājakēsarivarman (Rājarāja I)[68] recording the making over of the reservoir called Araiyan-ēri and the paddy growing land served by it, tax-free in favour of God Tiru-Anantiśvaramuḍaiyār of their *ūr*, by the *Ūrār* of Vaḍavūr in Vadavūr-nāḍu in Veṇkuṇṛa-kkōṭṭam, also seems to indicate the authority of the *ūr* to dispose of the irrigation facilities in the village at their discretion. Another inscription of Rājarāja I dated in his year 18 (1003) from Ārppākkam (Kanchipuram taluk, Chingleput district)[68a] records the purchase of a tank and land made tax-free for endowment for food offerings to God Tiruvīraviṇṇagar-Āḷvār by a certain Araṅgan Kodaṇḍarāman. The service was to be in the name of the queen Śembiyan Mukkokkiḷānaḍigal. Here again it was probably the *ūrār* of the place who made the sale of the tank and land.[69]

From the territorial division called Milāḍu (now in South Arcot district) neighbouring Toṇḍaimaṇḍalam comes another instance of the *ūr* selling irrigation rights. The inscription dated year 22 (929) of Parāntaka I from Siddhaliṅgamaḍam[70] records that the *ūr* of Marudūr in Kurukkai-kk*ūrram* in Milāḍu sold for a specified sum the right of taking water through the sluice of the tank in their village for irrigating the *bali-ppaṭṭi* (land endowed for providing for *śrī-bali* in the temple) to one Iṛaiyāṇ-kuḍi kiḷavan who probably endowed that land for the temple. An inscription dated in the reign of Pārthivēndravarman from Mōraṇam (North Arcot district)[71] records an agreement between the *ūr* of Pulvāypattur and the *ūr* of Moraṇḍattūr regarding the utilisation of the irrigation facilities.

There are two other instances where some individuals on their own are seen to have made grants for maintaining the local reservoir attached to villages about which it is not known if they were being administered by *sabhā, ūr* or *nagaram*. In the year 17 (887?) of Kampavarman, for the upkeep of the reservoir at Kīraippāttur one Diśaṅkan made a modest gift of 20 *kuli* of land.[72] In the year 17 of the Rājakēsarivarman, the wife of one Kumarandai Iravaṇaṇ. of Nāyaṛu in Nāyaṛu-nāḍu in Pulaṛkōṭṭam made a gift of a levy *vāl-amañji* due on the lands belonging to her husband at Kīraippāttūr for the upkeep of the reservoir at Kīraippāttūr.[73] Both the records are from Kīrappākam in Chingleput taluk and district but it is not known what sort of village organisation was in charge of the village. In the same way in Peramanur, in Seṅgunṛa- nāḍu in Kalattūr-kōṭṭam (the village is in the modern Chingleput taluk and district), one Pālikkāranār of that village made an annual grant of 70 (*kāḍi* of paddy)and land as *ēri-paṭṭi* along with the right to the trees therein in the year 15 (923) of Parantāka I.[74] Though in these two cases there is no mention of an *ūr* having been in charge of the villages, it is also observable that there is no indication as to who was made responsible for taking over the endowment and carrying out the maintenance. Hence it seems it was implied that those villages were under *ūr* and that it was to take over the responsibility automatically.[74a]

There is no evidence to the *nagaram* organisation undertaking to maintain the reservoir with the help of donations. The *nagaram* emerged in the field of landholding only about the end of the 10th century. It has also been seen that very often it was the members of the merchant community who made the donations for the upkeep of the irrigation works in the *sabhā* and *ūr* villages. So in respect of villages under their own control they could not have hesitated to use their resources. But this *nagaram* is also seen to have had rights similar to the *sabhā* or *ūr*.

For such rights exercised by the village organisation nagaram, there is the example from Mēlpāḍi (Chittoor taluk and district). Dated year 29 (1014) in the reign of Rājarāja I this record[75] states that the *nagarattār* of Mélpāḍi alias Rājāśrayapuram allotted a total of 5136½ *kuḷi* of land to enable the king to raise a temple of God Mahadeva in that village as a memorial to his grandfather Ariñjaya[76] and provide the various facilities for that temple. Apparently for such land of the God to be utilised for agricultural purposes which included a grove of *iluppai* trees (tree yielding oil-seeds for utilisation in lamps) the *nagarattār* authorised a channel of ¼ *kōl* width to be taken from the river *Nugā*.

It has been seen that the brahmins villages, were also given several irrigation rights to help in the extension of cultivation as also in controlling the locality. The landholders in some other villages are also seen to have been enjoying certain rights. All of them had taken steps to maintain the system and if possible to expand it. But in due course the system seems to have weakened as inscriptions of the tenth century and later evidence the diversion of the funds made available for the upkeep of the system. The Tiruppāṛkaḍal inscription of the time of Parāntaka I[77] as cited above while recording that a deposit of 120 *kaḷañju* of gold by Śenippēraraiyan had been made for defraying the cost of the maintenance of the operators of the boats engaged for dredging also says that the interest from the amount should be utilised for feeding four brahmins in the *śālai* of the temple in memory of four persons who died when they accompanied the above said Pēraraiyan to a battle. An inscription of the time of Tribhuvanachakravartti Kulōttuṅga (year 30-1100?) from

Tīruppāchchūr, Tiruvallur taluk, Chingleput district)[78] also says that a merchant purchased the land which was *ērippaṭṭi* meant for carrying out repairs to the tank at Koḍutalaiyūr, a *dēvadāna* of the temple and endowed it for feeding pilgrims in the temple.

However the irrigation system was such that came into existence during the period was effective enough that the famines noted in the earlier periods of late Sangam (*Maṇimekhalai*) and of Narasiṁhavarman I (middle of 7th century) are not evidenced to have visited the region during the period under study.[78a] Obviously so long as the *sabhās* and other village organisations were well knit and committed to their duties the irrigation system must have been well maintained.[79] Probably it is a tribute to the system that later when the village organisations seem to have degenerated, the irrigation system in Toṇḍaimaṇḍalam is noted to have become forlorn and uncared for. The North Arcot District manual[80] notes that the tank at Kāvērippākkam was found much silted up in the 19th century obviously due to the neglect of dredging during the course of years. The *Chingleput district Manual* written in the 19th century which noted the findings of the administrators of the Chingleput district (then Jagir) at the beginning of the 19th century contains enough indications of the efficient irrigation system that was once there in the region of which only some vestiges were left then to stand witness to the enlightened approach to this problem that the monarchs of the earlier period had.[81]

NOTES:

1. The background for the irrigation in the region and the various irrigation works mentioned in the records of the period are detailed in two appendices to this chapter.
2. Croele, (*Manual of the Chinglepu District,* p. 74 f) says that the river Pālār fills a chain of tanks in its course. In the Chōḷa country the Uyyakkoṇḍan channel feeding several tanks was named after the Chōḷa king (as uyyakkondan). The inscriptions from Pudukkottai state also frequently mention channels named after

the titles of the Chōḷa kings. These were probably provided at the initiative of those kings. Also Gunavardhanae, IHR, Vol. IV, No. 2.

3. Several records refer to provisions made for the dredging of the reservoirs. An inscription dated year 16 (923) of Parāntaka I *(SII.,* VI, 292) indicates that a channel also got silted up and became useless.

4. *EI,* IV, p. 152-153.

4a. Probably this was meant as *ūṭṭukkāl*—the channel which fed (the fields) cf. *SII.,* XIX, 169. From the context it appears that the word could not have meant the spring *(ūṟṟu)*—channel. Apart from *āṟṟukkāl ūṭṭukkāl* and *veḷḷakkāl* which seem to have referred to different types of channels cut from rivers, the Uttaramallūr inscriptions indicate that the term *vati* also indicated a feeding channel from the river to the reservoirs. The same source also refers to *kaṇṇāṟu* or channels drawn from the kaṇ(eye) or sluice on the reservoir and to the arrangement of the fields in squares (*chadukkam*) bordering on these *kaṇṇāṟus*.

4b. In the Kaśākkuḍi and Pullur plates *puḷudipāḍu* is mentioned as a right conferred on the donees. It seems to have meant the right to deposit the mud dug from the channel in the adjacent land and also utilise the mud (as manure?). In the Kūram grant, such land utilised for such purpose seems to have been indicated. cf. Minakshi, c. *op. cit.,* p. 110 also.

4c. Talaivāy (talai-head: vāy = mouth) (*SII.,* VI, 353, 365, 370; *SII.,* III, 187) and *talai—ppēḷai (pēḷai-box)* seem to refer to two parts of the head-water works where from the main channel from the reservoir was drawn. These items also seem to have occupied some land. The Rōyakōṭṭāh plates of Skandaśishya lists *talai-peḷlai* among the different types of land included in the village granted. cf. Minakshi, c, *op. cit.,* p. 106. Probably there was a committee in charge of such *talai-vāy* who were designated as *talaivāy-chachānṟōm*-elders of the *talaivāy.* In Allur, Tiruchirappali district in the time of Parāntaka I, they numbered eleven and held land that was *vett(i)-ppēṟu (SII.,* VII, 689) Also see *Ibid,* 570, and *SII.,* XIX, 49.

5. Apparently the land was in high ground and in consideration of this the authorisation for the picottahs seems to have been incorporated in the grant itself.

6. On one side there was also a road going north from Lōhita-griha.

7. *Yathōpapādam* meant the same thing as *nīr-īnda-valiyāl*
8. Cf. Iyer, KVS, Mannārkōyil inscription of Jaṭāvarman Sundara chōḷa -pāṇḍya *EI.*, XI, p 292 f. He refers to two types of tanks—*punal-kuḷam* (tank fed by rain) and *kāl-varattu-kkuḷam* (Tank fed by a channel) from the river

8a. cf. Little Kanchipuram inscription of the year 37 (944) of Parāntaka I (*AREp.* 1921, 21). A temple of Ananta-nārāyana itself had been built as a dam on the river Tiruvehka.

9. As per the Tamil text the reservoir was named after Tiraiyan. As pointed out above this name was borne by several chiefs from ancient time onwards. One Tiraiyan, the chief of Pavittiri, is referred to in an *Ahanānūru*-poem of the Sangam period. One IḷanTiraiyan (Junior Tiraiyan—probbaly the senior Tiraiyan was his father or grandfather—cf. the title *yuvamahāraja* borne by Vishṇugōpa, a member of the early Pallava dynasty) ruler of Kanchipuram is described in *Perumbānāṟṟuppaḍai* another Sangam work. *Tiraiyan* might also have been a group of people (cf. Mahalingam, T.V., *Kanchipuram in Early South Indian History,* p, 16-17). But as the Tiraiyams or *Tiraiyaṟ* of the Sangam period are not credited anywhere with having made any significant contribution to the irrigation system it is more likely that the reservoir was named after the Pallava kings of the 7-8 century, probably Nandivarman II, The issuer of the Kaśākkuḍi plates, himself or one of his predecessors. However the naming of the reservoir as Tīralaya-taṭāka in the Sanskrit text makes one doubt if the name applied to it in the Tamil text was just fortuituous. An inscription from Tennēri (Kanchipuram taluk, Chingleput district) *AREp.* 1922, 233 seems to refer to the place as Tiraiyanūr and to the lake as Tennēri. This suggests that even a village was named after Tiraiyan. Incidentally this record as well as some inscriptions of the 17th century (*Ibid*, 221, 222, *AREp* ending 31st March 1922, Pt. II, p. 118) evidence the vulnerability of the tank, Tennēri breaching its banks during heavy rains. Each time,a gift of land was made to those who closed the breaches. In the 17th century the reservoir had 23 sluices. Tiraiyan-eri of the Kaśākkuḍi plates might have been the same as Tennēri as the grant village was in Ūṟṟukkāṭṭu-kkōṭṭam near Kāñchīpuram.

10. *Kōlgalam* seems to be an erroneous reading. Considering that several inscriptions recording gifts of land to temples authorise the taking of a channel of ¼ kōl width (*SII.*, III, 15) or one *kōl*

width (*SII.*, VII, 440) and an inscription of the time of Parāntaka I, from Uttaramallūr (*SII.*, VI, 292) records the arrangements made by the *sabhā* to dig a channel of 2 *kōl* width it seems reasonable to read the word as *kōl-agalam* (in the writing on the inscriptions the word can be read both ways). (i. e.) the right granted to the brahmin of Ēkadhīramaṅgalam to have a channel of a *kōl* width dug to serve his irrigation purposes, cf. Minakshi, C. *op. cit.*, p. 110.

11. It would appear that it was envisaged that there would be some old channels which could not serve the purpose of the donees or which would come in the way of the donees and hence they were authorised to fill up these old channels as necessary. Probably it was in the same context that the donees in the Taṇḍantōṭṭam, Vēlūrpāḷaiyam and Chiṭṛūr plates were authorised to fill up water courses (*turavu*) and wells.
12. cf. note 8 above.
13. Obviously bailing with baskets, setting up picottahas and drawing subchannels were the prevalent methods of taking the irrigation water to the fields. Several records speak about the provision of picottahs as benefactious ((*AR Ep.* 1921, 372; *SII.*, III, 10). The picottah seems to have been a simple mechanism which did not call in for the expertise of a class of *odyantrikas*(cf. CII, IV, p. 1-4) who were probably necessary for operating the *araghattas* used in western and central India. The southern-most point where *araghattas* are heard of is Dharwar (EI, XVI, p. 277). *Ēttappulam* (*SII.*, XIV, 102) AREp. 1923, 116), *ēttappāḍu* (Royakottah plates of Skandasishya,) mentioned as types of land were either land fed by picottahs or land set apart to pay the expenses on account of the same. cf. Pillai, K.K., A *Social History of the Tamils*, p. 188, citing the Sangam work, *Madurai-kkanchi* (89-93), he says that even in those early times buckets made of reeds were used to bale water from tanks and reservoirs.
14. Of the four charteṛs issued by the Pallavas of the period outside Toṇḍaimaṇḍalam the Paṭṭattāḷmaṅgalam and Bāhūr plates do not refer to the grant of irrigation rights but refer to tanks, wells, streams etc. as included in the village granted and just say that the donees were entitled to all land cultivated by the supply of water *(nīr-pūśi neḍumbaramberindadu-ellām)*. This absence might have been due to the fact that the former recorded only the confirmation of what was already granted and that the latter

extended a blanket privilege to the grantees of the three village of enjoying whatever they were entitled to in respect of *brahmadēyam* Bāhūr. The other two record the grant of irrigation rights to the donees akin to that granted in the Toṇḍaimaṇḍalam charters the grant villages in both the Taṅḍantōṭṭam plates and the Kumaraḍimaṅgalam plates seem to have had the benefit of the water from the river Kāvēri, so the set of rights was adjusted to the necessities of the situation in those villages. In the former portions of the record having been last in missing plates, the extant portion probably only refers to the drawing of water by a channel direct from the river. This channel was exclusive to the brahmin donees and none could transgress into their channel. In the Kumaraḍimaṅgalam grant significantly only channels already existing are mentioned on the boundaries of the grant village. Again the rights accompanying the grant regarding irrigation conferred on the donees are seen to have been: they could take a channel (from the main channels), they were not needed to do *śennir-ppoduvinai* but could block that water and enjoy it. Others (than the donees) could not bale water with the basket, set up small picottahs and cut subchannels to the channels taken by the donees. "The clause *sennīr-ppodivinai seyyādadāgayum, annīr adaiṭṭu-uṇṇ-pperuvadāgavum,* apparently refers to the grant of an exemption on the one hand and a right on the other. When it is seen that some inscriptions include *sennīr-veṭṭi* (*SII.,* III, 24, 150, 151) and *sennīr-amañji* (*SII.*, VII, 947, *SII.*, VI, 324) among exemptions *(vetti* , *amañji* being free labour), it will be obvious that *śennīr-ppodivinai* must have been an obligation to provide free labour with regard to irrigation facilities. [Among the royal charters granting *dēvadāna*, though the Vēlūrpāḷaiyam plates do not refer to any irrigation rights, Tiruvālaṅgāḍu, plates of Rājēndra I authorised irrigation rights very similar to those granted to *brahmadēyams* in respect of Paḷaiyanūr granted as *dēvadāna* after bringing it under *veḷḷānvagai* from its former status of *brahmadēyam*. A. 13th century inscription from Tīrthanagari, Cuddalore taluk, South Arcot district (*SII.*, XVII, 143) also refers to the grant of the right to the water of the reservoir and channel along with land to a temple by a Pāṇḍya king]. There is no ground to understand the phrase to mean "good water should not be used (*SII.*, III, 24 translation). Minakshi's contention (*op-cit.*, p. 110) on the basis of a mutilated inscription from Kaṇḍiyūr

(SII., V, 572) that *sennīr-ppodivi* was an item of taxation is also untenable. *Sennīr* might have had reference to red or alluvium loaded water.

15. *SII.*, XII, 113, Introduction; though Rāshṭrakuta Dantivarman the grandfather of Dantivarman Pallava as also a ruler of late 9th century had the title Vairamēgha, as the earliest inscriptions at Uttaramallūr are dated in the reign of Dantivarman Pallava, it is likely that the reservoir was named after him or his father. (Cf. Mahalingam, T.V., *Kāñchīpuram* in *Early SI History*, p. 165. He has not given any reference for the inscription of the 2nd year of Dantivarman).

15a. In the light of the title Vairamēgha borne by Dantivarman it can be surmised that the title *Chitramēgha* must have been borne by one of the Pallava rulers. It is not known if one of the two Narasimhavarmans (I—630-668, II, 700-728) bore this title.

16. *SII.*, IV, 137.

17. *Nandikkalambagam*, Verses 18, 44, 46.

18. Dikshitar, VRR, "A History of Irrigation in South India," Indian Culture, Vol. XII, p. 74.

19. *SII.*, III, 181. In the Pāṇḍya country two *nāḍus* were named after reservoirs as Rājēndrachōḷa-kkuḷakkīḷ and Māḍakkuḷakkīḷ.

20. cf. *SII.*, VI, 292. This record from *Uttaramallūr* dated in the reign Parāntaka I detail, the purchase of strips of land from the brahmin members by the *sabhā* for taking out a channel.

21. See note 8 above. It is quite likely that the tanks and wells stated to have formed part of the village granted were those meant for house-hold purposes.

22. *SII.*, XII, 34.

23. The *gaṇattār* appears to have been an earlier version of the *sabhā* as the transaction is stated to have been concluded in the *kuṛi*.

24. *SII.*, VI, 359.

25. cf. Ramesh, KV., A History of South Kanara, p. xxv It appears that this was meant to be a perennial source of income for the purpose.

26. Several records from *Uttaramallūr* evidence the interest in the place shown by merchants from Kāñchīpuram. The cow-shed indicated seems to have been owned by that merchant.

26a. *SII.*, VI, 344.

26b. The record refers to one Muyandin Agambaḍi-uḍaiyān, the *pon* he could get as per the rule *milkavaril-nyāya,* the inability of the *kuḍi* for doing *bhaṭṭa-sāmantu,* to the *sabhā* arranging for the same with the help of the gold due to the individual and finally to the benefit accruing to the reservoir. The signficance of this relation of details seems to be explained by the editor of the *Annual Report* of *Epigraphy* (p. II, p. 128) who remarks, "According to a record of Dantivarman confiscated land (for default) was set apart by the *sabhā* for the tank". If this explanation pertained to the record under discussion, it is very inadequate.

27. *SII.*, III, 5.
28. The phrase used in "*eri-kaṭṭi-ikuttuvippōmānōm*" which has been translated as "shall close (the sluice of) the tank (to collect water for irrigation)" is misleading. The part of this expression i-*kuttuvippōmānōm* can be compared with *kuḷi-kuttuvippōmānōm* meaning digging a pit to describe the act of dredging used in the other records. The initial—*i* in the word as used in the record may be a redundant addition to the preceding word ending in *i*. Also cf. *SII.*, V, 489. Here *ēri kaṭṭi* has been used in the sense of tapping the reservoir.
29. *Ibid.*, VI, 244.
30. *Ibid.*, 348.
31. *Ibid.*, 369
32. *Ibid.*, 375.
33. Probably the person mentioned was the son of the king (cf. the newly discovered Tiruttaṇi plates),
34. *Ibid.*, 325
35. *Ibid.*, V, 1371.
36. As paddy is not known to have been used as currency, the depositors of the paddy in these two instances were either big landlords in the locality or persons, who could or had collected the paddy locally as their entitlement (cf. *SII.*, III,6, 30). If they were persons having a right over the village their investment of a part of their income in works for the betterment of the village might have been in expectation of some return out of this investment. However an inscription dated year 16 of a Parakesarivarman (Uttamaachōḷa?) from Kiḷiyanūr (Tindivanam taluk, South Arcot district) (*SII.*, XIX, 398) says that the *mahāsabhā* of Kiḷinallūr in Ōymā-nāḍu took *vilai-dravyam* (price) from one Śāttan Mallaḍi had sold an undertaking to collect a *tūṇi* of paddy per crop from each *cheṛuvu* (field) growing paddy with irrigated water *(eṅgaḷūr-nīr pūśi-nel-viḷaindānilam)* for the benefit of the reservoir of their

village. The *mahāsabhā* also undertook to pay a fine to *annaḷ-kō,* if they failed in their duty. Probably such of these persons who made deposits for the maintenance of reservoirs were officials of the king and the paddy or price-money given to the *sabhā* for maintenance of reservoirs was part of the royal income, collected from the village or of their own fee authorised to them for the performance of their function. If the former was the case, the depositing of a part of the collection for local betterment might have been part of the royal policy. That this was more likely is indicated in some more records. A Tiruppāṛkaḍal (Walajahpet taluk, North Arcot district) inscription dated year 12 (919) of Madirai-Koṇḍa Parakēsarivarman (Parāntaka I) (*SII.*, III, 99) says that the *Mahāsabhā* of Kāvadippākkam was given 120 *kaḷañju* of gold of 9½ carat *(māṛi)* by Dhīran Śennippēraraiyan, the Araiśūrudaiyan as the capital to pay the operators *(nāyanmār)* of the boats operating in the big reservoir of their village (the boats were to dredge in the various areas of the lake and bring the mud collected to the shore). He was probably an official cum general as he went to the battle when his king was attacked. Also the Tiruvallam inscriptions of the period of Rājarāja I say that another Araiśur-uḍaiyān was an official of the *perundaram* class of royal service-*AREp*, 1921, 218). The official stamp of the transaction is clearly indicated when the record goes on to say that the interest on the amount deposited should be utilised to feed four brahmins in memory of those that fell in the battle. An inscription of the year 4 (1016) of Rājēndra I from Ukkal (North Arcot district) (*SII.*, III, 10) also evidences the purchase of *3000 kuḷi* of land measured by 16 span rod, by Kōmuḷān Araiyan Baladevan of Kuvalaikkōḍu alias Anavaradachōḷanallūr in Kuvalaikkōḍu-nāḍu in Venkunra-kkōṭṭam, a servant of the king, from the *sabhā* of Ukkal, a *tankūṛṛu* for endowment for the maintenance of two boats for the reservoir of the place. Edirvāyir Kaḷumbaruḍaiyār who purchased land from the *sabhā* in an auction and endowed the same for the maintenance of five picottahs as referred to in the same record was also probably acting in an official capacity. He also paid the *sabhā* for making that land tax-free. Two inscriptions from Naṅgāvaram, Tiruchirappalli district, dated in the reign of a Rājākēsarivarman (*SII.*, VIII, Nos. 651 and 652) record the sale of a portion of their common land by the *sabhā* to an official (?) for being endowed for desilting operations in the *kuḷam* of their *ūr*. The land was to yield enough paddy (about four hundred and odd *kalam*) to pay for the maintenance of an *ōḍam,* six labourers to collect silt and deposit it on the shore, a carpenter to keep the boat in repairs, a blacksmith probably for the same purpose and a fisherman to supply the timber (?) and a supervisor to manage the show. The *sabhā* was left in charge of the land and were to cultivate it and contribute the paddy. Also see *AREp*., 1908, p. 49 which also says that fishermen were put in charge of the tank. But such endowments could have been motivated by munificence is also indicated in two undated inscriptions from Uttaramallūr (*SII.*, VI, 353, 357) which record the endowment of 100 *kaḷañju* each by one Anduraiyāvar Dāni Puttaḍigal and his mother respectively. The former is described as our son (*eṅgaḷ maganār*) by the *sabhā*. The former's endowment was for two boats for the dredging operations. His mother endowed for one boat. It is noteworthy that in the last two instances, the *sabhā* took over the gold for the administration of the endowment.

37. *AREp*. 1921, 156. A fragmentary inscription from Kaḷañjūr in the same taluk and district also records that the *sabhā* of the place set apart 780 *kuḷi* of land to be endowed as *ēri-paṭṭi* (land for the reservoir). On the other hand another inscription dated year 24 (931) of Parāntaka I from Veppanganēri in the same taluk and district (*Ibid*., 166) records that the aforesaid *sabhā* of Kāvanūr granted 100 *kuḷi* of land as *ēripa*ṭṭi, probably as generous gesture for helping a neighbouring village to maintain the local reservoir of that place.

38. cf. *SII*., VI, 291. This record from Uttaramallūr seems to say that the *sabhā* sold land earmarked for services in local temples to raise gold to pay the taxes.

39. *SII*., III, 12.

40. cf. Mukhia, Harbans, Presidential Address (Medieval India) *Proc*. IHC, 1979 (Waltair), p. 238.

41. e.g. Tiruppāṛkaḍal (Walajahpet taluk, North Arcot district) inscriptions of the time of Parakēsarivarman (*SII*., XIX, 84, 121, 160, 297).

42. e.g. Guḍimallam inscription of the time of Rājarāja I *(SII*., VIII, 521); also an inscription of the time of Kulōttunga I from Tiruvoṛṛiyūr (*AREp*, 1912, 131). An inscription from Tiruvaṇṇā-malai (Tiruvannamalai taluk, North Arct district) dated year 18 (1030) of Rājēndra I (*SII*., VII, 67) refers to *nīrkk-iṛai* exempted

by several *ūrs* in respect of land endowed to the temple. The Bāhūr (Pondicherry state) inscription of the time Rājarāja I (*SII.*, VII, 805) records the assignment of *ēri-āyam* collected at the rate of a *padakku* of paddy per mā of land by the *peruṇguṛi-sabhā* of that village for the maintenance of the big lake of that *ūr*.

43. *SII.*, VII, 64.
44. e.g. *Ibid.*, III, 24, 150; VIII, 696 (This term occurs in the records of the Chōḷa country),
45. *Ibid.*, V, 572; VIII, 570.
46. cf. *SII.*, III, 24. This inscription from Karūr (Tiruchirappali district) belonging to the early 13th century refers to the grant of the exemption from doing *śennīr-veṭṭi* and right to utilise *punnīr* in respect of land granted to God. Though *punnīr* seems to be differentiated here from *śennīr* the translation of the clause by the editor, "shall not be permitted to waste good water, shall use dirty water" is untenable though in *pun-chey* also, *pun* apparently indicated a contrast from *nan-chey. pun* is not seen used to indicate what is bad.
47. *Ibid*, VII, 805.
48. *SII.*, VI. 365.
49. It has been pointed above how *vati* in these inscriptions seems to have indicated the main channel, either the one connecting the reservoir to the river or the one that emanates from the reservoir. Paramēsvara vati was probably one such and the reservoir mentioned was fed by that channel. It is possible that this land was meant for the maintenance of this reservoir and had been endowed by some one and that it has not been provided for through a share in the charter creating the village. This possibility is indicated when it is seen that in an inscription dated year 49 (845) of the same king from Guḍimallam (Chittoor district), as endowment of *ēri-chcheṛuvu* for the tank Veḷḷēri in Tiruvippiram-bēḍu, a *sabhā* village, was made by a kiḷār belonging to the body of governors of that village. Probably Veḷḷēri was an additional reservoir of the village in need of private endowments.
50. *SII.*, VI, 292.
51. The term used *vati-aṭṭu* seems to have signified such cutting of a channel, cf. *Ibid.*, 316. This inscription of the time of Parakēsari Rājēndra refers to a channel which was Vikramachōḷa-vati. Also *AREp.* 1922,7. However the other term used in these inscriptions *bhaṭṭa-sāmantu* is not capable of explanation.

52. Usually the land occupied by the path of channels was exempted from taxes (cf. *SII.*, II, 4,5 etc.).
52a. *SII.*, VI, 370
52b. It is observable that wherever possible provision was made for the local reservoir. It is not known if Ullayakkūli mentioned in the Kaśākkuḍi plates and *Ugappārpon* (*SII.*, III, 54) had any relevence for the irrigation system.
53. *SII.*, VIII, 9. The name of the king in the epigraph has been obliterated and only Madirai, probably constituting the beginning of Madiraikoṇḍa Parakēsarivarman (Parāntaka I) has been doubtfully read.
54. *SII.*, III, 181.
55. *SII.*, III, 161.
56. *AREp*, 1909, 328. As the record does not provide details about the king the king Rājendra is not, identifiable.
57. *SII.*, XII, No. 97.
58. *Ibid.*, No. 102.
59. Also see *SII.*, III, No. 11 which mentions *Veḷḷakkāi*. The Kaśākkuḍi plates mention the grant of the privilege of digging the *āṛṛukkāl* from Tiraiyaneri and *veḷḷakkāl* (channel to catch the overflow of water) from river Chēyāṛu, Vehkā and Tirayanēri. The Gazetteer of Coimbatore District says that apart from the river Noyyal which when in floods fills up many irrigation tanks there are many rain-fed tanks and large number of wells which rarely go dry.
60. *SII.*, XII, 110.
61. *AREp.*, 1937-38, 380.
61a. *Erippaṭṭi* means a *paṭṭi* of land or some plot of land given for the reservoir. Such attachment of a *paṭṭi* extent of land for any purpose connected with the local reservoir seems to have been the original practice. But it appears that in many of these cases *paṭṭi* did not indicate any definite extent but only land. An inscription from Oḍḍantāṅgal, Gudiyattam taluk, North Arcot district, dated year 23 (930) of Parāntaka I also refers to the grant of *ērippaṭṭi* for closing the breaches of the tanks in *Tū-nāḍu*. Probably here also the intention of the endowment was that the income from the land should be utilised for closing the breaches as and when they occurred.
62. *SII.*, XII, 93.
63. cf. *SII.*, III, 64. This record from Tiruvoṛṛiyūr dated year 2 (1072) in the reign of Rājakāsari Rājēndra (Kulōttuṅga I) reflects that Igaṇaiyūr had an *ūr* organisation.

64. cf. *AREp*. 1922, 7. This inscription dated śaka 1408 (1486) from Tīruvāmāttūr (Viluppuram taluk, South Arcot district) records that the residents of several villages sold small bits of land to the temple treasury for digging a feeder channel from the river to the irrigation tank at Tiruvāmāttūr. Probably the sellers expected the temple to invest the capital in the works for their benefit.
65. *SII*., VII, 440.
66. The land *(cheruvu)* so reclaimed through the efforts of the endower veḷḷāḷan was named after him as Vēṅkaḍan-*mayakkal*.
67. The price paid included the cost of another plot of 187 *kuḷi* also endowed for the same purpose which probably did not need the efforts for reclamation as also the capital for making all the land endowed from *iṛai*. (In inscription dated year 22(929) of Parāntaka I from Siddhaliṅgamaḍam, Tirukkoyilur taluk, South Arcot district in the region adjacent to Toṇḍaimaṇḍalam).
68. *SII*., XIII, 199.
68a. *AREp*. 1923, 139.
69. cf. *Ibid*. 145.
70. *AREp*. 1909, 376.
71. *AREp*. 1965-66, B-154.
72. *AREp*. 1934-35, 20.
73. *Ibid*., 21. Obviously Kamarandai Irāvanan was a person who had a right to collect some levies in that village, cf. *SII*., XII, 86.
74. *Ibid*., 38.
74a. It is noteworthy that none of the records from Toṇḍaimaṇḍalam indicate that in a *ūr* village committees especially the one to take charge of the irrigation reservoir had been formed as in a *sabhā* village. Excepting the inscription dated year 18 (1030) of Rājēndra I from Tiruvaṇṇāmalai, which actually lay in the middle region beyond Toṇḍaimaṇḍalam. (*SII*., VIII, 67), the inscription referring to the exemption from *ūr-kkiṛai* (tax on amount of water) granted in favour of temple-land by several *ūrs* and the two inscriptions from Kīlppudūr and Pōṛpandal referring to adhoc levies authorised to be taken by the *ūrs* there is no other evidence of *ūrs* in Toṇḍaimaṇḍalam having been entitled to take *ēri-āyam* or *ūr-nīr-vilai*. Hence it appears that the *ūr* in Toṇḍaimaṇḍalam was an agency which rather coordinated the efforts in this matter in the village then took initiative on the basis of its being a corporation of the village landholder

75. *SII.*, III, 15.
76. Ariñjaya is referred to in the record as one who died at Āṟṟūr.
77. *SII.*, III, 99.
78. *AREp.*, 1929-30, 121.
78a. Minakshi, 6, op.cit., p. 112, 115. The late *Saṅgam* epic Maṇimēkhalai also refers to a famine at Kāñchīpuram, but the period when the epic was written is uncertain.
79. The hazards to the irrigation system in the region was caused both by excess rainfall and lack of rainfall. The liability of the lands getting sandlogged due to floods is evidenced in an inscription of the time of Pārthivēndravarman from Tiruppāṟkaḍal (Walajapet taluk, North Arcot district) (*SII.*, III, 156) and an Ukkal (North Arcot district) inscription of the time of Rājēndra I (*Ibid.*, 10). The Oddaṅtāṅgal (Gudiyattam taluk, North Arcot district) inscription of the time of Parāntaka I (*AREp*. 1921, 206) refers to the breaches in the tanks in Tūnāḍu and endowment of land made for closing the breaches. Late inscriptions from Tennēri, Kāñchīpuram taluk, Chingleput district) (*AREp*. 1922, 221, 222, 223) also evidence the breaches caused to the reservoir at that place due to floods. Apart from this, as the irrigation reservoirs brought into use during the period studied were based on the rainfed rivers which naturally brought in much mud and silt, they were constantly getting silted up and required periodical dredging and maintenance. While the former contingency had to be met only by ad hoc remedies, for the purpose of the latter the village organisations were indispensible in the absence of an official organisation. Hence when these village organisations lost their vitality, the irrigation system lacked the necessary attention and ran the risk of becoming useless.
80. *North Arcot District Manual* (Vol. 1-2nd edn., p. 438.) The same reference also states that the Mahēndravāḍi tank also was found contracted in size due to silting.
81. *op. cit.*, p. 65, 209, 250. The rulers of the later period are also evidenced to have shown their concern for the extension of cultivation and the upkeep of the irrigation system by extending concessions and making grants. Malaiyaḍipaṭṭi *(Pudukkottai)* inscription of the time of Vīrarājēndra (11th century) (Ins. *from* Pud. *State*, 116) says that lands cultivated by baling water from wells were to pay only half the *kaḍamai* (cf. Dikshitar, V.R.R., *op. cit.*, p. 76. He refers to the statement of Nunis as quoted by

Sewell that Krishnadēvavrya, the Vijayanagara ruler of the late 15th century had constructed a tank at Nāgalāpura and given away lands to people to bring them under the plough with the help of that tank, with an inducement to them in the shape of a concession that the lands would be taxed only after a particular period. He also cites another instance from the Karnāṭaka region (EC, III, Sr. 148) to say that there newly reclaimed land was entitled to a graded assessment, in the second and third years for reclamation, the full assessment being enforced only in the fourth year). But it appears that it was the temples which in the 13th century onward took the initiative in the matter of extending irrigation works and bringing more land under cultivation. An inscription from Vakkaṇāpuram (near Viriñchipuram), Velur taluk, North Arcot district, attributable to the 13th century (*SII.*, I, 65) records an arrangement made by the temple of the place to have a new reservoir (apart from Dēvanēri already existing at the place) constructed to have some land on high ground belonging to the temple reclaimed. The purpose was to have a portion of it set apart as *sarvamānya—iṛai-ili* to support the worship of a new deity set up, and to allot the rest of that and as *dēvadāna* to another deity. With regard to the latter bloc of the land it was stipulated that it could be reclaimed by *kuḍis* who would pay the dues to the temple as follows: in the first year, pay a consolidated levy including all *upādhis* per 100 kuḷi, one *kalam* and 4 *nāḷi* of paddy plus a cess *(viḷukkāḍu)* of ¼ *paṇam*, from the second year, they were to pay only a portion of what is called of the *variśai of kāla-paṛṛu-aṛṛa-magidāri,* (the phrase probably meant that the dues under the head *upādhis* were consolidated into a tribute without reference to the actual produce)—¼ in the second year, half in the third year and in the fourth year and onwards 3/4 of the *magidāri*. The authorities of another temple, as per an inscription of Rājēndra III (again thirteenth century) from Vālikaṇḍapuram, Tiruchirappali District, (*AREp*. 1914-15, B 302) are also evidenced to have fixed the contribution in paddy (obviously in respect of lands belonging to the temple and which had been leased out for reclamation) payable to them at progressive rates increasing every five years upto fifteen years. It is not known if such graded assessment was rendered necessary because the land concerned had to be reclaimed through the efforts of the tenants. Apart from these royal munificance in the later period is also seen to have been directed towards rewarding individuals for their efforts in safeguarding the irrigation tanks rather than in making provision for an enduring arrangement also. An Inscription from Tennēri (Chingleput district) records that an individual had arranged for the closing of the breaches in the tank bund at Tennēri and that Madhurāntaka Pottappichōḷan, the Telugu-chōḍa chief (13th century) ordered a grant of 3 *vēlis* of land to him (*AREp*. 1922, 233- cf. EC. IX., Bg. 77; *AREp*., 1917, 49—This sort of grant of land as reward for contributions to the irrigation system was termed as *dasavanda* or *kaṭṭukoḍage* in 17th century Karnāṭaka). But none of these sporadic efforts could compare with the earlier arrangement by which in situ village organisations were encouraged to take the initiative in the matter of safeguarding the irrigation facilities attached to their villages and maintaining them with constant attention to ensure that there was no disturbance in their agricultural efforts.

CHAPTER—7

TAXES ON LAND—LAND-PRICES

On the system of taxes on land that was in vogue in Toṇḍaimaṇḍalam during the period under study, definite information is available only in the records that pertain to the later half of the 9th century and later. They provide this information in the context of the grant of exemption from taxes in respect of land endowed to temples by several agencies. These taxes on land are seen to have been of two kinds, one, which was the entitlement of the king and the other which constituted the share of the expenses for the discharge of the burden on the whole village in respect of the payments to the local officials and governors like *kō* and in respect of the cost of running the local administration, maintenance of the irrigation facilities and carrying out common and public works which each villager had to bear. This scheme of taxation however could not have been newly introduced in the late ninth century as the records of even the earlier period contain hints about such a two-fold taxation policy. It has been seen that in the copper-plate charters, the list of exemptions or entitlements (*parihāras*) granted to the donees included some charges for local administration (*ūr-āṭchi*) *nāḍ-āṭchi, ūr-kāval? nāḍu—kāval)*. The charters do not indicate as to who was to pay these charges. They were probably payable by all inhabitants including landholders. In the same place some other levies on special utilisation of land by planting flower plants or laying cocoanut or arecanut groves are mentioned.[1] As such planting could have been done only on land. These charges must have been payable only by the concerned landholders. These are usually said to have been payable to the local governor *(kō)* for his enjoyment. Some stone records of the earlier period also refer to the undertakings given by village bodies to maintain the irrigation reservoirs with a *pro rata* levy from the landholders benefitting from those reservoirs. This again pointed to the prevalance of the practice of taking *ad hoc* levies from landholders by the local bodies.

While the charters issued in the 8th century all of which refer to only grants of *brahmadēyam,* indicate the existence of so many miscellanous levies collected from the villager, they do not clear by refer to any land-tax.[2] The few stone records pertaining to that century also do not mention about any land tax. The first such indication to a tax on land seems to be available only in a record of probably early eighth century. It refers to a term which on the basis of the context of its occurrence, is capable of being interpreted as the entitlements of the king from the land.

The record dated year 3 (673 or 731) of a Paramēśvara-varman[3] from Tiruvaḍi (South Arcot district) (i.e.) in the region around Toṇḍaimaṇḍalam,[4] lists the contributions from several pieces of land which are stated to have been granted for the maintenance of the services to the God Mahādēvar at Avinūr. The contributions both in paddy and gold are stated to have been either *talai* (head) or *talaichchemāḍu* (foremost charges?). The record does not refer to any endower of these pieces of land. However it appears that *talai* and *talai-chchēmāḍu* were taxes on the indicated plots which the king made over to the temple through this record. *Talai* in Tamil means head or 'foremost, and *talaichchan* eldest and hence the terms *talai* and *taḷaichacha-māḍu* might have been applied to the land tax, which was to be first charge on the land. If this was so, then these terms can be deemed to have been the earliest to be used in records to indicate the land-tax.[5]

A more definite indication to the land-tax seems to be provided by the Vēlūrpāḷaiyam- plates of Nandivarman III, year

6 (852) which for the first time among these records states that the *pañchavāram* of Tirukkāṭṭuppaḷḷi was 1000 *kāḍi* (of paddy). The *Chiṭṛūr* grant of Nṛipatuṅga (year 6, 865) also refers to the pañchavāram of 750 *kāḍi* payable by a newly constituted *brahmadēyam* village. In both these instances the *pañchavāram* is stated to have been payable to the temple and hence it may appear as if it was the designation by which contribution payable by villages to temples was known.[6] But in both the above instances the records do not state that the contribution to the temple would be paid as *pañchavāram* but that the *pañchavāram* of the village was such and such and that it would be paid to the temple. This indicates that the term *pañchavāram* referred to what had been assessed on the village concerned without reference to its having been gifted as *dēvadāna*. This interpretation seems to be justified when it is seen that an inscription of the year 21 (880) of Nripatunga from Kaṇḍiyūr in Tanjavur district[6a] used the term *pañchavāram* in the place of *iṛai* which is well-known as the main land tax in other records. This Kaṇḍiyūr record states that the *sabhā* of *brahmadēyam* Tirukkaṇḍiyūr sold some plots of land for being endowed to the temple and also mentions the levies *pañchavāram*, *echchōṛu*, *nervāyam*, *veṭṭi*, *vēdinai* etc.,[7] probably as such which had been exempted in respect of the land endowed. Here in the sequence of the list of levies *pañchavāram* is seen at the head. When such a sequence occurs in later records *pañchavāram* is seen replaced by *iṛai*. Tirukkaṇḍiyūr is also not stated to have been a *dēvadāna*. An inscription of the year 3 of Pārthivēndravarman from Tiruppāṛkaḍal (North Arcot district)[8] refers to the committee in charge of the collection of *pañchavāram* (*pañchavāra—vāriya -pperumakkaḷ*) as one of the committees in the *mahāsabhā* village Kāvirippākkam alias Amaninārāyaṇa—chaturvēdimaṅgalam. This village is not known to have been a *dēvadāna* village. This again indicates that *pañchavāram* was the land-tax levied from villages. The said committee in that village seems to have been in-charge of the collection of the main land tax which is otherwise known

as *irai*. On the basis of the above evidence, it can be concluded that about the middle of the 9th century the land-tax especially payable by and in the brahmin villages, was termed as *pañchavāram*.[9]

However it appears that the term came to acquire a specialised meaning as the contribution payable by *dēvadāna* villages to the temple in the tenth century. But even then from the contexts of its occurrence the term still seen to have had reference only to the land-tax. For instance an inscription dated year 10 of Parthivēndravaman from Takkōlam (North Arcot district)[10] refers to the *pañchavāram* paddy that was being measured to the temple by the *sabhā* of Rājamārttāṇḍa—chaturvēdimaṅgalam, the *puram* of Tiruvūral. An inscription of the year 22 (1007) of Rājarāja I from Tiruvallam[11] also refers to the *pañchavāram* paddy payable to the temple at Tiruttikkālivallam by the *Sabhā* of the *dēvadāna* village Mandiram *alias* Jayamēru-Śrikaraṇa-maṅgalam. In these cases also it can be deduced that *pañchavāram* constituted the assessment on account of the land in the village.

Further the records from the middle country as well as from Chōḷa-maṇḍalam refer to the *pañchavāram* payable both by plots of land as well as by whole villages to temples. An inscription from Tiruviḍaimarūdur (Tanjavur district) dated year 3 (959) of *Pāṇḍiyanaitalaikōṇḍa Parakēsari* (Sundara—Chōḷa refers to[12] the *pañchavāram* paddy being paid in respect of a bloc of land which was *dēvadāna- brahmadēyam* to the temple by the *sabhā* of *Tiraimur*.[13] An inscription from Kōnēri-Rājapuram (Tanjavur district)[13a] of the year 7 (977 ?) of probably Uttamachōḷa refers to the *pañchavāram* paddy of 600 and 200 *kalam* respectively payable to the temple by two villages. One of them, Pūṅguḍi consisting of 12 *vēlis* is stated to have been an old *dēvadāna* of God Mahādēva of Tiruvallam and the other was Muśiṭṭaikkuḍi (4 *vēlis*) which, is not stated to have been a *dēvadāna* but it was probably one. [14]Another inscription dated year 16 (1000-1001) of Rājarāja I from Tiruvakkarai (South Arcot district)[15] states that the *ūr* of Maṇali village, which was granted as *dēvadāna* to the God at Tiruvakkarai[16] would pay as *pañchavāram* 1000 *kāḍi* of paddy as also a *paḷḷippēṛu* of 96 3/4/ *kāḍi* of paddy. The manner of mention of the *pañchavāram* dues in these records also suggest that it was the tax-income from the land due to the king which had been diverted to the temple.

Pañchavāram seems to have been so designated either because it was the fifth portion (*pañcha*—five—fifth: *vāram*—turn, portion) due (to the king) or because it was paid in five instalments.[17] It is also noteworthy that in the records of 9th century and sometimes even in the tenth century the *pañchavāram* is quoted in round figures. This indicates that it was in the form of a tribute from land assessed at random without any careful assessment of the yield of the land. When in the Tiruvakkarai inseription the *paḷḷippēṛu* is seen added to the commitment of the village, and it is quoted in more accurate figures, it is indicated this might have been the additional amount found due from that village Maṇali as a result of the survey undertaken during the period of Rājarāja I. Whereas there is a suggestion in the records of the earlier period that *pañchavāram* was the due from brahmin villages, the Tiruvakkarai record designated the dues to the temple from an *ūr* village also as *pañchavāram*.[18]

Though as discussed above, the main tax on land due from some villages in Toṇḍaimaṇḍalam might have been designated as *pañchavāram* from about the middle of the 9th century, the other more well-known term, *iṛai* also seems to have come into use.[19] *Iṛai* is seen to have been used for the first time in an Uttaramallūr inscription dated year 24 (870) of Nandivarman III.[20] The record states that the *mahāsabhā* of Uttaramēru-chaturvēdimaṅgalam resigned (*oḷindom*) (their right to collect) *iṛai* in respect of 3 *pāṭakam* of land purchased and endowed for the God in the temple of Brahmīśvaram in their *ūr*. From that time onwards, this term came to be used more frequently mainly in the context of the freeing of land endowed to God from the liability.[21]

The meaning of the Tamil term, *iṛai* can be derived in two ways. It can be derived from the verbal root *iṛu* which means 'to pay' or from the noun *iṛai* which is applicable to both God and the king. The ancient didactic work in Tamil, *Tirukkuṛaḷ* says that the king can be considered as the *iṛai* of the people, as he regulates their life and protects them.[22] Hence it appears that the king originally charged *iṛai* on the land, as a fee for the protection he gave to the landholders. However the inscription of the year 29 (1014) of Rājarāja I from Tañjāvūr,[23] while referring to the contributions that the villages assigned to the temple were to pay says that the same was the "dues on account of the *kāṇi* which was assessed to pay *iṛai*" (*iṛai.—kaṭṭina-nilattāṟ-kāṇi-kkaḍan*).[24] The said contributions having been the royal revenue from the villages diverted to the temple the description seems to have been meant to explain the character of the *iṛai*. The reference to the *iṛai* as that which was due on account of *kāṇi* suggests that by the time of Rājarāja I, the king had asserted his right as the ultimate landlord and that during this period it was presumed that the several landholders in the villages were supposed to be holding the land as *kāṇi* or assignment against service from the king. This same theoretical basis behind the king taking the *iṛai* as the landlord's portion is again stressed in an inscription of the year 24 (1009) again of Rājarāja I, from Ukkal (North Arcot District)[25] which refers to the landholders in Chōḷa-nāḍu, Toṇḍai-nāḍu and Pāṇḍi-nāḍu as those holding *kāṇi*. Kāṇi having denoted an assignment against service, it is not known as to what service the landholders who held that *kāṇi* obviously from the king were supposed to render to the king apart from managing the land and getting it cultivated.[26] *Iṛai,* which is seen commonly used to denote the tax on land, in its character as the contribution paid to the king is also seen suffixed to words to indicate any tax. The category of the tax is indicated by the Prefix, like *chekk-iṛai*[27]—(tax on the oilpress), *taṛi-iṛai*[28] (tax on the loom) etc. in the records of 10th century and later.

Another term also began to be used in the records from

about the last quarter of the 9th century to denote the tax on land. An inscription dated year 4 (889 ?) in the reign of Aparājita from Satyavēḍu, Ponnēri taluk, Chingleput district[28a] refers to the *puravu* and *pon* due from the village Tuṟaiyūr. Another inscription from Tirupati dated śaka 820 (898)[89] speaks about the *puravu* of 1000 *kāḍi* due from the village Tiruchchoginūr. The Tirumālpuram inscription of the year 14 (984) of Uttamachōla[29a] again says that in the year 21 (892) of Āditya I, the village Śiṟṟiyāṟṟūr was paying a *puravu* of 6000 *kāḍi* of paddy. The Udayēndram plates of Parāntaka I stipulated while adding the village Kadaikkōṭṭūr to the *brahmadēyam* Udayachandramaṅgalam, that the *puravu* would be 1000 (kāḍi ?) (*āyira-ppuravināl*). The Shōliṅghūr (North Arcot district)—inscription of the year 9 (916) of Parāntaka I[30] states that the *puravu,* calculated at 1/6 (of the produce) *(aṟu-kūrināl)* on the field *mungilvari* as also other taxes on the same would be utilised for the maintenance of the reservoir, Chōḷavāridhi. Apparently, the *puravu* in these instances denoted the same thing as *pañchavāram* or *iṟai*. It is also observable that just as in the Vēlūrpāḷaiyam plates, in the above instances where the amount of the *puravu* is quoted it is seen given in thousands of *kāḍi* of paddy. But it is not known why in these cases this term was preferred to the other terms and whether this term had a regional significance. Under the Chōḷa administration there was an official designated as *puravu—vari—tiṇaikkaḷa—nāyakam*, (the head of the establishment, concerned with the *puravu*—taxes).[31] It is noteworthy that no such official was connected with *iṟai*. Hence it can be surmised that *puravu* was the official designation of the land-tax during this period and that *iṟai* was more a general term for indicating the taxes. The derivation of this word *puravu* however, is uncertain[32]. The Shōliṅghūr inscription cited above indicates that the *puravu* dues alone was collected at the rate of 1/6 of the produce.

These same references as cited above also indicate that the charge on land was not confined to *pañchavāram, iṟai* and *puravu*. The Satyavēḍu inscription of the time of Aparājita year

4 (889 ?) says that the village Turaiyūr had to pay *puravu* and also gold. The Tirumālpuram inscription of Uttamachōla (year 14 (984) says that in respect of the portion of *Śiṟṟiyāṟṟūr* attached as *dēvadāṇa-brahmadēyam* to the *sabhā* of *brahmadēyam* Puduppākkam in the time of Āditya I (year 21 and 22-891-892) the contributions due were fixed at 3000 *kaḍi* of paddy as *puravu*, 561 *kāḍi* of paddy as *iravu* (lit. what is begged for—benevolences?) and. gold, at 26½ *kaḷañju* and a *mañjāḍi* (ie) (26 *kaḷañju* and 11 *mañjāḍi*). The Shōlinghūr inscription of Parāntaka I, refers to the *āyadi* (the *āyam,* income other than the landtax) and *pon* payable on the field *mūṇgil-vari,* The Tiruvakkarai inscription of Rājāraja I records that the *ūr*. of Manali had to pay besides the 1000 *kāḍi* as *pañchavāram,* 96¾ *kāḍi* of paddy as *pallippēṟu* and *kāśu*(gold bullion by the weight)at 9 1/8 *kaḷañju* to which a *vāsi* half time over was added to make it 13 kaḷ*añju*, 13 *mañjāḍi* and 6 *mā*. The Tiruvālaṅgāḍu plates of Rājēndra I says that the *irai* payment due from Paḷaiyanūr was 3288 *kalam, 7 kuruni, 5 nāli* of paddy as also *pon*, 193 *kaḷañju* one *mañjā*ḍi and one mā. It is stated that this due included *palli* which term however is obscure.[33] It is apparent from these references that from about the last quarter of the 9th century the king began levying some 'additional charges in the shape of gold or even additional paddy from the landholders on the basis of their holding of land.[34]

Another term used in the records in connection with the assessment on land presents a puzzle. The term, *mudal*, is found used for the first time in the Tiruttani inscription of the year 18 (903 ?) of Aparājita.[35] It says that Nambi Appi, the donor purchased the *cheṟuvu* (field) to the north of the temple amounting to 100 *kuli* from the husbandsmen *(kuḍi-makkaḷ)* of Tiruttaṇiyal, sold the iṟaimudal accruing in respect of that land and paid gold to the *sabhā* to make the land *iṟai-ili*. Here the significane *of iṟai mudal* is not clear. Another inscription dated the year 7(963) of *Madirai-koṇḍa* Rājakēsari from Vēḷachchēri (Chingleput district).[36] It refers to the undertaking by the *sabhā* of the place to the effect that in respect of land they had sold after freeing it from taxes for endowment, if any one showed any *iṛai,* he could be fined 200 *kāṇam* as *dhanmāsaṇa-mudal,* by the *pan-māhēśvaras*. In the mention of *mudal* in this record there is a suggestion that it meant a fine or the income. However, the Tirumālpuram inscription of Uttama-chōḷa[37] refers to the assessment of 3000 *kāḍi* of paddy on the *kāṇi* of the *kiḷāṇ* of śaṅkarappāḍi as the *puravu* which was accruing (*varugira*) as *mudal*. When it is seen that the puravu payable by the land that was the kāṇi of the kiḷāṇ is stated to have been the *mudal* and not the payments due from the rest of the land in that village, it appears that in this case the *mudal* referred to the consolidated assessment combining the *iravu* and gold levies as well as the *puravu* assessment.[38] The inscription of the period of Rājarāja I from Tañjavūr[39] while referring to the dues payable by the village Tiruttēvankuḍi says that the same had been earlier allotted to Kaḍadēvar but was misappropriated and was at the time of the grant brought under *veḷḷānvagai* as a different *mudal* (*vēṛu-mudalākki*) and then the *mudal* was also excepted *mudal—ṭavirndu*). Thereafter the record says that the usual *iṛai-ili* land, the homesteads (*ūr-nattam*) and the cremation ground, was deducted from the total land as measured in the village and the tax payable to the temple was fixed. The Tiruvālaṅgāḍu plates of Rājēndra I also says that the village on being converted from *brahmadēyam* to *vellāṇvagai* was made into a different *mudal* (*veru-mudalāy)* with the *mudal* consolidated (*mudal-śurukki*) and with the *mudal* excepted (*mudal-tavirudu*) was assessed to pay a fixed tax *(ninriṛai*) to the temple. One more instance of the mention of *mudal* can also be quoted for whatever light it throws on the meaning of the term. As inscription from Tirunāmanallūr (Tirukkoyilur taluk, South Arcot district) dated year 18 (1003) of Rājarāja I[40] says that the officer Pallava-muttaraiyar while examining the affairs of the temple found that there was no *mudal* in respect of the paddy and gold payable, as the *mudalulvari* of the *ūr* and hence had the land in Tirunāvalūr measured and then fixed the paddy and gold payable and had the same entered in the register (*variyilidu*).

Hence in the light of these records it appears that originally *mudal* meant the total assessment on land on the king's account[41] and by the time of Rājarāja I at the end of the tenth century, when the administration was streamlined, the term began to indicate a classified head of account. This meaning will intelligibly explain the words *vēru-mudalāy* and *mudal tavirndu*[42] as indicating bringing of the tax under a different head of account and the deleting of it under the original head respectively.

Apart from the taxes due to the kind as mentioned above the charters of the period also reflect that the land was also burdened with several charges which were for local utilisation.[43] Among such charges the *ūrātchi* (charge on account of the administration of the *ūr*) *nāḍ-ātchi* (similar charge in respect of the nāḍu) and *nāḍu-kāval* (charge on account of policing of the nāḍu) mentioned among the *parihāras* in the copper-plate chartes do not figure in the transactions recorded on stones, either as those from which the temple lands were freed or otherwise. Probably these charges were not based on land alone but were leviable from all inhabitants of the village whether they were holding landor not.[44] Further these charges were not probably levied in each village which may explain the absence of mention of these charges in the villages wherein transactions have been recorded in stone inscriptions.

Information about the other local charges on land, actually find mention in the records in the context of the freeing of land endowed to temples from the various burdens. The earliest pointed mention of such freeing from several miscellaneous charges besides *irai* is probably found only in the record from the Chōḷa country.[45] As already mentioned above in the year 21 (880) of Nṛipatuṅga Kaṇḍiyūr Tanjavūr district) inscrip-tion referred to *echchōṛu, nervāyam, veṭṭi, vēdinai* and *śennīr—ppodivi* (*nai*) as levies in addition to *panchavāram* from which the *sabhā* of that place exempted the land endowed to that temple. This was in Chōlanadu. Among the records pertaining to Tonḍaimanḍalam, an inscription of the year 14 (884 ?) of

Kampavarman from Kāvantaṇḍalam (Kāñchīpuram taluk, Chingleput district)[46] mentions only *śōṛumāṭṭu* besides *irai*, which the *sabhā* of chaturvēdimaṇgalam undertook not to show against two *paṭṭi* of land purchased and endowed for a temple by a Mānasarppan, having recived a capital against those taxes (*irai—kāval*) from the endower. An inscription of the year 21 (891 ?) of the same king from *Uttaramallūr*[47] includes this *sōṛumāṭṭu* among *pura-irai* (external levies), which included other charges *manai-pon* (gold levy on homesteads) and *alp-iṛai*. The *sabhā* of the place was pleased to grant exemption from these levies in favour of one Mannipāk-kiḷān-kōyil, a resident of the southern merchant quarter at that place in appreciation of the several endowments, he had made for the upkeep of the local reservoir Vairamēgha-taṭākam. The *sabhā* however, decided to collect the bare *iṛai* from him. Of these three items of extra or external levies which the *sabhā* is seen to have been competent to dispose of at their pleasure, *manai-ppon* did not pertain to the agricultural land but the other two probably did. A*lp-irai* could be construed as referring to the minor or subsidiary *iṛai* like *iravu* or *pon* payable to the king but for the fact that it is reflected in the record to have been capable of being appropriated and also disposed off by the *sabhā*.

Inscriptions of the tenth century give more definite information on the charges leviable by the village organisations from landholders for local utilisation. An inscription of the year 37 (944) of Parāntaka I from Ukkal[48] records the grant of a hamlet for the conduct of the services in a local temple by the *sabhā* of Śivachūlāmaṇi-chaturvēdimaṅgalam alias Śrī-Vikramābharaṇa-chaturvēdimaṅgalam (Ukkal). The *sabhā* assured that they would not show *iṛai* against that hamlet and that they had issued an injunction *(niyōgam)* to the committees in charge of annual affairs, reservoir and gardens respectively to desist from taking *veṭṭi, vēdinai* and *vālakkāṇam* from the *kuḍis* colonising the *ūr*. Eleven inscriptions dated in the reign of Partihvēndravarman from Uttaramallūr[49] mention *echchōṛu, veṭṭi* and *amaṇji* besides *iṛai* as the levies from which the *sabhā* granted exemption in respect of land endowed to temples in that village. One of them[50] indicates that all the levies chargeable on account of the king were classed as *iṛai* by refering to "whatever *iṛai*" before mentioning *echchōṛu* etc. There is, however, no consistency in the listing of the charges other than *iṛai*. Whereas one inscription of the time of the same king from the same place[51] leaves out *amañji* from the list, another inscription of a Parakēsarivarman[52] from the same place leaves out echchōṛu from the list. An inscription of the year 7 (964) of *Madirai-koṇḍa* Rājakēsari (Sundara-chōḷa) from Vēḷa-chchēri (Saidapet taluk, Chingleput district[53]) adds *vēdinai* and *antarāyam* to the list. An inscription of the year 3 of a Parakēsarivarman from Śīyamaṅgalam (Wandiwash taluk, North Arcot district)[54] records the exemption from the levies *iṛai*, *echchōṛu*, *veṭṭi* and *amañji* in respect of two *cheṛuvu* granted as *dēvadāna,* which the *ūr* of the place undertook not to show the levies against those plots. Another record dated year 5 of a Parakēsarivarman from the same place[55] refers to the levies, *chilliṛai*, *sōrumāḍu, veṭṭi*, *muṭṭaiāl, śennīramañji* as the additional levies. The inscription of the year 23 (962) of Krishna III from *Uttaramallūr* again,[56] while listing the levies which the *sabhā* of the place state that it was eligible to collect from a hamlet of the village Uḷḷiyūr and to gift at their pleasure, mentions *tiṅgaṭchōṛu* (lit. monthly food) and *Senniramanji*[57] both of which levies seem to have had relation with the land and *ēr-kkāḍi* (a Kāḍi of paddy on the plough) and ēr-*ppon* (a gold levy on the plough) which seem to have been levies on the agriculturists. An inscription of the year 4 (898) of the period of Rājakēsarivarman Rājarāja I) from Guḍimallam (Chittoor district)[58] mentions only *aśuviṭpēṛu* (The enjoyment of *ājivika*s ?) and *nīr-vilai* (price of water) as the levies from which the *sabhā* of Tiruvippirambēḍu undertook to protect the land endowed to the temple. Of these two, while *nīr-vilai* as a charge for water could have been meant to be utilised for the maintenance of irrigation works, the destination and purpose of the levy, *aśuvippēṛu* are uncertain. The records pertaining to the period, tenth century, from the Uraiyūr and other regions[59] of Chōḷa-nāḍu also refer to similar levies in respect of the land.

Of the above-said levies *echchōṛu, śōṛu-māṭṭu* and *tiṅgaṭ-chōṛu* seem to have indicated either the same levy or at least similar levies. It has been surmised[60] that *echchōṛu* was a levy taken from the landholders for feeding the officials (of the king) visiting the village for the collection of the government dues. But when it is seen that this levy is found mentioned in the context of only a few villages it seems also possible that this might have had a local and restricted significance and was probably required by the village organisation to defray the expenses of feeding some people in the village itself. Probably the people who were, so fed were the ones engaged for carrying out the community works in the village.[60a] Even if it was so *echchōṛu* seems to have been only one of several levies taken on account of the obligation of the village organisations to manage the public works in the village. The levy *veṭṭi* in the list was obviously the Tamilised form of *vishṭṭi*—forced labour or *corvee*.[61] *Vēdinai* and *amañji* or *āl- amañji* are also understood as some form of labour required to be contributed by the landlords.[62] It is noteworthy that the Śīyamaṅgalam inscription of Parakēsarivarman (year 5)[63] mentions *sennir-amaṇji* and *muṭ ṭai-āḷ* and leaves out *amañji* and *vēdinai*. It is not known if the former two were the same as the latter two. It has been noticed that the Ukkal inscription of the period of *Parāntaka* I mentions *vālakkāṇam*, a *kāṇam* or cash levy in the same context as *veṭṭi* and *vēdinai*. The exact significance of the levy is not known but it might have been a compounded payment taken in cash.

But the puzzling point is that the village organisation stood in need of four kinds of free labour and there is no explanation as to the tasks against which each of the four kinds of free labour was and there is kno explanation as the tasks against which each of the four kids of free labour demanded. One task for which free labour must have been required was the maintenance of the irrigation works and regulation of water supply. It is not known as to which category of free labour was meant for this work. Whereas the Śīyamaṅgalam inscription by mentioning *śennīr-amañji* (*amañji* for goodwater) suggests that *amañji* was the category meant for the task, some Tiruchirappalli district inscriptions refer to *śennīr-veṭṭi* suggesting that it was *veṭṭi* which was required for the maintenance of irrigation works.[64] Ordinarily it can be imagined that one of these kinds of free labour would have been required to work the lord's land in the villages. But in the context of Toṇḍaimaṇḍalam during the period under study the records do not reflect the existence of royal demesne or lord's land in villages. It is also noteworthy that the plots of land involved in the transactions noted above, which were freed from the obligations were part of a *sabhā* village mostly and often the possessors of the land previous to the transfer to the temple were the brahmins, who had probably recieved the land as *brahmadēyam*. It is not imaginable that they were asked to provide free labour for a non-existant lord. It is possible, however, that at some earlier time there was such lord's land in villages, for cultivating which the landholders were obliged to provide *veṭṭi* or freelabour but in course of time such obligation was diverted to other channels and also probably compounded into cash payments and got attached as levies on land even when such lord's land ceased to exist in villages. From the evidence of the Ukkal inscription noted above it also seems that these local charges on land were earmarked for and appropriated by the reservoirs, gardens and annual committees of the village organisation for financing the execution of their commitments.

Besides the above two clear categories of levies, one meant for the king and the other for local appropriation, the records also reflect other charges on land whose destination has not been clearly indicated. One such charge was *antarāyam*.

Even among the records referred to above it has been noticed that the Vēlachchēri inscription of *Madirai-konda* Rajakēsarivarman (963) adds the levy *antarāyam* after mentioning *echchōru* etc. among the taxes which were exempted in respect of the land given over to the temple, suggesting that *antarāyam* was a levy for local utilisation. This is perhaps the earliest mention of the levy in Toṇḍaimaṇḍalam. Thereafter the records of 11-13th century frequently mention this *antarāyam* in the context of levies taken on behalf of the king or in the context of levies for local utilisation or as the designation of a group of levies.

Chronologically the next occurrence of the term among the records of Toṇḍaimaṇḍalam is in an inscription of the year 3 (1071) of Adhirājēndra from Tiruvallam[65] where it is stated to have been the nomenclature of a class of levies meant to be remitted to the king. *Antarāyam* is no doubt a term adopted from Sanskrit but the significance of the word even in Sanskrit is twofold depending on whether the word is taken as a single one or as a compound. The single word means obstacle—*badha*, *upādhi*.[66] The compound word consists of two words *antar* and *āyam* together meaning internal income. If the word is taken to have been derived from the compound, originally *antaṛāyam* could have meant only a charge for internal or local consumption.[67] But in the light of the above records it appears that in course of time the original significance of the word seems to have been lost sight of and the word came to signify any tax. However, from the above quoted instances it would also be apparent that there was no definiteness about what was intended to be signified.[68] This may be compared with the changes in the destination of the charges *echchōṛu*, *veṭṭi* which originally must have been charges for local utilisation and in course of time also had become like any other tax at the disposal of the king. Thus it can be concluded that as suggested by the Vēḷa-chchēri inscription of Madirairkoṇḍa Rājakēsariuarman, *antarāyam* was initially meant to be a tax for local utilisation and that in course of time the term came to signify a mere tax leviable on behalf of the king[69] or as the designation of a group of taxes.

Just like *antarāyam*, another word *pāṭṭam* is also seen

used initially as a tax-term indicating a levy for utilisation by the villages which in course of time came to signify a tax[70] that was to go to the king. An inscription of the year 11 (881 ?) of Kampavarman from Tiruvoṟṟiyūr[71] refers to several amounts of paddy payable by the village Muḍipaṭṭi and other villages. These contributions of paddy are termed as *pāṭṭa-nel* and the record seems to reflect that these contributions were payable to the village organisation *ūr* of Vaikkāṭṭūr, one of the *dēvadāna* village, as the village organisation probably showed this income as a guarantee for its carrying out a benefaction in the temple against gold taken over by it.

THE RATES OF THE TAXES ON LAND

It has been pointed out above that some records like the Vēlūrpāḷaiyam plates of Nandivarman III, the Chitṟūr plates of Nṛipatuṅga and the Udayēndram plates of Parāntaka I give an indication of the total amount assessed on villages involved in the grants. The Vēlūrpāḷaiyam plates say that the *pañchavāṟam*[72] due from Tirukkattuppalli was 1000 *kāḍi* (of paddy). The Chiṭṟūr plates enjoined on the new *brahmadēyam* Pirudi—Mādēvi-chaturvēdimaṅgalam to pay a *pañchavāram*[73] of 750. kāḍi to a temple. The Udayēndram plates of Parāntaka I merely state that the village Kaḍaikkōṭṭūr was added as a *brahmadēyam* to *brahmadēyam* Udayachandramaṅgalam with the stipulation of 1000 *puravu*[74] (i.e.) in respect of that village 1000 (*kāḍi or kalam*) of paddy should be paid as *puravu*. These records do not however give the total extent of land in these villages and hence it is not possible to know at what rate this total due had been computed. It is possible that the tax was fixed on the village as a whole without computing the taxes on each field contained in the village. The Vēlūrpāḷaiyam plates and the Chiṭṟūr plates enumerate several levies under the head of exemptions *(parihāras),* which were apparently not based on land. The charters do not however give the rate of collection of these levies. These were probably ad hoc levies and hence the amount of collection must have been uncertain. The Udayēndram plates do not refer to these levies at all.

The Tirumālpuram inscription of the time of Uttama-Chōḷa (year 14 (984)[75] which refers to the village *Śirriyārrūr* excluding the *kāni* of the *kiḷān* of Sankarappāḍi having been given over to *brahmadēyam* Puduppākkam in the year 21 (892) of Aditya I, as *dēvadāna brahmadēyam*, says that in respect of this portion of Siṟṟiyāṟṟūr made over as *dēvadāna- brahmadēyam*. A *puravu* of 3000 kāḍi, an *iṛavu* (benevolance ?) of 54 *kāḍi* both in paddy and gold amounting to 26 *kaḷañju,* 11 *mañjāḍi* would be paid to the temple. The record indicates that all the three *puravu*, *iṛavu* and *pon* levy were charges on land (the record also indicates that the land under the *kāṇi* of Sānkarappāḍi-kiḷān was exempt from *iravu* and *pon* levy) but as the record does not indicate the extent of land involved the data is incomplete to ascertain the rates of these levies.

However an inscription dated year 9 (916) of Parāntaka I from Shōliṅghūr (North Arcot district)[76] gives an indication of the rate at which the tax *puravu* was collected during that period. It records an authorisation to appropriate the *puravu* of the sixth part *(aṛu-kūrināl puravum*) as also other incomes (in paddy ?—*āyati*) and the gold (levy) from a field called *mūṅgilvari* for the maintenance of the local reservoir by the king. Though the record does not give the extent of the field, it is significant that it says that the *puravu* was computed at a sixth part of the yield, which seems to have been in conformity with an age-old norm.[77] But it is not known if the computation of *puravu* was done every year after ascertaining the total yield of the land or had been calculated on the basis of the yield in a normal year. The record does not also indicate the rate at which the other charges *āyati*[78] and *pon* were collected. It does not appear possible that the 1/6 norm applied in the case of these levies also as there is no indication that these levies were based on any yield.

In the light of the Sholinghūr record it appears that, during this period and possibly earlier and later also, in so far as *puravu* assessment was concerned, it was normal for the king to collect as his due a sixth of the produce of land. In the Udayēndram plates, where the tax due is again termed as *Puravu* there is a likelihood that instead of reflecting a random assessment, the 1000 (*kāḍi* or *kalam* of paddy) *puravu* that was due in respect of Kaḍaikkōṭṭūr, had been arrived at after a careful assessment of the yield of the land in the village in a normal year, which was rounded off to suit some convenience. Probably this sort of assessment on a village-wise basis was done in respect of such villages which were under the management of a village organisation.[79] However there seems to have been a difference in the mode of assessment as between the villages where in the plots of land were individually assessed and those which had been assessed as whole villages where those were managed by village organisations. While assessing the tax-dues for the whole village in the latter type of village, it appears that both the land already under actual cultivation as well as the land yet to be brought under the plough had been taken into account.[80] It is possible that this phenomenon was due to these whole villages having been those involved in the charters of the period and having been mostly virgin awaiting reclamation through the agency of the donees. The taxes paybale in the case of the latter type of villages seem to have been fixed on an approximation at a round figure at the outset. This will explain the various instances recorded in inscriptions wherein the *sabhā* or *ūr,* is stated to have taken a capital against the taxes before granting tax-free status to plots of land, which were still to be reclaimed before their grant to temples.[81] So even supposing that the 1/6 norm was kept in view while assessing the main land-tax (*puravu*) payable by these villages, the actual burden devolving on plots actually under cultivation in these villages might not have been restricted to the 1/6 of the produce. As the village organisation concerned had to collect from these holders of land under cultivation at a particular time, the whole amount fixed for the village including the cultivated and uncultivated parts, the tax-burden divided among the land-holders of the cultivated parts must have been higher than 1/6 of the produce.[82]

As said above, the Sholinghūr and Tirumālpuram records

or any other record of the period do not indicate either the total amount due or the rate of collection of the additional levies on land, *āyati* or *iravu* and *pon* due to the king and the other charges due to the local organisation. However, an inscription dated year 3 (1070) of Adhirājēndra from Tiruvallam[83] says that the rate of miscellaneous levies under the heads *antarāyam* and *kīlịrai-ppāṭṭam* which from the nomenclature of the levies included under each head[84] do not appear to have been related to land, was 25 *kāsu* per 1000 *kalam* of paddy. This paddy base for the extra levies was probably amount of paddy that was being paid as *pañchavāram*[85] as the record says that the total dues on this account from two *dēvadāna* villages, Mandiram and Kukkanūr were only 26¾ and 38 *kāsu* respectively, which indicate a base of 1070 *kalam* and 1530 *kalam* of paddy respectively. Thus this record supplies the useful information that at least the various miscellaneous levies chargeable originally on artisans, professionals and on other accounts in course of time, came to be related to the main tax on land, a pro rata tax in cash having been taken.[86] This inscription belongs to the third quarter of the 11th century and it is not known from when on this practice of relating the miscellaneous levies to the land tax had started. From this it also appears that the additional cesses based on land taken by the king were also related to the main land-tax.

ESCALATION OF TAXES ON LAND:

Though the information regarding the tax structure and quantum of the taxes on land during the period under study is meagre and incomplete, a scrutiny of the records even as available from Toṇḍaimaṇḍalam and cited above indicated that there was a gradual increase in the burden of the taxes, that the land had to bear.

It has been stated above that prior to about the middle of the 9th century, no record available clearly points to the system of the taxation on land and that the *taḷai-chchemāḍu,* a contribution in paddy, and gold which several plots of land were asked to pay to the temple as per the Tiruvaḍi inscription of the time of Paramēsvaravarman[87], (either the first 670-800 or the second 728-731) might be the earliest epigraphical reference to the tax on land. Whereas even this early inscription seems to indicate that there were paddy and a gold levy on land, the VēlūrPālaiyam plates dated more than a century later than the Tiruvaḍi record (852) seems to suggest that there was only a paddy levy on land termed as *pañchavāram*. But the Satyavēdu inscription of the year 4 (889 ?)[88] of Aparājita indicates again that there was a double levy, one in paddy *(puravu)* and the other in gold *(pon)* on the village land. Hence it can be said that upto that period the general practice was to take a tax in paddy and a tax in gold from the land with some exceptions like the village Tirukkāṭṭuppaḷḷi where only a levy in paddy was taken. Soon after the period of Aparājita when Chōḷa Aditya I stepped into the scene, an additional levy in paddy called *iravu* seems to have been imposed on land as the Tirumālpuram inscription of Uttama-chōḷa says that in the year 21 (892) of Aditya I, the *sabhā* of Puduppākkam was asked to pay *puravu iravu* and *pon* in respect Siṟṟiyāṟṟūr excepting the *kāni* of the *kilan* of saṅkarappāḍi attached to it as *dēvadāna-brahmadēyam*. Here again the *kāṇi* of Saṅkarappāḍi-kilān seems to have been an exception as it is stated that only *puravu* was due from that land. This record reflects that the number of levies and the rate held good in respect of at least Sirriyāṟrūr for nearly a century till 984 in the reign of Uttama-chola. The Shōliṅghūr inscription of Parāntaka I (916) refers to the second levy in paddy as *āyati*. Probably it was the same as *iravu*. It may also be the same as *siddhāyati* which is stated to have been due along with *puravu* and p*on* to the temple of Tiruv*ūr*al—Mahādēva from the *ūr* of Kayattūr, the *puṛam* of the temple. But this *siddhāyati* is said to have been a class of levies including *māṭṭukkaṛai* and *tokkai-kunṛi*. However there is no reference to *iravu* in these records. Thus though *āyati* and *siddhāyati* might have been different from *iravu*, it is clear that on account of the king or in his place the temple, during this period, only three kinds of levies *puravu iravu* or *āyati* or *siddhāyati* and *pon* were due from the land. It also appears that the rate of each levy remained constant. As the Tirumālpuram instription of Uttama-chōḷa (984) reflects that even until that year the barden on the land due to the taxes had not changed since the time of Aditya I (892), it can be presumed that generally there was no escalation in the tax-burden on the land during this whole period of nearly a century.

It appears that only in the subsequent period there was remarkable escalation in the burden on the land. As pointed out above the Tiruvallam inscription of Adhirājēndra (1079) indicates that there were two classes of levies, *antarāyam* and *Kīl-iṛai-pāṭṭam* due to the king. The rate of the levies had been based on the main land-tax and hence it appears that these levies had been added as the burden on the land. These two classes of levies seem to have been originally the taxes on artisans and the collections on account of fines, as *antarāyam* is stated to have included *taṛippuḍavai, vēli-kkāsu. daṇḍalir-kaḍamai and valaṅgai-iḍaṅgai-magaṇmai,* and *kil-iraippāṭṭam*, the levies, *ūrkkaḷañju, kumara-kachchāṇam, miṅ-pāṭṭam and taṭṭār-pāṭṭam.* The collections on these accounts must have been irregular when they were leviable from the classes of people indicated. On relating them to the main land-tax, the king had sought to ensure for himself a regular income and probably they were charged on the land as additional levies without any consideration of their original significance[89].

As this addition of the burden on the land seems to have been done only between the years 984 and 1070, it appears that during most of the period under study the tax-burden of the land was stable and escalations were done only in the succeeding period[90].

It may be observed from the foregoing discussion that it was the village organisations which were concerned with the taxes. As pointed out earlier the assessment of taxes on land due to the king was done on village-wise basis. The responsibility for its apportionment to and collection from the land-holders in the village were left to the corporate body of the village. Where the corporate body was not expected to be formed and the individual landholders had direct relationship with the king as it seems to have been case when the land was held under the *vellānvagai* tenure, probably a security against the taxes was taken from the landholder. This seems to have been excused if the corporate body of the village was there to be relied upon for the collection of the taxes in the village and its payment to the king[91].

PRICE OF LAND:

Though several of the records of the period refer to the purchase of land for endowment to temples, there is only scanty data available for deducing the general trend in the price of land during the period under study. The reasons for this phenomenon is not far to seek. For one thing the purpose of most of those records was to document the fact of endowment and not to highlight the process of purchase. As said above there is also a suspicious aspect about the term used to indicate the purchase, *viṟṟukoṇḍuuḍaiya* which might have been a polite couching of the process of confiscation or distriant, when the person involved was an honourable landholder. For, in most of the cases where there is mention of the purchase of land and on behalf of the temple, there is no reference to the price money at all. For another, usually where the records mention the amount exchanged in the transaction of purchase, the amount involved is stated to have been not only the price of land but also to have included the capital for yielding as interest commensurate to pay the taxes on the land. The taxes on the land being variable, it becomes difficult to distinguish the price paid for the land and the capital against the taxes. Moreover more often than not the records refer to the plot of land involved in the sale by its designation without giving its extent or area. Further the quality and gradation of the land sold for being endowed to temples are not specified, even in cases where the land was not common waste to be reclaimed.

All these drawbacks in the data available in the records can be illustrated by two records of the time of Māvali-vāṇarayar from Tiruvallam. Both of them record the setting apart of land in the *mañjikkam* (environs?) of the *ūr* after making the same tax-free by the *sabhā* of Tīkkālivallam against 40 *kaḷañju* in each case for being endowed to the temple. In one[92] the land involved was in three plots: *pāṛkuṭṭai* land-400 *kuḷi;* land under *paḷavēri*-720 *kuḷi* and *Nōṇiḍu-koḷḷi-2*; in the other case[93] also three plots were allotted as follows:

Vāgai-kkuṇḍil-500 *kuli, puṛavaḍu-kōllal*-800 kuḷi; *kuraṅgāḍi -2* -400 *Kuḷi*[94]—in both these sets of plots it will be observed that the area of the plot of one case is not given and that the fields mentioned were also of different types, one plot was a *kuṇḍil* and another was *kōllai* or garden land. The types to which the other plots belonged are not stated. In the latter case the total extent of the three plots was 1700 *kuḷis* and in the case of the former the extent was 1120 *kuḷis* plus the plot with only its designation. Even if it is assumed that the 40 *kaḷañju* of gold accepted against the land in each of the above two cases was of the same fineness and that the amount set apart as capital against the taxes in each case was identical, it will be hazarduous to conclude that the area of the plot where it was unspecified was (1700-1120) 580 *kuḷis* just because there is no indication that each plot was of the same grade and the price rate was the same in respect of all the plots irrespective of the land having been plantation land or *kuṇḍil* land[95]. There are also no data available to enable an apportionment of the 40 *kaḷañju* as price of land and as the capital against the taxes. However from the contents, of the above two inscriptions, it can be deduced that both were records pertaining to a period very near to each other. Further both records pertain to the same village. Hence it can be presumed that the element in the deposit of 40 *Kaḷañju* that constituted the capital against taxes must have been identical, the residue forming the price of the land of the extent as noticed above. But even this much inference is not possible in most of the other cases where the records mention the amount of money paid in the land transfer transactions, both as price as well as capital against the taxes[96].

In this midst, the records of the period from about the

reign of Uttama-chōḷa, enter a new complication by referring to current coins instead of gold bullion as hitherto, as having been paid in respect of the land. The comparative value of the coins of the various denominations, *kāsu,* old *kāsu (Paḷañ\-kāsu)* and *kāsu* of daily currency *(anṛāḍu-naṛkāsu)* is not known and hence their value for comparing the price of land is doubtful. For instance an inscription of the year 15 (985 ?) of a Parakēsarivarman (Uttama-chōḷa ?) from Kāñchīpuram[96a] says that 300 (Kuḷi ?) of land was purchased by a member of an army regiment from the *nagarattār* but does not mention the price of the land. The land was endowed for food offerings to a deity but was not got made tax-free. But the record states that the same donor also endowed 3 *pāḷāṅkāsu* for a *saṇdhi* lamp. Hence it is likely that the price he paid for the land may also have been in *paḷaṅkāsu*. These current coins find more frequent mention in the records of 11th century onward. An inscription of the year 4 (1016) of Rājēndra I from Tiruvallam[97] records the allotment by the *sabhā* of the place of 2000 *kuḷi* of land including a coconut grove measured by *chiṛṛambaḷattu-kkōl* after making the same tax-free (*iṛai-iḷichchi*) against 50 *aṇṛādunaṛkāsu* endowed to the temple by one Araisūruḍaiyān. A Tiruvoṛṛiyūr inscription[98] of the year 2 (1072) of Kulōttuṅga I records the purchase of 12 *vēlis* of land in five villages on the understanding that the village organisations which sold the land would themselves bear the *antarāyam* and *kuḍimai* dues on the land, for 240 *aṇrādu-naṛkāsu*. Of these three records the first does not provide firm data for calculating the price of land but the latter two provide some details which however are insufficient to draw conclusions. One has to assume that the taxes from which the land was freed in the Tiruvallam inscriptions of Rājēndra I and the *antarāyam* and *kuḍimai* dues of the Tiruvorriyur inscription of Kulōttuṅga I were of the same magnitude, and that the 2000 *kuḷi* of the former record was equivalent to a *vēli* and also that the *anrādu-naṛikāsu* in both the records was of the same value before comparing the data supplied by them and draw conclusions. On the basis of the above assumptions it can be concluded that the land in Tiruvallam in the period of Rājendra I was two and a half times more costly, than the land in Tiruvorriyūr in the early period of Kulōttuṅga I (i.e.) the land value had fallen considerably in the space of about 56 years[99].

The details supplied by the Tiruvoṛṛiyur inscription of Kulōttuṅga I can be compared with the set of data supplied by another inscription of the year (36) (1106 ?) of the same king from Takkōlam.[100] 5 *vēli* or 10,000 *kuḷi* of land measured by 16 span rod was sold by the *sabhā* of Rājamārttāṇḍa-chaturvēdimaṅgalam, after undertaking not to show *chill-antarāyam* including *vēlikkāśu* against the land and including the irrigation privileges in the transaction, at the rate of 2 *kāsu* per *vēli*. It is not known if this bare *kāsu* was the same as *anrāḍu-naṛkāśu* and if the taxes from which the land was freed in the last instance bore comparison with the *iṛai* or *antarāyam* and *kuḍimai* of the former records to arrive at any conclusion regarding the comparative prices of land at the different places mentioned.[101]

NOTES:

1. cf. Udgaonkar, Padma B, *The Political Institutions and Administration of Northern India during Medieval Times* (From 750 to 1200 AD), p. 187. She says that under the Paramāras, only the traders in coconuts and fruits were made to pay a tax.
2. cf. Ghosal, UN, The Agrarian System in Ancient India p. 46-48.
3. The equivalent date in the Christian era would have been 673 if he was the first king of that name or 731 if he was the second Paramēvaravarman.
4. *SII.*, VIII, 331.
5. An inscription of the year (11?—881?) of Kampavarman from Tiruvoṛṛiyūr (*SII.*, XII, 103) also mentions *talaichchēmāḍu* which had to be paid in paddy, in the context of a penalty for the non-observance of their contract to the temple by the *ūr* of Vaikkāṭṭūr in Tiruvoṛṛiyurppuṛam.
6. *Panchavāram* could not have meant the due to the temple as the record says that this was payable as *dēvadāna*. Cf. Sastri, K.A.N.,

Studies in Chola History p. 142-43. He connects it with the Tamil word, *pañcham,* meaning famine and thus surmises that *pañchavāram* might have been a levy against famines (for a famine fund). Sastri, H. K. (*SII.,* II, p. 509 and 512) thought that the word signified the five kinds of vārams (payments or portions) into which the produce of the land is apportioned like *mēlvāram, kuḍivāram* etc. But he does not explain how the *kuḍivāram* or the portion retainable by the cultivator for his maintenance could be deprived from him. Here it can be pointed out that later inscriptions refer to a tenure *'muṟṟūṭṭu'* which actually means feeding to the full. Here also it is unimaginable that the tenant holding *'muṟṟūṭ ṭu'* land was deprived of the entire produce.

Also cf. *AREp.*, 1913, pt. II, p. 105; Stein, Burton, "The Economic Function of a Medieval South Indian Temple", Jl. of *Asian Studies*, XIX (No. 2), p. 166 (see also note 13 below).

6a. *SII.*, V, 572.

7. The inscription breaks off after mentioning partly another levy *śennīr-ppoduvinai.*

8. *SII.*, III, 156.

9. However late in the 10th century the term was used in the context of the contribution to the temple from *ūr* also.

10. *SII.*, III, 190

11. *AREp.* 1921, 219.

12. *SII.*, III, 203

13. Some details given in the Tiruviḍaimarudūr record cited above seem to explain the term *pañchavāram* as a levy that was paid in five instalments *(pañcha* -five; *vāram* -time). One set of figures mentioned in the record refers to 160 *kalam* and to 800 *kalam* of paddy. The latter being five times the first figure, there is a suggestion that the latter was the total required to be paid and the former, the amount payable at each instalment. However the record supplies another set of figures which blurs this understanding. It is stated that the correct rate of payment (at each instalment?) should have been 256 *kalam* making a total payment of 2800 *kalam* by the special measure of the temple called Tiruvidaimarudan-marakkal. Five times 256 should have amounted to 1280 *kalam* and not 2800 *kalam*. It seems possible that the use of the special measure mentioned for measuring the paddy resulted in the inflating of the figure to 2800 from 1280. See *EI*, XXI P. 22f.

13a. *SII.*, III, 151.

14. The record seems to make out that these payments of *pañchavāram* were diverted by royal order to the God in the new temple raised by the king's mother. However the beneficiary deity does not appear to have been different from the one already existing in the Tirunallam temple which was now only raised in stone by the queen mother and at least one of the villages was already a *dēvadāna* of that deity.
15. *SII.*, XVII, 222.
16. This temple was also retained in stone by the mother of Uttama-chōḷa.
17. See note 6 above.
18. cf. AREp. 1912, 131, Intr, 1913, pt. II, p. 104. This inscription dated year 2 (1072) of Kulōttuṅga I, from Tiruvoṟṟiyūr refers to several taxes including *paṇcha-vāṛam* payable by five *dēvadāna* villages. Of these five villages only two, Maṇali and Vaḷsāṟu are known to have been under *sabhā* administration (*SII., VI, 374).*
19. In the middle country *irai* is heard of for the first time even in the year 3 (849) of Nandivarman III in an inscription from Kiḷiyanur (South Arcot district) (*SII.*, XII, 47). In the Chōḷa country, Epigraphically the term *iṛaī* is met with for the first time in an inscription of the year 22 (868) of Nandivarman III from Tiruvaigāvūr in Tanjāvūr district (*ibid*, 58).
20. *Ibid* VI, 356.
21. Eg. ibid., 84, 85, 102, ibid., VI, 285, 287, 314, 347, 369.
22. Tērukuṛaḷ ch. 39, verse 8 "*muṛai cheydu kappāṟṟu—mannavan makkaṭk-iṛai enṛu* vaikkappaḍum.
23. *SII.*, II, 4-5, also.
24. cf., Karur (Tiruchirappalli district) inscription of the year 3 plus 1 (1067) of Vīrarājeindra (*SII.*, III, 20). In this record also *iṛai kaṭ ṭina kāṇi kkaḍan* is employed in the context of a village under the status *veḷḷān—vagai* granted to a temple as *dēvadāna-tirunāmattukkāṇi*. The term *kaḍamai* employed by 11-13 century records to denote the tax (on land and on other items) cf. Sastri, KAN, The *Chōḷas*, p. 499) was probably derived from *Kaḍan* which also means "what is to be done.
25. *SII.*, III, 9
26. cf. Mahalingam, T.V., 'Village communities in South India', Readings in South Indian History (ed. Ramachandran, K. S.) p. 96.
27. *SII.*, XVII, 127, 169.

28. *SII.*, VIII, 68; *ibid*, III 61.
28a. *SII.*, XII, 86.
29. Tirumaḷai—Tirupati Devasṭhanam Epigraphicaḷ Series, Early Inscriptions—I No. 7.
29a. *SII.*, III, 142.
30. EI. IV, p. 221 f.
31. The reference to *puravu* and *vari* in the phrase may be indicative of the fact that the official was in-charge of the establishment dealing with the taxes *(vari)* on royal account (?).
32. Sastri, KAN, The *Chōḷas*, p. 469-70 and n. 94-95. He cites a *Puṛaṇānūru* verse to say that *purava* basically means the cultivated land'. But he goes further to say that *puravu* referred to all payments in kind and in cash, due from lands and supports this statement with the Tirumālpuram record of the time of Uttama-chōla among other records. It has been noticed that the last named record refers to *puravu* only as one of the dues from the land beside *iravu* and *pon* and not as the sum of the tax dues. But it is possible that in due course this term came to acquire an all encompassing meaning to cover the royal tax dues and to the tax register, reflecting these dues (e. g. *puravil-surukki*).
33. cf. ibid., p. 572 and 413. He has not, however, explained what this *paḷḷi* or *paḷḷi-ppēṛu* signified.
34. Probably some of the villages under the administration of *sabhās* as well as those under the *ṅagaram* were asked to pay the entire taxes in gold (Tiruvālangāḍu plates of Rājendra I; Taṅjavūr inscription of Rājarāja I *SII.*, II, 4-5).
35. *Ibid.*, XII, 95.
36. *Ibid.*, III, 116.
37. *Ibid.*, III, 142
38. An inscription of the year 40(947) of Parāntaka I from Kūram (*SII.*, VII, 35) indicates that *mudal* meant the totality. It refers to the *nila-mudal* including the waste and cultivated land in the village. It might have also meant the taxable land in the village. Also *SII.*, V, 702—this inscription of the year 4 (1122) refers to the land register of the village as *nila-mudal -pottagam*. Probably *nil-öpādi* (*SII.*, V, 705. Tiruviḍaimarudur inscription of the period (12 century) of Kulōttunga II) or *nell-ōpādi* (*ibid.*, XIV, 145—Mannārkoyil,Tirunelveli district—inscription of Sundar-chōḷa-pāṇḍya llth century) referred to total taxes in kind from the village, Also e.g. *SII.*, XVII, 235—an inscription of the year

24(1008-09) of Rājarāja I, from Mēlsēvūr also refers to what was accruing to the temple as *mudal* from several taxes.

39. *SII.*, II, 5.
40. Ibid., VII, 1000.
41. cf. *kāṇḍu-mudal*—the term used in the Tañjāvūr district nowadays to describe the operation for learning the exact total yeild from a crop.
42. cf. *SII.*, III, 20. This inscription of the year 3 plus one (1067) of Vīrarājēndra from Karūr (Tiruchirappalli district) also refers to a village pākkūr being granted as *dēvadāna Tirunāmāttukkāṇi* to the God with the Status of *veḷḷānvagaī* after deleting the *Iṛaī-mudal* (*veḷḷān*-vagaiyil-*iṛai-mudal—tavirndu)*. It is not impossible that, as the *mudal-tavirndu* is referred to in transactions involving a village under *Veḷḷānvagai*, the phrase referred to an exemption from a deposlt (*mudal*) as security for the taxes from such unorganīsed village, which was excused in these instanees on the ground that the village though under *veḷḷānvagai* had been glven over to the temple.
43. cf. Inscrīption of the time of Pārthivēndravarman from Uttaramallūr (*SII.*, III, 155) and Veḷichchēri (ibid., 191) which distinguish the charges payable by land to the king as all kinds of *iṛai* (*epperppaṭṭa iṛai*) in a separate category from the other charges payable for local consumption.
44. cf. *SII.*, XVII, 235. A 13th century inscription from Mēlsēvūr South Arcot district, mentions a levy payable on account of the administration of a hamlet (*sirūr- āṭchiyāl vandada*). Hamlets of cognisable size though attached to *sabhā* villages tended to have their own administration (For instance Dāmōdarachchēri and Tirttātil-hamlets of Uttaramēru-chatuvēdimangalam had their own *sabbā* and *ūr* respectively—*SII.*, III, 159, *ibid.*, V1. 286) and apparently in due course a charge was taken from the landholders to defray the expenses of local administration. Also cf. Tiruppārkadal (inscriptions of a Parakesarivarman (*SII.*, XIX, 121, 297) which refer to the person in-charge of the administration of Chirrūr.
45. From this feature it appears that the taxation system had been formalised earlier in the Chōḷa country. It is observable that in the Uttaramallūr record of Nandivarman III (year 24, 870) (*SII.*, VI, 356) the *sabhā* is stated to have freed the land endowed to temple from all kinds of *irai (eppēṛppaṭṭa iṛaiyum)*. On the other

hand the inscriptions of Pārthivēndravarman from *Uttaramallūr* (ibid., 155) mentions all kinds of *irai* but distinct from this adds the usual *echchōṛu veṭṭi* and *amañji* also *SII.*, III, 191).

46. *Ibid.*, VII, 420.
47. *Ibid.*, VI, 369.
48. *SII.*, III, 12.
49. *SII.*, III, 155, 157, 158, 164, 167, 168, 170, 171, 177, 182, 194.
50. *Ibid.* 155 cf. ibid. 116, 191.
51. *Ibid.*, 179.
52. *Ibid.*, VI, 297.
53. *SII.*, III, 116.
54. *SII.*, VII, 73.
55. *Ibid.*, 64.
56. *Ibid., VI, 324.*
57. *Śennīr-amañji* seems to have been free labour connected with the supply of irrigation water.
58. *Ibid.*, VIII, 521.
59. *Ibid.*, III, 150-151, ibid., VIII, 558, 570, 572, 605, 611, 620, 621, 623, 629, 631, ibid., XIX 54, 113, 127, 181, 290, 305 (Uḍaiyāṛkuḍi, South Arcot district) 309.
60. Minakshi, C., *op.cit.*, p. 82,83, Sastri, K.A.N. (The *Chōḷas*, p. 542-610) just refers to *echchōru* as a difficult term.

60a. It is also seen that the village organisations undertook to feed such persons who came to collect the interest on gold taken on deposit by them e. g. S11, XII, 90, 91, 99 (all from Tiruvoṟṟiyūr).

61. An inscription of the year (3) 7 (944?) of Parāntaka I from Allūr (Tiruchirappalli district) (*SII.*, VIII, 689) refers to a bloc of land as the enjoyment against *veṭṭi* (*veṭṭi-ppēṛu*) which was in the charge of the elders of the head-water-works *(talai-vāy-chchānrōm)* numbering eleven personnel. The land seems to have been quite adjacent to the River Kāvērī, as it is stated to have been flooded and sand-logged. Though this location of the land and the nomenclature of the committee (probably of the *ūr* of Allūr) suggest that the *veṭṭippēṛu* was an allotment against the *veṭṭi* in respect of the irrigation works, *veṭṭi* itself in this context seems to have indicated public works rather than forded labour. Also cf. *SII.*, I, p. 82, n 3 and p. 108 n. 6 -while editing the inscriptions of the 13th and 15th centuries the editor has drawn attention to the possibility of *veṭṭi* of these inscriptions having been the same as *veṭṭiyān,* the lowest category of village servant (scavenger)

known to the recent times. He has cited the *Tanjāvūr Manual* to point out that the *veṭṭiyān* as one of the village servants was enlisted to a share of the produce of the village.

62. Sastri, KAN, *The Chōḷas*, p. 531, 594 Cf. Minakshi, C, *op. cit.*, p. 110.
63. *SII.*, VII, 64.
64. Among the inscriptions from Tiruchirappali district an inscription of the time (970-985) of Uttamachōḷa from Tiruppalātturai (*SII.*, III, 150) mentions *śennīr-veṭṭi* as the only extra levy besides *iṛai*. Hence not only amañj*i* but also *veṭṭi* seems to have been connected with *śennīr* or irrigation water or irrigation works. This is also indicated by the list of the extra levies reflected in the Paṛakēsari-varman (year 18) inscription from Allūr (*SII.*, VIII, 696) which says that *śennīr-veṭṭi, vēdinai, īṛai* and *echchōṛu* will not be shown against the land endowed to a temple—*veṭṭi- ppēṛu* or land against *veṭṭi* connected with the head-water works, as discussed above also indicated the same fact. However another inscription of the year 4 of Parakesarivarman from the same place (*ībid.*, 692) mentions *śennīr-veṭṭi* as something which needed not to be done (not paid?) apart from non-payment of *echchōru, veṭṭi, vēdinai* and *iṛai*.
65. *SII.*, III, 57. This term occurs in a fragmentary inscription dated year 7, *śaka* 991 (1069-70) from Yōgimallavaram, Puttur taluk, Chittoor district (*SII.*, XVII, 301) but due to the fragmentary nature of the epigraph, no light is thrown on the character of the levy.
66. An inscription of the year 14 (1264) of *emmaṇḍalamum koṇḍaruḷiya* Sundara -pāṇḍya from Tiruppāṛkaḍal (North Arcot district (*SII.*, XVII, 759) lists the taxes remitted on temple land, as the *varis, kaḍmai*—and *upādhis* including *anṭarāyam* and *pon-vaṛi*. Another record of the year 36 of Yādavarāya (13th century) from Rāmagiri, Chingleput district) (*Ibid*, 705) says that the *ūr* of Arikāṇḍapuram exempted the temple land from the various *upādhis* including *ponvari*, *kaḍamai* and several (*pala*) *antaṛāyam*. An inscription of the year 13 (1033) of Sundara-chōla-pāṇḍya from Mannārkōyil, Tirunelveli district *(SII.*, XIV, 145) equates *nel-op*ādhi with the main land-tax, *iṛai*. An inscription of the year 9 (1142) of Kulōttuṅga II from Tiruviḍaimarudūr *(SII.*, V, 705) seems to equate *nila-opādhi* similarly with all the tax commitments on land.

67. cf. *SII.*, III, 61. This inscription of the 12th century from Tiruvallam seems to contrast *antarāyam* from *pura-āyam* (income or tax that went outside). Also Cf. *SII,* VI,369
68. cf. Ins. from Pudukkottai state, 126. This inscription of the year 46 (1116) of Kulōttuṅga I, from Irumba-nādu, Pudukkottai taluk, Tirunchirappalli district, suggests that in that region and at the particular period *antarāyam* meant an additional cess. The text runs—*ner—kaḍamai aḷandu antarāyam vaippadāga.*
69. This is made evident by the inclusion of the levies *nīrvilai, veṭṭi, muṭṭal-āl* and *echchōṛu* under *antarāyam* which was within the authority of the king as per the Tiruvoṛṛiyūr inscription of Kulōttuṅga I, cited above.
70. An inscription of the year 3 of a Rājakēsarivarman from Tiruviḍaimarudūr (Tanjavur district) (*SII.*, V. 716) seems to employ the word *pāṭṭam* to indicate land assigned for a specific purpose. The relevant text of the record runs *dēvadānam Vilāṅguḍi-ppāṭṭ am aṛupadu, nīkki nīnra nilattile vanda nellu*
71. *SII.*, XII, 103.
72. It has been explained above that *panchavāram* and to 74 *puravu* probably denoted the same thing as irai, the land-tax. The phrase *irai kattina-kāṇi-kkaḍan* also is used to indicate the due from villages to temples in records like the Tanjavūr inscription of the year 29 (1014) of Rājarāja I (*SII.*, II, 4-5). Probably this phrase indicated the consolidated *puravu* and miscellaneous dues from the village together.
73. *ibid.*
74. *ibid.*
75. *SII.*, III, 142.
76. *EI,* IV, p. 221 f.
77. Manu-smriti, ch. VII, V. 130. *dhānyānām = ashṭamō bhāgah. shashṭhō dvādasa ēva vā.* Vidyāraṇya, the theoretician for the Vijayanagar empire of the 14th century is also reported to have advised the 1/6 norm for the collection of the government dues from the yeild of the land (Mahalingam, T.V., *South Indian Polity*, p. 168).
78. It is possible that this *āyati* was the same as *iravu* occurring in the Tirumālpuram inscription noticed above.
79. It is noteworthy that Kaḍaikkōṭṭūr and Siriyārūr were handed over to the *sabhā* organisations, of Udayachandramaṅgalam and Puduppākkam respectively. In the case of Pirudi-Mādēvi-

chaturvēdimaṅgalam, the 53 *brahmadēyam* donees were probably expected to organise themselves into a corporate body. Tirukkāṭṭu-ppaḷḷi handed over to the temple of God Mahādēva was probably similarly organised already. The Tiruvālaṅgāḍu plates of Rājēndra I, however indicates that by that time (1018) there was also the practice of asking the *brahmadēyam* villages to pay the *iṛai* assessment in gold, where the assessment was not rounded off. probably the amount of gold 598 *kaḷañju* and one *kunṛi* which is said to have been *iṛaikaṭṭina-pon* was what the *brahmadēyam* Siṅgaḷāntaka-chaturvēdimaṅgalam was asked to pay in respect of both its main village and the village Paḷaiyūr attached to it. When the latter village was brought under *veḷḷān-vagai* tenure (the only characteristic of this tenure, known is that it was non-*brahmadēyam*), the assessment was re-fixed in paddy as was originally done and in addition a contribution in gold was also fixed. Both the payment in paddy as well as in gold as was assessed as due was termed *ninṛiṛai* (permanent *irai*). Hence apparently the assessment as *iṛai kaṭṭina-pon* under the *brahmadēyam* tenure had incladed not only the *puravu* but also the other charges includlng the gold levy. The *puravu* part of the assessment might have been fixed at the usual 1/6 rate. In the light of this, the *iṛai-kaṭṭina-kāṇikkaḍan* which is said to have been the tax due from villages transferred to the temple as per the Tañjāvūr inscriptions of the year 29 (1014) of Rājarāja I (*SII.*, II, 4-5) also seems to have been the consolidated amount of all the dues, *iṛai* and other charges in paddy as also the paddy equivalent of the *pon* levy. The Tañjāvūr inscriptions cited indicate that the levy only in paddy was due from *sabhā* and *ūr* villages and levy only in gold was due from *nagaram* villages, The data supplied by the Tañjāvūr inscriptions also point to the tax due per *vēli* having been either 100 *kalam* of paddy or alternatively 10 *kaḷañju*. The *puravu* portion of this consolidated amount might have also been fixed at the 1/6 norm. The dues as listed are said to have been payable by whole villages. The amounts might have been the sum of the dues payable by the individual fields in the village or an assessment on a village-wise basis. The amounts cited as due from villages as per the Tañjāvūr inscriptions were not rounded off. However an inscription of the year 4 (1016?) of Parakēsari Rājēndra I ?) from Allūr (Tiruchirappalli district (*SII.*, VIII, 677) states that *kaḍamai* alone when payable by land to a temple was fixed at 6 *kalam* per *mā* or 120 *kalam* per *vēlī* (20 *mā*). As discussed above this term *kaḍamai* seems to have indicated the total of dues payable to the king.

80. However the Tanjāvūr inscriptions of year 29 (1014) of Rājarāja I (*SII.*, II, 4-5) indicate that there were some special types of land in each village which were normally exempted from assessment of taxes. To cite some examples, one of these inscriptions says that there was Pālai-ūr in Iṅga-nāḍu in Ten-Kāḍuvāy alias Aṛumoḷidēva-vaḷanāḍu wherein the total land including *paḷḷi* and *kaṇi-murruṭṭu* as measured amounted to 134 (*vēli), 8 mā*, kīl 3/4-3, ½ kaṇi, *mundirigai*—kīl—4 mā. Of this,the land occupied by the following facilities -homesteads (*ūr-nattam*), temple-sites (sri-*kōyil*), tanks, channels passing through the *ūr* the quarters of artisans (*kammāṇa-chchēri*) , of the *paṛaiyas* (*paṛai-chchēri*) and of the un-approachables (*tīṇḍā-chechēri*) and cremation ground, all amounting to 9 *vēil.* 1 kāṇi, *mundirigai kī*l—½ was deducted as was the sanctioned practice as *iṛai-ili* land to give a balance of assessable land as 125 (*vēli*), 7½ *mā*, *mundirigai*, kīḷ—8 mā, ½ kāṇi mundirigai-kīḷ 4 mā. The *iraīkaṭṭinakāṇi-kkaḍan* assessment on this land was 12530 *kalam*, 2 tūṇi, 1 kuṛuṇi and 1 *nāḷi*, measured by the standard measure *āḍavallāṇ* (temple measure) equivalent to Rajakēsari (*SII.*, II, 4). Similarly in the *nagaram* village Tirutteṅgūr in the same nāḍu after excluding the usual *irai-ili* lands occupied by *nattam,* tanks (in general?—for drinking water?), tanks in fields (*pulam*), the *tīñḍāchchēri paṛai-chchēri* and cremation ground, the land assessed measured 29 Vēlī, 14 mā. This land was asked to pay 297 *kalañju* 4 *mañjāḍi,* 3 mā and 3 *kāṇi* (*ibid*).

81. For instance an Uttaramallūr inscription of the year 3 of Pārthivēndravarman (*SII.*, III, 162) says that a total of 1594 *kuḷi* of land in four plots, which was not paying *iṛai* was allotted to a temple by the *peruṅguṛi-sabhā* of that village which took *pūrvvāchāram* from a merchant to free that land from the taxes *iṛai*, *echchōṛu, veṭṭi* and *amañji*.

82. An inscription of the year 4 (1122), of Vikrama-chōḷa from Tiruviḷaimarudūr (Tanjāvür district) (*SII.*, V, 702) indicates how in that *sabhā* village, the members had to share the burden of the taxes in respect of land abandoned by the holder or cultivator (*kuḍi*).

83. *SII.*, III, 57.

84. This has been dealt with above.
85. That one of the villages involved in this transaction, Mandiram was paying *pañchavāram* to the temple of (Tiravallamuḍayār) is made known by an inscription dated year 22(1007) of Rājarāja I from Tiruvallam (*AREp*. 1921, 219).
86. This indicates that well into the 11th century the organisation of landholders of the village was made responsible for the taxes to be paid to the king and that instead of going to the trouble of assessing the dues from artisans and others individually, the king had fixed the total levy on this account in proportion to the land tax, leaving it to that organisation to apportion it among the artisans and professionals precent in the village. This course might have also been adopted because in the *brahmadēyam* villages these levies had been authorised to the brahmins holding shares of land in such villages.
87. *SII.*, VIII, 331.
88. *SII.*, XII, 86.
89. Of the above mentioned levies only *ṭarppuḍavai* among the levies under *antaṛāyam* is mentioned among the exemptions (*parihāras*) in the Rōyakōṭṭah plates and was probably a levy enjoyable by *kō* presumably the local lord. Probably the other levies under *aṇtarāyam* and *kīl-irai-ppāṭṭam* were also originally meant to be enjoyed by the *kō*. The king seems to have taken them over subsequently. Obviously when the concerned villages Mandiram and Kukkanūr were made over as *dēvadāna* to the temple to Tiruvallamuḍaiyār exemptions from or authorisation to these levies had not accompanied the grant as reflected in the Vēlūrpāḷaiyam plates., Sastri, K.A.N., (*The Chōḷas*, p. 537) details as to how during the 12-13 centuries, the local feudatories imposed several additional levies burdening the land to the breaking point.
90. This escalation during the 11th century is more clearly reflected in the amounts taken by the village organisations, as capital against taxes in respect of land endowed to temples in the Chōḷa country, a Tiruchchenduṛai (Tiruchirappalli district) inscription of the year (20 ?) of a Rājakēsarivarman (10th century ?) (*SII.*, VIII, 635) says that the *mūlaparuḍai* (*mūlaparishad*) took an amount equal to the price of the land as *Iṛai-kāval*. An inscription of the year 22 (1007) of Rājarāja I from Vēdāraṇyam (Tanjavūr district) (*SII.*, XVII, 470) also says that the capital against taxes taken was equal to the price of the land. On the other hand a record of the year 4

(1074) of Rājakāsari Rājēndra (Kulōttunga I) from Allur\ (Tiruchirappalli district) (*SII.*, VIII, 701) reflects that an amount equal to one and a half times the price of land was required as capital to free land from taxes. The *peruṅguri-sabhā* sold for endowment 7½ *mā* of land and took 4 *kāsu* as price of the land and 6 *kāsu* as *iral-kāval*. The tax burden of land seems to have gone still higher in the succeeding period. An inscription from Tiruchchenduṛai, in which of the king's name only *kēsaṛi* is readable but which probably belongs to the later period (12th century) (ibid, 636) records that the *mūlaparisbad* of Īśana-maṅgalam took 40 *kāḷañju* of gold (*tīy-ppokku-chchembon—tuḷaipaṭṭadu*) weighed by viḍēlviḍugūkal as cost of the land and 70 *kaḷañju* i.e. one and three quarter times the land *iṛai-kāval* to give *sarvvaparihāra* status to the land. Even when the cost of land and *iṛai-kāval* amount were equal (i. e.) in the period of Rājarāja I it seems to have been heavy enough to require coercion for collection (Sastri, KAN, the cōḷas p. 536-37). Hence the plight of the landholders in the 12th century when the capital requirement for making the land taxfree seems to have gone up to one and three quarters of the cost of land can only be imagined. An inscription of the year 4 (1122) of Vikramachōḷa from Tiruvidai-marudūr (Tanjāvūr district) (SII, V, 702) refers to the landholders running away abandoning the land without paying the taxes. Two inscriptions of the period of Rājādhirāja II (1163, 66-1179-1182) from Tirukkarugāvūr and Achchāpuram, 60th in Tanjavur district (AREp. 1918, 429, 538) record that the *sabhā* of the places concerned had to scale down and refix the contributions (*varisai-pparru*—dues as tribute and *vārapparru* dues as share of the produce due from the lands belonging to the temple. Two inscriptions dated (1239) in the reign of Rājarāja Ill record the complaint of the people of the *taniyūr* Rājādhirāja-chaturvēdi-mangalam (Mannārguḍi, Tanjāvūr district) (*SII.*, VI, 50, 58) regarding their difficulties in carrying on agriculture with the burden of the exactions on land (Subbarayalu, Y., *op. cit.*, p. 36, Sastri, KAN, *The Chōḷas* p. 538).

91. This seems to be suggested when the Tiruvālāngādu plates of Rājēndra I and the Tanjāvūr inscriptions of Rājarāja I, (*SII.*, II, 4-5) refer to the exemption from *mudal* granted in respect of villages, which had been brought under *veḷḷānvagai* from the status of a *brahmadēyam* and whose tax-income had been granted to the specified temples.

92. *SII.*, III, 45.
93. *Ibid.*, 48.
94. The editor of the record interpreted the expressions *Nōṇiḍu-Koḷḷi*—2 and *Kuraṅgāḍi*—2 as signifying that Nōnidu-koḷḷi and *Kurangadi* were plots with an area of two *vēli* each. But he has no explanation for the mention of 400 kuli following *Kuraṅgāḍi*. Obviously the figure 2 following the designation of the fields was part of the designation to indicate either that they were second fields of those names in the village or was indicative of the grade of the fields concerned.
95. It appears from the designation of the land as *kōllai* that it was at one time used for plantation purposes but that when it was allotted to the temple, it was meant for growing paddy. The significance of the designation *kuṇdil* is not clear.
96. It has also been observed that the tax-structure in each village was not also uniform. This might also have been based on the quality of the land and prosperity of the village.
96a. *SII.*, XIX, 365.
97. *SII.*, III, 54.
98. *AREp*, 1912, 131 also ibid., 1913, Pt. II, p. 104.
99. In this connection some inscriptions from the Chōḷa country provide more dependable data. As inscription of the year 20 of a Rājakēsarivarman from Tiruchchendurai (Tiruchchirappalli district) (*SII.*, VIII, 635) says that the *mūlaparuḍai* (*mūla-parishad)* of the village sold land for endowment (for a new shrine set up by himself) to a merchant and took 5 *kaḷañju* as price of the land and an equal amount as capital against the taxes (*iṛai-kāval*). In the year 22 (1007) of Rājarāja I at Vēdāraṇyam (Tanjavur district), the *sabhā* of Iṛaiyāṅmaṅgalam adjusted *20* Kāsu, equally, 10 *kāsu* as price of 10 *vēli* of the land *(vilai dravyam*). and 10 *kāsu* for freeing that land from taxes(*iṛai-kaḷippadaṛku) (SII.*, XVII, 470). It is clear that in the former case the 100 *pāttis* (rows in a plantation) had been sold for 5 *kalañju* and that in the latter, ten *vēlies* of land were sold at a *kāsu* each. On the other hand an inscription dated year 4 (1074 ?) of a Rājakēsari Rājēndra (Kulottunga I ?) from Allūr (Tiruchchirappalli district) (*SII.*, VIII, 701) says that the *perunguṛi-sabhā* of the place sold 7½ *mā* of land to a brahma-mahārajan, for endowment and took 4 *kāsu* as the price of land (vilai-pporuḷ) and took as capital against taxes *(iraī-kāval*), 6 kāsu, (i. e.) the capital required for freeing the land from taxes

was one and a half times the cost of land indicating the escalation of the tax burden of the land as between the time of Rajaraja I (1007) and the period (1074) of Kulōttuṅga I, (In the inscription of Kulōttuṅga I from Tiruvorriyur, there was no means to know if *antarāyam* and *kuḍimai* were terms comprehensive to cover all taxes on land of that period).

100. *SII.*, V, 1381.

101. An inscription of the year 13 (884 ?) of Rājakēsarivarman (Aditya I) from Lālguḍi (Tiruchchirappalli district) *EI,* XX, p. 53, the *sabhā* of Maṇakkāl took 30 *kaḷañju* of gold which combined the cost of ½ *vēlī* of land and the capital against taxes. Another inscription dated year 2 of a Rājakēsarivarman from Tiru-chchendurai (Tiruchchirappalli district—*SII.*, VIII, 611) records the charging of 100 *kaḷañju* for only freeing from taxes, 1 *vēlī* of land (half of it having been plantation land-ūr-pātti and half of it, wet land) already in the possession of the temple, by the *mūlaparishad* of Iśānamaṅgalam. Assuming that the necessary capital against the tax commitment was about the same as the cost of land, it would appear that at the pertinent time the cost of land in Maṇakkāl was 30 *kaḷañju* per *vēlī* and in Iśānamaṅgalam was about 65 *kaḷañju* per *vēlī*. This can be compared with an inscription of a Parakēsarivarman, year 22 from Tiruppālatturai in the same district (ibid., 570) which says that the *ṭalai-vāy. chchānrōm* of Talaivāyppāḍi, a locality in the village sold one veli, 3 *ma* and 1 *kāṇi* of land and received 130 *kaḷañju* which constituted the cost of land and the capital for making the land free from several taxes including *iṛai* and miscellaneous levies. Assuming again that the capital required against the taxes during this period also was equivalent to the cost of land, the latter at Tiruppālatturai during this period can be understood to have been about 55 *kaḷañju* per *vēlī* Another Parakēsarivarman (year 2) inscription from the same place (*ibid.*, 572) records the sale of 1 *mā* by the *ur*. of Pulivalam who received as price of the land sold and as the capital against taxes of 7 *kaḷañju* of *viḍēlviḍ*ugu-*tuḷai*. Here also the cost of land works out to about 50 *kaḷañju* per *veli*. Another inscription of the year 9 of a Parakēsarivarman from Tirchchendurai in the same district (*ibid.*, 605) says that the *paru*dai of Isānamaṅgalam took 28½ *kaḷañju* towards the cost of land as well as towards the capital required to protect it from taxes including *irai* in respect of 473 *kuḷi* of plantation *(pāṭṭi)*

land growing paddy including a tank. This also works out to about 50 *kaḷañju* per *veli* assuming that 2000 *kuḷi* made one *veli* in this village, and making a nominal allowance for the tank. But an inscription of the year 10 of a Parakēsarivarman from Naṅgavaram in the same district (*ibid*, 646) indicates that a *vēlī* in that village contained 4000 *kuḷis* as the record states that 14000 *kulis* constituting 3½ vēlis of land were sold by the *perung-uṛisabhś* of Aṛiṅjiya-chaturvēdimaṅgalam. In this case towards cost of the land and as the charge for making the same free from taxes including *iṛai* the *peruṅguṛi- sabhā* is stated to have tåken 1080 *kaḷañju* of gold of superfine quality (*māśili*). Thus in this case it is observable that the bare cost of the land, assuming again that the capital required against taxes was equal to the cost of land, works out to about 156 *kaḷāñju* which is at wide divergence from the trend of land price during the 10th century. Hence though the mere name Parakēsari gives no indication, it can be concluded that this inscription either belongs to a period far later than that of the foregoing or in view of the fact that the quotation of price is in *kaḷañju* weight of gold, a feature of the tenth century and earlier, it represents the standard of a different area based on some other factors like the quality of the land.

The price of land in the other eastern part of Cholamaṇḍalam, the present day Tanjāvūr district, as reflected in the records can also be seen. An inscription dated year 7 (963) of Pāṇḍiyaṇai-chuṛam-iṛakkina Sundara-chōḷa from Tirukkalittaṭṭai (near Tiruvidaimardur) (EI, XII, p. 121-126) says that for endowment to the God, ½ land nilam\vēli (?) (probably the land was called taliviḷ*āgam* which term literally means the residence around the temple but in this case it seems to have referred to agricultural land as it had been endowed for yielding produce for the *tirupponagam* service of the God) was purchased and got made tax-free from a consideration of 156 *kaḷañju* (i.e. by the above cited Standards this would mean that a full *vēlī* cost about 156 *kaḷañju* as price of land alone(The editor of the record had noted the high price charged for the land which was nearly three times over the price of land in the western portion of Chola-maṇḍalam except at Nangāvaram in the year 10 of Parakesari-varman, where the price of land was again 154 *kaḷañja* very similar to that at Tirukkaḷittaṭṭai). Another inscription dated year 2 of a Parakesari (Aditya II ?) from Kumbhakōṇam (SII, XIX, 6) records the allotment of ¼ *vēli* of land by the *mūlaparishad* against 25 *kaḷañju* of gold endowed by an Individual. There is no mention in the records of the land having been got made tax-free. It was probably because the land having been part of the land which the *mūlaparishad* had received as fee at the coronation (of king ?) (*abhishēka-dakshiṇ*ai) the land already was tax-free. If that was so, apparently 25 *kaḷañju* was the price of ¼ veli of land at Kumbhakōnam. That would amount to 100 *kaḷañju* per *vēli*. However an inscription which does not cite any king nor a date (but which probably belongs to an earlier period than the above two) from Tiruchennampūṇḍi (Tanjavur taluk and district) (*SII*., VII, 524 says that a merchant purchased from the *ūr*ār of Śuṛaikkudi ¼ (vēli) (for which one *mā* of nursery land (nārr*ukkal*) was added) for 8 *kaḷāñju*. He did not get the land made tax-free and hence the amount paid, 8 *kaḷāñju* for ¼ *vēli* (or 32 *kaḷāñju* per *vēli*) seems to have been the cost of land alone. The nursery land of one *mā* seems to have been standard accompaniment of agricultural land in the village for which no separate charge seems to have been taken. The quotation of the price in K*aḷāñju* in this record suggests that it belongs to the earlier period, earlier than the above two records from Tirukkaḷittaṭṭai and Kumbhakōnam respectively. If that was so, it can be concluded that the cost of land in the eastern region had trebled in the meanwhile.

CHAPTER- 8

CONCLUSION

Land System in Tamilnaḍu assumed a distinct shape during the period c. A.D. 800-1200. The characteristic feature of this land system was institutions having control of land. Of these institutions those based on brahmins occupied the pride of place. The rise of these brahmin institutions is traceable to Toṇḍai-maṇḍalam. It was in this region that the Pallavas started the practice of issuing *brahmadēyam* and *dēvadāna* charters in the 7th Century. They are seen to have done so under special circumstances. About this period this family of rulers began depending upon this region to back up their monarchy. Consequently, they had to get the area under agriculture therein optimised to give themselves a viable economic basis and as they seem to have been outsiders to the region they also had the problen of keeping the area under control. Apparently for the achievement of both these objects, they seem to have started giving villages as *brahmadēyam* to brahmins and to have developed the institution of temples where for the conduct of the rituals connected with the worship the brahmin was indispensible.[1]

The choice of the brahmins for this role might not have been due to their sturdiness to manually reclaim and work the land[2]. On the other hand they seem to have been engaged and expected to be engaged in pursuits connected with Vedic learning as the surnames of the brahmins favoured in the available charters testify. It is possible that they possessed the technical know-how for the efficient utilisation of land and working the land system with the kind of irrigation facilities provided. It also seems possible that they were chosen because their introduction into the localities would not cause resentment among the local population. For, the brahmin versed in the vēdas and adhering to his duties commanded respect and obedience in society[3]. The introduction of the brahmins into the localities might have also been intended to acculturise the local people already inhabiting these localities[4]. Further they were unlikely to organise themselves into rival loci of power (as the priestly bodies of the missionary religions of the west had done) and thus could be depended upon for continued loyalty[5].

It is also seen that the kings of the period preferred to associate groups of brahmins and probably encouraged them to organise themselves into corporate bodies in the control of land. These corporate bodies of brahmins referred to as *sabhāÿ* and as having been based on *brahmadēyam* villages are seen to have been inducted into the land system in the following different ways:

1. A single village or a cluster of villages combined into one was made into a *brahmadēyam* and entrusted to a single brahmin or in shares to a group of brahmins.
2. Some villages or hamlets were given the status of *brahmadēyam* and attached as a whole to neighbouring *brahmadēyams* of the first kind.
3. Villages granted to temples with a view to securing for them the royal income from these villages were more often than not associated with brahmin bodies. Such villages sometimes designated as *dēvadāna* and sometimes as *dēvadāna-brahmadēyam* were either held by a group of brahmins as *brahmadēyam* as in the *brahmadēyam* villages of the first kind or were attached as a whole to another *brahmadēyam* of the first kind.

The above picture is presented by the various land

transactions recorded during the period but the charters which could have explained how these brahmins or brahmin bodies were given control of the villages or that could have supplied information on the basis for their exercise of the sort of control evidenced,as available are only a few in number. However even these few available charters supply enough information on the intentions of the monarchs of the period in making the *brahmadēyam* and *dēvadāna* grants.

Through the *brahmadēyam* charters the king passed on to the brahmins, land in the village granted as *brahmadēyam* for their possession on the one hand and other rights and privileges to enable them to control the locality. That land had been given to the possession of the brahmins becomes clear from the records of land transactions in *sabhā-* controlled villages which could have been only *brahmadēyam* villages. While such grants of land evidenced the extent of control possessed by the king over land in his territory[6] these grants do not appear to have implied his snatching the land from those in the village already in occupation of that land. It has been pointed out how the charters refer to the exclusion from the purview of the grants, *dēvadāna* and *brahmadēyam* already under enjoyment as also *kuḍi* or *Pāḷaiyapāṛam*. In view of this it becomes clear that it was only the unoccupied portions of these villages which were given to the possession of brahmins. The Kaśākkudi charter says that only 2 *patti*s of land was excluded in respect of each of these categories, including *kuḍi* and thus indicates that these *kuḍis* had not interested themselves in bringing the land in the village under agriculture as, if they had shown such an interest they would have become eligible to more land than 2 *paṭṭi*s and would have become aware of their rights and would have resented the snatching of land from them to be given over to the brahmins. There is no reflection that the grants excited any resentment or opposition. Further the Kūram charter says that the brahmin donees were given the facility to draw a channel from the river Pālāru to Paramēsvara-taṭākam in the village and the Uttaramallūr inscriptions indicate that

Vairamēgha-taṭākam had especially been provided for helping the agriculture in that *brahmadēyam* village. Hence one is given to understand that these irrigation facilities were absent in those villages prior to the constitution of the *brahmadēyam*. While this must have been the reason why, this also demonstrated that the erstwhile inhabitants could not develop the land and assert their rights and had left the land available to the king to be granted to brahmins[7].

Thus though by issuing the charters the king does not appear to have trampled over the susceptibilities of people already inhabiting these villages, he is seen to have unhestitatingly nullified the control over those villages and localities exercised till then by *kō* who might have been the local chief or agent of the king[8]. This is made apparent by the reference in these charters to the changing of old possessors and the *kō* and seal. This control and authority was given over to the grantees of the brahmadēyam. This vesting of control and authority with the brahmins is reflected in the rights and privileges extended to the donees, in these charters. The Tamil text in these charters list several items of levies under the head 'exemptions' (*parihāra*, Leaving scope for the expansion of the list the texts say that all these and such were what the *kō* could take and thenceforward he could not levy the same in respect of the *brahmadēyam*. Sometimes they say pointedly that the donees could take these and enjoy. But apparently the implication in every case seems to have been that if they so wanted the brahmin donees could collect these levies and enjoy. Even while listing the irrigation privileges extended to the donees the charters say that the donees could collect fines from unauthorised poachers of the water in the same way as the *kō* could. These features in the chapters clearly enunciate how the control that might have been in the authority of *kō* till then was transferred to the brahmin donees in respect of the locality granted as brahmadēyam[9].

Apart from being given the position of *kō* in the land-control scheme the brahmins of these charters were also made supreme over the people of the locality who might or might not have been connected with land[10]. This is evident even from the exemptions which were often from levies that could be collected from tradesmen, artisans and professionals[11]. Through the non-mention of the rate of collection of these levies and the vagueness of list the *brahmadēyam* donees were enabled all the more to have these people under their authority. It is likely that the field for the exercise of this authority was not restricted strictly to the bloc granted as *brahmadēyam* but was wider, inclusive of the areas around[12]. The donees also could exercise discretion in the matter of allowing the toddy tappers to operate in the precincts of the *brahmadēyam*.

The other feature in the charters which highlights the control passed on to the *brahmadēyam* donees is the enumeration of types of land and facilities that could be deemed to have been included in the grant and the extension of exclusive privileges in respect of the irrigation facilities[13]. Though as per the exclusions referred to above the possession of land by *kuḍis* or others in the concerned villages was not disturbed the assertion in the charters that forests, pasture-ground, waste land high ground and low ground etc. in or in the precincts of the grant-village or that the donees could have the full and first use of the irrigation facilities, automatically placed the other inhabitants of the village in a position of dependence on the donees[14]. This is more pointedly driven home in some of the charters which say that *ūr* and *ūr-irukkai* apparently the residential sites and attached land of people probably other than *kuḍis* had been included within the grant. As under the "exemptions" the item fines (either mentioned as *maṇṛupāḍu* or *karaṇattandam* or *adhikarana-ttaṇḍam*) finds mention, it is obvious that the people from whom the fines could be collected, (i.e.) all the people of the locality had been placed under the judicial authority, probably in respect of minor offences, of the *brahmadēyam* donees[15].

Having thus associated the brahmins in the control of the localities the king extended to them the privilege of living in mansions of burnt bricks, the construction of which seems to have required royal permission issued only to the favoured controllers of land. The other privileges extended to these donees to utilise the land for raising flower and medicinal plants, for setting up coconut and arecanut groves, to set up the big oil press, to fill up ponds and wells probably at inconvenient places etc. further highlighted the extent of control that was vested in these donees.

While these *brahmadēyam* charters refer to the enlistment of the brahmins directly for the control of land the charters that refer to *devadāna* describe a variety of ways in which the brahmins were associated. The Kūram grant tells about the constitution of a *brahmadēyam* which the Sanskrit text of the charter says was a *devadāna-nimitta-brahmadēyam* for the purpose of the various services in the temple constructed by a feudatory at Kūram. The charter, however does not enlighten as to the way in which the *brahmadēyam* was to maintain the specified services in the temple. The Chiṭṛūr grant says that a newly constituted *brahmadēyam* would contribute the *pañchavāṛam* of 750 *kāḍi* of paddy as *dēvadāna* for maintaining a *chhatra* in a temple. The Vēlūrpāḷaiyam plates records the grant of the village Tirukkāṭṭuppaḷḷi as *dēvadāna* to a temple constructed in the same village by a brahmin belonging to the same village. Though here there is no indication if Tirukkāṭṭ uppaḷḷi was a *brahmadēyam* at the time of the grant, from the circumstances described it can be presumed that Tirukkāṭṭ uppaḷḷi was a *brahmadēyam*. Apart from this, late 9th century, 10th century inscriptions refer to some villages with *sabhās* in control, as those that were in the *puṛam* or *dēvadāna* of some prominent temples. As *sabhās* pertained to *brahmadēyam* villages it is again clear that these *sabhās* of *puṛam* villages were required to contribute the royal revenue to the concerned temples. Obviously these villages had been attached to those temples in the preceding epoch, possibly between the years c. A.D. 670-850. The Tiruvallam inscriptions of Nandivarman III actually records the attachment of a *dēvadāna* village to two other villages, one of which was probably already a *brahmadēyam* to constitute a new chaturvēdimangalam, the *sabhā* of which was asked to contribute to the temple a fixed amount of paddy and gold. While these instances demonstrate how brahmins or *brahmadēyams* to be exact, were associated with temples, they may be taken as suggesting that they were also subordinated to temples, which had been actually vested with the control of the land. But on closer look and on a consideration of the character of the temples concerned it will be clear that these *brahmadēyams* were meant to control the temple itself and its land and that the temple was only a pretext in the execution of the scheme for passing on the control of land to brahmins. When the Chōḷas took over the area, they do not seem to have required the *brahmins* for the control of land to the same extent as the Pallavas. There is no extant charter of the Chōḷa period recording the constitution of a new *brahmadēyam* except perhaps what was intended to be recorded in the Udayēndram plates of Vira-chōda which is incomplete without any certainty about its date.

Only two records pertaining to the period of Parāntaka I have any relevence to this subject. One of them, the Udayēndram plates (year 15-922) records the addition of a village to *brahmadēyam* Udayachandramangalam without making any mention of the *Parihāras* and privileges characteristic of the earlier period. The other the postscript as found in the Udayēndram plates of both Nandivarman I and II, only records the amalgamation of two *sabhā* villages of Kāñchīvāyil alias Igaṇmaṛaimangalam and Udayachandramangalam. Three other charters issued by members of the Bāṇa family who seem to have assumed independent control of the region for short periods when the Pallava and Chōḷa were in eclipse, also are in the nature of confirmatory grants only.

It has been mentioned above how in the year 21 (892) of Aditya I, that king adhered to the earlier practice and attached the major portion of a village granted as a *dēvadāna* to a *brahmadēyam* as *dēvadāna-brahmadēyam* and how subsequently in the year 36 (943) of Parāntaka I, when the bloc of land that was excluded in the earlier grant was also granted as *dēvadāna,* it was not handed over to the *brahmadēyam*. Not only that, early in the 11th century when Rājēndra I wanted to grant a village already attached as *brahmadēyam* to another *brahmadēyam*, as *dēvadāna,* he deliberately detached it from the *brahmadēyam* and brought it under *veḷḷānvagai* tenure before granting it to the temple. Further other information available in the records, that the Chōḷa king had sent his officials to watch over the proceedings of *sabhās* while they were enunciating regulations to govern the selections to committees that he arranged for an enhancement of the contribution of *pañchavāram* due from a *sabhā* village to a temple etc. all witnessed the direction in which the Chōḷa king was leading the land system. Not that the brahmin was discredited but there was no more dependance on the brahmin to control the localities. The Chōḷa king achieved this control of the localities through deputing his officials many of whom were apparently subordinate Chiefs.

While the records of the Pallava period indicate the extent to which these kings had passed on control of localities to brahmins, they do not throw any light on whether they had similarly associated the members of the royal family or feudatories in this control of land. Excepting the two records of the period of Nandivarnan III in the middle of the 9th Century which obliquely indicate that the king's mother and queen were in a position to exercise concurrent control over land where they wanted to make a religious donation, there is no reference to the members of the king's family having had anything to do with land. In so far as feudatories are concerned, several are mentioned but upto about the middle of the 9th Century there is no reflection in the records that any of them owed his position to the king or that the king had apportioned land to any one of them for control. In the only instance where the Udayēndram Charter of Nandivarman II says that the king wanted to recompense his feudatory who had steadfastly adhered to his cause he is seen to have only created a *brahmadēyam* in his honour and named it after him. However after the middle of the 9th Century some records indicate that the Pallava kings of that period, hardpressed as they were, had given a bloc of territory to a scion of the family of Gaṅga. One family of Prithvigaṅgaraiyar is stated to have had Paṅgala-nāḍu *(i-ṇnāḍu-uḍaiya)*. This family is also seen to have held the nāḍu hereditarily for a long time thereafter. But there is no information on the character of the control that had been passed on to this family. There is no indication in the records if more families like this had been associated in this land control. However during this same period there is an indication, that in the area of Paḍuvūr-kōṭṭam in Toṇḍaimaṇḍalam bordering on his territory, the Bāṇa who had his own home territory just to the north but had accepted the suzereinty of the Pallava, was gradually increasing his hold over that area. It has been seen that this feudatory was not in the picture when Nandivarman II made the Udayachandramaṅgalam grant in Mīyāṛu-nāḍu (referred to as Mēl-aḍaiyāṛu-nāḍu elsewhere) in that koṭṭam in the middle of the 8th century. But at the end of that century the Tiruvallam record pertaining to the same nāḍu indicated that the Bāṇa had some role in the land in that division as he is stated to have delimited the land granted to a temple by a private individual. Further on, in the middle of the 9th century another Tiruvallam record says a chief of that family made the supplication to the king regarding the constitution of a Chaturvēdimaṅgalam with a *sabhā* and that the same was named after him. This history of Tiruvallam evidenced the extent to which the Bāṇa's control over that territory had grown. It is not known if the Pallava king had consciously passed on control of the territory to any members of this family. It rather looks as if the initiative was that of the Bāṇa and the Pallava king had only to acquiesce after the Bāṇa had assumed that control. While in the above-mentioned records the Bāṇa still felt it necessary to acknowledge the sovereignty of the Pallava monarch in respect of that territory, at the end of the 9th century when the Pallava power had waned he dispensed with this formality. Two more records from Tiruvallam dated in that period refer to the Bāṇa as the ruler of the world.

Hence in the light of the case of the Bāṇa, it is difficult to say as to how far the Pallava monarch associated the feudatories in the land control scheme. Unless it was a local chief who had acknowledged the overlordship of the Pallava, to hand over the control of territories to those who did not belong to the locality could not have achieved the purpose of the king to secure the control by subtle means.

The records of the period make mention of a *kō* who from the contexts of the mention can be understood to have been a person in control of localities on behalf of the king. This *kō* is likely to have been such a local chief enlisted by the Pallava king for his own purposes, for exercising control and for collecting the royal revenue in respect of cultivated land from villages in the designated localities. Probably such a *kō* while he was a local chief, was used to collecting from the people certain levies unrelated to land and it appears that he was allowed to continue enjoying the proceeds from those levies.

While the *kō* could be deemed to have been an official of the Pallava king the records do not refer to any other person who could be *prima facie* recognised as an official of the Pallava king. Hence it is difficult to ascertain if the officials were associated in land control. However, a Kumārandai Kurumbar-ādittan of Chēra-nāḍu, who styled himself as *Kāḍu-paṭṭi*-pper-*araiyan* figures in an inscription of the time of Aparājita (year 4—889?). His title suggests that he might have been an official of the king in Toṇḍaimaṇḍalam though he might have been a chief in Chēra-nāḍu. In the Pallava's territory he seems to have been authorised to appropriate only the taxes both in kind and in gold payable to the king from one or more villages. In the record he is stated to have granted the same in respect of one village to the temple. The record does not say that he granted the village along with the taxes to the temple. The information not available is what for this authorisation was given to him, whether it was restricted to the period of service of the personage or if it was granted in perpetuity; whether it was partable (i.e.) bequeathable to heirs, whether it was capable of being sold or mortgaged; whether there were others who had been similarly authorised.

While the information on the place of feudatories in the land system of Toṇḍaimaṇḍalam under the Pallava regime is thus unclear, after the Chōḷa take-over some clear information on this aspect becomes available. In the light of the vigour and pervasiveness of the Chōḷa administration it could be expected that even if the feudatories had been exercising extraordinary land-control under the predecessor dynasty, that would have been curtailed. Actually as stated above the Chōḷas are seen to have tried to make each nook and corner feel their direct authority through their officials. However in the context of the period, the field of recruitment for the important positions in their official set up must naturally have been restricted only to the powerful landlords or chiefs. The records of that period refer to several persons sporting titles with suffixes, araiyaṟ (derivative of Rāja) and *nāḍuḍaiyāṇ* (he who had the nāḍu or merely uḍaiyān of an *ūr*.)[17] But such persons utilised by the Chōla king in the administration of Toṇḍaimaṇḍalam are mostly stated to have been araiya*n* or uḍaiyān of nāḍus or *ūrs* in Chōḷa-nāḍu. Hence it is obvious that the services of such chiefs or chief-like persons of Chōla-nāḍu were utilised in the administration but that there was no intention to pass on control of localities in Toṇḍaimaṇḍalam to them. Among these, even those who are known to have been chiefs, might have been such that were already there when the Chōḷas took over the control of both Chōḷa-nāḍu and Toṇḍai-nāḍu. If they continued to exist in that capacity, it seems to have been due only to the fact that this new dynasty of rulers did not think it necessary to displace them and found a way of utilising them without passing on control of localities to them.

Regarding the extent of control allowed to the chiefs under the Chōḷa administration the Pallaṅkōyil (North Arcot district) inscription of Uttamachōḷā (year 6—976) suggests that even in a territory (Paṅgaḷa-nāḍu) claimed by the feudatory (Uttama-chōḷa-Prithivī-gaṅgaraiyar) as in his possession *(uḍaiya)*, his control did not extend to the main land tax (iṛai) or to gifting land in that nāḍu to temples. The evidence of the Pañcha-pāṇḍavamalai (North Arcot District) inscription of the year 8 (A.D. 993) of Rājarāja I indicates that the feudatory had control over only the miscellaneous levies in the territory under his charge. It is not known if this restriction of the chiefs control had been imposed by the Chōḷas or if it had been the practice all along especially when a chief held or was given the control of territory within the proper domain of the king. It is probable that the above two chiefs belonged to the class of *kō* who is also seen to have been restricted only to the enjoyment of miscellaneous levies.

In the Chōḷa period some persons are stated to have had their maintenance *(jīvitam)* in a village each. An inscription of the year 4 of Rājakēsarivarman says that Kēraḷan Rājādittan alias Nanivichchādira-mārāyan had Valakkōn-maṅgalam as his *jīvitam*. It is not clear as to who he was, for what purpose he was given this village as maintenance and what he was entitled to in the village. On the other hand when a Maṇimaṅgalam (Chingleput district) record of the period of Vīrarājēndra (11th century) says that Jayaṅgoṇḍa-chōḷa-brahmādhirājar, a military commander *(sēnāpatigal)* had *jīvitam* in Maṇimaṅgalam, a *sabhā* village, it becomes evident that he could have had only the tax-revenue from the village as his maintenance. For, it is not conceivable that he could have had overall control over the land as the village was a sabhā village and it is the sabhā which is seen transacting in land therein.[18] Thus a person who was apparently a military commander and the other a brahmin military commander are seen to have received as their maintenance, the revenue of villages without any apparent connection with land. It is not known why among numerous other officials of the Chōḷa government none of the others is reflected to have had villages as their *jīvitam*.

Thus the records of the Chōḷa period indicate that the chiefs and officials, even where they had any connection with the territorial units in Toṇḍaimaṇḍalam they did not have any visible control of land.

However even during the Pallava period whereas the role of the feudatories in the control of land and people is found to be very vague, it is seen that such control was prominently exercised by communal organisations. The charters of Nandivarman II in the middle of the 8th century cite the *nāṭṭār* as an organisation depended upon by the king for the execution of details of the his grants. Significantly the king did not address himself to any feudatory, which fact by itself demonstrates that those territories were not in the control of any feudatory but under the charge of this body called *nāṭṭār*. The composition of this body is nowhere made clear but it can be surmised that influential persons probably landholders of the localities called nāḍu had formed this body to safeguard their own common interests and probadly also generally of the *nāḍu*. This body might already have been there when the pallava king began making grants of villages in those localities to brahmins. The Pallava king does not seem to have had a hand in its formation. The formation of such a local organisation seems to have been necessitated by the peculiarities of the region. However when the Pallava made grants of *brahmadēyam* often entrusting it to a group of brahmins, he seems to have had the intention of encouraging the formation of a compact local body with brahmins to displace the *nāṭṭāṛ* while such a formation might have been an answer to the necessities of the situation in the area, the apparent transfer of the control of localities from this *nāṭṭār* to these brahmin organisations, might have been impelled by his desire to have such people beholden to him and thus could be better depended upon, in the control of land. Whereas in the 8th century the *nāṭṭār* are reflected in the charters to have had conjoint control with the king in respect of at least the undeveloped portions of villages, and to have been a cognisable body with an establishment of its own, as the village organisations gained prominence subsequently, their role in the land system became truncated.

Probably it was the communal organisation, which owed its origin to the king and was envisaged while the king made grants to groups of brahmins as *brahmadēyam* in shares that came to be known as *sabhā* which finds very prominent mention in the records of the period. This *sabhā* seems to have been composed of only such brahmins in a *brahmadēyam* who were eligible to receive *brahmadēyam* on account of their antecedents and attainments. The formation of such a body seems to have been rendered necessary for the exercise of the control that was vested in the *brahmadēyam*[19] This body became so important in the land system of the period that, later, *dēvadāna* and other villages were attached as a whole to some of these *brahmadēyam*, with a *sabhā*.

In so far as land was concerned, the *sabhā* is seen to have held the common land of the main *brahmadēyam* village and to have taken measures to have it reclaimed. It had also the authority to entrust an attached village like Sōḍiyambākkam to a temple and authorise several rights to the temple but at the same time retain control over that village as made evident in the inscriptions from Ukkal pertaining to the 10th century. It seems to have been in charge of the collection of revenue in the *brahmadēyam* village as also in the attached villages and in that capacity it was in a position to accept deposits of capital against the taxes in respect of land endowed to temples and free the land from taxes. Some times it is seen that it could set apart common land in the village to a temple and grant tax-free status in respect of that land on its own. It could determine the items of levies which were to be paid for its own consumption[20]. It could also gift away for a temple purpose the levies due to it from an attached village[21].

The *sabhā* is also seen to have been in charge of the maintenance of the irrigation facilities pertaining to the village/ villages concerned and also in charge of the exercise of the rights connected with them conferred by the charter.

For the discharge of the various functions devolving on it, the *sabhā* in some of the villages is seen to have constituted committees as necessary. For meeting the expenses of the local administration, the *sabhā* is seen to have collected some charges. For maintaining the irrigation facilities and probably for meeting some capital expenses it accepted deposits of gold from temples.

Its control over people is also deduceable from the records. While it can be understood that the persons holding land in the attached villages as also the persons *(Kuḍis)* to whom the *sabhā* made common land available for reclamation must have come under its authority it can also be deduced on the basis of the details contained in the available charters that the persons other than those eligible to receive *brahmadēyam,* allotted shares in the *brahmadēyam* as per the charter must have come under the corporate control of the *sabhā*. Thus the *sabhā* got control over the priests in the temples within the *brahmadēyam* for which shares had been set apart as also over those employed for various services in the *brahmadēyam*. Only the Pullūr plates say that fifteen shares were allotted in Nayadhīramaṅgalam for arranging the various services in the village. However, though such allotment of shares for arranging the services is not seen in other charters, there must have been necessity for such services in other *brahmadēyam* also and persons must have been engaged under the authority of the *sabhā*.

Apart from these persons, the corporate body of the *brahmadēyam* brahmins, the *sabhā* was in a position to restrict the membership in the committees as also probably in the *sabhā* by laying down standard qualifications, like the possession of a minimum amount of land and of Vedic-scholarship. Thus the individual member in the group of *brahmadēyam* donees also became subordinate to the corporate body. On losing the eligibility to take part in the *sabhā* his position could not have been better than that of the non-*brahmadēyam* holders of the village. Thus it was the *sabhā*, the corporate body which was more important in a *brahmadēyam* than the individuals who were brought together originally to compose it.

Two other organisations *ūr* and *nagaṛam* were also seen to have been exercising communal control over villages. While the comnunal control exercised by *sabhā* is learnt to have been based on the intentions of the monarch to place different localities under the control of groups of brahmins, it is not known how these two bodies came to have control in the land system. Of these two even the composition of *ūr* is nowhere made clear. It might have been composed of landholders or of all the prominent inhabitants of a village and might have been part of the land system in Toṇḍaimaṇḍalam and around even before the start of the period under study. But from the fact that the type of *ūr* witnessed as exercising communal control is first heard of only in the beginning of the 9th century, more or less at the same time as *sabhā* began to be mentioned in the records, and as a Chintāmaṇi (Chingleput district) record of the period of Kṛṣṇa III (965) indicates that there was a periodical redistribution of land in that *ūr* village, it seems possible that this organisation also came into being as a result of charters of the period granting villages to a group of people, and that only a specimen of such a charter has not come up. However even if such a charter had been issued it could not have compared with a *brahmadēyam* charter, for, *ūrs* communal control is seen to have been limited.

In the records of the period, *ūrs* of different villages are stated to have (1) accepted deposits of gold or paddy from temples or individuals for contributing the stipulated interest to meet the expenses of specified services in temples and (2) to have been in charge of the maintenance of the irrigation facilities pertaining to their villages. They also probably possessed some special rights with regard to those irrigation facilities. However, if not all, at least some of the *ūrs* seem to have been in a subordinate position. Sometimes, as in the case of Paḷaiyanūr of the Tiruvālaṅgāḍu plates, *ūr* was administering a village attached as a whole with the status of *brahmadēyam* to the *sabhā* of a village where the *brahmadēyam* was shared by several individual brahmins. *ūr* is also found in charge of villages in the *dēvadāna,* or *puram* of temples. Their role in the temple complex could not have been the same as that of the *sabhās* in a similar position in those *dēvadāna* or *puram* complexes. In both the above instances the concerned *ūrs* must have been subservient to the brahmins of the *sabhā* or the temple which must have also been under the control of the *sabhā/sabhās* of some other village or villages in the concerned *dēvadāna* or *puṛam* complex. Apart from these, if the *ūrgaḷiḷār* who are stated to have represented some villages under special tenures, like *kāṇimuṛrūṭṭu, vēṭṭappēṛu*, *paḷḷichchandam* etc. were the same as the *ūr*s reflected to have been corporate bodies of villages, not specifically stated to have been under any special tenure, then also it becomes clear that the *ūrs* of these villages at least were subordinate to the beneficiary/beneficiaries of those special tenures.

The other body, *nagaram* is seen to be having a communal role in the land system only in the early eleventh century. The concerned inscriptions pertain to Māmallapuram and Mēlpāḍi. Though, again there is no charter available throwing light on how this body came to play a part in the land-system, the records from the two places mentioned give some significant information. The Māmallapuram inscription records a redistribution of land in that village in *kūrus* and refers to an earlier arrangement in this regard evidencing that the *nagaram* of that place had been in the land scheme of that place even before the date of the record (1010). It records further the rights pertaining to each bloc *(kūru)* into which the land of the village had been apportioned and makes a rare mention of the right to trees. It also lays down the rates of taxes payable by non-participants in the land-owning *nagaram*, though it is not made clear as to who was to be the beneficiary, from these levies the king or the *nagaram*. One Mēlpāḍi inscription dated just a few years thence gives the important, indication that the *nagaram* of Rājāśrayapuram too had got neighbouring villages attached to it but suggests that the land in the attached village was meant to be apportioned among the block *(kūru)*-holders of the main *nagaram* village. Another record from the same place of the same date indicates that the *nagaram* was in a position to extend to a temple the right to dig a channel of a specified width from the river to the field gifted to that temple by the same *nagaram*. Whereas in the case of *sabhā* and *ūr* villages. the records refer to the reservoirs attached to them, in the case of the two *nagaram* villages there is no such reference.

During most of the period under study, the temple is not indicated to have been concerned with land directly. Villages attached to temples are found under the control mostly of *sabhās* and sometimes of *ūrs*. The plots of land allotted to it on the strength of shares in *brahmadēyam* or otherwise endowed by interested persons were in the custody of one or two priests. However, towards the end of the 10th century and early in the 11th century it is found that in the case of the prominent temples where there were a number of priests in charge of the worship and where there were villages or land till then not attached to village organisations, such villages/land began to be held by the priests who had formed themselves into a corporate body. Apparently these priestly bodies were to contribute for the expenses of specified items of worship. This may suggest that this body of priests was also organised to exercise communal control over land like a *sabhā*. A Tiruvallam inscription of Rājēndra I (1016) indicates that the body of priests was also entitled to receive some miscellaneous levies from the occupants of the land. But this picture was illusory. The brahmin serving as a priest in a temple never enjoyed the prestige of the brahmins given *brahmadēyam*. During the year 7 (A.D. 992) of Rājarāja I the priestly body of the temple at Tiruvallam is found to have been hauled up when the worship in the Tiruvallam temple was in a poor state. The inscription from Tiruvallam dated year 4 (A.D. 1016) of Rājēndra I which refers to the priests of the temple of Tiruvallam-uḍaiyār as those possessing Kāṇi in a *dēvadāna* village also indicates that these priests were under the authority of the body of the administrators *(dēvakaṇmis*) of that temple. The latter body which might have been constituted with the influential members of the village is also seen to have had only a limited control of land belonging to the temple. Both these bodies the priests and *dēvakanmis* were helpless onlookers when the *sabhā* of Puduppākkam decided to take charge of the extra land in Sirriyarrūr when it was granted as *dēvadāna*. Hence while the *sabhā* was apparently untramelled in its exercise of communal control of land belonging to the temple on behalf of the temple, the bodies constituted especially in the temple were not vested with the same amount of control.

When it is seen that during the period the accent was on communal control, naturally the role of the individual in the control of land was correspondingly limited. It has been seen how the individual only in the *sabhā* villages gets mention among the records. These individuals, the brahmins, are evidenced to have enjoyed the right to gift, sell,and mortgage land. They also had the right to bequeath their possession in inheritance. But such transactions were governed by the limitations arising out of their possession having been a share or a part of a share in those *brahmadēyam* villages. Their position in the village was also determined by the quantum of land they held and their attainment of sufficient *vēdic* knowledge.

All the land system with a land-control scheme as devised in Toṇḍaimaṇḍalam during the period was made possible by the expansion if not introduction of a sound system of irrigation with reservoirs to store the runaway waters of the stormfed rivers of the region. Many of these reservoirs seem to have been constructed for the benefit of *brahmadēyams* at the time of their constitution. These *brahmadēyams* were in charge of the maintenance of the irrigation facilities pertaining to their villages. They also enjoyed exclusive privileges for the use of the water. They had also the right to make available these privileges to temples in respect of land endowed to them. Some other reservoirs also seem to have come up during the period, independent of *brahmadēyams*. It is seen that some *ūrs* were also supported by reservoirs. The *ūr* had the right to manage and maintain those reservoirs. Some other reservoirs which are not expressly stated to have been attached to villages are also mentioned in the records. Thus the development of the irrigation system which was originally meant to support *brahmadēyams* seems to have been expanded in due course to encourage cultivation of paddy which was the prestigious crop of the time in all possible areas. This effort of the time is very well brought out in the Tirumalai inscription of the year 21 (1006) of Rājarāja I which extols the achievement of a Jain teacher entitled *vaigai-kkō* in seeing to it that paddy was raised.

While these records of the period shed this much of light on those that held control of land, they do not indicate as to who worked the land. This might have been due to the character of the records.[22] It seems likely that the brahmins of the *brahmadēyams* never engaged themselves in the manual labour connected with cultivation At least some of the *kuḍis* might have been involved in this manual labour. But as even during the earlier saṅgam period, the groups, *Paraiyar, Eyinar* etc. are referred to and as these groups are found in later days in the position of serfs to brahmins and veḷḷāḷar, it can be surmised that even during the period studied, these groups might have been fitted into the agricultural society in a similar role.

The Pallava kings' efforts in the region were directed not only to secure control of the region but also to make his economic position sound which would have been possible only if he received his due share of the proceeds from land. Hence it is seen that he had not exempted even villages granted as *brahmadēyam* from the taxes payable to him. Howver it appears that he had not taken the trouble of getting the land assessed plot-wise. He seems to have been content to fix his dues, on a village-wise basis at a round figure. This is understable in the light of the evidence which indicates that he was prone to hand over the control of the territories to communal bodies. *Pañcha-vāram* which is seen to have been authorised to temples seems to have been such dues from these villages to him. This *pañchavāram* might have been what was paid in five instalments or what was the fifth portion of the produce. Initially the royal dues seem to have been restricted to a collection in kind but by the middle of the 9th century a gold levy seems to have been added. The dues in kind also seems to have been redesignated as *puravu* at about this time. This due in kind was probably fixed at 1/6 of the produce[23]. Soon after when Chōḷa Aditya I had taken over the region he seems to have added an *iravu* or what was demanded (benevolence) to the dues. Though this is cited in the case of only one village it might have had a general application. Probably the other tax term that is found used about this time *irai* included this as the latter is no more heard of. Thereafter the king's demand from land seems to have been steady. Apart from the king's taxes, the land is seen to have been burdened with some further levies meant to defray the expenses of local administration. This seems to have included the proportionate cost of the maintenance of the reservoir pertaining to the village, though during the period there is no evidence of the king having collected any levy against the provision of irrigation facilities. No information is available on the rates of these levies. There is not much evidence to indicate the price of land during the period but from the scraps that can be pieced together it appears that it was maintained at a steady level.

The land system in Toṇḍaimaṇḍalam shaped during the period studied is seen to have been generally beneficial. This is reflected in the enormous increase in the number of agricultural settlements. Whereas in the earlier period the available evidence points only to Kāñchīpuram and some area around as having been settled probably with an agricultural base, the records of the period studied refer to some 346 villages not counting some of the sub-villages and blocs of settlements attached to some main villages, spread over almost all the areas that was known as Toṇḍaimaṇḍalam. Of these, 190 villages have produced inscriptional records. Of the total villages mentioned 73 are stated to have been under the administration of *sabhā,* the brahmin organisation, 51 under the enigmatic *ūr* and 7 under the *nagaram*, the corporate body of merchants.

NOTES:

1. cf. Kesavan Veluthat, "The Temple-Base of the Bhakti Movement in South India", *Proc. IHC,* 1979 (Waltair), p. 188 etc. The first epigraphical evidence regarding grants to temples is provided only by the Tirukkāḷukkuṉṟam inscription of Narasimhavarman I (630-668). Though while stating that the king granted *Vāḷippāṭ-ṭuppuṟam* the record does not indicate what was given, as pointed out above, it can be deduced that Tirukkaḷukkunram itself had been granted as *puṟam*. It has also been pointed out that apart from the statement in the charters that shares had been allotted to temples in the newly constituted *brahmadēyams*, there is no epigraphic evidence of plots of land having been granted to temples before the time of Nandivarman III (846-869). When villages were attached to temples, the temples entitlement was restricted to the royal revenue from those villages and when plots of land began to be endowed, they were usually entrusted to the priests.
2. Though the *dharma—sāstras* conceded that a brahmin could wield the plough when necessary (*Brihaspati-smriti-Āpad-dharma-kāṇḍa*, V. 3, 7, 19), he could never have been expected by the king to mannually work the land. The British administators of the 19th century found that a concession in land tax termed as *brāhmaṇa-minaha* was allowable to brahmana landholders as they were told that the *sāstras* distinctly forbid a brahmin to plough (Croele, *Manual* of *the Chingleput District*, p. 50). Also Marc Bloch, *op. cit.,* (1974), p. 346.
3. Also cf. March Bloch, *op. cit.,* (1974), p. 347. Cf. Sharma, RS, *Ind. Feud.* (1980), p. 215,224; Yadava, BNS, *Society and Agriculture in Northern India in the 12th century*, p. 26-27.
4. cf. Sharma, RS., *Ind. Feud*, p. 285. Also ibid. Material Milieu of Tantricism, *ISHP*, p. 187.
5. The clerics of the Christian religion in the west like the brahmins in India were known to have been repositories of knowledge during the middle ages. But the similarity stopped there. The clericalism of the Christian religion was not hereditary and was very different from the brahminism of the Hindu religion. For instance the ecclesiastical hierarchy and extra territorial loyalties characteristic of the Christian religion was absent in the Hindu religion.

   Further, in the Hindu religion unlike in Christianity the brahmins conducting worship in temples came to form a class distinct from the brahmins engaged in scholarly pursuits. The brahmin renouncing the wordly life and becoming a sanyasin unlike a Christian monk was not expected to hold or manage properly. The brahmin engaged in scholarly pursuit if granted land in reeognition of his merit held it on his own. The brahmin engaged in temples could be deemed to have been some-what similar in position to a clergyman where he held land of the religious institutions and managed it on its behalf. But there was a tendency for that land becoming more personal to him as unlike in Christianity, he got a portion of the land, allotted to the temple, against a stipulated service both the service and land becoming a hereditary possession. There was also a vast difference between the hold of a Christian priest and of a brahmin or Hindu Temple priest, over the king and the others. cf. Marc Bloch, *op. cit.*, (Chicago, 1974), pp. 82, 346.

6. Lallanji Gopal, *Aspects of the History of Agriculture in Ancient India*, p. 68-69; p. 80-81.
7. It is not known if the *kuḍi* was part of the *nāṭṭār* the body which the king associated in the grant by addressing it regarding the grant, asking it to delimit the grant land and give the release order. If they were part of the *nāṭṭār* they must have enjoyed some vague right over the land. They were probably utilising the land for cultivation haphazardly whenever the facilities were available and favourable. cf. Stein, Burton, *Peasant State and Society in Medieval South India,* p. 17, Pillai, KK, *op. cit.,* p. 187.
8. Marc Bloch, *op. cit.,* p. 157.
9. *Ibid.*
10. cf. Yadava, B.N.S., *op. cit.,* p. 170.
11. cf. Jha, D.N., Presidential Address (Ancient India) Proc, IHC, 1979, (Waltair) p. 26-27.
12. cf. Stein, Burton, Social Mobility and Medieval South Indian Sects, *Social Mobility in the Caste System in India.* ed. James Salverberg, p. 82; ibid Integration of the Agrarian System of South India, *Land Control and Social Structure in Indian History,* ed. R. E. Frykenberg, p. 184.
13. Sharma, R.S., *Ind. Feud.* (1980), pp. 215, 222.
14. cf. Jha, D.N., *op. cit.,* p. 28.
15. Marc Bloch, *op. cit.,* pp. 109, 115, 129, 149, 192.
16. This phenomenon can be compared with that presented by the records of Bāṇa-Rēṇāṇḍu, the Bāṇās original territory, Where

the inscriptions pertaining to early 8th century indicate on the one hand the *Bānā's* subordination to the Western Chālukya through reference to his suzerein's regnal year, on the other hand they refer to the Bāṇa as the ruler of the area *(AREp.* 1958-59, B 15, 16, 17, 26.

17. Udaiyān sometimes is seen to indicate a person who Possessed land or where he is hailing from. Kumārandai-Kurumbar-ādittan of the Satyavēḍu inscription of Aparājita, aforecited described as (Chēra-nāḍu-uḍaiya could not have been the chief of *Chēra-nāḍu*. *Ūroḍeya* may have also been an official designation of persons in charge of the collection of revenue in a village (cf. *EI,* XXXVI, p. 118, 120; Udgaonkar, Padma, B., *The Political Institution and Adminis-tration of Northern India During Medieval Times* (From 750-1200 AD) (Motilal Banarsidass, Delhi, 1969), pp. 159-164; Sastri, K.A.N., *The Cola*, p. 466).
18. The brahmādhirājar, the military commander of this record could not have been an equivalent of the brahmādhirājar who was allotted four shares in *brahmadēyam* Nayadhīramaṅgalam as per the Pullur plates. The latter, though apparently a brahmin seems to have been distinct from the brahmins eligible to receive *brahmadēyam* as his name, gotra etc are not detailed. The *brahmadēyam* donees were probably expected to enlist a brahmin whose only qualification was robustness and utilise him as the strongman of the village. The military commanders designated as *brahmādhirājar* in the king's army might have been chosen from the ranks of the *brahhmadhirājar* of villages.
19. Sharma, RS., *Ind. Feud.* (1980), p. 219.
20. *SII.*, VI, 345
21. *Ibid.*, 324.
22. Jayasvāl, Suvira, "*Studies, in the, Social Structure* of the Early Tamils", *ISHP,* p. 151.
23. cf. Lallanji Gopai, *Aspects of the History of Agriculture in Ancient India,* p. 81 n.

BIBLIOGRAPHY

Original sources

Annual Reports on Epigraphy (1887 to 1921-22)

Annual Reports on south Indian Epigraphy (1922-23 to 1944-45)

Annual Reports on Indian Epigraphy (1945-46 to date)

Epigraphia Indica, Vols. I, II, III, IV, V, VII, XXXIII, XXXVI

Indian Antiquary. Vol. III

Butterworth A.and Venugopal chetty, V. ed. *Inscriptions on Copper-Plates and Stone in the Nellore District*—Vol I (1905)

Subrahmanyam, R. ed., Sri *Mallampalli Somasekhara* Sarma Commemoration Volume (Journal of the Andhra Historical Research Society, Vol. XXXV-1975-76, Hyderabad, 1976).

Ramesan, N. ed., *Copper-plate inscriptions of A. P. Govt.* Museum, Hyderabad Vol I, Vol III (studies in Medieval (1962) Deccan History) (1972).

Transactions of the Archaeological Society of south India 1955, 1956- 57; 1957-58; 1958-59; 1959-60; 1962.

Subramanian, TN. ed. *South Indian Temple Inscriptions* - (Madras, 1953, 1954, 1955).

Sadhu Subrahmania Sastri, ed. *Sri Tirupati-Tirumalai Dēvasthaṇam Epigraphical Series* = Vol. I (Early Inscriptions) (1931)

South Indian Inscriptions:

I to VIII, XII-XIV, XVII, XIX, XXIII.

LITERARY

Sanskrit

Iyengar, KV Rangasvami, ed. *Brihaspati-smriti-Āpad-dharma-kāṇḍam* (Baroda)

Vitthala Sarma, and Gore, ED. *Manusmriti-with Kullūka-bhatta's Commentary*—Bombay, 1887).

RP Kangle ed. Kautilya's Arthasāstra, Part I Bombay, 1970).

Tamil

Nandikkalambagam	Madras, 1968.
Tiruttondar-Mākkādai (Periya-pūrāṇam)	Madras, 1970.
Silappadigāram	Madras 1975.
Tirukkuraḷ—with the commentary of Parimelalagar.	Madras 1973.

SECONDARY SOURCES

Adhya, G. L., *Early Indian Economics*—Bombay, 1966).

Appadorai, A., *Economic conditions in South India* (1000-1500 A.D.)—1936,

Arokiasami, M., *The Kongu country* (Madras, 1956)

The Early History of Vellar Basin (Amuda Nilayam, Madras 1954).

Baden Powell, B.H., *Land Systems of British India*, (Oxford, 1892).

Balambal, V., *Feudatories of South India*. 800-1070 A.D., Allahabad, 1978.

Basham, A.L., History and Doctrines of the *Ajivikas* (Luzac and Co. Ltd., London, 1951).

Bloch, Marc, tr. LA Manyon—*Fedudal Society*, London, 1961)

Cantor, Leonard, M.A., *World Geography of Irrigation* (Oliver and Boyd, 1967).

Chopra, P.N., Ravindran, T.K., and Subramaniyan, N., *A History of South India,* Vol. I (Ancient period), New Delhi, 1979.

Cox, Arthur, F., Revised by Herold, *A Smart Madras District* Manual, North Arcot, Madras, 1880, 1895

Croele, Charles Smart, *A Mannual* of the *Chingleput District* (Madras, 1879).

Das, Dipak Ranjan, *Economic History of the Deccan* (Delhi, 1969).

Desai, P.B., Jainism in South India and, some Jaina Epigraphs (Sholapur, 1957).

Dikshitar, V.R.R., *Hindu Administrative Institutions* (Madras, 1929).

Dobby, E.H.G., *Monsoon Asia*, Vol. 5 (London, 1970).

Eugene, F., Irschich, *Politics and Social conflict in South India*, (OUP, 1969).

Forbes, R.J., *Studies in Ancient Technology*, Pt. I-III (Leiden, 1955-57)

Frykenberg, Robert Eric, ed. *Land Control and social Structure in Indian History*, "Integration of the Agrarian system of South India" (Milwaukee, 1969).

Ganguli, B.N., ed. *Readings in Indian Economic History-Proceedings of the First All-India Seminar on Indian Economic History,* (Bombay, 1964).

Ghosal, U.N., *The Agrarian System in Ancient India* (Calcutta, 1930)

——— *Contributions to the History of Hindu Revenue system* (Calcutta, 1929).

Ghosh, K.K., *Agricultural Labourers in India* (India Publications, 1969)

Gopal, Lallanji, *The Economic Life of northern India*, c. A.D. 700-1200 (Varanasi, 1965).

——— *Economic History of India, Aspects of the History of Agriculture* in Ancient India (Bharati, Varanasi, 1980).

Gopalan, R., *History of the Paḷḷavas of Kañchi* (Madras, 1928).

Govindaswami, M.S., *The Role of Feudatories in Pallava History* (Annamalainagar, 1965).

Gupta, K.M., *Land System in South India*, c. 800-1000, A.D. (Lahore, 1933)

Heintzelmann, Oliver, H. and Highsmith, Richard, M. Jr., World Regional Geography, Fourth Edition (New Jersey, 1973).

Iyer, K.V. Subramania, *Historical Sketcnes of Ancient Dekhan* Vol. II (Coimbatore 1967).

Jha, D.N., *Revenue Systems in Post-Maurya-Gupta Times,* Calcutta, 1967).

Kanaka*sabhāi*, V., *The Tamils Eighteen Hundred years Ago* (1904-Reprint by Asian Educational services, New Delhi, 1979).

Kosambi, D.D. *An introduction to the Study of Indian History* (Popular Book Depot (Bombay, 1956).

Krishnamurthy, Vaidehi, *A Social and Economic conditions in Eastern Deccan*—1970.

Kumar, Dr. Dharma, *Land and Caste in South India: Agricultural labour in Madras Presidency in 19th century* (Cambridge University Press, London, 1965).

Lyon, White Jr., *History of Technical and Social Change in Middle Ages*.

Mahalingam, T.V., *ed. Report on the Excavations in the Lower Kavēri Valley* (TirukkāmPuliyur and Alagarai (1962-1964, Madras 1970).

——— *Kāñchīpuram in Early South Indian History*—(Madras 1969).

——— *Readings in South Indian History* (ed. Ramachandran, K.S.)—Delhi, 1977.

——— *South Indian Polity*—Madras, 1955.

Maiti, S.K., *Economic Life in Northern India in the Gupta Period* (Cir. A.D. 300-550) (Revised Second Edition, Motilal Banarsidas, 1970).

Majumdar, B.P., *Socio-Economic History of North India* 1030-1194 A.D. (Phakaṭ Prasad Mukkopadhyaya, Calcutta, 1901).

Majumdar, R.C., *ed. The Classical Age*, (Bombay, 1962)

——— *Corporate Life in Ancient India* (Calcutta, 1918)

——— *The Age of Imperial Kanauj*, Bombay, 1964 (2nd Edn.)

——— *The Struggle for Empire*, Bombay, 1966 (2nd Edn.)

Minakshi, C., *Administration and social Life under the Pallavas*—Madras 1938.

Mukherjee, Radhakamal, *Land Problems of India*—Calcutta University Readership Lectures, London, 1933.

Mukherjee, Radha Kumud, *Local Government in Ancient India* Delhi, 1958.

Nagasami, R., *ed. Seminar on Inscriptions* (Madras, 1966).

Nandi, Ramendra Nath, *Religions and cults in the Deccan* c.A.D. 600-1000 (Delhi, 1973).

Narasimhamurthy, A.V., and Gururaja, B.K., Rao, *ed. Rangavalli-Recent Researches in Iṇdology* (Sri S.R. Rao Felicitation Volume) Delhi, 1983.

Narayanan, M.G.S., *Reinterpretations in South Indian History* (College Book House, Trivandrum—1977).

Parker, H., *Ancient Ceylon* (Reprint: Asian Educational Services, New Delhi -1981).

Pillay, K.K., *A Social History of the Tamils* (Madras, 1969).

——— *Early History of Nancinad*, (Madras, 1950).

Pirenne, Henri, *Economic and Social History of Europe* (London, 1936).

Ramachandran, K.S., ed. N. *Ramesan Radio-carbon dates of Archaeological Sites in India* (Hyderabad, 1975).

Raman, K.V., *Some aspects of Pandyaṇ History in the Light of Recent Discoveries* (Sir Subramanian Ayar Edowment lecture—1971-72) (Madras)

——— *Sri-Varadarājasvāmi Temple—Kānchi A study of its History, Art and Architecture* (New Delhi, 1975).

——— *The Early History of the Madras Region* (Madras, 1959).

Ramesh, K.V., *A History of South Kanara- From the Earliest Times to the Fall of Vijayanagara* (Dharwar, 1970).

Sarma, I.K., *coinage of the Satavahaṇa Empire,* Agam Kala Prakashan, Delhi, 1980.

Sastri, K.A.N., *A History of South India—From Pre-historic Times to the Fall of Vijayanagar* (Madras, 1966).

——— *Foreign Notices of South India*—From Megasthenes to Fahien, Madras, 1939).

——— *The Pandyan Kingdom—From the Earliest Times to 16th century* (London, 1929).

——— *Sources of Indian History*-with special reference to South India (Bombay, 1964).

——— *South Indian Influences in far-east* (Bombay 1949).

——— *Studies in Chōḷa History and Administration* (Madras, 1932).

——— *The Colas* (Madras—Reprint 1975).

Satyanatha, Iyer, R., *Studies in the Ancient History of Tondai-maṇḍalam* (Madras, 1944).

Sharma, R.S., *Ancient India*. (NCERT, 1977)

——— *Indian Feudalism* c. 300-1200 (University of Calcutta, 1965) second Edn. Macmillan, 1980).

——— ed. *Indian Society Historical-Probings* (in memory of D.D. Kosambi (New Delhi, 1974, 1977).

——— *Light on Early Indian Society and Economy* (Bombay, 1966).

——— *Sudras in Ancient India* (Delhi, 1958).

Shastri, K.R.R., *South Indian Guilds* (Madras, 1925).

Singh, Ram Gharita Prasad, *Kingship in Northern India,* Delhi, 1968.

Sircar, D.C., *Landlordism and Tenancy in Ancient and Medieval India as revealed by Epigraphical Records* (Dr. RK Mookerji Endowment Lecture, University of Lucknow, 1964) (Lucknow, 1969).

——— *Land system and Feudalism in Ancient India,* (Calcutta, 1966).

——— *Select Inscriptions* (Bearing on Indian History and civilisation), Vol. I Calcutta, 1965.

Slater, Gilbert, *Southern India. Its Political and Economic problems* (London, 1936),

Spellman, John W., *Political Theory of Ancient India,* Oxford, 1964.

Srinivasan, C.R., *Kanchipuram Through the Ages* Delhi, 1979.

Stein, Burton, *ed. Essays on South India* (Asian studies Programme, University of Hawaii, The University Press of Hawaii, 1975)

——— *Peasant State and society in Medieval South India* (OUP, Delhi, 1980).

Subbarayalu, Y., *Political Geography of the Chōḷa country* (State Department of Archaeology, Tamilnadu, Madras, 1973).

Subramanian, N., *History of TamilNadu* (To A.D. 1936) Madurai, 1972.

——— *Sangam Polity* Bombay, 1966.

——— *Pre-Paḷḷavan Index* Madras, 1966.

Subramanian, T.N., *Thirty Pallava copper-Plates (Tamil)* Madras.

Thomas and Ramakrishnan, *South Indian Villages—A Resurvey* Madras, 1940.

Thompson. J.W., *Economic and Social History of the Middle - ages,* Newyork, 1959.

Udgaonkar, Padma B., *The Political Institutions and Administration of Northern India During Medieval Times* (From 750-1200 A.D.) Delhi, 1969.

Warder, A.K., *An introduction to Indian Historiography,* Bombay, 1972.

Watters, Thomas, ed. T.W. Rhys Davids and S.W. Bushell, *On Yuan Chwang's Travels in India*, A.D. 629-645 (Munshiram Monoharlar, New Delhi, 1973).

Yadava, B.N.S., *Society and Culture in Northern India,* Allahabad, 1973.

Select Articles:

Chatterjee, K.R., "The Joint Villages of South India and communal Tenure".

——— *Journal of Andhra Historical Research Society,* XXVII, Pts 1-4, July 1961-April 1962, pp. 107-113.

Chaudhri, K.K., *"Some Aspects of Feudalism in South* India", JIH, Vol. 53,1.

Dikshitar, V.R.R., *"A History of Irrigation in South India",* JIH, Vol. 53, 1

——— , *"A History of Irrigation in South* India", *Indian Culture*, XII, p. 71 f.

Frykenberg, Robert, "Traditional Processes of Power in South India: An Historical Analysis of Local Influence, *JAS* XIX, (Aug. 1960).

Gopal, Lallanji, "On Feudal Politics in Ancient India", *JIH*, 41, p. 405-13.

Hanumanthan, K.R., "The *Valaṅgai* and Id*aṇgai* Factions of the Imperial Chola period *Proc.* IHC, 37th session (Calicut), 1976, p. 107-111.

——— "Was there Untouchability in the Early Tamil society", *Proc. IHC*, 38th session (Bhubaneswar) 1977, p. 90-99.

Hjejle, Benedicte, Slavery and Agricultural Bondage in South India in 19th Century, *The Scandinavian Economic History Review*, (1967), p. 83 f.

Irfan Habib, "The social Distribution of landed Property in Pre-British India,"

——— *International Economic History Congress*, 3, Munish, 1965.

Jaisval Suvira, *Presidential address to ancient India section, Proc. IHC*, 38th session (Bhubaneswar), 1977, pp. 23-48.

——— 'Studies in the social structure of the Early Tamils, *Indian Society : Historical Probings* ed. R.S. Sharma (Peoples Publishing House, New Delhi, 1974, pp. 124-155).

Karashima, N., The Power Structure of the Chōḷa Rule,' *International conference Seminar of Tamil* Studies, II (Madras, 1971) Proc, pp. 233-44.

Allur and Isanamaṅgalam-Two South Indian Villages of Chōḷa Times—*Indian Economic and Social History Review* III (1966), pp. 150-62.

Kesavan, Veluthat, 'The nature and Administration in the Brahmadēyams under the Pallavas and Pandyas (Summary)—*Proc*—IHC, 37th Session (Calicut), 1976, p. 106 f.

Kosambi, D.D., 'Indian Feudal Trade Charters' *JESHO*, ii, Pt. III (1959), p. 281-293.

Krishnan, K.G., Literary and Epigraphical References to the coinage in the Ancient Tamilnad, *JNSI.*, XX, pp. 9-14.

——— Chola Rājendra's Expedition to South-east Asia, (Seminar on Medieval Inscriptions—Aligarh, February, 1970) *JIH*, Golden Jbilee Volume, pp. 109-116.

Krishnaswami, S.Y., Major Irrigation systems of Ancient Tamilnadu'—*Proc. of The International Conference Seminar of Tamil Studies*, Kuala Lamapur, 1968, pp. 451-61.

Kumar, Dharma, Land Ownership and Inequality in Madras Presidency, *IESHR*. XII, 3, July-5 1975, pp. 230 f.

Liceria, A.C.M., 'The Migration of Brahamnas to Karnataka —Proc. IHG, 35th session (Jadavpur), 1974, pp. 80-86.

Mannithamby, L., Village and Temple Administration in the Allur Inscriptions', *International conference Seminar of Tamil Studies*, IITS, (Madras, 1971), *Proc*, pp. 245-50.

Mitchell, Will P., 'The Hydraulic Hypothesis—A Reappraisal, *Current Anthropology*, XIV (Dec. 1973).

Morris, David Morris, Stein, 'Burton, The Economic History of India; A Bibiliographic Essay' *Journal of Economic History*, pp. 179 f.

Nandi, R.N., Some Social Aspects of *Nalayira-Prabandham'*, *Proc. IHC*. 37th Session (Calicut) 1976, p. 138f.

——— Family and Inheritance in Early South India', *Proc. IHC* 35th (Jadavpur) 1974, p. 72 f.

Narayanan, M.G.S., *'Cattle Raiders of the Sangam Age' Proc. IHC*. 38th Session (Bhubaneswar), 1977, pp. 70-82.

Puri, B.N., "Irrigation and Agricultural Economy in Ancient India" *Annals of the Bhandarkar Oriental Research Institute*, Vol. 48-49 (1968), pp. 383-90.

Sharma, R.S., Forms of Property in the Early Portions of the Rig-Veda, *Proc. IHC*, 34th session (Chandigarh), 1973, pp 93-103.

——— "Indian Feudalism Re-touched", *Indian Historical Review*,. Vol. 1, 2.

——— "Problem of Transition from Ancient to Medieval in Indian History, *Indian Historical Review*, Vol. I, 1.

——— "Class Formation and its Material Basis in the Upper Gangetic Basin (c. 1000-500 B.C.] *IHR*, II, No. I (1975) pp. 1-13.

——— Rajasasana, Meaning, Scope and application, '*Proc-IHC*, 37th Session (Calicut) 1976, p. 76-87.

——— and Jha, D.N., 'The Economic History of India upto, A.*D*. 1200: Trends and Prospects', *JESHO*, XVII (Part I), pp. 48-80.

Sitaraman, B., As'ivika and Ajivika', *Studies in Indian History and Culture* (Prof. P. B'. Desai Felicitation Volume (Karnatak Education Board, Dharwar-1), pp. 483-86.

Stein, Burton, "The Economic Function of a Medieval South Indian temple" *The Journal of Asian Studies*, Vol .XIX, No. 2, February, 1960 pp. 163-176.

——— "Integration of the Agrarian System of South India", *land Control and Social structure in Indian History*, ed Robert Erik Frykenberg (The University of Wisconsin, 1969), Chapter VIII, pp. 175-216

——— "Social Mobility and Medieval South Indian Hindu sects", s*ocial Mobility* in *the* Caste *system* in *India*, ed. James Silverberg (Mouton Publishers), pp. 79-94.

——— and Morris David Morris "The Economic History of India"—A Bibliographic Essay", *Journal* of *Economic* History, June, 1961, pp. 179-207.

APPENDIX—I

THE APPENDIX DETAILS OF THE GRANTEES OF BRAHMADĒYAM IN TOṆḌAIMANḌALAM DURING THE PERIOD 670-900

Sl. No.	*The Villages they hailed from*	*The qualifications of the grantees— No. of brahmins with those qualifications (in brackets).*	*Udayēndram*	*Pullūr*	*Chitrūr*
1	**2**	**3**	**4**	**5**	**6**
I. Grantees whose original homes were in Andhra.					
1.	Kārambi	Sarmman	2	-	-
2.	Abhundi (see No. 12)	Sarmman	2	-	-
3.	Kulaputtira	Trivedi	-	1 each	
		Shadangavit (2)	-	1 each	
		Chaturvedi	-	1	
4.	Pipara	Sarmman		1	
5.	Nimbai	Shadangavit (3)		1 each	
6.	Kumaṇḍūr	Shadangavit		1	
7.	Tangār	Shadangavit-Somayaji	1		
8.	Vaṅgi-paru	Shadangavit Trivedi		1	

The 20 *Chaturvedins* who were given shares probably equal in *brahmadēyam* Paramēśwaramaṅgalam were probably meant to be chosen from the 108 *chaturvedi* brahmins of Kūram. The Single brahmin donee of the Kasākkudi plates hailed from Puniya in Toṇḍaimaṇḍalam itself.

1	2	3	4	5	6
9.	Angarai	Sarmman	-	1	
10.	Māngaḷūr	Sarmman	-	1	
11.	Muṅgaṇur	Sarmman	-	1	
12.	Abhyaṇṭi	Sarmman (3) (see No. 2).	-	1 each	
		Trivedi	-	1	
13.	Seṛuppāḷi	Sarmman	-	1	
14.	Pādagam	Shadangavit	-	1	
		Sarmman (2)	-	1 each	
15.	Ilakkanduru (Ilakkandiram)	Sarmman Das' apuriya	-	1	
16.	Kombaru	Sarmman	-	1	
17.	Kochchanañjeru	Bhatts	-	2	
18.	Tūrppil	Trivedi	-	1	
		Sarmman	-	1	
19.	Karambichchēḍu	Kramavit (1+1+1)	-	1 for one	½ each for two
		Trivedi (2)	—	1 each	
		Sarmman (3) + (1+1)	-	1 each	½ x ½
		Dasapuriya	-	-	
20.	Paṭṭangi	Trivedi	-	1	
21.	Vanganūr	Sarmman (2)	-	1	
22.	Venjēdu.	Shadangavit	-	1	
23.	Cheṇḍoṛu	Somayaji	-	2	
24.	Veingi	Shadangavit	-	1	
		Bhattan	-	1	½
25.	Guṇṭūr	Kramavit	-	-	1
26.	Krāñchi	(Kramavit) (1+1+1)	-	-	1 each for two ½ for one

1	2	3	4	5	6
27.	Kongoṭṭi	Chaturvedi	-	1	
28.	Iruṅgaṭṭi	Kramavit (1+1)	-	1	½
	(Irungānd)	Bhatta	-	1	½
		Trivedi	-	-	½
29.	Angārai	Dasapuriya	-	-	1
30.	Adambam	Sarmman	-	-	½
31.	Eṭṭukūr	Kramavit	-	-	½
32.	Kakkaṇḍūr	Kramavit	-	-	½
33.	Nanguḷḷai	unspecified	-	-	½
34.	Jattal	Kramavit	-	-	½
35.	Uruppiṭṭūr	Sarmman	-	-	½
36.	Koḍanur	Unspecified	-	-	½
37.	Kuravasiri	Kramavit	-	-	½
38.	Pambutinṛi	Kramavit	-	-	½
39.	Kumuṇḍili	Kramavit	-	-	½
40.	Ālikonrai	Unspecified	-	-	½
41.	Aṭṭakūr	Bhatta	-	-	½
42.	Bhavakuṛi	Chaturvedi Bhatta	-	-	½
43.	Panganūr	Bhatta	-	-	½
44.	Tiruchchogunūr	Chaturvedi (?)	-	-	½
45.	Chepakai	Chaturvedi (?)	-	-	½
46.	Pulliṭṭa	Kramavit	-	-	½
47.	Irāyūr	Kramavit	-	-	½
II. Grantees whose original homes were in Tamil-nadu :					
1.	Kāvanur	Trivedi (2)	-	1 each	
		Shadangavit	-	2	
		Somayaji	-	1	
		Sarmman (8+1)	2 for 1	1 each for 8	
		Chaturvedi	—	2	

1	2	3	4	5	6
		Chaturvedi	-	1	
		Krmavit	-	1	
2.	Kāyaṟu.	Kramivit	-	1	
3.	Arūr	Shadangavit	-	1	
4.	Sōlaiyūr	Sarmman (3)	-	1 each	
5.	Vanpākkam	Sarmman	-	1	
6.	Ārkkāḍu	Sarmman	-	1	
7.	Kaḷanjur	Sarmman	-	1	
8.	Uḍumbur	Sarmman	-	1	
9.	Kunjanūr	Sarmman	-	2	
		Sarmman	-	2	
10.	Teṅgaḷur	Kāṭhaka-Sōmayāji	-	2	
11.	Paṉṟikudi	Sarmman	-	1	
12.	Kovarangil	Sarmman	-	1	
13.	Vasukūr	Sarmman	-	1	
14.	Oḻukkaippākkam	Sarmman	-	1	
15.	Saṭṭipuram	Sarmman (2)	-	1 each	
16.	Sanūr	Sarmman	-	1	
17.	Irekkur	Sarmaan	-	1	
18.	Kāmappuḷḷūr	Unspecified (2)	-	1	
19.	Āṛrūr	Sarmman	-	2	
20.	Kāṭṭūr	Trivedi	-	1	
21.	Vāsalur	Sarmman	-	1	
22.	Saṭṭur	Kramavit	-	1	
23.	Kiḻinallūr	Sarmman	-	-	¼
		Kramavit (1+ 1+1 +1+1)	-	-	½ each to four ¼ to one
		Bhattan	-	-	¼
24.	Perumbarrappuliyūr	Chaturvedi (?)	-	-	½

1	2	3	4	5	6
25.	Aḷundur	Kramavit	-	-	½
26.	Ninṛayil	Kramavit	-	-	½
27.	. . . ndur	Bhattan	-	-	½
28.	Ōṭpuṛai	Chaturvedi	-	-	½
29.	Chendiram	Shadangavit	-	-	½
30.	Cheruppur	Kramavit	-	-	¼
III. Original homes quoted but those location is uncertain:					
1.	Chaṭṭipura	unspecified	2		
2.	Uḻāppur	Somayaji-Trivedi (2)	-	2 to one 1 no another	
3.	Kumandūr	Kramavit-Sarmman	-	1	
4.	Chirekkur	Bhatta	-	1	
		Sarmman (2)	-	1 each	-
		Unspecified	-	1	-
5.	Viṇṇūr	Sarmman (2)	-	1 each	-
6.	Uviyūr	Sarmman (2)	-	1 each	-
7.	Pāgai	Sarmman	-	1	-
8.	Usanam	Sarmman	-	1	-
IV. Grantees whose original home is not specifled:					
		Sarmman (10)	3 each		
		Sarmman (23)	2 each		
		Sarmman (1)	1		
		Bhatta	3		
		No surname (20)	2 each		
		Kramavit	-	- ¼	-

APPENDIX—II

The items of exemptions and entitlements listed under the *parihāras* in the Pallava charters during the period 670-900 belong to several categories and can be classified as under:—

	The items of Parihara	The charters where each occurs
I.	**Facilities or services of artisans etc. of the village authorised to the donees:**	
1.	Chekku (oil press) [1]	*Kūram*, Kasakkudi, Pullur, Tandantottam.
2.	Tari (loom) [2]	As above and also Royakottah, Chitrur, Kumaradimaṅgalam.
II.	**Right of the *kō* to take the best in the village and his expectancy of services from the villagers,**	
1.	Nallā (good cow)	Kasakkudi, Velurpalaiyam Chitrur, Tandantottam Pattattaḷ maṅgalam Kumaradimaṅgalam.
2.	Nallerudu(good bull)	-do-
3.	Nallāḍu(good sheep)	Velurpalaiyam
4.	*Pudu-kkudirai-kku*rra *tuvaiyam pullum* (grass for the new horse)	Kasakkudi
5.	*Nāyādigal*	Kasakkudi
6.	*Duhituvar*	-do-
7.	*Kaṇikārttigal*	-do-
8.	*Paṇṇuppāl-eḍuppar*	-do-
9.	*Paḍaṅgaḻi*	Kasakkudi
10.	*Kaiyāl*	-do-

	The items of Parihara	The charters where each occurs
11.	*Neḍumbuṛai*	-do-
12.	*Paṇambākku*[5]	-do-
III. Levies as charges for local administration.		
1.	*ūr-āṭchi* (administration of *ūr*.	*Kūram*, Pattattal maṅgalam, Velurpalaiyam, Kumaradimaṅgalam, Chitrur.
2.	*Nādu*-ātchi (administration of the nāḍu)	Velurpalaiyam, Kumaradi maṅgalam, Chitrur.
3.	*Nattu-vagai*[6] (on account of nadu)	Kasakkudi
4.	*nāḍu-kāval* (police of the nadu)	Pattattalmaṅgalam, Velurpalaiyam, Kumaradi-maṅgalam, Chitrur.
5.	*Visakkāṇam*[7]	Kasakkudi
IV. Levies for services provided (?)		
1.	*Tirumuga-kkāṇam*[8] (kānan charge "for letters)	Velurpalaiyan, Tandantottam
2.	*Pattigai-kkāṇam*[9] (kāṇam for paṭṭigai)	Kasakkudi a Pullur
3.	*Pattur-chchāu*[10]	-do-
V. Levies on professions/professionals		
1.	*Kuśa-kkāṇam*[11] (kanam levy on potters)	Kasakkudi, VelurPālaiyam, Chitrur, Tandantottam, Kummaradimaṅgalam.
2.	*Navida-kkāṇam* (Kaṇam levy on barber)	Puttur
3.	*katti-kkāṇam*[12] (kanām levy on knife)	*Kūram*
	Vannāra-kkāṇam[13] (kanam levy on washerman)	Puttur
	Pārai-kkāṇam (kanam levy on rock)	Velurpalaiyam

	The items of Parihara	The charters where each occurs
4.	*Taṭṭa-kkāṇam*[14]	Royakkottah
5.	*Tāṛikkūrai*[15]	Velurpalaiyam Royakkottah.
6.	*āṭṭukkāṇam*[16]	Pullur
7.	*Ulliyakkūli*[17]	Kasakkudi, Pullur, Tandantottam.
8.	*Ēttakkāṇam*[18]	Pullur
9.	*Paṭṭina-sāri*[19]	Velurpalaiyam
10.	*ūḍu-pōkku*[20]	Pattattalmaṅgalam, Velurpalaiyam, Kumaradimaṅgalam, Chitrur.
11.	*Cheyivu-pōga*[21] *chchiranda-pon*	Pullur
VI. Levies on trades/traders/bazar		
1.	*Taragu* (brokerage)	*Kūram*, Pattattalmaṅgalam, Velurpalaiyam, Kumaradi-maṅgalam, Chitrur.
	Taragri-ppāṭṭam	Tandantottam
2.	*Kūlam*[22]	This occurs in association with *taragu,* whereas that is mentioned only in the Royakottah plates it occurs alone.
3.	*Vatti-nali*[23]	This is also mentioned in the charters where taragu is mentioned.
4.	*Pudā-naḷi*[24]	-do-
5.	*Paṛi-kkāṇam*[25]	Pullur
6.	*Uri-kkāṇam*[26]	Pullur
7.	*Puṭṭaga-vilai*[27]	Kasakkudi, Pullur
8.	*Neyi-vilai*[28]	Kasakkudi
9.	*Kaḍai-aḍaikkāy*[29]	Tandantottam
10.	*Ari-kōḷi*[30]	Kasukkaḍi
VII. Levies due on occasion or for occasions		
1.	*Kaḷḷāṇa-kkaṇam*[31] (Kāṇam for marriage)	Kasakkudi, Kumaradimaṅgalam, Chitrur.

	The items of Parihara	The charters where each occurs
2.	*Kann-ittu-kkanam*[32]	Kasakkudi, Pullur
3.	N%vÈyam[33]	Pattāttalmaṅgalam
4.	*Taṭṭukkāyam*[34]	Velurpalaiyam, Kumaradi-maṅgalam, Tandantottam
5.	*Taṭṭukkāy*[35]	Chitrur
6.	*Brāhmana-rāsa-kkānam or Brahma-nichcha-kkāṇam*[36]	Kasakkudi
7.	*Vīra-tūkka-kkāṇam*[37]	Pullur
8.	*Īḷam-pūṭchi*[38]	Tandantottam, Pattattalmanga-lam, Velurpalaiyam, Kumaradi-maṅgalam, Chitrur.
9.	*Iḍaippūṭchi*[39]	-do-
10.	*Viśa-kkāṇam*[40]	-do-
11.	*Uppu-kkō-chcheygai*[41]	Tandantottam and Pattattal-maṅgalam.
VIII. Levies based on land-utilisation		
1.	*Kālkoṭṭu*[42]	Kasakkudi, Pullur
2.	*Kal-koṭṭu-kkāṇam*[43]	Pullur
3.	*Kuvaḷai-naḍu-vari*[44]	Kasakkudi
4.	*Kuvaḷai-kkāṇam*[45]	Kasakkudi, Pullur
5.	*Cheṅgoḍi-kkāṇam*[46]	Kasakkudi, Pullur
6.	*Kadir-kkāṇam*[47]	Kasakkudi
IX. Mines-treasures		
1.	*Sāḍippon*[48]	Pullur
2.	*kāṛun-ṭenga-ppon*[49]	Pullur
X. Fines		
1.	*Karaṇa-ttaṇḍam*	Kasakkudi
2.	*Upa-karana-ttaṇḍam*[50]	Pullur
3.	*Adhikarṇa-ttaṇḍam*	Pullur
4.	*Arappuṛa-ttaṇḍam*[51]	Pullur
5.	*Maṇṛupāḍu*[52]	Velurpaliyam

	The items of Parihara	The charters where each occurs
XI. Miscellaneous		
1.	*Ulayai-paḷḷi-vasṭu*[53]	Kasakkudi
2.	*Kōvil-vastu*[54]	Pullur
3.	*Pannīr-āṭṭai-kkarai*[55]	*Pullur*

APPENDIX—III

LAND-MEASURING RODS

It has been mentioned above that the records refer to measuring rods of different standards as having been used to determine the extent of land. The earliest reference to such a measuring rod (*kōl*) is found in the Kasākkuḍi and Pullūr plates which say that the donees of the grant were given the privilege of *Kōl-agalam* or a channel of a *kōl* width from the irrigation reservoir, to take the water to their fields.[56] However the size of the *kōl* is not indicated. Probably it was a standard length *kōl* widely in use at the time. Mention of the *kōl* with reference to measurement of land is found mentioned first only in a record of the year 17 (876), of Pallava Nṛipatuṅga from *Kūram*.[57] This record mentions a *kōl* of 12 span length. The *kōl* of the same length is also mentioned in an inscription of the year 19 (889) of Kampavarman from Tiruvorriyūr.[58] However, whereas this record of Kampavarman says that a *kōl* of 12 span length was used to measure land sold by the *sabhā* of Maṇali, it also states that when the residents of Tiśaimaṇgalam sold land, a measure of 16 span length was used to determine the extent of land. This indicates that *kōls* of different standard lengths were in use aṭ the same time even in neighbouring villages. An inscription probably of Parāntaka I from Vēppangulam (Kanchīpuram taluk, Chingleput district)[59], tells of a ka. . . . . *kkalattukkōl* used to measure the land involved in a transaction without however specifying the scale of the *kōl*. The name of the *kōl* which is damaged in the epigraph was probably *kadigai-kkaḷattu-kkōl* a *kōl* is mentioned again without any indication of its length, in two records of the period of Pārthivēndravarman (late 10th century) from Kāvanūr, Gudiyattam taluk, North Arcot district[60], and in a fragment probably belonging to the tenth century from *Kaḷañjur*, same taluk and district.[61] An inscription of the year 4 (989) of Rājakēsarivarman (Rājarāja I) from Gudimallam (Gudiyattam taluk, North Arcot district)[62] also mentions the same *kōl* but also gives the length of the rod as of 16 span.In this context *Kadigai-kkalam* was apparently the office of the ghaṭika[63], (the registry ?) (which seems to have been the same as *āvanakkalam*[64] referred to in later records. This agency seems to have prescribed the authentic measuring rods. Probably a specimen of the standard rod was kept there. *Ghaṭika* having been known as an official institution at least from the time of Nandivarman II (731-796), it is possible that this establishment instituted this standard measuring rod for computing the extent of land.It appears that the rod of this length was in normal use.[65]

That this 16 span rod was the normal standard, is also indicated when some records suggest that Chōḷa Rajarāja I (985-1014), who for the first time is said to have undertaken a thorough survey of the land in his empire,[66] had adopted this rod in his survey. An inscription of the year 19 (1004) of the king from Sīyamaṅgalam, Wandiwash taluk, North Arcot district[67] records a sale of land by the *ūr* of the place and says that the land was measured by the 16 span rod. Underneath the record there is an engraving of a linear representation, 12 feet 9 inches in length, which is labelled as *nilam aḷavu-kōl*. "The rod for measuring land". These details found in this record definitely indicates that during the period of Rājarāja I, the measuring rod for the land which was of 16 span length was standarised at 12 feet 9 inches according to modern scale.[68] This scale seems to have been used in the survey that was done for the first time in the reign of Rājarāja I.[69] This rod seems to have been the standard during the subsequent period also. The intention behind the engraving of the specimen rod in temples must have been that the people should compare any rods that might have been in local use with this standard rod and adjust it to accord with the official standard.[70]

While all the above evidence points to the 16 span rod as having been adopted as the standard with its length determined officially some deviation also seems to have been approved in particular regions probably in deference to local usage. Even during the reign of Rājarāja I, in his year 18 (1003) when an inscription from Mēlsēvur, Gingee taluk, South Arcot district[71] describes the king's official getting the land belonging to the temple measured for apportionment of the income from them it is stated that an 18 span rod was for the measurement. Another inscription dated year 29 (1014) of the same king from Mēlpāḍi, Gudiyattam taluk, North Arcot district[72] says that the land in that *ūr* administered by the *nagarattār* was measured by the 18 span rod for allotting the blocs (*kūru*).[73] Later inscriptions, one dated year 3 (1015) of Rājēndra I from Tirumullaivāyil (Saidapet taluk, Chingleput district)[74] and another dated year 5 (1075) of Kulōttuṅga I from Cheyyūr, (Madhurāntakam taluk, Chingleput district)[75] also mention the 18 span rod as having been used in measuring land. Though this variant from the standard seems to have been allowed to be used in transactions in some areas it is likely, that the length of this rod also had been standarised.

Some inscriptions refer to a few measuring rods with special attributes. The *sabhā* of Tiruvallam when they made over land to a temple in Mēlpāḍi alias Rājāsrayapuram against gold, in the year 14 (999) of Rājarāja I,[76] they are stated to have measured the land with *Chirrambala-kkōl*. The *kōl* of the same description was again used by the *sabhā* of the same place in the year 4 (1016) of Rājēndra I.[77] It is likely that though this measuring rod had special relevance used in the case of land-transactions connected with the Siva temples in the area. It might have had special relevence to that village also. For a *Siṛiyārūr-kōl* is also mentioned in an inscription of the time of Pārthivēndravarman from Tirumālpuram,[78] which shows that this rod was special for the village *Siriyārūr* which was also a *dēvadāna*.[79] A Tiruppāṛkaḍal (Walajahpet taluk, North Arcot district) inscription of the time of Pārthivēndravarman[80] refers to the *Kaḷanikōl* or the measuring rod of the field. A Shōliṅghūr (Walajahpet taluk, North Arcot district) inscription (the beginning portion of the epigraph containing the details of the king and date is damaged)[81] amplifies and mentions *iv-vūr-kaḷani-aḷakkum kōl* (i. e.) the rod used for measuring the fields of this village. A Maṇimaṅgalam (Sriperumbudur taluk, Chingleput district) record of the year 5 (1068) of Vīra-Rājēndra[82] simply refers to the *kōl* of the *ūr*. In these cases the records do not indicate the length of the measuring rod. It appears that these rods were those kept in the villages for local measurements, they must have conformed to the official standard rod. The standardisation of the measuring rod and the survey with it seems to have enabled the Chōḷas to correctly assess the land already reflected in the books.[83] It must have also brought to light all the land reclaimed in the meanwhile and which had remained unassessed till then. This is seen to have brought in increased revenue—contributions from the villages. A record from Tiruvallam dated year 22 (1007) of Rājarāja I[84] refers to an agreement by the *sabhā* of Mandiram to pay an enhanced contribution of paddy to the temple. It is noteworthy that a *perundaram* officer of the king is cited as witnessing this transaction. An inscription from Tiruvorriyūr also records the action taken on the finding of errors in measurement of land when in the 11th century following Rājarāja I his successor Rājēndra I also had the land in the empire resurveyed.[85]

The efficacy of having the land survey conducted periodically was appreciated and in the 11th and 12th centuries in almost[86] every reign one survey, is reported to have been conducted.

APPENDIX—IV

-KŌ-

In the copper-plate charter granting *brahmadēyam* or *dēvadāṇa* or *paḷḷichchandam* mention of *kō* is made in two contexts. While describing the mode of grant it is stated that it was made after changing or doing away with *kō* and seal indicating that the grant village was taken off the charge of *kō*. Again the items in the list of *parihāra* are stated to have been such which could be enjoyed by the *kō*. The Pullūr and Kasākkuḍi plates refer to fines that could be levied by the *kō* from transgressors and trespassers into the irrigation facilities granted for the exclusive enjoyment of the donees in the grants. It is apparent that this *kō* could not have been the king for the reason that whereas the text of the record is in the form of an order of the king mentioned, in the first person, addressed to the *nāṭṭār*. The reference to the *kō* is in the third person.[87] There is also no mention of the main land tax payable to the king in the list of parihāras. later evidence indicates that the grant village had never been sequestered from the control of the king.

So this *kō* must have been someone different from the king. The *kō* is also referred to in some stone inscriptions recording transactions. A Tiruttaṇi inscription of the time of Aparājita (year 18= 903)[88] states that on failure to fulfil their commitment to the temple, the *sabhā* would pay a fine to the *kō* in charge at the time *(anṛāḷ-kō)*.[89] An inscription of the year 11 (881) of Kampavarman from Kīlpputtūr (Chingleput district)[90] invoked the protection of the *kō* of the day (anṛal-kō) to the arrangement made for maintaining the local reservoir with a *pro-rata* levy from the cultivated lands of the village. An inscription of the year 12 (997) of Rājarāja I from Bāhūr (Pondicherry)[91] invoked the protection of the *kō* ruling that *ūr*, for an endowment of tax-free land made by the *sabhā* for a deity probably set up at the mint *(por-chāḷai)*. Another inscription from the same place dated year 27 (966) of Krishna III[92] refers to the great men (*Perumakkaḷ*) ruling the *ūr* as also to the *kō* of their choice *(tāṉ-vēṇḍu-kō)*\ to whom the *puṇyagaṇa-pperumakkaḷ* would pay the fine on failure to maintain a benefaction. An inscription of Pārthivēndravarman (10th century) from Pāḍi-Tiruvalidāyam (Saidapet Taluk, Chingleput district)[93] not only refers to the *sabhā* undertaking to pay a fine in the form of the due *(mudal)* of *dharmmāsaṇam* to the *kō* of their choice if they transgressed the terms of an endowment of land to the temple which land had been purchased and got made tax-free on payment to the *sabhā* but also to an assurance by the *sabhā* (to the-temple) that they would resolve any obstruction *(vighna)* arising from the *kō* ruling the *ūr*. A fragmentary inscription of the year 15 of a Parakēsari-varman (10th century) from Kāñchīpuram[94] refers to an undertaking by an *ūr*. to pay the fine to the *kō* of their choice including *uḷḷiṭṭa dharmmāsanam* (or who would be at the *dharmmasaṇam*?) An inscription of the year 23 (962) of Kṛishṇa III from Uttaramallūr[95] recording the making over of the miscellaneous levies due to them from an *ūr*. by the *mahāsabhā* of Uttaramēru-chaturvēdimaṅgalam, contains an assurance by the *sabhā* that no kind of *kō* (*ēppērpaṭṭa-ko*) would get an entry into the *ūr*. The aforesaid Kīlputtūr inscription which invokes the protection of the *kō*, of the day also says that both the *kō* and the *kuḍi*, (inhabitants) were together responsible for the contribution of paddy from the fields for the maintenance of the reservoir to which effect the *ūr* of the place gave an undertaking to Mādēvanār, son of Permubāṇan Sakkaḍi-araiyar. Finally an inscription of year 21 (1006) of Rājarāja I from Tirumalai (Polur Taluk, North Arcot district)[96] refers to the head of the Jain establishment at Vaigāvur as the *kō* of *Kuḷir-vaigai*.[97] *Kō* in Tamil meaning 'lord'. It is both applicable to god (kō-il—temple) and king (cf. kō-nēr- inmaīkoṇḍān- the lord without peer; also kō-il-palace).[98] However in all the above,contexts of the copper plate grants of land made over as *brahmadēyam* or as a religious benefaction, the records indicate that the land had been taken away from the control of the *kō* or the local lord by the king and placed instead the miscellaneous entitlements of the *kō* were also made over to the donees under the guise of the grant of *parihāṛas*, which contains only items of the miscellaneous levies. The function of the *kō*, might have consisted of the exercise of control over the region on behalf of the king and the safeguarding of the interests of the king. The fact that the king could take away land from his authority suggests that it was the king who had invested the concerned person with kō-ship or that the *kō* whom the king could disturb with impunity were the petty local chiefs whom the king had subdued but had allowed to continue therein in their original small principalities with an allowance to continue to levy and enjoy some miscellaneous levies.[99] Some of the chiefs like Ilāḍarāyar mentioned above might have been such *kōs*. It is also possible that the designation *kōs* was applied to the person, (he might have been a local chief) who was the king's agent in the different localities in the interior.

NOTES:

1. cf. Minakshi, C. *op. cit.*, p. 77.
2. *Ibid*.
3. The phrase actually means the *tuvai* (mashed feed: compare modern Tamil, *tuvaiyal*) grass for the new horse. Though not indicative of the *kō* expecting to appropriate the best in the village, this charge might have been such that was taken from the villagers to maintain the stable of the *kō* the horses wherein were ostensibly meant for use in the protection of the villagers. The editor (*SII.*, II, p. 361, m. i) connected this with the phrase *paṇṇuppāl-eḍunpār* preceding this in the text and surmised that both stood for the eliphant-stall and the horse-stable. It is noteworthy, that of all the charters of

the period only the Kasākkudi plates mention the list of the exemptions and concessions under several groups, which might have indicated that each group reflected different kinds of charges with different kinds of utilisation. This might have led the editor of the Kasākkuḍi plates to interpret both the phrases the way he did. Of the Guṇṭur-Nellore region charters, the Viḷa-veṭṭi grant which gives a similar list of levies also groups them into two, one *karas* and the other the king's portion *(asmad-bhōgyāni)* (cf. *EI*. XXIV, p. 298, n 5).

4. Items 4 to 8 are grouped together in the Kasākkuḍi plates and hence seem to have belonged to a particular class of charges. If that was so the presence of *dūtuvar* in the group may be significant. *Dūtuvar* were obviously messengers and hence the levy might have been meant for the maintenance of the messengers either king's messengers or those that were available to carry the messages of the villagers. In the light of this it appears that *pudu-kkudi-irai*-kkuṟṟa-tuvai, *kaṇikārttigal* and *pannuppāḷ-eḍuppāṟ* though the exact significance of these terms is obscure seem to have also had reference to the maintenance of some classes of people whom the citizens were expected to supply for the service of the *kō* or whom the *kō* had made available for the service of the villagers.
5. These four items are grouped together in the charter and so seem to have belonged to a particular class of contributions from the citizens, taken by the *kō*. *Paḍāṅgaḷi* has been interpreted as a tax on spinner's thread (*SII*., II, p. 361: Minakahi, C., *op. cit.*, p. 78 *Kaiyāḷ* means "handy man" and *neḍumbuṛai* actually means "what has been in a recess (puṛai) for long". *Panambakku* means nut or juice of the palmyrah. (cf. Minakshi, C., *op. cit.*, p. 79). Having been mentioned separate from the preceding group, these four items may have had reference to different kinds of services provided by the *kō*, against which the contribution was taken from the villagers.
6. cf. Minakshi, C., *op. cit.*, pp. 80-81.
7. In the context of the occurrence of this in the group pertaining to local administration *visa* seems to have meant the *viśavaṇ* or *viyavan*. This might have been a levy on account of *viyavan* or on *vivayan*. The former is more likely. However as it could have also meant a tax on *viyavaṇ* this has been included under the tax on professions also. Whether *viyavan* was an accountant or not it is certain that he was an official of the *nāḍu* (cf. Pullūr plates, line

120). However it is also doubtful if *kāṇam* could have denoted a levy on professions, This levy does not also occur in the context of levies on local administration.

8. Probably the *kō* used to provide some facilities for the transmission of letters and messages of the citizens and charged a fee for that. It does not appear that it was payment made for the service of bringing the royal writ as such writs cannot be expected to be frequent, cf. Minakshi, C., *op. cit.*, p. 79.
9. Minakshi says that it was a toll taken at ferries or a tax on the ferryman (*op.cit.*, pp. 76-77). It is possible that it was a levy against the provision of the facility taken from the citizens. Hultsch opines that it was a tax on cloth *(SII.*, II, p. 361)
10. It means announcement to ten or more *ūrs* (around). This occurs in the context of the mention of fines and so this announcement might have had judicial significance (cf. Mahalingam, T.V., *op. cit.*, p. 151) Minakshi (*op. cit.*, p. 80) thinks that it was a tax on toddy yielding trees of Pattūr, a probable neighbour of the grant village.
11. Minakshi, C., *op. cit.*, p. 75.
12. *Ibid.*, p. 81. She connects the levy with the sword but it is more likely that it was connected with the barber's knife.
13. *Ibid.*, p. 76. She seems to be correct in saying that this refers to a tax on washermen, who use the rock for beating the clothes. Probably it is the same levy which is referred to as *vaṇṇara-kkāṇam* in the Pullūr plates.
14. This is probably a levy on *taṭṭār-gold,* or silversmith. However Minakshi's and others' opinion that *taṭṭukkāyam* also denoted such a levy on goldsmith seems to be erroneous because the *taṭṭ ār* could have been taxed only on the basis of his profession and not on the basis of his hammering. Moreover the construction of the word itself denotes that it was an *āyam* for *tattu* (emergency ?) and not on *tattu,* (hammering).
15. This means cloth on the loom. Either the levy was based on the price of cloth finished on the loom or was a general tax on the weaver (Minakshi, C., *op. cit.*, p. 77.
16. This was probably a levy on the herdsmen on the basis of the sheep.
17. This was probably a tax on the wages earned by water-diviners, cf. *SII.*, II, 360. Here this has been interpreted as a tax on well-diggers.

18. This might have been a *kāṇam* levy on the picottahas or picottah operators. However as the text in the charter runs as *ulliyakkūliyum mettakkāṇamum* and it is also possible that the levy was termed *metta-kkāṇam* as in no other case the final m of the previous word is seen combined with the vowel beginning of the following word. If it was so the meaning of *metta-kkāṇam* will be obscure.
19. This was obviously a levy on fishermen (Minakshi, C., *op. cit.*, p. 79). The suffix *sāri* can be compared with the tax-term *sāṛigai* occurring in later inscriptions. However it is noteworthy that *paṭ ṭinam* was a word used to denote a habitation on the see coast and Tirukkāṭṭuppaḷḷi of the Vēlūrpalaiyam plates is far away from the sea. However *paṭṭinavar* applied to the fishermen on the coastal belt might have been applied to fishermen in general, in due course and *paṭṭina-sāri* could have indicated the levy on fishermen resident in *Tirukkāṭṭuppaḷḷi*. But still it will be intriguing why this levy is not mentioned among the *parihāras* in the other charters of the period.
20. The term actually means "removal of impurities or mixtures" and so might have referred to a levy on those engaged in refining gold. Minakshi's argument (*op. cit.*, pp. 78-79) that it meant a tax on the mixture of grains is not convincing.
21. This means to have meant the same thing as *ūdūpōkku* as the term means gold excelling after removal of *chevivu*. *Cheviva* might have meant admixtures. cf. Mahalingam, T.V., *op. cit.*, p. 150.
22. This has been taken to have meant "bazar" (*SII.*, II, p. 155, Minakshi, C., *op. cit.*, p. 77).
23. This seems to mean a *nāḻi* measure of whatever commodity was sold in baskets at the rate of a *nāḻi* per basketful. (Minakshi, C, *op. cit.*, p. 78). An inscription of the year 24 (1008-09) of Rājarāja I from Mēlsēvur, South Arcot district (*SII.*, XVII, 235) refers to the levy of a *nāḻi* per or on *vaṭṭi* on those dealing in *vaṭṭi* (*vaṭṭi-vāṇiyam*), indicating that either *vaṭṭi* was a commodity marketed or it referred to the profession of usury *(vaṭṭi-vṛiddhi)*.
24. This has been interpreted as a levy of a *nāḻi* measure on commodities sold by special measures (Minakshi, C., *op. cit.*, p. 78).
25. This could be interpreted as a. levy at the rate of a *kāṇam* at the time of plucking (fruits like cocoanut, arecaunt etc.) (cf. Mahalingam, T.V., *op. cit.*, p. 150).
26. This seems to have meant a levy of a *kāṇam* per sling (where the goods were sold by carrying in slings) (cf. Mahalingam, T.V., *op. cit.*, p. 150).

27. This is interpreted as a levy on the sale of cloth (Minakshi, C., *op. cit.*, p. 76).
28. On the face of it, it seems to have been a levy on the sale of ghee. But Minakshi (*op. cit.*, p. 81) thinks that it was a tax in lieu of the supply of ghee, required to be contributed to the king's palace by the people.
29. It means arecanut in the shop (i. e. marketed cf. *SII.*, XVII, 236). This inscription refers to two levies, *veruṅgāy*, *alagu-kāy* (unripe plant and tree products-plucked straight or brought down with the help of a crook) as some of the levies made over to the temple. Subsequently the Kasākkuḍi record refers to the levies on commodities sold by capacity or by linear measure (*kāl-āḷavalum kōḷlavāḷum vandadu*). Other records of the period of Rājarāja and Rājēndra I (*SII.*, XVII, 223; AREp. 1921, 395) mention *kāl-aḷavu* and *kōl-aḷavu-kūli* which were probably consolidated levies on merchandise.
30. This means fowl-cut. Probably this denoted a levy on fowl-meat marketed.
31. This might have been a charge payable to the *kō* or king on the celebration of marriage by the citizens or as a tribute to the *kō* or king for similar occasions in his household. (cf. Vilavetti grant—this refers to dues on *vivāha* or marriage; Minakshi, C., *op. cit.*, p. 74). *Kallāl-kkāṇam* as included in the list in the Kasākkuḍi plates probably was the same as *kallāṇa-kkāṇam* though the editor of the plates *(SII.*, II, p. 360 n. 7) says that it was indicative of the share *(kāṇam)* of *kallāi*. a kind of fig tree.
32. The significance of this is not clear and none has tried to explain it. It may be translated as "*kāṇam* on applying or extending the eye" and might have been a levy on engagements.
33. This could be split up as *nērvu āyam* (i.e.) cess on happenings or incidents in the citizen's life or to meet the exigencies as may happen in the locality. Minakshi, C., (*op. cit.*, p. 109) however thinks that it was a levy on excessive use of water.
34. This might have been a charge similar to *vaṭṭināḷi*. *vaṭṭīnāḷi* might have meant a levy on unripe fruit sold on plates as the following levy seems to clarify. However, this could be understood as *āyam* for *taṭṭu* as *taṭṭu* also means emergencies. Minakshi, C., *op. cit.*, p. 75 says that it was a levy on goldsmiths like *taṭṭar-pāṭṭam* which occur in the Tiruvālangāḍu plates of Rājēndra I. But *irai āyam* and *kāṇam* seem to have been the designation of

the levy on different categories. *Āyam* does not seem to have been indicative of a tax on professionals.

35. This might have been the same as *taṭṭu-kkāyam.*
36. This seems to have been a cess payable by a brahmin on a particular occasion in his life. It is possible that it referred to a levy on the occasion of the *upanayana* or initiation of a brahmin boy as *Kumāra-kachchāṇam* or *Kumāra-gadyāṇa*. This latter levy is mentioned in an inscription from Tiruvallam dated year 3-1070 of Adhirājēndra *(SII.,* III, 57) as also in an inscription from Tiruvaṇṇāmalai dated year 27-1039 of Rājēndra I *(ibid.*, VIII, 68). cf. Mahalingam, T.V., *op. cit.,* p. 151. Minakshi, C., *op. cit.,* p. 73). This might also have been a levy on brahmin teachers *(āsa-āchārya)* (cf. Subrahmania Iyer, K.V., Historical Sketches of ancient Dekhan, p. 344).
37. The editor of the Pullūr plates reads this as *nīr-tūkka-kkāṇam* but has left it uninterpreted. *Vīra* means soldier, *tūkka* means (sleep) and *kāṇam* referred to the coin. Hence this might have been a levy on the citizens towards the maintenance of the king's troops when not in service.
38. This was probably a cess charged on the young *Iḷavar* on initiation into his profession of toddy-tapping, cf. Minakshi, C., *op. cit.,* 72-73.
39. This might have been a cess on the initiation of the young *iḍaiyar*-herdsmen. cf. ibid., p. 73.
40. See note 7 above, cf. *Ibid.*, p. 75-76.
41. Probably it was a royalty on the manufacture of salt paybale to *kō* (cf. *ibid.*, p. 71-72). Probably the manufacture of the salt was a prerogative of *kō* and the citizens paid the royalty for the use of his prerogative.
42. Kaśākkuḍi plates refer to the *kāl-koṭṭu* on the planting *(? iṭṭaṇa)* of all fruit trees including arecanut and Pullūr plates refer to the *kāl-koṭṭu* on the planting *(iṭṭana)* of cocoanut and arecanut (trees) in saline soil *(veṇṇilam)*. The word *kāl-koṭṭu* seems to have meant digging a channel or laying the rows in a grove and if it was so the designation of levy indicates that it was charged even initially on the planting of the trees. (cf. *SII.,* II, p. 361) Mahalingam, T.V., *op. cit.,* pp. 151-152) The Sivakāsi plates of Vīra-pāṇḍya (Tr. Arch. Soc. of *SI.,* 1962-65, p. 341) refers to *vāḷai-kkoṭṭu*, or *vāḷai-kkōḍu* as a grove of planting trees,
43. See above. As this levy is placed under the group of *kāṇam* levies,

it might have been a levy on an occasion different from that of planting the trees.

44. This was a tax for planting the flower plant, *kuvaḷai*.
45. Like *Kalkoṭṭu-kkāṇam* this might have been a further tax in respect of raising the *kuvaḷai* plant.
46. A tax on another plant, *chengoḍi*. Probably there was no tax for planting *chengoḍi*.
47. *Kadir* means the ear of corn. It is also seen as part of the word *kadir-pachchai* which refers to a plant with aromatic leaves. The levy was probably on such a plant. *Kuvaḷai*, *cheṅgoḍi* and *kadir-pachchai* no doubt are used in worship but might also have been used as luxury items by ladies. The tax was probably on account of their latter use.
48. This word actually means jar-gold. It is possible that it denoted buried treasures or right over the same. The *kō* seems to have had a right to such unaccounted treasures that may turn up while the field is being prepared for cultivation cf. Mahalingam, T.V., *op. cit.*, pp. 150-151.
49. This term occurs immediately after *sāḍippon* which also might have indicated the same class of treasures. Word for word, the phrase means cloud, cocoanut, gold. It might have meant gold exposed due to the erosion of the soil in rains.
50. *Karaṇam adhikaraṇam* and *upakaraṇam* seem to have been different official establishments, where fines on account of offences were levied and had to be deposited. (cf. *SII.*, II, p. 361 and n 2; Mahalingam, T.V., *op. cit.*, p. 150)
51. *Aṛa-ppuṛam* seems to have been connected with religion or charitable establishments. The *kō* seems to have been entitled to get a portion of the fines, which the establishments concerned might collect. cf. Mahalingam, T.V., *op. cit.*, p. 150.
52. Manṛu was the forum. *Manṛupāḍu* must have been fines imposed as per decisions therein. Minakshi, C., *op. cit.*, p. 83.
53. Among the three words constituting the phrase, the middle one *paḷḷi* is usually indicative of the Jain establishment. As this term occurs among the group of fines, it might have indicated a sort of fine or some other collection connected with a Jain establishment. It is also interesting that in both the charters where this term occurs, *Ulavai-paḷḷi-vastu* follows *pattūr-chāru*. It is possible that both the terms together indicated a single item or *pattūr*-chāru which means announcing to ten villages was connected with the

collection of the fine of this type. cf. Minakshi, C., *op. cit.*, p. 80; Mahalingam, T.V., *op. cit.*, pp. 149-50.

54. *Kōyil* denotes the temple as well as the residence of the *kō (kō-il)*. The suffix in this phrase *vastu* also occurs in the other item *uḷavai-paḷḷīvastu*. The latter occurs immediately after the items denoting fines. But *kōyil-vastu* occurs at the head of the list of *parihāras* in the Pullūr plates just before *chekku*. It is possible that as interpreted by Mahalingam, T.V. (*op. cit.*, p. 149), this term combined with *chekku* formed a single item *(koyil-vastu-chekku)* and indicated a levy on account of the oil-press set up on temple premises. But in the light of the occurrence of the item *chekku* independently in the other charters and in consideration of the fact that for utilisation of temple premises, it would have been the temple which would be entitled to levy any charges not the *kō*. This interpretation seems untenable. It is possible that this item denoted a special tribute to the *kō*.

55. This means the *karai* of twelve years. *Kaṛai* as well as *kaṛai* are both used to denote the tax (Subrahmaniam, N. Sangam Polity, p. 198 *kaṛai-ppaḍu-mākkaḷ*-subjects liable to landtax also; *SII.*, VIII, 68 This inscription of the time of Rājēndra I from Tiruvannāmalai refers to an undertaking by the *ūr* of Āḍaiyūr to themselves pay all the *karai* in respect of land endowed to the temple which they had freed from *Iṛai.)* In this context, this might have been a tax generally payable by all, and that the donees of Nayadhīramaṅgalam were exempted from it or were enabled to collect it from the other residents for their own benefit. The periodicity of the tax, twelve years, is reminiscent of the Jupiter cycle. So it seems possible that this levy had something to do with *mahāmagha* or *kumbh-mēḷa* celebrations. It may also have something to do with the periodical reallocation of plots among the shareholders of the *brahmadēyam* under the *karai* system. So it is to be construed that the *brahmadēyam* holders were exempted from it which also seems to be indicated by the use of the term *iṛāmaiyum* in the context, (cf. Mahalingam, T.V., *op. cit.*, 148).

56. cf. SII, VI, 292, This inscription of the year 16 (923) of Parāntaka I from Uttaramallūr records the acquisition of strips of land of two *kōl* width by the *sabhā* to cut a channel *vati-aṭṭu)*. An inscription of the year 19 (1004) of Rājarāja I from Sīyamaṅgalam, Wandiwash taluk, North Arcot district (ibid.,VII, 440) also records an authorisation to take a channel of an internal width of one *kōl*

of 4 span length, from a branch channel to irrigate the fields sold to the temple of the place. Again another inscription of the year 29 (1014) of the same king from Mēlpāḍi (Chittoor taluk and district) (*ibid.*, III, 15) refers to an authorisation to cut a channel of ¼ *kōl* width from the river Nugā to irrigate the land allotted to a temple by the *nagarattār* of the place.

57. *SII.*, VII, 33. It seems that this rod of 12 span was devised in accordance with the age-old practice which was coming down from the time of the *Arthasāstra* (II, 20-*Shaṭ-kamśō daṇḍō-brahmadēy-ātithya-mānam—the rod of 6 kamśa (cubit?)* length is the measure of *brahmadēya-ātithya)* cf. Ramesan, N., cp. Ins. of Govt. *Museum*, AP II, p. 2.
58. *Ibid.*, XII, 105.
59. *Ibid.*, VIII, 9.
60. *AREp.*, 1921,160.
61. *Ibid.*, 191.
62. *SII.*, VIII, 521.
63. cf. *Kaḍigaiyār* (the members of the *ghaṭikā*) are mentioned as one of the bodies which was important enough to participate in the anointment of Nandivarman II when he was chosen as king (*SII.*, IV, 135); also cf. *SII.*, III, p. 94. One official is referred was the chief executive of the *ghatika*. For some fresh opinions about the *ghaṭikā*, see Narayanan, MGS, "Kandalur-sālai-New Light on the History of Aryan Expansion in South India", *Proc*, *IHC*, 32nd session (Jabalpur, 1970) p. 125 f. Also Jayasval, Suvira, ISHP., p. 152-53.
64. cf. *SII.*, XII, 105, this inscription of Kampavarman (889?) from Tiruvorriyūr contains the rare early reference to the establisnment *āvaṇakkuṛi*.
65. Rods measuring fifteen and 7½ span are also mentioned in an inscription of the year 16 (923) of Parāntaka I from *Uttaramallūr* (*SII.*, VI, 292). But *kōl*s of these lengths are not otherwise mentioned.
66. An inscription of the year 16 of the king from Tirukkarugāvur (Tanjavur district-(AREp., 1961-62, B 393) which credits the king with the title *Toṇḍai-nāḍu-vagai-sayda-uḍaiyār* (The lord who brought order to Toṇḍai-nāḍu) indicates that the survey in Toṇḍai-nāḍu must have been completed by that year. Probably the operation in respect of Chōḷa-nāḍu took a litle longer time as an inscription dated year 19 (1004) of the king from Tiruchcheṅga-

ttāṅkuḍi (AREp., 1913-59) states that the survey was completed by the year 17.

67. *SII.*, VII, 440.
68. As normally one and one third span make one foot, the 16 span rod should have been only 12 feet long by modern standards. But if it is shown to have been 12 ft. 9 inches, it shows that the hand span and feat of a man slightly oversize was adopted at the time to determine the standard length. An inscription of the year 4 (1122) of Vikramachōḷa from Tiruviḍaimarudūr, Ṭanjāvūr district (*SII.*, V, 702) refers to a *kōl,* 12 ft. *(aḍi)* in length as the one that was used for the survey of the world. (*tiru-ulag-aḷanduruḷina-paḍi*).
69. An inscription of the period of Rājēndra I from Mannārkōyil, Tanjāvūr district refers to the survey done with Rājarājan-kōl *(AREp.*, 1916, p. 107).
    An inscription of about the 11th century from Tiruvālaṅgāḍu also refers to the rod used for surveying the world' *(tiru-ulag-alanda-kōl)* (AREp., 1926,97).
70. The Tiruvālaṅgāḍu inscription as mentioned above (AREp., 1926, 97) says that the rod used in the transaction accorded with the one mentioned in the inscriptions in the Tanjavur temple. An Andanallūr (Tiruchirappalli district) inscription of the year 7 (992) of Rājarāja I *(SII.*, VII, 660) also guarantees the genuineness of the rod used in the concerned land transaction by saying that it compared with the rod engraved on the *srī-vimāna* of the temple at Tiruchchenduṛai (also in Tiruchirappalli district), specimens of the standard rod (16 span) are also found in the temples at Tiru-kkaḷukkunṛam (Chingleput district) *(AREp.*, 1932-33, 167—There is no indication as to when this was got done) ; Also (Iḍaiyāḷam-South Arcot district) *ibid.*, 1938-39, 3ḷ3 -here again the engraver authenticated the correctness of the length of the rod engraved by stating that it accorded with the rod of Tiruvūragam. The *Annual Report* of *Epigraphy* for the concerned year says that the engraving at Iḍaiyāḷam was done in the reign of Rājēndra I), at Vēlūr (North Arcot district) (*AREp.*, 1933-34, 66)—the remarks column of the *Annual Report* of *Epigraphy* contains the gist of the purport of an inscription of the time of Parāntaka I and also contains a subsidiary entry, "states that the mark on the *upāna* represents the *padinārūsān* -kōl and the (square measure of) this length is equal at *mā-kkāṇi,*" Apart from the apparent misinterpretation of the latter part of the epigraph there also seems to be some mixing up. There is no

evidence pointing to any survey or standardisation of the measuring rods during the time of Parāntaka I. Linear markings (length is not cited in the *Annual Report* of *Epigraphy*) described as *Gaṇḍar-gaṇḍan-kōl* and *Amaitta-nārāyaṇan-. kōl*, at a later period are also found engraved on temple walls at Kunnattūr (Chingleput district) (ibid. 1929-30, 228). One *Muvāyiravan-kōl*, represented by a line 15 ft long is also found in the temple at Peṇṇāḍam (South Arcot district) *(ibid.*, 1928-29, 249).

71. *SII.*, XVII, 243.
72. *Ibid.*, Ill, 15.
73. Two inscriptions from Ukkal (North Arcot district), a *sabhā* village dated year 13 and 14 respectively of Rājarāja I (ibid., 2,3) mention the rod used while apportioning the share (*paṅgiṭṭa-kōl*) but do not indicate whether this *kōl* measured 16 or 18 span.
74. *Ibid.*, XVII, 741.
75. *SII.*, VIII, 16.
76. *SII.*, III, 19. The inscription is from Mēlpāḍi (Chittoor taluk and district).
77. *Ibid.*, 54. This inscription is from Tiruvallam itself.
78. *Ibid.*, 198.
79. cf. *Ibid.*, 142.
80. *SII.*, III, 156.
81. *Ibid.*, V, 373.
82. *Ibid.*, Ill, 30.
83. The Tiruviḍaimarudūr inscription of Vikrama-chōḷa referred to above (*SII.*, V, 702) says that the extent of land which as per the records of the village (*nila-mudal-pottagam*) was stated to have amounted to one *vēli*. 11 *mā* 1 *kāṇi* and 1 *mundirigai* but when measured by the *kōl* of 12 feet used for the survey, and computed on the basis that 100 *kuḷi* constituted one *mā* was found to have consisted of 2 *vēli*.
84. AREp., 1921, 219.
85. cf. *Ibid.*, 1912, 104, ibid., 1913, p. 96. An inscription of the year 27 (1012) of Rājarāja I from Mēlappaḷuvr, Udaiyarpalaiyam taluk, Tiruchirappalli district *(AREp.*, 1924, 385, ibid., 1923, p. 101) states that as a result of the survey about 900 *kalams* of paddy was collected as surplus to the state. Also cf. ibid., 1921, p. 101-102.
86. *AREp.*, 1908, para 55 (survey done during the reign of Rājēndra I)*; ibid.*, 1922, para 18 (survey done during the reign of

Rājādhirāja I); *Ibid.*, 1906 para 22; *ibid.*, 1968-69 B 113 (survey done during the reign of Kulōttunga 1); *Ibia.*, 1925, para 10 (survey done during the reign of Kulōttuṅga II).

87. This must be compared with the Viḷaveṭṭi grant of Simhavarman (6th century) pertaining to the Guṇṭūr-Nellore region, wherein the miscellaneous levies are referred to as "what could be enjoyed by myself" (*asmad-bhōgyāni*) by the king in his order addressed to the officers stationed in the locality *(sarvv-ādhyakshas* and *tat-samchāriṇah* ~).
88. *SII.*, XII, 95.
89. This can be compared with other inscriptions like those from Tiruvoṟṟiyūr which say that the *sabhā* would pay the fine at *dharmmāsanam* (*Ibid.* 88, 90) or that the interest on gold taken over by the *sabhā* with an undertaking to contribute for the maintenance of services in the temple would be paid at Tiruvoṟṟiyūr-āṇi (*Ibid.* 88, 90 etc.)
90. *Ibid.*, 102, Also *SII.*, III, 125.
91. *SII.*, VII, 809.
92. *Ibid.*, 810.
93. *SII.*, III, 181. Also cf. *Ibid.* 167, 187. In this record of the period of Pārthivēndravarman from *Uttaramallūr*, the *sabhā* undertook to pay the fine at the place of their choice as the *mudal* of *dharmmāsanam*.
94. *SII.*, I, 148.
95. *SII.*, VI, 66.
96. *SII.*, I, 66.
97. The Jain establishment?
98. In the Kaśākkuḍi plates the Tamil text is prefaced by the statement that the following was the communication from *kōn* (*kōn-olai*). Hence *kōn* here might have referred to the king as in all the other grants. But it is also possible that it referred to Brahmasrirāja, the *mukhya mantri* or chief minister who according to the Sanskrit text got the village Kotukōlli for the grant of *brahmadēyam* from the king. The Sanskrit text further on names the *vijṅapti* as Brahma-yuvarāja and not Brahmasrī-rāja. The Tamil text does not mention Brahmasrīrāja but only cites Brahmayuvarāja as one at whose *viṇṇappam* the grant was made. Unless both Brahmasrīrāja and Brahmayuvarāja were identical the Sanskrit text seems to indicate that the former issued the grant with Brahmayuvarāja making the *viṇṇappam*.

99. It is likely that these *kōs* were originally (i.e.) before their subjugation by the king, collecting only what have been termed as miscellaneous levies, as the land had not been brought under agricultural economy during their independent sway over that territory. It is also possible that the *kō* in these contexts referred to the collector of taxes appointed by the king who was allowed to retain the miscellaneous levies as his fee. An inscription of the period of Parāntaka I from Uttaramallūr (*SII.*, VI, 291) uses the term *kō-chcheydu* in the context of the efforts of the *sabhā* to raise gold. Here 'doing the kō' might have meant the collection of taxes or doing what the *kō* does. cf. Sastri, K.A.N., *The Cōḷas*, p. 545, n. 81.

APPENDIX—V

THE BACKGROUND FOR IRRIGATION IN THE REGION

Regarding the irrigation potential in the whole of Tamilnāḍu it is worthwhile to quote the observations of recent authors who have made a special study of the subject, EHG Dobby in his *Monsoon Asia*, writes To the west and to the east of the Western ghats lie belts of alluvial soils which are of critical importance for local farming; they are smallest to the west, where the streams are short and greatest to the east where the rivers Cauvery, Vaijal and Ponnaiyār have built large deltas, Cape Comorin isolates these two alluvial belts. Complicating the surface are large areas of poor laterite soil on low in land platforms rising above the alluvials—East of these hills (Western ghats) is Tamilnād, the greater southern part of the old Madras Presidency, lying in rainshadow during the south-westerlies; local relief is so low and so aligned that during the north-easterlies rains are light and there are rainshadow effects, especially round Salem beneath the Deccan scarp. In Tamilnad, the larger easterly part of the Dravidian Parallelogram rains are thus both light and come chiefly in November with north-easterly winds establishing a special agricultural cycle and producing a prolonged draught which largely off sets the greater area of farmable land. The contrast between Kerala and Tamilnad, the Western and Eastern coastal zones, has led to great contrast in the way of life indicated by considerable tea and rubber growing to the west and cotton and groundnuts to the east by preoccupation with irrigation in the east except that the padi to the east must be irrigated and in consequence innumerable shallow tanks cover substantial area of the landscape even though it is only now and then that they contain equally large areas of water.[1] Further he says that the driest part of Tamilnad is around Tirunelveli with an average rainfall of 25 inches per annum but in spite of this the soil of the region being regur (*karisal*) developed upon a gneiss substructure, which though less retentive than in the Deccan, is easily worked and so at least a quarter of its surface is planted with cotton. Here tanks are rarely seen on the *karisal* and the dependence is on direct rainfall. To the north-east of this is the re-markable terrain of the Valgai (Vaigai) delta, "where the flat drought ridden countryside of poor laterite soils has been reshaped manually over many generations into a fantastic number of saucer-like tanks which are linked by small channels to the rivers, whose occasional storm-water they conserve. Very little run off from the ground or from the river reaches the sea; the Vaigai distributaries are almost dry. This region of innumerable tanks represents a probably unique degree of water control. In some localities tanks occupy one-eighth of the land. Only by this strict control has it been possible with an unreliable rainfall averaging 34 inches per annum and much reduced in efficiency by high evaporation, to maintain padi farming (which occupies about a quarter of the cultivated area) and to grow cotton (on a fifth of the area) and by this means support from one annual crop over 1300 people per sq. mile. Despite this effort, farmers have an exceptionally low standard of living. " "The Cauvery Delta, supporting a similar high density of farmers with an equally long history of cultivation is elaborately irrigated. Cauvery water below Trichinopoly is diverted to a fan of man-made distributaries stretching 75 miles from north to south. Without barrage or dam, old inundation canals overflow directly to the fields, but diversion to storage tanks is also done so that water is available for most of the year as against the brief occasional water in Vaigai tanks. On the Cauvery delta there is a time-lag in water availability. The eastern parts receive the water much later than the western where, in consequence, the farming cycle is considerably earlier. Its large catchment in the western ghats gives the Cauvery a steadier regime than most local rivers." "Padi dominates Cauvery farming and at Tanjore occupies three-quarters of the farmed area." He refers to the Salem-Erode through where the cauvery enters the lowland as dry poor soil supporting millets and to the Coimbatore plateau as having natural drainage which is well incised, with half the cultivated area remaining under millets with dependence on direct rains. (He says that "Tamilnad while an agricultural region has many market towns)". He does not deal with the other regions. As it is, he gives a good picture, though incomplete.

Leonard M. Cantor[2] also notes the importance of tank irrigation in the Tamil country even in the Cauvery delta. He says that "South of Madras in the Cauvery delta a modern canal network and an old tank system provide water for more than 1,300,000 acres on which rice, groundnuts and sugar are grown." The authors of World Regional Geography[3] after noting the requirements of rice cultivation, rice being the highest yielding member of small grains (i.e.) that it is grown on wet fields with 3-8 inches of water, on smooth soils with impervious sub-soil, supplemental fresh water supply and warm temperatures, say that in the monsoon tropics for the growth of rice, irrigation is supplemental to natural rainfall to the levels needed and for this irrigation through the long history of production, a great many techniques have developed,some depending upon shallow wells with water drawn by various fulcrum and windless arrangements but that most of the irrigation development was co-operative effort of villages which depended upon small streams diversions. They also say that canals are the most important type of irrigation providing water for at least half the acreage and on the plateau, tanks are the principal means of irrigation, in which system the rain run off the wet monsoon is impounded in drainage channels by simple dams for diversion to the fields at the end of the rainy season. Forbes said,[3a] "Old brooks and rivers were dammed in India and water was tapped from the artificial lakes or reservoirs thus formed. If they are silted up, a new weir is constructed in the river below or above the old one. This system first in use in Rajputana and central India gradually spread southwards where there are now no less than 53,000 reservoirs in the Madras Presidency[4] alone with a total of 30,000 miles of embankment." Thus, it will be seen that all the modern authors have drawn attention to the relatively poor water resources of Tamil-nadu. Even the most favoured areas in this region receive only a moderate rainfall and the rivers as there are carry water only at fixed periods. This rendered the development of irrigation works like tanks, lakes etc. inevitable for achieving any progress in the agricultural field.[5]

The above cited authors did not pointedly deal with Toṇḍaimaṇḍalam. About the character of the rivers and rain-fall pattern in the region reference has already been made in the chapter on physical background. While the statistics collected by the India Meteorological Department and published in their Memoirs[6] indicate that the North Arcot district, inland, has a moderate amount of rainfall OHK Spate and AT Learmonth (India and Pakistan: *A General and Regional Geography*, p. 743) say that the rainfall is less effective than its amount. In the same place they also point to the fact that the rivers in the region contain hardly any water for nine months, necessitating a recourse to tanks and spring channels. Hence it can be said that this region receives a moderate amount of rainfall and has some rivers carrying water during a short period only as they take their source either in the rain shadow of the South-West monsoon or in the Eastern Ghats. This has necessitated a technology for storing water as and when made available and distributing it evenly during the year for agriculture. As the Chingleput District Manual while noting the poor quality of the soil in that district[7] pays glowing tributes to the initiative shown by ancient Hindu monarchs in setting up a successful irrigation system with great hydraulic skill[8] and bringing the area into a flourishing state,[9] it is seen that such a technology was introduced in ancient times. Though one cannot be too positive as O.H.K. Spate and Learmonth that the Pallavas introduced this technology,[10] there are reasonable grounds to assume that they might have been responsible for the fashioning of the reservoirs fed from streams through channels and laying out distributory channels as it was they who first set up a strong kingship based on this region.

NOTES:

1. *op. cit.,* Vol. 5, p. 274 f. The author also says (*op. cit.,* p. 62) that wet paddy has been most cultivated on coasts of seasonally heavy rain, in flood plains and delta locations—the crop doing well in low lying clay land which is inimical to most other crops, which peculiarity tends a rice field to be used for that purpose alone. Double cropping of rice, a possibility related to continuous growing temperature necessitates a considerable control of water and less dependence on local rains.
2. Leonard M. Cantor, A World Geography of Irrigation, p. 117 f.
3. Oliver, H. Heintzelman and Richard M. Highsmith Jr., *world Regional Geography,* Fourth Edn., p. 144. Also see *SII.,* I, No. 66. An inscription of the time of Rājarāja I from Tirumalai (near Pōlūr), Polur Taluk, North Arcot District, states that a Jain teacher set up a *kaliṅgu*, or sluice (to the lake of the village) and thus ensured the cultivation of paddy there.

3a. Forbes, Studies in Ancient Technology, Pt. II, p. 12.

4. The Madras Presidency of British times included the whole of Tamilnāḍu, major portions of the present day Andhra Pradesh and some portions of Kerala, Karnāṭaka and Orissa. See *EI,* XVI, p. 277 f. Some Rāshṭrakūṭa inscriptions from Dharwar District, Karṇataka refer to *aṛaghaṭṭa*, the water wheel used in Central and Western India. But this method of drawing water was unknown
5. There seems to have been some *punsey* crops raised on the (i. e.) crop depending on rainfall alone. The crop was called *vānpayir* (*SII.,* XVII, No. 127, Inscription from Tiruchchōpuram, Cuddalore Taluk, South Arcot District, belonging to 13 th century)
6. *op. cit.,* Vol. XXVII, Pt V. cf. *North Arcot District Manual,* p. 199-200. It is stated that rain fall in that district was precarious.
7. *op. cit.,* p. 65.
8. *Ibid.,* p. 250.
9. *Ibid.,* p. 209.
10. *op. cit.,* p. 210

APPENDIX—VI

THE IRRIGATION FACILITIES

In Tamilnāḍu construction of irrigation works for efficient long term use had started even in very early times.[1] Some archaeological excavations stand witness to it. The vestiges of the earliest work were found in the excavation at Koṛkai near the Tāmbraparṇi river delta in the Pāṇdya country. It is said that small sections of many ancient bunds were seen rising upto twelve feet above the rice fields.[2] The excavation at Vāṇagiri near Kāvērippaṭṭinam about a mile south of river Kāvērī in the Chōḷa country has also exposed a fine example of irrigational construction of the first or second century" in the shape of a beautifully constructed and paved inlet channel flanked by semicircular walls built into the earthern embankment of a tank which was evidently fed by a channel from Kāvērī.[3] That construction of such irrigational works was in vogue in the first few centuries of the Christian era is also indicated in the Saṅgam poems which refer to the utilisation of water stored in tanks and reservoirs, drawn through small channels to the fields, with sand mounds to divert water, buckets of reeds being used occassionally to bale in water.[4] The same source also tells about how the kings of the period took the initiative in providing these facilities. Several of the Saṅgam works relate that the king Karikāla-chōḷa constructed an embankment for the river Kāvēri excavated a number of irrigation channels from that river and dug tanks to conserve water and finally earned the title *Peruvaḷattān*-promoter of great fertility.[5]

In respect of Toṇḍaimaṇḍalam reference do not indicate

if in the earlier period such constructions were undertaken. The Mahēndravāḍi inscription of Guṇabhara (7th century) contains the first reference to the construction of a reservoir in the region. It says that Mahēndra-taṭāka was excavated by the king. Thereafter the charters issued by these Pallava kings and the stone inscriptions pertaining to their period refer to several reservoirs and irrigational facilities. Some of these bear names of titles of the Pallava kings of the period reflecting that they might have been responsible for their coming into being. In so far as such reservoirs are found associated with *brahmadēyam* and *ūr* villages the details about them have been dealt with in the main chapter. The records of the period also refer to several other reservoirs and irrigation facilities in different contexts and provide interesting information as to who put up these facilities and with what purpose. Here it is proposed to discuss this information available.

Though the records do not expressly say so, the names of some reservoirs mentioned in these records indicate that the Chōḷa monarchs who conquered Toṇḍaimaṇḍalam by the end of the 9th century also had caused the construction of some reservoirs in Toṇḍaimaṇḍalam. An inscription from Shōlinghūr, North Arcot district dated year 9 (916) of Parāntaka I[6] mentions Chōḷavāridhi (Chola reservoir) and says that the king granted the revenues from a field for this reservoir. The execution of this order was left to his subordinates chief Gaṅga Prithivīpati II. Probably the king had constructed this reservoir.[7] It is noteworthy that the name of the place, Chōḷaliṅgapura (corrupted into modern Shōlinghūr) also indicates that Parāntaka I might have formed that settlement and constructed the reservoir for its support.

In the same way the records from the village Madhurāntakam (it is now called so and the taluk also bears the same name—it is situated in Chingleput district) which was known as Vīranārāyaṇavati in earlier days was supported by a reservoir Madhurāntaka-ppērēri of which the feeder canal was called Vīrachōḷa-vāykkāl.[8] Each of the prefixes of the geographical details, Vīra-nārāyaṇa, Madhurāntaka and Vīra-chōḷa were the titles of Parāntaka I. Hence it appears that Parāntaka I had also founded this village and the attached irrigation facilities.[9] Some reservoirs mentioned in the records of Toṇḍaimaṇḍalam also bear the names of some chiefs who are known to have been feudatories of the Pallavas and later of the Chōḷas. These might have been constructed by the chiefs to please their kings. However it is also possible that these reservoirs came to bear thier names just because the territories concerned had come under the control of the respective chiefs. They might have constructed a reservoir to benefit the people within this territory under their control or might have just got an already existing facility renamed. For instance one Bāṇasamudram is mentioned for the first time in an inscription quoting the reign of a Mahābali-vāṇarāja from Tiruvallam.[10] From the fact that the *sabhā* of Tīkkāli-vallam allotted land which was *mañjikkam* under Vāṇasamudram against gold received for contributing to the food offering and a perpetual lamp in the temple, it appears that the reservoir was meant to serve the land in their village. As another inscription from the same place quoting the reign of Mahābali-bāṇarāja[11] is dated *saka* 810 (888),[12] it can be presumed that the above cited inscription also belonged to the same period. Further as the *sabhā* of Tiruvallam finds mention only in these inscriptions, it would also appear as if that *sabhā* village was founded at that time and the reservoir was put up for their convenience by the Bāṇa. Another inscription dated year 14 (999) of Rājarājā from Mēlpāḍi (North Arcot district)[13] also refers to the *mañjikkam* land under the authority of the *sabhā* of Tiruvallam being served by the same reservoir. But Tiruvallam in Miyāṛu-nāḍu in Paḍuvūr-kōṭṭam was within the territory of the Pallava and has produced earlier records also. However even the earliest of them dated year 62 (793)[14] in the reign of Nandivarman II[15] refers only to the village Vāṇapuram obviously named after the Bāna but neither to a sabhā of Tiruvallam nor to Bāṇasamudram. The next in date, that of the year 17 (863) of Nandivarman III[16] speaks about the formation of a *brahmadēyam* named Vidēlviḍugu

Vikramāditya-chaturvēdimaṅgalam by the king at the request of the Bāṇa and a *sabhā*" of that village. Though the village was named after the Bāṇa who had assumed a title of the Pallava to show his subordination, there is no reference to the Bāṇa-samudram having been constructed to help that *brahmadēyam*. It is not known if the *sabhā* of Tiruvallam was the same as *sabhā* of Viḍēlviḍugu-Vikramāditta-chaturvēdimaṅgalam. Further the name Vāṇapuram mentioned in the earliest inscription figures again in inscriptions[17] of 1001 as an important village with *tankūru* status and it is reflected that Bāṇasamudram served this village also. The Bāṇa's influence in the area was pronounced even from the earliest times and hence all this evidence suggests that Bāṇasamudram might have been constructed by him without any particular reference to any village in the locality, but to benefit several villages around. The other water storages, Pāṟkuṭṭai and Paḷavēri mentioned in the context of the *sabhā* of Tiruvallam making over land to the temple might have been existing in the locality since time immemorial.

In the same way there is a village in Toṇḍaimaṇḍalam, which is now known as Tippasamudram (Velur taluk, North Arcot district). This village name was apparently derived from that of the reservoir of the place which had gained prominence.[18] But the earliest inscription from this place dated year 17 (887) in the reign of Kampavarman[19] refers to Valivalakka-maṅgalam which was probably the earlier name of the village. The record also refers to the reservoir of that village but does not indicate its name. Tippasamudram was in Paṅgaḷa-nāḍu and later records say that there was a feudatory family in charge of this nāḍu. Members of this family bore the title Prithvīgaṅgaraiyar and one of them in association with his wife is stated to have set up a river channel to the reservoir in memory of their daughter. There is no indication, however, about the construction of the reservoir itself though the circumstances of the record makes it appear that the village had already been existing along with the reservoir even before the time of this record. They might have been founded by the same or an earlier member of the same family. The present name of the village and also apparently of the reservoir probably came to be applied to them at a far later date after some Tippa got associated with the village as no member of the Paṅgaḷa-nāḍu family bore that name.[20] An inscription from Brahmadēsam, Cheyyar taluk, North Arcot district, dated in the year 20 of the reign of a Rājakēsarivarman (probably Āditya I)[21] refers to one Tigaittiṟal-ēri. The name of the reservoir suggests that it was constructed by the Tigaittiṟal, who was associated with the area at that time. Probably he was identical with or belonged to the family of Tigaittiṟalār, who figures in an inscription of the time of Nandivarman III from Kiḷiyanūr, Tiṅdivanam taluk, South Arcot district[22] as one who constructed a temple *(vishnu- griham)* and endowed some land free of taxes for the same. It is not known if Tigaittiṟal was a chief of the locality and if he had constructed the reservoir to benefit the village. It may be pointed out that Brahmadēsam where the record concerned is found seems to have been known as Rājamalla- chaturvēdimaṅgalam and is surmised to have been founded by a Gaṅga chief. Hence it is clear that this reservoir was not constructed at the time of the founding of the *brahmadēyam*.[23] One reservoir is referred to as Araiyanēri in an inscription of the year 9 of a Rājakēsarivarman from Bādūr, Wandiwash taluk, North Arcot district.[24] The *ūr* of that village Vaḍavūr,declared that land accommodating the reservoir and lands irrigated by it, taxfree, probably at the instance of that Araiyan who seems to have contributed the reservoir exclusively for the benefit of lands belonging to a temple. The identity of this *araiyan* is however, not clear. The name of the reservoir suggests that it was connected by the *araiyan*. The title *araiyan* was borne by chiefs and officials. It is not known in what context he had constructed the reservoir and if it was a small affair meant to serve the purposes of temple lands only. It is noteworthy that another *araiyan*, Konēri-araiyan of Seṟuppāṟai in Vilaiyūr-nāḍu on the northern bank of the river Peṇṇai in Vāṇagōppāḍi is also recorded to have dug a tank and to have given a field for its upkeep, according to an inscription of again a Rājakēsarivarman (year 5—Āditya I) from Mēlvāḷai, Tirukkoyilur taluk, South Arcot district).[25]

While the above instances evidence the construction of reservoirs by kings and chiefs either to enable the settlement of a village or to help the extension of cultivation in an already existing settlement by adding an irrigation facility, which ultimately would work to their own benefit the atomosphere of the period itself was built up to such an extent that provision of irrigation facilities came to be considered as an act of merit, and chiefs are witnessed to have put up reservoirs as memorials.[26]

An inscription of the year 23 (893 ?) of Kampavikramavarman from Chōḷavaram (near Vēlūr), North Arcot district[26a] refers to a reservoir as Kanakavalli-ēri in Paṅgaḷa-nāḍu in Paḍuvūr-kōṭṭam. Some land under this reservoir was granted for the worship and for the maintenance of the worshipping priests in the temple Kanakavalli-vishṇugṛiham constructed at[27] Kāṭṭuttumbūr. Unfortunately the portion of the epigraph containing the details about the land and as to who was responsible for all these benefactions, is lost. However this much is clear that some one constructed a temple for the benefit or in memory of one Kanakavalli and granted land for the same. The record also indicates that the reservoir was big enough as it is referred to as having belonged to the *nāḍu* rather than to the village. It might have been constructed at the time in honour of that lady or an existing reservoir might have been renamed after her. Kāṭṭuttumbūr and the reservoir were situated in Paṅgaḷa-nāḍu, which is known to have been under the control of the Prithivīgaṅgaraiyar chiefs at the time.[28] Hence it is reasonable to assume that it was the chief at that time who had built the temple reservoir and christened both the reservoir and the temple after Kanakavalli who might have been closely related to him, as a memorial. Such construction of a tank by a Prithivīgaṅgaraiyar in the memory of a lady, probably his daughter who was also the grand-daughter of a Vāṇakovaraiyar through her mother is also witnessed in another inscription from the same place dated saka 871 (949), which is stated in the record to have been the year in which Rāshṭrakūṭa Kṛishṇa III, entered Toṇḍaimaṇḍalam after over throwing Rājāditya-chōḷa. The tank was excavated and named after the lady as Kaḷḷinaṅgai-kkuḷam.[29]

Sometimes queens, wives and daughters of chiefs are also seen to have contributed irrigation reservoirs. One Vairamēgha-vāṇakovaraiyar's wife Aṇikōvan Oṛiyūr-piraṭṭi, who was the daughter of a Ilāḍarāya also is stated to have constructed a reservoir (*ēri*) with a sluice (*tūmbu*) at Nichchavinīta-maṅgalam according to an undated inscription from Mānampūṇḍi in Tirukkoyilur taluk of South Arcot district.[31] She seems to have carried out these charitable deeds in her father's territory as two inscriptions of a Rājakēsarivarman and Kṛishṇa III from Mēlvāḷai in the same Tirukkoyilur taluk[32] refer to the region as having been held by an Ilāḍavaraiyan, though the region is referred to a Vāṇagōppāḍi in the same place.[33]

A Chōḷa princess Kundavai is seen to have been commemorated by the construction of a big lake called after her in Pudūr, a hamlet of Brahmadēsam,[34] Cheyyar taluk, North Arcot district. There were several princesses of the Chōḷa family named Kundavai. It is not known who of these was associated with this reservoir, whether she was responsible for this construction or if it was put up as a memorial to her.[35]

Apart from kings, chiefs and members of their families, the records of the period also inform that members of the villages also showed their interest in adding to the irrigation facilities in villages. The earliest inscription from Uttara-mallūr, which is dated year 7 (803) of Dantivarman[36] records the sale of five *pāṭakam* of land set apart for a reservoir by the *peruṅguri-sabhā* of the place, to one SvāmiKumāra-chaturvēdi-sōmayāji who had hailed from Muḍumbai originally, for digging a lake and making an embankment. Apparently this brahmin was a member of that *brahmadēyam*. The brahmin got the tank dug[37] and named it after himself as Śvami-Kumārakuṭṭam. But that it was a facility meant for general and not his personal use is indicated by the condition laid down by the *sabhā* that on the strength of the purchase the brahmin should not presume exclusive rights with regard to the new tank. As has been pointed out above, Uttaramēru-chaturvēdimaṅgalam was probably constituted some time before the date of this inscription and Vairamēgha-taṭākam which seems to have supported the land in this *brahmadēyam* village was also probably constructed at the same time. However this record suggests that even while constituting the *brahmadēyam* some provision of land had been made for the digging of additional reservoirs as found necessary. Apart from Svāmi-kumāra-kuṭṭam one Āsuriyār-ēri is referred to in an inscription of the year 16 (923) of Parāntaka I.[38] Apparently it was named after one of the members of the village who had originally hailed from Āsuri as one Āsuri RudraKumāra-kramavittan is also mentioned in the same place. He had probably excavated the tank If it was so this must have been another such tank dug by another member of the same village on the same terms as recorded in the earlier inscription. The inscriptions from Uttaramallūr also refer to a Kārigai-kkuṭṭam in the main village[39] and also to a reservoir at Malliyankarāṇai, (a hamlet of the village (?).[40] Whereas these two also are mentioned as subsidiary irrigation facilities in the same *brahmadēyam* complex, it is not known if they were already there when the *brahmadēyam* was formed or were put up by the efforts of the *sabhā* or members of the *sabhā* subsequently.

Apart from Uttaramallūr, Tirumalai (near Pōḷūr) Polur taluk, North Arcot district is seen to have had two reservoirs Kaḍappēri and Madagēri[41] and Tiruvallam had besides Bāṇa-samudram, three other reservoirs, Pāṛkuṭṭai,[42] Pāḷavēri and Kīl-ēri.[43] These reservoirs seem to have been moderate affairs and might have been constructed by members of the villages concerned.

The reservoirs that were constructed during the period required the digging of necessary channels to and from the reservoir and the fitting of devices to draw the water from the same. It has been seen that the grantees of *brahmadēyam* as per Kūram charter were made responsible for taking the channels from the river to the reservoir and thence to the fields. Hence whoever might have contributed the reservoir, the execution of the further works to utilise the reservoirs was left to local initiatives, village corporations or individuals. However the records reflecting the contribution of such works during the period are only a few. These few records indicate that such works were provided usually by persons who seem to have had an interest in improving the prospects in the land.

An inscription dated year 6 (865) of the reign of Nṛipa-tuṅga from Vaḷuvūr (Wandiwash taluk, North Arcot district)[44] records the setting up of a sluice[45] at Vaḷukūr by some one whose name is not clear. The short epigraph is more or less in the form of a label probably inscribed on the sluice-stone itself and hence does not provide any details. It does not even refer to any reservoir. However another record dated year 12 (871) of the same king from Marudāḍu (same taluk and district)[46] is more informative. It indicates that there was a reservoir already at Marudāḍu fitted with a sluice but it lacked a weir *(kaliṅgu)*.[47] One Koṅgaraiyar Ninṛaperumān, whose name suggests that he was a local governor, provided the *kaliṅgu* and renovated the sluice. In the year 17 (887 ?) of Kampavarman, another Prithivī-gaṅgaraiyar and his wife, who was called I lāḍapperundēvi (obviously she was the daughter of a Lāṭa chief who were then ruling portions of the present day South Arcot district) founded a river-channel (ārukkāl-channel from the river to the reservoir) to the reservoir at Valivalakkamaṅgalam as a charity *(dharmmam)* in the name of their daughter Ayyakkuṭṭi-aḍigaḷ but named it Viḻupēraraiyan.[48]

Another inscription dated year 4 of a Rajakesarivarman (10th century ?) from Veṇpākkam Kāñchīpuram taluk, Chingleput district)[49] says that one (Kēraḷan) Rājādittan alias Nanivichchādara-Mārāyan, who set up a sluice (to the local reservoir) had Valakkōnmaṅgalam as his *Jīvitam* (maintenance). The inscription dated year 21 (1006) from Tirumalai (Polur taluk, North Arcot district)[50] records that a religious teacher of a Jain establishment, who is also described as the *kō* of Vaigai (the hill containing the establishment) set up a *kalingu* and enabled paddy to be grown on both sides of the hill.[51]

Two inscriptions form the adjoining South Arcot district also record the setting up of sluices by persons who appear to have been those with some authority. One inscription dated year 3 (959) of *Vīrapāṇḍiyaṇai-talai*-koṇḍa Parakēsari (Āditya II) from Meyyūr (Ponniyāṇḍāḷ) (Tirukkoyilur taluk)[52] says that one Sirigattaraiyan built a sluice (to the local reservoir) and gifted land for the maintenance of a reservoir *(ēri-ppatti)*. Another from Parindal (same taluk) dated year 7 (977) of Uttama-chōḷa[53] points to the sluice having been constructed by Vēṅkaṭa-ppēraiyan on behalf of (in memory of?) his son Semalan.

The irrigation reservoirs in Toṇḍaimaṇḍalam being subject to much silting due to their being fed by rivers carrying storm water, the records reflect that during this period several provisions were also made for arranging for the maintenance of the reservoirs. As discussed above maintenance was a perennial necessity and the village organisations are seem to have been entrusted with this responsibility. The provisions of capital were made by individuals to meet the expenditure on the equipment necessary, like boats etc. Some such provisions made, have been dealt with above and it has been pointed out that usually the continuing expenditure on maintenance in such cases was met from ad hoc levies from the users of the irrigation water. However the records of the period also refer to the endowment of levies due to them by kings and chiefs even for meeting the recurring expenditure.

An inscription dated year 21 (867) of the reign of Nandivarman III, from Avilāla, Chandragiri taluk, Chittoor district,[54] records that Vikramāditya-mahābali-Vijayakkanār,[54a] granted the taxes *kallāṇa-kkāṇam and viḍā-nāḷi* due to him from the village for the maintenance of the reservoir at Avilāli. The record dated year 9 (916) of the king from Sholinghur, Walajapet taluk, North Arcot district,[55] says that the king granted the main levy on land *(puravu)* at the rate of 1/6 (of the produce), other levies *(āyadi)* and gold levies due to him from a field named *muṅgil-vari* for the reservoir Chōlavāridhi, which from its name appears to have been constructed by a Chōḷa king. The record is engraved on the bank of this tank. The local chief Hastimalla is stated to have made the request for the grant and he was entrusted with the execution of the benefaction.

Another inscription dated year 17 of a Rājakēsarivarman from Kīrappākkam, Chingleput taluk and district,[56] records that Kaṇḍi, wife of Kumārandai Irāvanan of Nāyaṟu in Nāyaṟu-nāḍu of Puḷaṟ-kōttam[57] gifted the levy *vāḷ-amañji* due on the lands at Kīraippāttūr belonging to her husband for the upkeep of the local tank. In Siṅgapura-nāṭṭu-kkīḻ-vaḷi, adjoining Toṇḍai-maṇḍalam also, the son of the local chief is seen to have made a gift of the chief's entitlement from the village for the maintenance of the reservoir. This inscription dated year 24 (895?), of Rājakēsarivarman(Āditya I?) from Neṛkunṛam, Wandiwash taluk, North Arcot district[58] records that Nambiya. Mallanar, son of Nṛipatuṅga-maṅgala-ppēr-aṛaiyan granted, *marudaṅ-jeruvu, koḍu-māḍi-and kaḷuval.* and also the fines that could be levied in the village *(manṛupādu* including *aṇavāy-tadaṇḍam*)[59] for the reservoir at Neṛkunram.[60] The execution of the benefaction was entrusted to the *ūrar* of the place.

The picture drawn above describing the construction of reservoirs, big and small, equipping them with necessary inlet and outlet channels after providing weirs and sluices, and making of provisions for their maintenance by kings, chiefs and other typifies the great expansion activity witnessed during the period (700-1000). This flurry of activity with regard to irrigation is not recorded either earlier or later in Toṇḍai-maṇḍalam.

NOTES:

1. cf. Gunavardhana, Ralh, "Social Function and Political Power: A case Study of State Formation in Irrigation Society" *Indian*

Historical Review, Vol. IV, No. 2 (Jan 1978). He refers to such works undertaken in Sri-Lanka even two centuries prior to the dawn of the Christian era,

2. Maloney, Clarence, "Archaeology in South India: Accomplishments and Prospects" *Essays on South India* ed. Burton Stein, p. 12. He says that on the basis of archaeological evidence, irrigated rice cultivation must have spread from Bengal down the east coast to Tamilnāḍu and further to Srilanka where ancient irrigation facilities are present. The author, however, traces the linguistic connections of Srilanka from North-West India along Maharashtra. This latter statement justifies Forbes' view quoted above that this sort of irrigation was first in evidence in Rajputana and Central India and only from there it gradually spread southwards,
3. Rao, S.R., "Kaverippaṭṭinam Excavations Tr. *Arch*. Soc S. I. 1962-65, p. 164-65. The dating is stated to have been done on the basis of a punchmarked silver coin and rouetted ware found nearby.
4. Pillai, K.K., A *Social* History of the *Tamils* Part I, p. 189. He cites the Saṅgam works *Maduraikkāñchi* (verses 89-93), Puṛanānūru (33: 4-6) and Padirruppattu (30: 18-19) and 27. 9).
5. *PaṭṭinapPālai* (283-86); *Porunar-āṛṛuppaḍai* lines 42-48 *Silappadigāram* (X, lines 107-109) and *Padiṛṛuppattu* (29. 9) cf. Pillai. KK, *op. cit.,* p. 15, 126; Subramanian, N., *A History of Tamilnadu,* pp. 75, 323. Such constructions by ancient Pandya kings have also been referred to. One Pāṇḍyan king is stated to have created a river, Pahruḷi (probably a channel from river Tāmraparṇī) and taken the title *nilam-taru-tiruvil-pāṇḍiyan* (ie.) the Pāṇḍya who promoted prosperity by making more land available (for cultivation with the help of the irrigation work created). It is noteworthy that there are also channels from the same river, Porundan (latter known as Mudikoṇḍa-śōḷa-ppērāṛu) and Ghaṭanā (later known as Rājēndra-śōḷa-ppērāṛu) in that region which along with Pahruḷi- evidence the efforts in this direction taken by the ancient Pāṇḍyan kings (Subrahmanian, N., *op. cit.*, p. 85; *EI,* XI, p. 272 f). It has been said that the construction of these major irrigation works could have been possible only for kings (Gunavardhana, Ralh., op. *cit.* ; Forbes, op. *cit.* Pt. II, p. 12).
6. *EI,* IV, p. 221 f.

7. It is not unlikely that an already existing reservoir probably constructed by the Pallavas was renamed as Cholavāridhi. Such renaming seems to have been done in the case of Bāṇasamudram by Bāṇa on their conquest of or encroachment in the area. An inscription of the period of Rājamahēndra seems to refer to it as Rājēndra-Chōḷa-ppērēri-*SII.*, III, 56.
8. The earliest available inscription from that place is dated year 7 (914 ?) Parāntaka I but it does not give these details. It is only an inscription dated year 6 (1124) in the reign of Vikramachōḷa (*SII.*, V, 993) from the place which supplies the above-noted information. According to the Manual of the *Chingleput district* the Madhurāntakam tank is one and a half miles long with a circumference of seven miles. It feeds five villages.
9. Cf. AREp. 1921, pt. II, Para 24. In Chidambaram taluk of South Arcot district, the same king Parāntaka I seems to have founded an *agrahāram* and a supporting reservoir, both named after his title Vīra-nārāyaṇa (cf. Udayēndram plates of Parāntaka I year 15 (922)—the new *brahmadēyam* complex formed by the king after adding the village Kaḍaikkōṭṭūr to the already existing *brahmadēyam* Udayachandramaṅgalam was named Vīranārāyaṇachchēri). The tank is now called Virāṇam. About the same time a Pāṇḍya king who was also called Parāntaka-Vīranārāyaṇa, claimed to have raised the embankment of an *ēri* as an act of merit. He is stated to have followed in the footsteps of his ancestors who had constructed many *taṭākas* (Dalavaypuram plates of Parāntaka Vīrnārāyana—Tr. *Arch, of S.I.* 1962-65, p. I f). Also see Sastri, K.A.N., *The Chōḷas*, p. 234. He gives an excerpt from Ind. Ant., Vol. 17, p. 274 to describe the reservoir near Gaṅgaikondachoḷapuram fed by channels from two rivers, Koḷḷiḍam and Veḷḷār, which was probably constructed by Rājēndrachōḷa I, who founded the city after his northern victories.
10. *SII.*, III, 45.
11. The Bāṇa was the ruler of the territory lying to the north-west of Toṇḍaimaṇḍalam which was referred to as Vaḍugavaḷi-mēṟku in the Nandivarman II's inscription where he figures as his feudatory (*ibid.*, 42). Between these two records the former refers to him as the ruler of the earth and the latter makes no mention of the territory over which he was ruling. Neither of these mention any overlord of the Bāṇa.

12. *Ibid.*, 44.
13. *Ibid.*, 19.
14. It is this high regnal year which helps to fix the identity of the king.
15. *Ibid.*, 42.
16. *Ibid.*, 43.
17. *Ibid.*, 51.
18. cf. *EI,* IV, p. 223.
19. *EI,* XXXIII, p. 23 f. It is noteworthy that Tiruvallam is not credited with any alternate name ending in *maṅgalam* as other *brahmadēyams* created during the period were known.
20. cf. *AREp.* 1923, 89. This inscription in Tamil and Telugu from Vallappākkam, Kanchipuram taluk, Chingleput district, which does not quote any reign or date and which seems to be of a late period records the construction of a taluk called Tippasamudram at Veḷḷaippākkam by a Tipparasar. Veḷḷaippākkam was the *tiruvidaiyāttam* (land belonging to a vaishnavite temple) of the temple of Pēraruḷāḷar and the tank was meant to benefit that village. It is not known if he was the same as Mahāpradhāni Arasar who settled a dispute regarding the supply of water from a local tank between two villages in 1406 A.D. as per an inscription from Perunagar (Pennāgaram), Kanchipuram taluk, Chingleput district (AREp. 1923, 357).
21. *SII.*, XIII, 292.
22. *SII.*, XII, 47.
23. *SII.*, XIII, 322—introduction.
24. *SII.*, XIII, 199.
25. *AREp.* 1935-36, 52. The chief is also stated to have cut a mortar at the same place (*ibid.*, 53). In the Pāṇḍya country where again there was a dearth of irrigation facilities, local chiefs or governors contributed to the welfare of the land under their control by constructing reservoirs. According to one inscription of the time of Māṛañjaḍaiyan (9th century) from Ramanathapuram (Dindigal taluk, Madurai district) one Puḷḷan entitled Parāntaka-ppaḷḷivēḷān constructed a reservoir named after himself as Puḷḷan-ēri and set up a sluice (*Kumuḷi)* to the same. While he granted some land as *kāṇi* to the concerned stone-mason, there is no evidence of his having provided for the maintenance of the reservoir. Apparently Pandinadu reservoirs did not face the problem of silt to the same extent as did those of Toṇḍaimaṇḍalam (*EI,* XXXII, pp. 274-75)

Again in the reign of Saḍaiya-Māṛaṇ (9th century) one Eṭṭi-sāttan who was conferred the title Iruppaikkuḍi-kiḷavan by the king, also constructed a reservoir and named it kiḷavan-ēri (*SII.*, XIV, 44).

26. cf. *EI,* III, P. 88 f. Another inscription of a later date (1369 A.D.) quotes Hemādri to say that construction of a tank was one of the seven meritorious acts that a man could do.

26a. *SII.*, I, 53, *EI,* VII, p. 93; Minakshi, *op. cit.*, p. 99.

27. But the epigraph is now found in a ruined Iśvara temple at Choḷavaram.

28. cf. *SI.*, XXXIII, p. 23 f.

29. *EI,* VII, p. 194. The inscription is found on a rock near a pond now called Kaḷḷ(aṅguṭṭai) cf. *EI,* XXXIII, p. 23 f.

30. cf. *SII.*, XII, 87-88.

31. AREp., 1934-35, 233.

32. *Ibid.*, 1935-36, 52-53.

33. cf. Subbarayalu, Y., *Political Geography of the Chōḷa Country*, pp. 77, 83-84.

34. *AREp*. 1965-66 B. 158. This inscription is in characters of the 11th century.

35. Probably the princess was the elder sister of Rājarāja-choḷa I, who ia credited with several other benefactions (Sastri, K.A.N., *The Chōḷas* p. 643 etc.)

36. *SII.*, VI, 365.

37. The Phrase used, *ēri-tōṇḍavum, karai-aṭṭavum* could have been construed as "for dredging (the Vairamēgha reservoir) and for bringing the mud dug up to the shore" on the analogy of *kuḷi-kuttavum* which referred to the same process. This would have implied that the five *pāṭakam* of land had been set apart for the maintenance of the main reservoir of the place and by the sale the *sabhā* tried to raise some money by transferring its responsibility to a member by entrusting to him the land set apart for the purpose. But the record also says that the purchaser dug a tank and named it after himself.

38. *SII.*, VI, 292.

39. *Ibid.*, 370. This record dated in the year 8 of Kampavarman, refers to the sale by auction of land kōl broad around the same tank for putting up a pavilion (maṭham) to Kuravasiri Rāmadēvabhaṭṭan a member of the *āḷuṅgaṇattār* of the place and his two brothers, by

the *sabhā* of the place. The right for *bhaṭṭa-sāmaṇtu* (meaning of which is not clear was also conveyed to the purchaser. The *sabhā* ordered that those that infringed on the rights of the brothers would be fined 5 *kaḷañju* which would become the *veṭṭi-mudal* (capital against free labour?) for the Vairamēgha-taṭāka. Thus though this record indicates that there was another tank in the village, its status is rendered dubious by the sale of the strip of land around. Obviously the brothers did not dig the tank as the record opens with the statement that *kāriga+ikuṭṭam* was of the *ūr*.

40. *Ibid*. 288 (dated year 8-(878?) of Kampavarman).
41. *SII.*, I. 69, 75, 77. Also *Ibid.*, 66. It seems possible that the same tank was referred to by different names in different records.
42. *SII.*, III, 48.
43. *SII.*, V, 489.
44. *SII.*, XII, 62.
45. The word *tūmbu*,used to indicate this, actually means an outlet.
46. *Ibid.*, 65.
47. cf. *SII.*, I, 77. This record clarifies that *Kaliṅgu* had the purpose of raising the water to the reservoir.
48. *EI*, XXXIII, p. 23 f.
49. *AREp*. 1923, 419.
50. The word *tūmbu* used to indicate this, actually means an outlet.
51. Some other records from the place (*ibid.*, 69,77) which refer to the setting up of weirs (*kaliṅgu*) to Madag-eri and Kaḍappēri respectively indicate that several weirs to the local reservoirs were necessary to utilise the water from them.
52. *AREp*. 1937-38, 399.
53. *Ibid.*, 365.
54. *AREp*. 1937-38, 188.
54a. cf. *SII.*, III, 43.
55. *EI*, IV, p. 221 f.
56. AREp. 1934-35, 21.
57. cf. *SII.*, XII, 86, 89.
58. *SII.*, III, 93.
59. *Maṇṛu* was the forum, which was probably used as the hall of justice and hence the fines collected there were termed as *maṇṛupāḍu*. The exact meaning of *anayāy-tdaṇḍam* is not clear. It can be compared with *anyāya-vāva-daṇḍam* mentioned as a

levy foregone by a chief in an inscription of the period of Rājarāja I from Pañchapāṇḍavamalai (*EI,* IV, p. 139).

60. Whereas in the latter case it can be construed that Nambiya Mallanār was the actual person in authority even though it is his father who is seen attributed with the *aṛaiyan* title, in the former case it is interesting to note that a wife had the right to dispose of the levies which were due to her husband. She might have done so with his approval and permission though this part is not recorded.

APPENDIX—VII

ANTARĀYAM AND PĀṬṬAM IN 11-13 CENTURY

Among the records pertaining to Toṇḍaimaṇḍalam an inscription of the year 3(1071) of Adhirājēndra from Tiruvallam[1] refers to two classes of levies *antarāyam* and *kīliṟāipāṭṭam*. The record reflects that these levies were due to the king as it is stated that the income from these two classes of levies due from two *dēvadāna* villages were gifted to God Tiruvallam-uḍaiyār by the king. It is noteworthy that though the concerned villages were in the *dēvadāna* of the same God, the dues under these two heads were payable to the king even by these two villages till the date of the record as the king is stated to have granted them to the God. The first class of levies, *antarāyam* is stated to have included *taṟipuḍavai*[2] (cloth on the loom), *vēlikkāsu* (the kāsu-levy on fencing?)[3] *daṇdaliṟ-kaḍamai* (the duty on collections ?)[4] and *valaṅgai-iḍaṅgai-maganmai* (charge for recognition of the rights of the right hand and the left hand classes?).[5] The second class was *kīl-iṟai pāṭṭam*[6] the lower order of taxes?) which included *ūr-kkaḷañju* (a gold levy on the *ūr*?)[7] *Kumāra-kkachchāṇam* (*gadyāṇa* levy on *kumāras*)[8] , *mīn-pāṭṭ am* (levy on fish catches) and *taṭṭār-ppāṭṭam* (levy on goldsmith). All these were payable in gold to the king as it was the king who granted the income from these taxes to the God.

Though the designations of these taxes reveal that they were not related to land, the record reflects the interesting fact that the collection of these levies did not have to depended on the artisans and fishermen existing in the villages to pay the taxes.[10] The record says, that the total of dues on account of these levies was computed *proraṭa* on the amount of paddy either the total yield of the land in those villages or what was being paid to the temple as *pañchavāram* by those villages. Thus it appears that the levies under *aṇṭavāyam* and *kīl-irṇai-pāṭṭam* had by 1071 lost their original significance and had indirectly come to be based on land.[11] On the other hand an Inscription of the year 2 (1072) of Kulōttunga I from Tiruvoṟṟiyūr[11a] also refers to *antarāyam* as a class of levies based on land. It refers to two classes of levies, one *kaḍamai* and the other *aṇṭarāyam* including *pū-ppoṇ*, pañchavāram, vēlikkāsu, vaṭṭi, muṭṭai-āl, *echchōṛu* and kūṟṟu-nel. The villages that were to pay these taxes were, as per this record, were again *dēvadāna* villages but the collection from these taxes is stated to have been payable to the temple. The noteworthy feature of this inscription is that it has put together under the two heads *antarāyam* and *kaḍamai* such taxes which would normally have gone to the king but had been diverted to the temple-*pañchavāram vēlikkāśu* (cf. Adhirajeṅdra's inscription detailed above) and *pū-ppon* (?) as well as such which have been seen to have been the entitlement of the village organisation -*nīr-vilai*. ve*ṭṭi*, *muṭṭai- āḷ echchōṛu* and *kūṟṟu-nel*. It is not possible to distinguish which came under the head *kaḍamai* and which came under *antarāyam*. None of them is reflected to have been payable to any village organisation. Two other later inscriptions, from the same place safer to *antarāyam* as a levy by itself. Both of these inscriptions are dated in the reign of a Kulōttuṅga who might have been the second or the third *Chōla* king of that name. One of them dated year 8 (1141 or 1186)[12] mentions *antarāyam* along with *tiru-chchūlakkāsu*[13] and *kurra-ttaṇḍam*[14] as leviable from the temple of *Tiruvallam-udaiyār*. The second inscription dated year 11 (1144 or 1179) refers[15] to *antarāyam* payable by the temple as distinct from the groups of other levies—*puravāyam* (in contrast to *antarayam* ?) the collective designation for the tax in paddy *(nel-vari*) and in cash *(kasu-*

vari) leviable from specified fields;[16] the miscella-neous income (*āyam*) (i.e.) *tāri-iṛai* and *aśuva-kadamai*[17] leviable from the village Tīkkalivallam; the minor taxes (*chilvari*) (i. e.)ūr-kaṇakka-kkāṇi, *kōyil—kaṇakka—Kkāṇi*,[18] *kaḍamai* and lastly *kuṛa-ṭ teṇḍam* In both these instances *antarāyam* must have been collected from the temple on the basis of the temple possessing lands and due to its being treated as other landholders. An inscription of the reign-period-of Kulōttuṅga III[19] from Chōḷāpuram however says that *antarāyam, veṭṭi and tani-āḷ* constituted the *chil-varis* minor or miscellaneous charges. As *veṭṭi* is known to have been a charge on land meant for local utilisation, and *tani-āḷ* was also probably such a charge, by classing *antarāyam* with these two,the record suggests that in this instance *antarāyam* meant a charge for local utilisation. An inscription of the year 7 (1077) of Kulōttuṅga I from Tiruvorriyur[20] refers to *kāl -alavu-ppāṭṭam* imposed on those who measured grain in the temple granaries.[21] An inscription of the year 38 (1246) of Kulōttuṅga III from Tiruvorriyur[22] refers to the levy *antarāya-pāṭṭam* in the entitlement of king. It was based on land as the record says that the king ordered the exemption of taxes including *antarāya-pattam* in respect of 80 *vēli* of land endowed for a *vyākarana-matha-maṇḍapa* after purchase from the landholders of the village probably by an agent of the feudatory Yādavarāya. However a record of the year 39 (1216-17) of the same king from Tirumullai vāyil (Chingleput district)[23] indicates that *pāṭṭam* by isself signified, a tax that was to go to the king. The record says that the temple-lands were exempted from taxes, *aṇtrāyam. pāṭṭam. pon-āyam* (levy in gold)[24] and *nel-ayam* (levy in paddy.[25] Thus it appears that *anṭarāyam* and *pāṭṭam* were originally meant to be levies to be taken by the village organisations to pay the expenses of the local administration. By eleventh century when these village organisations began to lose their vigour, these levies were appropriated by the king. He thereafter probably doled out the requirements for local administration out of his own collection.[26]

NOTES :

1. *SII.*, III, 57.
2. This was probably a levy in lieu of cloth on the basis of the number of looms, due to the king. See above: *tari-kkūrai* occurs among the *parihāras* in the Vēlurpalaiyam plates and Royakkottah plates.
3. Probably on putting up fences to one's field a duty was payable to the king. The editor of the inscription does not explain the term cf. *SII.*, V, 1381. This inscription of the year (36) (1106?) of Kulōttuṅga I from Takkōlam says that *vēlikkāśu* was included in *chill- antarāyam*.
4. cf. *SII.*, III, 6. This record of the year 17 (1002) of Rājarāja I from Ukkal refers to "those that had the right of procurement (of paddy) in that *ūr* '*(iv-vūr daṇḍal-uḍaiyārgaḷ*
   The editor has understood the term to mean "a tax on collecting rents," It is not impossible that the term as given is a corruption of the term *daṇḍakkurram* or *kurra-ttaṇḍam*"(fines) as entered in some other records notified below.
5. The editor has understood the phrase to have meant "sonship of the right hand and left hand" cf. Minakshi, C., op. ct., p. 137.
6. This name of this class of levies is interesting as *irai* and pāṭṭam are other wise distinguished. Probably *chill-irai* (inscription of a Parakēsarivarman from Śīyamaṅgalam, *SII.*, VII, pp. 122, 143, 168n, 61; ibid., XVII, 590, 598 AREP, 1912, 343) meaning miscellaneous taxes was another term used to denote *kīl*-ir*ai ppāttam*
7. cf., *SII.*, VIII, 68.
8. This might have been a levy on behalf of the prince or on subjects on the attainment of majority, cf. Gopal, Lallanji, The Economic Life of Northern India c. A.D., 700-1200, p. 52-54. Also *SII.*, XIII, 68.
9. This designation of this levy may explain the term pāṭṭam ~ as share. This levy was probably in lieu of the king's share in the catches of fish.
10. The two villages involved were Mandiram and Kukkanūr, which are otherwise also known as *dēvadāna* villages of God Tiruvallam-uḍaiyār and the *pañchavāram* being paid to the temple by the former during the time of Rajarāja I as reflected in an inscription *(AREp.*, 1921, 219) has been referred to abdve. From the record of Adhirājēndra it transpires that unlike Tirukkāṭṭuppaḷḷi of the Vēlūrpāḷaiyam plates, when Mandiram and Kukkanur were granted

as *dēvadāna* for Tiruvallam-udaiyār, the king did not authorise the miscellaneous levies to the God but had retained them under his control.

11. Also cf. AREp, 1912, 343; ibid., 1913, pt. II, p. III. An inscription of the time of Kulōttuṅga III (12th century) from Cholapuram says that *antarāyam, veṭṭi, and tani-āḷ* were included under *chilvaris*.

11a. *AREp*. 1912, 131, *Ibid*., 1913, Pt. II, p. 104,

12. *SII*., III, 60.

13. The editor of the record says, (on the basis of the practice of marking of the boundaries of land belonging to Śiva temples with stones, bearing the trident (*triśhūla*) symbol of Siva) that this was a levy for safeguarding the boundaries of the temple land. But it does not stand to reason that the temple was burdened with a tax for guarding its own lands. It seems possible that in earlier days the *triśūlam* used to be passed around for making some collections for the temple of Siva and that there was a tax on the resultant collections. In due course this might have become a general levy and probably with the loss of its original significance this levy came to be charged on the temple-land itself.

14. It seems to reflect the system of those times whereby the village bodies were empowered to administer justice locally and pass on to the king the consolidated amount collected as fines. In the instant case the temple might have been asked to pay this in respect of the *kuḍis* in temple land. Again it is possible that this also had evolved into a mere levy.

15. *Ibid*., 61.

16. *Vaḍakaṇḍam* and *Kamugadiyal* were probably designations of fields.

17. Probably these were originally taxes on looms in the village and on behalf of *ājīvikas* respectively.

18. Originally these might have been levies from the accountant of the *ūr* and the temple in the form of a professional tax, or a cess collected from the villagers originally for maintaining these functionaries.

19. *AREp*., 1912, 343; ibid., 1913, Pt. II, p. 111.

20. *AREp*; 1912, 133.

21. *Ibid*., 1913, Pt. II, p. 105. This can be compared with an inscription of the year 24 (1008-09), of Rājarāja I Mēlśēvir. S11. XVII 235.

22. *AREp*., 1912, 201-02, cf. ibid, 434,—An inscription of the reign of Kulōttuṅga I from TirupPālatturai (Tiruchchirappalli district)

also records the remission of *antarāya-ppāṭṭam* and other taxes in respect of the *dēvadāna* village Tiruchchirrambalanallūr by the king as the same had proved very burdensome causing dimunition in worship (*ibid*., 1913, Pt. II, p. 105)

23. *SII*., XVII, 730.
24. cf. *Ibid*., 705.
25. cf. ibid., XIV, 145.
26. An inscription of the year 28 (1013) of Rājarāja I from Tirumukkūḍal (Madhurantakam taluk, Chingleput district) (*AREp*. 1915, 171; *ibid*, 1916, pt. II, p. 116) refers to two kinds of taxes, *ulav-irai and ur-irai*. the former was obviously based on the agriculture (*ulavu*) of the village and as such due to the king. The interpretation of the latter is however, difficult. It could have meant the group of taxes, which had no reference to land and was levied on account of the king from all the residents of the village, agriculturist and non-agriculturist, like the artisans and professionals. On the other hand it could have meant like *ūr-kkaḷañju* a levy on the whole *ūr* levied on account of the king (see above). It could have also meant the class of levies taken on account of the *ūr*, (i. e.) to defray the expenses of local administration. These taxes with these special designations are not met with together again among the records of the period. However, inscriptions of the year 3 (1073) of Rājakēsari Rājēndra (Kulōttuṅga I from Sōmaṅgalam (Kanchipuram taluk, Chingleput district) (*SII*., VII, 392) refers to *uḷaviṛai* as a tax leviable by the *Mahasabhā* of the place apparently for local consumption. On the other hand some inscriptions seem to refer to the same *ūrirai* when they refer to *ūrpaḍu kuḍmai* or *ur-paḍ marjadi*. An inscription of the year 4 (1016) of Rājēndra I from Tiruvallam (*SII*., III, 54) refers to the levies *nīrkkiya-vilai* (the price of water ?) and *ugappār-pon*—(gold payable by those that take water ?) as *ū-paḍ-kuḍmaī* (i. e.) dues on account of the *ūr*. An inscription of the year 12 of a Parakesarivarman from Kilaiyūr (Tanjavur district) (*SII*., XIX, 309) also refers to *ūr (paḍū)-kudimai* as a levy distinct from *iṛai echchōru* and *(vāśalil- ponda-kuḍimai*. On the otther hand an inscription of the year 10 (1142) of Kulōttuṅga II from Tiruvārur (Tanjavur district) *(SII*., XVII, 598) refers to *ur-paḍu-marjadi* and *antaṛāyam* as separate levies both due to the king as the record says that the *sabhā* of Rājarāja-brahma-maṅgalam undertook to bear these charges in respect of land granted to the temple. This class of

taxes beyond the main tax on land seems to be also referred to as *pura-irai* (outside *irai*) in an inscription of the year 21 (891 ?) of the reign of Kampavarman from Uttaramallūr (*SII.*, VI, 369). (The same record also says that *pura-irai* was a levy by itself). This *pura-irai* is reflected to have been in the entitlement of the *sabhā* as they are stated in the said record to have granted exemption from this class of levies on their own in favour of a merchant. Probably it is the same class of levies which is also referred to as *chil-vari* (miscellaneous taxes) in three inscriptions of the 12th century, one from Tiruvallam (*SII.*, III, 61), the second from Kāñchipuram (*ibid.*, 63) and the third from Chōlapuram (AREp. 1912, 343, ibid. 1913, Pt. II, p. 11). The last one says that *chilvari* included *antarayam*. *veṭṭi* and *tani-āḷ,* the taxes based on the land of that *ūr*. *Chil-irai* mentioned along with *chorumāḍu*, *veṭṭi*, *muṭṭai-āḷ* and *sennir-amañji*. might have also started as the designation of a class of levies of the miscellaneous kind but in course of time it might have denoted a tax by itself (*SII.*, VII, 64—An inscription dated year 5 (1017 ?) of Parakēsarivarman (Rājēndra I ?) from Śīyamaṅgalam, North Arcot district).

APPENDIX—VIII

LIST OF VILLAGES IN TONDAIMANDALAM AS MENTIONED IN INSCRIPTION OF C. A.D. 670-1000

The Epigraphs collected and reported by the Eigraphical branch of the Archaeological Survey upto the year 1968-69 have been utilised in preparing this list. The villages referred to as having been under the administration of one or the other of the corporate bodies are indicated as under:

* **Sabha :** It has been stated above that *sabhā* in its function as a corporate body of a village is first mentioned only in the records of the period of Dantivarman. However as in this list, only the earliest mention of the village among the records is cited, even though in the references cited the existence of *sabhā* in the village might not be evident, if in later records such fact is made known, against the entry, this mark to indicate that it was a *Sabhā*" village is shown. However in the case of many villages, even though their names and their having been *brahmadēyams* could lead to an inference that they were also *sabhā* villages, unless some record even though of a later period mentions that it was a *Sabhā*" village, they have not been indicated as such in this list.

** *Sabhā, and āḷuṅ-gaṇattār*

*** *Sabhā or mahāsabhā and committees*

**** *Sabhā. aluṅ-ganattar and committees*

*+ *Sabha and tankūrru*

@ *Ūr*

@+ *Ūr and tamlūrru*

Nagaram: This mark indicates only such *nagaram* or *nagarattār* which are stated to have been in control of whole villages. The *nagarattār* referred to as presiding over merchant quarters or streets in villages are not taken into account here as these apparently had no role in the land system.

King	*District*	*Name of Villages*	*Reference* (The findspot of the inscriptions in brackets).
1. Narasiṅgap-pottaraiyar (Narasimha-varman).	Chingle-put Veṇkuṟa-kkōttam	Magilamballi Porma lippūṅdi	*AREp.*, 1954-55 B 360
		Tuṇḍaṇūkka chchēri in Eyirkōṭṭam	(Kāñchīpuram)
		Tirukka lukkunram in Kaḷattūr-Kōṭṭam	*AREp.*, 1909, 65 (Tirukka ḷukkuṉṟam)
	North Arcot (Chengam tk)	Mēl-Vēḷūr (perruve-ḷūr) in mīkonrai-nāḍu	*AREp.*, 1933-34,69 (Vēlūr)
	(Gudiyattam tk)	Mukkuḍūr (Vadaka-rai-Mukkuṭṭūr)	*EI*, IV, p. 178 (Kīḻ-Muttugūr)
2. Simha-varman		Amaṉērkkai in perunagara nāḍu in Veṇkunṟa-KKōṭṭam	pallankoyil Plates.
3. Parame-svaravarman	Chungleput (Kanchupu-ram tk).	Namma ṉambākkam Kūram *** Nīrvēlūr-nāḍu in Ūṟṟūkkāṭṭam	*Kūram*-grant
4. Nandivar-man II	Chingle-Put	Māmallapuam	*SII*, XII, 34
		Kunṟattūr in Amūr-Kōṭṭam	*SII*, XII, 38 (Mahābalinpuram)
		Uḻalūr@ Kōṭukoḷḷi (Ēkadhīra-maṅgalām) pālaiyur	*SII*, VI, 453
		Maṇappākkam Koḷḷippākkam Veḷimānallūr	Kaśākkuḍi plates
	North Arcot (Gudiyattamtk)	Peṇ-kuḷi-kkōṭṭai Karkāṭṭūr	*AREp.*, 1921, 154 (Kuḷiḍikki)
	North Arcot	Vāṇapuram @+	*SII*, III, 42

King	*District*	*Name of Villages*	*Reference*	
	(Gudiyattamtk)	Aḻingaṇappākkam in Ūṟṟrkkāṭṭukkōṭṭam	(Tiruvallam)	
	North Arcot (Gudiyattamtk)	Kumāramaṅgalam Veḷḷaṭṭūr- koṟṟagrāmam Samudradatta-Chaturvēdi-maṅgalam Kañchidvāra(Kañchivāyil)* alias Igaṇmaraimaṅgalam	Udayachan-dra-manga-lam in Paśchima-śraya-nadi-vishaya	Udayen-dram Plates
		Nelli pullūr Kuḍiyūr Takkāṟu-(Maṇalaikkula-nādu) Śālainallūr Nēśalappūṇḍi Nāgaḍimaṅgalam paḻaṅ-gōḻūr	Kīḻvē-nāḍu-in palkuṉṟa-kkōṭṭam	Nayad-hīrama-ṅgalam Pullur
	(Wandiwash tk)	Śāttamaṅgalam (in Veṇkuṉṟa-nāḍu in Veṇkuṉṟa- kkōṭṭam@	*AREp.*, 1968-69 B 225 Kiḻśāttamaṅ-galam)	
	(Walajapet tk)	Pugaḻaimaṅgalam	*EI*, IV, p. 137. (Panchapāṇḍavama-lai)	
	Nellore dt. (Gudur tk)	Tiruvānpur in Paiyūr-iḻaṅgōṭṭam	*Ins. on CPs and stones in the Nellore* Dt. Vol. I, p. 429-30 *(Mallam) EI*, V, pp. 49-50.	
Skandas-ishya		Chāeukur (Shandaśishya-maṅgalam) in Mēl-aḍaiyāṟu-nāḍu in Paḍuvūr-kōṭṭam	(Royakkotah plates)	
Danti-varman	Chingleput Dt	Iṟaiyāncheri	*SII*, XII, 44 (Pillaipalaiyam)	
		Uttaramēru-chaturvēdimaṅgalam *(Tankūṟṟu in Kāliyur-kōṭtam)*	*SII*, VI, 365, 369 (uttanallūr)	
		Vayalaikka	*SII*, XII, 39 (Vayalaikkāvūr)	
	Sriperurm-brdur tk	Ninṟavūr* (in Prḻar-kōṭṭam)	*AREp.*, 1937-38, 168 (Tiṉṉanur)	
	Chittoor Dt. (Chandragiritk)	Tiruchchoginūr* in kuḍavūr-nāḍu in Tiruvēṅgaḍa-kōṭṭam	*SIII*, XII, 43 (Tiruchchanur)	
	Kalahasti tk.	Tiruvippirambēḍu ** (in Silai-nāḍu in Tiruvēṅgaḍa-kkōṭṭam	*EI*, XI, p. 225 (Guḍimallam)	
	North Arcot	Tiruppālaiyur in Perumbā-laiyūr in Uṟṟukkāṭṭu-Kōṭṭam	*AREp.*, 1956-57, B 131 (Siyamangalam)	

King	*District*	*Name of Villages*	*Reference*
	Madras	Tiruvallikkēṇi	*EI, VIII, p. 290 f* (Tiruvallikkēṇi)
Nandi-Verman III	Chingleput	Nayivaṭṭikuḷattūr	*SII*, IV, 827 (Kañchīpuram)
	(Chingleput tk)	Kalattūr in Kaḷattūr-Kōṭṭam	*SII, XII, 51* (Kaḷattur)
		Paḍuvūr in Paḍuvūr-nāḍu in Amūr-kōṭṭam	*AREp.*, 1934-35, 8 (Paḍur)
		Tirukkāttuppalli in Nayaṛu-nāḍu in Puḷaṛ-kōṭṭam	Velurpalaiyam plates
		Viḍāl (Vidāṛ-paḷḷi) (alias Mādēvi-Arānda maṅglam	*AREp.*, 1908, 82-84 (Vēḍal)
		Venkunṛam* in Veṇkunṛa-Kōṭṭam	*SII*, VII, 80 (Veṇkunṛam hill)
Nandi-Varman III	Kanchipuram taluK	Nallil-maṅgalam** in Mēṛ-paḷugūr-nāḍu in Maṇayiṛ-kōttam	*SII*, XII, 76
	Chingleput (Saidapet tk)	Nandiyambākkam* in Nayaṛu-nāḍu	*AREp.*, 1937-38, 162 (Tiruvoṛṛiyūr)
		Tiruveḷḷi-kiḻ	*SII*, XII, 53
		(māṅgāḍu)	*AREp.*, 1908, 351 (Māṅgāḍu)
	Sriperumbudur tk.	Tiruveḷḷi-kil*	*SII*, XII, 53 (Māṅgāḍu)
		Kunrattūr in Puliyūr-kkuḍi-kkōṭṭam	
	Chittoor	Veppambōḷappāḷ	*EI*, XIV, p. 224
	(Kalahasti tk).	Veppambōḷappāḷ	*EI*, XIV, p. 224 (Guḍimallam)
	North Arcot (Gudiyattam tk)	Tīkkālivallam (Tiruvallam)** in Mīyāṛu-nādu in Paduvūr-kōṭṭam (iṅ *karaivaḻi* of Perumbāṇa-ppāḍi	*SII*, III, 43 (Tiruvallam)
		Aimbūni Vilattūr Amarunṛi-maṅgalam Vidēlvidugu Vikramāditta Chaturvēdi-maṅgalam*	
	Velur tk	Vittūr	*SII*, XII, 45 (Paḷḷikoṇḍa)
Nripa-tuṅga	Chingleput Dt. (Kanchipuram tk)	Nallāyūr in Rērāyūr-nāḍu in Ōyma-nāḍu	*SII*, VII, 39 (*Kūram*)
		Paḷlavanārāyana- Chaturvēdi-mangalam*	*SII*, VII, 33 (*Kūram*)
		Tirumukkūḍai	*SII*, XII, 75

King	*District*	*Name of Villages*	*Reference*
		Siyapuram* in Ūṟṟukkāṭu-kkūṭṭam	(Tirumukkūḍai)
	(Madhurantakam tk)	Paramē Śvaramaṅgalam	*SII*, XII, 75 (Paramesvara-maṅg-alam)
	(Saidapet tk)	Manali* (in Tiruvorri-yurppuram)	*SII*, XII, 70 (Tiruvoṟṟiyūr)
	Sriperumbudur tk)	Pillaippākkam (in Māganūr-nadu in Cheṅgāṭṭu-kkōṭṭam)	*SII*, XII, 80 (Piḷḷaippakkam)
	(Tiruvattur tk)	Kanrigai.....* in Puḻalkoṭṭam	*AREp*., 1949-50, B 215
	Chittoor Dt (Chittoor tk)	Chiṟṟūr alias Prithivi-mahadevi-chaturvēdimaṅ-lam in Panmā-nādu in Maṅ-aiyiṟ kōṭṭam	*CP ins of state Museum Govt of AP*, Vol. III, p. 3f
	Chittoor Dt. (Tiruttani tk)	Aḻagam	*AREp*., 1943-44, 138 (Mathavaḷam)
		Tiruvālaṅgādu in Tiruvālaṅ palaiyanūr-nādu gāduplates	
		pulvelur* in Eyir-kottam	
		Tiruvālaṅgādu	*SII*, XII, 66 (Tiruvalaṅgāḍu)
		Pfurumulai-ūr, Brahmad esam* in kakkalūr-nāḍu in kakkalūr-kōttam	*SII*, XII, 64
Nripa-tunga	Njorth Arcot (Arkonam tk)	Kāvidippākkam alias Avaninārāyana-chaturvēdi mangalam** in paḍuvūr-ko-ṭṭam	*SII*, XII, 67, 79 (Kāvērippākkam)
		Viḍēlviḍugu..yamam in Māṅgāḍu-nāḍu in paḍuvūr-kōṭṭam	*SII*, XII, 82 (Kavērippākkam)
	Velur tk	Āmaiyūr in Mel-Adaiyāṟu-nāḍu in Paḍuvūr- kōṭṭam	*EI*, IV, P. 180-83 (Ambūr)
	(Wendiwash tk)	Marudāḍu	*SII*, XII, 65 (marudāḍu)
		Vaḻugūr@ (in Irumbēdu-naḍu in Veṇkunṟa-kkōṭṭam)	*AREp*., 1908, 68 (Vaḻuvur)
Apara-jita	Chinglepụt Dt. (Ponneri tk)	Tirumadaṅganpaḷḷi in Tekkūr-nāḍu in Paiyūr-iḷan-goṭṭam	*SII*, XII, 86 (Satyavēdu)
		Tuṟaiyūr (same nadu)	
		Pūvanūr (near Tirumadaṅ-ganpaḷḷi)	*SII*, XII, 89 (Satyavēdu)
	Saidapet tk	Ādambākkam* (in Tiruvoṟṟi-Yūrppuṟam) in Puliyūr-kōṭṭam	*SII*, XII, 87-88 (Tiruvo*ūṟ*ṟiyūr)

King	*District*	*Name of Villages*	*Reference*
		Oṟṟimudur Igaṅaimkudūr	*SII*,XII, 93 (Tiruvoṟṟiyur)
	Sriperumbudur tk	Māṅgādu*	*AREp*., 1908, 351; *SII*, XII, 85(Māṅgalam)
	Tiruvallurth	Parumūr in Perumūr-nadu in Ikkaṟṟukkōṟṟam	*AREp*., 1952-53, 3236 (Paṟṟaṟai-pperumtudur)
	Chittoor Dt (Tiruttani tk)	Kilāmbākkam	*AREp*., 1943-44,174 (Kaḷāmbākkam)
		Tiruttaniyal*	*SII*, XII, 959 Tirurrant)
Kampava-Verman	Chingleput	Aniyur* in Kaḷattūr-kōttam***...ngalam a *tankūṟṟu* in Kaliyūr-Kottam Kiraippāttūr@.........	*SII*, XII, 109 (Anūr)
	(Kanchipuram tk)	Chaturvēdi-maṅgalam Kōṭṭam	*SII*, XII, 102 (Kiḻputtur)
		Atiaraiya-maṅgalam in Mēṟkūr-nāḍu	*SII*, VI, 287 (*Uttaramallūr*)
		Śiṟupaḷuvūr	*SII*, VI, 314 (*Uttaramallūr*)
		Mēlūr in Mēlūr-kōṭṭam	*SII*, VI, 347 (Uttaramallūr)
		@Pōṟpondai in Kurumbuṟai-naḍu in Kalattur-kottam	*SII*, XII, 97 (Pōṟpandal)
		@ Ūṟṟu-kkaḍu (in Ūṟṟukkaṭṭu-kkoṭṭam)	*SII*, XII, 108 (Uttukkāḍu)
	(Saidapet tk)	Traiyāñchēri in Mayilārkppil	*SII*, XII, 99 (Tiruvoṟṟiōr)
		pulimāṟṟu in kalmāy-nāḍu in Puliyūr-koṭṭam Pudūr in Nāyarunāḍu in Puḻaṟ-kōṭṭam	*SII*, XII, 100 (Tiruvoṟṟiyur)
		@Vaikkāttūr (in Tiru-voṟṟiyūr-ppuṟam in Paḻa-nāḍu in Puḻaṟ-kōṭṭam Tachchanūr	*SII*, XII, 103 (Tiruvoṟṟiyūr)
		Kuḍi-ūr-Pōrūr panṟippākkam (near Tiru-voṟṟiyur) Tiśaimaṅgalam Pariyalūr Kaḍaṟpāttu	*SII*, XII, 105 (Tiruvoṟṟiyūr)

King	*District*	*Name of Villages*	*Reference*
	(Tiruvallurtk)	Śivanvayal* Ninṟaiyūr	*AREp.*, 1944-45, 13 (Sivanvayal)
Kampa-Varman	North Arcot Dt (Cheyyar tk)	Rājmalla-Chaturvēdi-mangalam**	*SII*, XII, 107 (Brahmadeśam)
		Utkar (Śiva-chūlāmaṇi-mangalam, Sri-Vikramā-bharana-chaturvēdi-maṅglam, Aparājita-chaturvēdi-maṅgalam)*+, *tankūṟṟu* in Kaliyūrkōṭṭam	*SII*, 5f. (Ukkai)
	(Gudiyattam tk)	Kavannūr* in Mīyāṟu-nāḍu in Paḍuvūr-Kōṭṭam	*SII*, XII, 101 (Mēlpatti)
	(Polur tk)	Kāmappuḷḷārs* (alias Raja-Chintāmaṇi-chaturvēdi-maṅgalam in Maṇḍaikuḷa-nāḍu in Pal-kuṅra-Kōṭṭam in Vasugūr-nāḍu	*AREp.*, 1938-39, 282 (Kappatur)
		Valivalakkamaṅgalam	*EI*, XXXIII. pp. 23-26 (Tippa-samudram)
	(Velur taluk)	Kāṭṭuttumbūr in Paṅgala-naḍu in Paḍuvūr-kōṭṭam	*SII*, I, 53 (Chōḷapuram)
	(Wandiwash tk)	Kāvidu@	*SII*, XII, III (Kaḍuṅgaḷūr)
		Kulattūr@ in Tennāṟṟūr-naḍu in Palkunṟa-kkōṭṭam	*SII*, XII, IIO (Maḍam)
Vaira-megha North	Chittoor (Tiruttani tk)	Takkōlam	*AREp.*, 1943-44, 178 (Kaḷambākkam)
	North Arcot	Palkalam@ in Dāmar-Kōṭṭam	*SII*, XII, 114 (Kilpulam)
	(Arkonam tk)	Perumbulippākkam@in Damar-kōṭṭam	*AREp.*, 1968-69,180 (Perumbulippākkam
		Poygainllūr* in Dāmaṟ-kōṭṭam	*SII*,XII, 113 (Poyyānur)
Bāṇa-Vidyādh-ara vana-rāya	Chittoor (Tiru-ttani tk)	Pudoṟṟūr	*AREp.* 1943, 44, 145 (Poddattūru)
Bana-Vik-ramaditya II	Chittoor (Kalhas-ti tk)	Viprapītha	*EI*, VII, P IF. (Guḍimallam)
Mahāli-Vāṇarāja	North Arcot	Vannipēḍu alias Iraṇa-Vikrama-chaturvēdimaṅ-galam* in Kārai-nāḍu in Paḍuvūr-kōṭṭam	*SII*, III, ·4 (Tiruvalla ı)
		Iraiyāñ-chēri-Ponpadu-kuṭṭam of Kachchippēḍu	*SII*,III, 45 (Tiruvallam)
Parān-taka I	Chingleput Dt	Kaṇṇamaṅgalam in Eyil-nāḍu in Eyil-Kōṭṭam	*AREp.*, 1921, 21 (Kāñchipuram)

King	*District*	*Name of Villages*	*Reference*
		Pulvēlūr in Eyir-Kōṭṭam	*AREp.*, 1923, 46 (Pul̤l̤alūr)
		Jinagirippal̤l̤i	*AREp.*, 1922, 430 (Anandamaṅgalam)
		Vel̤l̤ivāyil@ in Pul̤alēri-Kīl̤-naḍu in Pul̤al-kōṭṭam	*SII*, III, 105 (Tiruvoṟṟiyūr)
	(Saidapet tk)	Velichchēri** in Kōṭṭūr-nāḍu in Puliyūr-kōṭṭam	*AREp.*, 1911, 306, 315, (Vēḷañchri)
	(Sriperumbudur tk)	Ninṟavur* in Palkunṟa-kkōttam	*AREp.*, 1929-30, 176 (Pillaippākkam)
	(Tiruvattur tk)	Andanallūr*	*AREp.*, 1949-50, B 207 (Akkarappākkam)
	(Chingleput tk)	Pērakmanūr in Śeṅgunra-nāḍu in Kaḷattūr-kōṭṭam	*AREp.*, 1934-35, 38 (Peramanūr)
	North Arcot	Kaḍaikkōṭṭūr in Mēl-aḍaiyāṟu-ṅāḍu	Viranārā-yaṇacha-chēri *SII*, II, 76 (Udayen-dram plates)
	(Gudiyattam tk)	Udayachandramangalam*	
		Parakēsari-chaturvēdi-maṅgalam	*EI*, III, p. 79 (Udayendram plates of Vira-chōḍa)
	North Arcot	Sambul̤alai@ in the *kūrr* of the same name in Dāmar-kōṭṭam	*AREp.*, 1921, 246 (Takkōlam)
		Ūrāḍagam@ in Puriśai-nāḍu in Maṇayil-kōṭṭam	
		Parundūr* (*dēvadāna* village)	*AREp.*, 1921, 252, 261 (Takkōllam)
		Paśāli in Paśāli-nāḍu in Manayil-kōṭṭam	*AREp.*, 1921, 254 (Takkōlam)
		Anaikaraipudūr@	
	(Velur tk)	Vēlūr *alias* Paramēś-varamaṅgalam* in ......(ūr)-nāḍu.	*SII*, VIII, 9 (Chōl̤apuram)
		Niḍūr*	
	(Walajahpet tk)	Viḷappākkam in Perun-dimiri-naḍu	*SII*, VII, 56 (Viḷappakkam)
	Tanjavur dt	Velimānallūr in Ūṟrukkāṭṭu-kkōṭṭam	*AREp.*, 1907, 330 (Tiruviśalūr)
	Chittoor dt (Chittoor tk)	Māvalimaṅgalam* in Tū-nadu (of Parumbānappāḍi)	*AREp.*, 1931-32, 170 (Mahādēva-maṅgalam)
		Karuvili	
		Kīl̤aikkattamachchi@in Tūy-nāḍu	*AREp.*, 1907, 61 (*SII*, XXIII, 61) (Kaṟṟamañchi)
		Toṇḍaimān-Pērāṟṟūr* in Aṟṟūr-nāḍu in Tiruvēṅgaḍa-kkoṭṭam	*SII*, VII, 529 (Toṇḍamanāḍu near Kāḷahasti)

King	*District*	*Name of Villages*	*Reference*
	North Arcot dt (Gudiyattam tk)	Kaḻañjūr* (in Mīyāṟaiñādu)	*AREp.*, 1921, 189 *AREp.*, 1952-53, B-200 (Kalanjūr)
		Varikkiyam alias Chandrā-ditya-maṅgalam*	*AREp.*, 1921, 180, (Periyavarikkam)
Krishna III	Chingleput dt (Kanchipuram tk)	Vaḷśāru(*Āḷuṅgaṇattār)* in Viṟpēḍu-nāḍu in Kāliyūr-koṭṭam	*SII*, VI, 374 (*Uttaramallūr*)
	(Ponneri tk)	Karuṅgāli@	*AREp.*, 1933-34, 19 (Chintamani)
	(Saidapet tk)	Śērṇuppēḍu@ in Tuḍarmu-ninādu in Prliyūr-kōṭṭam	*AREp.*, 1912, 177 (Tiruvorriyur)
		Kuṛaṭṭūr alias Parāntaka-Chaturvēdimaṅgalam* in Ambattūr-eri-kiḻ-nāḍu in	*AREp.*, 1921, 179 (Tiruvorriyur)
		Puḻaṛ- kōṭṭam in Īkkāṛṛuk-koṛṛam	*AREp.*, 1944-45
	Tiruvallurraluk	Idaiyur-Nenmal in Perumur-nadu	1819 (Viḍaiyūr)
	North Arcot dt (Cheyyar tk)	Māmbākkam in Taraiyūr-nādu in Palkunṛa-kkōṭṭam	*SII*, VII, III (Tiruvottūr)
		Veṅgalattūr alias Śrī-Paṛamēśvara-chaturvēdi-mangalam in Kaḻumala-nāḍu in Kāliyūr -Kōṭṭam	*AREp.*, 1921, 93 (Veṅgaḷattur)
	(Gudiyattam tk)	Pugaḻūr	*AREp.*, 1921, 144 (Pogaḷūr)
	(Plur tk)	Vasugur in Vasugūr-nāḍu in Palkunṛa-kkōṭṭam	*AREp.*, 1938-39, (Puduppāḷaiyam)
		Vaigāvūr-Tirumalai (in Paṅgaḷa-nāḍu in Pal-kunṛakōṭṭam)	*SII*, XXIII, 65 (Tirumalai near Pōḷūr)
	Chittoor dt (Tiruttani tk)	Mēlmalai-Arumbākkam in Mellūrnaḍu in Mellur-kōṭṭam	*AREp.*, 1943-44,184 (Vyāsapuram)
	North Arcot (Wandiwash tk)	Śīyamaṅgalam@ (in Tennāṛṛūr -naḍu in Palkunṛa-kkōṭṭam)	*SII*, VII, 75 (Siyamaṅgalam)
Parthi-vendra-varman	Chingleput dt	Kaḷakkāṭṭ*ūr* alias Attita-nāma-chaturvēdi-maṅgalam in Kāl-iyūrkoṭṭam(said to have been in a Eri-kil-nāḍu and as a *Śālābhogam* in an inscription of Rajarajai *AREp.*1923-21	*AREp.*, 1923, 117, (Kaḷakkāṛṛūr)
		Tiraiyamaṅgalam@	*AREp.*, 1921, 17 (Kāñchipuram)
		Pannaippuram@	*AREp.*, 1921, 18 (Kāñchipuram)
		Pōndūr@	*AREp.*,1921, 19 (Kāñchipuram)
		Kunṛappākkam	*AREp.*, 1923, 417 (Kunnavākkam)

King	District	Name of Villages	Reference
		M-ẹṛpiḍavūr@ in Pukriśai-nāḍu in Maṇaiyiṛ-koṭṭam	*AREp.*, 1923, 68 (Poḍavūr)
	(Ponneri tk)	Kāṭṭūr@ in Paiyūr-kōṭṭam	*SII*, III, 188 (kāṭṭūr)
	(Saidapet tk)	Tiruvalidayil*(Kuṭṭattān) in* Tudamuni-nāḍu in Puliyūr-kōṭṭam	*SII*, III, 181 (Padi-tiruvalidayam)
		Villippākkam	
		Konṛūr	
		Nulappiyāṛṛūr (*Kūṭṭattān)*	
		Tirumullaivāyil in Vellaiyūr (Veṇṇaiyūr)-nāḍu in Puḻaṛ-kōṭṭam *(dēvadānam)*	*SII*, III, 196 (Tirumullaivayil)
		Kalikēsari-chaturvēdi-maṅgalam*+a *tankūṛṛu* in Puḻarkōṭṭam *(devadanam)*	*SII*, III, 174 (Tirumullaivayil)
	(Sriperumbudur tk)	Maḻaei-maṅgalam in Maṇaiyir kōṭṭam	*AREp.*,1909,189, 320,*SII*, III, (Maduramangalam)
		Vayinānallūr in Puliyūr-kōṭṭam	*AREp.*, 1952, 53, (Vayalnallur)
		Ayaṅdambakkam in Puḻal-kōṭṭam	
	(Tiruvallur tk)	Kāttuśemmalappākkam alias Kaḻikēsari Mañagaram in Śeṅgāṭṭu-kkōṭṭam...in	*AREp.*, 1947-48, B 39 (Aranvayal)
		Seṅgāḍu-nadu in Sengattu-kkottam	*AREp.*, 1947-48, B 60 (Mappēḍu)
		Talaiśayanapuram alias Taiyūr, a *tankūṛṛu* in Amūr-koṭṭam	*SII*, III, 180, 183 (Tiruvaḍandai)
		Vaiyodu	
Parthi-vendra-varman	North Arcot (Arkonam tk)	Pudūr (anai-akkarai-ppudūr-Pudur on the other side of the dam)@ Takkōlam	*SII*, III, 187 (Anaikkāṭṭūr)
			SII, III, 166 (Takkōlam)
		Rājamārttāṇḍa-chaturvēdi mangalam, a *tankūrru**+(in) Tiruvuṛalpuraml) in Manaiyil-kōṭṭam	*SII*, III, 190 (Takkōlam)
	(Cheyyar tk)	Moraṇḍattfur@ in Kāylisar-ambēḍunādu in nādu in Puivāypurrue@	*AREp.*, 1965-66, (Moraṇam)
	(Tiruppattur tk)	Vāṇiyanpāḍi alias Narasimha-chaturvedi-mangalam* in Aḍaiyā-ṛu-nāḍu in Paḍuvūr-kōṭṭam	*AREp.*, 1963-64, B 181 (Vāṇiyanpāḍi)
	(Walajahpet tk)	Ilaivallam in Dāmar-kōṭṭam	*SII*, III, 165 (Tirumalpuram)

King	*District*	*Name of Villages*	*Reference*
		Pattālam alias Eḻunūrrva-chaturvēdimaṅgalam* in Dāmar-nāḍu in Damar-koṭṭam	*SII*, III, 197 (Tirumalpuram)
		Ochchēri Udamadampaṭṭi	*SII*, III, 156 (Tirujpparkaḍal)
Madurai-konda-Rajakesari-Sundara-	Chingle put (Madurantakam tk)	Igaḷambākkam in Kanrūr-nāḍu in Manaiyir-kōttam	*AREp.*, 1922, 396 (Madhurantakam)
	North Arcot (Polur tk)	Puttud appāḍi-mādēvamaṅ-in Pal-kunra-kkōttam	*SII*, XIII, 1734 (Ten Mahaḍēva-manglam)
Uttama-chola	Chingleput	Ariyar-Perumbākkam* Atimana-ppūṇḍi Chōla-Niyamam Ekavira-ppāḍi Errrvali-chchēri Kambuḻān-paḍi Kañdchaka-ppāḍi Karuvuḻān-pāḍi	*SII*, III, 128 (Kanchipuram)
		Raṇajaya-ppadi Vamana-(Śankarappāḍi) Uḻaiyūr*	*SII*, III, 128 (Kanchipuram) Oḻukkai-ppākkam*
	(Saidapet tk)	Villipakkam in Ambattūr-nāḍu in Puḻar-kōṭṭam	*AREp.*, 1960-61, B 282 (Tirumullaivayil)
		Ambattūr* in Ambattūr-nāḍu in Puḻar-kōṭṭam Pāṇḍivayṭṭurai Kirainallūr-oḻugarai Munainallūr	*SII*, III, 141 (Tirumullaivāyil)
Uttama-Chola	North Arcot (Polur tk)	Pudanāḍappāḍi-Tiruppaḻaṅ-gōlūr in Paṅgaḷa-nāḍu in Palkunra-kkōṭṭam Pudanāḍi-odiyam-baḷḷam Tondaipūndi Taṭṭappaḍi	*SII*, XIX, 169 (Paḷaṅgōḷur)
		Puduppakkam, Brahmad-ēyam* in Puriśdsai-nāḍu in Maṇaiyilkcṭṭam	*SII*, III, 142 (Tirumalpuram)
Śaka 876	Chittoor dt (Puttur division)	Kurichchānūr in Pāṅkara-nāḍu in Kunṛavattana-kōṭṭam	*AREp.*, 1946-47, B 26, (Nagari)
S880	Chittoor dt (Tiruttani tk)	Uḻakkuṇipūṇḍi	*AREp.*, 1943-44, 128 (Chellāttūru)
S892	North Arcot dt (Arni tk)	Kaḷamūr*	*AREp.*, 1909, 246 (Kaḷambur)
S832	(Gudiyattam tk)	Chendattūr Igaṇṇaraimaṅgalam	*AREp.*, 1921, 168 (Chendattur)

King	*District*	*Name of Villages*	*Reference*
S880	(Velur tk)	Nandikampa-chaturvēdi-maṅgalam* in Pali-nāḍu in Paḍuvūr-kōṭṭam	*AREp.*, 1925, 469 (Paḷḷikoṇḍa)
S885		Vaippūr alias Arikulān-taka-chturved imaṅgalam (hamlet of Paḷḷikoṇḍa)	*AREp.*, 1925, 470
S835		Kalleḍuppūr-maryādi	*EI*, VII, p. 193f (Chōḷapuram)
Parakesari-	Chingleput dt	Kalluḍuppūr* in Virpēḍu-galam** in Perundarapuram in Purisainaḍu	*SII*, XIX, 353 (Parandur)
	(Chingleput tk)	Perumbālaiyūr in Perumbā laiyūr-nāḍu in *ūṟṟu* kkāṟṟu-kuāṟṟam	*SII*, XIX, 79 (Palūr)
		Kachchūr@ in Śeṅgunra-naḍu in Kallattūr-kōṭṭam	*SII*, XIX, 118 (Tirukkachchiyur)
		Nalvayal in Seṅgunṟa-nāḍu	
	(Saidapet tk)	Kulumanippākkam@ near Maṅgāḍu in Puliyūr-kōṭṭam	*AREp.*, 1912, 176 (Tiruvoṟṟiyūr)
	(Sriperumbudur tk)	Pudanmalli in Māṅgāḍunadu in Puliyūr-Kkoṭṭam	*AREp.*,1938, 39, 302 (Poonamalle)
	(Tiruvallur tk)	Kākkaḷūr	*AREp.*,1947-48, B 54 (Kākkaūr)
		Simhalantaka-chaturvēdi-maṅgalam*	*AREp.*,1952-53 B 235 (Kunnauaḷam)
		panṟiyūr@	*AREp.*, 1947,48, B 84 (Tiruppanduur)
Parakēsari-	North Arcot dt (Arkonam tk)	Iḷamaṇḍagam	*SII*, XIX, 177 (Kaverippākkam)
		Āṟalūr	*AREp.*, 1934-35, 57, *SII*, XIX, 177 (Kāvēvippākkam)
	(Velur tk)	Iṟaiyān-chēri in Kanchchippēḍu	*SII*, XIX, 310 (Paḷḷikonda)
	(Cheyyar tk)	Vāyinānallūr in Puliyūr-Kōṭṭam	*SII*, XIX, 101 (Brahmadesam)
	(Walajahpet tk)	Eśayanūr@ (Eydanūr) in Eśayanūr-nāḍu in Dāmaṟ-koṭṭam	*AREp.*, 1964-65, B 218-219 (Esaiyanūr)
		Tirumālpēṟr in Dāmankō-ṭṭam	*SII*, XIX, 341 (Tirumalpuram)
		Tirukkarapuram alias Śrikōyil	*SII*, XIX, 39 (Tiruppaṟkaḍal)
		Tavuśampalalai, *lankūṟṟu* in Dūmarkōṭṭam	*SII*, XIX, 446, (Tirumālpuram)
		Kaḍuvāykkuḍi	*SII*, XIX, 220 (Tirumalpuram)
		Chiṟṟiyāṟṟūr-Rāja-Kēsari-vati in Manaiyil-naḍu in	*SII*, III, 142, XIX, 318

King	*District*	*Name of Villages*	*Reference*
		Manaiyil-kōṭṭam Peruveṅgūr in the same nadu	(Tirualpuram) *SII*, XIX,(Tiruparval)
	(Wnddiwash tk)	Neḍuṅgunṟam in Kunṟa-nāḍu in Palkunra-kōṭṭam	*SII*, VII, 73 (Siyamangalam)
		Sri-daṇapuram-Perumbaḷḷi in Pannūr-nāḍu in Veṇ-kunṟa-koṭṭam	*SII*, XIX, 51 (Tirakkōl)
	Tanjavur dt	kumārapādi in Miyāru-Nādu in Kaḷattur-Kōṭṭam	*SII*, XIX, 30-31 (Tiruppaḷanam)
Rajakes-arivarman	Chingleput dt	Menalur@ in Ōgaḷa-nāḍuk in Kaliyūr-kōṭṭam (Tiru-kkaṟṟalippuṟam)	*SII*, I, 84 (Kanchipuram)
		(Uttaram in Ārvalakk*ūṟ*ṟam chōḷa-nāḍu)	*AREp*., 1921, 79 (Kāñchipuram)
		Manimaṅgalam* *alias* Lōka-mahādevi-chaturvēdi-maṅgalam	*SII*, III, 27 (Maṇimangalam)
		paṟamēśvara-chaturvēdi-mangalam** in Eyiṟ-kōṭṭam	*SII*,XIII, 121 (Puḷḷalūr)
		Pudukkuḷattūr-Kachchippēḍku	*SII*, XIII, 341 (Puḷḷalūr)
		Tenkaraiyūr-Kachchippēḍu	*SII*, XIII, 342 (Puḷḷalūr)
		Karupparaiyūr	*SII*, XIII, 342 (Puḷḷalūr)
		Velakkōnmaṅgalam in Kunra-naḍu in *ūṟ*ṟu-kkāṟṟku-kkōṟṟam	*SII*, XIII, 97 (Venpākkam)
		Kandalnallūr@	*SII*, XIII, 281A (Chintāmaṇi)
	(Tiruvattur tk)	Meyūr@ in Ikkāttu-kkōṭṭam	*AREp*., 1958-59, B 399 (Meyyūr)
		Tiruppāśūr*	*AREp*., 1929-30, 146 (Tiruppāchchur)
		Vengal(alias Satyāśraya-kulakāla-puram) in Veṅgāl-nāḍu in Paiyūr- iḷan-gōṭṭam	*AREp*.,1952-53, B 267 (Veṅgāl)
	Chingleput dt (C-hingleput tk)	Āmūr	*SII*, XIII, 80 (Amur)
		Kāyāṟr (*alias* Kamalanārāyaṇa Chatūrvēdi-maṅgalam)* in Kumiḷi-nadu in Amūr-kōṭṭam Pukkuḍaiyānpaṭṭi	*SII*, XIII, 302 (Kāyār)
		Venkudichchatu in Seṅgāṭṭu-kkōṭṭam	*SII*, XIII, 64 (Kāyār)
		Nāyaṟr in Nāyaṟu-nāḍu in Puḷaṟ-kōṭṭam	*SII*, XIII, 281B (Kirappākkam)

King	*District*	*Name of Villages*	*Reference*
		Kaḷakkāṭṭūr@ in Āmūr-kōṭṭam Maṇivalaichchēri	*SII*, XIII, 191 (Mānāmadi)
		Tiruppoṛiyūr in Kumuḷi-nāḍu in Amūr-kōṭṭam	*SII*, XIII, 157 (Tiruppōṛur)
		Tiruviḍavandai*@ in Paduvūr-nāḍu in Āmūr-kōttam (*devadānam*)	*SII*, XIII, 43 (Tiruvaḍandai)
		Māḍambākkam alias Aṇidhiramaṅgalam* in Neḍuṅgunṛa-naḍu in Puliyur-kottam	
		Neḍuṅgunram in neduṅgu-nṛa-nāḍu in Sembōṛ-kōṭṭam	*SII*, XIII, 79 (Virapuram)
	North Arcot dt (Arkonam tk)	Aparājita-chaturvēdimaṅga-lam (of Tiruvūralpuram)* in purisainaḍu in Maṇayiṛ-kōṭṭam	*AREp*., 1921, 255, *SII*, XIII, 294 (Takkōlam)
		Kirtti-mārttāṇda-kāḷapyam-aṅgāḍi	*SII*, XIII, 130 (Kavērippākkam)
	(polur tk)	Paḷaṅgōḷūr in Kāndaḷūr-*Kūṛ*ṛam in Kiḷ-vēmbu-nāḍu in Pal-kunṛa-kkōṭṭam	*SII*, XIII, 71 (Paḷaṅgoḷur)
	(Walajahpet tk)	Śri-Gōvindapāḍi in Vallava-nāḍu in Dāmar-kōṭṭam	*SII*, III, 17 (Tirumalpuram)
	(Wandiwash tk)	Vādavūr@ in Vādavūr-nāḍu in Venkunṛa-kkōṭṭam	*SII*, XIII, 185 199 (Bāḍūr)
		Nerkunṛam@ in Kīḻvaḷi of Śiṅgapura-nāḍu	*SII*, III, 93 (Neṛkunṛam)
		Śri-Rājakēsari-puram Paḷḷi-chchandam Tiruviḍaikkaḷḷi	*SII*, XIII, 297 (Tirakkōl)
Rajaraja	I Chingleput dt (Chingleput tk)	Karum-ūr in Kumiḷi-nāḍu in Āmūr-kōṭṭam	*AREp*., 1934-35, 46 (Karumbūr)
		Raṇachandra-chaturvēdi-maṅgalam*	*AREp*., 1934-35, 42 (Kāyarambēḍu)
		Kiḷāmbākkam in Neḍuṅgunṛa nāḍu in Puliyūr-kōṭṭam	*AREp*., 1934-35, 30 (Kiḷāmbākkam)
		Vallam in Kiḷāmbākkam	*AREp*., 1934-35,31 (Kiḷāmbāmbākkam)
		Māmbākkam in Kālvay-nāḍu Puliyūr-kōṭṭam	*AREp*., 1934-35, 19 (Mambakkam)
		Tirumukkūḍal, Northern hamlet of Madhurāntakda-chaturvēdimaṅgalam	*AREp*., 1932-33 13 (Pulippakkam)
		Śeṅgunram in Śeṅgunṛa-nāḍu in Kaḷattūr-kōṭṭam	*AREp*., 1956-57, B 137 (Singaperumāl-kōli)
		Narasimha-mangalam* in Āmūr-kōṭṭam	*AREp*., 1933-34, 81 (Śiṛuḍavūr)
	Chingleput dt (Kanchipuram tk)	Kuśippūr in Puḷaar-kōṭṭam in Toṇḍai-nāḍu	*AREp*., 1923, 118 (Kaḷakkārur)
		Araśāṇi-maṅgalam in Veṇkunṛakkōṭṭam	*AREp*., 1923, 343 (Arsanimangalam)

King	*District*	*Name of Villages*	*Reference*
	Ūṟṟukkāṟṟu-kkōṟṟam	Vanpākkam, in Tāmanūr-nāḍu in *(dēvadāna)*	*AREp.*, 1922, 210 (Aṅgambākkam)
		(Śirunanṟaiyūr@ in Ambi-nāḍu in Eyil-kōṭṭakm *(devadāna)*	*AREp.*, 1921, 79 (Kāñchipuram)
		Narasiṅga-maṅgalam in Kāliyūr-kōṭṭam (in Uttama-chōla ĪŚvarapuram of Tiruvekambam under chitra-mēgha-tatākam)	*SII*, IV, 137 (Kanchipuram)
		Śiṟupākkam in Nīrvēḷur-nāḍu	*AREp.*, 1923, 66 (Siruvakkam)
		Śandēr/Taṇḍaḷam in Puriśai-naḍu in Maṇaiyiṟ-kōṭṭam	*AREp.*, 1923, 71 (Srōtriyam-Taṇḍalam)
		Śrī-uttama-chōḷa-chaturvēdi-maṅgalam**, *Taṅkūṟṟu* in Ūṟṟkkāṟṟu-kkōṟṟam	*AREp.*, 1922, 240-41 *SII*, VII, 411, 412, 414 (Tennēri)
		Perunagar in Perunagar-nāḍu in Venkunṟakkōṭṭam	*AREp.*, 1923, 192 (*Uttaramallūr*)
		Arumbākkam	*AREp.*, 1922, 250 (Vayalaikkāvūr)
		Vayalaikkāvūr in Kāliyūr-kōṭṭam	*AREp.*, 1922, 254 (Vayalaikkāvūr)
	(Madurantakam tk)	Madhurāntaka-chaturvēdi-mangalam*	*AREp.*, 1922, 395 (madhuranrakam)
		Cheyyūr alias Jayaṅgoṇḍa chōḷa-nallūr	*SII*, VIII, 27 (Cheyyur)
		Vidāal in Viḍāl-nāḍu* in kōṭṭam	*AREp.*, 1961-62, B 175 (Vēḍal)
	(Saidapet tk)	Kiḷāñjēri	*AREp.*, 1961-62, B 210 (perumbākkam)
	(Sriperumbudur tk)	Ūrōdagam@ in Puriśai-nāḍu Śiṟppaḷḷiyūr	*AREp.*, 1959-60, (Śivapuram) *AREp.*, 1952-53, B 227 (Vavalnalllūr)
	(Tiruvattur tk)	Kaṭṭiyūr@ Peruñjēri@ Pondaippākkam@	*AREp.*, 1950-51, B 224 (Kachchūr)
		Punnaippākkam@ in Veṅga-nāḍu	*AREp.*, 1952-53, B 251 (Punnappākkam)
		Serumaṇi-Kārāṇai@	*AREp.*, 1929-30, 151 (Tiruppāchchūr)
		Nallāṟṟūr* in Mēlśeṅgāl-nāḍu in Śeṅgāṭṭu-kkōṭṭam	*AREp.*,1929-30,156 (Tiruppāchchur)
		Veṅgāl alias Satyāśraya....	*AREp.*, 1953-54, B 312 (Vengāl)

King	District	Name of Villages	Reference
		Kāvanūr in Veṅgāl-nāḍu in Paiyūr-iḷaṅgōṭṭam in Jayaṅgoṇḍachōḷa-maṇḍalam Mūvalūr	AREp., 1952-53, B 266, (Vengāl)
	(Chittoor dt) (C-hittoor tk)	Maṇaṟpākkam in Pērūrnāḍu Puliyūr-kōṭṭam	AREp., 1931-32,167 (Mahadēva-maṅgalam)
		mēlpāḍi alias Rājāśrayapuram in Tū-nāḍu in Perumbāṇappā-	SII, III, 15, 16, 17, 19 (Melpāḍi)
		(hamlet-Pulikkunṟam) Do@	AREp., 1921, 96, 99
	(Tiruttani tk)	Veḷḷigaram@	AREp., 1943-44, 157 (Veligaram)
	(Kalahasti tk)	Tirukkāḷatti in Āṟṟūr-nāḍu in Perumbāṇappāḍi Tiruvēṅgaḍakkōṭṭam in Jayaṅgoṇḍa-chōḷa-maṇḍalam	SII, XVII, 313, 328 (Kāḷahasti)
		Mummudi-chōḷapuram- *(a dēvadāna)*	SII, XVII, 327 (Kalahasti)
		Pēṭṭai alias Lōkamahādēvi-Puram in Karai-vaḻi of perumbāṇappāḍi	SII, XVII, 322
		Iraṇappākkam in Kanṟigai-nāḍu in Puḻar-kōṭṭam	SII, VIII, 508, 516, 516 (Gudimallam)
	(North Arcotdt.)	Śirūr (in Tiruvūralpuṟam) (hamlet of Takkōlam)	AREp., 1921, 257 (Takkōlam)
	(Arkonam tk)	Takkōlam alias Kshatriya-Śikhāmaṇipuram a *tankūṟṟu* in Maṇayir-kōṭṭam in Jayaṅgoṇḍa-chōḷa-maṇḍalam	AREp., 1921, 259 (Takkōlam)
	(Armonam tk)	puriśai@ in Puriśai-nāḍu in Maṇayiṟ-kōṭṭam	AREp., 1921, 244 (Takkōlam)
	(Cheyyar tk)	Kōvalūr* in Veṇkunṟa-	AREp., 1921, 438 (Kovalur)
		Kuḍiyāṟṟu-taṇḍalam (in Eri-Kiḻ-nāḍu in Kāliyūr-kāṭṭam)	AREp., 1954-55, B 294 (Kuṇḍiyāh-Tandalam
		Tiruvottur *(dēvadāna)*** *Tankūṟṟu* in Kāliyūr-Kōṭṭam	SII, VII, 110 (Tiruvottur)
	(Gudiyattamtk)	Eḷadaḷal@ in Kil-aḍaiyārai-nāḍu in Perumbāṇappāḍi in Jayaṅgoṇḍachōḷa-maṇḍalam	AREp., 1921,172 (Rajakkai)
		Jayaṅgoṇḍa-chōḷapuram in Andi-nāḍu in Perumbāṇap-padi in Jayaṅgondachōḷa-maṇḍalam	AREp., 1921, 149 (Chengunṟam)
		Naratuṅga-chaturvēdi-maṅgalam in Kārai-nāḍu in Paḍuvūrkōṭṭam	SII, III, 50 (Tiruvallam)

King	*District*	*Name of Villages*	*Reference*
		M-andiram alias Jayamēru-Śri-karana-chaturvēdi-maṅga-(*dēvadāna*) in Tūy-nāḍu	*SII*, III, 50 *AREp*., 1921, 271, 219 (Tiruvallam)
		Kurukāḍi	*AREp*., 1921, 213 (Tiruvallam)
		Arumbākkam	*AREp*., 1921, 153 (Vaḷattur)
	(Polur tk)	Tiruvachchiṟuppākkāḍu at Vasugūr in Vasugūr-nāḍu in pal-kunṟa-kkōṭṭam	*AREp*., 1938-290 (Kalaśappākkam)
		Uyyakkoṇḍān-chōḷapuram in Vankamugai-nāḍu north of Paṅgaḷa-nāḍu in Jayaṅgoṇḍachōḷa-maṇḍalam	*SII*, VIII, 7 (Choḷapuram)
	(Walajahpet tk)	Tiruppānmalai in Perum-Timirināḍu in Paḍuvūr-kōṭṭam Tiruppānmalai	*EI*, IV, p. 139 (Panchapāṇḍava-malai)
	(Wandiwash tk)	Ponnur	*AREp*., 1928-29, 406 (Ponnur)
		Cherukūr in Valla-nāḍu in Dāmar-kōṭṭam	*SII*, XIII, 29 (Tirumalpuram)
	South Arcot dt (Gingeetk)	Perumandai in Perumaṇḍai-nāḍu in Venkunṟa-kkōṭṭakm	*SII*, XVII, 243 (Melśēvūr)
Charaters 10 Century	Chittoor dt (Tiruttani rk)	Vēppūr in Tūyi-nāḍu	*AREp*., 1943-44, 132 (Chinna-nāga-pūṇḍi)

INDEX

✧✧✧